U.S. National Security

U.S. National Security

A Framework for Analysis

Edited by

Daniel J. Kaufman
U.S. Military Academy

Jeffrey S. McKitrick
U.S. Military Academy

Thomas J. Leney
U.S. Military Academy

Lexington Books
D.C. Heath and Company/Lexington, Massachusetts/Toronto

Library of Congress Cataloging in Publication Data

Main entry under title:

U.S. national security.
  Includes index.
    1. United States—National security—Addresses, essays, lectures. 2. National security—
Addresses, essays, lectures. I. Kaufman, Daniel J. II. McKitrick, Jeffrey S. III. Leney, Thomas J.
UA23.U225   1985   355′.033073   84–48809
ISBN 0–669–09812–4 (alk. paper)
ISBN 0–669–09851–5 (pbk. : alk. paper)

Published simultaneously in Canada
Printed in the United States of America on acid-free paper
International Standard Book Number: 0–669–09812–4 Casebound
International Standard Book Number: 0–669–09851–5 Paperbound
Library of Congress Catalog Card Number: 84–48809

For Kathryn, Myra, and Wendy

Contents

Foreword

Richard K. Betts

A modest renaissance in national security studies has occurred in the past half-dozen years. After turning their attention to economic interdependence and transnational relations for some time, many scholars have rediscovered the central importance of war, strategy, and deterrence in international politics. With the death of detente, the waning of trauma from the disaster in Vietnam, and increasing tensions in trouble spots around the world, citizens are also more conscious of how tenuous their safety may be.

Where do novices go to get a sense of the shape of the old general nature of the problem, its new specific manifestations, and the connections among them? This book is one good place to start. It fills a space in the literature available to students, educators, and general observers of international relations and foreign policy. Despite the importance of defense policy and the multitude of studies on its particular aspects, the range of comprehensive surveys in print is surprisingly limited compared to texts on other subjects. Of those that exist, many surveys are too superficial, too narrow, too broad, or too idiosyncratic to provide a sufficient foundation for someone entering the unfamiliar terrain of questions about why, how, when, and where the United States should use its power to protect its values and interests. This book avoids these limitations remarkably well and is marked by a balanced approach to analysis.

First, the book puts the complexity of the problem in appropriate focus. Many conceive of security in strictly military terms: the use of force or the threat to use it. This approach is common among professional strategists and was prevalent early in the cold war, before oil embargoes and ambiguous but crucial shifts in alliance relations (such as the U.S. rapprochement with China) highlighted the multifaceted nature of strategy. Others, in contrast, define security so inclusively that it becomes indistinguishable from foreign policy in general. The latter approach, which came into vogue in the 1970s, sometimes reflected the reluctance of academics to confront the continuing importance of force in the post-Vietnam era. Without resorting to a lengthy and indiscriminate compilation and commentary that could daunt all but the most compulsive of students, this book puts the relationship between essential and contextual elements of U.S. security in clear perspective.

Second, most literature on security tends to fall under two approaches that are seldom well integrated. Many analysts address security policy in terms of determinants that are either external and strategic or internal and political. Those who concentrate on the former often seem to see the relationships between threats and responses and between ends and means as clear and objectively calculable. This approach can convey an excessively rationalistic impression of how a nation operates strategically. Some who concentrate on the latter approach, on the other hand, sometimes overstate the impact of parochial interests and organizational games, as if policy were nothing but the residue of intragovernmental turf fights. Of course, it is impossible to appreciate the development of security policy without focusing on the international forest and the domestic trees. The book surveys both the forest and trees in a straightforward and coherent fashion.

This collection also avoids an overemphasis on novel ideas and new literature. Times change and new events or research do invalidate some old interpretations. What is remarkable when one looks back over the postwar era of U.S. policy, however, is how much continuity there is in the basic issues that have driven U.S. strategy and programs and how much wisdom is still to be found in earlier writings. The editors of this book have marshaled a representative array of essays from the 1950s, 1960s, and 1970s, as well as the current decade. The selection combines insights from trained analysts and academicians, experienced practitioners, and authors who—like the editors—hold both sorts of credentials.

Finally, neither the selected readings nor the editors' lucid essays that link them and place them in perspective will tell students what positions they should take on national security policy. This is as it should be but is no mean feat. Defense policy has always been contentious, but it has been especially so since the Vietnam war fractured the cold war consensus and the enterprise of arms control negotiations faltered. This book will not appeal to pacifists, isolationists, or radicals of any stripe (including ardent militarists), but it presents the broad mainstream of thinking on U.S. options for war and peace. Education about security is too important to be left to the polemicists. This book will not indoctrinate readers as to whether missile throw-weight, more or fewer aircraft carriers, or cuts in the defense budget are the most critical issues facing the body politic. It will, however, take them a long way toward learning how to think about the dimensions of security and the choices involved. Since so much debate about security reflects distressingly little serious thought, that alone establishes the worth of this volume.

Preface

For over twenty years, the U.S. Military Academy at West Point has offered a senior seminar in national security studies as part of its curriculum. Since no adequate textbook dealing with national security studies has been available, the professors in charge of that course have collected a set of readings from journals and books for students. That approach, however, has proved to be time-consuming and time sensitive, requiring annual updates. Further, such an approach left it up to each professor to develop a larger conceptual framework into which the readings would fit.

As a result, we undertook a project to develop a conceptual framework for analyzing national security and to identify the relevant literature that best elaborated on and clarified that framework. The articles sought were to be timeless (not trendy), analytical (not merely descriptive), and balanced (not biased). The aim was to develop an edited work that could serve as a textbook, not only in West Point's national security seminar but in courses of this nature at undergraduate institutions across the country. Additionally, we hoped that because of its uniqueness and utility, the conceptual framework would be of interest to practitioners in the national security field. To the degree that we were successful in these endeavors, *U.S. National Security: A Framework for Analysis* will fill an important void in the study and understanding of U.S. national security policy.

Chapter 1 describes in detail the analytical framework we developed. Each part is introduced by an original essay designed to set the readings in a larger context and to provide additional information on the issues. Finally, we provide an appraisal of U.S. national security policy since World War II to help students understand how it evolved and as an example of how to apply the analytical framework.

This book in no way represents an official policy position of either the U.S. Military Academy or any other agency of the U.S. government. The views expressed in it are those of the authors and do not purport to reflect the position of the U.S. Military Academy, the Department of the Army, or the Department of Defense.

We owe many thanks to the members of the Department of Social Sciences at the U.S. Military Academy for their help and encouragement as the project evolved.

The office staff, ably led by Barbara Thomas, provided outstanding support. Special thanks are due to Jacqueline Murphy for her skilled work on the word processor, her patience with our innumerable changes, and the expeditious way in which she implemented those changes. Finally, we would like to thank Jaime Welch of Lexington Books for guiding us through the publication maze and for her sincere commitment to this project.

All royalties from this book will be deposited in a fund for faculty research and development at West Point in order to provide additional opportunities for future efforts of this kind.

U.S. National Security

Part I
How to Analyze
National Security

1

A Conceptual Framework

The Editors

E very year the secretary of defense sends a report commonly known as the posture statement to the Congress. This annual report outlines in several hundred pages the secretary's assessment of U.S. interests around the world and the security threats facing the nation. It also identifies the policies and forces that the United States has, as well as those it needs, to protect itself against those threats. To the uninitiated, the discussion of strategy, programs, budgets, and weapons systems can be confusing. It is filled with new vocabulary terms—*counterforce, MIRV, triad, Backfire, START*—that roll strangely off the tongue. Though these words may have little meaning at first, students of national security affairs cannot help but be staggered by the resources and the costs involved and thus sense the significance of the subject being addressed. Even if an administration does not demonstrate adequately the importance of its requests for billions of defense dollars, the nation's national security is clearly at stake in the face of conditions such as assured destruction (the possibility that the United States could be totally destroyed).

Although most people concede the importance of national security and the need to establish an adequate security posture, a number of questions remain. How do we know our security policies effectively meet our needs? How can we best address the threats to our interests at the least cost? Before one can address these issues, even more fundamental questions must be answered: What are our interests? What are the threats to these interests? Often the government is accused of generating policies and forces that do not seem to achieve these interests effectively or efficiently. Newspapers and journals are filled with accusations concerning wasteful programs or charges that government policies have resulted in missile gaps, interest-capability gaps, or other shortcomings that degrade security. If we are to be able to judge the validity of these charges, we must have some method of analyzing national security policy and determining how well it meets national interests. Our objective in this book is to identify the important variables that shape national security posture and assist in understanding the relationship between ends and means.

Defining National Security

In spite of its wide usage, *national security* is a term that is ambiguous and thus has come to mean different things to different people. Traditionally national security has been defined as protection from external attack; consequently it has been viewed primarily in terms of military defenses against military threats. This view has proved to be too narrow, however; national security involves more than the procurement and application of military forces. Furthermore, such a view can delude one into believing that the way to increase security is merely to increase military power. Although military power is a very important component of security, it is only one facet; indeed history is filled with examples of arms races that resulted in less, rather than more, of this elusive commodity. Such races were often started by a nation strengthening its military power for defensive reasons in order to feel more secure. This action caused neighboring states to feel threatened and to respond by increasing their military establishments, which in turn made the original state feel less secure—and the race was on.

Today a much broader definition of national security is needed, one that includes economic, diplomatic, and social dimensions, in addition to the military dimension. Arnold Wolfers gives such a description: "Security, in an objective sense, measures the absence of threats to acquired values, in a subjective sense the absence of fear that such values will be attacked."[1] An analysis of this definition reveals important ideas that serve as a backdrop for the study of national security policy.

First, although security is directly related to values, it is not a value in its own right. It is a condition that allows a nation to maintain its values. Actions that make a nation more secure yet degrade its values are of little utility. Second, it is extremely difficult to measure security in any objective fashion. Therefore security becomes an evaluation based on perceptions of not only strengths and weaknesses but also the capabilities and intentions of perceived threats. Uncertainty about the true level of threat leads us to plan for the worst case, due to the drastic consequences of a security failure. Even if perceptions are accurate, security defies absolute measurement because it is a relative condition. We measure security relative to existing and potential threats, and since we cannot achieve absolute security against all possible threats, we must determine what levels of insecurity are acceptable. Last, it is important to realize that national security is not a static condition that exists in a vacuum. It is determined in the context of both the international and domestic environments, both of which are changing constantly.

National security policy is also a difficult concept to define. Frank Trager and Frank Simone have described it as "that part of government policy having as its objective the creation of national and international political conditions favorable to the protection and extension of vital national values against existing and potential adversaries."[2] Although this definition is not precise, it enables us to identify those actions that should be included in the study of national security. It also identifies some of the key elements (values, government, and the domestic and international environments) that must be examined in order to understand and evaluate policy. By organizing those elements into a conceptual framework that orders the relationship among variables, it is possible to explain and evaluate national security policy. Figure 1–1 outlines a framework that will enable students to understand these variables and to

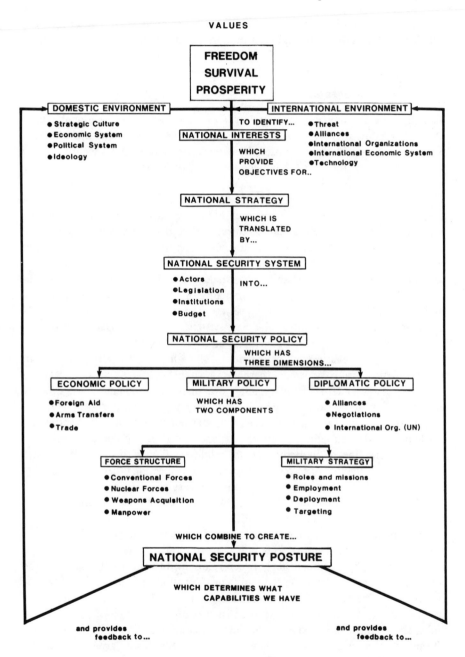

Figure 1-1. Framework for Analyzing National Security Policy

see the relationship between the major categories of analysis. In this chapter we establish the framework; we explore it in more detail throughout the book in order to provide a firm foundation for the analysis of national security policy.

Values and Interests

The objective of national security policy is to protect and extend national values. By their very nature, these basic values tend to be rather vague and abstract. Nonetheless, they are important for the determination of national security policy since values constitute the fundamental essence of a nation and determine the basic character of a society.

The most fundamental national value is survival. Without it, a nation cannot achieve any of its other values. Thus, the ultimate focus of national security policy is to ensure the survival of the nation. Survival includes protection of the population, territorial integrity, and sovereignty. Mere physical survival by itself is not enough, however; the society must maintain its other values in order to retain its basic character. Examples of other values held by the United States include concepts such as justice, freedom, and maintenance of a democratic society. These, in addition to such values as prosperity, prestige, and the promotion or protection of the nation's ideology, constitute the essential character of a society and as such provide the foundation for the development of national security policy.

Although national security policy often is thought to be logically derived from a clearly defined value structure, there are inevitable conflicts that arise between values. As Samuel Huntington so aptly describes the problem, "The crux of military policy, to be sure, is the relation of force to national purposes. But it is always national purposes in the plural, national purposes which are continually conflicting, and often being compromised, and seldom being realized."[3] For example, preservation of individual rights might conflict with desires to ensure public safety in the face of terrorist campaigns, or protecting other democratic nations might raise the threat to our own physical survival.

Further, it is difficult to determine with precision the relative importance of specific values, which in turn makes it difficult to determine precisely how they will influence policies a nation might adopt. Often when policies do not seem to support a particular value, it is because there are competing values to be considered.

Not only is there competition between values held by the nation, there may be competition between the value structures of the nation and those of the state or government. Therefore, it is important to examine who determines the values that are to be protected. We tend to assume that they are a reflection of the collective will of the people and consequently to view the nation-state as a unitary actor. The pluralistic nature of a democracy, however, ensures that not all groups within the nation have identical priorities. This pluralism results in a democratic nation's value structure being determined by competition and compromise among groups.

In a totalitarian society the state is not necessarily a unitary actor either. There may be a considerable disjuncture between the values held by the masses and the beliefs of the leaders who determine policy. In this case, national values may be determined largely by the ruling group. The result could be that survival of a particular regime is viewed as a more important objective than survival of the society as a whole. Hitler, for example, appeared willing to sacrifice German society to maintain the Nazi regime. Similarly, some people are concerned that the Soviet leadership, in an effort to maintain its political position, may be willing to sacrifice part of the Russian population.

Although protection of national values is the goal of national security policy, these values must be translated into something less abstract and related to specific situations if they are to serve as the basis for policy. By relating values to the domestic and international environments, policymakers can identify specific interests to serve as concrete objectives toward which policy can be aimed. Interests can be described as the conditions that the nation is attempting to achieve or maintain in both the international and domestic environments and, as such, provide the link between values and policies.

An example demonstrating the relationship between values and interests can be seen by examining the situation in the Persian Gulf. President Jimmy Carter declared that maintenance of the free flow of oil from the Persian Gulf region was a vital interest of the United States. This interest is a manifestation of the basic value of prosperity, since without oil the United States would be weakened economically. If the U.S. economy were weakened sufficiently, its national survival might even be threatened. Thus, it is apparent how interests are derived from national values.

There are three important points to consider in examining national interests. First, they are not important by themselves; they are important only if they contribute to the achievement of national values. Policymakers and analysts must take care to avoid focusing on interests as ends unto themselves rather than as intermediate objectives. To do so could result in policies that do not contribute to the achievement of national values and in fact may prove to be counterproductive. Second, interests, like values, can conflict with each other and need to be reconciled by determining priorities and by making acceptable compromises. Third, policy is often justified as protecting vital interests, which are those interests that relate to the most important values. Although some would define vital interests as those interests we would be willing to use force to preserve, this definition is backward. It is more appropriate to view the use of military force as justified only when in pursuit of vital interests.

Since national interests are identified as results of the interaction of values with the international and domestic environments, the next step in analyzing national security policy is to examine the environmental factors that combine with interests to shape national policy. Although these factors alone do not determine how a nation acts, they both constrain and stimulate security policy by precluding or reducing the benefits of some options while creating or advancing others.

The linkage between the domestic and international environments is stronger now than in the past since domestic policy contains greater international implications. For example, a decision to raise interest rates in the United States affects the economic well-being of nations in Western Europe by shifting investment capital from their markets. A decision to reduce U.S. defense spending in order to balance the budget affects European security and Europeans' confidence in the North Atlantic Treaty Organization (NATO). The international environment also has a greater effect than in the past on domestic interests. The 1973 oil embargo by OPEC (Organization of Petroleum Exporting Countries) restricted the flow of oil to the West, resulting in a dislocation of Western economies. Clearly the result of this greater linkage between the two environments is to increase concern about events occurring thousands of miles away.

International Environment

A number of the important influences on national security policy can be found by examining the international environment. These influences can be divided into two general categories: state specific (affecting relationships between the United States and other individual nations) and systemic (affecting the entire community of nations).

The relationships between nations are influenced by geography and ideology. Nations tend to be more concerned about states that are nearby or that are close to vital resources or lines of communication. For example, the United States is more concerned with what is happening in Central America than with what is happening in the Seychelles. A coup or revolution that deposes a democratic government and installs a communist regime generates a different set of policy concerns and responses than does a coup that topples a communist regime.

National security policy is largely a response to perceived threats in the international environment. The level of threat is determined by the capabilities and intentions of potential adversaries. The combination of powerful capabilities and aggressive intentions (one view of the Soviet Union) results in the perception of a high level of threat and receives the most attention from national security policymakers. Since it is difficult to determine intentions accurately and since intentions can change literally overnight, policymakers are forced to focus on capabilities, which, although somewhat more easily observed, may be difficult to measure precisely. The uncertainty that results from the inability to determine the precise level of threat affects policy by leading us to assume a worst case due to the potential costs of a miscalculation.

Although the threat to a nation's security is influenced by the capabilities and intentions of potential enemies, it is the perception of the threat that causes policy responses. Since perception is determined in large measure by the quality of the intelligence gathered about other nations, it is an important factor in policy determination. The degree of accuracy with which we can determine the level of threat will, in turn, determine how closely perceptions match reality, as well as the optimality of the response.

Many policy arguments derive from disagreements about adversaries' intentions. If we perceive that a state is aggressive in nature, then we may have to respond to an increase in its military capability or to actions that increase its military power. We must convince adversaries that we are both capable and willing to wage war over conflicts of interest. Disputes become tests of resolve, and concessions may be perceived as weaknesses, which could encourage future aggression. Although a demonstration of resolve may well be effective to deter an aggressive adversary, it could be counterproductive if the other state is not being aggressive but is acting only from a sense of insecurity. In this case, a nation's actions to increase its capabilities or even to expand its territory could be defensive actions designed to reduce its fear of potential enemies. As Robert Jervis points out, "The drive for security will also produce aggressive actions if the state either requires a very high sense of security or feels menaced by the very presence of other strong states."[4] His analysis identifies the root of the problem as the inability to distinguish offensive from defensive capabilities. Unless the forces required for defense and aggression differ, a nation desiring only to defend itself will acquire capabilities that resemble those of an aggressor. The tendency of policymakers to assume the worst case can result in other states increasing their arms as a result, causing an arms race that leaves both sides less secure.

Although the primary focus of national security policy is to counter military threats, not all threats take this form. States may threaten security by economic actions such as limiting access to vital natural resources. Ideological challenges from potential aggressors that export revolution or communism may be perceived as threats to the continued influence of the United States around the world and may result in the formulation of policies to counter such challenges.

The remaining factors in the international environment that influence national security policy can be considered systemic since they have a more general effect. In the absence of world government, nations exist in a state of anarchy. Although the degree of anarchy is limited somewhat by economic, political, historical, and cultural relationships among nations, ultimately each nation is the sole guarantor of its own security. In an anarchical environment, states are free to pursue their policy objectives as far as their interests and capabilities allow, and they usually are checked only by the strength of other countries.

Efforts to bring order to the international arena by establishing international or supranational organizations such as the League of Nations and the United Nations (UN) have had very limited success. National sovereignty defines the parameters of national freedom of action. Consequently nations avoid total reliance on collective security or supranational organizations since such reliance requires the surrender of a degree of sovereignty. Although efforts such as the UN have had limited influence in the development of security policy, other international relationships, such as alliances, play a major role.

Alliances are important to an understanding of national security policy because they are a method by which states augment their power and attempt to impose some order on the international environment. Alliances are formed out of mutual, though not always identical, interests. By promising to combine resources against a mutual threat, alliance partners hope to gain influence or meet interests that their individual resources would be insufficient to secure. Alliances also perform other functions besides simply expanding resources. They signal interests by making response to particular threats explicit, and they give legitimacy to a nation's involvement in particular areas of the world. Hans Morgenthau notes that "alliances are formed out of expediency not principles" in order to further interests.[5] One interest, credibility of commitments, is generated by the formation of an alliance. Once an alliance is created, a nation may be forced to respond to actions aimed at its partners. Membership in an alliance thus acts as a limit on options in some circumstances, since, even though the interests that created a particular alliance may have changed, we retain an interest in maintaining credibility of other alliance commitments. While alliances serve to define, extend, and even limit interests, they do not provide guarantees. Nations never can be completely confident that an alliance agreement will be kept until the *casus foederis* (an incident that triggers an alliance response) occurs. Thus, although NATO has been successful in deterring war to date, its members can never be sure if alliance commitments will be binding should an attack occur.

As the political dimension of the international environment is characterized by competition and cooperation, so is the economic dimension of the international environment dominated by competition for limited resources and a growing economic interdependence among nations. The United States is dependent for its economic well-being on resources imported from nations, as well as on markets for its own goods and services. These factors result in the United States having interests, such as access to oil and freedom of the seas, around the world.

Other systemic concerns, such as dwindling nonrenewable resources in an era of expanding demand, ecological deterioration, and population increases, also shape interests and influence policy. Responses to these concerns, which are essentially nonmilitary in nature, must compete for resources with the policies designed to respond to military threats.

Changes in the international and domestic environments can be caused by technology, since it shapes one's own security capabilities, as well as those of potential adversaries. The most important technological development affecting national security has been the advent of nuclear weapons. These weapons have greatly increased the capabilities to punish those nations that would threaten U.S. interests (thus increasing the risks to potential aggressors) and for the first time in its history put the survival of the United States at risk.

The ability to take advantage of technological change has enabled nations to prevail even when outnumbered. For example, the British use of radar in World War II enabled the Royal Air Force to defeat the vast air armada of the Luftwaffe. Failure to meet the challenges presented by changes in nuclear weapons technology could present decision makers with the stark choice between capitulation and annihilation.

The tremendous destructive potential of nuclear weapons makes the cost of fighting a nuclear war so prohibitive that deterrence has become the primary objective of national security policy. Prior to the development of nuclear weapons, the three primary objectives of military force—to punish the enemy, to deny the enemy territory (or take it away), and to mitigate damage to oneself—essentially were accomplished by the same weapons systems. Nuclear weapons, on the other hand, can punish an aggressor but do little to mitigate damage to oneself in the event of war. As a result, according to Glenn Snyder,

> a prospective aggressor may be deterred, in some circumstances at least, solely or primarily by threatening and possessing the capability to inflict extreme punishment on his homeland, assets, and population, even though he may be superior in capabilities for contesting the control of terrritory. Nuclear powers must, therefore, exercise a conscious choice between the objectives of deterrence and defense, since the relative proportion of "punishment capability" to "denial capability" in their military establishments has become a matter of choice.[6]

The key problem of deterrence is the determination of how much and what type of punishment a state must be able to inflict on an aggressor in order to deter it. The answer to this question is based in part on an evaluation of the opponent's values, which determine what level of suffering the opponent is willing to risk in order to gain its objectives. Although large numbers of nuclear weapons appear to represent a case of overkill, the difficulty in determining an opponent's values forces policymakers to plan for the worst case.

The advent of nuclear weapons has not ended war, as some had hoped, but it has altered the conduct of military conflict. The potential destructiveness of nuclear weapons creates a need and a desire to limit warfare. These limitations can be a function of geography, intensity, or objectives. While a desire to limit war reduces the threat of massive destruction, such a reduction actually could degrade the ability to deter aggression by making limited war appear to be a feasible alternative. Clausewitz stated that war, in theory, tends to escalate naturally to maximum levels of violence. With the availability of nuclear weapons, such a prospect could lead to national extinction. Thus, policymakers are faced with a dilemma: efforts to prevent escalation to nuclear catastrophe could reduce the deterrent value of nuclear weapons and make conventional war more likely.

Domestic Environment

The international environment influences the formation of national security policy, but there are also domestic factors that influence policy choices. In order to understand why policies are adopted, it is important to examine the way a nation views the world, the economic conditions that constrain defense expenditures, and the political constraints that structure interests and influence policy.

The domestic environment interacts with a society's values and shapes national interests. The domestic environment can be viewed in three broad dimensions: social, economic, and political. Within these dimensions exist the domestic variables that mold national security policy. These variables primarily affect the allocation of resources (people, money, material) and the degree of public support for security policies.

Clausewitz was one of the first strategists to draw attention to the social dimension of strategy by describing the social forces that distinguished Napoleonic warfare from warfare practiced in the previous century. Social factors are important because they are the source of commitment by the nation to national security endeavors. In a democracy, social factors provide the basis for political will and resource allocation decisions. Failure to account properly for social factors can have serious consequences, as may have been the case with the U.S. involvement in Vietnam. Military commanders repeatedly claim to have won the battles but to have lost the war due to the unwillingness of the American people to support continued conflict in South Vietnam.

The social dimensions of the domestic environment have their origin in the nation's historic experience, degree of national unity, geography, demography, and public mood. Public opinion about national security issues and willingness to use military force are manifestations of these societal factors.

In a democratic state, public opinion provides both an impetus to and a constraint on how resources are allocated to meet particular national security concerns. Although it is difficult to determine *a priori* the impact of something as diffuse as public opinion, the nature of the U.S. political process ensures a degree of responsiveness to public opinion. Authoritarian regimes may pay less attention to public opinion, but autocratic leaders still must be concerned about it. For example, to avoid losing popular support, Adolf Hitler did not put Germany on a full war production footing until more than four years of war had been waged. Public opinion identifies for policymakers the parameters of choices that are acceptable to the people. These parameters are quite broad, and public opinion is slow to mobilize on national security issues. As a result, public opinion has its greatest effect on security policy in the long term, after the policy has been enacted. Nonetheless, public opinion, when aroused, can exercise very real constraints on policy choices, as when U.S. policy in Vietnam was affected by public protests.

It is difficult, and perhaps unwise, to generalize about a U.S. approach to national security policy; however, it is possible to identify some common themes that influence the way the United States responds to the international environment. An analysis of such traditions helps to identify potential biases in U.S. policies and can help to explain certain actions the United States takes. Some of the traditions are a peacetime orientation on domestic affairs and limited interest in world events, an aversion to violence, an antimilitarism that distrusts standing armies, and a distrust of power politics and diplomacy. Although those attributes tend to mitigate against active involvement in world affairs, they are balanced by other

U.S. traditions, such as a crusading spirit and a sense of idealism, that have tended to result in U.S. intervention abroad.

U.S. traditions influence American's view of the world and color their perceptions of possible threats. They also limit the range of responses to the threats. Although the rise of Nazi Germany posed grave threats to world peace, the U.S. domestic orientation and aversion to violence made it reluctant to become involved in efforts to counter Hitler. Once the United States became involved in the war, however, other aspects, such as its crusading spirit and idealism, led its leaders to demand total victory and unconditional surrender. When World War II ended, there was a great cry for demobilization and a "return to normalcy" (both manifestations of U.S. traditions) despite the threat to Western Europe posed by the Soviet Union.

In addition to being influenced by cultural variables, public opinion is influenced by the mass media, important actors in the domestic environment. The media provide information from policymakers to the public and feedback from the public to the government. In addition to being a conduit of information, however, the media can exert influence for or against governmental policies. Investigative reporting and critical analyses, as well as favorable reporting, influence public opinion. While the pluralistic and fragmented nature of the press limits its influence, nonetheless it shapes (or even creates, according to critics) public attitudes.

Interest groups are another political force that exist in the domestic environment and influence national security policy. These groups use tools such as campaign contributions, votes, and their ability to energize public opinion. Interest groups, like the media and public opinion, do not determine policy directly. They affect policy through their ability to influence actors in the policy process, by marshaling support from the Congress, or by finding elements within the bureaucracy with complementary organizational interests. The success of interest groups in affecting policy has raised concerns over the appropriateness of that influence, such as President Dwight D. Eisenhower's warning against the coalition known as the military-industrial complex.

Economic variables in the domestic environment are important factors in the resource allocation decisions necessary in order to implement national security policy. The degree of industrialization and the strength of an economy determine the amount of resources available for defense programs. No nation has sufficient resources to provide for security against all possible threats. Further, there may be insufficient resources to support even the declared policies of the government. For example, in 1980, the Joint Chiefs of Staff (JCS) estimated that the United States would need 750 ships, 30 army and marine divisions, and 35 tactical air wings at a cost of $250 billion to execute the national security policies established by the Carter administration.[7] However, the fiscal year (FY) 1980 budget allocated only $125 billion for 458 ships, 19 divisions, and 26 air wings, a significant shortfall. Such discontinuities between interests and capabilities result from a scarcity of resources to meet multiple national objectives, which in turn forces trade-offs between national security objectives and other national objectives. The dilemma of guns versus butter is one that every president faces.

Not only does the economy affect the size of the defense budget, but defense expenditures can have an impact on the U.S. economy, affecting inflation, employment, and patterns of spending. Prolonged high levels of defense spending could have a serious impact on economic growth and degrade efforts to meet other interests and maintain other values. At some point the cost of achieving national security may outweigh the perceived benefits, especially when those benefits are difficult to define.

The political dimension of the domestic environment consists of factors that provide the foundation for the structure and process by which decisions about national security policy are made. The type of political system and the ideological orientation of the society determine to a large extent how the government is organized, which in turn influences how national security decisions are made. The democratic and pluralistic nature of the U.S. political system, typified by competition among groups for influence and the decentralization of power in the government (as established by the constitutional division of powers between the legislative and executive branches), establishes the parameters of the decision process.

National Strategy

National strategy is an attractive concept, but it has proved difficult to formulate and implement. National interests are derived from the interaction of values and the domestic and international environments. In theory, these national interests should provide the objectives for a national strategy. In practice, however, two significant difficulties act to hinder the formulation of such a strategy. First, the environmental factors that ought to influence strategy may be uncertain or ambiguous. For example, the nature and extent of the threats to national values may not be clear or may be perceived differently by different people. Second, there is no mechanism by which an explicit national strategy can be determined from national interests. Consequently, rather than having a cohesive, coherent, and integrated plan that would serve to secure the nation's interests and guide the formulation of national security policy, strategy tends to be shaped by the perceptions and beliefs of individual policymakers and the structures and processes of national security decision making. These structures and processes constitute the national security system.

National Security System: Structure and Process

An understanding of the decision-making structure and process is essential in order to explain how values and interests are translated into specific policies. As Samuel Huntington stated in *The Common Defense*:

Policy is not the result of deductions from a clear statement of national objective. It is the product of the competition of purposes within individuals and groups and among individuals and groups. It is the result of politics not logic, more an area than a unity.[8]

This competition determines who participates in policy decisions, what information is considered, which options are examined, and how decisions are implemented. Apparent discontinuities between interests and policy often have their source in the structures and processes of the national security system.

Structure refers to the institutions that make authoritative decisions on national security issues. Entities such as the National Security Council (NSC), the Office of the Secretary of Defense (OSD), and the Senate Armed Services Committee are part of the structure.

Several factors determine the structure of policymaking. Two of the most important determinants are the Constitution and legislation, which define the responsibilities and authority of the president and Congress in determining national security policy. Legislation supplements the Constitution and also determines to some degree the relevant actors and their roles in various policy processes. Legislation establishes access to the decision process and defines the authority for decisions. For example, the National Security Act of 1947 established the Department of Defense (DOD) and the NSC as important organizational players in the policy process. Subsequent amendments to the act have affected the roles of such actors as the JCS, the military services, and the NSC staff. The law gives the secretary of defense authority over all the armed forces of the United States, thus establishing his authority directly under the president. The National Security Act states that the JCS will advise the NSC, thus providing the JCS access to the policy process.

Process consists of the series of actions and interactions within the organizational structure that combine to create policy. The stages in this process can be identified as issue identification, planning, decision, implementation, and evaluation. How well these tasks are accomplished is influenced directly by the established structure. Since each policy has its own process, the national security system is the aggregation of these processes within the organizational structure.

The president's personal style is an important factor in determining structure and process. He will establish a policy apparatus with which he is comfortable, within the parameters defined by law. Examples of different approaches can be found by examining the NSC under various presidents. Although the National Security Act of 1947 established the composition of the NSC, the president has a great deal of latitude in organizing and using the NSC staff, headed by his assistant for national security affairs. Each president has set up and used the staff to fit his personal style.

The type of decision will affect the process and may alter the structure used. Due to the limited time that is available, crisis decisions often are made by a structure and process different from that used for routine decisions. Planning time is restricted, and options may be limited to those that have been prepared previously. Information may be incomplete or contradictory, and coordination could be hampered by time constraints or the need for secrecy. Routine decisions tend to be dealt with at lower levels, where standard operating procedures are important determinants of the policy processes and outcomes. The amount of time available, the need for secrecy, and the importance of a decision can influence which actors gain access to the process and how they participate. As a result, the type of decision, and the level at which it is decided, can influence whether an individual is the sole decision maker, one of several decision makers, or whether he or she is excluded from the process altogether.

Decisions may be categorized as strategic or structural, with a different process applicable to each. Strategic decisions determine the way forces are used; structural decisions focus on the procurement, allocation, and organization of those forces. Strategic decisions focus on the international environment and normally are within the purview of the executive branch. Structural decisions are oriented on domestic political considerations and economic conditions. Congress has much more influence, by virtue of its constitutional charter, in the structural decisions. Actors outside the government, such as interest groups and industry, are more influential in structural decisions.

In order to understand the policy process, it is important to know who the actors are and how they participate. We shall divide them into two basic categories, organizations and individuals. The array of international political, economic, and military issues with which the United States must deal requires the maintenance of a sizable institutional structure. Therefore decision makers must rely on organizations to a large extent for providing information, identifying issues, formulating options, and analyzing alternatives. Bureaucracies make many routine decisions within previously established parameters, and standard procedures affect how these tasks are performed, as well as how decisions will be implemented.

In order to understand the impact of organizations on policy, it is useful to examine several characteristics of these actors. Each organization is established with a mission designed to meet national interests. Organizations play a major role in dealing with routine events and therefore have ongoing responsibilities. These responsibilities are seldom sharply defined. Instead they are rather general and as a result create opportunity for conflict and competition. The structure set up by legislation often results in organizations with conflicting responsibilities, which in turn causes competition among agencies for turf. Consequently organizations tend to develop organizational interests in addition to the ones they were designed to achieve, the strongest of these being survival. Concomitantly, institutional success tends to be measured by size, growth, and degree of autonomy.

While organizational interests do not replace the national interests, they can bias an organization's perceptions of what is best for the nation. An organization's activities are designed to further its own, as well as national, interests. The organization may reach outside the governmental process to obtain support for its positions from interest groups, the media, or the public, believing that it is the organization best able to understand and achieve particular national goals. An organization's view of its primary role is called organizational essence, a view that influences attitudes within the organization. Those missions and activities that contribute to organizational essence receive strong support, while other missions may face apathy or even opposition within the organization, thus possibly hampering planning and implementation. An example of organizational essence can be found in the air force attitude toward manned aircraft. Manned aircraft are the raison d'être of the air force, and the service views its primary contribution to the nation's security as providing the best possible aircraft for accomplishing strategic and tactical missions. As a result, the air force attempts to ensure that manned bombers are maintained as a key part of the U.S. strategic deterrent, while supporting, less enthusiastically, long-range air transport programs.

By their nature, organizations dislike uncertainty and favor slow change. As a result, while organizations may provide continuity in programs, change tends to be incremental. This incrementalism can be a positive aspect of organizational behavior in that overcommitment or overexpenditure of resources may be avoided. However, it is easy for continuity to become inertia, which stifles creativity and decreases flexibility.

While bureaucracies play an important part in the decision process, decisions are made by people. It long has been recognized that an individual's position shapes not only his or her access to the process but also his or her power within it. Graham Allison's classic phrase, "Where you stand depends upon where you sit," indicates the degree to which individuals may reflect their organization's views, since many individuals participate only as a result of their positions in organizations, and these positions shape their perceptions and beliefs.[9]

Policy decisions made by individuals within large bureaucracies can be explained in part by pressures to conform, sympathy for organizational needs as opposed to national interests, and organizational inertia. These factors contribute to the difficulties bureaucrats have in making innovative decisions and the difficulty policymakers have in getting policies implemented when the bureaucracy opposes them.

Policy decisions also are influenced by the decision maker's values. Decision makers may favor a policy because of the benefits to a particular political party or the impact on the interest groups that are clients of their organization. Ideology and personal objectives, such as increasing one's prestige and influence, can have a significant effect on preferences. Finally, one should not discount the importance of the policymaker's perception of the national interest and the nature of the threats to those interests.

Attributes such as expertise, the ability to communicate, personal relationships with other decision makers, bureaucratic and political skills, and the ability and willingness to make decisions can affect the amount of influence individuals have in the system. For example, the assistant to the president for national security affairs is a key player, although he has no statutory authority and controls only a small staff. His influence is the result of his expertise and his personal relationship with, and access to, the president.

The role of individual and organizational actors may vary depending on the type of decision or stage of policy development. Issue identification and planning procedures tend to be standardized and routine and are handled by organizations. Implementation is also normally a routine organizational chore. The decision itself may be made at different organizational levels, depending on the sensitivity and importance of the issue, and may involve different actors at various stages in the process. For example, Congress plays a more important role in structural decisions than it does in strategic decisions. Even though organizations may have less influence than individuals in the formulation of policy, nonetheless decisions are implemented by organizations using existing procedures and capabilities.

National Security Policy

David Easton describes policy as the outputs of a nation's political system.[10] The system produces a large variety of policies that can be categorized as domestic or foreign, depending on the environment to which they respond. Since interests result from the interaction of national values with the domestic and international environments, there is considerable overlap between domestic and foreign policies. For example, trade policies affect our relationships with other nations and also have considerable impact on the well-being of domestic industries. At the same time, changes in domestic production affect our economic well-being and influence our relationships with other countries.

National security policy is influenced by both the domestic and international environments and as a result incorporates those elements of both domestic and foreign policy that affect a nation's security. Figure 1–2 illustrates the relationship between national security policy and the categories of foreign and domestic policy.

National security policy includes a broad spectrum of policy interactions. They vary from cooperation and persuasion, at one extreme, to violent coercion at the other. The importance of the interest, the degree of the threat, and the nation's own capabilities combine to determine where action will occur along the spectrum

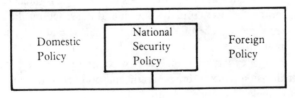

Figure 1–2. Policy Overlap

and what specific type of policy will be used. The relationship between the spectrum of interactions and the dimensions of national security policy is shown in table 1–1.

There are three dimensions of national security policy: diplomatic, economic, and military. Diplomatic policy concerns the handling of political relationships among nations. Economic policy focuses on the allocation of resources in society, as well as economic relationships with other nations. The military component consists of those policies that directly concern the armed forces and the use of military force.

While grouping policies into these three dimensions helps to organize our analysis, the dimensions should not be viewed as being completely exclusive. Specific policies may operate in more than one dimension. Aid, such as the shipment of U.S. military equipment to Israel, is an example of economic policy. Since these arms transfers also affect the readiness of the U.S. armed forces, they have an impact on the military dimension of U.S. national security as well.

Most discussions of security policy focus on the military dimension. While military policy is an important component of national security policy, its utility is limited by the costs and dangers associated with its use, especially in an era of possible nuclear confrontation. As a result, economic and diplomatic policy are the most commonly exercised dimensions of U.S. security policy.

Diplomatic Policy

Diplomacy is the primary means of developing and maintaining relationships among nations. It is the most frequently used mechanism of international interaction and is an important means of communication and persuasion. As table 1–1 demonstrates, diplomatic policy is the primary dimension of national security policy at the cooperation end of the interaction spectrum and is the preferred means of transacting business in international affairs. As such, it is an important complement to military and economic policy. The major elements of diplomatic policy include the development and maintenance of alliances, participation in international organizations, and the conduct of international negotiations.

A major objective of diplomatic policy is to maintain the strength of alliances and to ensure that they contribute to the achievement of national interests. Even a major power such as the United States does not have the resources to achieve its national security interests alone. While strong alliances are important for deterring aggression, they also can reduce international anarchy by circumscribing the activities of alliance partners. Due to the importance of Western Europe to U.S. economic well-being and to the balance of power between the United States and the Soviet Union, NATO is the most important alliance for the United States. This alliance is a major aspect of U.S. security policy, and consequently the United States should take into account the impact on NATO of U.S. policies throughout the world.

Table 1-1
Policy Interaction Spectrum

	Type of Interaction				
	Violent Coercion	Threats of Violence	Nonviolent Coercion	Rewards	Cooperation and Persuasion
Primary dimension of policy action	Military	Military	Economic	Economic	Diplomatic
Secondary dimension	Economic, diplomatic	Economic, diplomatic	Diplomatic	Diplomatic	Economic
Type of policy instrument	Nuclear warfare	Demonstration	Economic sanctions	Foreign aid	Alliances
	Conventional warfare	Blockade	Embargoes	Technology transfer	Diplomatic negotiations
	Military intervention	Deterrence	Boycotts	Arms transfers	International organizations
	Insurgent conflict	Explicit threat of war, intervention, subversion	Tariffs and quotas	Arms control agreements	Normal diplomatic intercourse
	Terrorism		Currency manipulation		

Source: K.J. Holsti, *International Politics: A Framework for Analysis*, (Englewood Cliffs, NJ: Prentice-Hall Inc., 1967), pp. 155–157.

Note: Diplomacy is an important complement to actions in other dimensions, as it is an important mechanism for transmitting threats (for example, threat of nonviolent coercion) or offers (for example, offers of reward), thus providing the opportunity for ends to be achieved without actually executing a policy.

Participation in international organizations provides an opportunity to seek cooperation with other nations in order to address common problems. Although international organizations, such as the UN, have not been very successful in eliminating conflict in the international environment, they do provide forums that can be used to communicate, persuade, and cooperate in areas where there are mutual interests. The UN also provides a mechanism for coalescing and communicating world opinion in an effort to influence the policies of a particular nation. It is through diplomatic efforts in such organizations that nations address systemic issues such as the development of accepted norms of international behavior.

International negotiations are another important element of diplomatic policy that contributes directly to national security. Negotiations may provide a substitute for military policy in terms of both military presence and the use of military force. Countries may attempt to improve their security by reducing the military threat rather than by increasing their own military power. Negotiations also can be useful to aid communications between adversaries in order to clarify intentions, identify mutual interests, threaten, gain information, or even deceive. Further, negotiations with adversaries provide an opportunity to demonstrate to allies that a nation is making every attempt to find alternatives to the use of force, thereby improving alliance cohesion and strengthening alliance resolve to employ force should it prove necessary.

Negotiations on arms limitations seek to reduce the risk of war, the cost of preparing for war, and the damage from war should war occur. For example, the Strategic Arms Limitations Talks (SALT) process was an effort to negotiate limits to a nuclear arms race between the United States and USSR, to reduce the threat of nuclear war, and to reduce the cost of strategic arms. Other arms control negotiations, known by such esoteric acronyms as MBFR (mutual and balanced force reductions), INF (intermediate-range nuclear forces), and START (strategic arms reductions talks), are aimed at increasing security through agreements to maintain a sense of balance across the spectrum of military capabilities.

Economic Policy

The major elements of economic policy that focus on the international environment are foreign aid, economic sanctions, arms transfers, and nuclear and non-nuclear technology transfers. There also are economic policies that focus on the domestic environment, such as protection of essential industries and stockpiling of strategic resources.

Foreign aid and arms transfers are economic policies designed primarily to meet national security interests. The United States can enhance the achievement of its own security objectives by strengthening the ability of its allies to defend themselves. Also, nations hope to gain influence by providing arms or economic support to other countries. However, the degree of political influence that results from economic aid is limited, as the Soviets discovered when the Egyptians accepted massive amounts of military assistance and then expelled all Soviet military advisers. Supplying arms also may degrade regional security by altering military balances within a region, encouraging local arms races, and providing the means of expanding a local conflict. For example, a transfer of significant amounts of U.S. military equipment to Pakistan in 1983, in hopes of deterring Soviet aggression against that country, heightened India's concerns, causing India to turn to the Soviet Union for additional military assistance in 1984.

Trade affects perceptions of national interests, hence policy, by creating economic relationships. It increases the level of interaction between states and creates or enhances mutual interests. If a major trading partner is threatened, our prosperity is affected, raising the possibility of conflict to protect that interest. The interdependency created by trade also provides opportunities to influence other states by the threat of economic sanctions.

Technology transfers are closely related to trade and are a useful component of economic policy because of the relationship between technology and military power. Acquisition of advanced technology can affect the military balance between nations. Consequently nations may attempt to retain the advantages that accrue from possessing technological superiority by limiting the transfer of technical knowledge to potential antagonists. While the primary focus is on military technology, such as missile guidance systems or weapons, a more difficult issue is the transfer of nonmilitary technology that may have military applications. For example, the Soviet Union may purchase computers from the United States ostensibly for the purpose of increasing its ability to manage its economy, but these same machines also might be able to break military codes or improve air defense coordination.

Military Policy

In many cases, diplomatic and economic policy will be adequate to meet threats to security. Nonetheless, a nation must be ready to employ military power either to coerce adversaries should efforts at persuasion fail or to defend itself against the use of force by other nations. The goal of using military force, or threatening to use it, is to develop a climate for political solutions. Therefore the use of military force should be designed to meet political objectives in addition to military ones, for, as Clausewitz pointed out, war is an extension of politics.

There are two major components of military policy: military strategy and force structure. Military strategy can be defined as the plan for the use of military force. Together with the doctrinal principles that guide how military forces will be used, military strategy determines the mission of military forces (what their objectives are), their employment (what they do), and deployment (where they are placed). Force structure refers to the organizations, soldiers, and equipment in the armed forces and their capabilities to execute military strategy.

Military strategy is the result of evaluations within the national security system of factors such as national interests, the nature of the military threats to those interests, and the contributions of allies. Ideally military strategy should determine the forces a nation builds; however, the inherent capabilities that result from existing forces cannot help but have an effect on what strategy is adopted. Further, the national security system can cause discontinuities between military strategy and military force structure.

Force structure decisions determine the capabilities that will be available to implement strategy decisions and as a result influence what can be done. Force structure decisions deal with issues such as weapons acquisition and manpower policy. Force structure is affected by the international environment through the medium of strategy. However, it also is influenced heavily by the domestic environment, since force structure decisions require resource allocation decisions.

Force structure and military strategy interact to produce a nation's military posture. (See figure 1–1.) This posture must be able to respond to a wide variety of threats, from strategic nuclear war to low-intensity insurgency.

Nuclear Posture: Doctrine and Forces. The primary goal of nuclear doctrine and its supporting force structure is to deter nuclear war. U.S. nuclear doctrine has evolved in part as a result of the correlation of forces between the United States and the Soviet Union. Whereas once the United States was able to threaten massive retaliation to counter limited aggression, the increase in Soviet nuclear capability has diminished the credibility of such threats. Today the threat to use nuclear weapons is credible only to protect those interests essential to national survival.

If the U.S. nuclear posture is to deter aggression successfully, it must pose the prospect of costs and risks outweighing any prospective gain. There are several requirements for a successful deterrent posture. First, the United States must have a secure nuclear force that cannot be destroyed before it can retaliate against an aggressor. Second, it must be able to identify the resources that an aggressor values the most so that any retaliation will result in unacceptable damage. Third, if nuclear force is to be used to deter anything other than a massive direct attack on the United States, the United States must be able to respond to aggression with an appropriate level of force in order to deny the enemy its objectives without risking total destruction. Finally, the credibility of threats to use nuclear force rests on the aggressor's perception of the capabilities and the determination of the United States to use them.

In order to meet these requirements, nuclear doctrine addresses issues such as how nuclear forces should be deployed and how they should be targeted. Force structure issues such as whether the United States must maintain a triad of nuclear capabilities comprised of bombers, land-based intercontinental ballistic missiles (ICBMs), and submarine-launched ballistic missiles (SLBMs) influence the strategy we adopt as well as strategies we can implement.

Both the United States and the Soviet Union maintain nuclear forces designed to bridge the gap between conventional and strategic nuclear forces. These weapons range from cannon-launched nuclear warheads designed for battlefield use, to intermediate-range ballistic missiles (IRBMs) such as the Soviet SS-20 and the U.S. Pershing II. In addition to enhancing deterrence by providing the link between conventional and strategic nuclear forces, these weapons provide an alternative to strategic nuclear war should conventional defense fail.

While strategic nuclear war is the most violent part of the conflict spectrum and the United States must have strategies and forces to deal with the threat of nuclear attack, there are other military threats that nuclear weapons have been unable to eliminate. As a result, the United States must have doctrine and forces to counter nonnuclear threats so that it is not faced with the unpleasant choice of using nuclear weapons and risking nuclear devastation in return, or acquiescing to aggression.

Conventional Posture: Doctrine and Forces. Conventional doctrine and forces address the levels of conflict below nuclear war. These range from high-intensity conventional war between NATO and the Warsaw Pact to low-intensity operations. General-purpose forces are the primary means of projecting power and thus must be flexible enough to respond to a wide variety of military threats anywhere in the world.

General-purpose forces consist of the nonnuclear components of the U.S. Army, Navy, and Air Force. The primary functions of the army are to prepare for prompt and sustained land combat, provide air defense, prepare for joint amphibious and airborne operations, and provide occupation forces. The primary functions of the navy, including the Marine Corps, are to prepare for prompt and sustained combat at sea, control vital sea areas, protect sea-lines of communications, and prepare for joint amphibious operations. The primary function of the air force is to prepare for prompt and sustained air combat operations, control vital air areas, gain and maintain air supremacy, establish local air superiority, provide air transport to the armed forces, and prepare for joint amphibious and airborne operations.

These missions, and others, when viewed in the context of U.S. interests and strategy, determine the force requirements of the United States. Thus, for example, President John Kennedy's military strategy of flexible response required 28 divisions, 41 fighter-attack wings, 600 ships, and an airlift capability of 300,000 tons (or 8 divisions); however, this total force structure never was deployed, in large part because of the tremendous defense expenditures that would have been required. Consequently, the United States has been forced to rely on the relatively cheaper reserve military forces and on mobilization in order to meet force structure requirements. The reduction of active military forces, as a result of the 1972 shift to an all-volunteer force, has placed even greater requirements on U.S. reserve forces. Thus, in the mid-1980s, 46 percent of the total army and 32 percent of the tactical fighter aircraft are found in the reserve.

Further, since national resources are finite, general-purpose forces compete for resources with nuclear forces. Since conventional forces are so much more expensive to develop and maintain, nuclear forces often appear to be a better bargain. There also is competition among the different types of conventional forces. The limitation on resources and the competition for those resources not only force trade-offs between guns and butter but also between nuclear and conventional forces and among land, air, and sea forces.

Conclusions

The need to formulate and implement a national security policy that achieves a nation's interests in the most efficient and effective way often results in formal efforts to rationalize the policy process. Yet the nature of the process can result in the existence of discontinuities in national security policy.

The first discontinuity exists between military strategy and force structure. In an ideal world, a military strategy would be developed to achieve specific interests and then a force structure would be developed to ensure that the strategy could be implemented. As we have seen, however, the national security process does not guarantee the formulation of a coherent, integrated, and accepted military strategy. Even in those instances where such a strategy is formulated, the process again can interfere in the development of the requisite force structure.

The second discontinuity exists between interests and capabilities, a spectrum that goes beyond military strategy and force structure. The same factors that contribute to the first discontinuity also contribute to the second. However, an interest-capability discontinuity also can result from the nature of the U.S. political system. Changes in administration can bring about redefinitions or reinterpretation of national interests. Given the nearly decade-long development process for new weapons systems and the length of time required to develop new economic and diplomatic policies, it is clear that changes in U.S. interests may cause a discontinuity as a result of this capability lag.

Nonetheless, U.S. national security policies are not characterized solely by discontinuities. Changes in administration, for example, do not necessarily result in changes in any, or all, national interests. The security of Western Europe has remained a defined interest of every U.S. administration for at least the last half-century. Our interest in deterring nuclear aggression has been with us since the dawn of the nuclear age.

National security, then, is a dynamic concept. Changes in the international and domestic environments can require new policies or revalidate old ones. Continuities and discontinuities can exist either vertically, between interests and capabilities, or horizontally, over time. It is for this reason that the analytical framework presented here has been constructed; it provides the means by which students can evaluate the U.S. national security policies of the past, present, and future. While an understanding of current security issues is important, unless they are viewed within a larger context, such an understanding of time-sensitive issues does little to prepare one for anticipating and understanding future issues.

The remainder of this book explores and develops the analytic framework constructed here. The framework has been divided into various parts to facilitate comprehension. Each part is preceded by an essay that explains how the chapters in the part fit together to illuminate the major points of the part. Finally, an examination of the evolution of U.S. national security policy since World War II is provided so that the student can see how the framework can be applied to analyze and evaluate policy. The concluding chapter poses some of the potential national security issues of the future and suggests some factors that might be considered in analyzing them should they occur.

Notes

1. Arnold Wolfers, *Discord and Collaboration, Essays on International Politics* (Baltimore: Johns Hopkins University Press, 1962), p. 150.

2. Frank N. Trager and Frank L. Simone, "An Introduction to the Study of National Security," in *National Security and American Society: Theory, Process and Policy,* ed. Frank Trager and Phillip S. Kronenberg (Lawrence: University of Kansas Press, 1973), p. 36.

3. Samuel Huntington, *The Common Defense* (New York: Columbia University Press, 1961), p. 2.

4. Robert Jervis, *Perception and Misperception in International Politics,* (Princeton: Princeton University Press, 1976), p. 64.

5. Hans J. Morgenthau, *Politics among Nations* (New York: Alfred A. Knopf, 1948), p. 175.

6. Glenn Snyder, *Deterrence and Defense: Toward a Theory of National Security* (Princeton: Princeton University Press, 1961), p. 9.

7. George Brown and Lawrence Korb, "The Economic and Political Constraints on Force Planning," *American Defense Policy,* ed. John Reichart and Steven Sturm (Baltimore: Johns Hopkins University Press, 1982), p. 581.

8. Huntington, *Common Defense,* p. 2.

9. Graham T. Allison, *Essence of Decision* (Boston: Little, Brown, 1971), p. 176.

10. David Easton, *A Framework for Political Analysis* (Englewood Cliffs, N.J.: Prentice-Hall, 1965), chap. 7.

Discussion Questions

1. What are the purposes of the analytical framework?

2. What are the three components of national security policy and how are they related?

3. What is meant by (a) *horizontal discontinuities* and (b) *vertical discontinuities*? Give an example of each.

4. One of the most famous quotations from Clausewitz is his statement that war "is merely the continuation of policy by other means." What are the implications of this statement for the relationship between military power and national security?

Part II
The National Security Environment

T he national security environment provides the context within which national strategy and national security policy are formulated. National interests are identified as a result of the interaction of values with the international and domestic environments. What are the characteristics of the national security environment that influence strategy and policy? How do the international and domestic environments affect the development of a nation's security policy? A more thorough analysis of the nature of the national security environment is needed in order to answer these fundamental questions.

Ambiguity

Few would argue with the premise that national security is one of the most important objectives of states, yet the ambiguity of the concept complicates the formulation or implementation of policies and makes the achievement of absolute security an unattainable goal. As Robert Osgood has noted, national security, "like danger, is an uncertain quality; it is relative, not absolute; it is largely subjective and takes countless forms."[1]

Given the ambiguities inherent in the search for security, how can nations develop coherent policies and programs that will result in a sense of national well-being? There is no precise formula available; nations are faced with the problem of choosing among the values that deserve protection, the level of security necessary to protect those values, and the means by which to achieve that level of security.[2] The attainment of these objectives involves some degree of judgment and choice. While there may be general agreement on the values that should be protected (independence, justice, peace), there will be much less certainty about the degree of security necessary to protect them. Since absolute security is unattainable, inherent in choosing an acceptable level of security is the acceptance of a tolerable level of insecurity. Further, the finite resources available for the establishment of the means designed to achieve the desired level of security impose limits on the number of programs which can be instituted.

The quest for security, then, is not (and should not be viewed as) deterministic. There is no simple and clear-cut set of objectives that will yield an unambiguous level of security if pursued diligently.

International Environment

The international environment can be characterized as an anarchic system, that is, one in which national interests conflict and no supranational organization exists as the final arbiter of national disputes. The absence of a legitimate central government means that each state must be responsible for its own security. Some of the traditional means by which states have attempted to protect their interests, preserve the peace, and regulate the behavior of other states include international law, diplomacy, and alliance arrangements. Recent innovations in the management of international behavior include collective security organizations such as the UN, regional organizations such as NATO and the Organization of American States (OAS), and extranational organizations such as the European Economic Community (EEC) and OPEC.

The structure of the international environment is shaped by the number of major actors involved in the system and the distribution of power among them. Today the international system can be described as militarily bipolar and politically multipolar. The military power of the United States and the Soviet Union is unmatched by any other nation or group of nations. The nuclear forces of the United States and the USSR provide each nation with overwhelming military capabilities. However, the traditional advantages associated with military superiority are being muted by the destructiveness of nuclear weapons. The desire of the superpowers to avoid direct military confrontation means that nuclear weapons would be used only in situations involving the preservation of the most vital national security interests. As a consequence of this restriction on the utility of nuclear force, the traditional link between military strength and positive political achievements has been loosened.

An international system that is politically multipolar has resulted from the limitation on the use of force, the development of independent centers of economic power such as Western Europe, Japan, and the OPEC countries, and the emergence of newly independent states of widely varying degrees of political and economic influence to which the nuclear balance is of little relevance. In such a system, the military superpowers do not exercise the degree of influence over many weaker states that the imbalance of military power might suggest. Indeed, the nuclear balance of terror may have given new freedom of action to middle-sized and small powers.

The primary danger in a politically multipolar system is that the superpowers may become involved in local disputes, either directly or through the use of proxies. The proliferation of nation-states increases the prospects of international instability, and the development of regional centers of political and economic power could create new areas of conflict. Therefore the politically fragmented nature of the international system may be conducive to the increased likelihood of superpower involvement in local or regional disputes, which could result in a direct confrontation between the United States and the Soviet Union.

Given the international environment characterized here, how do nations define interests and develop strategies and security policies designed to contribute to the preservation of national values and the maintenance of an international political system amenable to them? The first step in the development of a national strategy is to determine potential threats to national interests. Accurate threat assessment is problematic, however, since it is as much a matter of perception as of objective reality.

Threat Assessment

Threat assessment is not nearly the exact science that the development of modern reconnaissance and surveillance means would seem to make it. There is still a great deal of uncertainty involved in measuring the intentions and capabilities of a potential adversary, a situation unlikely to be alleviated because of two intrinsic difficulties associated with the problem of threat perception.

First, threat assessments rest on estimates of the past and present. Those estimates are inferences from usually fragmentary, ambiguous, and sometimes contradictory bits of information subject to interpretation. In the face of uncertainty, decision makers will tend to fit incoming information into their predetermined expectations and beliefs. In other words, actors tend to perceive what they expect.[3]

The second inherent difficulty involved in evaluating threats is that the perceptions based on past and present estimates must be projected into the future, and there can be no reliable information about the future.[4] Two distinct consequences result from this uncertainty. First, assumptions about future enemy capabilities tend to be based on straight line projections of past and present activity. These projections are used particularly when a potential opponent has been increasing its military inventory. Estimates based on assumptions about future activity can lead to threat inflation, a perception that the improvements in an adversary's military capabilities will continue inexorably. Further, uncertainty about the exact nature and extent of an adversary's programs can lead to the acceptance of a worst case analysis, the presumption being that it is more dangerous to underestimate risks and dangers than it is to overestimate them.[5] Security policies developed in response to such assessments may be more extensive than necessary, resulting in misperceptions on both sides and becoming self-fulfilling prophecies.

The second consequence that results from uncertainty about the future is the tendency to concentrate on enemy capabilities rather than intentions. The improving precision with which the United States can measure the Soviet Union's military inventory reinforces the tendency to concentrate on capabilities rather than intentions, which do not lend themselves to precise measurement. The prudent military planner will argue that intentions can change rapidly, whereas capabilities evolve much more slowly. Since even the best of intentions can be reversed quickly as a result of internal domestic political factors or a sudden change in leadership, the argument is that threat assessment must be based on capabilities, not intentions.

The major difficulty with this view of threat perception is that an opponent's military force structure can be the result of a number of factors. Internal bureaucratic influences may lead to the extensive production of certain items of equipment. An even more significant consideration is that an adversary may not perceive threats in the same way. For example, U.S. military planners tend to discount the role that the Chinese threat plays in the development of Soviet conventional (and, to a lesser extent, nuclear) forces.

Despite the inherent difficulties and uncertainties involved in threat assessments, the first step in the development of security policy must be to identify those nations or other actors inimical to one's values and that possess the ability to threaten one's national interests. The Soviet Union poses the greatest political threat to U.S. national interests because of its opposing political philosophy and its substantial military capabilities. Edward Warner III in chapter 2 describes the nature and sources of Soviet power, the Soviet perception of the international environment, Soviet security objectives, and the strategy designed to achieve those objectives.

Alliances

A second factor in the international environment that affects a nation's interests and security policies is the nature of alliances. Alliances are an integral feature of political life among interacting sovereign states.[6] They are an important factor in the national security environment because alliances can create inducements for action, as well as constrain a nation's freedom of action.

As the most binding and far-reaching type of obligation among states, alliances not only integrate the interests of alliance members within the geographic limits of the alliance, they also can weave together the interests of alliance partners in areas outside the geographic limits of the alliance. Consequently alliance relationships can expand the scope of interests and commitments of alliance partners. For example, longstanding French interests in Indochina shaped U.S. perceptions of the importance of the region. When the French withdrew from Indochina in 1954, the United States felt compelled to become involved in order to promote stability and oppose communist influence in the region. Similarly, when the British withdrew from the Middle East following World War II, the alliance relationship between the United States and Great Britain had created a community of interest such that the United States assumed the burden of protecting Western interests in the region.

Alliances can create inducements for action that might not otherwise exist. For example, the Soviet alliance with Cuba makes it possible for the Soviet Union to use Cuban troops for the furtherance of Soviet interests in central Africa. On the other hand, alliances can constrain national policy. The nations of Western Europe generally favor expanding economic ties with the Soviet Union, but U.S. opposition has prevented the development of a more extensive trading relationship.

Prior to 1945, the international system was characterized by multiple centers of military and political power. Alliance relationships tended to be flexible; they changed frequently as changes in the balance of power made old alignments obsolete and required a new lineup of partners for a stable military balance. The benefits of alliance membership tended to be mutual because most important nations were roughly equal in power. The balance of power system that operated in Europe from the defeat of Napoleon in 1815 until the outbreak of World War I in 1914 relied on flexible alliance arrangements to prevent one nation from attaining a position of dominance.

Today, alliances remain very much an important aspect of a nation's security environment. However, the technological changes brought about by the development of nuclear weapons and the emergence of two military superpowers have had an effect on the traditional rationale for alliance formation and on the distribution of benefits within an alliance.

The enormous disparity in power between the superpowers and their allies means that the distribution of military benefits is unequal. The rationale for alliance membership remains essentially unchanged: a sense of common threat. However, the tremendous difference in military power within each alliance means that each superpower is, in effect, providing a unilateral guarantee for the security of its allies.

The principal function of each superpower's alliance structure is to define as clearly as possible the areas that it considers vital and to protect them against encroachment by the other superpower. For example, the United States established alliance relationships with forty-three nations around the Sino-Soviet periphery in the decade following World War II. The purpose of this "pactomania" was to prevent what the United States perceived as the expansionist tendencies of the communist governments of the USSR and the People's Republic of China. While most of these alliance partners contributed only marginally to the military power available to the United States, their membership in a formal alliance served to draw the line beyond which the United States was prepared to resist the expansion of communist influence.

The nuclear stalemate between the United States and the Soviet Union has had a paradoxical effect on the nature of the postwar alliances, particularly in the West. Formally, the alliances have been much less flexible than the alliance systems of the nineteenth century; there have been relatively few major changes in membership; however, the political latitude available to the middle-level powers such as France and Great Britain has been increased significantly. Differing perceptions about the nature and degree of the threat posed by the Soviet Union may lead to substantial disagreements within NATO on what constitutes appropriate national policy. For example, the nations of Western Europe may see increased trade with the USSR as both prudent politically and advantageous economically, whereas the United States may be reluctant to see the West European economies tied more closely to the Soviet Union.

The growth of European and Japanese economic strength and political independence means that the United States cannot hope to maintain the position of political dominance it occupied following World War II. The United States must develop an alliance management strategy cognizant of the fact that alliance members may, on certain issues, have different perceptions of what is in their national interest. Differences are to be expected; however, these differences should be accepted within the context of the much larger areas of fundamental agreement on political, economic, and military issues.

In chapter 3, Robert E. Osgood examines the reasons for alliance formation and describes what he believes are the principal functions of alliances. His discussion of the evolution of alliances highlights their importance as instruments of international politics and supports the conclusion that alliances remain as important today as they have been in other periods of history.

Technology

The national security environment is one of complexity, uncertainty, and change. Among the chief factors responsible for this condition is technology. National security policy provides a major stimulus for technological development. National security is not always improved by advances in technology, however. Scientific advancement knows no nationality, and few frontiers are impermeable to the diffusion of knowledge. Thus, while it offers the possibility of improving significantly human control over the environment, technology may also increase both the risk and the cost of its misuse.

Technology affects the political, economic, and military aspects of relations among nations, thereby contributing to the increasingly complex international environment. Advancements in communications have had a direct influence on diplomacy, making it possible for national leaders to talk directly to their allies and adversaries alike, thereby reducing the possibility of delay or confusion that might result from the use of intermediaries. The reliance of defense and other high-technology industries on relatively rare minerals that must be imported has made the stability of the nations producing these strategic materials a matter of interest and concern to the importing nations. The economic interdependence that results from the need for raw materials and energy means that no nation can be isolated from the international environment. In sum, technology has made the world smaller and more complex and has made all nations more susceptible to the consequences of events in once distant lands.

Technological change presents a two-fold challenge: to direct changes into channels that improve security and to develop structures of control over new technology. For national security policy, these requirements translate into the need for the effective application of technology and the careful development of strategies consistent with the resulting capabilities.

The effective application of technology for national security purposes requires the careful balancing of two contradictory imperatives, for technology is a double-edged sword. On the one hand, the effective use of new technology can result in significant improvements in military capability. New technology is transformed into new equipment with improved capabilities, thereby increasing the effectiveness of a nation's military forces. However, attempts to incorporate every new technological advancement can add unnecessarily to the complexity, fragility, and cost of a new system.

The second problem associated with technological change is the need for the development of strategies and policies consistent with the capabilities resulting from technological advancements. Unfortunately, as Bernard Brodie has observed, the speed and extent of technological changes "have not usually been closely coupled with the strategic and political implications of the relevant changes."[7]

History is replete with examples of the failure of strategy and doctrine to keep pace with technology. The carnage that resulted in World War I is a graphic illustration of what can happen when technology outpaces strategy. A century of relative peace in Europe led to the stagnation of doctrinal development, while the Industrial Revolution had provided weapons of dramatically increased lethality. The military strategies of 1914 were not capable of exploiting the technology at hand. The stalemate that developed along the Western Front was due in large part to the inability of the leadership of either side to adopt new military strategies and tactics that recognized the realities of war imposed by technological change. Thus, in 1915, after over a year of war, Sir Douglas Haig, commander of British forces in France, "delivered himself of the opinion that the machine gun was a much overrated weapon."[8]

The need for strategy to keep pace with the implications of technological innovation raises another difficult question: What impact does technological advancement have on the development of national strategies? Do national interests and strategies determine the direction of technological advancement in order for the nation to carry out its policies more effectively, or do programs determine what is possible and thereby affect significantly the direction of national strategy? Put simply, do policies determine programs, or do programs determine policies?

Ideally, policies should determine programs. National security programs should be developed to produce the capabilities needed to carry out national policies; however, the relationship between policies and programs is not always so clearly defined. Technological advancements in military capabilities can create certain conditions of fact, regardless of national policy. For example, improvements in missile accuracy can create the fact of a counterforce capability, whether policymakers desired or required such a capability. At the conventional level, does the ability to project military power over extended distances lead to a U.S. policy of interventionism in the Third World, or does the capability reflect the reasoned decision that the United States has important national interests in many areas of the world and must be prepared to protect those interests?

There is a tendency to regard technology as one of the most important sources of influence in the development of national security policies. Certainly in the era of nuclear weapons, the impact of technology on the well-being of all nations cannot be overemphasized. However, there are two important points that must be recognized concerning the role of technology in the formulation and execution of national security policy. First, technology alone is seldom a determining factor. In 1940 the French had technologically superior tanks, machine guns, and armored vehicles, but they were defeated quickly by a numerically and technologically inferior German force that had developed a doctrine ideally suited to the use of mechanized forces. The U.S. experience in Vietnam demonstrated vividly that technological dominance does not guarantee military victory independent of political circumstances.

Second, if technology is to contribute to the development of an effective national security posture, technological means must be matched to the political ends that such means will serve. Military capability must not be regarded as an end unto itself; it must be integrated into a national security policy that incorporates the economic and diplomatic, as well as the military, dimensions of policy into a coherent strategy for protecting vital national interests.

In chapter 4 Harold Brown addresses the problems associated with the incorporation of technology into effective military capabilities. Brown argues that the United States has a comparative advantage over the Soviet Union in the development and application of modern technology and that this advantage is an important means by which the United States can counter Soviet numerical advantages, particularly in conventional forces, at a lower cost.

Domestic Environment

While the international environment constitutes the arena from which threats to national values and interests are perceived and toward which national security policies ultimately are directed, the development of national strategies, policies, and programs takes place within the crucible of domestic politics. As Samuel Huntington noted, national security policy "exists in two worlds . . . one is international politics, the world of the balance of power, wars and alliances. . . . The other world is domestic politics, the world of interest groups, political parties, social classes, with conflicting interests and goals."[9] The impact of domestic politics on the formulation and execution of national security policy is both clear and substantial. National security policy will never be the result of deductions from a clear statement of national objectives. Because of the domestic environment, national security policy will be the result of politics, not logic.[10]

How do domestic structures influence the determination of national interests and the development of security policy and programs? What are the internal characteristics that can affect a nation's perceptions of the international environment and its role within that environment?

Ideology

Ideology can be a particularly important domestic factor that contributes to the definition of a nation's interests and development of its security policy. Indeed, the protection or promotion of ideology can be a primary objective of a nation's strategy. Revolutionary ideologies that call for the complete transformation of the state system and profess to transcend traditional political boundaries may provide their followers a strong sense of commitment. Opposition to such ideologies can provide an equally strong domestic basis for national strategy. When different domestic structures are based on fundamentally opposing conceptions of what constitutes an acceptable international order, the results likely will be suspicion, hostility, and conflict.

Nationalism

A strong sense of nationalism can be an important element of a nation's domestic environment, with a corresponding effect on its international policies. Pride in a nation's accomplishments or a belief in the establishment or maintenance of cultural or territorial integrity can lead to expansionist policies, particularly if there is no major opposition. The manifest destiny doctrine espoused by some in the United States helped to foster the acquisition of significant amounts of territory. Traumatic historical experiences also can influence a nation's perceptions. The invasions of Russia and the Soviet Union from Western Europe in the past two centuries certainly have influenced the Soviet Union's perceptions of what is necessary to protect its homeland.

National Leaders

The personalities and perceptions of national leaders can play an important role in the determination of security policy. Ideological fervor or early political experiences can influence the way a leader views and responds to world events. For example, the perceived lesson of the 1938 Munich agreement reached between British Prime Minister Neville Chamberlain and Adolf Hitler was that appeasement only whets the appetite of aggressors. Subsequent events seemed to support the conclusion that the only way to deal with an aggressor was with firmness and strength. When Harry Truman was faced with the decision of whether to commit U.S.

troops following the North Korean invasion of South Korea in June 1950, the lesson of Munich no doubt influenced his decision. When decision makers who came to political maturity during the U.S. involvement in Vietnam reach positions of influence in later years, one can surmise that the lessons of Vietnam may be an important experience that will influence their views on the use of U.S. forces in revolutionary wars where the lines are less than clearly drawn.

Organizations

Institutions are an important source of domestic influence on national security policy. Increasing bureaucratization is a characteristic of all modern societies. As a society develops and becomes more complex socially, economically, and politically, the number of administrative agencies needed to deal with various problems grows as well. As organizations grow and mature, officials become increasingly concerned with maintaining the welfare of their agencies. Bureaucracies play an important role in the national security process, for institutions, such as the military services, advise policymakers during the formulation of policy, and these same organizations must implement the adopted policies. Therefore they have a vested interest in the nature of the policies and will attempt to influence them accordingly. The role of organizations is so important that the impact of institutional influence will be examined in more detail in part IV.

Politics and Economics

The extent to which public opinion, the media, interest groups, and economic considerations play an influential role in the development of national security policy depends on the nature of the individual nation and the salience of the issue involved. Obviously the media and public opinion are less influential in a totalitarian society than they are in a democracy. Even in a democracy, not all policy decisions are made in a public forum. Adverse public opinion can be an important source of restraint on policy. On the other hand, public support can be a valuable asset in implementing policies to deal with one's adversaries.

What conclusions can we draw about the importance of the domestic environment for the determination of national security interests and policies? First, it is the domestic environment that determines the amount of total social effort devoted to national security policy.[11] The need to promote economic welfare at home prevents national leaders, be they kings, dictators, or presidents, from spending all of the national treasure on security programs. On the other hand, when the nation is threatened, a supportive public makes it possible to raise the forces and provide the equipment necessary to defend the national interests. The allocation of resources for purposes of national security is rooted firmly in the domestic environment.

A second conclusion is that the domestic environment affects the way in which the international environment will be perceived and interpreted. For example, the perception that the international system is composed of states hostile to a nation's ideology or interests is derived from the nature of the domestic society. The desire of the Soviet Union to protect itself with buffer states in Eastern Europe is the result of both history and ideology.

Finally, the domestic environment is decisive in the elaboration of national goals.[12] If national interests are to be achieved and protected, they must reflect the values the nation seeks to protect. In the end, national strategy and national security policy must be based firmly in and reflective of the domestic environment.

Every nation has its own perspective on the problems of national security. The U.S. approach toward these issues is reflected in a number of basic public attitudes. In chapter 5, Robert Osgood identifies a number of characteristics he believes define the U.S. public's approach to questions of national security. Osgood concludes that the nature of the U.S. domestic political environment inhibits the ability of the United States to exercise self-restraint once it is committed to a conflict.

Notes

1. Robert E. Osgood, *Ideals and Self-Interest in America's Foreign Relations* (Chicago: University of Chicago Press, 1953), p. 443.

2. Arnold Wolfers, *Discord and Collaboration* (Baltimore: Johns Hopkins University Press, 1962), pp. 163–164.

3. Robert Jervis, "Hypotheses on Misperception," *World Politics* 20, no. 3 (April 1968):455.

4. Klaus Knorr, "Threat Perception," in Klaus Knorr, ed., *Historical Dimensions of National Security Problems* (Lawrence: University Press of Kansas, 1976), p. 84.

5. Raymond L. Garthoff, "On Estimating and Imputing Intentions," *International Security* 2, no. 3 (Winter 1979):22.

6. Robert E. Osgood, *Alliances and American Foreign Policy* (Baltimore: Johns Hopkins University Press, 1968), p. 4.

7. Bernard Brodie, "Technology, Politics, and Strategy," *Adelphi Paper No. 55* (London: International Institute for Strategic Studies, March 1969), p. 22.

8. Bernard Brodie, "Technological Change, Strategic Doctrine, and Political Outcomes," in Knorr, *Historical Dimensions*, p. 289.

9. Samuel P. Huntington, *The Common Defense* (New York: Columbia University Press, 1961), p. 1.

10. Ibid., p. 2.

11. Henry A. Kissinger, *American Foreign Policy* (New York: W.W. Norton, 1974), p. 13.

12. Ibid., p. 14.

2
Defense Policy of the Soviet Union

Edward L. Warner III

International Environment and Perceived Threats

The Soviet Union enters the 1980s as one of the world's two superpowers. After over sixty years of Communist rule, the aging leaders in the Kremlin are bound to view the nation's domestic and international accomplishments with considerable satisfaction. Within their lifetime the country has weathered the self-inflicted human losses of Stalin's forced collectivization campaign and bloody purges of the 1930s as well as the catastrophic devastation of the Second World War. They have seen the Soviet Union come back from the very brink of defeat at the hands of Hitler's armies in 1941–42 to become the most powerful nation in Europe and Asia.

The current leaders have also witnessed the realization of many of the most cherished foreign policy goals of their czarist predecessors. These include: (1) the expansion of the country's frontiers during the course of World War II and its immediate aftermath with the forcible annexation of the Baltic states, portions of Poland, Czechoslovakia, and Rumania in the West, and the southern half of Sakhalin Island and the Kurile Islands in the Far East; (2) the establishment of subservient client regimes throughout most of Eastern Europe in the immediate postwar period; and (3) greatly increased Russian presence and influence in many other areas, including the Middle East, South and Southeast Asia, and Africa, as the result of sustained efforts since the mid-1950s. Finally, over the past twenty years, they have presided over a seemingly inexorable expansion of Soviet military power which has succeeded in establishing the Soviet Union as a coequal with the United States in this critical dimension of power potential and has helped them promote their foreign policy interests aggressively throughout the world.

Relative Power Position

It has become commonplace to attribute the superpower status of the Soviet Union almost exclusively to its massive military might. Indisputably, defense efforts enjoy unrivaled primacy within the Soviet economy. Moreover, military

Reprinted with minor revisions from Douglas J. Murray and Paul R. Viotti, eds., *The Defense Policies of Nations: A Comparative Study* (Baltimore: Johns Hopkins University Press, 1982). Reprinted with permission.

power has played a critical role in the growth of Soviet influence in the world. Yet, Soviet claims to superpower status are not based solely on the country's obvious military prowess.

The Soviet Union is one of the world's leading industrial nations. With a gross national product of approximately $1.2 trillion in 1978,[1] the USSR ranks second in the world, behind the United States. Moreover, the Soviet Union leads the world in several economic categories, including annual production of iron ore, steel, cement, petroleum, lumber, and machinery, and trails only the United States in coal and natural gas production and electrical power generation.[2] Soviet economic achievements, however, are considerably less impressive when computed on a per capita basis. Viewed from this perspective, the Soviet Union, much like czarist Russia on the eve of the Revolution in 1917,[3] ranks behind not only the United States but also most of the industrial nations of Western Europe and Asia.[4]

Soviet superpower status has a substantial political and ideological component. Undoubtedly, the international appeal of the Soviet political system has dimmed somewhat in recent years as the shortcomings of the system in individual freedoms and the standard of living of the general populace have become widely known. Nevertheless, the USSR still enjoys considerable influence, particularly in the Third World, as the leader of the world Communist movement and the self-proclaimed champion of the fight against Western imperialism.

Threats Facing the Soviet Union

The Soviets have a deep-seated and historically well-founded concern about foreign military invasion. As former U.S. Ambassador to the Soviet Union Malcolm C. Toon has noted, "Centuries of invasions from both East and West have left their mark on the outlook of the Russian people and its rulers."[5]

Soviet concern about foreign invasion is not based simply on bitter Russian historic experience at the hands of such aggressors as the Mongol hordes of Genghis Khan and Napoleon's *grande armée*. This wariness also reflects direct experience during the Soviet period. The Soviets assiduously keep alive the memory of several foreign incursions: the invasion by imperial Germany just weeks after the Bolsheviks seized power in November 1917; the military interventions of Britain, France, the United States, and Japan on behalf of the rival "White" forces, who battled the Bolsheviks during the Russian Civil War, 1918–20; the border clashes with imperial Japan in 1938 and 1939; and most significant, the devastating effects of the Nazi invasion and brutal occupation in 1941–44.[6] This Soviet "siege mentality"[7] is further intensified by the strong emphasis in Marxist–Leninist ideology on the inevitable hostility of the capitalist powers toward the socialist states and by the Soviets' own repeated warnings about the dangers posed by "capitalist encirclement."

Soviet statements since the end of World War II have left no doubt that the United States has become the USSR's principal enemy. Soviet propaganda has consistently identified the United States as the leading force of "imperialist reaction," dedicated to the defeat of socialism and eagerly poised to attack the Soviet Union at the first opportunity. The only other Western nation that has merited such Soviet concern is the Federal Republic of Germany. The regular Soviet attacks on the "revanchist" goals of the West Germans reflect the deep scars left by two devastating German invasions in this century.

Since the mid-1960s, the Soviets have increasingly come to describe the People's Republic of China as a dangerous external threat. Soviet concern about China has several roots. These include historical distrust that can be traced back to the Mongol dominance of medieval Russia, racial antipathy, intense rivalry for leadership of the international Communist movement, and strongly conflicting foreign policy aspirations, particularly in Asia. This concern also reflects justifiable Soviet anxiety about the long-term threat posed by a mammoth neighbor with whom they share a 4,500-mile frontier and that has a population of over a billion, a growing nuclear capability, and a decidedly hostile attitude toward the USSR.

Having noted the Soviet obsession with defense and the threat of foreign invasion, we must not overlook the degree to which the Soviets and their czarist predecessors have successfully employed offensive military power to promote their foreign policy interests and to expand their frontiers. Neighboring countries such as Finland, Poland, Bulgaria, and Turkey, to say nothing of the formerly independent Baltic states of Lithuania, Latvia, and Estonia, and, most recently, Afghanistan, periodically have been the victims of Russian coercion and invasion. Buoyed by the apparent political utility of their growing military power, the Soviet leaders today almost certainly view the international scene more as an arena of substantial opportunity for the advancement of their interests than as a source of threats to the security of the USSR.

The national security concerns of the leaders in the Kremlin are not limited to external considerations. They also take very seriously the threat of internal political opposition. Their anxieties in this regard include concerns about oppositional political movements and the nationalistic aspirations of several of the minorities within the Soviet multinational state. Soviet spokesmen have traditionally attributed such opposition to the "diversionary activities" of foreign adversaries. Harsh internal security measures to deal with the subversive activities of so-called rotten capitalist elements were especially prominent in the early years of the Bolshevik regime. Fears of "class enemies" were manipulated by Stalin in particular to justify the ruthless suppression of political opposition groups in a series of bloody purges in the 1930s.

These fears of subversion and the attendant internal security measures to deal with this threat are still present today, although in much attenuated form compared with the days of Stalin's paranoia and terror. Nevertheless, the Soviet leadership remains vigilant and determined to deal ruthlessly with serious internal opposition, as evidenced in the wave of repression in the 1970s against dissidents of various persuasions undertaken by the secret police, the KGB. Despite its determined pursuit of détente with the West since the late 1960s, the Soviet regime has made it absolutely clear that there will be no relaxation of ideological or political controls on the domestic scene. Rather, it is precisely in such an atmosphere, with its attendant increased contacts with foreigners and their culture, that the Soviet leaders have insisted that tight social controls are most necessary and thus must be intensified.

Self-perception of the Soviet Leadership

The Soviet perspective on world affairs contains an amalgam of traditional Russian and Marxist–Leninist ideological elements. Much has been written about the relative weight of these two factors in Soviet foreign policy. These discussions are of limited value, since to a considerable extent the two traditions reinforce Soviet inclinations toward expansionism on the world scene.

Both the Russian imperial heritage and the Marxist–Leninist tradition provide support for a highly centralized, authoritarian government and a heavily regulated economy. Both traditions also call for defense of the ruling regime as the most fundamental objective of the Soviet state. Both are also marked by strong messianic strains. The Russian tradition included a centuries-old belief that the Russian Empire was the "Third Rome," the successor to Byzantium, and the defender of the true orthodox Christian faith. Moreover, Russia was viewed as having a special right to exercise hegemony throughout the Slavic areas of southeastern Europe. The imperial tradition was also marked by a paradoxical mix of attitudes about Russia and the West. It combined an almost mystical veneration of things Russian with a nagging sense of inferiority regarding the economic and technological achievements of the industrially advanced West.

Marxist–Leninist ideology provides the Soviets, as the leading Communist power, with a similar sense of being historically chosen. It also provides an element of long-term optimism by positing that communism will inevitably triumph over capitalism. This ideological self-confidence was well captured in Nikita Khrushchev's famous boast that Soviet communism would eventually "bury" the capitalist West.

Both the Russian imperialist tradition and Marxism–Leninism reinforce Soviet tendencies toward an expansionist foreign policy. The czarist pattern of territorial aggrandizement was largely characterized by the forcible incorporation of contiguous areas along Russia's lengthy European and Asian frontiers. The imperial Russian regimes were not, however, without longer-range ambitions, as evidenced by various diplomatic initiatives and involvements in Western Europe, the Far East, the Middle East, and even Africa.[8] Moreover, it is perfectly reasonable to expect that any twentieth-century Russian government, having industrialized and thus begun to realize the country's immense geopolitical potential,[9] would have broadened its horizons and sought to extend its influence on a global scale.

Some observers nevertheless attribute Soviet expansionist international behavior almost solely to a Marxist–Leninist drive for world domination. This school of thought asserts that the fundamental teachings of Marx and Lenin about the inevitable defeat of capitalism and the global triumph of socialism remain the key operative foreign policy goals of the Soviet leadership. From this perspective, the Communist leaders of the USSR are viewed as thoroughly committed to a protracted life-and-death struggle for power and as determined to expand their influence at every possible opportunity.

Regardless of whether one is inclined toward the traditional Russian great-power or ideological interpretations of Soviet motivations in the world, there is little doubt that the Soviet leadership today perceives the USSR as a major international actor with a right to be heard, if it chooses, on virtually any issue. Moreover, proud of its status as one of the world's two nuclear superpowers and the recognized leader of the world Communist movement, the Soviet leadership is virtually certain to believe that the Soviet Union should play an even greater role in world politics in the 1980s and beyond.

Interdependencies

The Soviet Union has an extensive series of treaty commitments, as befits a superpower. The most prominent of these is the multilateral Treaty of Friendship, Mutual Assistance, and Cooperation, signed in Warsaw, Poland, on May 14, 1955. This alliance, commonly known as the Warsaw Pact, commits the Soviet Union and the Communist regimes of Poland, Hungary, East Germany, Czechoslovakia, Bulgaria, and Rumania to the joint defense of their European territories. [The USSR also has close ties with these countries and Cuba through the Council for Economic Mutual Assistance (usually abbreviated as CEMA or COMECON).—Ed.] Originally conceived as a response to the rearmament of the Federal Republic of Germany and its admission into NATO, this treaty has become, over the years, a major policy instrument for the Soviets' domination of their Communist client states in Eastern Europe.

The common-defense commitments of the Warsaw Pact are reinforced by bilateral treaties of friendship and mutual assistance between the Soviet Union and each of the other member states. The Soviets have also signed bilateral status-of-forces agreements with East Germany, Poland, Hungary, and Czechoslovakia that provide for the stationing of Soviet troops in these countries. Soviet military forces permanently deployed in Eastern Europe include two tank divisions and a tactical air army within the Northern Group of Forces in Poland; five divisions (three motorized rifle and two tank) and a tactical air army within the Central Group of Forces in Czechoslovakia; four divisions (two motorized rifle and two tank) and a tactical air army in Hungary; and twenty divisions (ten motorized rifle and ten tank) and a tactical air army in the Group of Soviet Forces Germany (GSFG).[10]

There are a series of high-level military and political consultative bodies associated with the Warsaw Pact. All are thoroughly dominated by the Soviet Union. The most important are the Political Consultative Committee (whose membership includes the Communist party first secretaries, heads of governments, and defense and foreign ministers from each member state) and the Council of Defense Ministers. Both of these bodies convene on an average of twice a year. The military command structure of the Warsaw Pact is led by the Joint High Command, headquartered in Moscow. This command is headed by a senior Soviet officer, who serves as commander-in-chief of the Warsaw Pact. This post is currently occupied by Marshal V.G. Kulikov, who is also a Soviet first deputy minister of defense. The military commander also includes a chief of staff (currently General of the Army A.I. Gribkov), who traditionally serves simultaneously as a deputy chief of the Soviet General Staff. In addition, general officers from each of the member states represent their nations at the Warsaw Pact headquarters in Moscow.

The Soviets have bilateral "friendship" treaties with several other states. The oldest is with the Mongolian People's Republic, which has been allied with the Soviet Union since the creation of this vassal state under direct Soviet sponsorship in 1921. Soviet military cooperation with the regime in Ulan Bator is currently governed by a treaty of friendship, cooperation, and mutual aid signed on January 16, 1966. This pact provides for the permanent stationing of several Soviet divisions in Mongolia.[11] Over the past decade, the Soviets have signed ten other treaties of friendship and cooperation. These treaties have allied the Soviets with several Third World countries, including Egypt (May 1971), India (August 1971), Iraq (April 1972), Somalia (July 1974), Angola (October 1976), Mozambique (March 1977), Vietnam (November 1978), Ethiopia (November 1978), Afghanistan (December 1978), and South Yemen (October 1979). The treaties with Egypt and Somalia are no longer in effect, having been terminated by those countries in March 1976 and November 1977, respectively, after their relations with the Soviet Union had deteriorated severely.

Most of these treaties contain provisions calling for military cooperation between the parties, the only exceptions being the pacts with India and Vietnam. All ten were accompanied by varying degrees of Soviet military assistance, Soviet utilization of basing facilities, and, in some cases, the substantial presence of Soviet military personnel. Most recently, the treaty with Afghanistan was invoked by the Soviets in December 1979 to justify their invasion that toppled the Amin regime. It is likely that the treaty will also be utilized as the legal basis for the prolonged stationing of several Soviet divisions within Afghanistan. The eight treaties of friendship and cooperation remaining in effect provide dramatic evidence of expanding Soviet involvement in Africa, the Middle East, and Asia.

National Objectives, National Strategy, and Military Doctrine

National Security Objectives

The most fundamental security objectives of the Soviet leaders are the defense of the Communist regime and the territorial integrity of the USSR. The bitter experience of the Nazi invasion during World War II and the deap-seated patriotism of the Russian people provide a solid basis for a shared commitment between the Communist party leadership and the Soviet people regarding the primacy of defense considerations.

The Soviet near-obsession with defense has provided a powerful impetus for the accumulation of military power and for the steady expansion of Soviet political and military control beyond the nation's political frontiers. Motivated by what some observers have called a quest for "absolute security," the Soviets have, for over sixty years, accorded the highest investment priority to defense. In addition, they have sought to establish and enlarge a territorial buffer, particularly in Europe, between themselves and their prospective enemies. This drive to erect a *cordon sanitaire* lay behind the Soviet establishment of its first Communist satellite regime in Outer Mongolia in 1921 and the Soviet absorption of the Baltic states and eastern portions of Poland, Finland, Czechoslovakia, and Rumania in 1939–40. It also lay behind the subsequent westward expansion of this buffer zone via the forcible establishment of "baggage train" Communist regimes, which were imposed throughout most of Eastern Europe in the wake of the advance of the Red Army at the end of World War II.

Retention of subservient Communist governments throughout Eastern Europe has remained a high-priority Soviet security objective throughout the postwar period. This unrelenting Soviet determination has been visibly demonstrated in the Soviet army's brutal suppression of would-be defector regimes in Hungary in 1956 and Czechoslovakia in 1968. The Soviets demonstrated a similar willingness to employ armed force to maintain a "friendly" Communist regime in power in neighboring states in Asia, as evidenced by their 1979 invasion of Afghanistan. This apparent application of the so-called Brezhnev Doctrine, which justifies Soviet armed intervention to defend allied "socialist" regimes endangered by "counterrevolution,"[12] beyond the previous bounds of Eastern Europe does not augur well for other Third World states that have allied themselves with the Soviet Union.

Soviet national security objectives are not confined to these broadly construed "defensive" concerns. As noted earlier, Russian great-power and Marxist–Leninist drives combine to underwrite a strong impulse to expand Soviet influence in areas adjacent to the USSR and throughout the world. Soviet leaders, like their Russian predecessors, have evidenced consistent interest in gaining increased influence in Western Europe, the Middle East, and the energy-rich Persian Gulf. Moreover, during the past two decades, Soviet political and military spokesmen have increasingly come to speak about and utilize military power as a primary instrument for the promotion of their state interests.[13]

The Soviets are intensely concerned about their relative position in the international arena. They regularly assess their overall position in the world in terms of what they call the "correlation of forces" (*sootnosheniye sil*). In Soviet usage, this correlation refers to the overall balance of economic, military, scientific, and sociopolitical capabilities between two competing states or coalitions of states. Soviet analysts frequently calculate the correlation of forces both between themselves and their leading rival, the United States, and between the socialist and capitalist camps.

The Soviets are invariably optimistic about the long-term trends in the correlation of forces. This optimism reflects the basic tenet of Marxism–Leninism that socialism/communism will inevitably triumph over the capitalist order. Since the close of World War II, the Soviets have consistently claimed that the correlation of forces is shifting inexorably in the favor of the socialist states led by the Soviet Union. Given their relentless accumulation of military power over the past fifteen years, the Soviets have considerable basis to support this contention.

Undoubtedly, the Soviet leaders aspire to be the world's dominant political, military, and economic power. Soviet military experts frequently analyze the narrower military balance, which they describe as the "correlation of military forces and means," between themselves and their prospective enemies.[14] Discussions in this regard range from simple quantitative comparisons of the East–West balance of strategic nuclear or general purpose forces to sophisticated dynamic analyses of relative military capabilities in various scenarios, often using complex mathematical force-effectiveness calculations.[15]

Soviet declarations regarding the state of the military balance and Soviet objectives in the military competition with the West have varied considerably. For several decades, dating as far back as declarations accompanying the early five-year economic and defense plans of the 1930s, the Soviets openly declared their intention to acquire military superiority over their prospective enemies. Moreover, in the late 1950s and early 1960s, Soviet political and military figures asserted that Soviet military capabilities were superior to those of the West. The most prominent example of such claims was the series of outspoken assertions by Party First Secretary Nikita Khrushchev in the late 1950s that the Soviet Union was superior to the United States in strategic missile strength. These boasts, made against the backdrop of dramatic Soviet Sputnik launches, helped spur the United States to make determined efforts to overcome what was later revealed to have been an illusory "missile gap."[16] The fact that the resultant surge of U.S. strategic missile deployments placed the Soviets at a distinctly inferior position throughout the 1960s may help explain the Soviet avoidance of such bold claims of military advantage since that time.

The Soviets have exhibited increased circumspection in public declarations regarding their goals in the East–West arms competition over the past decade. Military figures wrote openly in the 1960s and on into the mid-1970s of the need to attain military-technological superiority over their adversaries.[17] Nevertheless, Soviet claims of the possession of such superiority tapered off significantly in the early 1970s and virtually disappeared from Soviet public discourse in the latter half of the 1970s. This occurred at the very time when the unrelenting momentum of Soviet arms programs was leading many Western observers to argue that the Soviet Union was, in fact, embarked upon a drive to attain clear-cut military superiority. The Soviet declaratory stance since 1977 has become, instead, one of strongly rebutting these Western charges and of asserting that the Soviet Union seeks nothing more than military parity with the West.[18] Whatever their public position, the combination of military doctrinal incentive, residual siege mentality, and their apparent conviction regarding the political utility of vast military power are such that the Soviet leaders are almost certain to continue to seek and to attain substantial military advantage over their capitalist foes.

The Soviet armed forces make important contributions to the fulfillment of the regime's internal objectives as well. The military forces of the Ministry of Defense have infrequently been involved in the maintenance of domestic order. Over the past two decades their activity in this regard has been limited to occasional use in extraordinary circumstances, such as their reported involvement in the forcible suppression of striking workers in Novocherkassk in 1962[19] and the quelling of rioters protesting food shortages in Rostov in 1963.[20]

The regular troops of the Ministry of Defense are unlikely to see this type of action often because such incidents occur extremely infrequently in the Soviet Union. Moreover, responsibility for the maintenance of public order rests primarily with the Ministry of Internal Affairs (MVD) and the Committee of State Security (KGB), both of which have sizable forces organized in regular military formations available for such contingencies. These internal security troops are, interestingly, included by the Soviets as an element of the Soviet armed forces.

By far the most important domestic political role played by the Soviet military establishment occurs in the area of political socialization. Some two million young men are inducted into the Soviet armed forces annually for terms of service of one and a half to three years.[21] During their stints in the military, these young men are exposed to an intensive indoctrination effort supervised by the political officers of the Main Political Administration. . . . Compulsory attendance at five hours of weekly political instruction conducted by the political officers and mandatory participation in the activities of the Young Communist League, the Komsomol, are utilized in a determined effort to inculcate the desired domestic and foreign policy perspectives. These experiences within the armed forces represent the final phase of a sustained, Party-controlled political indoctrination campaign, begun in the nursery schools and elementary schools, that is designed to meet the regime's long-term objective of developing properly oriented "new Soviet men."

The Soviet armed forces also contribute in various ways to the functioning of the Soviet economy. Soviet army personnel stationed in agricultural regions within the USSR are regularly called upon to aid in the harvest. In addition, contingents of the 400,000-person Construction Troops, although predominantly involved in the construction of defense-related facilities, are also employed to build a variety of civilian projects, such as Moscow State University, Sheremetovo Airport, and multistory apartment buildings in Moscow.[22] Both the Construction Troops and the Ministry of Defense's Railroad Troops are working on the Soviet showcase construction project of the late seventies and early eighties, the new rail line, called the Baikal-Amur Magistral (BAM), which will run parallel to the legendary Tran-Siberian Railroad through Siberia and the Far East to the Pacific.

National Security Strategy

Despite the Soviet penchant for authoritative programmatic statements and the voluminous output of their sizable communities of political commentators and professional military theoreticians, there is no single, publicly available document or group of documents that sets forth the Soviet strategy for pursuing its national security objectives. It is quite likely that even within the inner councils of the Kremlin no such document exists. Nevertheless, on the basis of the statements of Soviet political and military spokesmen and the many defense-related activities of the Soviet government, it is possible to piece together what appear to be the broad guidelines of the Soviet national security strategy.

The central element of the Soviet national security strategy is quite straight-forward: the Soviets relentlessly expand and improve their large and diverse military arsenal and then utilize these capabilities to protect and advance their interests on the world scene. First and foremost, the Soviet leaders rely upon their steadily growing military power to deter attack on the Soviet Union itself and on its allies and friends. They accomplish this by maintaining a full spectrum of strategic and general purpose forces.

The Soviets assign the highest priority to the deterrence of nuclear war. Over the past three decades, Soviet spokesmen have repeatedly made deterrent threats, directed primarily at the United States and its NATO allies. Their approach to deterrence has a decidedly traditional military tone. Soviet military and political figures have consistently warned that any state that dares to attack the Soviet Union or its allies will receive a "crushing rebuff" and suffer certain military defeat.

Soviet military doctrine fully supports this war-fighting approach to deterrence. It commits the Soviet armed forces, in the event of a war, to a combination of offensive and defensive operations designed to allow the Soviet Union to survive and prevail in any conflict, including a worldwide nuclear war. Moreover, Soviet force deployments—from the fielding of large numbers of accurate ICBM weapons, which are increasingly capable of successful "counterforce" strikes against U.S. silo-based ICBMs, to the steady upgrading of their vast active and passive defenses, which are designed to limit damage to the Soviet homeland—are consistent with this war-fighting orientation.

This victory-oriented Soviet approach differs markedly from the American perspective on strategic deterrence, which has consistently emphasized a threat to punish any aggressor by devastating his urban-industrial base with retaliatory strikes.[23] This is not to say that the Soviet war-fighting perspective lacks a substantial punishment dimension. Soviet military writings on general nuclear war clearly assign the highest priority to attacks on the enemy's military forces, in particular his nuclear delivery systems. Yet, at the same time, Soviet doctrinal writings also call for extensive strikes against key industrial and political facilities throughout an enemy's homeland with the stated objective of disrupting and devastating his economy and political-administrative apparatus and breaking the morale of his people.

The Soviets have evidenced little interest in restraining their strategic programs in the interest of maintaining a stable nuclear deterrent standoff based on mutual societal vulnerability. From time to time, Soviet diplomats, civilian academics, and even military writers have acknowledged the existence of such a state of mutual vulnerability.[24] Nevertheless, Soviets' doctrinal pronouncements, their unwillingness to constrain significantly their growing hard-target counterforce capabilities in SALT, and most important, their unrelenting drive to acquire survivable forces with comprehensive war-fighting capabilities all point toward an abiding concern for the security of Soviet deterrent capabilities. Nevertheless, the Soviets show little interest in exercising restraint that would assist the United States in maintaining its assured retaliatory capability.

This is not to say that the Soviets have succeeded or are close to succeeding in denying the United States its very substantial nuclear retaliatory capabilities. But it is to recognize that their periodic disclaimers notwithstanding, the Soviets show strong inclinations to do so. The Soviet view of strategic nuclear stability appears to be, quite simply, that the more powerful the USSR is, the more stable the international situation.

The threat to defeat any aggressor in a general nuclear war is the cornerstone of Soviet deterrent policy. It is complemented by a clear determination to acquire the capabilities to fight and win lesser conflicts in major theaters of war along the periphery of the Soviet Union. Soviet preparations to fight successfully in such theater conflicts include a readiness to engage in conventional, chemical, or nuclear warfare supported by the combination of a well-developed combined-arms force-employment doctrine and a panoply of impressive military capabilities.

Throughout their history, the Soviets have confronted a serious "two-front" security challenge due to the presence of hostile, militarily significant adversaries on their extended European and Far Eastern borders. Consequently, the Soviets have long adhered to a "two-war" policy in the sense that they have sought to maintain sufficient forces in both theaters with the capability, at a minimum, to defend these areas independently. This "two-war" policy, or "two-major-contingency approach" in the language of contemporary American defense policy planning, has become increasingly evident since the severe deterioration of Sino-Soviet relations in the early 1960s. Over the past fifteen years, Soviet forces facing China in the Far East and Central Asia have more than doubled in strength. Yet this was accomplished at the same time that Soviet forces stationed in Eastern Europe and the western portions of the Soviet Union were being significantly expanded and upgraded.

In the 1970s, the Soviets dramatically improved their capabilities to project forces by air and sea far beyond the traditional peripheral reach of the Red Army. In this same period, Soviet military writers increasingly touted the role of the

Soviet armed forces in advancing Soviet foreign policy interests throughout the world. These enhanced Soviet force projection capabilities, combined with the Soviet occupation of Afghanistan and its resultant strengthening of Soviet forces in Southwest Asia, suggest the emergence of a new "half-war" or lesser-contingency objective in Soviet national security strategy. This new strategy and attendant capability appear to be directed primarily toward possible operations in the Middle East and the Persian Gulf, with further potential for supporting longer-range projection of Soviet military power into Africa or Southeast Asia as well.

Soviet national security strategy is not confined to the accumulation of military power to support its deterrence and theater-warfare objectives. It also includes the utilization of arms control negotiations and military assistance programs of various types to support the achievement of Soviet foreign policy goals.

The Soviets have participated in virtually all of the important international arms control negotiations since the close of World War II. A major objective of this participation has been the Soviet determination to gain widespread recognition as one of the world's two leading powers. The Soviets have also used these negotiations to support their claims of peace-loving intent on the international scene.

The Soviets' pursuit of what they call "military détente" became a central element in their broader policy of promoting political détente with the West during the 1970s. In addition to the motivations cited above, Soviet arms control efforts have been designed to foster mutual East–West commitments to avoid nuclear conflict. Despite the clearly stated war-winning objectives of their doctrine and the periodic claims by military figures that victory is possible in a nuclear conflict, Soviet military and political commentators have repeatedly acknowledged the catastrophic consequences of general nuclear war and are certain to support its avoidance. The Soviets also seek to use arms control negotiations and agreements to constrain the military activities of their adversaries while maintaining maximum flexibility for themselves. Arms control efforts in pursuit of these objectives are likely to remain a fundamental element of the Soviet national security strategy.

For over fifty years, the Soviets have employed military assistance programs to aid factions struggling to gain power and to support friendly regimes in power against internal opposition or international foes. These programs have frequently proven useful as a means to gain political influence in the recipient nation and, in many cases, to maneuver the recipient into a position of dependence on the Soviet Union for economic support or for maintenance and logistic support of the military equipment provided.

Since the mid-1950s, the Soviets have had considerable experience in this area. Major infusions of military assistance have by no means guaranteed success for the Soviets in their dealing with Third World countries. Despite extensive Soviet military aid programs over several years, the Soviets suffered major setbacks in their dealings with Indonesia in the mid-1960s and Egypt in the mid-1970s. Nevertheless, the Soviets clearly intend to continue to use this instrument to strengthen their ties and create further dependencies with old clients and to seek to move other countries into the Soviet sphere of influence.

Soviet military assistance programs complement growing Soviet capabilities for long-range power projection activities discussed earlier. Arms aid has frequently facilitated initial Soviet acquisition of basing, staging, and transit rights that are critical to operations in distant areas. Military assistance efforts often result in the establishment in distant areas of substantial stockpiles of modern Soviet weapons that can readily be utilized in short order by Soviet-sponsored surrogates like the Cubans or East Germans or directly by Soviet military personnel. Regional and internal tensions that appear inevitable in the Third World in the years ahead suggest that military assistance diplomacy will remain a vital element of Soviet foreign and defense policy.

Domestic Determinants

The Soviet national security strategy is the product of many diverse influences. These include not only the aspirations and concerns derived from Imperial Russian and Soviet historical experience and Marxist–Leninist ideology noted above, but also the geographical character of the USSR and various aspects of the Soviet political and economic systems.

Character of the Political System. Defense is clearly one of the highest-priority policy issues within the Soviet system. As such, it is carefully overseen by the top Soviet leadership. Consequently, all key defense decisions are apparently made (or at least reviewed) by the twenty-three-member Party Politburo, which sits atop the combined Communist party and Soviet government hierarchies. The priority of defense matters is also evident in the fact that each time a single dominant Soviet political leader has emerged, he has personally taken charge of defense matters. Josif Stalin, Nikita Khrushchev, and Leonid Brezhnev all chose to confirm their personal responsibility for defense by assuming the post of supreme commander-in-chief of the Soviet armed forces.[25]

This centralization of authority at the top regarding defense matters has several important consequences. First, it means that there are no significant checks built into the system once the decision is taken within the Politburo. Second, given the lengthy tenure of the senior Soviet political leaders—Stalin dominated the Soviet political scene from the mid-1920s until 1953, Khrushchev from 1957 to 1964, and Brezhnev from 1964 until this article was written (early 1980)—this centralization has provided a pronounced element of continuity in Soviet military policy. Third, the reverse side of this highly personalized pattern is that when a period of leadership transition occurs, it clearly carries with it considerable potential for significant change in defense policy. Consequently, during these struggles for power, which are inevitable due to the absence of a regularized procedure for Soviet leadership succession, the leading contenders are virtually certain to be particularly attentive to defense issues. Conflict over defense matters was evident in the struggle between Khrushchev and Malenkov during the post-Stalin succession in 1953–54, and it appears to have surfaced briefly in 1965 following Khrushchev's political demise.[26] Fully aware of this, the constituencies with substantial stakes in defense matters, the professional military and their allies in the defense production ministries, are certain to defend and promote their interests actively during such succession periods.

The closed nature of Soviet political processes is another aspect of the Soviet political system that influences both the formulation of Soviet defense policy and our understanding of it in the West. Soviet policy making in all issue areas is conducted in considerable secrecy. This pattern is most pronounced with regard to national security matters. U.S. suspicions about the strict compartmentalization of defense-related information within the Soviet system were dramatically confirmed in an often-recounted incident that occurred during the early phases of the Strategic Arms Limitation Talks. At that time, the leading Soviet military representative, then Colonel General N.V. Ogarkov (he is now a marshal of the Soviet Union and chief of the General Staff), asked the U.S. negotiators not to discuss the details of Soviet strategic weapons deployments with Soviet civilian representatives, who, he said, were not authorized access to such information.[27] This denial of information to those outside the professional military establishment and a small circle of senior Soviet leaders is similarly evident in the limited knowledge of Soviet defense information found among the civilian national security policy analysts of the world affairs institutes of the Academy of Sciences.[28]

The consequences of this closed policy-making pattern and compartmentalization of defense information are twofold. First, in such an environment, those with access to the controlled information, in this case for the most part officers of the Ministry of Defense, are in an excellent position to influence decisively the formulation and implementation of defense policy. This new monopoly of relevant information and expertise is a crucial factor that strengthens the hand of the armed forces on the Soviet political scene. Second, this secrecy effectively limits the data available to both internal Soviet and foreign observers about defense policy making. It compels Western analysts to rely upon a variety of partial sources, including a smattering of memoir accounts, observable activities such as major weapons deployments, and Kremlinological analyses of various Soviet official publications, in order to piece together plausible explanations of Soviet defense policy.

The Economic System. The Soviet defense effort has long been the primary beneficiary of the Soviet command economy. The extent of this priority has been such that some have been prompted to argue that the accumulation of military power has been the primary social product of the Soviet economic system, while the production of other goods and services is nothing more than necessary social overhead.[29] Although this may be somewhat overstated, there is no doubt that military weaponry has consistently been accorded the highest priority in a host of inputs, including direct budgetary support, the infusion of the highest-quality equipment, such as advanced computers and machine tools, and the recruitment of talented scientific and technical personnel.

Throughout the Soviet period, the economy has been largely autarkic. Consequently, questions of access to imports or markets for exports have had little influence on Soviet foreign or defense policy. In recent years, however, various difficulties in the functioning of the Soviet economy have begun to surface that may alter this situation. These problems include: a steady decline in the overall rate of economic growth, the prospect that Soviet oil production will peak in the early 1980s and then decline for the next several years, while domestic energy demand is projected to rise steadily,[30] continuing poor performance in agriculture (the economy's endemically weak area), and declining worker productivity.[31]

Many of these problems have been evident for several years. They were almost certainly major factors behind the decision of Mr. Brezhnev and his colleagues to pursue a "policy of selective economic interdependence" as a key element of Soviet détente with the West throughout the 1970s.[32] While by no means abandoning their pronounced tendency toward economic self-reliance, the Soviets have significantly expanded their involvement in the world economy over the past decade. However, substantial technology imports, joint ventures in the expansion of motor transport, and major grain imports have failed to reverse the adverse trends in the performance of the Soviet economy. Thus, it appears that if the Soviets are to address these deficiencies effectively, they must reexamine both their external trade relations and the structure and working of their highly centralized command economy.

Continuing economic difficulties could, of course, have significant impact on Soviet defense policy. Some have suggested that these difficulties will prompt the leaders in the Kremlin to reduce their investments in defense. Soviet defense expenditures are estimated by the Central Intelligence Agency to have run at approximately 13–14 percent of the Soviet GNP for the past several years and to have increased steadily at an average of 4–5 percent per year.[33] Barring a very dramatic downturn in the performance of the overall economy, however, cuts in defense spending do not appear likely, at least over the next several years. Ever since the fall of Khrushchev in 1964, the Brezhnev-led leadership has proved itself prepared to accept declining overall economic growth and to continue to suppress the consumer demands of the Russian people in order to sustain the relentless expansion of Soviet military strength. And they are very likely to continue to do so.

Geography. The Soviet Union occupies a central geographic position, straddling the continents of Europe and Asia. Spanning approximately 170 degrees of longitude, the USSR directly borders on twelve neighboring states and looks out across enclosed seas at an additional seven. Thus, Soviet interests and concerns range from their Scandinavian neighbors Norway and Finland in the northwest, through the Communist client regimes of Eastern Europe, on to Turkey, Iran, and Afghanistan in the Near East, to Pakistan and India in South Asia, and China, North Korea, and Japan in the Far East. The majority of these frontiers are marked by no significant geographical barriers, thus contributing to the historical perceptions and reality of Russian vulnerability to overland invasion. From the critical "heartland" location, the leaders in the Kremlin, like their czarist predecessors, confront a multitude of challenges and opportunities along this lengthy frontier.

The Soviet Union is richly endowed with natural resources. Its deposits of precious metals, petroleum, natural gas, coal, iron, and several other minerals are among the largest in the world. However, many of these deposits are located in relatively inaccessible regions of Siberia, thus significantly complicating successful exploitation. Another important geographic characteristic is the northerly latitude of the Soviet Union. Most of the country lies above 40°N. Consequently, the amount of arable land available for sustained civilization is quite small for a country of such vast size and has proven consistently inadequate to meet the needs of the nation's more than 260 million people.

Public Opinion. The authoritarian character of the Soviet political system is such that public opinion plays no direct role in the shaping of the nation's foreign or domestic policies. Nevertheless, the prevailing views of the Soviet citizens on defense matters are not without importance.

By all evidence, the Russians are an intensely patriotic people with a genuine commitment to the defense of the *rodina*, the motherland. Whatever their views about the domestic policies of the Soviet regime, the vast majority of Soviet people are intensely proud of their nation's political, economic, and military accomplishments and are prepared to support the Kremlin unquestioningly in the name of the defense of Mother Russia. This is not to say that many Soviet citizens would not prefer a reduction in defense spending—Soviet dissident literature has periodically included calls for this. But such matters are not the business of the Soviet people, who are expected to (and largely do) accept their nation's massive defense exertions silently.

Nationality Issues. The Soviet leaders, like the czars before them, face a significant "nationalities problem." The USSR is a multinational state composed of over 130 national groups. This polyglot population can be usefully divided into two major ethnic groupings: the European nationalities, including the Great Russians, Ukranians, Byelorussians, Moldavians, Latvians, Lithuanians, and Estonians; and the non-Europeans, such as the Uzbeks, Tartars, Kazakhs, Azeri, Turkmen, Kirgiz, Tadzhiks, Armenians, and Georgians.

The multinational character of the Soviet state is reflected in the federal structure of the Union of Soviet Socialist Republics, with its fifteen union-republics, organized along national lines, and a host of smaller nationality-based autonomous republics and autonomous regions. Yet despite the formal lip-service paid to the rights and traditions of the constituent nationalities, the Soviet leadership has always demanded full subordination of these groups to the will of the Communist party center in Moscow. This Party core has been and remains thoroughly dominated by the Great Russians, with substantial assistance from the other Slavs, the Ukranians and Byelorussians.

Nevertheless, the national identities have persisted and remain a substantial concern to the regime. The primary problem posed by the nationalities to the Kremlin authorities today is not one of incipient political separatism but rather a demand from many of the nationality groups for a larger voice within the national system and for somewhat greater autonomy in the handling of local issues. These matters have no clear-cut impact upon defense matters.[34]

However, in recent years the Soviet nationalities issue has taken on a new dimension due to the pronounced disparities in the population growth rates of the European and non-European groups. The non-European nationalities of Central Asia have produced far higher birth rates over the past few decades, and this disparity is virtually certain to continue in the years ahead. This trend is bound to have significant impact on Soviet economic choices in the years ahead. It has already raised what one author calls the specter of the demographic "yellowing" of the Soviet population as the Asiatic peoples become a larger and larger share of the populace. The leaders in Moscow must either succeed in encouraging a migration of the more numerous Asiatics into the labor-short manufacturing centers of the Urals and European Russia or take the necessary steps to expand greatly the industrial facilities of Central Asia.[35]

The increased numbers of Asians within the annual cohorts that are inducted into the Soviet armed forces will be likely to necessitate major adjustments in assignment policies within the armed forces. Up to this time, Central Asians, whose mastery of the Russian language is often rudimentary, have generally been excluded from most prestigious, high-technology military career fields. They are commonly found, instead, to make up the majority of pick-and-shovel soldiers of the Construction Troops as one encounters these units in Moscow and other major cities.

In sum, despite the various problems raised by the nationalities issue, it currently does not appear to pose a significant threat to the political integrity or military preparedness of the USSR.

Force Employment Doctrine

Over the years, the Soviets have developed a distinctive style of warfare that reflects a variety of influences. These include: imperial Russian military tradition (transmitted to the Red Army by a sizable core of former czarist officers who were particularly active in the development of Soviet military doctrine in the 1920s and 1930s), the geographic setting of the USSR, the numbers and types of weapons made available by the pampered defense sector of the Soviet economy, and a unique Soviet approach to theater war that emerged from the military scientific specialists working in the General Staff and the prestigious senior military academies in Moscow beginning in the early 1930s.[36]

The Soviets devote enormous attention to the study and elaboration of military doctrine. This activity falls fully within the purview of the professional military establishment. Successive generations of officers attached to the Military Science Directorate of the General Staff and the military science and history faculties of such academies as the Voroshilov Academy of the General Staff and the Frunze Academy have developed an elaborate and highly formalized body of military doctrinal concepts. These concepts are presented in a host of journals and books that steadily pours out of the Ministry of Defense's military publishing house (Voenizdat), and in classified publications such as the General Staff's *Military Thought (Voennaia mysl')*.

The contemporary Soviet approach to theater war and, to a considerable extent, to intercontinental conflict as well clearly reflects key elements that were already evident in the Soviet doctrine for massed, armored warfare called the theory of operations in depth, developed almost fifty years ago.[37] These guiding principles include a commitment to seize the initiative at the outset of hostilities and to conduct bold offensive operations with massed, armor-heavy forces at high tempo in order to annihilate completely the enemy's military forces. At the same time, Soviet doctrine calls for all possible offensive and defensive efforts to limit the damage that the Soviet Union itself would suffer in a war. Soviet military theory categorically rejects the dominance of a single weapon or branch of the service in the conduct of these operations. It calls instead for the reinforcing efforts of all ground, sea, and air forces to achieve victory via the so-called combined-arms concept.[38]

Contemporary Soviet military writings deal primarily with various facets of a complex scenario for general nuclear war. This literature describes several aspects of this global clash between the opposing socialist and capitalist social systems, including: (1) a major theater land and air battle; (2) war at sea; (3) both regional and intercontinental missile and bomber exchanges; and (4) extensive efforts to defend the Soviet homeland. While a comprehensive review of these variegated operations is beyond the scope of this study, some of the highlights of the distinctive Soviet force employment doctrine are given below.

Theater War. Soviet doctrine exhibits a readiness to conduct massive ground-air offensive operations against NATO and, presumably, the People's Republic of China, using only conventional weapons for an opening period of indeterminate length. The Soviets say they are prepared to initiate, at the same time, extensive nuclear operations either at the very outset of the conflict or at any time during its conduct. For the latter case, the Soviets maintain a high state of nuclear readiness and clearly intend to preempt any enemy resort to the use of nuclear weapons with massed missile and aircraft strikes of their own throughout the depth of the theater.

In either a conventional or a nuclear environment, the Soviets plan to mass their armor-heavy forces along selected main axes of attack and to make a series of simultaneous breakthroughs of the enemy's defenses. These breakthroughs are to be exploited immediately by the continuous introduction of additional echelons, which are to advance rapidly in order to encircle and destroy the enemy's main formations and occupy his territory in a matter of days.[39]

This land offensive is to be supported by extensive "air operations" that combine units from tactical ("frontal") and strategic ("long-range") aviation to destroy enemy forces, especially nuclear delivery systems, throughout the theater.[40] In a nuclear conflict, these air forces will be supplemented by operational-tactical and regional strategic missile forces in the conduct of massive strikes both on the battlefield and throughout the enemy's rear area.

War at Sea. Primary emphasis will be devoted to efforts to destroy enemy naval combatants, in particular aircraft carriers and ballistic missile submarines, that are capable of striking Soviet forward-deployed forces or targets on Soviet territory. These efforts will involve coordinated attacks by cruise-missile-equipped surface ships, submarines, and land-based bomber aviation.

Over the past decade the Soviets have also developed a concept calling for the employment of combined antisubmarine warfare assets—attack submarines, surface ships, and aircraft—in a "bastion defense" or "strategic support mission" to help protect their own strategic ballistic missile submarines, deployed in nearby waters, from U.S. attack submarines.[41]

The forces of the Soviet navy are expected to conduct amphibious operations using naval infantry and ground force units along the maritime flanks in support of theater land offensives. They must also be prepared to execute coastal defense operations to deny the enemy the ability to mount successful amphibious assaults against the Soviet Union.

Soviet naval air and submarine forces are also tasked to interdict enemy sea lines of communications, although this appears to be a secondary mission.

Intercontinental Nuclear Warfare. In the event that a strategic nuclear exchange occurs, Soviet doctrine includes a strong predisposition to launch a preemptive strike against U.S. strategic forces if U.S. preparations to commence nuclear operations can be detected.[42] If preemption is not achieved, there are hints that the Soviets might employ a "launch under attack" tactic[43] or, failing this, simply retaliate after absorbing the U.S. strike.

In any case, Soviet ICBMs, SLBMs, and strategic bombers would be employed to strike simultaneously such targets as U.S. strategic forces (ICBMs, SSBNs in port, and bombers), key military command and control facilities, major groupings of general purpose forces, and a variety of economic and political objectives, including electrical power systems, stocks of strategic raw materials, and large industrial and transport centers.[44]

These strikes, executed in the so-called initial period of a general nuclear war, are said to be capable of having a decisive influence upon the outcome of a war, although "final victory" is said to be achievable only with the combined efforts of all arms and services.

Soviet doctrinal writings have displayed no interest in the possibility of limited nuclear warfare at either the central strategic or theater level. The Soviets have expressly rejected U.S. concepts of limited nuclear war as artificial "rules of the game" and continue to embrace instead a concept of massive nuclear strikes for maximum military and political effectiveness. Nevertheless, growing Soviet capabilities could support a wide spectrum of controlled nuclear operations, which they could choose to employ in a crisis.[45]

The Soviets also speak of their intentions to conduct active antiair, antimissile, and antispace (antisatellite) measures in combination with extensive civil defense activities to reduce the damage inflicted on the USSR by those enemy forces that survive the vigorous Soviet counterforce attacks.

Notes

1. *Handbook of Economic Statistics, 1979* (Washington, D.C.: Central Intelligence Agency, 1979), p. 10.

2. Ibid., pp. 11, 128, 130, 150.

3. This point has been documented in the modernization research of Professor Cyril Black, of Princeton University.

4. *Handbook of Economic Statistics*, pp. 10, 11. Today the Soviet Union and the industrialized nations of the West have been surpassed in GNP per capita by a few of the oil-rich states of the Middle East.

5. Statement of Ambassador Malcolm C. Toon, in U.S., Congress, Senate, Committee on Foreign Relations, *The SALT II Treaty: Hearings*, 96th Cong., 1st sess., pt. 3, p. 6.

6. The efforts of the Soviet regime to perpetuate popular awareness of the massive suffering of the Great Fatherland War, as the Soviets call their involvement in World War II, is well captured in the title of Hedrick Smith's chapter on this subject, "Patriotism: World War II Was Only Yesterday," in his *The Russians* (New York: Quadrangle, 1976), pp. 303–25.

7. Helmut Sonnenfeldt and William G. Hyland, *Soviet Perspectives on Security*, Adelphi Paper 150 (London: International Institute of Strategic Studies, 1979), p. 9.

8. See Ivo J. Lederer, ed., *Russian Foreign Policy* (New Haven: Yale University Press, 1962).

9. An especially prescient observation about Russia's power potential was made almost 150 years ago by Alexis de Tocqueville, who predicted that Russia and the United States were destined to be the world's dominant powers, with the Russian position resting primarily on Russia's military capabilities.

10. International Institute of Strategic Studies, *The Military Balance, 1979-1980* (London: International Institute of Strategic Studies, 1979), p. 13.

11. The Soviets maintained two divisions in Mongolia until 1975, when they increased the number to three divisions, which it has remained until now (*The Military Balance, 1974-1975* and *1979-1980* [London: International Institute of Strategic Studies, 1974 and 1979]).

12. The so-called Brezhnev Doctrine, justifying Soviet intervention in the "defense" of socialism, first appeared in a *Pravda* editorial on September 26, 1968, a month after the Soviet invasion of Czechoslovakia in August 1968. It was repeated by General Secretary Brezhnev at the Polish Party Congress in Warsaw on November 12, 1968.

13. The most outspoken military figure in this regard has been the commander-in-chief of the navy, Fleet Admiral of the Soviet Union S.G. Gorshkov. Over the past fifteen years, he has regularly touted the navy's ability to serve Soviet foreign policy, as, for example, in his assertion that "the Navy is, to the greatest degree, capable of operationally supporting the state's interest beyond its borders" (S.G. Gorshkov, *Morskaia moshch' gosudarstva [Sea power of the state]* [Moscow: Voenizdat, 1976], p. v).

14. M. Ellen Jones, "The Correlation of Forces in Soviet Decisionmaking" (Paper delivered to the 1978 Biennial Conference, Section on Military Studies. International Studies Association, November 1978).

15. For example, Maj. Gen. I. Anureyev, "Determining the Correlation of Forces in Terms of Nuclear Weapons," *Voennaia mysl'* [Military thought], no. 6(1967):35- 45.

16. See Arnold L. Horelick and Myron Rush, *Strategic Power and Soviet Foreign Policy* (Chicago: University of Chicago Press, 1966).

17. Cf. Lt. Col. V.M. Bondarenko, "Military Technological Superiority—The Most Important Factor in the Reliable Defense of the Country," *Kommunist Vooruzhennykh Sil* [Communist of the armed forces], no. 17 (September 1966):7-14; and *Sovetskaia voennaia entsiklopediia* [Soviet military encyclopedia], vol. 2 (Moscow: Boenizdat, 1976), p. 253.

18. Brezhnev himself keynoted this campaign to refute Western assertions that the Soviet Union seeks military superiority over the United States and its NATO allies in his major address at Tula in January 1977 (*Pravda*, January 19, 1977). Marshal N.V. Ogarkov, first deputy minister of defense and chief of the General Staff, has lent the authority of the professional military to this claim in various public statements and in his authoritative article "Military Strategy," in *Sovetskaia voennaia entsiklopediia*, vol. 7 (Moscow: Voenizdat, 1979), p. 563.

19. Timothy Colton, *Commissars, Commanders and Civilian Authority: The Structure of Soviet Military Politics* (Cambridge, Mass.: Harvard University Press, 1979), p. 251.

20. Harriet Fast Scott and William F. Scott, *The Armed Forces of the USSR* (Boulder: Westview Press, 1979), p. 176.

21. For most Soviet draftees the period of compulsory military service is two years. However, this term is three years for certain naval components, while most deferred students who have received institute or university degrees serve for a year and a half (ibid., p. 305).

22. A.I. Romashko, *Voennye stroiteli na stroikakh Moskvy* [The military builders in the building of Moscow] (Moscow: Voenizdat, 1972).

23. For an excellent comparison of many aspects of U.S. and Soviet military doctrines, see Fritz Ermarth, "Contrasts in American and Soviet Strategic Thought," *International Security* (Fall 1978).

24. Cf. Raymond L. Garthoff, "Mutual Deterrence and Strategic Arms Limitation in Soviet Policy," *International Security* (Summer 1978):112-47.

25. Stalin assumed this position after the German invasion in 1941. Khrushchev apparently did so in the late 1950s or early 1960s as he sought to impose his will on the military regarding doctrinal and budgetary issues. Brezhnev's accession to the post, date unknown, was acknowledged in the course of a routine article in the military press in the fall of 1977.

26. There were signs of disagreement on defense investment priorities within the Brezhnev-led collective leadership that succeeded Khrushchev in early 1965 (see T.W. Wolfe, *The Soviet Military Scene: Institutional and Defense Policy Considerations*, Rm-4913 [Santa Monica: RAND, 1966], pp. 64–67).

27. John Newhouse, *Cold Dawn: The Story of SALT* (New York: Holt, Rinehart & Winston, 1973), p. 192.

28. Personal observations in contacts with Soviet staff members of the Institute for the Study of the USA and Canada and the Institute of World Economics and International Relations, Moscow, 1976–78.

29. This point has been made to the author by William E. Odom and Robert G. Kaiser in *Russia: The People and the Power* (New York: Pocket Books, 1976), p. 380.

30. J. Richard Lee and James R. Lecky, "Soviet Oil Developments," in Joint Economic Committee, *The Soviet Economy in a Time of Change: A Compendium of Papers*, 96th Cong. (Washington, D.C.: U.S. Government Printing Office, Oct. 10, 1979), pp. 581–99.

31. Paul K. Cook, "The Political Setting," in ibid., pp. 38–50.

32. John P. Hardt, "Soviet Economic Capabilities and Defense Resources," in *The Soviet Threat: Myths and Realities*, ed. G. Kirk and N.H. Wessell (New York: Academy of Political Science, 1978), p. 124.

33. *Estimated Soviet Defense Spending: Trends and Prospects*, SR-78-10121 (Washington, D.C.: Central Intelligence Agency, 1978).

34. Jeremy Azrael, *Emergent Nationality Problems in the USSR*, R-2172-AF (Santa Monica: RAND, 1977), p. v.

35. S. Enders Wimbush and Dmitry Ponomareff, *Alternatives for Mobilizing Soviet Central Asian Labor: Outmigration and Regional Development*, R-2476-AF (Santa Monica: RAND, 1979).

36. For an excellent review of these and other factors, see Benjamin S. Lambeth, "The Sources of Soviet Military Doctrine, in *Comparative Defense Policy*, ed. F.B. Horton, A.C. Rogerson, and E.L. Warner III (Baltimore: Johns Hopkins University Press, 1974), pp. 200–215.

37. See Marshal M.V. Zakharov et al., *Voprosy strategii i operativnogo iskusstva v sovetskikh voennykh trudakh, 1917–1940* [Problems of strategy and operational art in Soviet military works, 1917–1940] (Moscow: Voenizdat, 1965), pp. 17–24; John Erickson, *The Soviet High Command: A Military-Political History, 1918–1941* (New York: St. Martin's Press, 1962), pp. 349–54, 404–11; Marshal N.V. Ogarkov, "Deep Operations (Battle)," in *Sovetskaia voennaia entsiklopediia*, vol. 2, pp. 574–78.

38. Cf. Ogarkov, "Military Strategy," pp. 559–63; Marshal A.A. Grechko, *Vooruzhennye sili Sovetskogo gosudarstva* [The armed forces of the Soviet state] (Moscow: Voenizdat, 1976); Marshal V.D. Sokolovskiy, ed., *Voennaia strategiia* [Military strategy], 3d ed., rev. (Moscow: Voenizdat, 1968); and commentaries such as Benjamin S. Lambeth, *How to Think about Soviet Military Doctrine*, p-5939 (Santa Monica: RAND, 1978).

39. Cf. A.A. Sidorenko, *Nastuplenie* [The offensive] (Moscow: Voenizdat, 1970); and John Erickson, "The Soviet Concept of Land Battle," in *The Soviet Union in Europe and the Near East*, ed. John Erickson (London: Royal United Service Institution, 1970), pp. 26–32.

40. Y.G. Veraka and M.N. Kozhevnikov, "Air Operations," in *Sovetskaia voennaia entsiklopediia,* vol. 2, pp. 281–82; Robert P. Berman, *Soviet Air Power in Transition* (Washington, D.C.: Brookings Institution, 1978), pp. 11, 66–73; Chief Marshal of Aviation P. Kutakhov, "The Conduct of Air Operations," *Voenno-istoricheskii zhurnal* [Military history journal], no. 6 (June 1972):20–28.

41. Michael McGwire, "Naval Power and Soviet Global Strategy," *International Security,* Spring 1979, pp. 170–73; and Robert P. Berman and John C. Baker, *Soviet Strategic Forces: Requirements and Responses* (Washington, D.C.: Brookings Institution, 1982), pp. iv-80 to iv-86.

42. Soviet doctrinal writings in the 1950s spoke openly of such preemption. Since that time, however, the Soviets have not expressly stated their intention to strike preemptively but have often used suggestive euphemisms such as claiming a readiness to "nip in the bud" any Western nuclear missile attack (see Edward L. Warner III, *The Military in Contemporary Soviet Politics: An Institutional Analysis* [New York: Praeger Publishers, 1977], p. 151).

43. Cf. Marshal N.I. Krylov, "The Nuclear Shield of the Soviet State," *Voennaia mysl',* no. 11 (November 1967):20; General S. Ivanov, "Soviet Military Doctrine and Strategy," ibid., no. 5 (May 1969):48; and Maj. Gen. N. Vasendin and Col. N. Kuznetsov, "Modern Warfare and Surprise Attack," ibid., no. 6 (June 1968):46–47.

44. Maj. Gen. V. Zemskov, "Characteristic Features of Modern Wars and Possible Methods of Conducting Them," ibid., no 7 (July 1969):20; and Joseph D. Douglas and Amoretta M. Hoeber, *Soviet Strategy for Nuclear War* (Palo Alto: Hoover Institution Press, 1979), pp. 14–33.

45. Benjamin S. Lambeth, *Selective Nuclear Options in American and Soviet Strategic Policy,* R-2034-SSEW (Santa Monica: RAND, 1976).

Discussion Questions

1. How does a nation determine what is a threat to its national interests?

2. Can one nation's security be another nation's threat? What are the possible policy implications as they relate to force structure and strategy?

3. How does Soviet defense policy threaten the United States?

4. What are the major factors that shape Soviet defense policy?

3
The Nature of Alliances

Robert E. Osgood

Why Alliances?

Alliances are an integral part of international politics. They are one of the primary means by which states seek the co-operation of other states in order to enhance their power to protect and advance their interests. This instrument of co-operation is so pervasive that every state must have an alliance policy, even if its purpose is only to avoid alliances.

The subject of this analysis, however, is broader than alliances. Alliances are only one kind of commitment by which states enhance their power. Moreover, there are many kinds of alliances, and alliances serve a variety of purposes. One cannot properly assess the value and the prospects of alliances without examining the alternatives to alliances and distinguishing between the various kinds of alliances.

In this study an alliance is defined as a formal agreement that pledges states to co-operate in using their military resources against a specific state or states and usually obligates one or more of the signatories to use force, or to consider (unilaterally or in consultation with allies) the use of force, in specified circumstances. It differs in principle from a "collective security" agreement. Strictly speaking, such an agreement obligates its members to abstain from recourse to violence against one another and to participate collectively in suppressing the unlawful use of force by any member. It may also obligate its members to resist aggression by a nonmember against any of them, but what distinguishes it from a mere collective defense agreement is that it presupposes a general interest on the part of all its members in opposing aggression by any of them and entails the procedures for the peaceful settlement of disputes among the members.

A defensive alliance presupposes only a common interest in opposing threats from specific states or groups outside the alliance and does not necessarily or usually entail provisions for settling disputes among its members. An offensive alliance aims at forcibly changing the international status quo, territorially or otherwise, to increase the assets of its members.

Osgood, Robert E., *Alliances and American Foreign Policy* (Baltimore: Johns Hopkins University Press, 1968). Reprinted with permission.

A defensive alliance may also be a local or regional collective security agreement. The OAS, for example, is both. Alliances, although ostensibly or actually directed against an external threat, may additionally or even primarily be intended to restrain a member, limit its options, support its government against an internal threat, or control its foreign policy in some fashion. In this respect, many alliances have actually been as much concerned as a collective security agreement would be with organizing relations between allies, although national sensitivities may have counseled against making such concern explicit or public. The internal concern of alliances tends to increase with their duration and with the diminished perception of an external threat.

Alliances commonly reflect more than a single, explicit, and identical interest between members. Allies may wish to support a variety of interests that include merely complementary or parallel interests and even divergent ones. Some of these interests may be specified in the agreement, but some are more prudently left unspecified, whether they are mutual or not. In any case, the full substance and significance of an alliance is seldom revealed in the formal contract or treaty for military co-operation, any more than the essence of marriage is revealed in the marriage certificate. The contract is simply an attempt to make more precise and binding a particular obligation or relationship between states, which is part of a continually changing network of interests and sentiments. An alliance, therefore, reflects a latent war community, based on general co-operation that goes beyond formal provisions and that the signatories must continually cultivate in order to preserve mutual confidence in each other's fidelity to specified obligations.

As a formal contract for military co-ooperation, however, an alliance may be difficult to distinguish from other kinds of military contracts such as military subsidies, military assistance agreements, or military base agreements. Most alliances specify (if only in a general phrase) the contingencies under which force will or will not be used by the members and against whom it will be used, but they may be worded so broadly that these particulars can only be inferred. Conversely, other kinds of military contracts may contain explicit political provisions concerning the use of weapons and facilities. In any case, like alliances, they are based on definite understandings and expectations (whether shared by both partners or not) about the purposes and circumstances of the specified military co-operation.

Even in the absence of formal contracts for military co-operation, unilateral declarations of intentions can go far to commit states to the use of force in behalf of other states. Such declarations are particularly important now that the communication of military intentions for the sake of deterrence plays such a prominent role in international politics. Their importance is indicated by their extensive use to reinforce and refine formal reciprocal commitments.

But military commitments need not depend even on unilateral declarations. They are often established and conveyed indirectly by countless official and unofficial words and actions, creating understandings and expectations that are no less significant for being implicit. These understandings and expectations are the substance of alignments of power and interest, and alliances and other explicit commitments would be useless without them.

Why, then, do states make alliances? Generally, because alliances are the most binding obligations they can make to stabilize the configurations of power that affect their vital interests. Alliances add precision and specificity to informal or tacit alignments.

More than that, the fact that alliances are *reciprocal* and *formal* agreements increases the obligation of signatories to carry out specified commitments and co-operation. The ceremony and solemnity accompanying the formation of an alliance signify that sovereign states have surrendered important aspects of their freedom of action and obligated themselves to an interdependent relationship.

Moreover, the obligation of alliance relates directly to the response of signatories to contingencies that call for a possible resort to war. Alliances impinge more fundamentally upon the vital interests of nations and more broadly upon the whole range of their foreign policies than agreements designed merely to provide for the use of goods and facilities. For this reason alliances are also more likely to provoke rivals and adversaries and lead to countervailing combinations, which may further limit the political options and enhance the interdependence of allies.

The political significance of alliances is all the greater in this era of popular (including undemocratic) governments because alliances generally presuppose national or ideological affinities that go beyond the matter-of-fact expediencies involved in more restricted contracts.

Thus, whatever its benefits, an alliance tends to cost more than other kinds of military commitments because it limits a member's political options and freedom of action more. For this reason the signatories of an alliance feel entitled to continual assurance of each other's fidelity and their own net benefit. Consequently, an alliance of some duration encourages further claims upon its members and tends to require repeated regeneration through adjustments of their liabilities and assets. Lacking recourse to supranational instrumentalities to enforce an obligation that could involve their very survival as nations, states must rely on diplomatic co-operation against an adversary and on other manifestations of good faith and common interest. These by-products of alliance may entangle states in each other's affairs to an extent that is not always easy to anticipate when an alliance is formed.

As an investment in future returns of national security and welfare, an alliance is apt to be more open-ended and consequential than other kinds of military contracts. Therefore, although alliances are a pervasive element of international politics, the capacity and incentive for states to engage in alliance are far from universal. Relatively few states have the resources, the internal cohesion, or the coherence of national interests to become effective allies. Some states that will freely seek and accept military assistance or base agreements may regard even the most limited alliance as an unwise political entanglement.

The Functions of Alliances

There are four principal functions of alliances, and they are not necessarily mutually exclusive: accretion of external power, internal security, restraint of allies, and international order.

The accretion of power entails increasing the military power of allies by combining resources and eliciting positive co-operation. This has been the basic and the most common function of alliances. The ultimate purpose of accretion is to enhance the relative power of one or more allies against another state or states for defensive or offensive ends (although some states, especially the smaller ones, may want power largely in the form of status).

Internal security is sometimes a more important function of alliance for a weak state than accretion of its external power. In recognition of the international significance of internal threats and developments, which are often supported covertly from outside, alliances may be intended principally to enhance the security or stability of an ally's government or regime, often by legitimizing material assistance or military intervention against internal opposition. This purpose is usually not made explicit, however, since intervention in the domestic affairs of another state, even at that state's invitation, has acquired a stigma in the age of popular national governments.

Next to accretion, the most prominent function of alliances has been to restrain and control allies, particularly in order to safeguard one ally against actions of another that might endanger its security or otherwise jeopardize its interests. This function may be accomplished directly by pledges of nonintervention or by other reassurances that one ally will not contravene the interests of another, or it may be the by-product of commitments that limit an ally's freedom of action and provide its partner with access to, and influence upon, its government.

International order is the broadest and the least attainable function of an alliance. An alliance may aim to preserve harmony among its members and establish an international order—that is, a stable, predictable, and safe pattern of international politics—within an area of common concern. In its ultimate form, this function of an alliance becomes collective security. In different ways, the Quadruple Alliance after the Napoleonic Wars and the OAS have exercised this function of maintaining order. Before the onset of the cold war, the United States expected the Big Three, as the core of the United Nations, to be guarantors of a new world order. Some people believe that NATO has served indirectly as a framework for a new Western European order or even an Atlantic Community.

The Determinants of Alliances

Among the numerous factors that may affect the creation, continuation, or decline of alliances in various parts of the world, several "determinants" (in the nondeterministic sense) seem particularly important. These determinants also affect the characteristics of alliances and the nature of their functions, but they are principally relevant to the elementary questions of the existence or nonexistence, utility or disutility, and vitality or impotence of alliances. They are:

The Pattern of Conflicting and Converging Interests

If states have no interests that they need to support by military power against other states, they lack sufficient incentives to form alliances. If two or more states feel no need for each other's assistance in improving their military capacity to protect or advance their interests against other states, an alliance is not likely to be created, and an existing alliance is likely to erode.

Even if mutual military needs exist, the creation or maintenance of an alliance often requires a convergence of interests that goes beyond a common interest in security. Most notably, there must be sufficient affinity and harmony of policies. The importance of this convergence is directly proportionate to the comprehensiveness and mutuality of the alliance's obligations and to the duration of the alliance; it is inversely proportionate to the intensity of the security threat.

In the case of existing or prospective alliances in which interallied control or order is an important function, the urgency of a commonly felt threat to security may be less determinative, but then the pattern of conflicting as well as converging interests among allies becomes crucial.

The Distribution of Military Power

The formation and preservation of an alliance depends on the military capacity of states as well as their political incentive to co-operate militarily (even though one state may only provide bases and facilities or promise to remain neutral). The capacity of states to help each other depends on the relationship of their concerted power to the power of potential adversaries.

The interaction of this distribution of power with the pattern of interests among states affects not only the desirability and feasibility of alliances but also the characteristics of alliances and the nature of alliance policies. For example, it establishes the polarity of power, or, more specifically, the number of states that are engaged in a dominant international political conflict, are projecting decisive military power, and are undertaking independent military commitments. Whether there are two, or many, "poles of power," has many implications for alliances. . . .[1]

The changing distribution of power between an alliance and its opponents may affect the cohesion of an alliance. For example, adverse changes in the external distribution of power may create dissatisfaction with the distribution within an alliance. Such dissatisfaction and the effort to overcome it may change alliance policies and even alliance functions.

Alliance Capability

Even if the preceding determinants should support the creation or maintenance of an alliance, the states that are concerned may lack certain minimum military and political prerequisites of alliance. Most important among these prerequisites are: (a) enough internal stability, executive authority, and economic strength, along with a sufficiently coherent and predictable foreign policy, to enable a state to be a reliable collaborator and (b) adequate capacity of a state to dispose its military power effectively for the benefit of an ally. (Again, the capacity of one state may be confined to a relatively passive role.)

Alliance-mindedness

Related to the preceding determinant, and also of special significance for the future of alliances among the small and newer states in the Third World, is the subjective attitude of governments toward alliances. For example, some small, recently independent states are averse to alliances with the chief protagonists of the cold war. The subjective inclination or disinclination to enter alliances may be closely related to considerations of expediency; yet it goes beyond sheer reasoned calculations of security requirements and reflects hopes, suspicions, and ideals that are deeply rooted in the national culture and experience. In America's period of physical invulnerability and political insulation, its high-principled denigration of alliances was as important as its glorification of them in the cold war.

These determinants should be considered as a whole because they reinforce, qualify, or offset each other. None of them is sufficient by itself to account for the past, present, or future of alliances. The first two determinants, however, are particularly important.

The Evolution of Alliances

All the functions and determinants of alliances that I have cited apply to contemporary alliances, but the context and methods of application have changed throughout modern history as basic changes occurred in the military and political environment. One way of comprehending these changes is to note the shifts of emphasis among several contrasting types of alliances: between offensive (or revisionist) and defensive (or status quo), wartime and peacetime, bilateral and multilateral, guarantee and mutual assistance, institutionalized and noninstitutionalized alliances. The distinctions among them should be apparent in the brief description of the evolution of alliances that follows.

In the eighteenth century, alliances were the primary means by which states tried to improve their military positions, since the strength of their armed forces are relatively fixed. The typical alliance was a bilateral agreement, or several interlocking bilateral agreements, made during a war or in anticipation of war, after which it was terminated or became inoperative. It usually involved one or several of the following kinds of commitments: a subsidy to support another state's troops; a guarantee to fight on the side of another state (often with a specific number of troops) under stated circumstances; a pledge of nonintervention or mutual abstention from war in the event that one or both of the signatories should become engaged in war with other states; or a division of the territorial and other spoils of war.

Before the last part of the nineteenth century, alliances entailed no extensive military preparations or co-ordination. The undeveloped state of technology, the limited economic capacity of states to carry on war, and the small scale of warfare made such arrangements infeasible and unnecessary. Moreover, states had few of the inhibitions against going to war that arose later when modern war revealed its awesome potential for civil destruction, and they lacked the need and the capacity to sustain alliances as peacetime instruments of military deterrence. War was not yet so terrifying as to create this need and capacity. It was a more or less normal recourse.

Consequently, although there were a few multilateral defensive alliances of long duration, there were scores of offensive alliances – chiefly bilateral – that were intended to acquire territory by means of war. Both offensive and defensive alliances aimed as often at restraining an ally by limiting his political options and deflecting him from an opposing alliance as they did at aggregating military power. The ideal was to keep alliances flexible and commitments limited. Toward this end secret alliances and secret clauses in published alliances were commonly arranged, not only to conceal aggressive designs, but also to increase diplomatic options by making deals with other states without giving offense to allies.

The eighteenth and the first half of the nineteenth centuries were notable for the large number of alliances that were formed and unformed; but a more significant feature of alliances at that time was their limited and flexible nature, which enabled them to adjust readily to shifting interests with little regard for the later contraints of sentiment and ideology or the imperatives of aggregating power in peacetime. The flexibility and secrecy of alliances created a good deal of diplomatic turmoil, but, because there was a fairly equal division of power among the several major states of Europe, these qualities helped to sustain a working equilibrium that restrained and moderated ambitions and acquisitions and kept any single state or coalition of states from dominating the others. The politics of alliances were punctuated by frequent wars, but the limited scale and destructiveness of warfare made it a tolerable instrument for maintaining an equilibrium.

The Napoleonic Wars revealed the new scope, intensity, and dynamism that war could attain when based on the mobilization of manpower and popular enthusiasm. This revelation compelled the European states to combine in a grand coalition to defeat Napoleon's bid for hegemony, just as they had combined against Louis XIV and earlier aspirants to hegemony. This time, however, a wartime alliance became a novel peacetime coalition. In 1815 the victors formed the Concert of Europe, which combined the eighteenth century conception of equilibrium (insofar as the territorial-political settlements and the Quadruple Alliance were aimed at checking France) with the new conception of a multilateral combination of states pledged to concert their power and to consult among themselves in order to preserve the international order against further liberal and nationalist revolutions as well as against divisions among themselves. Therefore the Concert might be called the first modern experiment to form an organization for international order—a forerunner of the League of Nations and the United Nations.

The Concert of Europe was undermined by differing national interests, especially by Britain's refusal to join in suppressing revolutions. After 1822, when the British left the Quadruple Alliance, nothing remained of the Concert except the habit of consultation during crises. International politics returned to flexible, limited, and mostly offensive alliances in a multipolar international system. Taking advantage of the fragmented structure of power, Bismarck acquired territory at the expense of Denmark and Austria, and he rounded out Germany's boundaries with a quick victory over France in 1871. He shored up his accomplishments with a complicated network of bilateral and trilateral alliances designed to keep power fragmented and to prevent combinations that could revise the status quo by setting up balanced antagonisms. Primarily his alliances were intended to limit the options of allies while keeping Germany's commitments to them equally limited.

Yet Bismarck actually helped to undermine his own system of alliances and to set the stage for a different kind of alliance system. The suddenness and decisiveness of Prussia's victories demonstrated the efficacy of its continuing peacetime military preparations, particularly the conscription system, the use of railroads, and the professional planning and direction of war under a general staff. To withstand such an assault, a state would have to be as well-prepared during peacetime as during wartime. Furthermore, military preparedness would require advance arrangements for the co-operation of other states and the co-ordination of military plans and operations. (The French defeat was partly due to France's mistaken calculation that she could acquire allies after the war broke out.) The dramatic development in the last quarter of the nineteenth century of the technological and economic capacity of major states to advance their military positions by quantitative and qualitative arms increases indicated that the internal development of military capacity might replace shifting alliances as the dynamic element of power.

In these circumstances Bismarck's alliance system led to counteralliances that, under the growing pressure of military preparedness through arms races, tended to polarize international conflict between two opposing coalitions, the Triple Alliance and the Triple Entente. These two alliances were far from being tightly knit diplomatically, and they were only partially co-ordinated militarily by military conventions and staff conversations. Nevertheless, they provided the political frameworks within which military commitments were consolidated; and the consolidation of military commitments in turn tightened the alliances. Thus alliances evolved from a means of fragmenting military power to a means of aggregating it.

The consolidation of defensive alliances before World War I, combined with the build-up of military power, made states more susceptible to being triggered into war by an ally (as Austria's war against Serbia entangled Germany). This consolidation encouraged a chain reaction of involvement, once war began, and practically guaranteed that any war involving one ally would become a general war. Nevertheless, if states had been primarily concerned with military deterrence rather than simply with preparing to fight, and if they had not permitted military plans (especially those for total mobilization) to take precedence over diplomatic opportunities to accommodate disputes short of war, the polarization of alliances need not have been incompatible with the peace and security of all. In fact these were not primarily deterrent alliances but rather alliances formed in anticipation of war. Unfortunately, statesmen deferred to their general staffs, who were absorbed in preparing maximum offensive striking power for a war that they expected to be as short and decisive as the Franco-Prussian War.

Contrary to prevailing expectations, World War I turned out to be a devastating war of attrition, and modern firepower chewed up the manpower and resources of Europe. This grim surprise led to a widespread reaction in the victorious countries against alliances, which were regarded as one of the principal causes of the war. Woodrow Wilson caught the popular imagination by proposing an "association" of power, in opposition to the discredited balance of power system. According to his conception of the League of Nations, all states would be organized against aggression from any quarter. He expected the chief deterrent to aggression to be the power of world opinion rather than the threat of force. Other American proponents of the League idea thought the United States should concert its power with that of Britain and France to preserve a new postwar order. However, it is doubtful that the nation as a whole was prepared to participate in power politics to the extent required of a major ally, for Americans still retained the sense of physical security that underlay their isolationist tradition. Until they became convinced by America's involvement in World War II and the onset of the cold war that aggression abroad impinged directly upon American security, they would not enter a peacetime alliance.

The ascent of Hitler's Germany showed that a peacetime deterrent coalition, whatever its effects in other circumstances might be, was essential to peace and order in the face of the most dangerous bid for hegemony since Napoleon. Unfortunately, the major democratic countries failed to form such a coalition. Although Wilsonian collective security would have been unworkable as a universal supranational order, even if the United States had joined the League, this ideal served as an excuse for avoiding an alliance, especially for Britain, which turned down France's bid for a defensive alliance against Germany. Yet World War II led the major democratic states to draw a lesson from this interwar experience that became the psychological foundation of America's postwar system of deterrent alliances. This system came to dominate the postwar history of alliances.

In the cold war, alliances have been as important in international politics as in any other period of history. But among the advanced states several developments have reduced their flexibility (but, by the same token, enhanced their stability). Their primarily deterrent function, the inhibitions against major states going to war in the nuclear age, the increased importance of peacetime military forces, the sensitivity of governments to public sentiment and ideological positions, the persistence of a dominant international conflict and structure of power that have been essentially bipolar – all these developments have tended to restrict the number of alliances and the frequency of shifts of alliance among major states. At the same time, the emergence of many new states in previously colonial and politically inactive areas has meant that the great majority of states lack the basic external and internal prerequisites for engaging in alliances. One consequence of these new constraints on alliances is that other forms of military commitments have come to play a proportionately greater role in international politics. Another is that intra-alliance functions have assumed greater importance.

Note

1. Reference to poles of power may involve an awkward geometrical analogy, but common use of the concepts of bipolarity and multipolarity in discussions of international politics has nevertheless established this analogy.

Discussion Questions

1. How do alliances affect a nation's flexibility and capability in meeting threats to its security?

2. How do alliances shape strategy? Are alliances more a function of strategy, or is strategy more a function of alliances?

3. What are the four principal functions of alliances?

4
Technology, Military Equipment, and National Security

Harold Brown

Just about everything that has to do with national security, in both foreign and defense policy, has been a matter of substantial controversy since the mid-1960s. But since about 1979 what was formerly a minor theme in the usual dissonant symphony of views has become perhaps the most popular of all. It has to do with the place of advanced technology, and of the military equipment that incorporates it, in the U.S. defense posture. Discussions of this matter have become as adversarial as discussions of U.S.-Soviet relations or of the proper U.S. policy towards the Middle East.

The Simple Myths and the Complex Facts

There are three main complaints about the development and procurement of military weapons and equipment.

U.S. military equipment has become too complex over the past couple of decades. It incorporates too high a level of technology and aims for too high a level of performance. Because of this, the equipment is too expensive and is unreliable and unsuitable.

The effort put into the technology of modern weapons is one reason, perhaps the major reason, for the decline of the United States' relative position in modern civilian technology and productivity, because it detracts from efforts that would otherwise go into civilian functions.

There is an iron triangle of Congressional committee members and their staffs, military and civilian officials in the Department of Defense, and contractors that works to produce this overambitious, unreliable, colossally expensive, and dangerous armament.

Brown, Harold, *Thinking about National Security* (Boulder: Westview Press, 1983). Reprinted with permission.

These concerns are expressed by a variety of commentators. Their numbers include people who have participated in weapons development programs, experienced members of Congress, and middle-level or (more rarely) senior military officers. They also include journalists and other commentators, whose less thorough familiarity with the intricacies of defense procurement does not necessarily make their allegations less worthy of serious attention.

These arguments are set forth here in their most extreme and therefore least defensible form. In fact, there is at least a little truth and sometimes a substantial truth in more moderate expressions of each. But the facts do not support the allegations. The conclusions that are in turn drawn from these allegations, and the remedies proposed, are often wildly out of line. The situation can be more realistically summarized as follows.

The United States has no real choice but to adopt advanced technology for its weapons systems, given the relative advantages it can provide over potential adversaries, and the fact that the American public and its political leaders are willing to maintain only a certain level of defense spending. Moreover, if correctly handled, U.S. reliance on advanced technology is likely to produce a more effective military capability.

There is less spinoff from defense-oriented research and development to the civilian sector today than there was in the 1950s. That is, the civilian sector profits less from military research and development (R&D). In fact, U.S. military research and development now rides, to a considerable extent, on the back of civilian technology, especially in the areas of advanced electronics and integrated circuits. But military R&D still contributes to civilian technology substantially. And the deficiences of U.S. industry in productivity and in competition with other countries, notably Japan, are very much less a consequence of the division of technical talent to military R&D than they are of a variety of cultural factors, of business organization and labor union practices, and of government regulatory, employment, tax, and antitrust policies. The relationships between military and civilian R&D differ in the Soviet Union, Western Europe, and Japan. None of these is a better model for the United States.

Institutional, operational, and industrial forces create pressure to use insufficiently mature technology in military weapons systems and, more often, to use mature technology to achieve peak performance while slighting the features of low cost, reliability, and maintainability. These forces typically cause contractors to overpromise performance and military user agencies to push for the higher performance that the contractor offered in the brochure that won the contract, to the detriment of those other factors. Together the contractor and the operator often push the developing agency and the program manager into an impossible situation. When the program manager is squeezed, so are the virtues of reliability and affordability. It takes a strong program manager, backed by the most senior military and civilian officials in DOD, to withstand those pressures. Some have— and these are not always the ones who are given credit for being great program managers. The Congressional role in this matter is equivocal. Sometimes knowledgeable legislators (or their staffers) without a constituent interest or personal ax to grind will side with sensible management. More often, contractor pressure expressed through Congress, or the lure of power without responsibility combined with a Congressional staffer's whim, will exacerbate the problem.

The Lessons of History

Historians can speak of the advantage of the then inferior but less expensive (and therefore more numerous) iron swords over bronze ones to the Dorian invaders of Mycenaean Greece, of the iron-beaked prow to the Roman navies, of "Greek fire" in prolonging the life of the Byzantine empire, or of the rate of fire of the longbow to the English at Agincourt. There is some question of how relevant any of these examples is to the choices the United States faces today or to the appropriate criteria in deciding which technologies to choose and how to employ them for military purposes. The lessons of World War I and World War II are more applicable.[1]

During World War I, the United States was behind both its allies and the Germans in technology, in aircraft, in tanks, in artillery, and probably even in naval design. During World War II, the United States was again behind at the start in quality and sophistication of most military equipment. Never during that conflict did the United States outdistance the Germans in quality of basic military hardware—tanks, artillery, or aircraft. The antisubmarine warfare problem remained unsolved, although the combination of technology and tactics that went into U.S. aircraft carriers came to dominate the naval war in the Pacific. Moreover, in jet aircraft and guided aerodynamic (V-I) and ballistic (V-II) missiles the Germans remained ahead to the end of the war. It was primarily the quantity, not the quality, of equipment that gave the United States its advantage.

But there were some notable exceptions. These proved critical, at least in limiting the duration of the war, both by preventing the Axis powers from making even greater gains at the beginning and by terminating the war in the Pacific. The critical developments included radar, the proximity fuse, the atomic bomb, and cryptanalysis. The British did the initial work on radar, but during the last three years of the war the United States carried out most of its application. Neither the Germans nor the Japanese were able to match it in quality or quantity. U.S. researchers were also responsible for developing the proximity fuse and nuclear weapons. Great Britain and the United States cooperated in using cryptanalysis for major military gain.

The Situation Today

The present situation differs in two important ways from that of World War II. First, the number of troops and the amount of equipment available by 1943 clearly favored the United States and the Allies. Second, as in World War I, the United States had a period of years between the time that U.S. participation was clearly envisioned, or at which it entered the war, and the time the crucial battles were fought.

If one considers the likely combat scenarios in which the United States today might find itself engaged, neither of these conditions would be fulfilled. In the first place, the United States and its allies would not have an advantage in numbers of personnel or quantity of materiel. Even cursory examinations of the current economic, political, and social situation make it clear that the United States would enter any such confrontation with the Soviets with a much smaller active-duty and reserve military force. The active-duty forces of the Soviet Union are about double the size of those of the United States. U.S. and European allied forces do not fully balance those of the Warsaw Pact on the central front, and if Soviet reserves are counted, the Soviet numerical advantage is substantial. In East Asia, the United States would be at a disadvantage relative to the Soviets, even after U.S. reinforcements arrived. The overall ratios would depend on the belligerent status of other major nations or of various proxies. In Southwest Asia, the United States would find it difficult to bring forces to bear comparable in size to those of the relatively nearby Soviets.

An even more important difference in a prospective conflict is that the United States could not expect to have a year or two to prepare before the critical battles were fought. The United States must be prepared to fight from a standing start against what would undoubtedly be Soviet blitzkreig tactics, whether in Europe, in East Asia, or in Southwest Asia. Had that been the case in World War II, the Germans and the Japanese would have won. But the United States then had the good fortune to be allowed three years to build up its capabilities.

Technological quality, quantity of materiel, and size of forces are all important factors in the military balance. But there are many examples of military victory by numerically inferior forces with proper doctrine and tactics. Neither technology, quantity of materiel, nor numbers of troops can be counted on to substitute for morale, political and military strategy, and superior generalship. The incorporation of advanced technology into U.S. weapons systems must not, and need not, preclude its integration into such a political and military strategy for execution by innovative military strategists and commanders.

Can greater quantities of military hardware substitute for technological superiority in U.S. strategy, as it did in World War II? The amounts of materiel the United States now deploys are appropriate to the size of its peacetime forces. Those forces will not be much increased. If the United States were willing to raise and rely on very large reserve forces, it might be willing to pay the immense price of stockpiling the corresponding quantities of equipment for their use—tanks, planes, ships, and so on. But even that would make sense only if the United States could be sure of bringing those military forces to combat readiness and of transporting them to the theater of combat before the critical battles were fought.

It now takes two years from initial order to produce a tank, three to produce an aircraft, and at least five to produce a ship. Most personnel can be trained in a short time, so it would make sense to buy and stockpile the equipment beforehand if the U.S. anticipated (as I do not) that a global or even a European war could last for years. It does make sense, within economic constraints, to shorten those procurement lead times so that the United States could increase its forces during a period of much higher tensions lasting two or three years.

If the United States looks for comparative advantages against a potential Soviet adversary with superior numbers of forces, one of the most obvious is the relatively lower cost of incorporating high technology into U.S. military equipment. The same is true for U.S. allies. In contrast, a low technology–high manpower mix is more advantageous to the Soviets, who are behind on technology but have greater numbers. What follows is a discussion of a few areas in which U.S. high technology can and must be applied to counter Soviet numerical advantages.

Tanks

The Soviets have 40,000 tanks in their inventory, as compared to about 10,000 first-line U.S. tanks. On the NATO central front, which is a more relevant measure of what might be encountered in a combat situation, the ratio is about 2.5 to 1 in favor of the Warsaw Pact. If the United States were to try to redress this difference by manufacturing and deploying a comparable number of tanks, the initial equipment cost (not the total systems cost) for 30,000 tanks would probably be about $50 billion (1982 dollars). Over ten years, such an inventory buildup might be economically feasible. But it would also be necessary to provide crews for those tanks. Given pipeline and training figures, that would probably require 150,000 to 200,000 additional troops in the tank crews alone, and given the U.S. support ratios (or even the much more austere Soviet support ratios), it would probably require an increase in the U.S. Army of 300,000 or 400,000. There is no prospect that this will happen in peacetime, even if the United States returns to conscription.

The United States and its allies must therefore counter this advantage with some combination of innovative tactics and technology. One way to do this would be to have much better tanks. But in technologies for ground forces the Soviets are able by and large to match the United States. In fact, they produce new variations of armored vehicles at about twice the frequency of NATO, so that most of the time the best of their deployed technology tends to be ahead of NATO's. The Soviet T-72 is at least a match for our most modern versions of the M-60 tank. The U.S. M-1 tank is better than the T-72, but the Soviets will follow that up within a few years with a successor probably more advanced than the M-1. In some areas of tank technology, such as materials for armor protection, stability as a platform for target acquisition and firing, and crew comfort, the United States is ahead. In others, such as tank guns and low tank height to make the tank more difficult to see and to hit, the Soviets have advantages. In view of the claims that Soviet systems are less complex, it is interesting to note the presence of an automatic gunloader on the T-72. One more mechanical system to go wrong—but for lack of it the M-1 needs one more crew member (four, as opposed to three on the T-72) to lift and insert the 50-pound shells. The M-1 turret must also be bigger, and it must frequently revolve for loading and again to retarget.

The appropriate comparison, especially in a situation in which NATO would be defending against a Soviet attack, is that between Soviet tanks and NATO antitank capability. This is where the technology of the industrialized democracies, and specifically of the United States, can play a critical role. The United States took the lead in antitank guided missiles in the mid-1960s. Since then, the Soviets have made gains. But the United States has now introduced laser-guided artillery shells and bombs, and infrared imaging systems to guide air-to-ground ordnance. It is developing ground-launched and air-launched missiles that will contain submissiles guided by millimeter waves to acquire tanks as targets and penetrate the thinner armor on their tops from above. Such technological innovations, based on U.S. capabilities in sensor technology and in data processing, can be expected to make a major contribution to the allied ability to stop Soviet tank attacks.

Air-to-Air Missiles

A second example of the uses of technology in offsetting numerical deficiencies is in air-to-air combat capabilities. U.S. tactical air forces now hold a distinct advantage because of the longer range of U.S. air-to-air missiles, coupled with longer-range radars, more advanced data processing systems, and the ability of shorter-range, heat-seeking, infrared-guided missiles (such as the AIM-9L version of the Sidewinder) to home in on opposing aircraft from the side or even from the front, as well as from the rear. The ability to fire such a missile and then have it home in on its own, without continued attention by the firing aircraft, will inevitably be incorporated into the next generation of air-to-air missiles, thanks again to U.S. advantages in integrated circuits and data processing.

There are, as always, limits to how far such advantages can be pushed. Extensive tests in simulated air combat indicate that even the best air-to-air combat system cannot overcome a ten-to-one numerical advantage when combat takes place in an adversary's air space, with ground radar controlling the adversary's aircraft. And much of the advantage of long-range air-to-air missiles is lost if the air-to-air combat doctrine does not include firing at long range on any aircraft that fails to give the correct IFF (identification friend or foe) signal. U.S. military doctrine has in the past been at best ambiguous on this point, and restrictions have been placed on the use of long-range missiles in air combat tests. As a result, some analysts have drawn incorrect conclusions, overvaluing the advantages of superior numbers of fighter aircraft engaged (say, two-to-one or three-to-one ratios) as compared with the advantages of superior long-range air-to-air radars and missiles.

The United States must pay more attention to the competition in electronic countermeasures and counter-countermeasures, in which the Soviets have by no means lagged behind. But overall, U.S. capability in air-to-air missiles is one area in which U.S. technology has paid off.

Precision-Guided Air-to-Surface Missiles

A third general area in which U.S. technological sophistication has become to a substantial degree a substitute for large numbers is precision-guided munitions. The ability to destroy military targets is greatly dependent on the accuracy of delivery of ordnance. In many cases only a tenth or even a hundredth as many sorties by tactical aircraft are needed to accomplish the same mission, provided that they carry such precision-guided munitions. The cost and complexity of the munitions is therefore repaid many times over, not only in the reduced numbers of rounds of ordnance that are needed, but also in the reduced loss of aircraft and pilots, which constitutes the most severe price paid to accomplish a given military mission.

The U.S. Technological Lead

The three examples given share the common features of advanced electronics, integrated circuitry, and computers and data processing. In that area the United States and its European and Japanese allies maintain a five-to-seven-year lead over the Soviet bloc. This is perhaps the most solid single technological advantage possessed by the industrialized democracies. They have a much smaller, though real, lead in aircraft engines and aerodynamics and a substantial lead in antisubmarine warfare capabilities, which again results largely from advantages in data processing and sensors. As for new applications of materials science, the Soviets are ahead in some and the industrialized democracies in others.

There are thus several critical areas in which U.S. technology leads that of the Soviets. To a considerable extent these leads now offset and will continue to offset some of the Soviet numerical advantages. There are limits, however, to the numerical disadvantages they can offset, and they are not a substitute for wise strategy, effective tactics, strong leadership, trained personnel, or any of the other elements of military strength, let alone for the nonmilitary aspects of national security policy. But to fail to take advantage of them would be to throw away a major equalizing factor, much of whose cost has already been paid in any event because, for other good reasons, the United States has a large civilian and a relatively small military sector in its industrial economy. Among the technological areas in which the United States can expect in the future to enjoy such an advantage are precision-guided munitions, cruise missiles, air-to-air missiles and their associated sensors, low-observability "stealth" technology, technical systems for intelligence to offset the Soviet advantage of tighter military security, and antisubmarine warfare capabilities. Without these advantages, the comparative military position of the United States and the other industrialized democracies would be much more precarious than it is.

There is some experimental evidence that supports this assessment of U.S. military technology. When U.S.-equipped forces have engaged Soviet-equipped forces in recent years, U.S. tanks and antitank equipment, advanced fighter aircraft, air-to-air missile systems, and U.S.-inspired air battle and antiaircraft suppression tactics have worked well. These results were not against the most modern Soviet equipment or against Soviet forces, and factors other than equipment have played an important part in the outcome. But even making allowances for those factors, U.S. military equipment and doctrine for its use acquitted themselves well in both the Iran-Iraq War and the Arab-Israeli conflicts of 1973 and 1982.

The Horrible Examples

Whenever a new weapons system reaches the testing stage, a predictable pattern emerges. Test failures occur and are highly publicized. No one explains that tests would not be necessary if it were not expected that some of them would result in failures, or that these failures illuminate the changes that need to be made in the system's design. Cost overruns are announced by officials or Congressmen or discovered by investigative journalists. One source from which the cost overruns are unearthed is the so-called Selected Acquisition Report program cost summary, mandated by Congress for military systems (though not for civilian entitlement programs or for Congressional office building construction). These include as overruns the effects of overall cost inflation in the economy, for which some think Congressional actions bear part of the responsibility.[2] The General Accounting Office conducts investigations and finds that some characteristics of the system are not (or might not be) what was advertised or are (or might be) disliked by some of the people in the testing organization or the potential user organization. The new system is compared unfavorably to an existing system a few years older, now in the inventory. Exactly the same negative comments were being made about the existing but now praised program by the same critics a few years earlier: Compare the situation of the F-18 in the early 1980s with that of the F-16 five years before. It is all great sport, but it is not a very useful contribution to decision making or to national security policy.

The cycle of research, development, systems design, testing, and procurement is an extremely complex one. Judgments are difficult to make about when a technology is ripe for incorporation in a weapons system, what performance trade-offs should be made, and what degree of concurrency there should be in the development, testing, and procurement schedule. The need to balance such factors and to make such trade-offs naturally produces differences of judgment, even from those who have spent their professional lives considering such matters. The people of the United States are trusting both their money and their lives to these judgments. The decisions have often left much to be desired, resulting in high costs, delayed schedules, and imperfect performance. But the American public should not place more trust in the conclusions drawn about these matters by journalists and television personalities.

Some defense critics conclude from the problems they find in new systems that what is needed is a return to the good old days of wooden ships and iron men, or of spit and baling wire. Such an attitude is dangerous nonsense. Large numbers of low-technology weapons cannot be counted on to outfight smaller numbers of modern weapons. Even if they could, the United States cannot, as explained above, expect to have enough troops to operate larger numbers of weapons. The United States would almost surely end up with about the same numbers of weapons as at present, but of much less capable systems. The United States does need the cruise missile, it does need the F-18 fighter aircraft, it does need the M-1 tank.

It is a sensible management practice on the part of the Secretary of Defense to have the production of each new system carried out at only a low rate until the development and operational testing have adequately demonstrated performance and reliability, thus encouraging the contractor to meet those requirements before going into a high rate of production. In peacetime, a crash program substantially telescoping development and production is justified only when the availability of some single weapons system at a particular time is seen as representing the difference between peace and war or between victory and defeat. With the present multiplicity of weapons systems, such a situation almost never arises. But caution in approving high rates of production early in a program is quite different from concluding, as some critics have, that the modernization of U.S. systems has caused reduced military capability, or that more modern systems are necessarily more complex to operate or even to maintain. The jet engine goes longer between overhauls than the piston engine. The F-4, much older than the F-16, requires more hours of maintenance for each hour of flight time. And modern electronic technology has made radar and guided missiles more reliable than they were in the 1940s or 1960s.

A new generation of "smart bombs" allows the operator to designate the target and then have the munition itself hold to that designation while the operator turns his attention elsewhere. This requires less training for the operator, not more. A "joystick" approach, in which a bomb or antitank missile is flown into the target, requires much more training and experience on the part of the operator than does a system in which the operator keeps the crosshairs on the target. The electronic and control systems that in the latter case automatically steer the munition to the target will be more complex. In both of these systems the operator must watch the target until impact. The "fire and forget" approach will require still more design complexity, and will cost more, but it does not require operator attention after target designation, and it does not expose the launcher or operator to counterfire after target designation.

There is much to be said for separating the responsibility for operational test and evaluation of a new system from the developing agency when making the decisions on whether to proceed with procurement. But those who advocate separation of this responsibility from the military service that will use the system go too far. Moreover, development objectives and the needs of operational evaluation must often be met in the same test. Efficiency therefore dictates that the developer be involved in some operational testing. But there should be an operational organization to evaluate the performance of systems before they are bought in large numbers. It should consist not of personnel specially selected for their technical skills, but of ordinary troops. And it should report to the Service Chief outside development channels. The Navy's Operational Test and Evaluation Force does just this.

How Some Others Do It

It is often alleged that the Soviets have solved all these problems of judgment, while the United States has not. There are cases in which the Soviets have emphasized simplicity with some success. Moreover, they tend to keep a much larger number of development programs going at one time in a given area. By and large they introduce about twice as many models of tanks, armored personnel vehicles, aircraft, and air defense systems, and they tend to blanket all the fields of technology more completely. They can do this because they are willing to devote to military expenditures more than double the percentage of GNP and to spend about 50 percent more on military research and development than the United States does and to pay their troops and workers much less. Massive Soviet military development and production place a substantial premium on the United States's making correct judgments both on which technologies to push and on which weapons to develop and produce. Because U.S. military R&D funding is smaller, the United States has chosen to concentrate on a few choices rather than playing the entire field. Inevitably this leads to a few big systems and leaves less room for errors. If U.S. judgments are generally correct, this approach is more efficient than the Soviet approach; if incorrect, less effective than theirs.

There is another alternative. The United States could adopt the Soviet approach and pursue almost everything of interest in technology, doubling the number of full-scale systems brought through development and production. That would require the United States to augment by about 50 percent its present military R&D expenditures—now more than $20 billion a year and growing at a rate of more than 6 percent a year in real dollars.

In my view, such a switch would probably be a mistake, even if it were politically and economically feasible. There is more to be gained by achieving a more efficient and rational allocation of development and production tasks with U.S. allies. Major steps in that direction have been taken since the mid-1970s.

Allied defense-oriented R&D spending, at a current level of about 40 percent of that of the United States, helps offset the Soviet advantage, despite the existing inefficiencies. Furthermore, there is a large civilian R&D infrastructure in the United States and the other industrialized democracies, especially in microcircuitry and data processing and to a lesser extent in aerodynamics and even in materials, that is not duplicated in the Soviet Union.

One generally unrealized sign that the U.S. development approach is comparable in its effectiveness to that of the Soviets is that U.S. systems take about as long to develop and procure as do theirs, though the United States could probably shorten this if some changes were made in the industrial base and in our Congressional appropriations and executive procurement procedures. For the Soviets, the time from initiation of development to achievement of an operational capability is limited by the level of their managerial efficiency, which is better in their military than in their civilian sector, and sometimes by their technological shortcomings. Soviet decisions to proceed through the key stages of development and production for major systems are made at the top level of the party and government. Once that decision is made, resources are assured and programs are seldom modified—even when they should be.

Development times in the United States benefit from the advanced state of U.S. technology and the support of an efficient civilian sector, though competition from the civilian sector has lately lengthened the lead time for some components. Delays result from the number of levels of government that can delay execution after development is initiated and from the stop-and-go funding associated with multiple reviews.

The Real Problems

If the widely heralded criticisms are often off the mark, what are the real problems in choosing technologies to push and in applying them to the weapons systems needed by U.S. military forces to give them an edge against potential adversaries?

One problem is the tendency to try to achieve the best possible performance (speed, payload, range) in systems and to take full advantage of the newest technology only for that purpose. The operating commands have often insisted, for example, on the highest possible speed for a given aircraft design, without asking what value the last 100 knots provides and what it sacrificed, to achieve that capability, in other desirable performance characteristics or in reliability. In other cases, fleet air-defense missiles have been given ranges considerably beyond those at which the radar associated with them could provide reliable target information. This situation is reversed in the new Aegis fleet air-defense system: There the radar outperforms the missile. Almost always, these unnecessary increments of performance have been paid for in unreliability, demonstrated in either more frequent equipment failure or more frequent maintenance requirements. Accepting a performance 5 percent or 10 percent lower than the peak that could be obtained from new technology and using the design freedom thus achieved to operate engines at lower temperatures, structures at lower stresses, or circuits at higher redundancy pays rich dividends in reliability. Moreover, it is better to achieve higher reliability by using for that purpose part of the capabilities of advanced technology (for example, the redundancy made possible by microelectronics) than it is to seek reliability by using older technology or older equipment beyond its time. Failure to use modern technology to get the right combination of performance and reliability creates a high risk that the Soviet materiel will be superior. Given the inevitable Soviet advantage in numbers, that is an unacceptable risk.

A second real problem is the need to train U.S. military forces, both the combat forces who will operate the equipment and the support personnel who will maintain it. The increasing unit cost of weapons has reduced their use for practice and training. More realistic simulators provided by modern technology can ease this problem.

It is U.S. practice to do much of the equipment maintenance in the field, as opposed to the Soviet system of maintaining large stocks of equipment and replacing complete units from replacement depots. There has been a real erosion since World War II in the mechanical experience of military recruits and in their technical education. The decline in the mathematical and technical course work in the high schools and even in the universities over the last fifteen years, after the brief renaissance engendered by Sputnik, is alarming. One new craze may help: The generation raised playing computer games may find that experience as useful in operating some kinds of military equipment as the World War II generation found its experience repairing a simpler generation of automobiles in dealing with the materiel of World War II, the first really mechanized large-scale combat operation.

It will take a variety of skilled and educated personnel to conceive, design, manufacture at acceptable cost, operate, and maintain the advanced and complex weapons and support systems that will be needed. These personnel include research scientists, design and production engineers, technicians, and technically trained military people. The erosion of training of technician-level personnel in the civilian educational system, the poor mathematics and science curricula in U.S. elementary and secondary schools, the declining proportion of students in science and engineering at the undergraduate and graduate levels, and the lack of growth or even the shrinkage in federal support for research, teaching, and equipment in these fields during recent years are real and serious problems.

Distinctions must be made among complexity of function, complexity of design, difficulty of maintenance, and difficulty of operation. The first is inevitable; the United States has often overdone the second, which has led to the third; U.S. equipment usually avoids the fourth. Reliability and ease of maintenance must be emphasized from the time requirements are set and design begins, even at the expense of performance. Greater automaticity will inevitably involve greater complexity, which will reduce reliability and increase maintenance requirements. The former can be compensated for, to some degree, by providing redundancy of subsystems where that is made possible by the lower weight and smaller size associated with advanced technology. Very-high-speed integrated circuit technology and designs now being developed under DOD sponsorship are one example of a way to achieve this capability.

The extra maintenance that complex equipment may require is best split. One segment of a maintenance program could include the replacement of modular sections in the field. If the design is modular and the equipment is self-testing, equipment replacement would not require highly-trained personnel, but it would require that replacement modules be available at field maintenance facilities. The other segment should include rear-echelon repair of faulty modules and of subsystems or systems that cannot be either replaced or repaired in the field.

Another real and serious problem is the inflation of major defense systems costs at a rate higher than the general inflation rate in the economy. This phenomenon was experienced from 1978 to 1980. Its effect was to cut the quantities of major systems procured by 10 or 15 percent below what had been planned. This is a separate phenomenon from the increase in unit costs as a result of reductions in the rate of procurement. It can be traced instead to competition for resources with a then-healthy part of the economy. The civilian aerospace industry had a brief boom as a consequence of the need to replace an earlier generation of jet aircraft with a new generation that is quieter and consumes much less fuel per ton-mile. At the same time, the airlines projected an increase in passenger traffic, largely as a result of the airline deregulation scheduled to be phased in from 1978 to 1985. This increase has since proven illusory. Simultaneously, a growth in consumer electronics products using integrated circuits (video games, pocket calculators) increased the demand for the same kind of electronic components that are used in major weapons systems. This competition for air frame, engine, and electronic components drove up prices for those items more rapidly than the average prices in the civilian economy. There emerged correspondingly and simultaneously a shortage of engineers, which drove up their salaries. There was also a rapid increase in the price of certain strategic materials heavily used in defense systems.

All of these phenomena were exacerbated by the shrinkage in the defense subcontracting structure that had taken place over the previous fifteen years. The decline in levels of defense procurement, the uncertainties in the program as a result of the cycles of increased and decreased defense procurement, the relatively low profit, and the opening up of new civilian markets all pushed some subcontractors (especially the second-tier and third-tier subsubcontractors) entirely out of defense subcontracting and caused most of the others to reduce the percentage of their business given over to defense. These factors made it more difficult for the prime contractors on defense systems to get competitive bids from subcontractors for the components of their systems. This in turn raised prices. As a result, major defense systems rose in price at an annual rate 5 percent or even 10 percent higher than the budgetary figures assumed by the Office of Management and Budget in its government-wide projections for those years. Inflation in overall defense procurement, about half of which is in major systems, corresponded rather closely to the producer price index.

This phenomenon suggests a more general problem connected with the fact that the political process tends to produce unsteadiness in programs, with an off again–on again cycle. At the very least there is likely to be a four-year cycle, corresponding to Presidential elections. But there are also annual budget cycles. Defense spending is set forth as a five-year program, but even during the 1960s, when more stability in programs was politically possible, the funding for a given weapons systems such as the F-111 could be seen after the fact as five one-year segments of five different five-year programs. Such unsteadiness in funding clearly makes for inefficiency and cost escalation; it is compounded by the instability of personnel assignments, especially for program managers. This complex of deficiencies is far more serious in its effects than the allegations of the new generation of defense critics that are listed at the beginning of this chapter.

Solutions

If these are the real problems, what are some of the real solutions? There are no panaceas, and few really new ideas. Fundamental solutions must be contingent on fundamental changes not only in the management structure of the Department of Defense but in the way that the Federal Government does business, including such basic issues as the relations between the executive and legislative branches. But there are some important palliatives that suggest themselves strongly.

One is stable management. Broad policies, whether in international relations, military strategy, or procurement practices, change slowly even when administrations change. Individual weapons systems are considerably more subject to the attitudes of subordinate officials who, at the political level, change even more rapidly than administrations. The predilections, right or wrong, of individual legislators and their staffers also have a significant effect on the stability of programs, usually a bad one because programs become an element in political bargaining. Multiyear contracting, urged on Congress by previous administrations and pushed to partial adoption in the Reagan administration, should help to ease this problem. But what hurts most of all are the changes in program managers that tend to occur every two or three years as part of the normal military rotations. Continuity of assignments and holding program managers accountable would have a big payoff. Major program managers should be kept at the head of a given systems program office for six or seven years, allowing them faster-than-normal rates of promotion if they manage their programs well. This would be a change from the usual situation, which is that an officer at the colonel or Navy captain level who is not moved around among assignments has reduced chances for promotion. In such programs as the Special Projects Office of the Navy (which ran the Polaris and Poseidon missile programs), the ballistic missile division of the Air Force, and more recently the joint service Cruise Missile Program Office, this pattern has been followed. These programs have been among the most successful, although in their later phases all encountered production cost overruns.

A second measure that would improve the application of technology and the effectiveness of modernized weapons systems would be to give the systems contractors performance specifications rather than technical specifications. Performance specifications indicate the performance to be achieved; technical specifications detail the way to achieve it. To the extent that technical specifications are used, they inhibit contractor creativity. The prime contractor needs to have some leeway for trade-offs among the various performance specifications, giving substantial weight to maintainability and reliability. The development of the F-16 was a successful example of such an approach.

A third prescription, to avoid making inflation rates higher in defense than in the rest of the economy, is to have defense procurement grow at a modest rate in real dollars. Real growth of 10 percent a year in military systems procurement is not likely to cause inflation in unit prices. Overall procurement expenditure growth of 20 percent to 30 percent in a year will increase unit prices significantly. In extreme cases, more of the increased funding can end up in higher unit costs than in larger output of units.

One desirable change would be to use the profit incentive more effectively and to give more weight to past performance and less to the quality of the brochures that prospective contractors prepare as part of their bids in choosing among contractors. A larger return on investment than what has become common in defense work may be required to bring more subcontractors to bid on defense programs and to encourage both subcontractors and prime contractors to invest more of their own resources. This is not a popular idea. Such defense critics as John Kenneth Galbraith have argued that the defense industry ought to be nationalized, because it takes no risks and is not responsive enough to direction from the Federal bureaucracy. Professor Galbraith lauds the flexibility allowed by federal shipyards and arsenals. Such an attitude could be held only by one who has never tried to close down or reduce the size of a federal shipyard or arsenal. In my experience, that is enormously more difficult to do than to cancel a contract or allow a contractor to go into bankruptcy. There was much criticism of the famous "golden handshake," a government guarantee of bank loans to the Lockheed Aircraft Corporation in connection with the C-5 aircraft contract. That arrangement levied a $200 million loss on Lockheed, from which the company has not fully recovered, though the government has never had to pay out any money on the guarantee. The settlement was harsh but just. It is difficult to imagine treating a government facility as sternly. Because the private sector is by and large more efficient than the government sector, that sector should be encouraged to use on defense programs the efficiencies of which it is fundamentally capable.

Summary

There are real problems in employing modern technology in defense weapons systems—although they are not the ones set forth by the current crop of popular critics—and the solutions to those real problems are not easy. But the United States cannot afford to abandon the advantages that modern technology offers. It also needs to keep its lead in military technology by employing in the military sector advanced technologies available in the U.S. civilian economy but not in that of the Soviets. There are alternatives to this reliance on technology: doubling the number of U.S. personnel under arms to approach Soviet levels, increasing defense procurement budgets by 50 percent over what they would otherwise be to compete with the Soviets in quantities of equipment, and substituting purchase of production by allies for much of the current U.S. production of military equipment. None of these would be acceptable to the American people. The defense procurement budget will have to continue to grow. The United States will have to share more rationally the task of defense development and procurement with its allies. U.S. defense personnel requirements will prove a difficult problem in any case. But to exacerbate the difficulty of all these choices by abandoning the advantages of technology is an unnecessary, unintelligent, and self-defeating course.

The military balance between the United States and its allies and friends, on the one hand, and the Soviet Union and the states subordinated to them, on the other, is not nearly so unfavorable as the denigrators of U.S. military capability have been proclaiming for the last few years. But it is precarious enough. The United States must not fail to take advantage of the advantages that it has—economic, political, ideological, or any other. And among all of these, the U.S. technological advantage is one of the most important and valuable.

Notes

1. The Korean War showed that superior technology and materiel resources can compensate for inferior numbers of personnel. The Vietnam War showed that technology, along with an enormously superior GNP, larger forces, and more materiel, will not win a war in the absence of an adequate political infrastructure in the nation being defended, a determination comparable to that of the forces on the other side, or a willingness to use those advantages.

2. The costs of defense systems or of decisions made about them have come to be expressed publicly in terms of lifetime acquisition costs or overall system costs (including operation), because the analyses in the Department of Defense are sufficiently detailed to take a stab at such numbers. Defense critics sometimes object (correctly) when only acqui-

sition, not personnel, spares, or maintenance costs, are included. For a social program, the annual costs are given, often for the first year (before full implementation). Presumably this is because, the program being likely to go on forever, there is no systems "lifetime" cost. The result is that some legislators and analysts will press for a choice between a new weapons system and a domestic social program. In principle, the comparison may be feasible. They announce that the weapons system, estimated at $40 billion current dollars, will probably cost $80 billion considering inflation and overruns. They may well be right. The social program will cost only $3 billion. Right again—and the comparative cost (and by implication, the priority) seems clear. But the cost of the weapons system is a twenty-year cost and includes the effects of inflation. The cost of the social program is an estimated first-year cost. In fact, the social program is likely to cost $5 billion in current dollars the first year, $10 billion the fifth year (because eligibility will be expanded and because benefits are indexed to inflation), and even more thereafter. At the end of twenty years, the weapons system will have cost $80 billion in current dollars, and a new one will be in process. The social program will have cost, over the same twenty years, say, $300 billion in current dollars and will be spending $40 billion a year. It can be expected to be continued, at an ever-increasing rate, thereafter. Comparisons are not easy.

Discussion Questions

1. What role does technology play in shaping the international environment? Give examples.

2. How does technology affect the domestic environment? Give examples.

3. Has there been a traditional U.S. approach to technology as it relates to national security policy? If so, what is it, and is it likely to change?

5

The American Approach to War

Robert E. Osgood

Dissociation of Power and Policy

Notwithstanding these general principles concerning the relation between military power and national policy, some of the strongest American traditions in foreign policy run counter to the fundamental requirements of a strategy of limited war. Although America's military policies have been revolutionized during the past decade, her basic propensities, formed during the protracted period of nineteenth-century innocence, remain in effect. Under pressure of the Soviet threat, the American people have learned that military power is an essential element of foreign relations; but they are only beginning to learn that military power must be strictly disciplined by the concrete requirements of national policy.

Dissociation of power and policy is in some measure common to all democracies. A democratic people—or the influential portion that cares what the nation does in international politics—associates itself morally and emotionally with national policies and actions, and demands that the government reflect its sentiments. This inevitably inhibits a democratic government from acting upon the kind of dispassionate calculation of ends and means that a rational adjustment of power and policy requires. For popular sentiment does not always coincide with the imperatives of power; and once the public has invested its emotional and moral capital in a particular position, it is reluctant to withdraw it—especially if this is tantamount to a defeat—even though the investment proves a bad one from an objective standpoint. These democratic propensities are especially strong when the people's spiritual commitment to their nation is heightened by the stress of war.

For many reasons it will always be difficult for modern democracies to put Clausewitz' dictum into practice. Therefore, few of the following observations apply exclusively to the United States. However, among all democratic people, Americans are bound to find it particularly difficult to use military power as a rational instrument of power. More than any other great nation, America's basic predispositions and her experience in world politics encourage the dissociation of power and policy.

This dissociation is most marked in America's traditional conception of war and peace as diametrically opposite states of affairs, to be governed by entirely dif-

Osgood, Robert E., *Limited War* (Chicago: University of Chicago Press, 1957). Copyright © 1957 by the University of Chicago. Reprinted with permission.

ferent rules and considerations without regard for the continuity of political conflict. With the country at peace, foreign policy has been formed and executed with
little regard for considerations of military power; but with the country at war,
foreign policy has been largely suspended, and immediate military considerations
have been dominant. Typically, during war the determining objective has been to
obtain a clear-cut, definitive military victory in the most effective manner as
quickly as possible; but when peace has returned, the determining objective has
been to get rid of the instruments of victory and to return to "normal" as fast as
possible. In neither case have national actions been governed by careful regard for
the international political consequences. With power and policy so dissociated,
America has been notoriously slow to anticipate war or prepare for it, but it has
been shocked into single-minded determination to overwhelm the enemy once war
has broken out. This basic propensity confirms the observation that Alexis de
Tocqueville made on the basis of his American tour more than a century ago:

> When a war has at length, by its long continuance, roused the whole community
> from their peaceful occupations and ruined their minor undertakings, the same
> passions that made them attach so much importance to the maintenance of peace
> will be turned to arms. War, after it has destroyed all modes of speculation,
> becomes itself the great and sole speculation, to which all the ardent and am-
> bitious desires that equality engenders are exclusively directed. Hence it is that
> the self-same democratic nations that are so reluctant to engage in hostilities some-
> times perform prodigious achievements when once they have taken the field.[1]

The results of this approach to war are manifest in the record of America's
foreign relations since the turn of this century. On the one hand, the United States
has demonstrated an impressive ability to defeat the enemy. Yet, on the other
hand, it has been unable to deter war; it has been unprepared to fight war; it has
failed to gain the objects it fought for; and its settlements of wars have not brought
satisfactory peace. The blame for these failures must be shared by circumstances
beyond American control; but to the extent that they were avoidable, they must be
attributed not to a weakness in the basic elements of national power but to a deficiency in the political management of power. And this deficiency stems not from
lack of intelligence or diplomatic skill but from the faulty habit of mind that
regards war as a thing in itself rather than as a continuation of political intercourse. War as something to abolish, war as something to get over as quickly as
possible, war as a means of punishing the enemy who dared to disturb the peace,
war as a crusade—these conceptions are all compatible with the American outlook.
But war as an instrument for attaining concrete, limited political objectives,
springing from the continuing stream of international politics and flowing toward
specific configurations of international power—somehow this conception seems
unworthy to a proud and idealistic nation.

Surveying some of the most successful American military efforts, one is struck
by the extent to which the United States ignored or deliberately excluded concrete

political considerations. The Spanish-American War and World War I had momentous political consequences; in both of them American intervention had a decisive effect in shaping the configurations of national power. Yet the reasons for which the nation entered and fought these wars had scarcely anything to do with the conduct of military operations or the political results. Avenging the sinking of the *Maine,* liberation of the oppressed Cubans, and Manifest Destiny; the vindication of neutral rights, banishing autocracy, and the establishment of universal peace—these issues and goals excited powerful sentiments of national honor and righteousness, but they did not direct the great military power, which they generated, toward feasible political objectives serving America's vital interest amid the changing configurations of national power. In fact, Woodrow Wilson specifically proscribed such self-interested objectives as being incompatible with America's mission to serve humanity impartially. It is little wonder that, having pursued its wars in a political vacuum, the country was unprepared to assume the vast political responsibilities that followed war and that, disillusioned over the disparity between high expectations and the wars' disappointing results, America tried to withdraw from the world of conflict into an illusory isolation.

Somewhat differently, the United States entered and fought World War II primarily for the sake of its security. Yet so far as the nation as a whole and almost all its leaders were concerned, World War II was waged with virtually no consideration of the impact of military operations upon the international political conditions of American security in the postwar world, aside from the one overriding condition of destroying the Fascist powers. When the war was won, America overwhelmingly ignored the continuing need of supporting foreign policy with adequate military power and wholly neglected to prepare for the new forms that the continuing struggle for power assumed in the aftermath of war.

The same dissociation of power and policy characterizing America's approach to war has, quite naturally, infused the whole realm of military planning concerned with preparedness for war. Before World War II strategic thinking was dominated by the assumption that the only legitimate purpose of the military establishment was to protect American rights and to ward off direct attacks upon American soil. This assumption seemingly obviated the necessity of calculating military policies in terms of American interests abroad and their relation to the interests and power of other nations. Although there were repeated controversies over the size and composition of the military establishment, these controversies were almost barren of any fundamental discussion relating military policies to concrete objectives of foreign policy. In fact, they usually revolved around issues of military organization, as though these issues were unrelated to questions of national strategy. To be sure, defense appropriations were customarily justified as being necessary for "the protection and the promotion of national policy," but this stock phrase had no more practical import than "the general welfare" would have had. In effect, defense policies were formulated and legislated in a political vacuum; one of the chief criteria of their acceptability seemed to be that they should not be entangled with considerations of international politics, the very stuff of national policy.

The dissociation of military policy from political policy was reflected in the almost complete absence of collaboration, informal or organized, between military and political leaders until the eve of American intervention in World War II.[2] Military policies were formed without knowledge of their political ends or consequences. Political decisions were made without information or professional advice about military capabilities. We can hardly speak of a coherent national strategy of the United States, as opposed to purely military strategy, until the rudiments began to appear under the pressure of the cold war. The traditional American approach to military policy is epitomized in the Chief of Staff's defense of the War Department's program for a large regular army in 1919, when in reply to Senator Hiram Johnson's futile inquiry about the nature of the international situation that required such an army, General March stoutly assured the Senate that the program "was framed on its merits, without any relation whatever to national politics or international politics."[3]

Aversion to Violence

The traditional American approach to war and, more generally, to the use of military power is a product of certain basic conceptions and predispositions concerning international relations, combined with American experience in international relations. The basic conceptions and predispositions are not peculiar to Americans; they are shared, in some measure, by all peoples under the influence of the Western liberal tradition. However, they have assumed a distinct form and emphasis in the American environment by virtue of the distinct nature of America's relations with the outside world.

The typical dissociation of military power and national policy in the American approach arises, in the first place, from a profound moral and emotional aversion to violence. This aversion springs, ultimately, from the great liberal and humane ideals of Christianity and the Enlightenment, which look toward man's progressive ability to resolve human conflicts by peaceful settlement—by impartial reference to reason, law, and morality.

Among Americans these ideals have a distinct sense of immediacy. They are not content to leave the ideals as mere aspirations. They assume that ideals have the power to transform the human and material environment in remarkable ways, if only they believe in them strongly enough. And, perhaps more profoundly than any other people, they are convinced that these ideals are an integral part of the national mission and creed. In American domestic politics the liberal and humane ideals grow somewhat ambiguous amid the competing claims upon them put forth by scores of groups and individuals caught up in the contest for power; but in the sphere of international relations, where the issues are comparatively remote from everyday experience, ideals carry great and unembarrassed conviction.

The American aversion to violence in international relations is not the sort of aversion that results in absolute pacifism. It does not prevent participation—in fact, enthusiastic participation—in war when war cannot honorably be avoided. However, it does inhibit indulgence in the enormous evil of war for limited, prosaic ends of national policy. This kind of war strikes Americans as cynical and ignoble. It is as though they conceived of war as such a denial of normal relations among states as to be beyond ordinary political intercourse among nations. In this sense, they regard war as a social aberration, in a category by itself, to which it seems incongruous to apply ordinary rules of reason and restraint. Like Prince Andrew in *War and Peace,* struggling on the eve of the Battle of Borodino to make sense of of the chaos of war, they feel, as Tolstoy himself is said to have felt, that war is too serious and too terrible to be fought with anything but war's own self-sufficient rules. "War is not courtesy," the Prince exclaims, "but the most horrible thing in life; and we ought to understand that and not play at war. We ought to accept this terrible necessity sternly and seriously. It all lies in that: get rid of falsehood and let war be war and not a game."

However, if moral sensibilities forbid the use of war as an instrument of national policy, they do not prevent the use of war as an instrument of ideology, once war has become unavoidable. In a sense they encourage this; for tender consciences find in broader, more exalted goals a kind of moral compensation for the enormity of war and a rational justification for their contamination with evil. Thus the very ideals that proscribe war become the incentive for fighting war. An aversion to violence is transmuted into the exaltation of violence.

Nothing defeats the political limitation and control of military power like the transformation of war into an ideological contest. However, we should not suppose that the aversion to war, which induces this ideological transformation, is purely an abstract moral sentiment. Quite aside from the moral odium of war, the fear of violence and the revulsion from warfare are bound to be strong among a people who have grown as fond of social order and material well-being as Americans. War not only kills and maims; it not only separates friends and families. War upsets the whole scale of social priorities of an individualistic and materialistic scheme of life, so that the daily round of getting and spending is subordinated to the collective welfare of the nation in a hundred grievous ways—from taxation to death. This accounts for an emotional aversion to war, springing from essentially self-interested motives, which is quite as compelling as the moral aversion to war. And, like the moral aversion, it tends to put a premium upon military considerations at the expense of limited, political objectives in the conduct of war. For the natural reaction to war's threat to the security and happiness of the individual is to try to end the war as soon as possible by destroying the enemy. Therefore, it is difficult to countenance any restraint or diversion of the maximum military effort for the sake of some limited, prosaic political objective, such as the establishment of a local balance of power in some remote geographical area. Moreover, because American society places such a high value on the life of each individual,

Americans are disposed to demand that the sacrifice of life serve some purpose of commensurate value; and total victory seems like the minimum compensation.

Pugnacity

The more one examines the American approach to war, the more it seems to spring from contradictory motives. Certainly, the nation's moral and emotional aversion to violence is joined by a strong streak of pugnacity. There broods in the American mind a fighting spirit that recalls the days when the United States was a bumptious young nation trying to prove itself to the world, as well as the more recent days when the populace boasted that the country had never lost a war. The predisposition to exercise force to the utmost is rooted in America's consciousness of the great material power it has gained by "thinking big" and by applying all the vast resources of technology to the conquest of nature.

It is important to note that American pugnacity is not cunning and premeditated; rather it is a romantic impulse that erects boldness and initiative into patriotic tenets, but only in response to provocation. It is true that in the expansionist years the fighting spirit was strong enough to precipitate at least two wars—the Mexican War and the Spanish–American War—and to sustain a powerful strain of aggressiveness, which, but for the internal divisions created by the slavery question, might have fostered more extensive military adventures. America's profoundly peaceful instincts since her coming of age, however, have suppressed this overt aggressiveness to the point where only the strongest provocation will arouse it. Yet American pugnacity is perhaps all the more passionate for that reason, because it springs from righteous indignation rather than from design. As George Kennan has observed:

> Democracy fights in anger—it fights for the very reason that it was forced to go to war. It fights to punish the power that was rash enough and hostile enough to provoke it—to teach that power a lesson it will not forget, to prevent the thing from happening again. . . . It does look as though the real source of the emotional fervor which we Americans are able to put into a war lies less in any objective understanding of the wider issues involved than in a profound irritation over the fact that other people have finally provoked us to the point where we had no alternative but to take up arms.[4]

If American pugnacity had ever been the kind that springs from the pure egoism of national aggrandizement, it might have been accompanied by a more rational and calculating approach to the use of military power. But because it was always impassioned, always tinged with outrage, moral fervor, or sheer animal exuberance, American wars have been governed less by expediency than by the kinds of broad goals and exhilarating emotions that override the rational control of force for limited objectives.

In reality, pugnacity and hatred of war, here separated analytically, are commonly fused into one explosive emotional coalescence that gives the American approach to war its characteristic preoccupation with military operations and its contempt of considerations extraneous to victory. In both words and action no one has expressed this approach to war in all its passionate ambivalence more poignantly than General Douglas MacArthur. In his congressional testimony in 1951 on his relief from command in the Far East, MacArthur went out of his way, as he has on several occasions, to stress his profound hatred of war and his belief that it should be outlawed. "I am just one hundred per cent a believer against war," he said.

I believe the enormous sacrifices that have been brought about by the scientific methods of killing have rendered war a fantastic solution of international difficulties. In war, as it is waged now, with the enormous losses on both sides, both sides will lose. It is a form of mutual suicide; and I believe that the entire effort of modern society should be concentrated on an endeavor to outlaw war as a method of the solution of problems between nations.[5]

On the other hand, if war could not be outlawed and if the United States became involved in war, MacArthur was equally convinced that such a war should be fought all-out to a clear-cut victory; and he condemned political considerations that might hinder the utmost military efforts to destroy the enemy forces quickly and effectively as being contrary to all the rules of war and the simple dictates of humanity. On this ground he severely criticized the Truman administration's restrictions upon the military effort in Korea. The administration's policy, he declared,

seems to me to introduce a new concept into military operations—the concept of appeasement, the concept that when you use force, you can limit that force. . . . To me, that would mean that you would have a continued and indefinite extension of bloodshed, which would have limitless—a limitless end. You would not have the potentialities of destroying the enemy's military power and bringing the conflict to a decisive close in the minimum of time and with a minimum of loss.[6]

Although the American people, as a whole, were probably unwilling to follow MacArthur's specific program for achieving victory, there can be little doubt, judging from their spontaneous emotional reaction to his return to the United States and from the whole disturbing impact of the Korean War, that the General's words expressed something that is deep and compelling in the nation's attitude toward war even now.

Depreciation of Power

America's non-political approach to war must also be ascribed to a depreciation of the factor of power in international relations. In order to employ military power as a rational and effective instrument of national policy, a nation must first have a foreign policy that is defined in terms appropriate to power. But Americans have traditionally depreciated "power politics" as the tool of wicked statesmen or the last recourse during occasional crises. American policy has been preoccupied with two extreme levels of objectives: on the one hand, the level of technical performance—as in the realm of arbitration treaties or, more recently, economic aid—and, on the other hand, the level of philosophical generalities concerning the highest ideals of mankind. Too often it has left unattended the intermediate realm of politics that is concerned with the translation of national power into concrete situations of fact.

A nation that does not attend to this intermediate realm of objectives as an aspect of the continuing contest for power among nations cannot comprehend war as a continuation of political intercourse; for power is the raw material of international relations, from which the need for continual political direction arises. By depreciating the role of power the traditional American conception of international relations excludes the most important link between war and peace. Without this link, war and peace appear to be antithetical situations calling for entirely different standards of national conduct. Therefore, Americans have shown scant interest in the military instruments of national power during peace, but they have been preoccupied with them during the war, to the virtual exclusion of national policy. In effect, they have identified power politics with war while dissociating it from national policy, as though they could thereby keep policy-making inviolate by excluding power politics from peace and confining it to the self-evident demands of war. Not understanding the continuity of power, they have customarily met each military contingency as a separate emergency unrelated for all practical purposes to an unceasing political process in terms of which the nation might rationally plan a continuing program of power and policy.

America's depreciation of power and hence its lack of planning spring naturally from the same ideals and sentiments that underlie the aversion to violence. Like all people, Americans tend to envision the reality of international politics in the image of their desires. Consequently, they have envisioned international society as the product of a natural harmony of interests. In this ideal society there are no lasting rivalries or deep conflicts of interests; for it is a universal society of equals, in which all members normally subordinate their special interests to the good of the whole and settle their differences by peaceful and legal means. For this reason peace is supposed to be the normal expression of the international collective interest; and the only wars are collective wars against criminal states that rebel against law and order. Power politics is therefore thought to be an abnormal state of affairs, the product of misunderstanding, faulty legal and institutional arrangements, or the exceptional wickedness of a few statesmen or particular nations rather than a pervasive and continuing element of international relations. Thus international society is cast in the image of domestic society, where the struggle for power is supposedly absorbed in the automatic processes of the free market place, which peacefully reconcile all conflicts of interest within a system of liberal values shared by everyone.

Perhaps Americans instinctively realize that the true international society does not conform to this model and that in fact their own actions do not conform to the model. Nevertheless, they are compelled to regard the struggle for power, which perverts the ideal, as wrong, abnormal, and transitory; and so they have not granted recognition to this malevolent influence by dealing with it according to its own methods. As Walter Lippmann has observed:

> Our foreign policy throughout the last forty years has been dominated by the belief that the struggle for power does not exist, or that it can be avoided, or that it can be abolished. Because of this belief our aim has not been to regulate and to moderate and to compose the conflicts and the issues, to check and to balance the contending forces. Our aim has been either to abstain from the struggle, or to abolish the struggle immediately, or to conduct crusades against those nations that most actively continue the struggle.[7]

Actually, by depreciating the struggle for power, Americans have neither avoided it nor abolished it. They have simply forfeited the opportunity to use power—conspicuously military power—as an effective instrument of national policy.

Dissociation of Diplomacy and Power

Since diplomacy is the pre-eminent instrument for controlling and limiting warfare, America's approach to diplomacy is as important a source of its antipathy toward the primacy of politics as it is the American approach to entering, fighting, and preparing for war. Just as the nation has traditionally approached war in a political vacuum, so it has regarded diplomacy as something apart from power. Consistent with the ideal image of international relations, Americans have commonly regarded diplomacy fundamentally as an instrument for realizing an underlying harmony of interests rather than as an instrument for directing national power toward limited objectives.

This dissociation of diplomacy and power has resulted in a certain ambivalence toward diplomacy. On the one hand, Americans have sometimes thought of diplomacy as a purely rational process whereby national conflicts are ironed out on their merits and a meeting of minds is reached. The assumption here is that all nations, whether they recognize it or not, have an equal interest in peace and the status quo and that therefore diplomacy is simply a means of making all parties aware of the common interest. It follows from this assumption that agreement in itself is a desirable thing, as evidence of reason and good will; and that agreement upon general principles of national conduct is especially valuable. This positive approach to diplomacy is exhibited in countless diplomatic ventures—for example, Cordell Hull's repeated enumerations of the articles of international virtue as a basis for resolving the conflict with Japan—and in a number of documents that have struck the nation as notable diplomatic achievements—such as the Fourteen Points, the Atlantic Charter, and the Declaration on Liberated Peoples.[8]

On the other hand, Americans have combined with this sanguine approach a profound distrust of diplomacy, as though it were incompatible with open and forthright relations among nations. The latter view is probably the obverse side of the former; for one instinctively perceives that diplomacy is in reality involved with power politics and therefore that it contravenes the ideal image. Its secrecy and deviousness are the trappings of an occult art, compatible, perhaps, with the ways of the Old World but certainly the very antithesis of the Wilsonian model of "open covenants openly arrived at." In this way distrust of diplomacy reflects the contradiction between ideals and the reality; and the distrust has seemingly been confirmed by the disparity between high expectations and the bitter results of the postwar settlements and wartime agreements of two world wars.[9]

Whichever strain—the positive or the negative view of diplomacy—has been dominant in foreign relations at different periods, both of them, consistent with their common origin in the depreciation of power, have militated against the use of diplomacy as a flexible instrument of national power—as a means of moderating, balancing, limiting, and controlling power. Instead, they have disposed Americans to envision diplomacy as an instrument for transcending power conflicts and realizing universal moral principles. Consequently, it has been difficult to countenance the compromises and accommodations which are the lifeblood of political intercourse without seeming to violate principles. And this has been markedly true when the passions of war have rendered compromise and accommodation particularly repugnant. In wartime especially, concession comes to seem like appeasement, and a limited settlement like humiliation.

Considering the premium imposed by the potential destructiveness of modern war upon limited political settlements, it is evident that the dissociation of diplomacy and power, like the dissociation of power and policy which it exacerbates, is a formidable obstacle to the control of war as a rational instrument of national policy.

The Antimilitarist Tradition

One cannot fully appreciate the American approach to war without taking into account the nation's long antimilitarist tradition. To oversimplify the matter, this tradition originated in the early fear of standing armies as a threat to democratic liberties, but it persists even though that threat is no longer a serious problem. Although the fear of military subversion or usurpation has subsided, the fear of undue military influence in the counsels of government has grown in recent decades, and Americans commonly suspect the "military mind" of being somehow antithetical to democratic principles and institutions.

To guard against undue military influence of any kind, the nation has traditionally relied upon the principle of "civilian supremacy," which is imbedded in the Constitution, implemented in legislative statutes, and reflected in the administrative structure of the federal government. However, the legal and institutional embodiments of this principle—largely originating in the fear of usurpation—have little relevance to a vast number of contemporary situations in which civilians have to make decisions that rest upon military considerations beyond the sphere of civilian competence. In practice, Americans have approached this contemporary problem with another honored principle: the principle of military supremacy over purely military matters. The military must not interfere in political matters, but the civilians should not interfere with purely military matters, the nation seems to have decided. This arrangement is intended not only to keep the military from usurping civilian functions but also to guard against civilians arrogating military authority—a contingency believed to be as contrary to democratic principles as to military efficiency. Thus the two principles together purport to define a division of labor that preserves civilian supremacy while securing the highest degree of military competence.

The trouble with this theory of separation is that military and nonmilitary considerations are inextricably entangled, and "purely military matters" have important political consequences. Therefore, as national security has become increasingly dependent upon military considerations, the theory of separation has not only exacerbated the evils of making political and military policies in a vacuum but has also tended to create such great reliance upon military considerations as to subordinate national policy to military policy. The deference of political leaders to military advice has not been matched by a corresponding capacity of military leaders to acquire political guidance, although military men have frequently been more conscious of the need for such reciprocity than the civilians. Naturally, in wartime this civilian deference to military advice is even more marked, in accordance with the view that, when the civilians have failed to keep the peace, the conduct of war becomes a purely military matter. By this devious route the fear of the influence of military personnel upon civilian affairs has contributed to the domination of national policy by military considerations.

The American Experience

It is impossible to understand America's basic conceptions and predispositions concerning foreign relations apart from her historical experience in foreign relations. When one seeks an explanation of the American approach to war and military power, the central fact emerging is that for the greater part of their national history the American people have not come to grips with the difficult problem of combining military power with foreign policy. Their prolonged enjoyment of relative isolation and security in the period from the War of 1812 to World War II spared them the necessity.

Americans were under no pressure to balance military power with political objectives, because military and political policies seemed to be in perfect harmony. Thanks to a fortunate geographic position, the protective presence of British sea power in the Atlantic, the strife among potential adversaries, and the weakness of actual adversaries, the United States was able to realize its two preeminent political objectives, continental isolation and continental expansion, either without resort to war or else with resort to relatively short and easy wars that involved no political complications in the conduct of military operations. The United States likewise was spared the necessity of securing its power positions through the kind of tortuous diplomatic bargains that were necessary in the Old World. Thus America's major political objectives were simple and attainable. They neither conflicted with her view of immediate military necessities nor complicated her policy with diplomatic concessions. Although the political conse-quences of the wars against Spain and Germany bore little relation to the nebulous and grandiose objectives for which the nation fought, this fact raised no question in American minds about harmonizing power and policy, because American security was never seriously threatened—and, after all, the United States did win striking victories. The fortunate political circumstances that made security and victory possible were concealed from America because they existed independently of any effort on her part.

American strategy began and ended with the overriding objective of continental security, conceived in the image of first acquiring and then protecting a vast fortress from enemy assault. This simple and appealing conception seemingly obviated the necessity of forming military or political policies in terms of the configurations of national power abroad. It concealed the extent to which American security was actually interwoven with the power and interests of other nations. It sustained the flattering analogy of the militiaman taking down his gun from the wall when the enemy approached and putting it back when the danger had passed. This conception seems hopelessly unrealistic to many Americans now, but pragmatically and on the face of things it was the very essence of realism until the fall of France in 1940. Although the nation did not seriously prepare for war, did not calculate the political configurations of power in waging war, and quickly abandoned its arms after war, it nevertheless won wars handily; and that seemed to be sufficient proof that a strategy of continental isolation suited American needs. Until unmistakable evidence to the contrary should arise, there was no incentive for entangling military policies with national policy or national policy with power politics.

As American experience encouraged a dissocation of power and policy, so it was equally congenial to that quality of pugnacity which overrides the political limitation of force. For America's relative isolation relieved the nation of the sobering experience of foreign occupation or defeat, which injected a note of precaution and design into the military preparations and activities of European nations. Americans could feel confident that, no matter what direction the fortunes of war might take, their security would be guaranteed so long as the insular fortress was protected. Thus instead of tasting defeat or the fear of defeat, the United States enjoyed an unbroken string of military successes, which encouraged the notion that her geographical position and her natural endowments made her invincible. There is no greater stimulus to unreasoning pugnacity than the notion of invincibility.

At the same time, America's relative isolation from the mainstream of international politics also encouraged that compelling commitment to liberal and humane ideals which underlay her moral and emotional aversion to violence. If these ideals carried more weight in the American approach to foreign relations than in the external relations of other democratic nations, this must be attributed, in large part, to the circumstances that saved the nation from having to test them against the unpleasant realities of international politics. Virtue comes easily to those who do not have to put it into practice under adverse conditions. The American people were spared the education of adversity, while events confirmed their basic assurance that the national mission of bringing a universal society of peace and order to the world—even if this had to be done by a crusading war—was perfectly compatible with national self-interest.

By the same token, America's conception of an international society governed by a natural harmony of interests is a product of the circumstances that shielded her from the actual conflicts of interest. Not having experienced the immediate necessity of participating in the struggle for power, Americans found it easy, as well as gratifying, to imagine that the natural state of international politics is harmonious. Because they did not themselves have to balance the claims of universal moral principles against the claims of national security, Americans attributed the indulgence of other nations in the compromises of power politics, as well as their own abstinence, to innate moral qualities rather than to transitory political circumstances in a continuing struggle for power.

The impact of international experience upon the American approach to foreign relations becomes clearer when one compares it with the impact of internal experience upon the American approach to the domestic sphere of human relations. The same basic ideals that Americans brought to international affairs produced no comparable innocence of the role of power in national affairs. In business affairs, labor relations, or party politics Americans have taken the struggle for power pretty much for granted. The very principle of the balance of power is imbedded in the Constitution. And it is noteworthy that American domestic reformers have customarily dealt with conflicts of interest by compromise and accommodation, by moderating and controlling power, rather than by trying to abolish it. It seems likely that if America had contended with the conflicts of power among nations as intimately as it contended with power conflicts among groups and individuals within the nation, the nation would have developed a conception of international relations more compatible with the political limitation of military power.

The Transformation of the American Approach

If the American approach to war and the use of military power is so largely a product of experience, we may expect the recent radical changes in the nature of America's international experience virtually to transform her traditional approach. Undoubtedly, just such a transformation has been taking place, but it is by no means completed.

World War II destroyed America's sense of geographical isolation and produced a widespread consciousness that American security could be seriously jeopardized by disturbances in the distribution of national power overseas. This momentous alteration in America's traditional image of its position in world politics has been accompanied by radical departures in the nation's military policies and political commitments since the war. Yet World War II was fought in the pattern of America's traditional preoccupation with military objectives. Proceeding through the cycle of unpreparedness, mobilization, overwhelming offensive, total victory, and demobilization, the nation paid little attention to concrete political objectives. It ended the war scarcely more conscious of the interdependence of military power and national policy than before.

It is primarily the cold war that is transforming America's traditional approach to the relation between power and policy; for the cold war confronted the nation, as World War II never did, with the practical necessity of balancing military means with political ends within the framework of national strategy. The cold war is neither war nor peace in the orthodox sense, but a continuing struggle for power, waged by political, psychological, and economic means as well as by a variety of military and semimilitary means. There is no way of fighting the cold war to a clear-cut decision without precipitating a total war; but the American people know that total war with nuclear weapons would be an incredible disaster and that the enemy may never offer the provocation for such a war. In the meantime, the United States is forced to consider the means to protect and promote its far-flung interests against unrelenting Communistic pressure and the ever-present possibility of limited war.

Therefore, in some measure, the United States has had to alter its traditional approach to war and military policy and subordinate military considerations to considerations of high policy. In some measure, it has had to combine diplomacy with "situations of strength." In some measure, it has had to harmonize military power with all the other elements of national power according to a national strategic plan for achieving its basic security objectives. The very existence of the National Security Council testifies to this fact. If it had not accomplished this much, in all probability the nation either would have precipitated a total war or suffered disastrous losses of positions vital to survival.

Taken as a whole, the American record in foreign policy since 1945 is a remarkable adaptation to novel and challenging circumstances. However, the most cursory examination of the evolution of American strategy in the past decade must reveal that the adaptation has been partial and on an *ad hoc* basis. The record of the United States does not show a real adjustment, either in its underlying conceptions of force and politics or in its concrete policies, to the imperatives of a strategy capable of resisting limited aggression by limited means. Such an adaptation is bound to be encumbered by the weight of traditional habits of mind resisting the pressure of unprecedented events.

Notes

1. Alexis de Tocqueville, *Democracy in America,* trans. Bradley (New York: Vintage Books, 1954), II, 292–93.

2. Ernest R. May, "The Development of Political-Military Consultation in the United States," *Political Science Quarterly* 70 (June 1955):161–80.

3. Quoted in William T. Stone, "The National Defense Policy of the United States." *Foreign Policy Reports,* August 31, 1932, p. 151.

4. George F. Kennan, *American Diplomacy, 1900-1950* (Chicago: University of Chicago Press, 1951), pp. 65–66, 84.

5. Hearings before the Joint Senate Committee on Armed Services and Committee on Foreign Relations, *Military Situation in the Far East,* 82d Cong., 1st sess., Part I, p. 145; cf. pp. 223–24, 302.

6. Ibid., pp. 39–40.

7. "The Rivalry of Nations," *Atlantic Monthly* 171 (February 1948):19.

8. The Declaration on Liberated Peoples, part of the Yalta settlement, applied the principles of democratic self-determination to the peoples of Central Europe, who were liberated from German occupation. The image of diplomacy transcending power politics gleams through President Roosevelt's report upon the Yalta settlement shortly after his return: "The Crimean Conference was a successful effort by the three leading nations to find a common ground for peace. It spells the end of the system of unilateral action and exclusive alliances and spheres of influence and balances of power and all the other expedients which have been tried for centuries—and have failed. We propose to substitute for all these a universal organization in which all peace-loving nations will finally have a chance to join." Address on March 1, 1945, *Department of State Bulletin,* March 4, 1945, p. 361.

9. A good explicit expression of assumptions which are ordinarily only implicit in the American distrust of diplomacy appears in C. Hartley Grattan's book *The Deadly Parallel,* which was written in the atmosphere of disillusionment following World War I: "Diplomacy is one of the black arts. Its practitioners are always a select minority, even of the governmental bureaucracy. Out of the mumbo-jumbo of a highly formal and specialized vocabulary, they snatch at advantages for the nation they represent. The line between victory and defeat is so narrow—so dependent upon interpretation of ambiguous statements—that it flickers before the eyes of the uninitiated to their utter bewilderment. The language employed is so specialized that the possibility of saying one thing and meaning another is always present. Vast consequences flow from the order of 'weasel' words in a sentence; the lives and fortunes of men are juggled within subordinate clauses. The influence of diplomacy on their destiny is something ordinary men are quite unable to control. Its results are a fatality like weather." Grattan, *The Deadly Parallel* (New York: Stackpole Sons, 1939), p. 74.

Discussion Questions

1. What characteristics define the U.S. approach to war?

2. From what sources do those characteristics derive?

3. Which of these characteristics have received more emphasis than others through the past? Why?

Suggestions for Additional Reading

Almond, Gabriel A. *The American People and Foreign Policy.* 2d ed. New York: Frederick A. Praeger, 1977.

Betts, Richard. "Analysis, War, and Decision: Why Intelligence Failures Are Inevitable." *World Politics* 31, no. 1 (October 1978): 61–89.

Brodie, Bernard. *Strategy and National Interests.* New York: National Strategy Information Center, 1971.

——. "Technological Change, Strategic Doctrine, and Political Outcomes." In Klaus Knorr, ed., *Historical Dimensions of National Security Problems.* Lawrence: University Press of Kansas, 1976.

Dyson, Freeman. *Weapons and Hope.* New York: Harper & Row, 1984.

Gaddis, John L. *Strategies of Containment.* New York: Oxford University Press, 1982.

Garthoff, Raymond L. "Estimating and Imputing Intentions." *International Security* 2, no. 3 (Winter 1978):22–32.

Howard, Michael. *The Causes of War.* Cambridge: Harvard University Press, 1983.

——. "The Forgotten Dimensions of Strategy." *Foreign Affairs* 57, no. 5 (Summer 1979): 975–986.

Huntington, Samuel. *The Common Defense.* New York: Columbia University Press, 1961.

Jervis, Robert. "Hypotheses on Misperception." *World Politics* 20, no. 3 (April 1968): 454–479.

——. *Perception and Misperception in International Politics.* Princeton: Princeton University Press, 1976.

Kissinger, Henry A. *American Foreign Policy.* 3d ed. New York W.W. Norton, 1977.

Knorr, Klaus. "Threat Perception." In Klaus Knorr, ed., *Historical Dimensions of National Security Problems.* Lawrence: University Press of Kansas, 1976.

Morgenthau, Hans J. *Politics among Nations.* 5th ed. New York: Alfred A. Knopf, 1973.

Osgood, Robert E. *Ideals and Self-Interest in America's Foreign Relations.* Chicago: University of Chicago Press, 1953.

Part III
Strategy in the Nuclear Age

 One of the most famous quotations from Clausewitz's classic work *On War* is his statement that war "is not a mere act of policy but a true political instrument, a continuation of political activity by other means."[1] In an era in which the physical power available to some nations is essentially limitless, Clausewitz's dictum serves to remind us that the use of force is not, and should not be viewed as, an end in itself. The use of force must be regarded as one policy instrument among many, one way in which a nation can achieve its interests.

Strategy and Politics

The concept of war as an act of policy traditionally has been rejected by the American public. Robert Osgood pointed out in chapter 5 that the predispositions and experiences of the United States in world politics encourage the dissociation of power and policy. War is not regarded by Americans as political activity or a normal state of affairs; it is an extraordinary measure to be used only in extraordinary circumstances. War and peace are viewed as diametrically opposite states of affairs, to be governed by entirely different rules and considerations. The dissociation of power and policy is reflected in the United States's historical inability to prepare itself for war and its single-minded pursuit of total victory once it has been committed to war. As Alexis de Tocqueville observed, "The self same democratic nations that are so reluctant to engage in hostilities sometimes perform prodigious achievements once they have taken the field."[2]

The effect of the attitude that separates power and policy is profound. War is regarded by Americans as a crusade, an extraordinary venture requiring the commitment to a swift and complete victory. President Franklin Roosevelt's refusal to discuss postwar political considerations just weeks before the capitulation of Germany in 1945 reflects this view.[3] During war, the overwhelming objective is a definitive military victory, obtained as quickly as possible. When peace returns, the instruments of victory are discarded, and political interaction returns to a normal state of affairs.

The strong tradition that dissociates power and policy would seem to run counter to the fundamental requirements of modern strategy. Unconditional surrender is a concept that is not relevant in a nuclear war. On the opposite end of the spectrum, how can a nation wage war against terrorists or revolutionary groups that have no territorial base?

Strategy must be based on an appreciation of the fact that war is an instrument that serves political ends and that war therefore is an act of policy. As Clausewitz correctly noted, "The political object is the goal, war is the means of reaching it, and means can never be considered in isolation from their purpose."[4] Military power cannot be used in isolation from political objectives, for the use of military power as an end in itself makes no sense. Consider the claim made by some U.S. military officers that the United States was not defeated on the battlefield in Vietnam and therefore the United States did not really lose the war. The crucial point is that U.S. national objectives were not achieved in Vietnam. To view the success or failure of U.S. arms in isolation from this result is to see the use of military force as an end in itself, unrelated to the accomplishment of national political objectives.

Deterrence and Defense

Given the dangers associated with the use of force in the nuclear age, how can a nation prevent political adversaries from threatening vital national interests? There are two ways in which a nation can obtain what is desired or protect what is valued. A nation can use its military power to repel an attack or to seize and occupy an adversary's territory. Force can be used to project power and to protect interests, to disarm and disable, or to deny access to critical territory.[5]

The alternative means of influencing an adversary's behavior is by coercion. Rather than relying on brute force, coercion works on an opponent's intentions rather than capabilities. Coercion is based on the threat to use force to inflict pain and damage. It is the threat of violence that influences an opponent's decisions and persuades the opponent to comply or to yield.

The use of brute force focuses on capabilities, while coercion works on intentions. As Thomas Schelling noted, the threat of pain is used to structure an opponent's motives, while brute force tries to overcome his strength.[6]

The difference between coercion and brute force is the difference between deterrence and defense. Deterrence works on an adversary's intentions, while defense works against its capabilities. Deterrence, as Glenn Snyder points out in chapter 6, means discouraging an opponent from taking military action by posing the prospect of cost and risk outweighing any prospective gain.[7] Defense is the capability to deny your enemy the ability to take items of value from you.

Nuclear weapons have changed the relationship between deterrence and defense. Traditionally a strong military capability could prevent an opponent from seizing your territory or inflicting significant levels of damage on your society. Further, battles usually took place along some relatively well-defined fighting front, which was as far as possible from one's major population centers and important territory. The traditional distinctions between the winner and the loser and between the homeland and the battle front have been eliminated by nuclear weapons. The possession of nuclear weapons now makes it possible for the nation that is losing a conflict to inflict enormous damage not only on the military forces but also on the society of the side that is winning. Victory is no longer an assurance against having terrible destruction inflicted on one's nation. The consequence of these distinctions is that deterrence has become a much more important part of a nation's security concerns.

Traditional conceptions of victory are no longer relevant when faced with an opponent armed with nuclear weapons. Military forces represent a threat of latent violence. Deterrence is based on the influence and bargaining power that are derived from the capacity to hurt rather than on the direct consequences of military action. As Schelling concluded, military strategy can no longer be based on the pursuit of military victory. Military strategy is now the art of coercion, of intimidation and deterrence, where the instruments of war are more punitive than acquisitive.[8]

How is a credible deterrent achieved? There are two important contingencies against which one's deterrent posture is aimed: deterrence of a direct attack on a nation's homeland and deterrence of an attack or major provocation against one's allies (sometimes referred to as extended deterrence).

Both the United States and the Soviet Union possess a vast arsenal of strategic nuclear weapons, which includes bombers and land- and sea-based intercontinental missiles. Since all of these weapons could not be destroyed completely by a surprise attack, a retaliatory strike would inflict enormous damage on the homeland of the attacker. These secure retaliatory capabilities are the basis of deterrence against a direct attack. (The ability to unleash a second strike capable of destroying the attacker's society is referred to as assured destruction.) Although there are periodic concerns about the vulnerability of certain elements of the strategic forces, the uncertainties associated with launching any massive nuclear attack, coupled with the thousands of warheads that would survive any conceivable attack, make the deterrent posture of the United States and the Soviet Union seem relatively stable.

A much more difficult problem for deterrence is how to protect one's allies. Given the destructiveness of nuclear weapons, how can a nation credibly threaten to use such force not for defending one's homeland but for protecting one's allies? The key to the success of extended deterrence is commitment. A nation must commit itself to the protection of its allies in such a way that potential adversaries must assume that a provocative move against a particular nation would trigger the involvement in the conflict by the threatened nation's allies.

In order to make such a deterrent posture believable, a nation must commit its honor, its prestige, or its forces to the protection of its ally. For example, the pledge of the United States to defend Western Europe against an attack by the Soviet Union is codified in the NATO charter and in the public pronouncements of every president since Truman. U.S. presidents have proclaimed that an attack on Western Europe would be considered an attack on the United States. Further, the presence of over 200,000 U.S. troops in Western Europe is visible evidence of U.S. resolve to protect this area of great national interest. Linking the protection of Europe (or any other major U.S. ally such as Japan) to the deterrent power of U.S. strategic nuclear weapons is the manifestation of extended deterrence.

Two criteria must be fulfilled in order to establish and maintain deterrence. The first criterion is capability. A nation must be capable of carrying out the retaliatory strikes it has promised if an adversary commits an act of aggression. The deterring nation must have the ability to make the costs of aggression appear to outweigh any prospective gain or at least create sufficient uncertainty as to the outcome that an aggressor cannot have high confidence of success. Nuclear weapons provide an unambiguous capability to inflict damage on an aggressor. In order for deterrence to be successful, however, the threat to use this capability must be believable.

Credibility is the second prerequisite for successful deterrence. The threat to respond militarily to certain acts of aggression must be believable. The requirement for credibility means that a nation cannot threaten to use nuclear weapons in areas that are not of vital national interest. Threats of punishment must be related to the value of the objective being protected. The very destructiveness of nuclear weapons limit the credibility of threats to use them. Therefore a credible deterrent posture must include both nuclear and conventional capabilities.

Nuclear Strategies and Flexibility

In the years immediately following the development of nuclear weapons, the strategy envisioned for their use was similar to that of the strategic bombing campaigns of World War II. The few existing weapons were large and unwieldy, meaning they would have to be carried to their targets by large bombers. Since the number of atomic weapons available to either side was limited, they would have to be used against the highest-value targets, population and industrial centers.

The development of intercontinental missiles and relatively small warheads that could fit into the nose cone of a missile meant that weapons could be delivered rapidly from thousands of miles away. Although the accuracy of the early missiles would be considered low by today's standards, the ability to deliver a thermonuclear weapon within a mile or two of a target meant that the weapons could be used against a much broader array of targets than just cities.

As a result of these technological developments, two different nuclear warfighting strategies were possible. A countervalue (sometimes called countercity) strategy would concentrate on the destruction of an opponent's population and industrial centers, inflicting as much damage on the society as possible. A counterforce strategy would focus on the destruction of the adversary's military capabilities, thereby limiting the damage it could inflict in return and reducing its ability to use military forces for any meaningful political gain.

As the United States and the Soviet Union expanded their nuclear arsenals, there began to be increasing concern about what would happen should deterrence fail. The possibility that war might occur by accident or miscalculation meant that some controls on the escalation of nuclear conflict needed to be established. Further, the continuing buildup of Soviet nuclear forces reduced the credibility of U.S. reliance on a doctrine of assured destruction. In the event of nuclear war in Europe or Asia, an attack by the United States on Soviet cities would ensure a retaliatory strike against U.S. population centers. Decision makers concluded that greater flexibility in the targeting of U.S. nuclear forces was necessary to improve the credibility of the deterrent. As President Richard Nixon phrased it in 1970, "Should a president, in the event of a nuclear attack, be left with the single option of ordering the mass destruction of enemy civilians, in the face of the certainty that it would be followed by the mass slaughter of Americans?"[9]

As the Soviets began to match the United States in strategic nuclear forces, some U.S. analysts worried that the Soviet Union might fire, or threaten to fire, a limited number of nuclear weapons against U.S. military targets while holding U.S. cities hostage to future destruction. If the only choice open to the United States was to respond massively against enemy cities or do nothing, in a crisis the Soviets might be tempted to threaten or carry out a limited attack on the assumption that the United States would be forced to do nothing; however, if the United States had the ability to respond in a controlled and selective way against Soviet military targets, the Soviet calculation of the U.S. response would have to change since a limited attack would precipitate a response in kind.[10]

A second concern related to the failure of deterrence was the problem of escalation control. If deterrence failed, how could the conflict be terminated without resorting to unrestricted nuclear war? At issue here is the question of whether a nuclear war can be controlled and terminated once even a few nuclear weapons have been detonated. Would the pressures for retaliation be so intense that such a war would escalate rapidly to a general nuclear war, or is it possible to control escalation and limit the damage in such a conflict?

Proponents of flexible nuclear response (alternatively called limited nuclear options, limited nuclear war, and flexible nuclear options) argue that the selective and controlled use of nuclear weapons offers the prospect of terminating a conflict before nuclear weapons are used against population centers. In this view, the controlled use of nuclear weapons would provide the United States with a means of tailoring its response to the nature of the aggression. Further, the use of limited nuclear strikes could prevent the adversary from achieving its immediate political objectives while holding its countervalue targets hostage and force the enemy to change its perceptions about the potential risks involved in pursuing its intended course of action. Once the United States has demonstrated its willingness to respond with nuclear weapons, the enemy would recognize the potential costs involved and would cease hostilities. The assumption here is that there are limits to the losses rational political leaders are willing to accept in order to achieve their objectives and that faced with the prospect of escalation to a wider nuclear war, such leaders will not take actions that would precipitate such an event.[11]

Inherent in this concept of flexible nuclear response is the notion that there are a number of discrete steps in the escalation ladder and that the use of a few nuclear weapons does not mean that there will be an automatic progression to general nuclear war. While the nuclear-nonnuclear firebreak is obviously the most salient point in the spectrum of conflict, it is possible to impose other thresholds that will provide the opportunity for limiting nuclear war. The concept of intra-war deterrence is at work here; that is, even if deterrence fails, for whatever reason, it can be reestablished by observing certain restraints on the numbers of weapons used or the nature and location of targets attacked.

Critics of the strategy of flexible nuclear response argue that the concept of limited nuclear attacks undermines deterrence by making nuclear war more likely. If each side was confident that the war could be controlled and that limited strikes would not lead automatically to general war, there might be less reluctance to initiate the use of nuclear weapons.

Further, the notion of limited nuclear war connotes an acceptable level of destruction. If the anticipated costs of the war are lowered, then the perceived horror of nuclear war might be lessened. If nuclear war is made to seem less costly, it might be made more likely. Once such strikes were launched, what if the escalatory pressures could not be controlled? The result would be a devastating nuclear exchange.

A second criticism of the flexible nuclear response strategy is that the force structure designed to carry out such a strategy is indistinguishable from a force designed to carry out a preemptive first strike. The procurement of highly accurate weapons would threaten the survival of land-based missiles, thereby reducing the opponent's secure retaliatory capability. This vulnerability might prompt a first strike in a crisis in order to avoid the destruction of strategic forces before they could be employed. Fears about the survivability of nuclear forces can foster a "use'em or lose'em" philosophy—an outlook that does not contribute to stability during a crisis.

Regardless of one's views on the utility of flexible nuclear response, the ability to attack a variety of targets exists and is reflected in the nuclear targeting policies of both the United States and the Soviet Union. The specific tenets of U.S. nuclear doctrine will be described in greater detail in part VI.

U.S. nuclear strategy reflects the requirement for deterrence across a spectrum of possibilities. The need to deter a direct attack on the United States and to extend nuclear deterrence to a number of important allies remains the primary purpose of U.S. nuclear strategy. Flexible nuclear response is designed to enhance the credibility of the U.S. nuclear deterrent through the ability to respond to a threat to a vital national interest with an appropriate level of force.

Chapter 6 is a classic exposition on the nature of deterrence and defense and the fundamental conceptual differences between the two. Glenn Snyder's analysis there of the differences between the traditional balance of power and the nuclear balance of terror identifies a number of significant points distinguishing security considerations in the nuclear age from those of an earlier era.

Limited War

What does the concept of limited war mean in the nuclear age? To say that all wars short of general nuclear war are limited may be accurate, but such a notion is analytically unsatisfactory. Indeed, the very destructive potential of nuclear weapons appears to have undermined their utility. Although the threat of nuclear war remains a central element of international diplomacy, the inhibitions against using nuclear weapons may be growing stronger with each year.

The threat of nuclear war has not, as some once hoped, made war itself less prevalent. Paradoxically, the nuclear stalemate and the lack of utility of nuclear force as a useful instrument of policy may have increased the likelihood of the use of conventional forces in limited conflicts. Stability at the nuclear level may well have produced instability at the conventional level.

What distinguishes limited war from total war? The most important characteristic that separates limited war from general war is that limited war involves an important kind and degree of restraint, deliberate restraint. This deliberate restraint can be thought of in terms of self-imposed limitations by the belligerents. As Robert Osgood discusses in chapter 7, these limitations are imposed on the political objectives for which the war is being waged and on the military means employed to achieve the political objectives.

In the nuclear age, when the military power available to one or both contenders may be physically limitless, there must be a degree of self-restraint imposed on political objectives. Both sides must be willing to tolerate an outcome neither had foreseen and in which the objectives of both are achieved imperfectly or not at all. The total effort undertaken by the belligerents depends to a significant degree on the political objectives at stake, that is, the magnitude of the political gains and losses involved. Political objectives may change throughout the course of a war, or they may be undefined. Internal domestic political considerations may become just as important as international political objectives, particularly in a democracy.

Political stakes may not be symmetrical in a limited war. One side may be willing to bear exorbitant costs in order to achieve its objectives. Unless one side capitulates or abandons the war effort, it takes two to end a war. The willingness of one side to bear high costs may make it extremely difficult to negotiate a settlement acceptable to both sides. An opponent whose war aims require only that the enemy not win is formidable, even for a major power, as the U.S. experience in Vietnam and the Soviet experience in Afghanistan have demonstrated.

The central political question in limited war is how a nation can maximize its wartime objectives and yet negotiate a settlement that its adversary will find acceptable. Pressures to improve the military outcome must be balanced against the costs that such escalation might engender. Attempts to maximize payoffs, taking both the political gains and the associated military costs into account, are difficult at best, for there is no common measure between political values and war losses. A willingness to accept limited military objectives and reduced political aims requires a convergent political reorientation of the two sides. The losing side must believe it is better to accept an unfavorable outcome than to risk escalation to a larger conflict, and the prevailing side must avoid the temptation to press for a settlement so favorable as to cause the other side to prefer continued fighting and escalation. Limited war requires the willingness of each side to recognize, and hence legitimate, the other's claim to an interest in the outcome. Successful limitation thus presumes, paradoxically, a relatively high degree of cooperation between the belligerents.

The deliberate limitation of war assumes a conception of the relation between power and policy which is, as noted in chapter 5, antithetical to U.S. ideas and predispositions about the nature of war and the use of force. A cause noble enough to justify the use of force cannot be pursued by limited, self-restrained means. Paradoxically, the U.S. aversion to violence leads to the demand that force, once accepted as necessary, be applied without restraint. War is to be ended as soon as possible by destroying the enemy. As Osgood notes, it is difficult for Americans to countenance any restraint of the military effort for the sake of some limited, commonplace political objective, such as the establishment of a local balance of power in some remote geographical area. Americans are disposed to demand that the sacrifice of life serve some purpose of commensurate value, and total victory seems like the minimum compensation.[12] Political objectives based on less than total victory runs counter to the powerful American tradition that the justification for violence can be nothing less than the complete achievement of the objectives toward which the nation's efforts were committed.

The implications and consequences of these attitudes toward the use of force are significant. Americans will accept and even enthusiastically support the use of national military power, but only for suitably noble and just causes. If U.S. policymakers are to build public consensus, they must identify a threat that warrants a significant response. How can U.S. decision makers ensure public support for their policies? The answer, to use Theodore Lowi's term, is to oversell the threat.[13] To engender public support for a particular course of action, policymakers are driven to paint the enemy in the harshest possible manner, to create a sense of crisis that requires an immediate and vigorous response by the United States. Public support for a president habitually increases following a major international crisis, and substantial public support is a major political resource for any president.[14]

The most common method of generating a sense of crisis is to invoke the spectre of advancing international communism. This technique was used by President Harry Truman to justify economic aid to Greece and Turkey in 1947. In explaining the need for the economic aid program, President Truman argued that the United States would be unsuccessful

> unless we are willing to help free peoples to maintain their free institutions and their national integrity against aggressive moves that seek to impose upon them totalitarian regimes. This is no more than a frank recognition that totalitarian regimes imposed on free peoples, by direct or indirect aggression, undermine the foundations of international peace and hence the security of the United States.[15]

Senator Arthur Vandenburg had advised President Truman to "scare hell out of the American people."[16] President Truman's rhetorical escalation succeeded dramatically, and his rationale for U.S. action has been used by all subsequent U.S. presidents as justification for their efforts to attempt to prevent the expansion (or perceived expansion) of communist influence.

The concept of containment enabled U.S. policymakers to allege that all local wars, guerrilla actions, and revolutionary wars were interrelated and cumulative. It has become an established procedure in U.S. security policy to invoke the threat of communist takeover whenever support for U.S. actions seems divided. The domino theory of communist advances in Southeast Asia was designed to engender support for U.S. policies in that region by raising the prospect of an entire region's subjugation to communism if the U.S. response were not sufficiently vigorous (an argument that was repeated concerning the appropriate U.S. response to instability in Latin America). President Johnson justified the deployment of U.S. forces to the Dominican Republic in 1965 as necessary to prevent a communist takeover of the government. Regardless of the issue, generating public support requires invoking a perceived threat to national security or to the security of an ally.

In order to generate public support for their policies, decision makers often oversell the threat. By so doing, they may become victims of their own rhetorical excesses. In order to deal with oversold threats, policymakers must oversell the remedy. The efficacy of the U.S. response must be praised in order to satisfy expectations about the adequacy of the U.S. response. Once the necessity for military action is accepted, Americans believe that the campaign should be waged with sufficient ferocity to accomplish objectives completely and rapidly. Overselling the remedy, however, may lead to two less than satisfactory results: overcommitment or lack of public support.

The escalation of meaning led to the escalation of conflict in Southeast Asia. Having described the preservation of noncommunist Laos and Vietnam as vital national security interests, U.S. policymakers hardly could say in 1965 when a communist victory seemed imminent that the issue really was not very important (even if they believed it). The remedy of the commitment of U.S. combat forces was oversold. Lights at the end of the tunnel began appearing as early as 1966. The lack of progress led inevitably to frustration and public dissatisfaction with

U.S. policy in Vietnam. Even if U.S. policymakers sought only to stabilize the situation in Vietnam, as Daniel Ellsberg and others have suggested, limited or partial responses are very difficult to justify when threats have been described in demonic terms. Overselling the threat may preclude pursuit of limited objectives by limited means.

The U.S. approach to war influences significantly the formulation and execution of U.S. limited war strategies. Wars are to be waged totally; the use of force for limited political objectives is antithetical to U.S. philosophy and historical experience. Americans will respond to a sense of threat, leading policymakers to oversell potential threats and demonize potential opponents in order to ensure public support. Having oversold the threat, it is then necessary to oversell the remedy, raising expectations of the complete and rapid accomplishment of objectives when the process of limitation involves negotiating with the ultimate evil represented by the enemy. Oversold threats and remedies make negotiated settlements difficult to achieve. Responses perceived as inadequate ultimately cause widespread public dissatisfaction. The inherent conflict between *a priori* limitation of objectives and the U.S. style of going to war makes the accommodation process between the government and the public often intractable.

The international environment in the post–World War II era has challenged traditional U.S. conceptions about the separation of power and policy, and U.S. policy in the postwar period indicates that the nation has accepted, at least to a certain degree, the necessity of balancing military means with potential ends within the framework of national strategy. The presence of a significant number of U.S. military forces in Europe and elsewhere since the end of World War II indicates that the United States has accepted partially the need for a degree of military readiness if U.S. interests are to be protected. This acceptance of the use of military force as a means of furthering national policy has altered in some measure the traditional approach to war and military policy. Although the separation of power and policy may no longer be as distinct as it once was, the difficult U.S. experiences in Korea and Vietnam indicate that the adjustment to the imperative of a strategy capable of waging limited war by limited means for limited objectives is still incomplete.

Notes

1. Carl von Clausewitz, *On War*, trans. Michael Howard and Peter Paret (Princeton: Princeton University Press, 1976), p. 87.

2. Alexis de Tocqueville, *Democracy in America* (New York: Alfred A. Knopf, 1963), p. 228.

3. John Lewis Gaddis, *The United States and the Origins of the Cold War, 1941–1947* (New York: Columbia University Press, 1972), p. 102.

4. Clausewitz, *On War*, p. 87.

5. Thomas C. Schelling, *Arms and Influence* (New Haven: Yale University Press, 1966), p. 1.

6. Ibid., p. 3.

7. Glenn H. Snyder, *Deterrence and Defense* (Princeton: Princeton University Press, 1961), p. 3.

8. Schelling, *Arms and Influence*, p. 34.

9. Richard M. Nixon, A Report to the Congress, *U.S. Foreign Policy for the 1970s, A New Strategy for Peace*, February 18, 1970, p. 122.

10. Lynn E. Davis, "Limited Nuclear Options," *Adelphi Paper No. 121* (London: International Institute for Strategic Studies, Winter 1975), p. 5.

11. Ibid., p. 7.

12. Robert E. Osgood, *Limited War* (Chicago: University of Chicago Press, 1957), p. 34.

13. Theodore J. Lowi, *The End of Liberalism* (New York: W.W. Norton, 1969), p. 180.

14. Ibid., p. 184.

15. James M. Jones, *The Fifteen Weeks* (New York: Harcourt, Brace and World, 1955), p. 272.

16. Walter LaFeber, *America, Russia, and the Cold War 1945–1971* (New York: John Wiley, 1972), p. 45.

6

Deterrence and Defense: A Theoretical Introduction

Glenn H. Snyder

National security still remains an "ambiguous symbol," as one scholar described it almost a decade ago.[1] Certainly it has grown more ambiguous as a result of the startling advances since then in nuclear and weapons technology, and the advent of nuclear parity between the United States and the Soviet Union. Besides such technological complications, doctrine and thought about the role of force in international politics have introduced additional complexities. We now have, at least in embryonic form, theories of limited war, of deterrence, of "tactical" vs. "strategic" uses of nuclear weapons, of "retaliatory" vs. "counterforce" strategies in all-out war, of "limited retaliation," of the mechanics of threat and commitment-making, of "internal war," "protracted conflict," and the like. Above all, the idea of the "balance of terror" has begun to mature, but its relation to the older concept of the "balance of power" is still not clear. We have had a great intellectual ferment in the strategic realm, which of course is all to the good. What urgently remains to be done is to tie together all of these concepts into a coherent framework of theory so that the end-goal of national security may become less ambiguous, and so that the military means available for pursuance of this goal may be accumulated, organized, and used more efficiently. . . .

The central theoretical problem in the field of national security policy is to clarify and distinguish between the two central concepts of *deterrence* and *defense*. Essentially, deterrence means discouraging the enemy from taking military action by posing for him a prospect of cost and risk outweighing his prospective gain. Defense means reducing our own prospective costs and risks in the event that deterrence fails. Deterrence works on the enemy's *intentions;* the *deterrent value* of military forces is their effect in reducing the likelihood of enemy military moves. Defense reduces the enemy's *capability* to damage or deprive us; the *defense value* of military forces is their effect in mitigating the adverse consequences for us of possible enemy moves, whether such consequences are counted as losses of territory or war damage. The concept of "defense value," therefore, is broader than the

Glenn H. Snyder, *Deterrence and Defense: Toward a Theory of National Security.* Copyright © 1961 by Princeton University Press Excerpts, pp. 3–16, 42–46, reprinted by permission of Princeton University Press.

mere capacity to hold territory, which might be called "denial capability." Defense value is denial capability plus capacity to alleviate war damage.

It is commonplace, of course, to say that the primary objectives of national security policy are to deter enemy attacks and to defend successfully, at minimum cost, against those attacks which occur. It is less widely recognized that different types of military force contribute in differing proportions to these two objectives. Deterrence does not vary directly with our capacity for fighting wars effectively and cheaply; a particular set of forces might produce strong deterrent effects and not provide a very effective denial and damage-alleviating capability. Conversely, forces effective for defense might be less potent deterrents than other forces which were less efficient for holding territory and which might involve extremely high war costs if used.

One reason why the periodic "great debates" about national security policy have been so inconclusive is that the participants often argue from different premises—one side from the point of view of deterrence, and the other side from the point of view of defense. For instance, in the famous "massive retaliation" debate of 1954, the late Secretary of State Dulles and his supporters argued mainly that a capacity for massive retaliation would deter potential Communist mischief, but they tended to ignore the consequences should deterrence fail. The critics, on the other hand, stressed the dire consequences should the threat of massive retaliation fail to deter and tended to ignore the possibility that it might work. The opposing arguments never really made contact because no one explicitly recognized that considerations of reducing the probability of war and mitigating its consequences must be evaluated simultaneously, that the possible consequences of a failure of deterrence are more or less important depending on the presumed likelihood of deterrence. Many other examples could be cited.

Perhaps the crucial difference between deterrence and defense is that deterrence is primarily a peacetime objective, while defense is a wartime value. Deterrent value and defense value are directly enjoyed in different time periods. We enjoy the deterrent value of our military forces prior to the enemy's aggressive move; we enjoy defense value after the enemy move has already been made, although we indirectly profit from defense capabilities in advance of war through our knowledge that if the enemy attack occurs we have the means of mitigating its consequences. The crucial point is that *after* the enemy's attack takes place, our military forces perform different functions and yield wholly different value than they did as deterrents prior to the attack. As deterrents they engaged in a psychological battle—dissuading the enemy from attacking by attempting to confront him with a prospect of costs greater than his prospective gain. After the enemy begins his attack, while the psychological or deterrent aspect does not entirely disappear, it is partly supplanted by another purpose: to resist the enemy's onslaught in order to minimize *our* losses or perhaps maximize *our* gains, not only with regard to the future balance of power, but also in terms of intrinsic or nonpower values. That combination of forces which appeared to be the optimum one from the point of view of deterrence might turn out to be far inferior to some other combination from the point of view of defense should deterrence fail. In short, maximizing the enemy's cost expectancy may not always be consistent with minimizing our own. Thus we must measure the value of our military forces on two yardsticks, and we must find some way of combining their value on *both* yardsticks, in order accurately to gauge their aggregate worth or "utility" and to make intelligent choices among the various types of forces available.

Before launching into a theoretical analysis of the concepts of deterrence and defense, it may be useful to present a sampling of policy issues involving a need to choose between deterrence and defense; the examples will be treated in more detail in subsequent chapters.

Examples of Choices and Conflicts between Deterrence and Defense

A strategic retaliatory air force sufficient only to wreak minimum "unacceptable" damage on Soviet cities—to destroy, say, 20 cities—after this force had been decimated by a surprise Soviet nuclear attack, would have great value for deterring such a surprise attack and might be an adequate deterrent against that contingency. But if deterrence were to fail and the Soviet attack took place, it would then not be rational to *use* such a minimum force in massive retaliation against Soviet cities, since this would only stimulate the Soviets to inflict further damage upon us and would contribute nothing to our "winning the war." If we are interested in defense—i.e., in winning the war and in minimizing the damage to us—as well as in deterrence, we may wish to have (if technically feasible) a much larger force and probably one of different composition—a force which can strike effectively at the enemy's remaining forces (thus reducing our own costs) and, further, either by actual attacks or the threat of attacks, force the enemy to surrender or at least to give up his territorial gains.

The threat of massive nuclear retaliation against a Soviet major ground attack in Western Europe may continue to provide considerable deterrence against such an attack, even if actually to carry out the threat would be irrational because of the enormous costs we would suffer from Soviet counterretaliation. Strategic nuclear weapons do not provide a rational means of defense in Western Europe unless they not only can stop the Russian ground advance but also, by "counterforce" strikes, can reduce to an acceptable level the damage we would suffer in return. We may not have this capability now and it may become altogether infeasible as the Soviets develop their missile technology. For a means of rational defense, therefore, NATO may need enough ground forces to hold Europe against a full-scale attack by Soviet ground forces. This does not mean, however, that we necessarily must maintain ground forces of this size. If we think the probability of attack is low enough, we may decide to continue relying on nuclear deterrence primarily, even though it does not provide a rational means of defense. In other words, we might count on the Soviet uncertainties about whether or not nuclear retaliation is rational for us, and about how rational we are, to inhibit the Soviets from attacking in the face of the terrible damage they *know* they would suffer if they guessed wrong.

An attempt to build an effective counterforce capability, in order to have both a rational nuclear defense and a more credible nuclear deterrent against ground attack in Europe, might work against the *deterrence* of direct nuclear attack on the United States. Since such a force, by definition, would be able to eliminate all but a small fraction of the Soviet strategic nuclear forces if it struck first, the Soviets might, in some circumstances, fear a surprise attack and be led to strike first themselves in order to forestall it.

Tactical nuclear weapons in the hands of NATO forces in Europe have considerable deterrent value because they increase the enemy's cost expectation beyond what it would be if these forces were equipped only with conventional weapons. This is true not only because the tactical weapons themselves can inflict high costs on the enemy's forces, but also because their use (or an enemy "preemptive" strike against them) would sharply raise the probability that the war would spiral to all-out dimensions. But the defense value of tactical nuclear weapons against conventional attack is comparatively low against an enemy who also possesses them, because their use presumably would be offset by the enemy's use of them against our forces, and because in using such weapons we would be incurring much greater costs and risks than if we had responded conventionally.

For deterrence, it might be desirable to render automatic a response which the enemy recognizes as being costly for us, and communicate the fact of such automation to the enemy, thus reducing his doubts that we would actually choose to make this response when the occasion for it arose. For example, a tactical nuclear response to conventional aggression in Europe may be made semi-automatic by thoroughly orienting NATO plans, organization, and strategy around this response, thus increasing the difficulty of following a non-nuclear strategy in case of a Soviet challenge. But such automation would not be desirable for defense, which would require flexibility and freedom to choose the least costly action in the light of circumstances at the time of the attack.

The Continental European attitude toward NATO strategy is generally ambivalent on the question of deterrence vs. defense; there is fear that with the Soviet acquisition of a substantial nuclear and missile capability, the willingness of the United States to invoke massive retaliation is declining, and that therefore the deterrent to aggression has weakened. Yet the Europeans do not embrace the logical consequence of this fear: the need to build up an adequate capacity to defend Europe on the ground. A more favored alternative, at least in France, is the acquisition of an independent strategic nuclear capability. But when European governments project their imaginations forward to the day when the enemy's divisions cross their borders, do they really envisage themselves shooting off their few missiles against an enemy who would surely obliterate them in return? One doubts that they do, but this is not to say that it is irrational for them to acquire such weapons; they might be successful as a deterrent because of Soviet uncertainty as to whether they would be used, and Soviet unwillingness to incur the risk of their being used.

Further examples easily come to mind. For the sake of deterrence in Europe, we might wish to deploy the forces there as if they intended to respond to an attack with nuclear weapons; but this might not be the optimum deployment for defense once the attack has occurred, if the least-cost defense is a conventional one. For deterrence of limited aggressions in Asia, it might be best to deploy troops on the spot as a "plate-glass window." But for the most efficient and flexible defense against such contingencies, troops might better be concentrated in a central reserve, with transport facilities for moving them quickly to a threatened area.

As Bernard Brodie has written,[2] if the object of our strategic air forces is only deterrence, there is little point in developing "clean" bombs; since deterrence is to be effected by the threat of dire punishment, the dirtier the better. But if we also wish to minimize our own costs once the war has begun, we might wish to use bombs producing minimum fall-out, to encourage similar restraint in the enemy.

For deterrence, it might be desirable to disperse elements of the Strategic Air Command to civilian airfields, thus increasing the number of targets which the enemy must hit if he is to achieve the necessary attrition of our retaliatory power by his first strike. However, this expedient might greatly increase the population damage we would suffer in the enemy's first strike, since most civilian airfields are located near large cities, assuming that the enemy would otherwise avoid hitting cities.[3]

The Technological Revolution

The need to *choose* between deterrence and defense is largely the result of the development of nuclear and thermonuclear weapons and long-range airpower. Prior to these developments, the three primary functions of military force—to *punish* the enemy, to *deny* him territory (or to take it from him), and to *mitigate damage* to oneself—were embodied, more or less, in the same weapons. Deterrence was accomplished (to the extent that military capabilities were the instruments of deterrence) either by convincing the prospective aggressor that his territorial aim was likely to be frustrated, or by posing for him a prospect of intolerable cost, or both, but both of these deterrent functions were performed by the *same* forces. Moreover, these same forces were also the instruments of defense if deterrence failed.

Long-range airpower partially separated the function of punishment from the function of contesting the control of territory, by making possible the assault of targets far to the rear whose relation to the land battle might be quite tenuous.

Nuclear weapons vastly increased the relative importance of prospective *cost* in deterring the enemy and reduced (relatively) the importance of frustrating his aggressive enterprise. It is still true, of course, that a capacity to deny territory to the enemy, or otherwise to block his aims, may be a very efficient deterrent. And such denial *may* be accomplished by strategic nuclear means, though at high cost to the defender. But it is now conceivable that a prospective aggressor may be deterred, in some circumstances at least, solely or primarily by threatening and possessing the capability to inflict extreme punishment on his homeland assets and population, even though he may be superior in capabilities for contesting the control of territory. Nuclear powers must, therefore, exercise a conscious choice between the objectives of deterrence and defense, since the relative proportion of "punishment capacity" to "denial capacity" in their military establishments has become a matter of choice.

This is the most striking difference between nuclear and pre-nuclear strategy: the partial separation of the functions of pre-attack deterrence and post-attack defense, and the possibility that deterrence may now be accomplished by weapons which might have no rational use for defense should deterrence fail.

Deterrence[4]

Deterrence, in one sense, is simply the negative aspect of political power; it is the power to dissuade as opposed to the power to coerce or compel. One deters another party from doing something by the implicit or explicit threat of applying some sanction if the forbidden act is performed, or by the promise of a reward if the act is not performed. Thus conceived, deterrence does not have to depend on military force. We might speak of deterrence by the threat of trade restrictions, for example. The promise of economic aid might deter a country from military action (or any action) contrary to one's own interests. Or we might speak of the deterrence of allies and neutrals as well as potential enemies—as Italy, for example, was deterred from fighting on the side of the Dual Alliance in World War I by the promise of substantial territorial gains. In short, deterrence may follow, first, from any form of control which one has over an opponent's present and prospective "value inventory"; secondly, from the communication of a credible threat or promise to decrease or increase that inventory; and, thirdly, from the opponent's degree of confidence that one intends to fulfill the threat or promise.

In an even broader sense, however, deterrence is a function of the *total* cost-gain expectations of the party to be deterred, and these may be affected by factors other than the apparent capability and intention of the deterrer to apply punishments or confer rewards. For example, an incipient aggressor may be inhibited by his own conscience, or, more likely, by the prospect of losing moral standing, and hence political standing, with uncommitted countries. Or, in the specific case of the Soviet Union, he may fear that war will encourage unrest in, and possibly dissolution of, his satellite empire, and perhaps disaffection among his own population. He may anticipate that his aggression would bring about a tighter welding of the Western alliance or stimulate a degree of mobilization in the West which would either reduce his own security or greatly increase the cost of maintaining his position in the arms race. It is also worth noting that the benchmark or starting point for the potential aggressor's calculation of costs and gains from military action is not his *existing* value inventory, but the extent to which he expects that inventory to be changed if he refrains from initiating military action. Hence, the common observation that the Russians are unlikely to undertake overt military aggression because their chances are so good for making gains by "indirect" peaceful means. Conceivably the Soviets might attack the United States, even though they foresaw greater costs than gains, if the alternative of not attacking seemed to carry within it a strong possibility that the United States would strike them first and, in doing so, inflict greater costs on the Soviet Union than it could by means of retaliation after the Soviets had struck first. In a (very abstract) nutshell, the potential aggressor presumably is deterred from a military move not simply when his expected cost exceeds his expected gain, but when the net gain is less or the net loss is more than he can expect if he refrains from the move. But this formulation must be qualified by the simple fact of inertia: deliberately to shift from a condition of peace to a condition of war is an extremely momentous decision, involving incalculable consequences, and a government is not likely to make this decision unless it foresees a very large advantage in doing so. The great importance of *uncertainty* in this context will be discussed below.

In a broad sense, deterrence operates during war as well as prior to war. It could be defined as a process of influencing the enemy's *intentions*, whatever the circumstances, violent or non-violent. Typically, the outcome of wars has not depended simply on the clash of physical capabilities. The losing side usually accepts defeat somewhat before it has lost its physical ability to continue fighting. It is deterred from continuing the war by a realization that continued fighting can only generate additional costs without hope of compensating gains, this expectation being largely the consequence of the previous application of force by the dominant side.[5] In past wars, such deterrence usually has been characteristic of the terminal stages. However, in the modern concept of limited war, the intentions factor is more prominent and pervasive; force may be threatened and used partly, or even primarily, as a bargaining instrument to persuade the opponent to accept terms of settlement or to observe certain limitations.[6] Deterrence in war is most sharply illustrated in proposals for a strategy of limited retaliation, in which initial strikes, in effect, would be *threats* of further strikes to come, designed to deter the enemy from further fighting. In warfare limited to conventional weapons or tactical nuclear weapons, the strategic nuclear forces held in reserve by either side may constitute a deterrent against the other side's expanding the intensity of its war effort. Also, limited wars may be fought in part with an eye to deterring future enemy attacks by convincing the enemy of one's general willingness to fight.

The above observations were intended to suggest the broad scope of the concept of deterrence, its non-limitation to military factors, and its fundamental affinity to the idea of political power. In the discussion following, we shall use the term in a narrower sense, to mean the discouragement of the *initiation* of military aggression by the threat (implicit or explicit) of applying military force in response to the aggression. We shall assume that when deterrence fails and war begins, the attacked party is no longer "deterring" but rather "defending." Deterrence in war and deterrence, by military action, of subsequent aggressions will be considered as aspects of defense and will be treated later in this chapter.

The Logic of Deterrence

The object of military deterrence is to reduce the probability of enemy military attacks, by posing for the enemy a sufficiently likely prospect that he will suffer a net loss as a result of the attack, or at least a higher net loss or lower net gain than would follow from his not attacking. If we postulate two contending states, an "aggressor" (meaning potential aggressor) and a "deterrer," with other states which are objects of conflict between these two, the probability of any particular attack by the aggressor is the resultant of essentially four factors which exist in his "mind." All four taken together might be termed the aggressor's "risk calculus." They are (1) his valuation of his war objectives; (2) the cost which he expects to suffer as a result of various possible responses by the deterrer; (3) the probability of various responses, including "no response"; and (4) the probability of winning the objectives with each possible response. We shall assume, for simplicity's sake, that the deterrer's "response" refers to the deterrer's entire strategy of action throughout the war precipitated by the aggressor's move—i.e., not only the response to the initial aggressive move, but also to all subsequent moves by the aggressor. Thus the aggressor's estimate of costs and gains is a "whole war" estimate, depending on his image of the deterrer's entire sequence of moves up to the termination of the war, as well as on his own strategic plans for conducting the war, plans which may be contingent on what moves are made by the deterrer during the war.[7]

Obviously, we are dealing here with factors which are highly subjective and uncertain, not subject to exact measurement, and not commensurate except in an intuitive way. Nevertheless, these are the basic factors which the potential aggressor must weigh in determining the probable costs and gains of his contemplated venture.

Certain generalizations can be made about the relationship among these factors. Factor 3 in the aggressor's calculus represents the "credibility" of various possible responses by the deterrer. But credibility is only one factor: it should not be equated with the deterrent *effectiveness* of a possible or threatened response, which is a function of all four factors—i.e., the net cost or gain which a response promises, discounted by the probability (credibility) of its being applied. An available response which is very low in credibility might be sufficient to deter if it poses a very severe sanction (e.g., massive retaliation) or if the aggressor's prospective gain carries very little value for him. Or a threatened response that carries a rather high credibility but poses only moderate costs for the aggressor—e.g., a conventional response, or nuclear retaliation after the aggressor has had the advantage of the first strategic strike—may not deter if the aggressor places a high value on his objective and anticipates a good chance of attaining it.

The credibility factor deserves special attention because it is in terms of this component that the risk calculus of the aggressor "interlocks" with that of the deterrer. The deterrer's risk calculus is similar to that of the aggressor. If the deterrer is rational, his response to aggression will be determined (within the limits, of course, of the military forces he disposes) largely by four factors: (1) his valuation of the territorial objective and of the other intangible gains (e.g., moral satisfaction) which he associates with a given response; (2) the estimated costs of fighting; (3) the probability of successfully holding the territorial objective and other values at stake; and (4) the change in the probability of future enemy attacks on other objectives which would follow from various responses. Variations on, and marginal additions to, these factors may be imagined, but these four are the essential ones. The deterrer will select the response which minimizes his expectation of cost or maximizes his expectation of gain. (As in the case of the aggressor's calculus, we assume that the deterrer's estimates of cost and gain are "whole war" estimates—i.e., the aggregate effects not only of the deterrer's initial response, but also of all the aggressor's countermoves, combined with the deterrer's counter-countermoves, over the entire progress of the war.) The credibility of various possible responses by the deterrer depends on the aggressor's image of the deterrer's risk calculus—i.e., of the latter's net costs and gains from each response—as well as on the aggressor's assessment of the deterrer's capacity to act rationally.

The aggressor, of course, is not omniscient with respect to the deterrer's estimates of cost and gain. Even the deterrer will be unable to predict in advance of the attack how he will visualize his cost-gain prospects and, hence, exactly what response he will choose once the aggression is under way. (Witness the United States' response to the North Korean attack in 1950, which was motivated by values which apparently did not become clear to the decision-makers until the actual crisis was upon them.) Nor can the aggressor be sure the deterrer will act rationally according to his own cost-gain predictions. Because of these uncertainties, the aggressor's estimate of credibility cannot be precise. More than one response will be possible, and the best the aggressor can do is attempt to guess how the deterrer will visualize his gains and losses consequent upon each response, and from this guess arrive at a judgment about the likelihood or probability of each possible response.

The deterrer evaluates the *effectiveness* of his deterrent posture by attempting to guess the values of the four factors in the aggressor's risk calculus. In estimating the credibility factor, he attempts to guess how the aggressor is estimating the factors in *his* (the deterrer's) calculus. He arrives at some judgment as to whether the aggressor is likely to expect a net cost or net gain from the aggressive move and, using this judgment and his degree of confidence in it as a basis, he determines the probability of aggression. Happily, the spiral of "guesses about the other's guesses" seems to stop here. In other words, the aggressor's decision whether or not to attack is not in turn affected by his image of the deterrer's estimate of the likelihood of attack. He knows that once the attack is launched the deterrer will select the response which promises him the least cost or greatest gain—at that point, the deterrer's previous calculations about "deterrence" of that attack become irrelevant.

Denial vs. Punishment

It is useful to distinguish between deterrence which results from capacity to deny territorial gains to the enemy, and deterrence by the threat and capacity to inflict nuclear punishment.[8] Denial capabilities—typically, conventional ground, sea, and tactical air forces—deter chiefly by their effect on the fourth factor in the aggressor's calculus: his estimate of the probability of gaining his objective. Punishment capabilities—typically, strategic nuclear power for either massive or limited retaliation—act primarily on the second factor, the aggressor's estimate of possible costs, and may have little effect on his chances for territorial gain. Of course, this distinction is not sharp or absolute: a "denial" response, especially if it involves the use of nuclear weapons tactically, can mean high direct costs, plus the risk that the war may get out of hand and ultimately involve severe nuclear punishment for both sides. This prospect of cost and risk may exert a significant deterring effect. A "punishment" response, if powerful enough, may foreclose territorial gains, and limited reprisals may be able to force a settlement short of complete conquest of the territorial objective. However, there are some differences worth noting between these two types or strategies of deterrence.

Apart from their differential impact on the cost and gain elements of the aggressor's calculations, the two types of response are likely to differ also in their credibility or probability of application. As a response to all-out nuclear attack on the deterrer, the application of punishment will be highly credible. But for lesser challenges, such as a conventional attack on an ally, a threat to inflict nuclear punishment normally will be less credible than a threat to fight a "denial" action—assuming, of course, that denial capabilities are available. While the making of a *threat* of nuclear punishment may be desirable and rational, its *fulfillment* is likely to seem irrational after the aggressor has committed his forces, since punishment alone may not be able to hold the territorial objective and will stimulate the aggressor to make counterreprisals. The deterrer therefore has a strong incentive to renege on his threat. Realizing this in advance, the aggressor may not think the threat a very credible one. A threat of denial action will seem more credible on two counts: it is less costly for the deterrer and it may be effective in frustrating the aggressor's aims, or at least in reducing his gains. A denial response is more likely than reprisal action to promise a rational means of *defense* in case deterrence fails; this consideration supports its credibility as a deterrent.

A related difference is that the threat of denial action is likely to be appraised by the aggressor in terms of the deterrer's *capabilities;* threats of nuclear punishment require primarily a judgment of *intent.* It is fairly certain that the deterrer will fight a threatened denial action if he has appropriate forces;[9] the essential question for the aggressor, therefore, is whether these forces are strong enough to prevent him from making gains. In the case of nuclear reprisals, however, the capability to inflict unacceptable punishment is likely to be unquestioned, at least for large nuclear powers; here the aggressor must attempt to look into the mind of the deterrer and guess whether the will to apply punishment exists. Thus a denial threat is much more calculable for the aggressor than a reprisal threat—assuming that a comparison of military capabilities is easier than mind-reading. This may make a denial strategy the more powerful deterrent of the two if the deterrer has strong denial forces; but if he obviously does not have enough ground and tactical forces to block conquest, the threat may be weaker than a nuclear reprisal threat. Even if there is doubt in the aggressor's mind that the reprisals will be carried out, these doubts may be offset by the possible severity of his punishment if he miscalculates and the threat is fulfilled.

Differences between the Balance of Terror and the Balance of Power

The traditional balancing process continues to operate as a balance between conventional forces (and the potential for building such forces) in all situations in which there is no significant possibility that nuclear weapons will be used. Hereafter, we shall refer to this balance as the "tactical" balance of power, differentiating it both from the strategic balance of terror and from an over-all balance of power involving interactions between the strategic balance and the tactical balance. Some significant differences between these two balancing systems in their "pure" form are worth noting.

One difference is that, in the strategic balance, quantitatively matching the enemy's capabilities is virtually irrelevant as a criterion for balance. A balance of terror exists when neither side can eliminate enough of the other's forces in striking first to avoid an unacceptable retaliatory blow. Depending chiefly on technological conditions, especially the degree of vulnerability of the opposing forces, a potential attacker may be balanced with a force only a fraction of the size of the attacker's forces; or balance may require having more forces than the potential attacker. The proper criterion is to be able to inflict unacceptable retaliatory damage.

By contrast, in the modern tactical balance centering on conventional ground forces, as in the traditional balancing process, simply equaling the strength of the enemy's forces is still the most plausible balancing criterion, although of course a sophisticated calculation would require that it be modified to take account of factors such as a possible advantage of the defense over the offense, possibilities for post-attack mobilization, geography, asymmetries in supply capabilities, etc.

The balance of terror is primarily a *deterrent* balance rather than a *defensive* balance. That is, a "balance" is said to exist when a potential aggressor faces the prospect of retaliatory damage sufficient to deter him, not when he faces the prospect of defeat or frustration of his aims. Conceivably, a balance of terror could exist in the defensive sense, if the forces on both sides were so invulnerable that the side which absorbed the first blow could still retaliate with sufficient force to destroy or prostrate the attacker. But the forces required for winning the war after being attacked would be considerably larger in number and probably different in kind from the forces required to deter the attack.

The tactical balance of power, on the other hand, centers primarily on the function of defense. A balance of power exists when the defending side has enough forces to defeat the attacker or at least to prevent him from making territorial conquests. Deterrence is the consequence of this defensive capability, not of a capacity to inflict unacceptable costs. In the tactical balance, the requirements for deterrence and for effectively fighting a war more or less coincide; this is not the case in the balance of terror.

Another difference concerns the strategic value of territory and of territorial boundaries. In the tactical balance, the strategic value of territory and of the human and material assets associated with territory continues to be high. The traditional elements of national power, such as manpower, natural resources, industrial strength, space, geographic separation, command of the seas, and so on, remain the primary sources of power and they are important criteria for determining the existence or non-existence of a tactical balance.

These territorially based elements are also a source of power in the balance of terror, but their significance is less and considerably different than in the tactical balance. Strategic nuclear weapons have reduced the importance of geographical separation of the opponents in the balance of terror, since ICBMs can reach from continent to continent. However, distance still retains some significance in the strategic balance of terror. An aggressor can reduce the required range and hence increase the accuracy and possible payload of his missiles by obtaining control of territory between himself and his prospective nuclear opponent. He may also increase the points of the compass from which he can attack, thus complicating the opponent's warning and air defense problem. He may increase the space available for dispersal of his striking forces, and he may obtain useful staging bases and post-attack landing points for his long-range aircraft.

The acquisition of industrial and resource assets by conquest may increase a nuclear power's capability to produce additional strategic weapons. While "raw" manpower is not a significant source of power in the balance of terror, an aggressor may turn to his own uses the scientific brainpower of a conquered nation.

On balance, however, the strategic value of territory and its associated assets is probably smaller in the balance of terror than in the tactical balance.

Overconcentration on the strategic balance and the contingency of all-out war has caused us, in recent years, to downgrade excessively the importance of industrial potential for war. War potential continues to be a source of power in the tactical balance not only prior to war but also after the war has begun. Stockpiles of raw materials, stand-by war production plants, and the like can be translated into actual military power during the progress of a limited war, provided of course that the forces ready in advance of the attack can hold off the enemy until the additional power can be mobilized. However, in the balance of terror, industrial potential provides only pre-attack power, not post-attack power. Once the war has started, if such potential were not destroyed, its usefulness probably would be limited to survival and reconstruction. Even in a very restrained war, involving only counterforce attacks on military installations, with minimum damage to economic assets, a decision probably would be reached before industrial potential could be brought into play.

In the tactical balance, alliances are useful for both deterrence and defense, in roughly equal proportions; the costs of war are low enough and the incentives to prevent the conquest of an ally are high enough that allies are likely to see a net advantage in coming to each other's aid. The conquest of an ally means a very serious erosion of one's own power and security position, and such erosion may be prevented at bearable intrinsic costs, if the necessary forces are available. Since the potential aggressor is aware of this, the credibility of alliance obligations tends to be high.

In a world of many nuclear powers—i.e., in a "multipolar" balance of terror—alliances are likely to have less utility and credibility for protection against nuclear attack. Obviously, a country which could mount a completely unacceptable retaliation to a nuclear attack on itself would not need allies for security against this contingency. (It might, of course, enter into an alliance for security against non-nuclear attack.) Countries which doubted their individual capacity to deter a nuclear attack might feel they could gain security by combining. In combination, they might be able to muster enough retaliatory power to deter either an attack on the whole alliance simultaneously or an attack on a single member.

The alliance's capacity to deter attack on a single member would depend critically on the amount of his forces which the aggressor would have to use up in attacking the first victim. It is conceivable that the attacker would so deplete his own forces that the other members of the alliance could strike without fear of serious retaliation; at least the prospect of this would limit the amount of force which the attacker could use against the initial victim and might deter the attack. But if the aggressor could retain substantial and invulnerable forces while successfully attacking a single member, the supporting allies would feel powerful incentives to renege. Fulfilling the alliance obligation would mean accepting severe destruction. These costs might be suffered in vain, for there would be little chance

of saving the attacked ally by nuclear retaliation. And, in retaliating, the supporting allies would be using up forces which they would need for their own future
protection. Thus the alliance pledge may not seem very credible to a prospective
nuclear aggressor.

Nevertheless, alliances might have some deterrent value in a multipolar
balance of terror, because of the aggressor's uncertainties, because an alliance
would limit the amount of force which an aggressor would be free to apply against
a single victim, and because deterrence does not depend on absolute credibility. A
nuclear attack on a single country would be a very momentous act which might
stimulate enough emotional reaction and irrationality among the victim's allies to
trigger retaliation on their part. The aggressor would have to realize that the *possible* damage he might suffer at the hands of the whole alliance would be very much
higher than the value he placed on conquest of a single member. The magnitude
of the possible retaliatory damage might very well offset in his mind the low
credibility of an alliance response.

Notes

1. Arnold Wolfers, " 'National Security' as an Ambiguous Symbol," *Political Science
Quarterly* 67, no. 4 (December 1952):481ff.

2. Bernard Brodie, *Strategy in the Missile Age* (Princeton: Princeton University Press,
1959), p. 295.

3. This particular choice between deterrence and war costs has been analyzed by
Thomas C. Schelling in an unpublished paper which I have been privileged to read.

4. Other treatments of the theory of deterrence include Bernard Brodie, "The
Anatomy of Deterrence," *World Politics* 11, no. 2 (January 1959):173–92; Morton A.
Kaplan, "The Calculus of Deterrence," *World Politics* 11, no. 1 (October 1958):20–44;
William W. Kaufmann, "The Requirements of Deterrence," in W.W. Kaufmann (ed.),
Military Policy and National Security (Princeton: Princeton University Press, 1956);
Thomas W. Milburn, "What Constitutes Effective Deterrence?" *Conflict Resolution* 3, no.
2 (June 1959):138–46; Glenn H. Snyder, "Deterrence by Denial and Punishment,"
Research Monograph No. 1, Center of International Studies, Princeton University, January
2, 1959; and Glenn H. Snyder, "Deterrence and Power," *Conflict Resolution* 4, no. 2 (June
1960):163–79. Robert E. Osgood has allowed me to read several of his manuscripts on the
subject which were unpublished at this writing.

5. For an excellent extended discussion of this point, with case studies, see Paul
Kecskemeti, *Strategic Surrender* (Stanford: Stanford University Press, 1959).

6. See Thomas C. Schelling, *The Strategy of Conflict* (Cambridge: Harvard University
Press, 1960), chap. 3.

7. By way of example, NATO capabilities might raise the prospect of the following
possible reactions to a Soviet attack on West Germany: massive retaliation, limited retaliation with nuclear weapons on the Soviet homeland, a tactical nuclear response confined to
the local theater of battle, a conventional response, or no response at all. Theoretically, the
Soviets would assign a probability and a net cost or gain for themselves to each possible re-

sponse (the net cost or gain representing the summation of their territorial gains, other gains, and war costs as a consequence of the entire war following the initial response), calculate an expected value for each response by multiplying the probability times the assumed net cost or gain, and determine an expected value for the aggression by summing the expected values for all possible responses. If the expected value were negative, or positive but less than the positive expected value of non-military alternatives, the Soviets would be deterred.

8. This distinction is discussed by Robert E. Osgood in "A Theory of Deterrence," mimeographed, 1960, and in my own "Deterrence by Denial and Punishment."

9. It is possible that the aggressor may be able to deter "denial" resistance by threatening to take punitive action if resistance occurs. This is perhaps most feasible with respect to allies of the country attacked whose troops are not deployed on the territory of the victim.

Discussion Questions

1. What is the relationship between defense and deterrence?

2. If deterrence can never be absolute (or can it?), are deterrent forces useless if they do not increase defense? Are defense forces useless if they do not increase deterrence?

3. Which do you think U.S. military policy should emphasize, defense or deterrence? Why?

7
Toward a Strategy of Limited War

Robert E. Osgood

The Need for Reappraisal

It is easier to discern the inadequacies of American strategy than it is to prescribe a remedy, but it is also easier to be contented with the status quo than it is to venture alternatives. For the most practicable alternatives to current policies seem to promise a larger military and economic effort, although they carry no compensating guarantee of improving America's position in the cold war. As long as no conspicuous catastrophe befalls us, the status quo has at least the appeal of something known, whereas the feasible alternatives to the status quo seem at best untested measures of avoiding speculative dangers.

Yet the history of America's foreign relations in recent decades is a succession of unanticipated crises preceded by general complacency and followed by widespread alarm and recrimination. One does not have to entertain an apocalyptic view of history to believe that the present international situation is replete with opportunities for a repetition of this pattern. Common prudence requires not only a critical reappraisal of existing military and political policies but also a systematic examination of possible alternatives.

The suggestions that follow are not intended to comprise a detailed military program or a strategic blueprint. They are of a general nature—partly because of the limited technical information available to the layman, and partly because the most important factor determining the adequacy or inadequacy of American strategy has been our ideas about basic strategic principles rather than our technical capacity for implementing these principles. The general requirements of an American strategy must necessarily be set out in terms of the military technology known at the present time, but one can try to analyze the important elements of this strategy broadly enough to allow for alterations of policies within the general requirements in response to unforeseen technological developments and a great variety of possible military contingencies.

Osgood, Robert E., *Limited War* (Chicago: University of Chicago Press, 1957). Copyright © 1957 by the University of Chicago.

Containment—A Question of Method

The logic of the cold war and the concrete experience of the last decade indicate that America's over-all strategy should be the containment of the Communist sphere of control by our readiness to oppose aggression with a variety of means under a variety of circumstances. Containment is based upon assumptions about the nature of Communist conduct that have been confirmed in practice. It is a feasible strategy, compatible with our basic political objectives and our power to attain them. No other strategy, under present circumstances, will fulfill the requirements of American security as adequately. The nation has tacitly acknowledged this fact by rejecting every opportunity to pursue an alternative.

The important question concerning American strategy is not its general objective, which is best described as containment, but rather the method of attaining that objective. Assuming that the capacity to oppose aggression—which includes the willingness as well as the physical capability—is the most effective deterrent to Communist military expansion, the real question that has faced us since 1947 is: By what means should we be prepared to oppose different forms of Communist aggression in different areas under a variety of circumstances?

In the most general way, we can answer the question by saying that containment requires a capacity to wage both total and limited war. The capacity to wage one kind of war is insufficient without the capacity to wage the other.

Capacity for Total War and Limited War

America's capacity to wage a total war should be adequate to serve the following ends: to deter the Communists from undertaking major aggression in areas essential to our security; to induce them to refrain from taking measures that would be incompatible with limited war; and, if these deterrents fail, to fight a large-scale war in a manner that will maximize our chance of achieving basic security objectives at the end of the war.

In order to command a military capacity adequate for these purposes the United States must maintain at least offensive and defensive parity in strategic nuclear weapons and delivery capabilities with the Communist bloc. However, effective parity does not require numerical equality. Moreover, unless defensive techniques should attain an overwhelming superiority over offensive techniques, gains in our strategic nuclear weapons and delivery capabilities seem likely to reach the point of diminishing returns before long, since neither the United States nor the Soviet Union will be able to prevent the other from imposing intolerable destruction upon its tactical and strategic facilities, regardless of how the enemy's blows are countered.

It can be argued that for this reason ground forces will come to play a more decisive role in the military balance. But considering the extent of destruction that would follow a total nuclear war, even if we assume that the adversaries quickly eliminated each other's capacity to maintain such a war, increases in our capacity for ground war are not likely to contribute much toward preventing the deliberate resort to total war. On the other hand, if all deterrents proved ineffective and a total war, a war of desperation, actually did occur, then the side with a military superiority on the ground would be in a much better position to occupy and control territory; and to that extent it would have a substantial advantage in achieving its own political objectives and obstructing the enemy's.

Nevertheless, in terms of the relative urgency of military dangers confronting the United States, there can be little doubt that the greatest strategic dividends to be derived from a given expansion of our ground forces lie in the direction of preparing the free world for the contingency of limited war. In view of the superior numbers of trained manpower available to the Communist bloc, our capacity for total war is likely to be promoted most effectively and at a tolerable cost by maintaining an offensive-defensive superiority—or, at least, parity—in the ability to strike directly at the tactical and strategic capability of the Soviet Union. As the offensive capabilities of the Soviet Union increase, the relative importance of American and allied defensive capabilities—both in terms of air defense and a dispersed base system—will increase, unless or until both nations attain offensive capabilities so vast as to be beyond the power of the defense to nullify in any significant measure.

Assuming that the United States maintains an adequate capacity for total war and that the Communists continue to conduct a rational and cautious foreign policy, designed to gain their ends by indirection and limited ventures rather than by massive military assault, the chief function of our capacity for total war will be to keep war limited and to strengthen our diplomacy against the blackmail that a strong and unscrupulous power can wield. However, the fulfillment of this function will not be sufficient for the purposes of containment unless it is accompanied by a ready capacity to resist lesser aggressions by limited war. Otherwise the Communists can confront us with the choice between total war, non-resistance, and ineffective resistance; and the results of that situation would probably be piecemeal Communist expansion, the paralysis of Western diplomacy, and the further disaffection of uncommitted peoples.

Therefore, preparation for limited war is as vital to American security as preparation for total war. It is a matter for thorough and systematic planning, not for improvisation. After all, in developing our capacity for total war we are preparing for the least likely contingency; its principal justification lies in the fact that it may never be used. But in developing a capacity for limited war we would be preparing to meet the most likely contingency; we would be maintaining the only credible military deterrent to Communist advances in the most vulnerable areas of the world.

The Limitation of Political Objectives

The specific requirements of a strategy that will enable the United States and its allies to deter and fight limited wars must be determined in the light of the many forms such wars can assume and the great variety of circumstances under which they may occur. These wars may vary in character from guerrilla actions to a massive clash of modern arms. They may result from clandestine Communist support of an indigenous revolution, from the intervention of Communist "volunteers" in a war between smaller powers, or from a direct invasion across a well-defined boundary. As an increasing number of smaller powers acquire the will and strength to act according to their independent designs, the United States may have to consider intervention in wars that do not directly involve Communist powers at all. One can readily imagine the different means by which limited wars might have to be fought in the Formosa Straits, the jungles and swamps of Southeast Asia, the mountains of Afghanistan, or the deserts of the Middle East.

The detailed military plans to meet these varied requirements are beyond the scope of this study; but we can properly formulate the essential guidelines for these plans. These guidelines extend from the framework of the two general prerequisites of limited war: the limitation of political objectives and the limitation of military means. What do these prerequisites mean in terms of a strategy of limited war under contemporary military and political conditions? Let us examine the question of limited objectives first.

Clearly, the over-all strategic objective of containment requires that the specific political objectives for which the United States must be prepared to fight limited wars will not entail radical changes in the status quo. The very fact that a war remains limited although the belligerents are physically capable of imposing a much greater scale of destruction assumes that neither of the belligerents' objectives constitutes such a serious challenge to the status quo as to warrant expanding the war greatly or taking large risks of precipitating total war. However, this does not mean that we must necessarily confine our war objectives to the exact territorial boundaries and the other political conditions that existed prior to aggression. This kind of mechanical requirement, making no allowance for the dynamic, unpredictable elements of war, would impose rigid political constraints, unrelated to the actual balance of military power and the enemy's response. Moreover, if potential aggressors could count upon ending a war in at least no worse position than they began it, they might come to regard this situation as an irresistible invitation to launch a series of limited incursions at a minimal risk in proportion to the possible gain.

In the final analysis the precise objectives of a war can be determined only in the light of the specific circumstances in which it occurs. However, this does not mean that the objectives should be left entirely to improvisation. They should be derived from a pre-existing framework of concrete political aims, expressing the particular power interests of the United States throughout the various strategic areas of the world. This is a matter of balancing power and commitments, of combining force with policy, in advance of crises, so that when crises occur, the government will not be forced to formulate under the pressure of the moment the kind of basic judgments of strategic priority and enemy intent that are essential to the rational conduct of war.

The Korean War illustrates the dangers of ignoring this rule. Although we did manage to improvise limited objectives once the war broke out, these objectives had no clear relation to our strategic planning before the war. Throughout the war the government gave the unfortunate impression of being in doubt about its own aims, as well as the aims of the adversary. Our objectives during the war suffered unnecessary ambiguity because they seemed to be more the product of intuition and changing military fortunes than of firm military and political policies formulated in the light of an over-all national strategy. Clearly, our general commitment to the Truman Doctrine and the principle of collective security was no substitute for strategic forethought; in fact, our reliance upon these generalities tended to obscure rather than to clarify the determining objectives of the war.

This is not to say that wartime political objectives should or can be formulated with the precision of legal documents prescribing binding rules in perpetuity. What is necessary is that the government establish concrete, feasible objectives, sufficiently well defined yet flexible enough to provide a rational guide for the conduct of military operations, and that it communicate the general import of these objectives—above all, the fact that they are limited— to the enemy. The importance of this requirement is evident in view of the fact that one of the essential elements of limited war is the operation of some kind of system of mutual self-restraint based upon the belligerents' observance of a reasonable proportion between the dimensions of war and the value of the objectives at stake.

Political objectives need not be made explicit at all times in order to serve their proper function of limiting and controlling war. The method of conducting military operations, especially the particular military restraints observed, may convey the nature of determining political objectives more effectively than explicit announcements. But since the political character of limited war is all-important, diplomacy—the public statement of positions, the private exchange of official views, the bargaining over terms—is an indispensable instrument of limitation, not only for communicating objectives but for terminating hostilities on the basis of accommodation. However, diplomacy is not something that nations can readily turn on and off. It operates best when it is in continual use. Diplomacy is not apt to serve its moderating function during war unless there exists in advance of war an expectation that neither side will push things too far without recourse to political accommodation.

Admittedly, there are grave difficulties in conducting useful diplomatic relations with Communist powers. The Communists do not regard diplomacy as a means of ironing out conflicting positions among nations sharing a fundamental harmony of interests. They regard it, rather, as a device and a tactic for pursuing an inevitable conflict of interests. Nevertheless, there is nothing to indicate that they are unwilling to strike bargains of mutual advantage. They neither make nor accept concessions as a tender of good will, but we should not on that account exclude compromises that advance our interests as well as theirs. They understand better than we that diplomacy, like force, cannot properly be divorced from power; rather it is a function of power. If we were to comprehend the function of diplomacy as an instrument for attaining limited political objectives in conjunction with military force, rather than as an alternative to force, we would be in a better position to cultivate useful channels of communication for keeping the present struggle for power cold and limited.

When one considers the general requirement of the formulation and communication of limited objectives, one must also take into account the method of promulgating strategic objectives. For the impression of its objectives that the government seeks to convey through diplomacy can be undone by the way in which it publicly announces its strategy. The essential requirement here is that the government announce its strategy in such a way as to make credible its limitation of objectives and its ability to back them up with proportionate force. This is not a matter of giving fuller publicity to the details of American strategy but rather of publicizing strategy in words that correspond with capabilities and intentions and that avoid raising false expectations. It would be foolish to try to relieve potential aggressors of all their doubts about our intentions under every conceivable circumstance, even if we could know those intentions ourselves. But it would be dangerous to leave them with the impression that our conduct is reckless, capricious, and unrelated to our words. And the point is equally applicable to the impression we convey to allied and uncommitted nations.

Unfortunately, much of the hyperbole we use to convince ourselves that we are conducting our strategy in the American way convinces others that we are incurably aggressive. Foreign states are peculiarly sensitive to our emphasis upon military considerations and the ideological aspects of the cold war. The bold phrases which, presumably, give us courage make our allies shiver. It is ridiculous that we should be the ones to bear the onus of militarism and imperialism when it is the Communists who have the huge armies and who have been the determined expansionists while we have had to be begged and frightened into making the minimum effort necessary to defend even the positions essential to our security. But if our bellicose talk is the obverse of our pacific inclinations, we cannot expect other nations to appreciate that paradox. Sometimes we even fool ourselves into taking this talk at face value. Perhaps if we were clear in our own minds about the limited nature of our strategic objectives, we would be in a better position to clarify the thoughts of others. And then we could place the onus of militarism and imperialism where it belongs.

The Limitation of Military Means

The problem of limiting the political objectives of war and national strategy is inseparable from the problem of devising limited military means. Unless we have military policies, weapons, techniques, and tactics capable of supporting limited objectives, we cannot have an effective strategy of limited war; for containment depends less upon what we say than upon what we are ready to do. An effective strategy requires more than the mere formulation of objectives; it requires a balance between objectives and means, such that the objectives are within range of the means and the means are commensurate with the objectives. Otherwise, we shall have to intrust our security to bluff, improvisation, and sheer luck.

One great difficulty in developing a military establishment and a military strategy and tactics capable of meeting the threat of limited war lies in the fact that the requirements for limiting war do not necessarily correspond with the requirements of fighting limited wars effectively; and yet the fulfillment of one requirement is incomplete without the other. Therefore, nations must be ready to weigh the risk of expanding wars against the need for military success. In balancing these two factors the importance of the political stakes must be the crucial determinant.

At the same time, the requirements of both military limitation and effectiveness are, in themselves, complicated by the great variety of circumstances under which limited wars might have to be fought. The kind of measures that would be effective in fighting a limited war in the Formosa Straits might be ineffective in Thailand or incompatible with limited war in Iran. Moreover, both the limitation and the effectiveness of military operations embrace a number of separate but related criteria, which are not susceptible to precise measurement. The scale of war, for example, can be limited in area, weapons, targets, manpower, the number of belligerents, the duration of war, or its intensity. And military effectiveness must be measured not only by physical capabilities on the battlefield but also by the political and psychological consequences of various measures and the relation of these measures to the general resources of the United States and its allies, especially manpower and economic potential.

The proper blending and balancing of all these considerations in a coherent strategy assumes an accurate anticipation of the response of potential adversaries to a wide range of measures and circumstances. Such an anticipation will depend upon calculating the value that the potential adversaries attach to various objectives and the proportionate effort they are willing to expend upon achieving them or upon preventing us from jeopardizing them. And this sort of calculation must rest upon a sound appraisal of their intentions, strategy, and general international behavior.

Moreover, we must anticipate the response to our policies and actions in terms of a two-way interaction, calculating that the adversary will respond on the basis of his own anticipation of our counter-response. In other words, the course of action—the means of resistance and deterrence—upon which we plan to rely under different circumstances must be determined in the light of the same kind of complex calculation of response and counter-response that chess players or boxers must make. Therefore, it is too simple to operate on the principle that successful deterrence depends merely upon letting potential aggressors know that they will suffer damage outweighing any possible gains from aggression; for the same measure might also cause the potential aggressor to respond in a way that would impose intolerable penalties upon our own interests. Calculating the deterrent effect of this risk upon our own actions, the aggressor might well conclude that he could safely ignore our threat. The Chinese Communists seem to have done this very thing in supporting the Vietminh seizure of Dienbienphu.

Thus the first requirement of deterrence is that it be credible to the potential aggressor; and credibility, in turn, requires that the means of deterrence be proportionate to the objective at stake. This commensurability may be difficult to achieve in practice, but the underlying principle is simple enough: it is the principle of economy of force, without which the reciprocal self-restraints essential to limited war cannot exist.

Even this elementary outline of general considerations concerning the limitation of military means should leave no doubt that the different factors involved and the complexity of their relationship to one another confront American strategists with a perplexing problem of military planning. Nevertheless, if we are at least aware of the various elements that enter into the military equation, it should not be beyond our ingenuity to devise means of preparing the nation for the most serious contingencies of limited war. After all, there are only a limited number of areas in which such wars might occur, and there are only a limited number of circumstances, or kinds of circumstances, from which they are likely to arise.

The history of American strategy since 1947 strongly suggests that we have excluded from our military planning some of the central elements in the equation of limitation, that we have obscured them with handy but misleading generalizations, simply because our aversion to the very idea of limited war has inhibited us from approaching the problem objectively and systematically. One might almost say that the things we have failed to consider in the realm of military preparation have been less of a handicap than the things we have taken for granted; for it is the major unexamined premises of our approach to force and policy that have established the pattern and focus of our strategic thinking.

Geographical Limitation

Under the military and political conditions of the foreseeable future the decisive limitations upon military operations that are within the power of belligerents to control would seem to be limitations upon the area of combat, upon weapons, and upon targets. Without these three kinds of limitations, it is difficult to imagine a war remaining limited. With them, the other limitations would probably follow, and wars might remain limited even if they did not follow. Therefore the heart of the problem of developing a strategy of limited war lies in devising methods of conducting military operations that are compatible with these three limitations and yet militarily effective in terms of supporting America's security objectives.

The importance of geographical limitation is obvious. Without the localization of war, hostilities involving the United States and the Communist bloc, directly or indirectly, would almost certainly exceed the scale of practicable limitation, given the existing military potentials of major powers. For a war not fought within well-defined geographical limits would probably pose such a massive threat to American and Russian security that both powers would feel compelled to strike at the center of opposition. The same thing can be said of the simultaneous occurrence of several local wars, for both the Soviet Union and the United States would probably regard such wars as the sign of a general contest that it could not afford to counter on a local and piecemeal basis. Geographical limitation is all the more important because it is the easiest, most practicable limitation to establish, to observe, and to communicate.

However, like any other limitation designed to control the dynamics of warfare, limitation of the area of combat must not be construed in an absolute sense. Thus it need not under all circumstances preclude naval action or tactical air retaliation beyond the immediate area of attack. Whether the extension of a war by air and sea action is warranted must be judged in the light of the danger of enlarging the scope of war beyond the bounds of control, balanced against the political urgency and the military efficacy of the measures involved. For example, if important political objectives are at stake in a peripheral contest supported by Communist China, and if they can only be attained by bombing Chinese bases and supply lines supporting the aggression, then this measure might be worth the additional risk of enlarging the scale of war that it would entail. However, if the military efficacy of such a measure is dubious, if bombing Chinese bases would probably lead to retaliation by countermeasures that would nullify the anticipated military advantage or that would entail a risk of total war disproportionate to the importance of the objective at stake, then the least objectionable course might be to adhere to existing limitations and make the best of them.

Ideally, we should like to be able to contain every possible Communist aggression on a strictly local basis, for then we could avoid the choice between undertaking ineffective resistance and risking total war or, at least, war on a scale beyond our ability to sustain at a tolerable cost—a dilemma that would probably result in non-resistance unless aggression occurred in the most vital strategic area. However, we must recognize that in some highly industrialized and economically integrated areas—certainly the core of the NATO area—even limited military incursions would constitute such a serious threat to our security interests (and would be so difficult to check on a purely local basis) that we could not afford to confine our resistance to the immediate combat area. This might be true even if the topography, the industrial and transport linkages, and other physical features made restriction theoretically feasible. Therefore, in these areas, except in cases of insurrection and minor military coups, we shall have to continue to rely primarily upon our capability to strike at the center of aggression to deter Communist advances.

But the American government, especially under the Eisenhower administration, has frequently argued another reason for the unfeasibility of relying upon purely local defense, a reason with much less claim to validity. It has argued that because of the Communists' central geographical position and their numerical superiority in manpower the free world cannot afford the expenditure of men and money necessary to resist aggression locally at every possible point along the Sino-Soviet periphery. American strategists have been frightened by this theoretical situation ever since the inauguration of containment. What they have envisioned is the Russians and Chinese, secure in the heartland of Eurasia and enjoying the advantages of inexhaustible manpower and interior lines of communication, striking out at will at a series of soft spots along the periphery, remote from the center of our own strength, while the American coalition dissipates its precious manpower and resources in endless futile efforts to hold a kind of Maginot Line against assaults initiated by the Communists at places and with weapons of their choosing. The prospect is, indeed, a disturbing one; but how realistic is it?

In the first place, the image of trying to hold every point on a 20,000-mile Maginot Line is, to say the least, exaggerated. It is true that in the European sector of such a line we would certainly operate at an irrevocable disadvantage in trying to contain Communist assaults on a local basis, since the West suffers such substantial numerical inferiority in mobilizable manpower.[1] But, as we have observed, the defense of the part of the Communist perimeter that adjoins the NATO area does not depend primarily upon local resistance. Furthermore, other sectors of the perimeter are less vulnerable than a simple line drawn on a map suggests. India and Pakistan are protected by a formidable mountain barrier. Political considerations may protect other segments equally effectively. For example, India's close interest in Burma and the reluctance of Communist China to turn India from a neutral power into a dangerous competitor in Southeast Asia may deter an attack on Burma—and, perhaps, on Laos, Cambodia, and Thailand too—far more effectively than a large local garrison, providing that these nations have a minimum capacity to police their territories.

The Middle Eastern and Asian rimlands are undoubtedly vulnerable but not so vulnerable as the purely spatial relation between the heartlands and the rimlands implies. We shall deal with the methods of defending these rimlands when we examine the specific problem of applying containment to the gray areas; but it can be noted now that the image of Sino-Soviet interior lines of communication facilitating the rapid transfer of great masses of troops from one peripheral point to another is not supported by the logistical realities of the situation. The tremendous length of those lines, their distance from major supplies, their sparseness, and the poor transportation facilities refute any analogy with our own elaborate and highly developed network of communications. And as for transferring troops rapidly from one peripheral point to another, the Communists are in no better position to do that than we are; for the Asian rimland is not a continuous open field but actually a series of terrain compartments, between which communication is far easier by sea and air than by land. In a contest with the Sino-Soviet heartland for this Asian rimland we and our allies have the tremendous advantage of easy access to the sea and control of the sea, as well as a large number of naval and air bases encircling Eurasia and the technical capability of transporting great quantities of men and equipment to various points on the Sino-Soviet periphery. The Korean War was an impressive illustration of this fact.

As for a number of more or less simultaneous attacks on the periphery of Communist power, there is no reason to think that the Communists are in a better position to fight more than one local war at a time than we, providing that we take full advantage of our superior mobility, our geographical position, and our logistical advantages. Moreover, assuming that the Communists continue to conduct a strategy of caution and limited risk, they will realize that a series of small wars could constitute such a serious threat to our prestige and security as to incur an inordinate risk of precipitating a full-scale war; for their simultaneous attacks would be a signal to us that they had deliberately accepted the grave risk of a general war, and we would have to accept the same risks. If we could not contain these attacks locally, we probably could not afford to confine our resistance to the combat area; nor would the American people tolerate piecemeal defeat under this circumstance. Presumably, the Communists would know this.

Therefore, with the exceptions and qualifications noted above, it seems both feasible and essential that the United States develop its strategy around the conception of local defense that has been implicit in containment from the first. Of course, the particular geographical restrictions upon a war must be determined in the light of such factors as the direction and scope of the aggression and the geographical features of the area. Clearly, island and peninsular wars will be easier to localize than wars in areas with no clear physical demarcations; and small-scale attacks directed at well-defined territorial objectives will be easier to localize than large-scale assaults or general insurrectionary activity unaccompanied by clear indications of military and political intent.

However, we must also recognize that alliances may inject a complicating factor into geographical limitation of warfare; for by creating an obligation for many nations to come to the aid of one, they also create the danger that an attack on one country will result in spreading the war to several. Thus we might find it difficult to resist the demands of an ally under attack that other allies share the burden of the war in their own territories. We must remember that such an ally will not feel the same restraints as we. For the war which we strive to confine geographically may, in effect, be unlimited from the standpoint of the ally whose country happens to be the scene of battle. He may already have reached that stage of desperation that we are trying to avoid. This situation will afford him considerable bargaining power, especially if the adversary offers him conditional surrender. If this hard-pressed ally should also have a nuclear capacity, he could increase his bargaining power that much more by threatening to expand the war on his own.

For this reason alone, it would be a mistake to seek in other parts of the world, where local resistance is both feasible and essential, the kind of tight, inflexible commitments that the North Atlantic Treaty embodies. By the same token, we should avoid trying to make every local action in which we are involved a UN action. At least we shall have to weigh whatever onus may attach to unilateral action against the advantage of controlling the scope and conduct of war more readily. And that calculation should not be colored by a false assumption of the moral superiority of "collective security." If the divergent interests and the growing independence of the non-Communist powers should preclude their joining rigid alliances or UN defense commitments anyway, that is all the more reason, then, to avoid needless irritations and misunderstandings by importuning them to participate in conflicts in which we shall have to bear the lion's share of the fighting.

Weapons and Targets Limitation

Before the momentous economic and technological expansion of the Industrial Revolution, the severely restricted physical capacity for war which states could draw upon made limited war virtually an automatic by-product of limited objectives. But, with the tremendous capacity for destruction available to modern nations, the limitation of war demands a deliberate restriction not only of the area of combat but also of weapons and targets. For it is doubtful that any war could be controlled for limited political purposes, no matter how narrowly and precisely a belligerent might try to define his objectives, if all the present means of destruction were employed indiscriminately, even though they were employed initially within a narrowly circumscribed area.

At the same time, it would be a mistake to assume that there is a mathematical correlation between the destructiveness or firepower of weapons and the scale and scope of warfare. The effect that use of a certain weapon exerts on the dimensions of warfare depends largely upon the seriousness with which the enemy regards the resulting threat to national values. The careful limitation and clarification of objectives can go far to keep that threat ordinate, even when the most powerful weapons are employed. Therefore, nothing inherent in a wide range of atomic weapons renders them incompatible with limited war, apart from the targets toward which they are directed and the political context in which they are employed. For this reason it is a serious mistake to equate nuclear warfare with total warfare and oppose them both to "conventional" warfare. Of course, we must reckon with the fact that weapons as destructive as the multi-megaton nuclear bombs are pre-eminently instruments for obliterating large centers of population. Consequently, the employment of these weapons under almost any conceivable circumstance would be a signal that a general war upon strategic targets had begun. But there is a vast difference between the multi-megaton bomb and the variety of "low-yield" kiloton weapons—a much greater difference than between the most powerful World War II "block-busters" and conventional artillery shells. A two-kiloton bomb has a maximum damage radius of several hundred yards; its radioactive fallout is negligible. A twenty-megaton H-bomb, by no means the largest available, would virtually obliterate everything within a radius of ten miles and dust a downwind area with deadly or harmful fallout for hundreds of miles (unless it were exploded at a great height). Since the enemy's exact response to the use of certain weapons against certain targets under particular circumstances is difficult to anticipate, it would be dangerous not to allow for a considerable margin of error in planning our weapons system and our military strategy and tactics; but it would be equally dangerous to assume that the powerful new weapons that have recently become available are necessarily and under all circumstances less compatible with limited war than the conventional weapons of World War II.

The essential requirement in adapting weapons to a strategy of limited war is that we have a flexible weapons system and flexible military strategies and tactics capable of supporting limited objectives under a wide variety of conditions. Clearly, all the weapons and measures that are suitable for total war are not suitable for limited war. For example, it is almost inconceivable that any war in which air power were employed against major strategic targets would remain limited; nor would the indiscriminate employment of air power necessarily promote local defense even if the war did remain limited. The special technological requirements of limited war are particularly marked in the realm of mobile, airborne troops capable of employing low-yield nuclear weapons and the most advanced conventional weapons with precision against military targets. Therefore, we cannot simply devise our military policies to meet the threat of major aggression and total war and expect to deter and repel lesser aggressions by improvising resistance with whatever can be spared from the total-war arsenal. Precisely because the requirements of reconciling the limitation of war with military effectiveness are so varied and complex, we cannot afford to rely too heavily upon any single weapon or any single tactic. We need to have a weapons-and-delivery system as flexible as the probable military contingencies are varied, lest the range of measures from which we can select our response in the event of an attack be so narrow as to deprive us of an intermediate response between total war and non-resistance. For, even though the Communists may never force us to choose between nuclear suicide and acquiescence, we shall have to act as though they might; and our diplomatic position will profit or suffer in proportion as we are prepared or unprepared to avoid the dilemma. By same token, in proportion as our range of military capabilities increases, the flexibility of our diplomacy will be enhanced;

and as the flexibility of our diplomacy is enhanced, we shall be that much better able to advance our bargaining power with Communist nations and to promote our relations with non-Communist nations.

Ground Troops

Under existing technological conditions, one essential requirement of a flexible military establishment is sufficient numbers of ready combat troops to check Communist aggression locally. If we cannot check aggression locally, we shall be compelled to run larger risks of total war by striking at targets beyond the area of combat that support the aggression, unless, of course, we choose to acquiesce in defeat. It follows that the greater our capacity for local military containment, the better we shall be able to minimize the risk of total war. Some advocates of tactical air power notwithstanding, there is little military support for the view that "mobile striking power" can provide this capacity in the absence of substantial ground strength—except, perhaps, in a very few island and peninsular positions, such as the Formosa Straits, with naval support. The Korean War is only the latest war to demonstrate this fact.

However, if we recognize the desirability of possessing ground strength capable of checking aggression locally, we must also recognize that we cannot realistically expect to achieve this condition of limitation in all areas of potential aggression, since we cannot count on the free world mobilizing sufficient manpower for the purpose. However, this drawback is rendered somewhat less significant by the fact that western Europe, the area in which local ground defense is least likely to be feasible, is of such great strategic importance and so uncongenial to limitation on other grounds that we shall have to rely primarily upon the deterrent of massive retaliation for its defense anyway.[2]

At the same time, we need not conclude that our relative numerical deficiency in ready, mobilized manpower precludes successful local ground defense in all areas. That would be true only if we had to match the Communists man for man. But the experience in Korea confirmed the lesson of other wars that troops with superior firepower, technical skill, and logistical support can hold forces several times as numerous. Throughout the gray areas our superior mobility and our superior ability to train, equip, and supply troops can go a long way toward compensating for numerical inferiority. Indeed, in the light of this superiority, considered in conjunction with the growth of Communist air power, some students of military strategy have suggested that we may actually enjoy our greatest potential advantage in ground warfare.[3]

Tactical Nuclear Weapons

In considering the requirements of a flexible military establishment, the role of tactical nuclear weapons looms large; for the adaptation of these weapons to limited war is probably the most crucial problem of weapons and targets limitation that American strategists face today.[4] At some future time the role of other kinds of weapons—perhaps weapons that have not as yet been designed—may be equally important, but for the foreseeable future the peculiar importance of tactical nuclear weapons lies in the fact that they carry greater promise than any other weapon of enabling us to fight limited wars on an equal basis against numerically superior forces. And yet we know very little about their actual effects on the battlefield. Therefore, what follows, in an attempt to assess the role of tactical nuclear weapons, is necessarily speculative.

In official statements dealing with the military efficacy of tactical nuclear weapons, it has frequently been claimed that they will compensate for our numerical inferiority in ground troops. When the Truman administration made this claim, it seemed to be thinking primarily in terms of supplementing the firepower of the ground troops in Europe; whereas the Eisenhower administration stressed the substitution of "mobile striking power"—that is, air and sea action—for ground forces in Asia. We have just observed that the validity of the latter conception is dubious, except under very special circumstances. As for tactical nuclear weapons being used in conjunction with ground troops, it is undoubtedly true that they will provide a given number of troops with more firepower than conventional weapons; and to this extent they compensate for our numerical inferiority in comparison with Communist ground forces. However, they do not obviate the necessity of having a minimum number of troops available to compel the enemy to concentrate his forces, to cover the routes of attack, to provide for a strategic reserve, and to perform many other tactical functions that conventional forces would have to perform. Although the tactical employment of atomic weapons is still in an experimental stage, the experience so far does not indicate that the minimum number of troops needed to defend any particular theater of operations will be substantially smaller than would be necessary in the absence of atomic weapons;[5] and some authorities, like General Ridgway, even believe that the successful exploitation of these weapons will require more, not fewer, troops.[6]

Aside from these considerations, there are other reasons for taking a qualified view of the military efficacy of tactical nuclear weapons. For one thing, they are no answer to irregular warfare—to the kind of insurrectionary and guerrilla activity upon which the Communists prefer to rely in the early stages of a campaign of expansion. Nor do they meet the needs of intervention in a war fought by non-Communist powers, such as might occur in the Middle East. Furthermore, even in the case of orthodox, direct Communist assaults it is by no means certain that it will always be to our advantage to use tactical nuclear weapons if, by doing so, we lead the enemy to use them also. There can be no doubt that the Soviet Union and perhaps China as well will acquire a large and varied arsenal of tactical nuclear weapons. When that time arrives, even though we shall probably still retain quantitative superiority, we shall face the serious question of who has the most to gain by using these weapons. Who would be more vulnerable to these weapons in the event of a Chinese attack on Formosa? Who would have most to gain or lose by using them in a war in Southeast Asia? Here again we encounter questions that are difficult for even the military expert to answer with any assurance. But at least it seems safe to say that the questions are not foreclosed by what little is known in the absence of battlefield experience. And precisely because it is so difficult to gauge the exact military efficacy of tactical nuclear weapons, it would be foolhardy to rely on them to solve all the problems of limited war. That would be committing the same mistake that we committed in our over-reliance on the atomic bomb.

Much of the recent discussion of tactical nuclear weapons has started by assuming that they will necessarily give us a great military advantage and then has addressed itself to the question of their compatibility with limited war. But the two questions cannot properly be separated, because if these weapons cannot be used in ways commensurate with limited objectives, then, regardless of their superior firepower, they will not meet the standards of flexibility that an effective strategy of limited war demands.

Clearly, weapons with a range of destructiveness extending as high as the explosive power of the bombs dropped on Hiroshima and Nagasaki must be used in a highly selective fashion in order to remain compatible with limited war. Of course, it is conceivable that a war in which these weapons were used indiscriminately could still be settled for limited objectives before the belligerents reached the stage of utter exhaustion or mutual annihilation; but the physical, economic, and social impact of a war like this would almost certainly extend beyond the limits within which it could be controlled as an instrument for attaining predictable political results. Therefore, given the tremendous destructive potential of even the smaller tactical nuclear weapons, their utility as rational and effective instruments of national policy will depend upon the belligerents' observing rules of self-restraint that relieve them of the fear of the extreme devastation and the radical alteration of national power which would occur if these weapons were employed indiscriminately.

The possibility of using tactical nuclear weapons in a manner proportionate to limited objectives would seem to depend largely upon the feasibility of two methods of limitation: (a) confining the use of these weapons to a limited geographical area and (b) using them with precision against military targets without destroying strategic targets and the large centers of population. Geographical limitation without target restrictions would be effective in keeping warfare limited only under three conditions: (a) if the battle area is one within which the United States and its Communist adversary are willing to accept virtually total destruction of all physical facilities without retaliating upon targets beyond the area; (b) if the Americans and the Communists believe they can fight the war effectively enough by confining their operations to the area without striking at targets beyond the area which facilitate these operations; (c) if the area does not belong to a nation that possesses an independent atomic arsenal, the use of which it would be unwilling to confine to its own territory at the cost of what would amount to total national destruction. The last condition may exist for a decade or longer, but we cannot safely count on the other two even now. It follows that in the use of tactical nuclear weapons geographical restrictions must be combined with target restrictions in order to fulfill the minimum requirements of limitation.

The successful restriction of targets depends largely upon the feasibility of distinguishing between tactical and strategic targets—that is, between targets directly related to military operations (such as the actively employed armed forces, the supporting air bases and naval units, and the supply and transportation facilities of direct service to the field armies) and targets directly related to the economy and the civilian morale of a nation (principally, industrial facilities, central supply depots, and urban population centers). For if this distinction were feasible, it could be the basis for a rule of mutual self-restraint that would minimize the threat to national values and enable the belligerents to employ a graduated scale of force proportionate to a wide range of objectives and contingencies.

Theoretically, the distinction is feasible on three major conditions: (*a*) if tactical targets can be distinguished logically and physically from strategic targets in a manner that both belligerents recognize as legitimate; (*b*) if nuclear weapons can be used with sufficient precision to destroy specific tactical targets and those targets only; (*c*) if the belligerents are willing to tolerate strikes upon occasional strategic targets as accidental or as incidental to attacks upon legitimate tactical targets.

There is a good prospect that the condition of precision could be met by the smaller nuclear bombs and missiles and by further development of low-yield atomic artillery weapons of from two to ten kilotons' power, designed for use against enemy troops on the battlefield. The low-yield weapons, which were designed but not in production in 1956, seem especially well suited for limited warfare; for they promise not only great mobility and firepower but also the requisite accuracy to confine destruction to well-defined military targets.[7]

The condition of mutual definition of tactical targets is more doubtful. Certainly, in heavily industrialized areas and areas with great concentrations of population it will be difficult to draw a distinction between tactical and strategic targets—especially with respect to supply depots and the communications and transportation network—that both sides will recognize as legitimate in the heat of battle; and even if the distinction is logically feasible, the two kinds of targets may be so closely associated in physical space as to preclude the destruction of tactical targets without also devastating large urban centers. The great number of tactical targets (consider merely the 150 or so airfields) that would be subject to attack in an area like western Europe would, by itself, almost preclude the possibility of establishing significant limits upon the scale of destruction. On the other hand, areas like this are unlikely scenes of limited war anyway, because the strategic stakes are so high and the interdependence of the geographical components renders localization so difficult. In the areas of less immediate strategic importance, where Communist military incursions are most likely and area limitation is more practicable, the distinction between tactical and strategic targets is a good deal more feasible, because of the relatively undeveloped state of the indigenous economies. Moreover, the distinction between targets does not require the logical clarity of a legal document in order to serve as a practical basis for limiting warfare. The important requirements are two: first, every belligerent involved should believe that the other belligerents intend and are able to limit military destruction in a manner commensurate with the limited objectives at stake; and, second, on the basis of this belief every belligerent should observe definite target restrictions, which will serve as effective tokens of limited intentions, however difficult it may be to formulate those restrictions in terms of discrete strategic and tactical categories.

But this raises the question of the condition of tolerating accidental or incidental destruction; for since it would be too much to expect the belligerents invariably to be capable of confining destruction to tactical targets with complete accuracy and precision, the limitation of war may depend upon the willingness of the belligerents to tolerate occasional destruction of non-tactical targets on the assumption that such destruction is contrary to the intentions of the adversary. The existence of this requisite degree of tolerance is plausible, provided the belligerents share a confidence in each other's willingness and ability to discriminate between different kinds of targets. Therefore, where other conditions of target and area restriction exist, the limitation of war may depend upon the ability of each belligerent to establish in the mind of the others a presumption that it is conducting the war according to definite and practicable restraints that are contingent upon the adversary doing likewise. Indeed, without the existence of this fundamental condition, it is hard to conceive of the successful operation of any other condition for target or area restriction.

Considering the incentive for avoiding thermonuclear war, and assuming that the belligerents possess flexible military capabilities, the public announcement of a general policy of so-called graduated deterrence might well promote the measure of confidence needed to sustain effective mutual restraints.[8] This would simply amount to a public acknowledgment of our adherence to the principle of the economy of force, according to which we would employ a range of military measures proportionate to the enemy's threat to our security, as determined by the kind of targets he attacks and the weapons he uses against us. An advance declaration of our intention to observe, on a reciprocal basis, a distinction between tactical and strategic targets (except perhaps in the NATO area) would be a reasonable way of giving this general policy sufficient content to make it susceptible of verification. We might also state that we had no intention of dropping nuclear bombs on large cities in the event of a war in any area unless our own cities were bombed first.

These advance commitments would go no further than recognizing the restrictions which we could count upon being to our advantage and, with the possible exception of the implicit restriction upon bombing our large port cities, to the Communists' advantage as well. Any further explicit commitments to specific self-imposed restrictions would be of doubtful value, because we could not be sure of adhering to them; and a violated commitment would be infinitely worse than no commitment at all, since it would undermine confidence in the whole system of reciprocal restraints. Plainly, if self-imposed restraints turned out to jeopardize national security, neither we nor the Communists would feel bound to observe them in the heat of war. The diverse circumstances of war, the multitude of unpredictable elements, including the rapid rate of technological change, would seem to preclude advance knowledge of specific restrictions that we could safely observe in the event of war, beyond the minimum ones mentioned above. And it is doubly difficult to foresee what reciprocal restrictions the Communists might feel that they could safely observe; for, clearly, the same restrictions that were to the advantage of one belligerent might be a serious disadvantage to the other.

An examination of the role of tactical nuclear weapons would be incomplete without considering their psychological consequences, which are so closely related to the requirements of effectiveness and limitation. We cannot doubt that the strange and terrible power of any nuclear explosion raises a peculiar moral revulsion in the popular mind today. If the Communists launched an attack for limited objectives with conventional weapons and we retaliated with nuclear weapons, we would incur the onus of initiating nuclear warfare. If the people of the world were convinced that any kind of nuclear weapon is so horrible that the nation that uses it first is worse than an aggressor, then the military advantages of using tactical nuclear weapons to check Communist aggression by conventional means might be outweighed by the political disadvantages—especially if we initiated their use in Asia, where the cold war turns so largely upon a struggle for the respect and allegiance of the inhabitants.

On the other hand, if these weapons are really a vital military asset to our capacity for limited war, we cannot afford to renounce them simply because of widespread misunderstanding of their effects. Instead, we should find ways of counteracting their adverse psychological impact. Actually, there are no rational grounds for regarding low-yield atomic battlefield warheads as any more horrible and inhumane than napalm or, for that matter, TNT. To the extent that the world has come to regard nuclear weapons as a peculiar form of terror, that popular impression is derived from the devastation of Hiroshima and Nagasaki and from the well-publicized American tests of even more powerful atomic and thermonuclear bombs. But the apprehensions raised by these instruments of total war need not be irrevocably associated with all nuclear weapons. Of course, if we talk in words that suggest virtually an exclusive reliance upon massive retaliation and if our military establishment reflects this strategic imbalance, all nuclear weapons will be likely to carry the stigma of the super-bombs. But if the American government were to adapt tactical nuclear weapons to a well-conceived strategy of limited war, based upon a policy of graduated deterrence, then it should not be difficult to erase this stigma by publicizing the facts in a sober and candid fashion.

Finally, in considering the role of tactical nuclear weapons in a strategy of limited war, we must reckon with the fact that before long the Communists will also acquire an arsenal of these weapons. Their achievement will probably mark the time when nuclear weapons will be considered conventional. Then we may be compelled to plan our military policies on the assumption that tactical nuclear weapons will be used whether we desire their use or not; and once war is so planned, it is more than likely to be fought that way. If the Soviet arsenal is not yet as diverse and numerous as ours, at least it will soon be sufficient to compel us to plan our training, equipment, and tactics to fight wars in which both sides will use tactical nuclear weapons; for, although there may be circumstances in which it would not be to our advantage to meet conventional forces with nuclear weapons, it is hard to imagine circumstances in which we would not suffer serious disadvantages if the enemy used them and we did not. Indeed, the United States is already far advanced in this process of adaptation.

As the variety and quantity of tactical atomic weapons increase and the process of military adaptation is refined and elaborated, it will become increasingly difficult for troops prepared for nuclear war to fight strictly conventional wars effectively. The military materiel, the size and deployment of troop units, and other measures of preparedness suited to nuclear warfare will be ineffective and probably a positive liability in fighting purely conventional warfare.[9] This very prospect will make a war in which only conventional weapons are used increasingly unlikely, except in the case of insurrections, guerrilla activity, and police actions. Therefore, although there will still be sound reasons for withholding the use of nuclear weapons in some military and political situations—preeminently in the case of non-nuclear aggression in the gray areas—we must count upon these weapons becoming an integral part of our military policies and our national strategy.

In summary, tactical nuclear weapons, especially the low-yield battlefield weapons, can play a decisive role in supporting containment by giving the United States an adequate capacity for limited war at a tolerable cost. In anticipation of the Communists' growing tactical nuclear capacity, as well as our own needs, we shall have to plan our training, equipment, and tactics around the use of these weapons. However, in the light of the requirements of a flexible military establishment, we shall also have to retain a capacity to fight non-nuclear wars in areas and under circumstances in which the political and psychological disadvantages of nuclear war, as well as the added risk of total war, outweigh the possible military advantages of employing tactical nuclear weapons. Furthermore, we cannot safely assume that our growing nuclear capacity will enable us to reduce our ground forces; it may actually require an increase in ground forces.

But regardless of the composition of our military establishment, it is essential that American strategists plan the use of tactical nuclear weapons in accordance with a policy of graduated deterrence, based upon the distinction between tactical and strategic targets. Above all, these weapons must be employed within a carefully defined political context of limited objectives, susceptible to the process of diplomatic accommodation.

Notes

1. Thomas R. Phillips has pointed out that on the basis of UN statistics the 15 NATO nations have a population of 436,060,000, whereas Russia and her European satellites have only 278,125,000 (*St. Louis Post-Dispatch*, November 21, 1954, p. 3 C). However, because of foreign policies and domestic economic and political considerations, the free world clearly suffers a great numerical disadvantage in terms of the troops it is willing to mobilize and maintain.

2. The possibilities of local ground defense are assessed in greater detail in the discussion of the application of a strategy of limited war to the NATO area and to the gray areas in Robert Osgood, *Limited War* (Chicago: University of Chicago Press, 1957), pp. 259–273.

3. See, for example, the observations of Roger Hilsman and William W. Kaufmann in Kaufmann (ed.), *Military Policy and National Security* (Princeton: Princeton University Press, 1956), pp. 182, 250.

4. As of 1956, the less powerful nuclear weapons suitable for tactical use depended upon atomic fission for their explosive power. However, the general term "nuclear" is used so as not to exclude suitable hydrogen or fusion weapons that may be developed.

5. Kaufmann, *Military Policy*, pp. 72–73.

6. Matthew B. Ridgway, *Soldier: The Memoirs of Matthew B. Ridgway* (New York: Harper, 1956), pp. 296–97.

7. A.T. Hadley deals with the characteristics, the potentialities, and the cost of these weapons in "Low-Yield Atomic Weapons: A New Military Dimension," *Reporter*, April 19, 1956, pp. 23–25. As against Hadley's hope that tactical nuclear weapons might be a boon to our capacity for limited war, Hanson Baldwin concluded on the basis of Exercise Sage Brush—in which a theoretical total of 275 tactical atomic projectiles, ranging from two to forty kilotons' power, were expended in a war game in western Louisiana during October and December, 1955—that such large-scale devastation would have resulted that "there probably can be no such thing as a limited or purely tactical nuclear war," at least not in similar areas. However, he did not say what proportion of low-yield weapons were expended or how much of the theoretical devastation was caused by the twenty- to forty-kiloton bombs (*New York Times*, December 5, 1955, p. 12). The theoretical results of Operation Carte Blanche the NATO tactical air force exercises held in western Europe during June, 1955, were similar to the results of Exercise Sage Brush. According to unofficial calculations 1,700,000 Germans were "killed" and 3,500,000 "wounded." However, these calculations were based on the explosion of 335 bombs, presumably of the same power as the ones "dropped" on Louisiana, in the area between Hamburg and Munich (ibid., June 29, 1955, p. 4; Kaufmann, *Military Policy*, pp. 225–26).

8. Rear Admiral Sir Anthony Buzzard has, perhaps, done the most to publicize the policy of graduated deterrence. See his articles in the *Manchester Guardian Weekly*, November 3, 1955, p. 5, and in *World Politics* 8 (January 1956):228–37. For an earlier and fuller expression of a similar idea, see Colonel Richard S. Leghorn, "No Need To Bomb

Cities to Win Wars," *U.S. News and World Report*, January 28, 1955, pp. 79–94. Both Buzzard's and Leghorn's plans are based upon a distinction between tactical and strategic targets, and both would rule out bombing cities unless the enemy bombs ours first. Both plans recognize that target and weapons restrictions must be contingent upon the enemy's observing similar restrictions.

9. Henry A. Kissinger has observed that "forces will have to deploy as if nuclear weapons might be used, because the side which concentrates its forces might thereby give its opponent the precise incentive he needs to use nuclear weapons. But if forces are dispersed, they will not be able to hold a line or achieve a breakthrough with conventional weapons, because the destructive power of conventional weapons is so much smaller" ("Force and Diplomacy in the Nuclear Age," *Foreign Affairs* 34 [April 1956]:356–57). Roger Hilsman believes that as nuclear weapons are integrated more closely with fighting units, "it is also likely to become more difficult for a unit to switch from one kind of war to another" (Kaufmann, *Military Policy*, p. 192). Thomas R. Phillips has argued that in our adaptation of equipment, transportation, and tactics to nuclear weapons we may be approaching the point beyond which we shall be unable to fight anything but a nuclear war ("Our Point of No Return," *Reporter*, February 24, 1955, pp. 14–18).

Discussion Questions

1. How have nuclear weapons limited the scope of warfare?

2. In what ways can war be limited?

3. Is the utility of military power reduced due to the limitations on war described by Osgood? Do these limitations apply equally to all actors on the international stage?

4. How do economic constraints and U.S. public opinion affect attempts to keep war limited?

Suggestions for Additional Reading

Brodie, Bernard. *Strategy in the Missile Age*. Princeton: Princeton University Press, 1959.

Clausewitz, Carl von. *On War*. Translated by Michael Howard and Peter Paret. Princeton: Princeton University Press, 1976.

Freedman, Lawrence. *The Evolution of Nuclear Strategy*. New York: St. Martin's Press, 1981.

Halperin, Morton H. *Limited War in the Nuclear Age*. New York: John Wiley, 1963.

Kahn, Herman. *On Escalation*. New York: Praeger, 1965.

———. *On Thermonuclear War*. Princeton: Princeton University Press, 1960.

———. *Thinking about the Unthinkable*. New York: Horizon Press, 1962.

Kissinger, Henry A. *Nuclear Weapons and Foreign Policy*. New York: Harper, 1957.

Mandelbaum, Michael. *The Nuclear Question*. Cambridge: Cambridge University Press, 1979.

Schelling, Thomas C. *Arms and Influence*. New Haven: Yale University Press, 1966.

———. *The Strategy of Conflict*. New York: Oxford University Press, 1960.

Wohlstetter, Albert. "The Delicate Balance of Terror." *Foreign Affairs* 37, no. 2 (January 1959):211–234.

Part IV
The National Security System: Structure and Process

The environment in which U.S. national security policy is formulated and executed has become increasingly complex since the end of World War II. The development of weapons of mass destruction, the fragmentation of colonial empires, the proliferation of nation-states, and the diminishing distinctions between diplomatic, military, and domestic issues and increasing international economic interdependence have placed critical demands on the formal decision-making structure of the U.S. government.

The structures and processes of national security decision-making constitute what we have defined as the national security system. The national security system performs the critical function of translating national strategy into national security policy. To this end, the national security system is the transmission belt by which the objectives of national strategy are translated into the diplomatic, economic, and military dimensions of national security policy. Further, the national security system administers the specific programs that constitute the various dimensions of security policy.

National Security System: Structure

The structure of the national security system is composed primarily of the formal institutions that participate in the national security decision-making process. Less formal participants such as the media and the general public also can be important players in the national security system. A review of the major participants in the national security system is necessary prior to analyzing the processes by which national security policy is formulated and implemented.

The President

The president is the focal point of the national security system. His constitutional authority and his institutional position as head of the executive branch dictate that the president will be the primary actor in the policymaking process. The president is responsible for the articulation of a coherent national strategy and the design of a national security system that can translate that strategy into an effective national security policy.

Four critical roles combine to make the president the initiator, the innovator, and the director of national security policy. As the chief of state, the president is the one person who represents the people and the government of the United States. As the commander in chief of the armed forces, the president can employ the military forces of the United States in the manner he considers appropriate for the protection of national interests. As the chief diplomat, the president is responsible for the state of relations between the United States and other nations. He appoints ambassadors and other official representatives of the government and is responsible for the conduct of diplomacy and negotiations. Finally, as the chief executive, the president is responsible for the operation of the executive branch.

In order to carry out these roles, the president must establish an effective structure and process to formulate and implement policies. Consequently the structures and processes of the national security system are determined, at least in part, by the president's management style and his preferences for how information and advice will be presented to him and how decisions will be carried out.

Patterns of presidential style have varied. Alexander George has identified three management styles that characterize the approaches taken by different presidents: the formal, the competitive, and the collegial models.[1]

The formal model is characterized by an orderly decision-making structure with clearly drawn lines of authority, well-defined procedures, and an orderly flow of information up through the various organizational levels to the president. The president relies on the system to provide him with the appropriate information. Consequently he seldom bypasses a cabinet official to get independent advice from a subordinate. While the differing views and judgments of the participants in the process are encouraged, the formal model discourages open conflict or bargaining among the participants. Presidents Truman, Eisenhower, Nixon, Ford, and Reagan used variations of the formal decision-making structure.

The competitive model deliberately encourages competition and conflict among the actors in the national security system. This model is based on organizational ambiguity, overlapping lines of authority, and multiple channels of communication to the president. The president feels free to communicate with subordinates in the various departments and to seek outside advice or information. Franklin Roosevelt used the competitive model, as did Lyndon Johnson.

The collegial model attempts to combine the advantages of the other two models. The president tries to assemble a team of cabinet officials, staff members, and advisers who can work together to identify problems and present policy alternatives in a way that incorporates divergent points of view as much as possible. The president is at the center of the process, with connections to the various advisers and agency heads. This approach encourages interdepartmental coordination and collegial participation in decision making while trying to avoid bureaucratic bargains and compromise. The president's advisers function as a debate team that considers information and proposals from all of the relevant players and attempts to develop creative solutions to problems. Presidents Kennedy and Carter used the collegial model.

The level of presidential involvement in the policymaking process will vary according to the president's style and experience; however, given the extent of presidential authority and the need for the effective supervision and coordination of the various actors participating in the national security process, the president inevitably will be the foremost actor in the national security system. I.M. Destler in chapter 8 examines the various decision-making structures presidents have used in the past and posits eight variables he believes are important in shaping the decision-making systems.

Executive Agencies

The president does not make national security policy alone. He must rely on a number of executive agencies for information and advice. Further, making decisions is only half of the process. These same organizations are responsible for implementing the president's decisions.

Department of State. The State Department is a major actor in the national security system because of the importance of the diplomatic and economic components of national security policy. Normal diplomatic interactions, negotiations, participation in international organizations and alliances, and the use of foreign aid are all integral aspects of national security policy. Diplomatic and economic instruments are the most commonly used policy tools (they will be discussed in greater detail in part V). Consequently, the State Department is involved to a significant degree in the national security system.

Despite its institutional responsibilities for diplomatic and economic policy, the influence of the Department of State depends largely on two conditions: the personal relationship between the president and the secretary of state and the degree of active presidential involvement in national security affairs. The more a president becomes directly involved in national security policy, the more difficult it is for the secretary of state to be the principal figure in the formulation of policy. Activist presidents tend to rely more on their personal advisers, such as the assistant for national security affairs, than on cabinet members who, in addition to advising the president, must devote much of their time and effort to managing large and diverse organizations. A succession of powerful national security assistants has reduced the secretary's traditional position as the president's principal adviser.

The State Department is organized along two lines, regionally and functionally. Each of the five regional bureaus is made up of country analysts who study and recommend U.S. policy toward individual nations. The bureaus are Africa, East

Asia and the Pacific, Inter-America, Near East and South Asia, and Europe. The European bureau includes offices dedicated to analyzing the Soviet Union and Eastern Europe.

The functional bureaus (such as policy planning, intelligence and research, economic and business affairs, and political-military affairs) oversee areas of responsibility that cut across geographic regions. For example, the Bureau of Economic Affairs is responsible for the preparation of economic analyses concerning economic issues related to all geographic regions.[2]

As might be expected, studies of the regional and functional bureaus are often at odds, requiring the secretary of state to sift through contradictory policy recommendations about what U.S. policy ought to be. Further, the individual bureaus rise and fall in influence depending on the particular administration's views and the capabilities of the individual who heads the bureau.

Department of Defense. The Defense Department is responsible for the execution of military policy. There are a number of important actors in this agency. The secretary of defense, the JCS, and the military services all bring different perspectives to bear on the problem of developing and implementing military policy. Therefore the Department of Defense should not be considered a unitary actor, since disagreements among the various elements of the organization can and do arise.

The secretary of defense, aided by the supporting offices that comprise the Office of the Secretary of Defense, is responsible for the management of the Defense Department. Resource allocation, weapons development, readiness, and force modernization are but a few of the issues for which the secretary is responsible. A series of defense reorganization acts since 1947 has greatly strengthened the secretary's authority and centralized management in the Defense Department.

A strong secretary serves several purposes. He ensures civilian control and provides a focal point for authoritative decisions. Further, the secretary must make the difficult trade-off decisions that cut across the various military services. The secretary reviews competing claims for scarce resources and allocates them in a way he believes best serves the interests of the nation as a whole.

The secretary of defense also has operational responsibilities. The president exercises his authority as commander in chief of the armed services directly through the secretary of defense to the operational commanders in the field. In this regard, the secretary of defense is second in command of U.S. military forces. The president and the secretary of defense together comprise what is known as the National Command Authority.

The JCS were established by the National Security Act of 1947, the same act that created the position of secretary of defense. Today the JCS include the chairman, the chiefs of staff of the army and air force, the chief of naval operations, and the commandant of the marine corps. By law, the JCS are the principal military advisers to the president. Like all other advisers, however, the influence of the JCS depends primarily on how much the president chooses to rely on them. Legally the Joint Chiefs are not in the operational chain of command. In practice, the secretary of defense normally exercises his operational control of deployed forces through the Joint Chiefs.

The membership of the JCS highlights the conflict of interest inherent in the structure of that body. As a corporate body, the Joint Chiefs are responsible for advising the president, the secretary of defense, and the NSC, planning for contingencies that might require the use of military force, and coordinating the activities of the various services and operational commands. Individually, however, the members of the JCS (excluding the chairman) are the chiefs of their respective services. Therefore they tend to reflect the parochial priorities of their service. One hardly can expect a service chief to recommend the acquisition of a major new weapon system and then become an objective critic of that system when he is sitting as a member of the JCS. Not surprisingly, this double-hatting makes it extremely difficult for the JCS to deal with contentious issues involving conflicting service interests. Critics argue that JCS positions tend to be the result of bureaucratic compromise more than objective analysis.

In chapter 10, John Kester examines in detail the functions of the JCS, their role in the policy process, and a number of criticisms made of them. His analysis includes a number of suggestions for reorganizing the JCS and reducing the structural deficiencies that hamper their effectiveness.

The individual military services are responsible for recruiting and training their forces, as well as for the administrative and logistical support of deployed forces. Further, each service is responsible for its own force planning and weapons acquisition (subject to supervision by the secretary of defense). In short, the individual services determine what forces, weapons, and capabilities will be available to carry out national military strategy. While the JCS and the secretary of defense do have some influence on these issues, the services generally have been able to develop their organizational structures with a minimum of interference. For example, the length of time necessary to conceive, test, produce, and deploy a new weapon system makes it very difficult for a secretary of defense, who serves for a relatively short time, to manage or control the process. Since all of the services have dozens of new systems in various stages of testing and development at any time, the management problem for the secretary of defense can be almost insurmountable.

In chapter 12, Graham Allison and Frederic Morris examine the influence of the military services, using the weapons acquisition process as the vehicle for their assessment. Their conclusions on the influence of the individual services have important implications for the analysis of how the national security system operates.

Intelligence Community. The assessment of threats is an important factor in the development of national strategy. The actors in the national security system who are responsible for threat assessment are referred to collectively as the intelligence community. While public attention tends to focus primarily on the Central Intelligence Agency (CIA), the intelligence community consists of a number of organizations whose task is to provide policymakers with the information needed to make sound decisions.

Although the CIA is the most visible member of the intelligence community, there are several other important members. The National Security Agency (responsible for electronic and communications intelligence), the Defense Intelligence Agency (responsible for providing military intelligence to the secretary of defense and the JCS), the Bureau of Intelligence and Research in the State Department, and the intelligence staffs of each of the military services participate actively in the intelligence process.

There are three phases of the intelligence cycle: collection, production, and consumption. While the popular image of intelligence collection pictures spies secretly photographing secret documents, the reality is quite different. Much intelligence information is gathered by electronic means from reconnaissance satellites and radar stations. Other data is gathered from local publications or mass media in the region of interest, conversations with public officials, scholars, refugees, and other individuals who have first-hand knowledge of an area, and observations of local conditions, troop movements, military parades, and the like. Clandestine agents are used, of course, but the data obtained from this source account for only a small percentage of the intelligence information collected.

Once information is collected, it is unlikely to be passed directly to policymakers. The amount of data collected can be staggering, and high-level officials do not have the time or the expertise to sort through and evaluate intelligence information. The information that is collected must be evaluated for timeliness, importance, accuracy, and credibility. Providing decision makers with unsubstantiated reports could lead to a decision based on faulty information. Therefore intelligence analysts review the data, evaluate them to determine their importance and credibility, and organize the information into a form that can be disseminated readily. Samples of intelligence products include daily and periodic intelligence estimates, technical intelligence reports, and ocean surveillance reports. The highest-level intelligence reports take the form of national intelligence estimates, which go from the director of central intelligence to the president.

Intelligence information is used by officials at all levels of the bureaucracy. Reports on Soviet military forces are disseminated to tactical units in the military services. Sensitive intelligence reports may be used by the president and cabinet officials in order to ascertain an adversary's intentions. The degree to which the products of the intelligence community are used depends on the degree of confidence that policymakers have in the product and the community that developed it. As we noted in part II, threat assessment is based on information about which there always will be a degree of uncertainty.

Assistant for National Security Affairs

The assistant to the president for national security affairs has become a prominent actor in the development of national security policy. Traditionally the secretary of state was the president's primary adviser; however, the fragmented structure of the bureaucracy, the nature of the interagency coordinating process, and the need for a presidential adviser divorced from institutional affiliations have made the assistant for national security affairs a permanent and influential participant in the structure of the national security system. The national security affairs adviser has three essential roles: policy coordinator, policy analyst, and presidential adviser. Each of these roles is an important source of influence in the national security system.

The role of policy coordinator is the formal basis for the influence of the national security adviser. This function stems directly from the National Security Act of 1947, which established the NSC. The complexity and diversity of issues facing any president requires a decision-making system that can integrate effectively the activities of the numerous organizations involved in the national security system. The national security adviser is responsible for coordinating the interagency process that prepares analyses and recommendations for the president and the NSC.

The role of policy analyst stems from the national security adviser's position as the coordinator of the interagency process and from the need to prevent the president from making decisions based on faulty or biased analysis. The national security adviser is responsible for ensuring that all agencies involved in an issue have the opportunity to provide input and that all reasonable alternatives have been aired and examined.

Perhaps the most influential role played by the assistant for national security affairs is that of personal adviser to the president. The national security adviser has two distinct advantages over other members of the national security policy apparatus: physical and philosophic proximity to the president and institutional independence.

As a presidential adviser, the assistant for national security affairs enjoys direct access to the president on a variety of security-policy-related issues. The national security affairs adviser and the NSC staff have been used by all presidents since Kennedy as a personal staff, responsive to presidential inquiries and relied on by each president for information and analysis.

Since the president appoints his national security affairs adviser, he naturally selects an individual who shares his political style and view of the world. The perspectives, attitudes, and personal relationship shared by the president and his national security affairs adviser are a major influence on presidential perceptions of national security.[3] The president feels comfortable with his adviser and therefore tends to respect his opinions and recommendations. The physical proximity guarantees numerous contacts daily between the president and his adviser.

The national security affairs adviser is not responsible for the management of a major executive department and therefore is not likely to be captured by an institutional point of view. His loyalty is only to the president.

Recent presidents appear to have opted for a trusted staff of personal advisers to play a primary role in the formulation of national security policy. The president feels confident that his national security affairs adviser will not present a biased organizational viewpoint but will provide balanced, analytical advice designed to inform and protect the president.

President Reagan's unsuccessful experiment in downgrading the position of national security adviser (discussed more fully in chapter 20) seemed to affirm the proposition that the assistant for national security affairs has become a permanent and influential player in the national security system.

While the actors and institutions discussed here are the most prominent executive branch participants in the national security system, they are by no means the only ones. The nature of the issue under consideration determines which actors will be involved. For example, the Commerce Department is involved in issues concerning export controls and technology transfer, while the Department of Energy is involved in matters related to the production of nuclear weapons.

Expanded Role of Congress

In recent years the Congress has been willing and able to play a much more active role in the national security policymaking process. The constitutional allocation of authority between the executive and legislative branches in dealing with national security issues created, in Richard Neustadt's phrase, "a government of separated institutions sharing power."[4]

Following World War II, the Congress generally acquiesced to presidential initiatives regarding national security policy. There was genuine bipartisan support for the national strategy of containment, and although there were debates over the most effective means to achieve the objectives of U.S. policy, there was little disagreement over the ends of that policy. The reassertion of congressional involvement in national security policy resulted from three important factors. First, the consensus on the ends of U.S. security policy collapsed. The failure of U.S. policy in Vietnam undermined the consensus that supported the tenets of containment. With the very basis of U.S. national strategy in question, the merits of every action, commitment, or response were open to challenge.

The second important impetus for the reassertion of congressional influence resulted from challenges to the notion of the imperial presidency. The mismanagement of the war in Vietnam shattered the myth of executive expertise. Congress no longer equated executive access to greater information with executive exercise of superior judgment.

Finally, abuses of power by the executive undermined the credibility of the president. Distorted information concerning the events that led to the Gulf of Tonkin resolution and the U.S. deployment of combat troops to the Dominican Republic in 1965 had a major impact, as did the relentlessly optimistic assessments of the progress being made against communist forces in Vietnam. Concerns about the illegal activities of the CIA and other intelligence organizations further damaged executive credibility. The pattern of abuse of power revealed during the Watergate affair alienated the Congress and the public, creating an atmosphere conducive to the reassertion of congressional involvement.

The breakdown of policy consensus, the erosion of the notion of executive competence, and the disclosure of widespread abuse of power each provided momentum to structural changes that gave Congress greater access to information and increased oversight over government policy. The size of congressional professional staffs has been increased significantly. The professional staff members provide expertise to individual members of Congress, as well as to the armed services, appropriations, and budget committees of both houses. These six committees, backed by dozens of qualified staffers, now are prepared to question the president and the executive agencies on all aspects of national security policy. The presumption that expertise and access to more complete information are centered in the executive agencies is no longer valid.

In addition to its professional staff, Congress has other sources of independent analysis. The Congressional Research Service, the Office of Technology Assessment, the General Accounting Office, and the Congressional Budget Office provide information and analysis on issues concerning national security policy. As a result, Congress does not have to rely on the executive agencies for information. It can get information, alternatives, and policy proposals from a number of sources.

What are the implications of increased congressional involvement in national security policy? Certainly the ability of every member of Congress to become an independent source of policy advocacy creates uncertainty in the United States and on the part of its allies as to what U.S. policy is likely to be on a certain issue. On the other hand, congressional access to authoritative sources of information and policy alternatives ensures that the debates over the development of national security policy will be more substantive. In chapter 11, Richard Haass describes the means by which Congress has reasserted its influence and analyzes six specific areas where Congress has used its legislative powers to gain greater authority in national security policy.

Public Opinion and the Mass Media

Not all of the important actors in the national security system are formal members of the government. Public opinion and the mass media must be included in any consideration of the policymaking structure.

Through long-held propositions, public attitudes can define the limits of acceptable action. For example, the "who lost China?" attitude in the 1950s reflected the belief that somehow unsuccessful U.S. policy was responsible for the communist victory in China. Public perceptions of the lack of legitimacy of the government of the People's Republic (PRC) prevented the normalization of relations between the United States and the PRC for thirty years after the Chinese revolution. It was not until 1972 that Richard Nixon, a conservative Republican president with impeccable anticommunist credentials, could begin the process of reestablishing relations between the two nations.

In the years following the Castro revolution in Cuba, a general public attitude of "no more Cubas" influenced U.S. perceptions of events in Central and South America. Lyndon Johnson was confident of public support for the deployment of U.S. troops to the Dominican Republic in 1965 because he was, after all, preventing "another Cuba."

The difficult U.S. experience in Vietnam fostered a new public attitude toward active U.S. involvement in limited and revolutionary wars. "No more Vietnams" is now a popularly held view, one that policymakers must consider when contemplating the use of U.S. forces. Although the attitude may be softening somewhat, the divisive public debate after the deployment of U.S. marines to Lebanon in 1982 indicates that there remains a good deal of reluctance on the part of the public to commit U.S. troops in situations where the issues are not clearly drawn.

The media are a critical nongovernmental actor in the national security system because of their role in disseminating information and interpreting events. The media have become almost a fourth branch of government; no significant government policy can be formulated without consideration of what the likely press response will be.

A president can use mass communications to mobilize public support for his policies; on the other hand, the media also can focus considerable attention on those who oppose government policy. In fact, one way in which a dissatisfied government official can attempt to change the direction of a particular policy is by leaking information to the press, thereby initiating a public debate on the issue. The public debate in 1977 over the production of the neutron bomb was initiated in just such a manner.

The National Security System: Process

In chapter 1 we characterized the national security process as the series of actions and interactions within the organizational structure that combines to create policy. How do the disparate organizations and actors operate to develop national security policy? What are the actions and interactions that comprise the national security policymaking process?

Analytic Model

The most common explanation of the development of policy is based on assumptions about national behavior. In this view, nations perceive threats to their interests from the international environment and develop policies and programs designed to deal with these threats. The nation's national security policy is conceived as the product of governmental choice aimed at achieving well-defined strategic objectives.

The conceptual basis for this view of national behavior is what Allison and Morris in chapter 12 term the "prevailing simplification," the shorthand way in which analysts tend to deal with governmental outputs, whether they are domestic welfare programs, weapons deployments, or any other activity inferred to be the result of the decision-making process. This conceptual simplification aggregates the various organizations and individuals that comprise a government into a single actor that, like individuals in the marketplace, is presumed to value maximize—that is, to make choices that optimize satisfaction within given constraints.

Despite the presumed rationality of this analytic model, it is readily obvious that the actual process by which national security policy is formulated and implemented differs significantly from the prevailing simplification. Governments are not unitary actors; they are composed of individuals and organizations with differing perspectives on what is in the best interests of the nation and with different priorities on how the limited resources available ought to be allocated.

The need for a more thorough explanation of the multiple determinants of national security policy leads to two alternative perspectives. One focuses on the political interactions that comprise decision making in the national security system. The other concentrates on the organizations responsible for the various aspects of national security policy. The former view sees security policy as a political resultant, with emphasis on the bargaining among bureaucratic players atop the organizational hierarchy. The latter perspective examines organizational behavior and its influence on the national security policy process.

Individuals and Influence

Since a variety of individuals and organizations—the president, the secretary of defense, members of Congress, and the military services, for example—are involved in national security policy decisions, differences of opinion among the participants in the process must be resolved by compromise, bargaining, and politics. The unitary rational actor of the analytic model is disaggregated in components represented by individuals in positions of authority in the various organizations involved in the national security system. This disaggregation does not automatically imply nonrationality; the individuals may pursue their interests quite analytically. However, decisions depend not only on the preferences of the participants but also on how the preferences are combined in influencing the decisions.

Discontinuities can result from the compromises of reasonable people participating in the decision-making process.

These reasonable people do not exist in an institutional vacuum. The decision-making apparatus consists of a multitude of elected and appointed officials, career bureaucrats, and military officers who tend to see the world through the perspective of their organization and endeavor to protect their institutional interests. As Morton Halperin observed:

> Organizations have interests. Career officials in these organizations believe that protecting these interests is vital to the security of the United States. They therefore take stands on issues which advance these interests and maneuver to protect these interests against other organizations and senior officials, including the President.[5]

Organizational interests therefore are a dominant factor in determining the stand policymaking bureaucrats will take in pursuit of what they believe to be the nation's security interests.

Organizational Influence

The recognition of organizational interests as a source of influence in national security policy is a critical aspect of the analysis of the national security system. Organizational interests often are dominated by the desire to maintain organizational autonomy and influence while pursuing what its members view as the essence of organization. In chapter 9 Morton Halperin defines organizational essence as the view held by the dominant group in the organization of what the missions and capabilities of the institution should be.

The concept of organizational essence is particularly pertinent to national security organizations. One impact of organizational essence is that it influences the way in which the organizations adapt to the changing technological environment. Subjective judgments about an organization's essence can make major institutional adjustments very difficult in the face of technological change. As Edward Katzenbach noted in 1958, "The military history of the past half century is studded with institutions which have managed to dodge the challenges of the obvious."[6] To the horse cavalryman who defended the usefulness of the fabled cavalry charge well into the era of tanks, trucks, and machine guns, the effectiveness of these new devices did not eliminate the need for soldiers mounted on horseback. In 1917, two years after the introduction of tank warfare in Europe, two of the hottest items of debate at the U.S. Army Cavalry School were the redesign of the saddle and whether the saber should be curved for slashing or straight for thrusting.[7] In a more modern version of the horse cavalry syndrome, the tenacity with which the air force defends the need for a manned penetrating bomber reflects the degree to which combat flying is seen as the essence of that service, ballistic warheads and cruise missiles notwithstanding.

Organizational essence further affects national security policy because it will determine which roles and missions the organizations regard as most important. The structure of the organization will be designed to carry out these important roles and missions, and organizational capabilities will be acquired to do so. In the case of the military services, these assumptions regarding required capabilities are the primary determinants of both force structure and weapons acquisition. If the air force assumes that a fighter-bomber must be capable of flying from bases in rear areas to attack targets deep in Eastern Europe at night in any weather and also must be able to identify and destroy high-speed Soviet fighters beyond visual range, then a highly complex, expensive aircraft like the F-15 will be "required."[8]

The consequences of organizational essence can lead to discontinuities between the requirements of national strategy and the capabilities developed to implement that strategy. This potential for discontinuity is why an understanding of the national security system is a critical aspect of the analysis of national security policy. If important discontinuities exist between what is required and what is acquired, then it may be that the national security system is not doing an effective job of translating national strategy into national security policy.

An important example of this type of discontinuity is the relatively low priority accorded by the air force to the mission of close air support of ground forces. Other tactical air missions, such as air superiority and interdiction, have higher priorities. Since resources are limited, the lower priority close air support programs receive less emphasis (and hence less funding). While this allocation of resources is rational from the air force perspective, the potential lack of close air support has forced the army to develop attack helicopters capable of supporting ground operations. Consequently both the army and the air force maintain forces and weapons designed to accomplish the same purpose.

In chapter 9, Morton Halperin describes in detail the characteristics of organizational behavior. In addition to the concept of organizational essence, Halperin describes the importance of an organization's view of its critical roles and missions, its desire for autonomy, and the importance of maintaining what it considers its fair share of the budget. Halperin's discussion has important implications for our analysis of how the national security system works.

Given the fragmented bureaucratic structure and the characteristics of organizational behavior described here, how does the policy process work? How are the various actors brought together to consider problems, analyze alternatives, and make decisions? The answer is the national security council system.

National Security Council System

The NSC was established by the National Security Act of 1947 to "advise the president with respect to the integration of domestic, foreign, and military policies relating to the national security." Further, the council existed for the purpose of "more effectively coordinating the policies and functions of the departments and agencies of the government relating to national security."[9] The extent to which different presidents have relied on the NSC is discussed by I.M. Destler in chapter 8. It is important to understand, however, that the NSC is an advisory body; it has no formal decision-making authority. The president can accept or reject its recommendations.

There are four statutory members of the NSC: the president, the vice-president, the secretary of state, and the secretary of defense. There are two statutory advisers: the director of central intelligence and the chairman of the joint chiefs of staff. The president may invite anyone else to participate in the NSC deliberations.

How does the NSC system work? Suppose the president decides that he wants to review the issue of the deployment of intermediate-range nuclear forces to Europe. The president, or his national security adviser, would issue a tasking document (called a national security study directive (NSSD) in the Reagan administration, a presidential review memorandum (PRM) by President Carter, and a national security study memorandum (NSSM) by Presidents Nixon and Ford), which specifies the issues the president wants considered and any specific questions the president would like addressed. The presidential directive would be sent to all relevant agencies.

An interdepartmental group, consisting of representatives of all the agencies affected by the study, would be given the task of preparing the initial response to the president's directive. Membership and chairmanship of the group vary with the issue; in our hypothetical case, the Department of Defense would chair the group. Given the issue under study here, the interdepartmental group would consist of representatives from the Office of the Secretary of Defense, the Department of State, the JCS, the Arms Control and Disarmament Agency, the Department of Energy, and possibly the CIA. The NSC staff also would provide a representative. The NSC staff has a representative on all interdepartmental groups.

The interdepartmental group will forward its report to a senior interdepartmental group composed of secretary- or deputy-secretary-level officials from the same agencies. The senior interdepartmental group will review the results of the report. Areas of agency disagreement will be reconsidered, but it may not be necessary for the departments to be unanimous in their recommendations. The result of the interagency process should be thorough analysis in which all pertinent information has been gathered and all relevant alternatives have been examined.

The report, including any dissenting views, will be forwarded to the president or the NSC for its deliberation. The president's assistant for national security affairs ensures that one organization does not dominate the policy process by eliminating or bypassing opposing points of view. It is the proper role of the president to resolve disputes that cannot be settled by the cabinet secretaries.

The NSC will consider the report of the senior interdepartmental group and make recommendations to the president. Again, it may not be necessary for the members of the NSC to be unanimous in their recommendations. The president will make the policy decision following his consideration of all points of view.

Once the president has made his decision, he will issue a decision document (called a national security decision directive (NSDD) by President Reagan, a presidential directive (PD) in the Carter administration, and a national security decision memorandum (NSDM) in the Nixon-Ford years). In this document, the president will announce his decision and make any adjustments to existing policy that are required. The document also may task various organizations to perform certain actions to carry out the president's decision. The presidential decision document becomes the formal statement of U.S. policy on that issue.

In a crisis, the time available for decision obviously is much more limited. Crisis management tends to be handled by ad hoc groups of advisers that make recommendations to the NSC and the president.

Policy formulation is only half of the process. Once a decision has been made, it must be implemented. Obviously the president cannot carry out his decisions himself. He must rely on the organizations that make up the national security system to carry out his directives. How accurately decisions get translated into outcomes depends on the execution of the responsible organization. If a decision supports an important organizational priority, one can assume that execution will be prompt and complete. If a decision conflicts with an organization's interests, then the ability of bureaucracies to delay, obstruct, and alter decisions may make the implementation of a decision much more difficult.

The structures and processes of the national security system are the critical elements in the formulation and implementation of national security policy. The efficacy of the diplomatic, economic, and military components of national security policy is related directly to the ability of the national security system to translate the requirements of national strategy into the capabilities for effective action.

Notes

1. Alexander L. George, *Presidential Decisionmaking in Foreign Policy: The Effective Use of Information and Advice* (Boulder: Westview Press, 1980), pp. 148–419.

2. Henry T. Nash, *American Foreign Policy* (Homewood, Ill.: Dorsey Press, 1973), p. 73.

3. Sam C. Sarkesian, ed., *Defense Policy and the Presidency: Carter's First Years* (Boulder: Westview Press, 1979), p. 10.

4. Richard E. Neustadt, *Presidential Power* (New York: Wiley, 1960), p. 33.

5. Morton H. Halperin, "Why Bureaucrats Play Games," *Foreign Policy* 2 (Spring 1971):88.

6. Edward L. Katzenbach, Jr., "The Horse Cavalry in the Twentieth Century," *Public Policy* 7 (1958):120.

7. Martin Blumenson, *The Patton Papers, 1885–1940* (Boston: Houghton Mifflin, 1972), pp. 380–381.

8. Laurence E. Lynn, Jr., and Richard I. Smith, "Can the Secretary of Defense Make a Difference?" *International Security* 7, no. 1 (Summer 1982), p. 68.

9. *United States Statutes at Large*, Public Law 80–253, 80th Cong., 1st sess. (Washington, D.C.: Government Printing Office, 1948), 61:496–497.

8

National Security Advice to U.S. Presidents: Some Lessons from Thirty Years

I.M. Destler

In large part, Presidents determine the range and quality of advice that they get. They choose their principal officials. They decide day-by-day, personally or through chosen aides, which of these officials will get into the Oval Office, how often, in what contexts. Their styles and preferences also do much to shape the sorts of advice that will reach them from further down in the government, and from people outside it. Clark Clifford once characterized the executive branch as "like a chameleon," taking its color from "the character and personality of the President";[1] certainly this is true of its senior levels. As Dean Rusk noted, "the real organization of government at higher echelons" is "how confidence flows down from the President."[2]

Yet, notwithstanding their power in shaping it, Presidents are sometimes frustrated by the advice they receive. Kennedy had his Bay of Pigs, of which he noted later—with less than full accuracy—that "the advice of every member of the executive branch brought in to advise was unanimous—and the advice was wrong."[3] Johnson pulled back from the multilateral force, but was moved to denounce his advisers vehemently for the counsel which had nearly won the day.[4] Each President may indeed have determined the advice he got by how he handled the issue and how he handled his advisers, but neither did so with that particular outcome in mind; each was shaken by what his advisory system had wrought. And even when Presidents pronounce themselves satisfied, large numbers of citizens may not be. They may find their President isolated from objective analysis and national sentiment (Cambodia), or caught up in an "inside" set of values and expectations that says more about himself and his advisers than it does about the world they seek to shape (Vietnam escalation as seen through the *Pentagon Papers*; Watergate as seen through the Nixon tapes).

I.M. Destler, "National Security Advice to U.S. Presidents: Some Lessons from Thirty Years," *World Politics*, Vol. 29, No. 2 (Jan. 1977). Copyright © 1977 by Princeton University Press. Reprinted by permission of Princeton University Press.

How Presidents get what advice, then, is an important if difficult subject for analysis. It is important in all areas of national policy. It is particularly important in the sphere alternatively labelled "national security" or "foreign" policy. Many Americans rightly reject the standard cold war belief that foreign policy *ought* always to have primacy over domestic. But it continues to receive priority attention from Presidents. There are enduring reasons—the President's particular constitutional authority and responsibility in foreign affairs; the absence of some of the domestic political constraints that affect other spheres; the opportunity to build a statesman's reputation among current voters and future historians alike; the fact that foreign policy remains, in Kennedy's oft-quoted words, the sphere where a mistake "can kill us."[5]

Presidents seek foreign policy advice from many sources. Much of it comes from persons outside of the executive branch—Congressional leaders whose judgment Presidents value or whose support they need; outside experts on specialized subjects; establishment "wise men" like the Senior Informal Advisory Group that urged Lyndon Johnson to change course on Vietnam in March 1968. Formal external advisory bodies also exist on such subjects as intelligence, arms control, and information policy. Presidents get reams of unsolicited advice as well—from policy critics motivated by strong substantive convictions and/or partisan political interest; from foreign leaders; from interest groups with particular economic stakes; from newspaper editorials and columnists.

Without denying the impact of advice from other sources, however, this essay will focus largely on advice provided by officials and institutions within the executive branch. It is such inside advice that any President gets the most of, and that responds most directly to particular problems as he must deal with them. It is, by all evidence, what influences Presidents most, most of the time, when they make particular foreign policy decisions. Too great a dependence upon senior administration insiders can cost a President dearly, particularly if these insiders are insensitive to broader national political currents. Yet, as Joseph Kraft noted ten years ago, the size and complexity of modern government have sharply limited the advisory influence of outsiders compared to the "trained intellectual bureaucrat" who is there, inside the government, to push his objective hour by hour, day by day.[6] In foreign affairs, official secrecy gives further advantages to insiders.

Every postwar President has gotten most of his inside national security advice from the occupants of some or all of a handful of senior line and staff positions: the Secretaries of State, Defense, and the Treasury; the Presidential Assistant (entitled *Special Assistant* until 1969) for National Security Affairs; the Chiefs of Staff of the military services (particularly the Chairman of the J.C.S.); and the Director of Central Intelligence. Important policy advice has also flowed from general White House policy aides like Clark Clifford for Truman, Theodore Sorensen for Kennedy, and Bill Moyers for Johnson, and from trusted political advisers like Attorneys General Robert Kennedy in 1961–1963 and John Mitchell during the early Nixon years. Some Presidents have given a regular hearing to sub-Cabinet officials in the

State Department; the Under Secretary (now Deputy Secretary) of State has sometimes been one and, less frequently, so have Assistant Secretaries with briefs of particular Presidential interest. The weightiest advisers, however, have usually been holders of senior official foreign policy and national security positions.

The role of these advisers was the target of the central postwar institutional reform in national security policy making, the creation of the National Security Council in 1947.[7] Since then, the formal "White House machinery for the resolution of major foreign affairs issues has remained remarkably stable," as the Murphy Commission report notes.[8] Yet structural continuity has not prevented considerable variation among Presidents and Administrations in how particular issues are typically treated. And how the N.S.C. has evolved over thirty years tells us much about the broader patterns of foreign policy advice to postwar Presidents— what they have desired, what they have received, and what choices present themselves for the future. Moreover, the story of the Council offers a sobering object lesson to would-be procedural reformers. Its proponents sought to constrain the President, to bind him more closely to his senior Cabinet advisers. But their creation ended up freeing him and lessening his dependence upon these advisers.

The National Security Council Since 1947: The Evolution of a Reform[9]

The Council has affected advice to Presidents in three major ways. It has served as an advisory forum of senior officials reviewing foreign policy issues for the President, usually in his presence. It has provided a focal point for the development of formal policy planning and decision processes. It has provided the umbrella for the emergence of a Presidential foreign policy staff. Its founders mainly conceived it as the first; the last is what is has most importantly become.

The N.S.C. as Forum

In form and in public imagery, the National Security Council is the most exalted committee in the Federal Government. Its statutory membership is now limited to four—the President, the Vice President, the Secretary of State, and the Secretary of Defense. The Assistant to the President for National Security Affairs is the senior staff official of the N.S.C.; the Chairman of the Joint Chiefs of Staff, the Director of Central Intelligence, and (since 1975) the Director of the Arms Control and Disarmament Agency serve as statutory advisers. Unlike many Cabinet-level committees, moreover, the N.S.C. actually does meet—more than 600 times since its inception. Thus, one way in which it provides advice to Presidents is through its actual debates and deliberations as a sitting body.

To provide advice to the President through a more orderly, even collegial institution was a major objective of the prime exponent of the N.S.C., James Forrestal.

His hopes may have been even greater—that the Council might, in practice, actually make the major U.S. policy decisions. A study which he commissioned in 1945 emphasized that, while the Council "would be formally described as advisory . . . the fact that the President himself heads the Council would for all practical purposes insure that the advice it offered would be accepted."[10] The conscious model was the British War Cabinet; the pattern to avoid was Franklin D. Roosevelt's highly personalized, *ad hoc* decision making during World War II, above and around his principal formal advisers. (The N.S.C. was quickly labelled "Forrestal's revenge.") The President was, to some, a "rogue elephant" who needed fencing in (or perhaps, in Truman's case, a "weak reed" in need of shoring up). Such concerns were widely shared. The report of the Hoover Commission Task Force of January 1949 saw Presidential participation in the conduct of foreign policy as "marked with many pitfalls," and emphasized that "the President should consult his foreign policy advisers in the executive branch before committing the United States to a course of action."[11]

The substantive objective of the N.S.C.—more effective coordination of advice and action in U.S. foreign and military policies—was widely applauded in the forties and has been since. But Forrestal's effort to control Presidential advisory processes, even to collectivize executive decision making, reflected, as Paul Hammond has noted, a "failure to understand the Presidency."[12] It also reflected a failure to understand particular Presidents. Thus, President Truman welcomed the Council as a "badly needed new facility" to bring together "military, diplomatic, and resources problems"[13] but, like all of his successors, firmly established its inability to bind him. One way in which he preserved his autonomy in practice was by attending only 12 of the 57 N.S.C. meetings held prior to the outbreak of war in Korea. Even Eisenhower, who convened the Council approximately as many times as all other postwar Presidents combined, and who almost always attended personally when his health permitted, felt moved to note his puzzlement that certain Congressmen couldn't understand that the N.S.C. itself had no powers but simply gave advice that a President could take or ignore as he pleased."[14]

The Council did nevertheless function as a major Presidential advisory forum through the fifties. Once the Korean War began, it met more frequently, and with Truman in attendance, dealing not only with Korean problems but with the more general U.S. political-military response to what was seen as a worldwide Communist challenge. Under President Eisenhower, the N.S.C. reached its peak as a sitting institution. Meetings had averaged two a month under Truman. During the Eisenhower Administration, the Council met on the average almost once a week, with Secretaries John Foster Dulles (State) and George Humphrey (Treasury) the most weighty voices.[15] When Eisenhower had a heart attack in 1955, and an operation for ileitis in 1956, Council meetings chaired by Vice President Nixon provided for useful continuity in national security policy deliberations, both actual and symbolic. Yet even under Eisenhower, the Council itself did not truly dominate

Presidential foreign policy advice. One reason was that its major mandate was to review general and relatively long-range policy; Eisenhower had other institutions and individuals for day-to-day crises and the many *ad hoc* decisions that inevitably arose. A second reason was the strong individual role played by his Secretary of State, and the strong direct relationship to the President which Dulles succeeded in establishing through assiduous efforts.

If the N.S.C. as a sitting, deliberative advisory body was of at least moderate importance to Eisenhower, his successor perceived it largely as an encumbrance. President Kennedy came to office influenced by the Jackson subcommittee's criticisms of Eisenhower's national security procedures as cumbersome and sterile; his personal penchant for informality meshed nicely with such criticism. Thus, he noted as early as 1961: "We have averaged three or four meetings a week with the Secretaries of Defense and State, [Special Assistant for National Security Affairs] McGeorge Bundy, the head of the C.I.A. and the Vice President. But formal meetings of the Security Council which include a much wider group are not as effective."[16] Formal N.S.C. meetings continued to be held—sixteen during the Administration's first six months, and less frequently thereafter. But they were seldom the place where really serious Presidential advice was solicited or conveyed.

The preference for less formal advisory meetings whose format and attendance were more susceptible to Presidential control continued under President Johnson. Bill Moyers noted that L.B.J. found the Council to be "not a live institution, not suited to precise debate for the sake of decision."[17] The Council did experience a modest re-emphasis under Special Assistant for National Security Affairs Walt Rostow, who replaced Bundy in early 1966; meetings were held, in Rostow's words, "primarily for generating and exposing a series of major problems on which decisions would be required of the President, not at the moment but in some foreseeable time period."[18] But the heart of Johnson's foreign policy advisory system was the Vietnam-dominated "Tuesday lunch," where he met informally with a small group of his top aides, including the Secretaries of State and Defense and the Special Assistant.

Nixon came to office in 1969 pledged to "restore the National Security Council to its pre-eminent role in national security planning"; he even made this the theme of a late-October campaign speech.[19] "Catch-as-catch-can talkfests" were to be supplanted by actual use of the Council as the "principal forum for the consideration of policy issues" requiring Presidential decision."[20] For a while in 1969, and more sporadically in 1970, Nixon did so employ it. But like other aspects of Nixon's proclaimed "open Presidency," it had by 1973 lapsed into unprecedented disuse, with advice to the President formulated and conveyed primarily by and through National Security Assistant Henry Kissinger, working with his staff and with interagency N.S.C. subgroups that he dominated.[21] Up to President Nixon's trip to China in February 1972, his Council had had 73 meetings—half of them in his first year. This twice-a-month average was nearly double that of the Johnson Administration. But when Kissinger stated that the controversial October 1973 military alert during the Yom Kippur War had been decided upon only after "a special meeting of the National Security Council," N.S.C. records did not support him. In fact, they showed only two meetings during the first ten months of 1973.[22]

Under President Ford, use of the N.S.C. as a convening forum has been revived somewhat (as of April 1976, the Council had met 31 times during his Presidency)[23] to a frequency slightly above that of the Johnson and Nixon Administrations. But overall postwar experience provides ample reason to conclude that Presidential use of the National Security Council was a regularized, major advisory forum is the exception rather than the rule. A major reason is that the Council's main virtues to its proponents—formality and regularity of membership and meetings; pre-established, well-disseminated agendas—prove to be drawbacks in practice. N.S.C. meetings tend to attract too many people for serious advice to be conveyed—senior advisers and Presidents are constrained to speak "for the record" notwithstanding the formal secrecy of the proceedings, since their remarks are likely to be passed on by word of mouth to a much wider audience inside the Government. Cabinet members consider themselves judged on how effectively they push their departmental briefs; Presidents must take care lest their tentative suggestions close off discussion or be disseminated after the meetings as clear Presidental preferences. These drawbacks can be reduced by limiting attendance, and all Administrations that took the Council at all seriously have made some efforts in that direction. The Nixon regime was particularly stringent in this regard. But security and frankness can be achieved even more effectively through informal meetings or "one-on-one" sessions, and it is these on which Presidents ultimately tend to rely for serious advice.

The Council as committee can nonetheless serve certain Presidential purposes. By calling them together collegially, a President can impress on officials that they share responsibilities for national security and foreign policy advice which stretch beyond their specific job descriptions. Thus the Council tends to meet most often early in an Administration, when the roles of senior advisers are still fluid and susceptible to being defined. But Presidents can build a sense of a collegial advisory team in other ways. In fact, well-conducted informal sessions may be more effective in this regard, since they can encourage the "real" debate that the Council itself inhibits. Indeed, the most widely praised example of collegial advisory practice was the informal group of his most important advisers that President Kennedy established to explore options during the Cuban missile crisis.

One way in which the Council has proved useful to all Presidents has been in public relations. Convening the Council in a time of crisis is thought to convey the impression of the most somber and careful high-level deliberation. Such meetings can protect the President from charges that he acts arbitrarily and raise the image of his Administration. Thus, Kissinger's insistence that the military alert of October 1973 had the "unanimous" support of the N.S.C. was aimed at combatting the widespread suspicion that Nixon was trying to divert attention from the domestic crisis brought on by his firing of Special Prosecutor Archibald Cox. Eleven years earlier, Kennedy had dubbed his chosen advisory group during the Cuban missile crisis the "Executive Committee of the National Security Council." And in May 1975, Press Secretary Ronald Nessen had a similar goal when he declared, "The President has met with the National Security Council," in the second sentence of his briefing revealing the seizure of the *Mayaguez*. Indeed, the Council did meet five times during that week.[24]

The N.S.C. as Formal Process

Most of those who have favored a major role for the National Security Council have sought to establish regular means for bringing important policy issues before it, supported by thorough staff work. Fundamental to the early activities of the Council, therefore, were procedures for interdepartmental reviews and policy papers aimed at putting particular issues into focus, and giving the Council documents on which to act. Under President Truman, a considerable number of policy papers were developed for N.S.C. consideration, dealing mostly with individual countries or regions. One of the most famous of all Council papers, NSC-68, was completed during this time; its call for much-increased defense spending was implemented once the Korean War made this possible domestically. NSC-68, however, was not so much instigated by Truman's N.S.C. system as by Paul Nitze and other State Department officials, who felt that the American military response to the Soviet challenge was seriously inadequate. The N.S.C. framework, however, was useful to these officials in gaining interdepartmental cooperation at a time when the Secretaries of State and Defense were not on speaking terms.[25]

The Korean War infused the policy studies process of the Truman Council with a greater sense of urgency. And the N.S.C.'s role was formally strengthened in July 1950 by a Presidential directive emphasizing that all major national security policies should be recommended to the President through the Council. Truman had stated this earlier, but his personal participation in Council sessions now gave it new significance. However, after a year of intensive activity, the Truman process, in one participant's words, "gradually drifted into the doldrums along with the rest of the government,"[26] as a lame-duck Administration struggled with a war it could not end.

President Eisenhower built upon procedures already established in the Truman Administration, but made them more structured, formal, and comprehensive. He and his Special Assistant for National Security Affairs, Robert Cutler, believed deeply in orderly deliberations based upon thorough staff work. Under them, the Council "Planning Board" (a committee of departmental assistant secretaries) presided over the development of papers that analyzed virtually every significant U.S. foreign policy problem and proposed, on each, a general "policy" for Council review and Presidential approval. The most comprehensive of these was the annual overview document entitled "Basic National Security Policy."

In the development of its structure and the scope of its ambition, Eisenhower's N.S.C. process was therefore unmatched. The aim was not just to get top officials to consider every issue of consequence; it was to have a set of written general policies approved by the President which would serve as guidance for the overall government. But the process proved to have three very serious limitations.

One of these limitations is endemic to all efforts aimed at statements of general policy: they frequently do not and cannot provide clear cues for responses to particular events unknown and unanticipated when the documents were written. The tendency of officials is therefore to deal with such events on their own terms without too much reference to policy statements framed earlier. A second limitation arose from its comprehensiveness: such a large number of papers was being drafted and cleared that the whole operation became, to many participants, a cumbersome, slow-moving "papermill." The third, perhaps most frequently expressed criticism was that because the process pressed the different agencies to reach agreement on paper prior to its submission to the Council, key policy issues and choices were suppressed rather than highlighted. Dean Acheson suggested that the way the system handled disagreements was to "increase the vagueness and generality" of the policies adopted.[27]

Defenders of the Eisenhower system argued that major issues were in fact frequently brought up for Council debate during the process; they pointed to the existence of "splits," or disagreements between agencies reflected by alternative language in the papers the N.S.C. reviewed. Eisenhower's Special Assistants for National Security Affairs seem to have been sensitive to this problem, and labored hard to be sure that fundamental issues were not buried in verbiage meaning different things to different people. Nevertheless, since Eisenhower's concept of interagency staff work was that it should, if possible, produce an agreed recommendation, such efforts seem to have had limited effect.

Finally, the Eisenhower process was limited by the evolution of the President's broader advisory system, above all the foreign policy predominance established by the Secretary of State. John Foster Dulles and his subordinates participated actively in the system, but he valued his own flexibility highly in particular negotiations and decisions, and worked very hard to keep it. He preferred to resolve tough choices by dealing privately with the President or, when necessary, in negotiations with other strong officials like Treasury Secretary George Humphrey. Such procedures limited the ability of the managers of Eisenhower's N.S.C. process to ensure that it was the place where the basic policy questions were really addressed.

President Kennedy's attitude toward this process was even more negative than his attitude toward Council meetings. He dismantled it completely, abolishing both the Planning Board and the Operations Coordinating Board whose role was to oversee implementation of policies developed through the N.S.C. framework. In National Security Assistant McGeorge Bundy's words, the new administration "deliberately rubbed out the distinction between planning and operation which governed the administrative structure of the NSC staff in the last administration."[28]

Believing that "policy" was shaped primarily through day-to-day decisions and actions, Kennedy put nothing in the place of the Eisenhower process; nor generally did his successor, Lyndon B. Johnson. There were some efforts at developing broad policy guidelines outside the N.S.C. framework, such as the "National Policy Papers" pushed by Rostow while he was State Department Policy Planning Chairman; some efforts were conducted under the auspices of interdepartmental committees (chaired by State Department officials) established by Johnson in March 1966. Also, a general counterinsurgency policy had been adopted in the wake of the Bay of Pigs fiasco. But these were exceptions to the informal, operations-oriented style that prevailed.

As already noted, Presidential candidate Nixon sharply criticized this Kennedy-Johnson informality. He was also, however, critical of the Eisenhower process as fostering illusory "concurrences" that limited active assertion of the President's power to choose. Therefore, the formal process for providing policy advice which he established—the so-called N.S.S.M. (National Security Study Memorandum) system—reflected his desire that policy papers drafted by interagency committees offer not agreed recommendations but real "options" from which the President might select. The focus shifted from establishing broad policy to providing an analytic basis for specific decisions. There was also an effort to avoid duplicating the encyclopedism of the Eisenhower period by being selective in the studies ordered. However, since many issues were in need of review, and since the memoranda were a major vehicle for the Kissinger staff in seizing the initiative, 69 studies were ordered in the system's first six months of operation. That volume was enough to convince some departmental officials (mistakenly, it appears) that the purpose of the system was simply to inundate the bureaucracy with paperwork so that Nixon and Kissinger could do their real business without too much molestation. And the number of completed studies soon did become far greater than the capacity of the Nixon Administration to review them and act seriously on them, especially considering the extreme centralization of power under the President and his White House National Security Assistant.

Ironically, the *de facto* Nixon-Kissinger "system" soon evolved into practically the opposite of the one advocated in 1968 and designed in 1969: the two chief officials tended to disregard or discount much of the advice they received from the broader Government. They not only made their own decisions based on their own analyses (or their own private sifting of other analyses), but often kept the bureaucracy in the dark concerning these decisions. And the Nixon Administration's N.S.C. "system" also demonstrated, rather quickly, another limitation of structuring procedures too much around broad policy studies aimed at a limited number of major decisions. Responses to various crises and to ongoing situations which the United States is seeking to influence require day-to-day operational choices by the President and lesser officials which are not easily managed through formal "options" studies that take weeks to prepare. Thus the most active institution in the Nixon system was frequently the Kissinger-dominated "Washington

Special Actions Group," which was not even a part of the original system, but was created in the aftermath of the downing of a U.S. intelligence airplane by North Korea. The Group was designed to coordinate advice and operations on similar fast-moving situations.

Nevertheless, N.S.S.M.s have continued to be employed; 35 new studies were initiated in Ford's first 21 months. And, notwithstanding how the real Nixon-Kissinger "system" evolved, their N.S.S.M. procedure seems a clear improvement over its predecessors in both its selectivity and its focus on Presidential choice. Its formal goal—that agencies reach agreement on a list of options through objective analysis uncolored by agency interest—is probably unrealistic, and may also be undesirable; Alexander George, for example, has argued that Presidents should nourish rather than suppress "multiple advocacy" founded upon the divergent perspectives and interests of different agencies.[29] But in practice, such advocacy is not eliminated, for agencies have frequently used the system to try to ensure that their own preferred options are presented in reasonably attractive form, so that their chiefs can argue for them effectively at high-level meetings. And as George and others have recognized, multiple advocacy works best when senior officials are acting not as narrow pleaders for their departmental briefs, but as senior governmental officials bound by obligations to their President and their colleagues to explore all possible choices in the most objective and thoroughgoing manner. The N.S.S.M. process is designed to push officialdom in that direction.

The N.S.C. as Presidential Staff

The third, and surely most important, way in which the creation of the National Security Council has shaped foreign policy advice to Presidents is that it has served as the institutional base for the establishment of a strong Presidential foreign policy staff. Unlike the generally declining use of the Council as a sitting committee and the intermittent use of it as a focal point for formal policy-making procedures, the use of the N.S.C. as staff has grown steadily.

All postwar Presidents from Truman to Nixon contributed to this development. Truman established the precedent of treating the Council as his body to be housed in his Executive Office, and adopted its staff as a useful addition to Presidential resources. He considered it, however, a career staff like that of the Bureau of the Budget, which would serve from administration to administration, providing continuity. His two N.S.C. Executive Secretaries, Sidney Souers and James Lay, were appointed with this criterion of "neutral competence" in mind.[30]

Support staffing was strengthened in the N.S.C. reorganization that followed the outbreak of war in Korea. It was both strengthened and enlarged in 1953, when President Eisenhower created the new position of Special Assistant for National Security Affairs.[31] This official was to serve as the President's personal staff aide in charge of managing the N.S.C. process, with the Executive Secretary's role now that of head of the career staff. The Council staff was also enlarged and strengthened in other ways, including an enhanced capability for independent analysis and review of agency positions. It remained, however, predominantly a career staff operating under the expectation that most of its members would (or at least could) stay on from administration to administration. The new Special Assistant, though a stronger, higher-ranking official than Truman's Executive Secretaries, was limited in his leverage over the senior national security officials and agencies by, among other things, his separation from the day-to-day processes of national security operations. In fact, Eisenhower had *two* staff aides with national security responsibilities. The Special Assistant was one; the other was his Staff Secretary, General Andrew Goodpaster, whose duties included providing daily intelligence briefings to the President, coordinating the flow of daily national security business, and acting as liaison in arranging for meetings and the communication of decisions on operational issues.

When President Kennedy assumed office, he preserved the position of Special Assistant for National Security Affairs, but abolished most of the formal policy planning system on which the position's previous occupants had lavished their attention. McGeorge Bundy inherited, however, most of the national security tasks of General Goodpaster, particularly the management of day-to-day Presidential foreign policy business. This gave him a new and very important source of leverage, particularly since he—unlike Goodpaster—was working for a President who was inclined to make a large number of specific decisions himself rather than delegate them to others. Moreover, Bundy's own instinct for power no doubt contributed to his ability to carve a major advisory and coordinating role for himself out of his position at the center of White House national security action processes. Moreover, the Bay of Pigs fiasco of April 1961 strengthened Kennedy's determination to exert control, with Bundy his principal vehicle.

Bundy recruited a small, aggressive, independent staff of intellectual operators who identified particularly with the current administration. They were inclined to seek out issues, to challenge departmental opinions, to press for surfacing of buried policy choices and for implementation of what they saw as Presidential desires. The staff was strengthened because Bundy was an apt delegator of authority, allowing staff members to operate rather freely as his agents. Another major innovation was direct access to information. The White House Situation Room was established, and equipment was installed enabling the White House to receive departmental cables to and from the State and Defense Departments and the Central Intelligence Agency; previously, Presidents and their White House aides had depended on the agencies to forward such communications.

Working for a President who tended to resist any firm sense of organizational structure and division of labor, Bundy and his staff met the need for an informal yet wide-ranging effort at central coordination. In so doing, they began increasingly to play one of the roles originally envisaged for the Council—developing and pressing a broad, government-wide "Presidential" view encompassing diplomatic, military, and frequently economic elements in foreign policy.

One indication that this staff reform was filling a real need was that it lasted, in modified form, under a very different type of President. Lyndon Johnson did not duplicate his predecessor's wide-ranging involvement in foreign policy, preferring to limit himself to a few issues (though he dominated these), and to lean predominantly on his chief line officers, the Secretaries of State and Defense. Over time, this reduced the power of the Special Assistant and his staff, as did the fact that Bundy's style did not mesh with Johnson's nearly as well as it had with Kennedy's. Nevertheless, Bundy's successor, Walt Rostow—though he was originally given a reduced mandate—ended up performing essentially the same formal functions: coordinating the flow of information and intelligence to the President; managing the flow of decision papers to the President; monitoring governmental operations to promote coordination and responsiveness to Presidential interests; communicating Presidential decisions and instructions to departments and agencies; acting as liaison with Cabinet officers and other high foreign policy officials; and serving as personal adviser and source of staff analysis for the President.[32]

But it was under Henry Kissinger, of course, that the N.S.C. and its staff became synonyms. And as the President's foreign policy adviser, now renamed *Assistant* for National Security Affairs, Kissinger achieved unparalleled personal dominance. If Kennedy's active involvement and preference for an open decision-making style created a need for coordination which a Bundy could fill, Nixon's combination of a desire to dominate foreign policy personally, and a preference for dealing with and through a very small number of people, gave Kissinger an even greater opportunity. Moreover, Kissinger—unlike Bundy—was to become identified as the architect (and actual builder) of a particular set of policies. Under him, the strength of other senior N.S.C. staff members proved less than it had been under Bundy. His own closed style disinclined him to delegate, and this, plus the President's closed style, limited the direct access of Kissinger's subordinates to the Oval Office. The staff grew to unprecedented size, however—over fifty professionals—giving Kissinger considerable issue coverage and analytic and operational resources when he chose to employ them. Kissinger's strength was further enhanced, during the early months, by his role as director of the policy studies program already described. He thus combined the role of Eisenhower's Special Assistants—directing a structured planning process—with that of Bundy and Rostow—managing the day-to-day Presidential process. Before his first year was out, he was to add a further role which became prominent in 1971 and 1972—that of the President's personal, secret envoy handling those negotiations about which Nixon cared the most.

In September 1973, however, Kissinger became Secretary of State. And although he retained his N.S.C. position until November 1975, he gave priority to the Secretaryship almost immediately in order to play a stronger role of public leadership and to gain a measure of separation from the Watergate-enveloped White House. The Council's staff remained in existence, with its day-to-day operations under Kissinger's N.S.C. deputy, Brent Scowcroft. But, with most of

Kissinger's chief aides now in State Department positions, it went into relative eclipse. Its formal neutrality vis-à-vis the departments was re-established in November 1975, when President Ford replaced Kissinger with Scowcroft as National Security Assistant. However, the staff did not return to its former power. The major reason, apparently, was that Ford was not playing the kind of assertive, initiating foreign policy role that most of his predecessors had played. Another important reason was the strong role that Kissinger had established and was loath to relinquish as long as he stayed in office. This waning of the N.S.C. staff has precedents in other election years—1952 and 1968 come to mind. In both cases, it rose to new importance after the Presidential inauguration the following January.

Lessons of the N.S.C. Experience

What can be learned from this decidedly mixed experience—the fluctuation and evolution of the N.S.C. as Council, as process, and as staff?

The first lesson is that the N.S.C. has taken a course very different from that envisioned by its original proponents. They sought coordination of policy advice and execution, and the development of a transdepartmental view of national security problems, and these the N.S.C. has, to varying degrees, provided. But James Forrestal would roll over several times in his grave were he to learn that Richard Nixon had been able to use the N.S.C. to shield himself from his advisers, as the institutional base for a Presidency of unexampled isolation and considerable flexibility in decision and action.

Nixon was able to do this, of course, because of what the Council did become. Hence, the second clear lesson: the Council's most consistent value to Presidents has been to provide them with a senior official and staff to coordinate their personal foreign policy business, and serve as a broader coordinator of decision and action processes. The Council itself has increasingly been treated as a bore, if not an encumbrance. Formal planning processes have risen and fallen with particular Presidents—or, as in the case of the N.S.S.M.'s—declined within the tenure of a particular President. But three consecutive, very different Presidents found the National Security Assistant and his staff to be of considerable personal value. A fourth, Gerald Ford, emulated them formally by re-establishing the separation of the positions of Secretary and Assistant, though he did not accompany this action with a systematic effort to use the Assistant to reduce his dependence on his chief Cabinet advisers.

Even the rise of the National Security Assistant has been the result of special circumstances, including the disinclination or inability of two Secretaries of State—Dean Rusk and William Rogers—to exert leadership and achieve predominance as Acheson and Dulles did before them and Kissinger after. The third broad conclusion therefore is that the N.S.C. in all its manifestations has reflected more than it has shaped the foreign policy making of particular administrations. Not only is the N.S.C. at the mercy of particular Presidents, to be used, reshaped, or ignored as they prefer. The impact of particular processes and the emergence of particular roles depends also on the broader pattern of relationships among top Presidential advisers. Eisenhower's planning process was limited by a Dulles determined to be Secretary of State in the maximum sense and a President quite willing to allow it. Both Bundy and Kissinger built the role of National Security Assistant into something much larger than envisaged because they met Presidential needs no one else was meeting. And when Bundy stayed on to serve a second President, his role came to shrink when Rusk increasingly met *Johnson's* criteria of performance for a Secretary of State.

Broader Presidential Advisory Systems

The foregoing underscores the need to think in terms of broader systems that shape national security advice to Presidents, systems that include the N.S.C. but many other things besides. The need becomes particularly dramatic in the case of a Nixon and a Kissinger: the "closed" system for foreign policy making and execution which they had developed in 1971 and 1972 was so completely at variance with the structured system built around the Council as forum, relatively open to inputs from other officials, which they had proclaimed with much fanfare in January and February of 1969. Other Presidential "systems" for decision and action on foreign policy may defy such brief characterization. But all administrations do develop recurrent patterns of how issues reach the President, with what range of analysis and advice, whose advice is most valued on which subjects, and what roles senior officials play vis-à-vis the President and one another. When a particular issue arises, the manner of handling it will be shaped, to a considerable degree, by the "system" already in place. This is particularly true of crises perceived as requiring a quick response.

What are some of the variations in broad Presidential policy-making systems that have appeared in the postwar period? What substantive, stylistic, or organizational preferences on the part of Presidents and other senior officials have helped to determine them? At least eight related variables among Presidents and their advisory teams seem important in shaping their broader foreign policy-making systems. No attempt is made here to rank them in importance, or to delineate all of the many relationships among them.

One basic variable is *whether a President has a particularly clear organizational sense*, especially a conception of the appropriate roles for occupants of particular positions, and how much he is prepared to insist on its implementation. Eisenhower had such a sense to an unusual degree—he clearly distinguished between staff and line functions, between planning and operations, and he expected his subordinates to keep to their proper roles. Indeed, he himself deferred frequently to others' roles rather than insisting on command over them, a habit that lent support to the view that he became his system's prisoner. At the other extreme was

Kennedy, who seems—perhaps by design—to have differentiated very little among individuals' roles. He dealt with those whom he found congenial and useful, handing them such assignments as he felt they could perform—much in the way some Senators handle their staffs. When a McNamara insisted on control of top Defense Department appointments and of his Department more generally, Kennedy could live with it and even came to welcome it. But such organizational order was not something he would have imposed himself, as evidenced by his choice of at least three other state appointees before he decided on Secretary Rusk. And his disorder had costs also, including confusion about who was responsible for what, about what "the policy" was, and who reflected the President's wishes.

A second, related variable is *how much particular Presidents have favored formality and regularity in the flow of analysis and advice to them.* Here Eisenhower similarly ranks as the most in favor of formal procedures, and Kennedy as the least. Truman inclines to the Eisenhower side, Johnson toward the Kennedy side. Nixon is an odd case. He certainly conceived of himself as preferring orderly procedures, but what he seems to have meant by this in practice was having an orderly, controlled personal environment. He ended up being served by highly informal procedures, though these were combined with very limited and controlled channels of access to his person.

A third important variable is *how much particular Presidents have had—and have wanted—*strong leaders in the major line positions, the Secretary of State above all, but also the Secretary of Defense. That is related, of course, to one of the most-discussed issues of foreign policy organization—whether a system of coordination and central management should be State Department-centered or White House-centered. It is related also to whether a President wishes to make a large number of decisions himself or to preside over a process in which decisions are largely made by others. All of this having been said, one is struck by the fact that most postwar Presidents have not perceived their Cabinet members as "natural enemies."[33] Truman and Eisenhower wanted and supported strong Secretaries of State and deferred to them. Johnson likewise deferred to Rusk. Even Kennedy, who was ambivalent on this point, was enthusiastic about Robert McNamara, the archetypal strong Cabinet member, and frustrated with Rusk. Richard Neustadt noted in 1963 that Kennedy "appears far less inclined than FDR to keep his senior ministers at arms length. . . . On the contrary, with those of his department heads whose work is most bound up with his from day to day—State, Defense, Justice, above all—he has sought a relationship as close and confidential and collegial as with his staff, and he has delegated tasks to them and their associates as though they all were members of his staff."[34] Gerald Ford seems particularly to have welcomed strong voices in his Cabinet—he retained some and appointed more. Only Nixon seems consistently to have preferred weakness in Cabinet positions, though he professed the contrary. His appointment of Kissinger as Secretary of State in 1973 seems attributable not to his stated desire "to get the work out in the departments where it belongs,"[35] but to his need to demonstrate renewed Administration vitality and distract attention from his personal plight in the first year of Watergate.

A fourth important variable, partly subject to a President's control but partly beyond it, is *how his principal advisers work out their own particular roles, jurisdictional boundaries, and relationships with one another.* Bundy, as National Security Assistant, deferred to Cabinet members much more than Kissinger did; Rusk accepted McNamara's primacy on military-strategic questions in a way Kissinger, as Secretary, would never have considered accepting Schlesinger's. Another dimension of the relationships among senior Presidential advisers is how much they are collegial and mutually supportive, and how much they are antagonistic.[36] There are always elements of both competition and cooperation, but the mix differs—as do the effects on foreign policy. On balance, considerable collegiality seems desirable, but it can cause officials to avoid the hard questions and the rigorous and perhaps wounding debate necessary to subject difficult policy choices to hard scrutiny. This proved to be a serious flaw in policy making toward the end of the Truman Administration, and also, recurrently, in the Kennedy and Johnson regimes. The generally antagonistic relations among senior advisers during the Nixon Administration were also quite damaging, however, reinforcing the lack of interpersonal trust emanating from the President personally, and reinforcing the closed, two-man character of that system.

A fifth important variable is *how widely Presidents have wished to cast their nets for advice.* By this measure, Nixon stood clearly at one extreme and Kennedy at the other, and their unusually "closed" and "open" systems reflected these conflicting tendencies. Ranking the other three Presidents is harder. Johnson seemed to be seeking a range of advice, but frequently came down hard on proponents of views he wished not to face. Truman was content to receive the bulk of his advice through line channels once he found congenial Secretaries of State; Clark Clifford's main impact seems to have been prior to the Marshall-Acheson regime. Eisenhower welcomed and sometimes sought advice from outside line channels, but would defer in action to his Secretary of State. (This and some of the earlier variables help to determine how many senior officials will have a strong personal relationship with the President, and will be able to act, in Washington and vis-à-vis foreign governments, with the weight that such relationships allow.)

A sixth variable is *how broad a substantive involvement a President seeks personally.* Inevitably, he will deal formally with a very wide range of matters, but over what range does he seek to make a strong personal mark? Here Kennedy with his global interests ranks at the broad end. Johnson, in contrast, took on only a few issues that were not forced upon him. Gerald Ford likewise seems to have dealt chiefly with issues brought before him by ongoing world events and by his Secretary of State.

A seventh important variable relates to the type of advice a President wants: *what is his attitude toward divided counsel and toward interpersonal disputes among his principal advisers?* Does he typically seek alternative views as a means of enhancing his choice and leverage, or does he want "agreed recommendations" from his advisers? Of the postwar Presidents, Eisenhower and Johnson explicitly pressed for concurrences—Eisenhower through his formal system, Johnson less formally. Kennedy and Nixon more frequently wanted the differences brought to them for decision, and Nixon was perhaps more willing than any of his postwar predecessors to *act* with divided counsel, though he shielded himself from personal exposure to advisory give-and-take. No President since F.D.R. seems to have welcomed personal rivalries among his chief aides.

An eighth variable is *how much a President seeks operational involvement—pre- and post-decision—as opposed to preferring his impact to come at a regular decision point*. How much is he a persistent intruder in the process, as opposed to a magistrate, seeing his role as deciding issues brought to him and having his wishes executed without further extensive personal effort? By this criterion, Kennedy and Johnson were "intruders," whereas Eisenhower and Nixon were "magistrates." Truman and Ford come closer to the latter role than to the former.

In addition to these variations, there is a whole range of personal Presidential characteristics that affect their systems. Do they prefer advice and information orally or in writing? If the former, do they prefer "one-on-one" or group sessions? How do they react to being confronted, personally, with a challenge to their policies? Can they "turn off" an adviser supporting a course they reject without discouraging him from such advocacy on other issues in the future? Nixon offers an unusual case here: a President almost incapable of delivering a strong no or rebuff to an aide, who—partly for that reason—dealt increasingly through staff aides who could.

Prescription—Problems and Choices

In view of the extensive postwar experience analyzed here, how ought Presidents to organize their advice-getting in the future? What can outside observers recommend to them? Given that the systems that evolve are so heavily dependent upon the personalities of Presidents and their chief aides, can general prescriptions be offered that are not tailored to fit a particular chief executive? The remainder of this article is a discussion of some such prescriptions.[37]

A Basic Dilemma: Choice versus Persistence

Most thinking and writing about foreign policy advice to Presidents focuses on ensuring the wisest, most fully informed Presidential *choices*, from among the widest possible range of reasonable policy alternatives. That was the purpose of the most sophisticated formal inside effort to date—Nixon's N.S.S.M. system. It is the purpose also of most of the best academic work, notably that of Alexander George and his colleagues. The model (usually explicit) is the chief executive as magistrate, *the President deciding.*[38]

Yet Presidents need advice and support not just in deciding what they want, but in making their choices effective. They need help in implementation. Since it takes considerable time and effort for most policies to be put across, Presidents need both the fact and the appearance of steadfastness of purpose, of knowing and communicating what they are after, and of being skillful in getting it. Neustadt quoted Truman to the effect that what the powers of the Presidency amounted to was the chance to persuade others to do what they ought to do anyway. The word "ought" implies that the President already knew—as when he mobilized his limited power resources in 1947–1948 to win Congressional support of the Marshall Plan. The model here is a different one—*the President leading.*[39]

Obviously, Presidential advisers and advisory institutions need to support the President in both of these tasks: careful deliberation prior to decision; effective pursuit of the goal chosen in a decision when its attainment depends on more than Presidential action alone. Fortunately, all Presidents do get support toward both of these goals. Unfortunately, the goals are frequently in conflict. For Robert McNamara in 1967, continued escalation in Vietnam was futile and foreclosed other possibilities. What was needed was to reevaluate the situation and consider other, more limited options. His President, however, believed—or dearly wished to believe—that what was needed above all was perseverance to prevail over adversaries at home and abroad. And when McNamara surfaced some of his arguments before the Senate Armed Services Committee, Johnson "drew the analogy of a man trying to sell his house, while one of the sons of the family went to the prospective buyer to point out that there were leaks in the basement."[40]

To use Vietnam as an example today hardly presents the best argument for perseverance. But Richard Nixon behaved similarly in a much more successful case—that of China policy. Once he had set his course, he gave the utmost priority to careful implementation—maintaining secrecy until the Kissinger visit (even though this foreclosed any very broad canvassing of alternative approaches), and placing very severe restrictions on intragovernmental consideration of China policy between his surprise announcement of July 15, 1971, and his visit the following February.[41] In both cases, consistency of purpose and execution were given priority; serious policy review was discouraged or prevented. And in both, the conflict between the two goals was real. The need for sending a consistent set of signals to Hanoi or China may have been exaggerated by Johnson or Nixon, but it was a real need and it stood to be threatened by any appearance of reconsideration or irresolution. The tension had other roots as well. Johnson needed unity among his advisers to sell a controversial policy at home; Nixon needed some degree of secrecy in approaching Peking.

The fact that there is a conflict between full consideration of all options (irresolution?) and perseverance in a policy course (tunnel vision?) suggests that Presidential advice must balance and trade off the two; unfortunately, it is hard to develop objective criteria that determine how the trade-off should be made. In practice, people tend to choose one value or the other, according to whether they like the current policy; it is a "conflict between coherence and change."[42] Another way the trade-off has been made in more than one Administration is by emphasizing choice early in the term, and execution thereafter. As Robert H. Johnson has written, "at the beginning of any administration" leaders tend to believe "that existing policy is defective" and that "the international environment is relatively malleable."[43] They are in search of alternatives, of ways to make an impact. Later on, they have a reduced sense of the possible and are hooked to their own choices. This helps explain the evolution of the Nixon-Kissinger system from an open process, oriented toward widening Presidential options, to a very closed implementation system, with the President's Assistant becoming predominantly a "line" officer engaged in making and carrying out decisions on policy execution.

Another basis for making the trade-off is one this author has suggested elsewhere—one's conception of how U.S. foreign policy is made. If one sees it as shaped predominantly by a manageable number of Presidential decisions, one advocates a system that spurs the broadest range of pre-decision analysis and advocacy. If one believes that the truly consequential Presidential decisions are exceptional, and that most policy evolves from day-to-day actions at several governmental levels, one emphasizes the advice and support Presidents need in pursuing effective policies over time, as well as the need for the government to act with coherence to achieve consistent impact. One would not favor this degree of emphasis on execution, however, if one felt—either because of a negative view of the Presidency or a skepticism about the prospects of strong policy initiatives in an uncertain world—that strong Presidential leadership were likely to bring more harm than good. In such a case, one might well emphasize care in choice and regularity in reconsideration of choices previously taken, with damage limitation as the goal. This face of the dilemma was highlighted by what Acheson told Neustadt after Johnson torpedoed the multilateral force: "I know your theory. You think Presidents should be warned. You're wrong. Presidents should be given confidence."[45]

Finally, some have argued that it is typically a President's subordinates who favor strong action, while the President's interests are usually served by a deferral of choice—"keeping options open." As Graham Allison has put it: "In policy making then, the issue looking *down* is options: how to preserve my leeway until time clarifies uncertainties . . . the issue looking *upwards* is confidence: how to give the boss confidence in doing what needs to be done."[46] The Neustadt "theory" denounced by Acheson is generally consistent with Allison's proposition—though not with Neustadt's celebration elsewhere of Truman's (and Acheson's) Marshall Plan leadership. In this view, Presidents not only want to have a range of options available, but want to retain them—to avoid choosing as long as possible. By contrast, foreign policy making systems built around options usually assume that a President's interest is often in making a choice; that includes not just the 1969 Nixon system, but George's multiple-advocacy proposal.

But to carry a system of "open options" to its logical conclusion is to forgo effectiveness of execution almost entirely. Thomas L. Hughes wrote ten years ago that any prolonged "attempt to keep all options open prevents the persistent pursuit of any one of them. . . . A foreign policy whose chief characteristic is a plethora of unclosed options is not much of a foreign policy at all."[47] Ultimately, a President's influence is not shaped by the choices he defers, though it may be protected by them. It comes from the choices he makes and perseveres in. Admittedly, Presidents do not wish to have subordinates force their hand on decisions. But some, like Truman and Nixon, have placed very positive value on being—to appropriate a phrase recently applied to a Japanese Prime Minister—"men of decision and action." Their historical reputations, for better or worse, will rest on the courses they persisted in following. To quote Dean Acheson again, "Flexibility in maneuver may be highly desirable in certain circumstances, but when it leaves one's own and friendly forces and commanders uncertain of the nature and purpose of the operations or of who has responsibility for what, it can be a handicap. Machiavelli was writing for weak princes."[48]

If one accepts the need to emphasize effectiveness of execution as well as care in decision in foreign policy making systems, and if one accepts further the elusiveness of general rules to establish which value should receive priority when, prescription must fall back upon a need to institutionalize both. This offers a marginally new way of looking at an old question of foreign policy making—whether the President's prime adviser should be the Secretary of State or the National Security Assistant, and what sort of balance should exist between the Secretary and the White House staff.

Notes

1. Clifford, "The Presidency As I Have Seen It," in Emmet John Hughes, *The Living Presidency* (New York: Coward, McCann, and Geoghegan 1973), 315.

2. Quoted in *Life*, January 17, 1969, p. 62B.

3. Quoted in Theodore Sorensen, *Kennedy* (New York: Harper and Row 1965), 305.

4. On the MLF decision, see Philip Geyelin, *Lyndon B. Johnson and the World* (New York: Praeger 1966), chap. 7; and John Steinbruner, *The Cybernetic Theory of Decision* (Princeton: Princeton University Press, 1974), esp. chap. 9.

5. Quoted in Arthur M. Schlesinger, Jr., *A Thousand Days* (Boston: Houghton Mifflin 1965), 426.

6. Joseph Kraft, *Profiles in Power* (New York: American Library 1966), 63–68.

7. Of course, one may argue that the establishment of the Secretary of Defense was of equal if not greater importance. Indeed, in the immediate postwar years the phrase "national security" was considered a near-synonym of "national defense"; James Forrestal, as Secretary of the Navy, originally backed the establishment of the N.S.C. as an alternative to defense unification. When both the Council and the Secretary of Defense were established by the National Security Act of 1947, the latter was described in the Act as the President's principal adviser in the field of "national security." In short order, however, the N.S.C.

became heavily involved in State Department and foreign policy business, an involvement reflected in Truman's early order that the Secretary of State chair the Council in his absence. "National security policy" then became a near-synonym of foreign policy, or at least of its "security" or "political-military" components. The latter usage is employed in this article.

8. *Report of the Commission on the Organization of the Government for the Conduct of Foreign Policy* (hereafter referred to as *Murphy Commission Report*) (Washington: G.P.O., June 1975), 4.

9. These pages on the N.S.C. draw particularly on the following sources: Stanley L. Falk, "The National Security Council Under Truman, Eisenhower, and Kennedy," *Political Science Quarterly* 79 (September 1964):403–34; David K. Hall, "The Custodian-Manager of the Policymaking Process," in Alexander L. George, "Toward a More Soundly Based Foreign Policy: Making Better Use of Information," Appendix D (Volume 2) to the *Murphy Commission Report*, 100–119; Paul Y. Hammond, "The National Security Council: An Interpretation and Appraisal," *American Political Science Review* 54 (December 1960), reprinted in Alan A. Altshuler, *The Politics of the Federal Bureaucracy* (New York: Dodd, Mead 1968), 140–56; Robert H. Johnson, "The National Security Council: The Relevance of Its Past to Its Future," *Orbis* 13 (Fall 1969):709–35; the early Jackson Subcommittee hearings and staff reports (U.S. Senate, Committee on Government Operations, Subcommittee on National Policy Machinery, *Organizing for National Security*, vols. I–III [Washington 1961]); James S. Lay, Jr., and Robert H. Johnson, "Organizational History of the National Security Council," August 1960; published ibid., vol. II, 411–68; Richard M. Moose, "The White House National-Security Staffs since 1947," in Keith C. Clark and Laurence J. Legere, eds., *The President and the Management of National Security* (for the Institute of Defense Analyses, New York: Praeger 1969), 55–98; I.M. Destler, *Presidents, Bureaucrats, and Foreign Policy* (Princeton: Princeton University Press 1972 and 1974), esp. chap. 5 and Epilogue.

10. Study by Myron Gilmore for the *Eberstadt Report*, quoted in Hammond, "National Security Council," 141.

11. Harvey H. Bundy and others, "The Organization of the Government for the Conduct of Foreign Affairs," Appendix H to the *Report of the Commission on Organization of the Executive Branch of the Government* (Washington, D.C., February 1949), 51.

12. Hammond, "National Security Council," 141.

13. Harry S. Truman, *Years of Trial and Hope* (New York: Doubleday 1956), 59.

14. Dwight D. Eisenhower, *Waging Peace* (New York: Doubleday 1965), 246n.

15. The Secretary of the Treasury has never been a formal member of the N.S.C., but was regularly invited to Council meetings under Eisenhower and most other postwar Presidents. The Murphy Commission proposed that he be added as a statutory member in view of the increased importance of economic relations in foreign policy. Congress passed legislation to this end in December 1975, but President Ford vetoed it, declaring that "adequate arrangements for providing advice to the President on the integration of economic and foreign policy already exist."

16. Quoted in Sorensen, *Kennedy*, 284.

17. "Bill Moyers Talks about LBJ, Poverty, War and the Young," *Atlantic* 222 (July 1968):35.

18. W.W. Rostow, *The Diffusion of Power* (New York: Macmillan 1972), 361.

19. Report in the *New York Times*, October 25, 1968.

20. Ibid., and White House Statement of February 7, 1969.

21. On the operations of the Nixon-Kissinger system generally, see esp. Chester Crocker, "The Nixon-Kissinger National Security Council System, 1969–1972: A Study in Foreign Policy Management," in National Academy of Public Administration, "Making Organizational Change Effective: Case Studies of Attempted Reforms in Foreign Affairs," Appendix O (Vol. 6) to the *Murphy Commission Report*, 79–99; and Destler, *Presidents*, chap. 5 and Epilogue. For an insider's account of how the system was established, see Morton H. Halperin, "The 1969 NSC System," unpub. paper prepared for the Murphy Commission.

22. *Washington Post*, November 9, 1973.

23. Information provided by the N.S.C. staff, covering the period through April 28, 1976.

24. *New York Times*, May 13, 1975; *The New Republic*, June 7, 1975, p. 8; and information provided by N.S.C. staff.

25. The standard account of this episode is Paul Y. Hammond, "NSC-68: Prologue to Rearmament," in Warner Schilling and others, *Strategy, Politics, and Defense Budgets* (New York: Columbia University Press 1962).

26. Johnson, "National Security Council," 714.

27. Acheson, "Thoughts on Thought in High Places," reprinted in Jackson Subcommittee, II, 292.

28. Bundy's letter to Senator Henry Jackson, in Jackson Subcommittee, I, 1338.

29. George, "The Case for Multiple Advocacy in Making Foreign Policy," *American Political Science Review* 66 (September 1972): esp. 753–56.

30. On the issue of neutral competence in U.S. public administration, see Herbert Kaufman, "Emerging Conflicts in the Doctrines of Public Administration," in Altschuler, *Politics*, 75–77; and Hugh Heclo, "OMB and the Presidency—the Problem of 'Neutral Competence,'" *Public Interest*, no. 38 (Winter 1975):80–98.

31. For a careful, illuminating account of the development of this role, and of conflicts among the Special Assistant's *roles*, see Hall, "Custodian-Manager."

32. On Rostow's functions, see Moose, "White House National Security Staffs," 85–86.

33. The quote is from the first federal Budget Director, General Charles G. Dawes, who used to brief his successors about the job and end with the following: "Young man, if you retain nothing else that I have told you, remember this: Cabinet members are Vice Presidents in charge of spending, and as such they are the natural enemies of the President. Good day." Quoted by Kermit Gordon, "The Budget Director," in Thomas E. Cronin and Sanford D. Greenberg, eds., *The Presidential Advisory System* (New York: Harper and Row 1969), 61. It should perhaps be noted that Dawes was probably referring mainly to Cabinet members in charge of *domestic* Departments, with strong program interests and supporting constituencies.

34. Neustadt, "Approaches to Staffing the Presidency: Notes on FDR and JFK" in Altschuler, *Politics*, 119.

35. Quoted in the *New York Times*, August 23, 1973.

36. On "competitive," "collegial," and "formalistic" management patterns in general Presidential decision making, see Richard T. Johnson, "Presidential Style," in Aaron Wildavsky, ed., *Perspectives on the Presidency* (Boston: Little, Brown 1975), 262–300.

37. The discussion will avoid duplication of the more comprehensive organizational proposals on foreign affairs presented in Destler, *Presidents*, chap. 9.

38. See, for example, George, "Case" and "Toward a More Soundly Based Foreign Policy"; Hall, "Custodian-Manager"; and Irving L. Janis, *Victims of Groupthink* (Boston: Houghton Mifflin 1972).

39. See above all Richard Neustadt, *Presidential Power* (New York: Wiley & Sons 1960 and 1964).

40. Quoted in Townsend Hoopes, *The Limits of Intervention* (New York: David McKay 1969), 90.

41. For one contemporary report, see Rowland Evans and Robert Novak, "Foggy Bottom Faces a Trauma," *Los Angeles Times*, August 30, 1971, cited in John S. Esterline and Robert Black, *Inside Foreign Policy* (Palo Alto, Calif.: Mayfield Publishing Company 1975), 231. It refers to an instruction by Secretary Rogers warning against "written memoranda raising questions about such dramatic policies as Mr. Nixon's approach to mainland China."

42. Destler, *Presidents*, 292.

43. Johnson, "National Security Council," 716.

44. Destler, "Comment: Multiple Advocacy: Some Limits and Costs," *American Political Science Review* 66 (September 1972): esp. pp. 787–89.

45. Acheson quoted in Steinbruner, *Cybernetic Theory*, 332.

46. Allison, "Conceptual Models and the Cuban Missile Crisis," *American Political Science Review* 63 (September 1969):711.

47. Hughes, "Relativity in Foreign Policy," *Foreign Affairs* 45 (July 1967):676.

48. Acheson, *Present at the Creation* (New York: Norton 1969), 734.

Discussion Questions

1. How does the structure that a president sets up constrain or enhance his ability to acquire accurate information and affect his ability to make informed decisions?

2. What roles does Destler say the NSC can perform, and what variables affect the determination as to the role chosen?

3. What NSC role would be most appropriate in the current administration? Why?

9

Organizational Interests

Morton H. Halperin

To the extent that participants come to equate national security with the interests of their organization, what stands do they tend to take, and how do these relate to organizational interests? Do organizations always seek to grow larger and do more things? This chapter attempts to specify in detail the organizational interests of the Defense Department, the State Department, the CIA, and their components.

Missions, Capabilities, and Influence

Most organizations have a mission to perform, either overseas or at home, and some organizations need to maintain expensive capabilities in order to perform their missions effectively. All organizations seek influence.

Organizations are formally charged with specific *missions*. Some of these can be accomplished entirely at home (such as maintaining good relations with Congress); others require actions abroad (such as deterring a Soviet attack on the United States).

Participants in a policy decision examine any proposal to gauge whether or not it would help their particular organization carry out its missions. For example, in examining ABM, the Budget Bureau and the Comptroller's Office in the Pentagon were concerned with how it would affect their ability to keep down the military budget. State Department officials were concerned with the impact of deployment on relations with European allies and with the Soviet Union.

The missions of some organizations in the national security field encourage them to maintain substantial and expensive *capabilities* which may be employed abroad. The armed services, for example, are responsible for creating very expensive military forces. Organizations with expensive capabilities will see the face of an issue which affects their ability to maintain what they view as the necessary capability for a variety of actions.

Organizations with expensive capabilities will be particularly concerned about budget decisions and about the budgeting implications of policy decisions.

Organizations with missions but low-cost capabilities will be relatively uncon-
cerned about the budget implications but highly concerned over the immediate
implications of specific policy decisions. This is an important difference between
the armed services and the State Department. The case of ABM illustrates this
point. For the Army ABM meant a bigger budget and a greater role in strategic
warfare. State Department officials, on the other hand, cared much less about
costs and capabilities than about how the decision would affect relations with allies
and potential adversaries. The fact that an ABM system might cost several billion
dollars while an alternative way of reassuring allies might cost very little does not
affect State Department interests, since State neither pays the costs nor operates
the capabilities.

All organizations seek to have *influence* in order to pursue their other objectives. Those that have large operational capabilities seek influence on decisions, in
part, to maintain the capability to perform their mission. Some organizations—the
Office of International Security Affairs in the Office of the Secretary of Defense,
for instance, and the policy planning staff in the State Department—have neither
large capabilities nor stable, clearly defined missions. Their *organizational* goal
tends to be that of gaining influence in pursuit of ideological concerns. Individuals
on these staffs share with their counterparts in other organizations the belief that
they can best judge the nation's security interests. One way or another, pursuit of
influence is felt to be in the national interest. Not only is influence necessary to
protect the organization's other objectives, but senior members of the organization
are considered by its junior members to be peculiarly qualified to advise the President on what is in the national interest.

Stands on issues are affected by the desire to maintain influence. This could
lead to support for certain policies which will require greater reliance on the
organization. Participants prefer courses of action which will require information
from them or which they will be asked to implement. They recognize that they
will gain in influence if such decisions are made. The desire for influence can also
lead organizations to avoid opposing particular policy in the belief that to do so
would reduce their influence on other issues. To develop a reputation for losing
reduces a group's standing with other groups.

Organizational Essence

Organizations have considerable freedom in defining their missions and the capabilities they need to pursue these missions. The organization's *essence* is the view held
by the dominant group in the organization of what the missions and capabilities
should be. Related to this are convictions about what kinds of people with what expertise, experience, and knowledge should be members of the organization.

Career officials generally have a clear notion of what the essence of their
organization is or should be. In some organizations the same view of the essence is

shared by all those in the same promotion and career structure. In other cases there will be differences of view. The differences may concern the particulars of a broader agreed essence or may reflect struggles for dominance. In either case there are often conflicts among subgroups within a single career structure to define the essence of the organization. Struggles over essence and the results for some of the major national security organizations are discussed below.

Air Force

Since its inception as a separate service in the early postwar period, the dominant view within the Air Force has been that its essence is the flying of combat airplanes designed for the delivery of nuclear weapons against targets in the Soviet Union.[1] More recently, this has been challenged by Air Force proponents of ICBMs.

The most serious internal challenge to this definition of the role of the Air Force has come from those officers involved in Tactical Air Command (TAC). Some officers in this group have argued that providing combat air support for the ground forces is an equally important mission. Others assigned to TAC have taken the line that their group can prosper only if it emulates the Strategic Air Command (SAC) by developing an overseas theater-based nuclear delivery capability, what Alain C. Enthoven and K. Wayne Smith have described as a "junior SAC."[2]

TAC officers seeking to enhance the role of their command have had a difficult problem. On the one hand they have been obliged to pay lip service to the formal missions for TAC, and on the other hand they have been tempted to seek to develop capabilities for the role seen as the essence of the Air Force—namely, the combat delivery of nuclear weapons against the Soviet Union. This dilemma shaped the arguments used by the Air Force in an effort to get a new tactical airplane at first called the TFX and in a later version named the F-111. The officer largely responsible for the design of TAC, General F.F. Everest, argued that the TFX was essential to meet the three missions of his command, which were to maintain air superiority, to disrupt enemy supply lines, and to supply close air support. However, the political scientist Robert J. Art in a careful study of the TFX decision reports that General Everest's underlying motives were, in fact, quite different:

> These three missions represented TAC's dogma, to which Everest had to pay lip service. It appears, however, that he was interested primarily in having his new aircraft penetrate enemy defenses at a low level at supersonic speeds while carrying nuclear weapons. The reason Everest wanted such an aircraft is self-evident. In the late 1950's American military doctrine still concentrated primarily on maintaining a strategic nuclear retaliatory capability in order to ensure that deterrence was a credible posture. Under such a doctrine, TAC, as well as the Army, suffered from a relative lack of funds. The Air Force received a large share of the military budget; but within that service, the Strategic Air Command (SAC) received

the preponderant portion of those funds. By trying to acquire a nuclear capability for TAC and by thus providing it with an ability to deliver nuclear weapons in a way that SAC's B-52 bombers could not (by low level, supersonic interdiction), Everest attempted to protect the present identity of and future role for TAC. (The Army did exactly the same thing when it stressed that the United States lacked an ability to fight limited conventional wars. It too used doctrinal arguments as a means of protecting its service identity and share of defense funds.)[3]

The most successful challenge to the Air Force definition of its essence arose because of the development of ICBMs. However, until fairly recently (when those concerned with missiles developed some influence within the Air Force) the impetus for development of missiles came largely from outside the Air Force and was bitterly resisted by officers who continued to give highest priority to the development of combat aircraft. Herbert F. York, former Director of Defense Research and Engineering, reports on the resistance within the Air Force to the decision by the Defense Department to give highest priority to the development of ballistic missiles, following the Soviet Union's successful testing of an ICBM and the launching of Sputnik:

> General Curtis E. LeMay, the man with the cigar, was the commander of the Strategic Air Command (SAC) at the time. As I recall his personal view of the priorities, he placed the B-52H first (it was then called the B-52 Squared) and the B-70 second (it was then called the WS-110). The nuclear airplane (ANP) was somewhere in the middle of his short list, and the long-range missiles were at the bottom. He and other leading Air Force generals managed to make it clear to the contractor that they personally considered the B-70 to be at least as important as the ICBMs, whatever the official priorities might be, and they ordered first flight by the end of 1961.[4]

Sitting in silos just cannot compare to flying bombers.

The high priority given by the Air Force to maintaining its strategic bomber role is shown not only by its resistance to ICBMs but also by its continuing campaign for a nuclear airplane, its advocacy of the B-70 and then the B-1 as a follow-on to the B-52, and its effort in every way possible to extend the flying effectiveness of the B-52.[5] It was this concern that made the Skybolt issue of such critical importance to the Air Force. Skybolt was designed as a missile that would enable bombers to fly toward the Soviet Union and then fire missiles which could penetrate Soviet defenses. In the face of the growing Soviet air defense capability, bombers without missiles were considered too vulnerable. While some argued that Skybolt was no different from an ICBM, in the Air Force view the difference was that Skybolt would be delivered from an airplane, thus enabling Air Force officers to continue their preferred role. The Air Force would continue to have a large intercontinental bomber fleet which was more important to it than the actual mechanism by which the bombs would be dropped.

In the 1960s, with the growing emphasis on non-nuclear forces and increased recognition of inhibitions against using nuclear weapons, the Air Force was forced to choose between continued reliance on nuclear delivery and its ability to play the dominant role as the deliverer of other kinds of weapons against enemy targets. After considerable initial resistance the Air Force finally came around to accepting a non-nuclear role, recognizing that this was the way to maintain its dominance in delivery of weapons by air.[6]

The part of the Air Force that has been least effective in challenging the dominant role of the SAC is the Military Airlift Command (MAC), charged with movement of men and materiel primarily for the Army. In the evaluation of possible alternatives to relieve the blockade of Berlin in 1948 the Air Force bitterly resisted the airlift concept because it would use up all of the planes believed to be necessary for the combat role of the Air Force.[7] After the successful airlift the Air Force failed to exploit this success to enhance its prestige, and the reasons for not capitalizing on the episode related to the top officers' view of the essence of the service, as explained by Paul Y. Hammond:

> Why did the Air Force thus fail fully to exploit the public relations value of the notable achievement of air power in the Berlin airlift? And why did the extraordinary and unexpected experience of the airlift have so little effect upon the developing dispute over roles and missions? Any answers to these questions must be wholly speculative, but some seem possible. The airlift was a freight-carrying operation which served to demonstrate the importance of air transport. But the Air Force has been paring its transport facilities to a minimum in order to maximize its strategic bombing forces. Supporters of strategic air power, the predominant strategic doctrine in the Air Force, might have viewed the airlift as a potential threat to the primary mission of the Air Force, and feared that airlift publicity would only give substance to the charges which had often been voiced in Army circles that the Air Force was neglecting its duty to provide air transport for Army troops. This answer to the first question suggests an answer to the second. Since the airlift was more relevant to Air Force–Army relations than to the Air Force–Navy relations, and since the latter were the ones which were currently raising the inter-service issue of roles and missions, the airlift had no direct relationship to the aviation controversy then developing. Moreover, as has been indicated, boasting about the airlift could have been shared by the British and even the Navy. Sharing of aviation responsibilities was not what the Air Force was trying to enlarge.[8]

Years later in the mid-1960s the Air Force did accept procurement of a large number of C-5A troop-carrying airplanes, but only because the move was forced on it by civilians. When given their own way, the priorities of the Air Force officers have always been clear. Hammond recalls a classic decision made in 1949:

> The Senior Board of the Air Force had convened in late December to consider in closed sessions the procurement program of the Air Force in the light of (1) the

existing situation in aircraft development in the Air Force, particularly the greatly improved performance of the B-36, and (2) the President's stand on the budget. Anticipating the severe cuts in existing and future force strength which the President was determined to make, the Board decided to concentrate the limited resources of the Air Force upon strategic bombing aircraft (i.e., long-range and heavy bombers), in order to make sure that the Air Force could at least fulfill what they regarded as its first responsibility, retaliatory capability. It recommended to the Secretary of the Air Force on January 6 that the procurement of medium bombers (B-45, RB-49), troop transports (C-125), and a new version of the F-86 jet fighter (F-93) be cut back and the money thus saved transferred to purchasing B-36's and B-50's.[9]

To sum up, in taking stands on many strategy and policy questions the Air Force has been guided by the effort to protect its role in the strategic delivery of weapons by air.

Navy

Naval officers agree on the general proposition that the essence of the Navy is to maintain combat ships whose primary mission must be to control the seas against potential enemies. Unlike the Air Force, with SAC usually dominating the other commands, the Navy has been affected by serious dispute among three groups: naval flyers (the brown shoe Navy) emphasize carrier-based air units; seapower advocates (the black shoe Navy) stress the surface Navy; submariners focus on attack submarines. In recent years a fourth group has come to be identified with the Polaris submarines. No senior naval officers see the essence of the Navy as involved in transport, and this function has received relatively little attention.

In the early postwar period, the Navy's struggle was to maintain its capability despite a tight budget and the rise of the Air Force. Naval aviators were locked in a struggle with the Air Force over the relative role of super-carriers and B-36 bombers and, within the Navy, over the relative role to be accorded to carriers in contrast with submarines and conventional ships. Though the carrier admirals argued in debate with the Air Force that the carriers could do a better job of firing nuclear weapons against targets in the Soviet Union, their primary interest was in targets connected with naval warfare such as submarine bases and air bases of planes directed at sea operations. Within the Navy, the struggle was about which kind of force could best carry out the role of dominating the seas. The victory of the carrier admirals was signified by the offer of the Navy to scrap many ships then currently under construction if in return the relatively modest naval budget in the late 1940s might be used to construct super-carriers for the delivery of nuclear weapons.[10] Such thinking has continued to play a large role in Navy calculations, leading to emphasis on aircraft carriers and their missions long after many outside observers concluded that carriers had been rendered obsolete by developments in Soviet naval capabilities.

The most serious challenge to the dominant role of the aircraft carriers came from the proposals first developed by small groups within the Navy to develop a submarine missile-launching capability. Superficially the two roles were the same, since both the carriers and the submarines armed with Polaris missiles could deliver nuclear weapons against the Soviet Union. However, the Polaris missiles, besides being "unpiloted," were primarily directed at the destruction of Soviet cities and played only a very limited role in control of the seas. Thus the carrier advocates in their opposition to Polaris, which would deprive them of aircraft, had the support of much of the rest of the Navy.

Senator Henry M. Jackson reports on his frustration in seeking to win support for the Polaris program within the Navy:

> I was interested in this program from the very outset, going back many, many years. I found that in trying to get the Navy to do something about it, I ran head-long into the competition within the Navy for requirements in connection with their day-to-day operational needs, whether it was anti-submarine warfare or limited war requirements; whatever it was . . . , I was told that this strategic system would just eat away and erode their limited funds. . . . The result was that Polaris was not pushed hard until Sputnik came along.[11]

When the program passed from the R&D stage to that of procurement, the Navy's resistance once again was aroused because of the large amount of funds necessary to procure a substantial number of Polaris submarines. In approaching this problem, the Navy took the stand traditionally taken by the services when civilians seek to force on them programs that they view as contrary to the essence of their activity. As noted by Enthoven and Smith:

> In its budget requests for fiscal years 1961 and 1962, the Navy budgeted for only three Polaris submarines in each year. One of the first things that President Kennedy and Secretary McNamara did when they came into office was to speed up the Polaris program and to authorize the building of ten Polaris submarines in each of these fiscal years. Nobody, to our knowledge, has since questioned the necessity or the wisdom of that action. But at the time, senior Navy officers, when confronted with arguments for increasing the Polaris program based on urgent national need replied: Polaris is a national program, not a Navy program. By this was meant: the Polaris mission is not a traditional Navy mission and therefore should not be financed out of the Navy's share of the defense budget.[12]

Army

Career Army officers agree that the essence of the Army is ground combat capability. They tend to deprive of funds those functions which they view as peripheral, such as advisory roles in Military Assistance Advisory Group (MAAG) missions, air defense, and the so-called "Green Beret" counterinsurgency forces.

In the 1950s, there was considerable dispute among career officers about the degree to which the Army should be organized primarily for nuclear warfare as opposed to conventional ground combat operations. In the early 1960s two battles raged. One, related to the conventional notion of the Army's mission, concerned the role of air mobility. The other concerned the Green Berets: the most determined challenge to the Army's definition of its essence since the separation of the Air Force from the Army.

In the case of air mobility, the issue turned on the degree to which the Army should depend on helicopters as opposed to heavy tanks and artillery. Outside groups pressing for air mobility found considerable support within the Army, particularly from paratroopers, and were able eventually to prevail.

The effort to enhance the role of the Green Berets, though it had much more active high-level support, was considerably less successful. President Kennedy came into office believing that American security would be challenged by guerrilla forces against whom American power would have to be used in limited and quite special ways. He therefore began an effort to develop such a capability within the Army. This ran contrary to the Army's definition of its essence, which involved ground combat by organized regular divisional units, and the Army by and large was able to resist.

Advocates of air and missile defense within the Army have not proclaimed that the element of warfare that interests them should become the dominant form of Army activity. They have merely said that it deserves a partial role, and they have made headway with the argument that the money for air and missile defense would not come from the Army ground combat forces. According to them, the funds would otherwise be spent on equivalent programs of the other services. In the 1950s, faced with growing priority for strategic delivery systems, some Army officers sought to get the Army involved in the deployment of medium-range ballistic missiles. In the 1960s, Army efforts of this sort focused on ABMs. Although these Army programs failed to elicit the all-out commitment aroused by issues believed to affect the organizational essence of the service, there was some steam behind them. The Army, a more eclectic group with many long and differing historical traditions, does have greater tolerance for diverse groups even though its essence remains that of ground combat.

Central Intelligence Agency

CIA career officials are split into three groups according to their notion of what the essence of the agency ought to be. Each group has looked to senior officials in the agency for support of its own notions.

One group, reportedly headed by Richard Helms, director of the CIA during the Johnson and Nixon administrations, emphasizes intelligence collection. This group believes that the primary function of the CIA should be to conduct clandestine operations designed primarily to get information about potentially hostile governments. It also believes the CIA should be involved in limited clandestine efforts in foreign countries to support movements such as labor unions or political parties friendly to the United States.

In contrast, a second group, long headed by Richard Bissell, a former senior CIA official, believes that the CIA should actively intervene in events abroad. This group led the CIA during a period in which it was involved in relatively large-scale operations in Iran and in Guatemala, as well as embarking on the U-2 program and the Bay of Pigs invasion. CIA involvement in Laos and in Vietnam also represents the influence of this group's notion of what the agency's function ought to be.

Still a third group, with considerably less influence, emphasizes intelligence evaluation. It has often been said that the CIA gets 90 percent of its information from public sources, and a large part of its staff is involved in the evaluation of material received from both clandestine and public sources. Members of the third group believe that the conduct of operations jeopardizes the CIA's claim to impartiality and reduces its involvement in policy issues.

Foreign Service

In contrast to career officials in the military services and in the CIA, Foreign Service officers are agreed on the essence of their profession, as they would call it. The basic function of the State Department and hence of the Foreign Service is seen as political reporting about the activities of foreign governments that bear relevance to the United States, general representation of American interests abroad, and negotiation of specific issues when directed by the government.[13] Charles W. Thayer, a Foreign Service officer, notes approvingly the views traditionally held: "Secretary Cordell Hull once said he required four things of his ambassadors: to report what was going on; to represent the United States before foreign governments and publics; to negotiate United States government business; and to look after American lives and property."[14]

Career Foreign Service officers view their enterprise as an elite organization composed of generalists, and they resist the introduction into the department of novel functions and of experts who might be needed to perform those functions. In the immediate postwar period, Foreign Service officers were appalled to discover that various agencies had been disbanded and their personnel assigned to the State Department. They were particularly concerned about the transfer of propaganda officials and intelligence analysts. Robert Murphy, a senior Foreign Service officer, commented on this:

> Meanwhile, in Washington, the weakened Department of State suffered a postwar influx of manpower from unexpected sources, some of it dumped by President Truman and Secretary Byrnes from liquidated war agencies such as the Office of War Information, the Office of Strategic Services, and others. The new employ-

ees arrived—certainly not at the request of the Foreign Service—without qualification examination or security screening, and they created an awkward situation. . . . At the same time greatly increased responsibilities were heaped upon the State Department. Foreign Service officers, no longer limited to orthodox consular and diplomatic activities, were allocated to propaganda, intelligence, and military government, and became involved in many of the conflicts arising from Soviet expansion.[15]

State has continued to resist the transfer to it of such agencies as USIA and AID and in so doing has demonstrated that organizations may oppose expansion instead of seeking it. Still today career officials tend to take the operations of USIA and AID less seriously than traditional functions and to disparage efforts to give State direction and control over them. Only in recent years have career ambassadors, particularly in the field, come to be at all concerned about operations. Many Foreign Service officers resisted the policy ordained in the letter from President Kennedy to ambassadors instructing them that they would have operational control over all programs in their bailiwick, including at least some of those of the Central Intelligence Agency.[16] These officers feared that control over such programs might prove to be embarrassing and would prevent them from focusing on the important functions of reporting and negotiation. A retired Foreign Service officer, Ellis Briggs, expressed this point of view with regard to the functions of an ambassador:

> In theory each ambassador is responsible for all government operations conducted within his jurisdiction. That is a good thing, but in practice it would be manifestly impossible for a chief of mission to accomplish, as ambassador, anything in the way of business with the government to which he is accredited, if in addition he tried personally to supervise all the programs operated in the name of the American government within his bailiwick. Liaison with other agencies is customarily delegated to the ambassador's overworked deputy, who in turn must rely on the senior members of the embassy staff, an appreciable part of whose time is devoted to preventing the representatives of other agencies, who invariably regard themselves as diplomats, from damaging the delicate machinery of international relations.[17]

Career Foreign Service officers view the regional bureaus of the State Department—those dealing with Europe, East Asia, the Near East and South Asia, Africa and Latin America—as the heart of the State Department operations. They believe that the Assistant Secretaries for these regions should be career officials and should have flexibility in managing relations with the relevant countries. They resist the growth of functional bureaus such as those dealing with economics and political-military affairs, in part because such bureaus tend to be dominated by civil servants or in-and-outers rather than by Foreign Service officers. In the early postwar period, State Department officials saw a threat from non-regional bureaus, and the United Nations Bureau in particular worried them because of an influx of non-career officers who had been planning for the UN during the war. After a brief struggle, State's Foreign Service officers were able to confirm their dominance of the department and uphold the regional bureaus, particularly the Bureau of European Affairs.[18]

To the extent that they differ over missions, career diplomatic officials contest the relative priority to be given to different geographic areas. Subgroups within the department do not rally around particular kinds of missions, as in the case of the CIA, so much as they take sides over the relative attention to be given to improving relations with different parts of the world or, in the case of potential enemies, effectively opposing them. There is a West European group, a Soviet group, an "Arabist" group, and groups concerned primarily with African and Latin American affairs. Internal controversy consists of disputes among these groups over particular policy issues.

Enhancement of Essence

An image of the essence of an organization shapes an organization's conception of its interests. The concern with essence is manifest in several ways. (1) An organization favors policies and strategies which its members believe will make the organization as they define it more important. For example, the Air Force some years ago favored the new look strategy which called for reliance on weapons of mass destruction, while the Army favored the strategy of flexible response which implied reliance on conventional ground forces. The State Department in the early postwar period, resisting efforts to rely on the UN and on economic cooperation if such efforts entailed reliance on experts outside the Foreign Service, fought for a policy which would involve direct bilateral diplomatic dealings with the Soviet Union and with the countries of Western Europe.

(2) An organization struggles hardest for the capabilities which it views as necessary to the essence of the organization. It seeks autonomy and funds to pursue the necessary capabilities and missions. Thus long after most experts had concluded that Skybolt was not technically feasible, the Air Force continued to seek the missile as a means of preserving the manned strategic bomber.

(3) An organization resists efforts to take away from it those functions viewed as part of its essence. It will seek to protect these functions by taking on additional functions if it believes that forgoing these added functions may ultimately jeopardize its sole control over the essence of its activities. The Navy and Air Force, for instance, insist on performing the troop transport role for the Army, and the Air Force rejects Army efforts to perform the close air support role. If the Army transported its own troops by sea, it might well build ships which would enable Army troops to come ashore firing—the (not previously discussed) essence of the Marine Corps' activity. In dread of such an "infringement," the Navy demanded that the Army's proposed fast-deployment logistics (FDL) ships be constructed in such a way that they cannot be used for amphibious operations. Failing to kill the medium-

missile program, the Air Force, to cite another example, fought to take on the program itself because it feared that the Army would use the missiles as a foot in the door on the strategic deterrence mission.

(4) An organization is often indifferent to functions not seen as part of its essence or necessary to protect its essence. It tends not to initiate new activities or seek new capabilities even when technology makes them feasible. Thus the Air Force did not press for the adoption of intercontinental ballistic missiles, and the program had to be forced on it from the outside. Similarly, career Foreign Service officers have not championed the use of such techniques as economic aid, propaganda, or military advisory missions. If assigned such functions, organizations will devote as few resources as they can to them. For example, the Air Force and the Navy have devoted limited resources to airlift and sealift techniques while insisting on performing the transport function. Ambitious career officers avoid serving in "unessential" activities. U.S. Army officers in Vietnam, for example, preferred leading troops in combat and serving on a combat staff over advisory assignments.

(5) Sometimes an organization attempts to push a growing function out of its domain entirely. It begrudges expenditures on anything but its chosen activity. It is chary of new personnel with new skills and interests who may seek to dilute or change the organization's essence. For example, the Army after World War II urged the creation of a separate Air Force in the belief that, if this were not done, flyers would come to dominate the Army, changing the conception of its role.[19] Similarly, Foreign Service officers resisted efforts to assign operational responsibility for aid, propaganda, and intelligence functions to the State Department.

In short, an organization will accept new functions only if it believes that to refuse to do so would be to jeopardize its position with senior officials or if it believes that the new function will bring in more funds and give the organization greatest scope to pursue its "own" activities. The military services describe functions not related to their essence as "national programs" rather than service programs and demand that the funding for them be counted outside their regular service budget. For many years, the Navy took this position in relation to the Polaris program, and the Army did so in relation to the ABM.

Roles and Missions

From what has been said so far, it follows that conflicts over roles and missions arise constantly in politics inside the government. Furthermore, fights over roles and missions are particularly acute when they impact on the essence of the contending organizations.

The three classic disputes which divided the military services in the 1940s and continue to divide them now are: (1) the struggle between the Navy and Air Force over naval aviation; (2) that between the Army and Air Force over combat support; and (3) that between the Army and Marines over Marine participation in ground combat operations. Two conflicts pitting the CIA against the older agencies have become equally familiar: (4) the struggle between the CIA and the military over control of combat operations; and (5) that among CIA, State, and the military over the domain of each in intelligence collection and evaluation. Because career officials feel so strongly about the essence of their respective organizations, the conflicts have been intense and have affected stands on issues as well as implementation of decisions. Each of the conflicts is discussed in turn.

Naval Aviation

The depth of feeling in the Navy and the Air Force about the role of naval aviation is reflected in Secretary of Defense James Forrestal's report of a conversation which he had with Air Force General Hoyt Vandenberg in 1948:

> I remarked that there were these fundamental psychoses, both revolving around the use of air power:
>
> (1) The Navy belief, very firmly held and deeply rooted, that the Air Force wants to get control of all aviation;
> (2) The corresponding psychosis of the Air Force that the Navy is trying to encroach upon the strategic air prerogatives of the Air Force.[20]

The intensity of the dispute comes from the fact that each service sees its essence being threatened by the presumed intentions of the other. The Air Force fears that the Navy will seek to expand its air power until it performs a dominant part of the strategic offensive mission. On the other hand, the Navy fears that the Air Force seeks to take over the entire air mission, controlling all airplanes whether based at sea or on land or, at a minimum, all airplanes based on land, even those involving the function of control of the seas.[21]

Some naval aviators trace the fight back to 1925, when the Army Air Force group headed by General William A. Mitchell sought to take over complete control of all air forces. This conflict has raised its head intermittently since then.

In the postwar conflict over unification the Air Force sought to get control over all land-based air operations. This struggle was further exacerbated by the fact that naval air enthusiasts, having recently won the struggle for dominance within the Navy, were not prepared to yield anything to the Air Force. In the end, the controversy over naval aviation became the stumbling block to naval support for unification—support which was necessary to get congressional approval. The issue was finally compromised by President Truman's allowing the Navy authority over aircraft to be used in conjunction with all matters related to control of the sea.

The controversy was not over, however. In 1948, the Air Force argued for the absorption of all naval air into its forces, while the Navy went on the attack by criticizing the effectiveness of Air Force strategic bombers and arguing that supercarriers could more effectively perform the strategic bombing mission. This led to the famous revolt of the admirals: when the Navy was denied authority to build super-carriers, several admirals resigned and took their case to the public.

In the 1950s Navy aviation commanders and the Air Force quarreled about the proposed nuclear-powered airplane. The Air Force, originally uninterested in the project, began to be concerned when the Navy pressed for a nuclear-powered airplane which could fly off aircraft carriers and perform the strategic mission. From then on both services vied for the nuclear-powered airplane despite the increasing evidence that such an aircraft was simply not technologically feasible.[22]

This dispute arose again in connection with the TFX. The Air Force sought a plane which would carry only nuclear weapons and which could carry them over long distances. The Navy, on the contrary, sought a short-takeoff plane with limited range. Robert Art explains:

> The Navy was so insistent because of its own perspectives. It had no real interest in seeing a plane built with such a long ferry range. If missiles had reduced the strategic and interdiction roles of aircraft, including naval aircraft, a plane that could fly across the Atlantic, nonstop, without refueling, and that could be deployed from semiprepared fields would be even more injurious to the Navy's interests: such a plane could only downgrade the role of the aircraft carrier. If it could fly over oceans, there would be no need to transport it over them. If it could operate from semiprepared fields, there would be less need for carriers to stand offshore to service it. On the other hand, the Missileer was the ideal aircraft for the Navy. It would protect the fleet, including the aircraft carriers, from an enemy air attack. It would thereby ensure the safety of aircraft like the F-4H, which were designed to perform tactical missions from aircraft carriers.
>
> Each service thus saw its future threatened by the other's TFX design. The Air Force wanted to extend the life of the airplane. The Navy wanted to do the same for the aircraft carrier. Both knew that the TFX program was going to be costly. Each knew that the supply of defense funds was limited. Neither wanted its future programs jeopardized by those of the other. The result of these opposing perspectives was three months of interminable discussion, delay, and disagreement.[23]

The controversy has also affected combat operations. In Korea and especially in Vietnam the Navy sought as large a role as possible for carrier-based aircraft in an effort to demonstrate that carriers could operate as effectively, if not more effectively, than land-based air power. The Air Force, on the other hand, sought to restrict the role of the Navy (arguing that it could deliver weapons more effectively and more cheaply). This controversy probably led each service to exaggerate the effectiveness of its bombing in order to outshine the other. Neither service has any doubt that in the post-Vietnam period the other service will go after a larger share of the air mission. Inasmuch as both the Air Force and the Navy aviators see as their essence the flying of combat air missions, the conflict between them has been inevitable and has shaped a good deal of the overall rivalry between the two services.

The conflict over missiles, discussed below, has been less intense because it has not touched the essence of either service.

Combat Air Support

In contrast to the Navy, which opposed reunification and favored the status quo, the Army was anxious in the late 1940s to divest itself of its air units in order to protect the essence of its ground combat mission. It was, therefore, in no position to argue very hard about its need to keep some air capability. Thus the Army came to depend on the Air Force not only for transport and interdiction but also for combat support—airplanes which could fly in the immediate vicinity of a battle to give support to infantry.

In the 1950s, the Army began to have second thoughts about its decision. It recognized that the Air Force was giving highest priority to strategic bombardment and therefore neglecting missions of concern to the Army. For the Army, autonomy (discussed below) was at stake, and for the Air Force a potential threat to its essence seemed to be developing. General Matthew B. Ridgway described the situation in the following terms in his memoirs:

> There is an understandable opposition in the Air Force to the development of those types and the procurement of those number of aircraft for which the Army has so vital a need. The helicopter and the converti-plane do not now fit into the pattern of the Air Force's primary missions, or the limitations of its budget. Nor does the young airman want to fly the close-support and assault aircraft—the dive bombers, cargo ships, the transport planes that carry the paratroopers. He wants to fly jets, for that is where the glamour and the glory lies. And I don't find it in my heart to blame him.
>
> But somebody must man these planes and the Army, of course, has considered seeking to relieve the Air Force of its unwanted burden. Plans have been advanced whereby the Army would develop its own specialized assault aircraft, and recruit and train its own pilots to fly them, and to a slight degree this has been done. If neither manpower nor dollars were to be considered, the prospect that the Army will be able to develop its own aviation in the near future is highly improbable.

Ridgway concluded:

> I think perhaps there is a balance to be found somewhere, a reasonable compromise. Of one thing, though, I am sure. To do its job on the battlefield, to gain its objectives in the least time with the least loss of life, the Army must have the support of combat aircraft that can fly in any kind of weather, under all conditions incident to enemy interference, both in the air and from the ground, and deliver its bomb load, or its rockets, on target with the accuracy of a field gun. If the Air Force should develop such planes, we would be deeply pleased. If they continue to ignore our needs in this respect, we eventually will have to develop them ourselves.[24]

Toward the end of the fifties, the Army was pressing an all-out assault on the Air Force control of tactical air. After his retirement as Army Chief of Staff, General Maxwell D. Taylor made public the Army position:

Since 1947, the Army has been dependent upon the Air Force for tactical air support, tactical air lift, and for long-range air transport. Throughout this period, the Army has been a dissatisfied customer, feeling that the Air Force has not fully discharged its obligations undertaken at the time of unification. The Air Force, having something which the Army wanted, has been in a position to put a price upon cooperation and to insist upon acquiescence in Air Force views on such controversial issues as air-ground support procedures, air resupply, and control of air space over the battlefield. As technical improvements in weapons and equipment offered the Army the possibility of escaping from dependence upon the Air Force, the latter has vigorously resisted these efforts and has succeeded in obtaining the support of the Secretary of Defense in imposing limitations on the size and weight of aircraft procured by the Army, on the ranges of Army missiles, and on the radius of Army activities in advance of the front line of combat.

As a result of the controversies arising from the dependence of the Army on the Air Force, the two services have been constantly at loggerheads. They have been unable to agree on a doctrine for cooperation in battle. They are at odds as to the adequacy of levels of Air Force support for the Army, and as to the suitability of types of Air Force equipment to furnish this support. Because of the very high performance of their airplanes, designed primarily to meet the needs of the air battle today, the Air Force is not equipped to discharge its responsibilities to the Army in ground combat. Having witnessed this unhappy state of affairs for over a decade, I am convinced that the Army must be freed from this tutelage and receive all the organic means habitually necessary for prompt and sustained combat on the ground. It should have its own organic tactical air support and tactical air lift, or rather the new weapons and equipment which will perform the functions presently comprehended under those two headings.

Special restrictions of size, weight, and in the case of weapons, of range should be abolished forever and the Army encouraged to exploit technology to the maximum to improve its weapons and equipment habitually necessary for prompt and sustained ground combat. It is essential to end the present fragmentation of the land force function, particularly at a time when the role of land forces should assume increased importance under the strategy of Flexible Response.[25]

In return, Taylor proposed that the Army cede the continental air defense mission to the Air Force. Since this was a mission that neither considered part of its essence, Taylor was not giving up very much, nor would the Air Force see it as much of a compromise.

The Air Force was nevertheless in a bind. Unwilling to devote substantial resources to developments of tactical air power and unwilling to adapt itself to Army requirements for tactical air support, the Air Force found itself without a convincing rebuttal from the national viewpoint.

By the time of Vietnam, the Army was persuading others that it needed to develop its own combat air support. Secretary of Defense McNamara had been pushing air mobility, thereby getting the Army into helicopters to carry troops. Improvements in helicopter technology enabled the Army to begin using support helicopters for combat missions as well as troop transport and so to reduce dependence on the Air Force. Despite the increased attention the Air Force gave to tactical combat operations in response to the Army's encroachment, the Army emerged from the Vietnam War with more pilots than the Air Force and with even greater determination to develop its own organic air capability.

The Role of the Marines

The Marine Corps sees itself as an elite combat unit primarily designed for amphibious operations—that is, the landing of shiploads of armed men under combat conditions against a hostile force. Some Marine Corps officers would like to see their service also take on specialized ground combat operations not involving amphibious operations.

The conflict between the Marine Corps and the Army like that between the Navy and the Air Force goes to the essence of each service. The controversy about the definition of the functions of the Marines and the size of the Corps was a major issue in the unification battle of the late 1940s.

Some Marine Corps officers feared that the Army desired to integrate the Marines into the Army as a specialized unit. If nothing else, the Army sought to limit the Marine Corps to the role of auxiliary to the fleet, with the job of accompanying landing parties to protect Americans during disturbances in foreign countries and in wartime and of providing expeditionary forces to attack bases that were of exclusive interest to the Navy and that could be overcome by small combat units.[26] The principal area of contention then was large amphibious operations. The Marines argued that such operations were more clearly within their scope of activity, while the Army suggested that such operations should come under Army control.

In the mid-1950s the Army, struggling for a limited war strategy, feared that the Navy and the Marine Corps together would seek to take over this mission. The Marines could argue that they were the only integrated force containing its own sea transport and combat air capability and therefore the most effective unit for limited war operations. General Taylor spoke out: "As for the Marines, the Army acknowledges their potential contribution to limited-war situations occurring on or near the coast but resists vigorously any suggestion that the Marines should become a second Army and take over any part of the Army's role of prompt and sustained ground combat.[27]

During the Vietnam War, the Marines were assigned to general combat responsibilities and occupied the I Corps close to the demilitarized zone. In conducting operations in I Corps the Marines were seeking to demonstrate that they could more effectively carry out counterinsurgency operations. The Army, on the other hand, sought to show that Marines because of their independence could not be effectively fitted into an Army chain of command. This debate probably affected the Army unwillingness to adopt the strategy of combined action patrols pioneered by the Marine Corps and may also have affected the decision by General Westmoreland to assign the Marines the highly difficult task of defending the Khe Sanh base, close to the demilitarized zone.[28]

The Question of the CIA

The CIA frequently collides with the military services over the conduct of relatively large-scale covert operations and intelligence gathering programs. These operations go to the heart of the CIA mission as conceived by many of its career personnel and yet arouse the misgivings of the Pentagon about creating an alternative military capability. The debate is largely carried on behind closed doors but came out into the open in the controversies surrounding the Bay of Pigs invasion, the Cuban missile crisis, and U.S. actions in Indochina.

The CIA had responsibility for training the Cuban forces to be used in the Bay of Pigs invasion and for planning the military operations. The Joint Chiefs gave only cursory review to the plans and later were in a position to argue that the operations had been botched by the CIA. As a result, President Kennedy turned responsibility for such operations over to the Pentagon.[29]

In the opening days of the Cuban missile crisis, the military services, particularly the Air Force, challenged the CIA's control of U-2 flights over Cuba. As long as U-2s were used in relatively peaceful situations in which the likelihood of combat was small, the Air Force was more or less content to have the CIA manage the program. However, as the possibility of conflict heated up in the Caribbean, the U-2 forays began to look more and more to the Air Force like a separate air arm, and a campaign was mounted which ultimately succeeded in taking the function way from the CIA.

The dispute over U.S. operations in Indochina centered upon CIA influence over the Montagnards and other irregular forces in Laos and South Vietnam. Early in the 1960s, the military apparently succeeded in having the Special Forces take over arrangements with the Montagnards, but the CIA seems to have counteracted by gaining substantial influence over the Special Forces themselves.[30]

Other Conflicts

From time to time, new technological developments have produced other role and mission conflicts among the services, often overlapping with the ongoing disputes described above. In the early postwar period the development of nuclear weapons produced a fight as to whom these weapons would be assigned. The Air Force originally had a virtual monopoly on nuclear weapons. This control was first challenged successfully by the Navy on the grounds that its carriers could effectively deliver such weapons; later the Army introduced tactical nuclear weapons which would be supplied to ground forces.

The development of strategic missiles also produced controversy over roles and missions, although it lacked the intensity of the other fights because it did not go to the essence of any of the services. The Air Force, however, did see some infringement on its strategic primacy. It tried for a while, but without success, to prevent the development of the Polaris submarine force (a program pushed by the civilian analysts and the scientists rather than by the Navy itself). The Air Force was more successful in resisting the Army's effort to enter into the strategic offensive realm through the development of medium-range missiles. For a time, both services had medium-range missile programs, but the Air Force was able to secure authority over the development of such weapons.[31]

All three services competed for a role in space exploration, with the Air Force first getting the upper hand and then losing status in regard to the newly created National Aeronautics and Space Administration (NASA) in 1957. The Air Force is now engaged in a conflict with NASA over the relative roles of the two agencies in the space program. It has also sought to recoup by infiltrating NASA itself with active duty Air Force officers.

Implications of Roles and Missions

The conflict over roles and missions, particularly as it relates to the essence of each agency's activity, produces several characteristic forms of behavior in the pursuit of organizational interest.

1. Disputes over roles and missions affect the information reported to senior officials.

For example, according to a former Air Force intelligence officer, both the Air Force and the Navy exaggerated the effectiveness of their bombing of North Vietnam. Both recognized that the postwar dispute over the Navy's bombing role would be affected by evaluation of their bombing operations in Vietnam. Each, believing (or fearing) that the other service would exaggerate, decided to emphasize the positive in order to protect its position.[32]

2. In implementing missions which they know to be coveted by another organization, organizations may bend over backward to avoid giving reason to increase their bureaucratic competitor's share of the responsibility.

Townsend Hoopes, who was then Under Secretary of the Air Force, reports that he saw this process at work in the Air Force request for an additional 17 tactical fighter squadrons as part of a proposed increase in American forces in Vietnam in March 1968 following the Tet offensive:

> Moreover, it was a matter of some delicacy in Army–Air Force relations because it touched the boundary line between the assigned roles and missions of the two Ser-

vices. If the Air Force did not provide close air support in a ratio satisfactory to the Army, that would strengthen the Army's argument for developing its own means of close support. Already, through the development of helicopter gunships of increasing power, speed, and sophistication, the Army had pressed against that boundary."[33]

3. In periods of crisis, career officials calculate how alternative policies and patterns of action will affect future definitions of roles and missions.

Participants have learned over time that changes in roles and missions frequently occur during crises. Thus an organization concerned about its mission and desiring either to expand it or prevent others from expanding theirs at its cost will be particularly alert to both challenges and opportunities during a crisis. Because this phenomenon is widely understood, organizations must be on guard: they cannot trust other organizations not to take advantage of a crisis situation. Frequently, an organization whose functions were expanded during a crisis tries to argue that it has now established a precedent and should continue to perform the new function. Thus organizations seldom put forward options which might lead to changes in roles and missions to their detriment. If suggested by other participants, they may argue that such options are infeasible. Participants may also feel obliged to distort information reported to senior officials in order to guard against the danger that it will in the future affect roles and missions. Disputes over roles and missions also affect policy stands and the way policy decisions are implemented.

During the Cuban missile crisis, for example, both the CIA and the military services were concerned with how intelligence operations during the crisis would affect future definitions of roles and missions. A key episode is described by Graham Allison:

> The ten-day delay between decision [to direct a special flight over western Cuba] and flight is another organizational story. At the October 4 meeting, where the decision to dispatch the flight over western Cuba was made, the State Department spelled out the consequences of the loss of a U-2 over Cuba in the strongest terms. The Defense Department took this opportunity to raise an issue important to its concerns. Given the increased danger that a U-2 would be downed, the pilots should be officers in uniform rather than CIA agents, so the Air Force should assume responsibility for U-2 flights over Cuba. To the contrary, the CIA argued that this was an intelligence operation and thus within the CIA's jurisdiction. Besides, CIA U-2s had been modified in certain ways that gave them advantages over Air Force U-2s in avoiding Soviet SAMs. Five days passed while the State Department pressed for less risky alternatives, and the Air Force (in Department of Defense guise) and the CIA engaged in territorial disputes. On October 9, COMOR [the Committee on Overhead Reconnaissance] approved a flight plan over San Cristobal, but, to the CIA's dismay, the Air Force rather than the CIA would take charge of the mission. At this point details become sketchy, but several members of the intelligence community have speculated that an Air Force pilot in an Air Force U-2 attempted a high altitude overflight on October 9 that

"flamed out," i.e., lost power, and thus had to descend in order to restart its engine. A second round between Air Force and CIA followed, as a result of which Air Force pilots were trained to fly CIA U-2s. A successful overflight did not take place until October 14.[34]

Autonomy

Career officials of an organization believe that they are in a better position than others to determine what capabilities they should have and how they should best fulfill their mission. They attach very high priority to controlling their own resources so that these can be used to support the essence of the organization. They wish to be in a position to spend money allocated to them in the way they choose, to station their manpower as they choose, and to implement policy in their own fashion. They resist efforts by senior officials to get control of their activities.

In particular, priority is attached to maintaining control over budgets. Organizations are often prepared to accept less money with greater control rather than more money with less control. Even with the smaller funds they are able to protect the essence of their activities. The priority attached to autonomy is shown by the experiences of two recent Secretaries of Defense. Robert McNamara caused great consternation in the Pentagon in 1961 by instituting new decision procedures which reduced the autonomy of the services, despite the fact that he increased defense spending by $6 billion and did not directly seek to alter the roles and missions of the various services. Melvin P. Laird, in contrast, improved Pentagon morale in 1969 by increasing service autonomy in budget matters while reducing the defense budget by more than $4 billion.

Organizations also seek total operational control over the forces required to carry out a mission of other organizations. To avoid encroachment by other agencies, they seek to report directly to the President, in hopes that this will mean infrequent interference in their affairs. For example, the Office of Strategic Services pressed hard at the end of World War II for the creation of a Central Intelligence Agency which would no longer be subordinate to the Joint Chiefs of Staff but would report directly to the President.

The quest for autonomy also leads organizations to resist operations in which control must be shared with foreign governments. This leads the military services to seek bases under U.S. control and to resist integrated forces.

We have already mentioned that the quest for autonomy on the part of the military services affected the unification struggle in the late 1940s. The Air Force drive for existence as a separate service was fundamentally a quest for autonomy. Air Force doctrine and strategy were stated in terms which would justify autonomy.[35] The Navy resisted the unification plan precisely because it saw the plan as a threat to its autonomy. Fearing that the Air Force would use the integrated structure in an effort to dominate the other services, the Navy argued that the Secretary of Defense should be coordinator of the services and not have operational control over them. The Army was in a dilemma: it had to choose between autonomy for its operations by maintaining an integrated combat air arm or give this up in order to prevent the Air Force officers from coming to dominate the Army. It chose to "let the Air Force go" in order to maintain autonomy over its favored field of action—ground combat operations; since then it has been struggling to regain some air capability.

The State Department's quest for autonomy has led it to reject White House interference in its ongoing operations and to resist non-career ambassadors as well as presidential envoys.

The quest for autonomy has a significant impact on the stands and actions of organizations. The following patterns show up repeatedly.

1. In negotiations among organizations about desirable actions, each prefers an agreement which leaves it free to pursue its own interests even if this appears to an outside observer to lead to an uncoordinated and hence inefficient policy. Thus both the Air Force and the Navy prefer the situation in which the Polaris missiles are controlled independently of the Air Force missiles and strategic bombers. Each service developed its own strategic doctrine and its own targeting. Both services, but especially the Navy, have resisted efforts to create an integrated command, and only with great reluctance did the Navy acquiesce in a joint strategic targeting organization set up under intense civilian pressure in the early 1960s. In Vietnam, the services conducted largely independent combat operations with each service getting a share of the target areas. Each preferred this to an overall plan that would limit its autonomy.

The State Department has frequently maintained its autonomy in the conduct of diplomatic negotiations and political relations with foreign governments by leaving the Treasury Department and the foreign aid agencies free to conduct their own bilateral negotiations and arrangements on trade and aid matters.

2. In devising options for senior officials, organizations tend to agree on proposals which exclude any joint operations and which leave each free to go its own way and continue to do what it prefers to do. As one keen student of the Washington bureaucracy has observed:

> Over time, each agency has acquired certain "pet projects" which its senior officials promote. These are often carried out by one agency despite concern and even mid-level opposition from others, as part of a tacit trade-off: "We'll let you do your thing, and you let us do ours." Such deals, or "non-aggression treaties," are almost never explicit, but are nonetheless well understood by the participants. The results from such arrangements obviously vary. Sometimes programs are in direct conflict. Waste and duplication are frequent; lack of information about what one's colleagues are doing is common. These are all direct costs of the multi-agency system, which is too large and scattered to come under one driver.[36]

In budgetary negotiations, organizations most often seek a compromise by which subordinate officials are committed to set limits but are free to spend money within that limit.

3. In presenting policy proposals to senior officials, organizations typically indicate that the proposed course of action is infeasible unless they are given full freedom to carry it out. During the 1958 Quemoy crisis the Joint Chiefs of Staff repeatedly pressed for freedom to use nuclear weapons on their own authority. They informed the President that they could guarantee to defend the offshore islands against the Chinese attack only if granted this autonomy.[37] In developing their preferred overseas base structure, the armed forces are particularly concerned with their freedom to conduct operations without the interference of allied governments. This leads them to insist upon the need for unambiguous U.S. control over bases, as they did in the case of the Trust Territories in the Pacific and for many years in the case of Okinawa. Where this is not feasible, the military press for bases in countries which they judge are unlikely to object to any operations they wish to conduct. This was apparently a major motive for the military's efforts to develop bases in Spain.[38]

4. Organizations seek to guard their autonomy by presenting to the President or Cabinet officials only a single option so that he cannot choose among options interfering with their preferred course of action. U. Alexis Johnson, for many years the senior State Department Foreign Service Officer, has said that he objected to President Kennedy's introduction of procedures that prevented the Secretary of State and the Secretary of Defense from conferring with each other and arriving at a consensus before meeting with the President.[39]

Organizational Morale

An organization functions effectively only if its personnel are highly motivated. They must believe that what they are doing makes a difference and promotes the national interest; that the organization's efforts are appreciated and that its role in the scheme of things is not diminishing (and preferably is increasing); and that the organization controls its own resources. Above all the career official must believe that there is room for advancement in the organization and that the organization is seeking to protect his opportunities for advancement. In order to keep open promotions to top positions, an organization resists efforts to contract the size of the organization (unless the contraction is necessary to protect the essence of its activities). It also strives to assure that top jobs are held primarily by career officials of its service. Thus the Foreign Service generally opposes the appointment of non-career ambassadors, although it has learned to accept some non-career appointees as inevitable. The military services struggle for the post of Chairman of the Joint

Chiefs as well as positions which put their representatives in charge of integrated commands (such as the Commander-in-Chief in Europe and the Commander-in-Chief in the Pacific). They oppose efforts to close out functions which would mean a reduction in the number of senior personnel.

Career personnel are assigned so as to appear to give everyone a reasonable chance of promotion rather than to put people in the slots where they are likely to do the most good. Military officers compete for roles in what is seen as the essence of the services' activity rather than other functions where promotion is less likely. Thus the commander of the ill-fated *Pueblo* tells us of his great disappointment at being appointed commander of that ship rather than of a submarine.[40] So, too, Army officers compete for roles in combat organizations rather than advisory missions. Foreign Service officers seek assignments in political sections and on regional desks in the department rather than in economic sections or in specialized bureaus.

An organization resists functions which it believes may interfere with career patterns either by bringing in people who would not be eligible for the top spots or bringing in people who would, because of their senior rank, fill the top spots and foreclose advancement for others. Both of these considerations affected the Air Force's decision not to fight for the air defense mission at the time of the separation of the Air Force from the Army.[41]

Organizations also seek to maintain morale by laying down modes of conduct for their staff members which avoid conflict within the group. Andrew M. Scott reports, for example, a series of injunctions about how Foreign Service officers are to deal with each other: "Play the game, don't rock the boat, don't make waves, minimize risk taking."[42]

Organizations may also seek to maintain morale by seeking a homogeneous group of career officials. According to research cited by Harold Seidman, both the military services and the foreign service are relatively homogeneous although the two groups differ in terms of the area of the country from which they incline to draw their personnel.[43]

Because they have learned the vital importance of morale for the effective functioning of an organization, bureaucrats give close attention to the likely effects of any change of policy or patterns of action on the morale of the organization, and they shun changes which they feel will have a severe effect on morale. Even changes which would probably improve the organization's effectiveness in carrying out its mission may be resisted if officials believe that such actions would severely affect the morale of the organization. In particular, they will be concerned about the effects on the promotion patterns of the organization. Short-run accomplishments of goals and even increases in budgets take second place to the long-run health of the organization.

For example, almost every observer of U.S. operations in Vietnam concluded that extending the tour of duty of commissioned Army officers from one year to two or three years would substantially improve the U.S. military performance. Yet the Army refused to make this change. This is not because the Army differed with the assessment that there would be an improvement in effectiveness. Rather, the Army believed that there would be immediate adverse effects on morale if officers were sent to Vietnam either for an indefinite period or for a prolonged period such as three years; and, particularly in the early stages of the war, Army leaders felt that there would be long-range morale problems if only a small percentage of career Army officers had combat experience in Vietnam, since those officers who did would have an inside track on the promotions. They believed it desirable not only for morale but also for improving the effectiveness of the service over the long run to give as many career officers as possible experience in Vietnam.[44]

Budgets

Career officials examine any proposal for its effect on the budget of their organization. All other things being equal, they prefer larger to smaller budgets and support policy changes which they believe will lead to larger budgets.

There is, however, a substantial asymmetry between the Department of Defense and the Department of State in regard to the impact of policy issues on budgets. The State Department budget is relatively small, and very few of the foreign policy matters with which the State Department deals have any direct effect on its budget. For the military services, most policy issues are likely to have important budgetary implications. For example, the ABM had no implications for the State Department budget, but it had very important consequences for the budget of the Army and the Defense Department as a whole.

An organization is usually quick to question whether a proposed change which generates a new function will in fact lead to a budget increase or merely add to its responsibilities without any corresponding increase in its budget. The calculation of whether or not a new function will lead to an increased budget depends in part upon the nature of the budget-making process. For example, during the 1950s the budgets for the military services were largely determined by allocating fixed percentages of an overall budgetary ceiling established by the President. In general, new responsibilities had to be financed out of existing budgetary levels. By contrast, during the 1960s there was at least no explicit budgetary ceiling. The budget was determined by the Secretary of Defense on the basis of functional categories and responsibilities. Thus the services believed that new functions tended to mean increased budget levels.

Whether a new function will lead to new funds, and hence should be desired, or to a reallocation of old funds, which may need to be resisted, depends in part also on whether the new function is seen as closely related to existing functions. For example, the Army was interested in acquiring responsibility for the deployment of medium-range ballistic missiles (MRBMs) in the 1950s, in part because this would justify altering the existing percentages so as to increase its share of the overall defense budget, since the existing allocation was based on the Army having no strategic function. On the other hand, the Air Force recognized that MRBM would simply be considered another strategic weapon and that it would be forced to finance development and deployment out of existing budget funds. Thus, in terms of budgetary interests, the Army sought the MRBM role, while the Air Force was reluctant to take it on. Concern with protecting its existing roles and missions, on the other hand, meant that if there was to be an MRBM program, the Air Force was determined to have it.

Organizations are vigilant not only about their absolute share of the budget but also about their relative share of a larger budget. This proposition applies particularly to each of the military services, although it may also apply to parts of the AID organization. They fear that once established levels change in an adverse direction, the trend may continue, leading to substantial reductions in the activities of a particular service, which could have substantial effects on morale.

As a precaution, each of the services tends to resist proposals which, though promising more funds, may lead to a less than proportionate increase in its budget as compared with other parts of the defense establishment. The services individually prefer the certainty of a particular share of the budget to an unknown situation in which budgets may increase but shares may change. For example, in 1957, the Gaither Committee appointed by President Eisenhower recommended substantial increases in the budgets of all three services, arguing the need for secure second-strike retaliatory forces and for larger limited-war capabilities. However, none of the services supported these proposals, in part because none was certain how the expanded budget would be divided.[45]

Organizational Stands

Participants who look to organizational interests to define national security interests seldom feel the need to engage in a full-scale analysis of a particular issue. Rather, their reactions reflect "grooved thinking"—responding to a particular stimulus in a set way. This leads to typical patterns of stands by organizations. We have already referred to the traditional State Department opposition to negotiations by presidential emissaries or the President himself and its opposition to proposals which would appear to require the State Department to involve itself in direct intervention abroad. In negotiations, State typically presses for the talks to be kept going and for concessions to be made to the other side in hopes that counterconcessions will be offered in turn.

Each military service supports foreign policies which will justify the forces it believes are necessary for the essence of the service and favors strategies which presume that precisely those forces will be the ones used in the event of hostilities. Each opposes mixed forces or combined service operations. The military usually also support proposals which will give them new equipment. They tend to emphasize the procurement of forces and of overall force structure even at the cost of combat readiness and real combat capability.[46]

The military view issues involving American bases overseas in terms of the interests of their own organizations. Each service favors the retention of the bases which it uses and which suit a military strategy that accords with its force structure. Senior officers are particularly sensitive to possible actions which might jeopardize their bases. According to Arthur Schlesinger, Jr., Secretary of State Dean Rusk discovered this when he proposed that the Bay of Pigs invasion be transferred to the American naval base at Guantánamo.

> He [Rusk] reverted to a suggestion with which he had startled the Joint Chiefs during one of the meetings. This was that the operation fan out from Guantánamo with the prospect of retreating to the base in case of failure. He remarked, "It is interesting to observe the Pentagon people. They are perfectly willing to put the President's head on the block, but they recoil from the idea of doing anything which might risk Guantánamo."[47]

In assessing what forces a friendly country should be encouraged to maintain, the military prefer an organization similar to their own. Thus the Army will be concerned about allied ground forces, the Navy with fleets, and the Air Force with the air arm. They urge the buildup of sister forces and the provision of aid for that purpose.[48]

The "sister service" approach extends to the composition of international forces. In the debates in the United Nations Security Council Committee on the Composition of an International Military Force, the American Air Force representative argued that the contribution of the great powers should be entirely in air forces, while the Army representative, General Ridgway, argued that the United States should contribute ground forces.[49] The same philosophy applies to estimates of enemy forces, each service stressing that the enemy has been building up in its area.

In the eyes of American officers, the best way to build up a "sister service" abroad is to supply American training and advisers. Without these, military aid may be useless, they feel.[50] As for the proper size of a military assistance program, in their estimation that depends upon whether military aid will be subtracted from their own service budgets or added on.

The attitude of the military services toward commitments and the use of force is surprising to observers who expect a bellicose outlook. In general, the military oppose new commitments for the United States and have in general been opposed to, or neutral on, postwar American interventions. (On the other hand, when interventions do occur, the services push for authority to employ the full range of available forces.)

The services are often reluctant to take on new commitments, feeling that their forces are already stretched too thin. With regard to allies, they tend to see the defense of Western Europe against a Soviet attack as the main commitment. The military have learned that the allocations given to them do not necessarily correspond to the number of commitments that the United States undertakes, and therefore they see new commitments as adding new obligations on them without yielding additional forces. Dean Acheson relates a typical example from the era when the French wanted help to hold on to Indochina:

> As the year wore on without much progress and we ourselves became bogged down in the negotiations at Panmunjom, our sense of frustration grew. A review of the situation in late August, before I left for a series of meetings in the autumn of 1951, brought warning from the Joint Chiefs of Staff against any statement that would commit—or seem to the French under future eventualities to commit— United States armed forces to Indochina. We did not waver from this policy.[51]

On the issue of American military intervention, the armed services have been in general quite cautious. At different times they have resisted proposals for intervention, remained neutral, or asked for authority to use all their existing forces to make the gamble of involvement less risky if taken at all. Professionally they prefer a conservative estimate of the readiness of forces, and they are sensitive to the danger of using forces where they might be defeated or where they would be drawn away from the primary theater of operations. This military attitude first manifested itself during the Berlin crisis of 1948. General Lucius Clay, who had direct responsibility for Berlin, favored the sending of an armed convoy down the road from the American zone of Germany to Berlin. President Harry S Truman was prepared to support this proposal if it won the endorsement of the Joint Chiefs. The Chiefs, however, refused to recommend such action. Moreover, the Air Force was itself opposed even to the airlift.[52]

At the time of the outbreak of the Korean War in June 1950, the military made no recommendation for intervention. Indeed, the top commanders were known to believe that though Taiwan was vital to the security of the United States, Korea was not. Consequently Truman was forced to agree to defend Taiwan as the price of gaining military acquiescence in the Korean intervention. The military were not the driving force in planning the Bay of Pigs operation, which was largely a CIA endeavor. In the case of the possibility of intervention in Laos in 1961, the military were opposed unless granted full authority to use all forces. They also pressed for an all-out strike if there were to be any action against Cuba in 1962. The services were not the driving force behind the American involvement in Vietnam.

Paradoxically, however, military reluctance to enter into half-hearted or ill-backed commitments leads to the opposite of caution once intervention begins. As soon as the United States committed itself to the defense of South Korea, the Joint Chiefs pressed for a rapid buildup of American forces. Similarly in the case of Vietnam, the Joint Chiefs pressed for a larger, quicker buildup and for attacks on North Vietnam.

In particular, the services have pressed for the right to use nuclear weapons in any military conflict. The first such effort came during the Berlin blockade when the military, supported by Secretary of Defense James Forrestal, pressed the President to agree that the atomic bomb would be used if necessary.[53] President Eisenhower did make a generalized decision that the armed forces could plan on the use of nuclear weapons in the event of conflict.[54] But he resisted pressure to delegate authority in any particular crisis. The military nonetheless continued to press him—for example, during the Quemoy crisis of 1958.[55] The Joint Chiefs pushed hard for advance authority to use nuclear weapons when the Kennedy administration was considering intervention in Laos in 1961.[56]

This chapter is [quite long], and the reader may feel somewhat uncertain as to why so much detail has been provided. Recall that our purpose was to explain organizational interests. Career officials, including those who will come to head organizations such as the Joint Chiefs of Staff, often develop their position largely by calculating the national interest in terms of the organizational interests of the career service to which they belong. Even in-and-outers are sometimes "captured" by the organizations which bring them into government. It is necessary to understand the details of these interests if one is to avoid the erroneous notion that organizations simply seek to grow in size. The details of organizational interests, the essence of groups as defined by the members, and the competition of groups over roles and missions are likely to be unfamiliar to readers, and they are important in understanding how a large number of participants come to see issues and what motivates the stands they take.

Notes

1. For an excellent description of the Air Force's push for autonomy and choice of the strategic delivery of nuclear weapons by air as its prime mission, see Perry McCoy Smith, *The Air Force Plans for Peace, 1943-1945* (Baltimore: Johns Hopkins Press, 1970), esp. pp. 23-25, 97.

2. Alain C. Enthoven and K. Wayne Smith, *How Much Is Enough?* (New York: Harper and Row, 1971), p. 9.

3. Robert J. Art, *The TFX Decision* (Boston: Little, Brown, 1968), p. 16.

4. Herbert F. York, *Race to Oblivion: A Participant's View of the Arms Race* (New York: Simon and Shuster, 1970), p. 53.

5. See ibid., pp. 60-74; W. Henry Lambright, *Shooting Down the Nuclear Plane* (Indianapolis: Bobbs-Merrill, 1967), p. 10.

6. Theodore C. Sorensen, *Kennedy* (New York: Harper and Row, 1968), p. 588.

7. Robert Murphy, *Diplomat among Warriors* (New York: Doubleday, 1964), p. 318.

8. Paul Y. Hammond, "Super Carriers and B-36 Bombers," in Harold Stein (ed.), *American Civil Military Decisions* (Birmingham: Univ. of Alabama Press, 1963), p. 485.

9. Ibid., p. 489-90.

10. Ibid., p. 470.

11. Senator Jackson, quoted in Michael H. Armacost, *The Politics of Weapons Innovation* (New York: Columbia Univ. Press, 1969), pp. 65-66.

12. Enthoven and Smith, *How Much Is Enough?* pp. 16-17.

13. John Ensor Harr, *The Professional Diplomat* (Princeton: Princeton Univ. Press, 1969), pp. 35–40, 43–44, 243–44; Smith Simpson, *Anatomy of the State Department* (Boston: Beacon Press, 1967), p. 3; and Andrew M. Scott, "The Department of State: Formal Organization and Informal Culture," *International Studies Quarterly*, 13 (March 1969), p. 3.

14. Charles W. Thayer, *Diplomat* (New York: Harper Brothers, 1959), p. 81.

15. Murphy, *Diplomat among Warriors*, pp. 451–52 (italics added).

16. (Jackson) Subcommittee on National Security Staffing, *Administration of National Security: Selected Papers*. Hearings. 87 Cong. 2 sess. (Washington: Government Printing Office, 1962), pp. 8–10.

17. Ellis Briggs, *Farewell to Foggy Bottom: The Recollections of a Career Diplomat* (New York: McKay, 1964), p. 166.

18. Martin Wishnatsky, "Symbolic Politics and the Origins of the Cold War," paper prepared for the 67th annual meeting of the American Political Science Association, 1971, pp. 3–5.

19. Smith, *The Air Force Plans for Peace*, p. 19.

20. Walter Millis (ed.), with E.S. Duffield, *The Forrestal Diaries* (New York: Viking, 1951), p. 66. Cited hereafter as *Forrestal Diaries*.

21. On the controversy between the Navy and the Air Force over air power, see ibid., pp. 222–26, 228–29; Demetrios Caraley, *The Politics of Military Unification* (New York: Columbia Univ. Press, 1966), pp. 79, 96; and Hammond, "Super Carriers and B-36 Bombers," pp. 488, 533–39.

22. Lambright, *Shooting Down the Nuclear Plane*, pp. 9, 13–14.

23. Art, *The TFX Decision*, p. 46.

24. Matthew B. Ridgway, *Soldier* (New York: Harper Brothers, 1956), pp. 314–15.

25. Maxwell D. Taylor, *The Uncertain Trumpet* (New York: Harper Brothers, 1959), pp. 168–70.

26. Caraley, *The Politics of Military Unification*, p. 67. See also *Forrestal Diaries*, pp. 224–25, and Hammond, "Super Carriers and B-26 Bombers," pp. 529–30.

27. Taylor, *The Uncertain Trumpet*, p. 100.

28. William R. Corson, *The Betrayal* (New York: W.W. Norton, 1968), pp. 77–80.

29. Sorensen, *Kennedy*, p. 630.

30. Roger Hilsman, *To Move a Nation: The Politics of Foreign Policy in the Administration of John F. Kennedy* (New York: Doubleday, 1967), p. 455.

31. Armacost, *The Politics of Weapons Innovation*, p. 63.

32. Morris J. Blachman, "The Stupidity of Intelligence," in Charles Peder and Timothy J. Adams (eds.), *Inside the System: A Washington Monthly Reader* (New York: Praeger, 1970), pp. 271–279.

33. Townsend Hoopes, *The Limits of Intervention* (New York: McKay, 1969), pp. 161–62.

34. Graham Allison, *Essence of Decision* (Boston: Little, Brown, 1971), pp. 122–23.

35. Smith, *The Air Force Plans for Peace*, pp. 14, 27, 28.

36. Richard Holbrooke, "The Machine That Fails," *Foreign Policy*, no. 1 (Winter 1970–71), p. 70.

37. Dwight D. Eisenhower, *The White House Years*, vol. 2: *Waging Peace, 1956–1961* (New York: Doubleday, 1965), p. 299. Cited hereafter as *Waging Peace*.

38. Theodore J. Lowi, "Bases in Spain," in Stein, *American Civil Military Decisions*, pp. 677–78.

39. U. Alexis Johnson, John F. Kennedy Library Oral History Interview, pp. 14–15. See also Arthur M. Schlesinger, Jr., *A Thousand Days: John F. Kennedy in the White House* (Boston: Houghton Mifflin, 1965), p. 557, and Scott, "The Department of State," p. 6.

40. Lloyd M. Bucher, *Bucher: My Story* (New York: Doubleday, 1970), pp. 2–3.

41. Smith, *The Air Force Plans for Peace*, pp. 101–2.

42. Scott, "The Department of State," p. 4. See also Chris Argyris, *Some Causes of Organizational Ineffectiveness within the Department of State* (Washington: Government Printing Office, 1967), pp. 1–9.

43. Harold Seidman, *Politics, Position, and Power: The Dynamics of Federal Organization* (New York: Oxford Univ. Press, 1970), p. 113.

44. Adam Yarmolinsky, *The Military Establishment* (New York: Harper and Row, 1971), p. 20; Seymour M. Hersh, *My Lai 4: A Report on the Massacre and Its Aftermath* (New York: Random House, 1970), p. 6.

45. Morton H. Halperin, "The Gaither Committee and the Policy Process," *World Politics*, 13 (April 1961), pp. 360–84.

46. Enthoven and Smith, *How Much is Enough?* pp. 10–11.

47. Schlesinger, *A Thousand Days*, p. 257.

48. For examples of this attitude, see Laurence Martin, "The American Decision to Rearm Germany," in Stein, *American Civil-Military Decisions*, p. 649; Arthur J. Dommen, *Conflict in Laos* (New York: Praeger, 1964), p. 101.

49. Ridgway, *Soldier*, pp. 169–70.

50. Dean Acheson, *Present at the Creation: My Years in the State Department* (New York: W.W. Norton, 1969), pp. 331, 661.

51. Ibid., p. 675.

52. Murphy, *Diplomat among Warriors*, p. 316; Truman, *Memoirs*, vol. 2: *Years of Trial and Hope*, pp. 124–26.

53. David E. Lilienthal, *The Journals of David E. Lilienthal*, vol. 2: *The Atomic Energy Years, 1945–1950* (New York: Harper and Row, 1964), p. 406.

54. Glenn Snyder, "The 'New Look' of 1953," in Warner Schilling, Paul Hammond, and Glenn Snyder (eds.), *Strategy, Politics, and Defense Budgets* (New York: Columbia Univ. Press, 1962), pp. 427, 433–35.

55. Eisenhower, *Waging Peace*, p. 299.

56. Hilsman, *To Move a Nation*, pp. 129, 133–34; Schlesinger, *A Thousand Days*, pp. 338–39.

Discussion Questions

1. How does the bureaucratic structure of the government enhance or limit the ability of the president to plan and implement foreign policy?

2. Do organizational interests always run counter to national security interests? Why or why not?

3. How would you characterize the organizational essence of the various actors in the national security system?

10

The Role of the Joint Chiefs of Staff

John G. Kester

The Original Understanding

The decline in JCS influence on national security policy can be dated from 1947, the year when the Joint Chiefs of Staff were established by law. There had been a JCS organization before, its genesis in the Combined Chiefs of Staff set up by Roosevelt and Churchill early in 1942 to coordinate the war effort of the two English-speaking allies. To parallel the British Chiefs of Staff Committee, Roosevelt created a U.S. group composed of the Chief of Staff of the Army, the Chief of Naval Operations, and as a third U.S. member, the Chief of the Army Air Forces. Admiral William Leahy, chief of staff to the President, soon was the de facto chairman of the U.S. chiefs. Roosevelt never issued a formal charter for these Joint Chiefs of Staff. Working directly under him, with minimal involvement by the secretaries of war and the Navy, the JCS soon became the central directorate of U.S. military strategy and operations.

Although the body's composition after 1947 continued as before, the role of the JCS was never again the same, for the same National Security Act which gave a statutory basis to the JCS also created a National Security Council and a secretary of defense responsible directly to the President. Each of these new entities was assigned some of the functions performed during World War II by the JCS, as was the new director of central intelligence. The JCS were made "subject to the authority and direction" of the new secretary as well as the president. Two years later, in 1949, the Congress established the Department of Defense and placed the Joint Chiefs of Staff within it, presided over by a chairman. Unlike Admiral Leahy, this chairman was not the president's personal representative to the chiefs. Though a descendant carrying the same name, the present organization called the Joint Chiefs of Staff is no more identical to its wartime predecessor than the Fifth French Republic is to the Fourth.

Reprinted with minor revisions from John G. Kester, "The Future of the Joint Chiefs of Staff," *AEI Foreign Policy and Defense Review* 2, No. 1 (February 1980). Reprinted with permission of the American Enterprise Institute.

The Joint Chiefs of Staff today still include the chairman, the chiefs of staff of the Army and Air Force, and the Chief of Naval Operations. The Commandant of the Marine Corps was authorized in 1952 to meet with the chiefs and vote on matters directly concerning the Marine Corps; in practice it became difficult to explain why nearly anything did not directly concern the Marine Corps, and he soon came to be treated in practice like another member of the chiefs—so much so that in 1978, after general chagrin in discovering he was ineligible to serve as acting chairman, the Congress routinely made him a full member.[1] Since 1967 the members of the JCS have been appointed by the president for terms of four years; the chairman's term is two years, renewable for an additional two. Four-year terms were intended to, and probably do, limit somewhat the political ease with which a president may replace a member in whom he lacks confidence, although constitutionally he may do so at any time.

The activities of the JCS fit conveniently into three obviously overlapping areas: (1) advice, both in immediate situations and for long-term national security policy; (2) planning—again, both for short-term crises and long-term "what-ifs"; (3) finally, serving as a central transmission and coordination point for our armed forces operating throughout the world, in peacetime or during hostilities.

Advice

By law the JCS "are the principal military advisers to the President, the National Security Council, and the Secretary of Defense." It is not clear, however, that those words mean anything concrete. Every president (fortunately) takes his advice where he chooses; there is no way to legislate its source. Moreover, the same law declares that the secretary of defense "is the principal assistant to the President in all matters relating to the Department of Defense" with "authority, direction and control over the Department of Defense"; in case anyone wondered, it adds that the JCS "are in the Department of Defense."

In trying to decide the scope of advice to give, the chiefs often are in a double bind: if they respond to questions simply in terms of military capabilities, they may be dismissed as parochial military officers who don't understand the bigger picture; but if they offer their own analysis of geopolitical relations, or domestic consequences, they may be accused of meddling in areas in which civilian officials are more expert. President Kennedy warned the chiefs after the Bay of Pigs episode "that he did not regard them as narrow military specialists."[2] Again in the Cuban missile crisis he was "disturbed by this inability [of the JCS] to look beyond the limited military field"[3] and signed a directive ordering the JCS to be "more than military men."[4] That directive was replaced by one of similar purport but less rousing tone issued by President Carter in 1977.[5]

In the end, of course, advice will be judged by its quality and persuasiveness, not just by the charter of its source. The chiefs are expected, first of all, to come up with good military advice, including strategic advice. To the extent that they venture beyond the purely military (granted that the borderline is not sharp), they will find themselves more and more in competition with other advisers. But the chiefs can have a role in policy formulation. The invitation to think broadly never has been withdrawn.

Planning and Staff Work

One thing everyone agrees the JCS should do is plan. Their work force for doing so is the joint staff of several hundred officers.[6] Planning for the middle- or long-range future, of course—strategic planning—necessarily must include assumptions as to the forces, weapons, and capabilities that will be available. But it is the individual military departments, not the JCS, which are assigned the task of developing what those forces will be.

Civilian leaders sometimes wonder whether the plans are current and how realistic are the assumptions.[7] Military leaders in turn may chafe at the lack of civilian policy guidance. One response—the most far-reaching organizational change of Harold Brown's tenure as secretary of defense, and so far the least understood—has been to create the new senior office of Under Secretary of Defense for Policy. The new under secretary, third-ranking official of the secretary's office, has a broad charge to consider the adequacy and currency of all planning, including JCS planning, for likely contingencies. The present chairman of the JCS, General David C. Jones, also has moved to improve the planning process. Soon after his appointment he lent his prestige to a major headquarters exercise which revealed gaps in mobilization plans and capabilities.

The joint staff also originates or comments on quantities of decision papers moving through the department of defense. In doing so the joint staff acts less as a player than as a broker among the staffs of the separate military services, each of which has a large contingent of officers assigned to press that service's views in "the joint arena." The process usually begins at a relatively low level and goes through several iterations as successively senior layers of officers from the joint staff and from each of the service staffs become involved. The requirement for "coordination" with the services nearly always is taken to mean not just that each service's staff will have an opportunity to comment, but also that an answer must be produced on which all services agree. Although a few splits of opinion survive all the way up to the chiefs themselves, and on rare occasions beyond, most individual ideas and controversial alternatives tend to be washed out along the way.

Operations: The Chain of Command

Misunderstanding persists—among many who should know better, including military officers—about the chain of military command which runs from the president and the secretary of defense to the U.S. military forces throughout the world. The confusion may stem in part from a discomfort about a situation in which the highest ranking officers of the armed forces, the Joint Chiefs of Staff, do not command any operating forces at all. Though that may seem paradoxical, it is without a doubt the arrangement presidents have established for some time. "The Joint Chiefs of Staff are not in the chain of command; they have a staff function."[8]

The members of the Joint Chiefs of Staff by JCS appointment did command the operating forces until 1953. In that year President Eisenhower directed that the chain of command for operations should run instead through the secretaries of the Army, Navy, and Air Force, respectively; he announced that the Joint Chiefs of Staff "are not a command body" and would thenceforth devote themselves to their planning and advisory role.[9] However, the individual chiefs themselves, as heads of their respective services and quite apart from their JCS role, remained in the chain with responsibility for execution of operations by their respective services.

By amendments in 1958 sponsored by President Eisenhower, however, the services (both service secretary and service chief) were also removed from the operational chain of command, and a new command structure was established that still exists today. The present chain of command for military operations runs from the president to the secretary of defense to the four-star commanders (CINCs) of five unified commands[10] and three specified commands,[11] and from them to the operating units of the armed forces.[12]

Confusion as to the JCS role persists in part because Secretary of Defense Neil McElroy issued a directive, also in 1958, which said that orders to the CINCs would be transmitted from the president or the secretary of defense through the Joint Chiefs of Staff; in that context it stated that the chain of command to the unified and specified commanders runs "through the Joint Chiefs of Staff," the body which is the agent by which the secretary's orders are transmitted to the field.[13] But the role is one of agency, not of command. Only the president or the secretary of defense can originate orders to the unified and specified commanders. The Joint Chiefs of Staff themselves cannot originate operational orders; the JCS can only transmit them. Although the Blue Ribbon Panel on Defense Organization in 1970 recommended that for clarity the 1958 directive be rescinded,[14] no secretary of defense has chosen to do so.

The distinction between one who commands and one who transmits the commands of another can be blurry. It is in the nature of bureaucracy for the transmitter to keep it so, as thousands of staffers all over Washington demonstrate every day. In this case the confusion has been so great that even some of the CINCs themselves seem to have shared it. Thus a former CINCPAC writes of serving in that assignment "under the direct authority of the JCS," and refers to the JCS as "commanders."[15]

How do the JCS perform in their staff role for operations? The secretary of defense has two principal duties by law and presidential direction: as a cabinet officer to head the Department of Defense and assure that the forces provided by the Congress are ready to fight; but also to command those forces, subject only to the direction of the president. In that second, command, role he has no substantial staff support except the JCS and its joint staff. The Blue Ribbon Panel in 1970 warned that the existing arrangement "provides a forum for inter-Service conflicts to be injected into the decision-making process for military operations" and "inhibits the flow of information to the President and Secretary of Defense, often even in crisis situations," and called the situation "a deficiency which can be tolerated only at high risk."[16] It recommended the secretary be given a whole new operations staff outside the JCS. Instead, another task assigned to the new under secretary of defense for policy was to try to help make JCS operational staff support more responsive. It still is too early to judge the results.

Avenues of Influence

Relations with the President

The JCS seldom are found in the Oval Office or the Situation Room of the White House arguing the pros and cons of strategy. Of necessity the Joint Chiefs offer their advice more often to the secretary of defense than to the president. The president simply cannot give the chiefs nearly as much time. The secretary of defense sees the president several times each week; often, as in NSC meetings, the JCS chairman is present.[17] But the Joint Chiefs as a body see the president only irregularly and—like many who see the president—no doubt seldom for as long as they would like. By tradition the chiefs can specially request to see the president singly or as a group on a matter about which they care deeply; that prerogative was not exercised under President Carter.

In reiterating President Kennedy's direction that JCS advice should come to him "direct and unfiltered," President Carter added, "after informing the Secretary of Defense."[18] As a practical matter this means that the chiefs' views either are summarized to the president by the secretary of defense, or are forwarded to the president in the chiefs' own words if the importance of the topic warrants, or if the JCS so request. None of the present participants seems to have experienced problems with the system.[19]

No adviser, of course, owns the guarantee that his advice will be taken. JCS advice was rejected, for example, in the decision not to produce the B-1 bomber. But the advice most often is taken, and even advice which goes against the grain of a presidential policy may succeed partly. For example, after the JCS initially objected to President Carter's 1977 plan to withdraw U.S. ground combat forces from Korea, the administration accepted three modifications proposed by the JCS and gained JCS approval. Similarly, JCS support of the SALT II treaty clearly is conditioned on a sustained enhancement of the overall U.S. defense effort; it is much more difficult, however, to hold the Congress or the president to such broader commitments.

The Joint Chiefs also have an opportunity to influence presidential policy through the JCS chairman's persuasiveness in meetings of the NSC and its sub-committees, meetings at which he may express his views (or those of all the chiefs) without restriction. But contacts with the president by the other chiefs are likely to be more meager and formal. Admiral Elmo R. Zumwalt, Jr., plaintively described his elaborate preparations for a meeting of the JCS with the president, and his surprise when it turned out to be "a ceremony, a ritual even, at which Mr. Nixon listened to things he already knew and made responses he and Kissinger had contrived beforehand."[20] Jimmy Carter often stated publicly that he had met with the Joint Chiefs of Staff more frequently than had any of his recent predecessors; however, former Chairman General George S. Brown judged that "the exposure of the Chiefs to President Carter on a routine basis on policy questions is, perhaps, less extensive than it was with President Ford."[21] And President Carter did not claim to have taken their advice more often.

No secretary of defense would find it easy to tolerate a channel of communication running around him from the JCS directly to the president, though apparently such has occurred in some administrations. President Nixon on occasion issued instructions to then Chairman Admiral Thomas H. Moorer, adding that the chairman should not inform the secretary of defense. Moorer in turn was accused of spying on Henry Kissinger's wastebaskets[22] and of receiving "bootleg" copies of documents directly from the NSC. Admiral Zumwalt, then chief of naval operations, saw these puckishly as "games people play" and chose to tell the secretary of defense of information he received out of channels; but shortly before retiring, Zumwalt defiantly criticized presidential policy and informed his superiors afterwards, and sent memoranda to the president without going through the secretary of defense.[23] There was no hint of such behavior by any JCS member under President Carter and Secretary Brown.

Nor did the chiefs in the Carter administration have a uniformed ally or rival—a Taylor, Goodpaster, Haig, or Scowcroft—on the White House staff. Obviously, such a person can be a source of concern both to the JCS and to the secretary of defense.

Relations with the Secretary of Defense

Because he is the only civilian other than the president with authority to command our armed forces,[24] the secretary of defense has a relationship to persons in uniform unlike that of any other civilian in the Pentagon. Yet it often has been observed that rather than striving to provide advice and analysis keyed to the secretary's needs and wishes, the JCS for many years offered advice "designed primarily to serve their interests rather than his."[25] Many in the joint staff probably still see the JCS as a semiautonomous fiefdom rather than an integral part of the defense bureaucracy. Agencies outside the Department of Defense often seem to view the JCS the same way.

No doubt the members of the JCS understand better than their staff that influence seldom is enhanced by failing to give one's boss what he needs. As a practical matter, the boss is the secretary of defense, unless a president wishes it otherwise. Confusion by JCS staff officers and unresponsiveness to the secretary's needs probably have been encouraged by the statutory designation of the JCS as "principal military advisers to the President," as well as by the reluctance of the JCS to challenge positions of the individual military services.

Personal ties, of course, are important. Melvin Laird, for instance, was able to voice sentiments which drew the chiefs' enthusiasm while at the same time he and President Nixon, with congressional urging, relentlessly pulled U.S. forces out of Vietnam and reduced defense budgets in real dollars year after year. The tradition of the secretary's visiting the Tank for a weekly meeting with the JCS began in the late 1950s with Secretary of Defense Thomas Gates and has continued—with varying results depending on the personalities involved. Secretary Brown used these meetings to address any topic the chiefs or he desired, including the secretary's frank explanations of administration policy and intentions and candid responses from the chiefs. These meetings on Tuesday afternoons offered a few-holds-barred chance to exchange views which only a handful in the Pentagon enjoy so regularly.

If a secretary of defense cannot find military guidance he needs from the JCS, he is bound to turn elsewhere. Secretary Robert S. McNamara's broadening of the role of the assistant secretary of defense for international security affairs reflected in some part a need for help in political-military activities which the chiefs were not supplying. McNamara's expansion of his civilian staff and designation of an assistant secretary for systems analysis clearly was designed to supply him with alternatives to programs urged by the services—alternatives he could not get from JCS.

Secretary Brown took office with a large—overly large—staff of civilian assistants in place. He initially cut it somewhat and tried to encourage greater participation by the JCS in policy making by prodding the joint staff, through the JCS, to do work useful to him. On many occasions he did not hesitate to accept uniformed military advice on program decisions in the face of contrary recommendations of his assistant secretaries. In short, he expressed a desire and willingness to listen to JCS advice and gave some evidence that he really would heed it when it was persuasive.

Relations with the Services

If the JCS have a natural rival for power in the Department of Defense today, it is not the secretary of defense. True, part of any secretary's job is to impose the president's budget limitations on the expected desire of the JCS for more capable forces.

But as long as those budget decisions meet some minimum military standards and are within a range of public and congressional acceptability, they are not likely to be too bitterly contested by the chiefs. On most other issues, the secretary and the chiefs are not pushed by opposing institutional forces.

Within the Department of Defense, the natural rivals of a departmentwide, supraservice body like the JCS are the departments of the Army, Navy, and Air Force. Yet the JCS do not behave like a supraservice body; most often they are controlled by the services, a control which is assured by having the JCS composed of the military heads of each service.

The largest question in the Defense Department in most years is the size of the defense budget and how it is to be allocated among programs. Budget and program decisions shape fighting capabilities and future strategy. Yet making recommendations on allocation of limited resources has been an almost impossible task for the JCS when one service's programs have competed against another's. Traditionally the chiefs collectively, as the JCS, have contented themselves with endorsing the programs that they themselves, wearing their chief-of-service hats, earlier proposed.

Someone, however, has to choose among competing claims on limited resources. Secretary McNamara turned to his civilian staff for advice on such questions. Secretary Brown, while keeping the systems analysts, also tried to encourage more meaningful JCS participation in his program and budget decisions.

On the other hand, the JCS often advise the secretary on matters where JCS participation is not needed or even wanted, in matters that do not involve operations, strategy, and planning and are clearly assigned not to the JCS but to the departments of the Army, Navy, and Air Force. Such topics as military compensation, retirement, and even health care for military dependents have been discussed at length, and opined upon, by the JCS, even though such concerns are properly those not of the JCS but of the military departments. Much JCS attention also is devoted to the preservation and filling of flag-officer billets, typically with each chief negotiating relentlessly and trading as necessary to preserve the interests of his own service in the outcome. Assignments of officers to three-star and four-star positions, even nonjoint ones, are submitted for recommendation of the chiefs even though already recommended by the secretary of the Army, Navy, or Air Force, and some writers have seen it as somehow sinister if JCS advice is not taken. The JCS also can provide a handy, though inappropriate, forum for a chief to reopen an issue on which he failed to obtain the support of the secretary of his service.

Relations with the State Department and the Assistant
for National Security Affairs

From the beginning of the Carter administration Secretary of State Cyrus Vance and Presidential Assistant Zbigniew Brzezinski dealt closely on a daily personal basis with Secretary of Defense Harold Brown. Each attended one or two JCS meetings by invitation, but they worked with the Department of Defense mainly through the secretary and at NSC or NSC subcommittee meetings; there also was staff level contact at many levels. Neither Vance nor Brzezinski evidenced a desire to deal directly with the JCS.[26]

The JCS often are invited to designate their own representatives on the delegations to international organizations and to negotiations with national security aspects, such as NATO, Mutual and Balanced Force Reductions, and the Law of the Sea. Usually these representatives have been active or recently retired senior officers, and sometimes they have been designated on behalf of the Secretary of Defense as well. The presence of such representatives can benefit the political leadership as well as the interests of the JCS; President Carter was able to remind audiences that the chiefs had had a delegate deeply involved in the negotiations of the Panama Canal treaties. On the other hand, there is political risk: the JCS delegate to the SALT II negotiations retired and denounced the treaty.[27]

Relations with the Congress and the Public

The attitude of the Congress toward the JCS has been essentially opportunistic. When it has appeared that there might be profit in it, members of Congress occasionally have tried to play off the chiefs against their civilian superiors, though usually without much success.[28] As a whole, the Congress has appeared happy to have the JCS remain a weak, compromise organization. The congressional debates on the National Security Act of 1947 and its periodic amendments clearly opposed a powerful central military staff or a single uniformed commander. While not very illuminating or precise, those comments do show a congressional attitude that probably is not much different today.

Grumbles are heard from time to time—sometimes expressed publicly by the more strident members of the House Armed Services Committee—that the chiefs have been emasculated by tight restrictions on what they may say in public. The two Singlaub incidents sometimes are cited as an example. They are not a good one. The statements of Major General John Singlaub (who of course was not connected with the JCS) were not even close to the border of propriety for a serving military officer. When he spoke to a reporter against the policy he was assigned to help execute in Korea, he was scolded and reassigned; when nevertheless a year later he gave a wide-ranging public denunciation of the president's national security policies, he was asked to retire. It is difficult to see how the general could have expected consequences much milder. Nevertheless, it probably is true that the public disgrace of General Singlaub may have had some *in terrorem* effect on other uniformed people, and since President Carter went out of his way to become personally involved the first time, it may well be that such an effect was what the President intended.

The rules on public statements by military officers have not changed. They were set forth simply and clearly by General Maxwell Taylor twenty years ago:

> Having made every effort to guide his civilian superiors in the direction which he believes right, the Chief of Staff must accept the decisions of the Secretary of his service, of the Secretary of Defense, and of the President as final and thereafter support them before Congress. The alternative is resignation.[29]

In short, the duty to civilians in authority is no different from what a military officer owes to a military superior, and what he rightfully expects from the military personnel under his command. General George S. Brown, characteristically, put it more succinctly: "We don't go public without leaving active duty first in doing so."[30]

Testimony before congressional committees, however, is a special situation. General Taylor's advice again is good: "I have found no way of coping with the situation other than by replying frankly to questions and letting the chips fall where they may," while at the same time also explaining the administration's position.[31] It goes without saying that an officer breaks the rules if he maneuvers to elicit a question as to his personal views;[32] nor should he be free to express personal views contrary to decisions of his civilian superiors in a noncongressional public forum.

Of course, disagreements can be highlighted or muted by the way questions are answered. It is doubtful that a chief who rebuked his civilian superiors in unrestrained terms before a congressional committee would retain much influence within the administration, nor should he as a chief. Civilian authority over the military requires no less. This has not greatly inhibited the chiefs from expressing disagreements in a sober way. Both military and civilian leaders agree generally on the ground rules. The chiefs do not appear to be unduly muzzled.

Unmuzzling the military, however, appeared in the first years of the Carter administration to be a greater potential problem. The administration was not bashful about displaying one or another of the chiefs (and other officers as well) at public gatherings to emphasize their support of the Panama Canal treaties, and in the view of the *Washington Post*, Chairman George Brown's "strong testimony in favor of the Panama Canal treaties was surely crucial to their approval."[33] Any practice, however, that tends to move the uniformed military into the political process grates on our traditions and should carry a heavy burden of justification. There also are potential costs to the military in becoming too entangled in seeking public support for a particular policy, even one in which the armed forces are involved: consider General William C. Westmoreland's 1967 acquiescence in making speeches in support of the Vietnam War, including addressing a Joint Session of the Congress.[34]

Moreover, for politicians there are some very practical reasons not to rely on the military for backing. Taking advantage of the chiefs' support when it is available risks emphasizing their lack of enthusiasm on other issues. And the seduction by vice that Alexander Pope described might also apply to generals pushed into political advocacy: "We first endure, then pity, then embrace." Some officers involved in public forums on the Panama Canal treaties were heard to remark afterwards that they rather enjoyed it. Any administration would do well to keep in mind the experiences of Pandora and of Dr. Frankenstein.

The potential impact of the chiefs' views on the public and the Congress can never be ignored by a president or a secretary of defense. On some issues, such as the amount of defense spending, their opinions may already be discounted; on others, like the Vietnam War, their views ultimately became discredited. But the chiefs no doubt retain power to influence national decisions to some degree on some security issues, and to add legitimacy to one view or another. Moreover, the chiefs as individuals know and converse with members of Congress, to an extent best known only to themselves. If they choose to withhold support for a major administration initiative, the chiefs face no difficulty in making their objections known, but, like other officials in Washington, they will if wise engage in policy battles limited in number and only proportional in intensity to the importance of the issues at stake. Such exercise of power and responsibility is not necessarily improper; the limits are not to be found in directives, but are traditional and prudential.

Criticisms of the Chiefs

Practically since the day they were established, the JCS as a body and their joint staff as an institution have been assailed from all sides. The brickbats have flown:

From secretaries of state: The JCS "is quite literally like my favorite old lady who could not say what she thought until she heard what she said"; such an organization is "extremely difficult for civilian officers engaged in foreign affairs to work with" and "all too often it produces for those looking for military advice and guidance only oracular utterances."[35]

From national security advisers: "The 'agreed' Joint Chiefs of Staff submissions were usually nonaggression treaties among the various services unrelated to a coherent strategy."[36]

From outside reorganizers: "The process militates against the likelihood of the Joint Chiefs of Staff clearly facing up to difficult and potentially divisive issues. The repetitious, committee-type negotiations tend to reduce issues to a level of compromise which will either avoid the potential conflicts or substitute a solution that can be accepted on a quid-pro-quo basis."[37]

Of course, from whiz-kid systems analysts: "The JCS staples together service requests. If forced to make hard choices, the JCS tries to negotiate a compromise—one that often bears little relationship to the best mix of forces from a national or military view."[38]

Even from former generals and presidents: "Had I allowed my interservice and interallied staff to be similarly organized in the theaters I commanded during World War II, the delays and resulting indecisiveness would have been unacceptable to my superiors."[39]

Some of the most pointed criticism has come from former members themselves. Admiral Elmo Zumwalt said of the Joint Strategic Objectives Plan, formerly the basic JCS planning paper, that "I found this particular document to be almost as valueless to read as it was fatiguing to write."[40] General Maxwell Taylor wrote that the JCS "have all the faults of a committee in settling important controversial matters."[41]

Of course, some who find fault may simply disagree with the positions the JCS are likely to take. Also, compromises seldom satisfy everyone, and the JCS represent one of the great compromises of the postwar era. Moreover, some tendency to ignore the JCS may have little to do with its actual performance. For several years the United States has been pulling out of the antimilitary feeling generated by the Vietnam War. The Congress is beginning to recognize that larger numbers of voters are developing defense concerns. As perception of decline of our relative military power in the world, and the costs of that decline, becomes more widespread, and the effects of that decline on political influence more apparent, the willingness of politicians to listen to uniformed advisers may increase.

Yet the smoke which has continued to drift upward for thirty years from the JCS corridors of the Pentagon suggests that there may be some fuel for the fire of criticism. Influence in the United States government naturally gravitates to those who can develop and express ideas articulately, persuasively, and promptly when asked. The contributions of the JCS to national security policy making and defense planning have been called slow, unimaginative, unhelpful and indecisive; the Joint Chiefs have been called a body devoted to logrolling and mutual back-scratching, prone to recommendations so sterile they are not objectionable to anyone, and to the development of grandiose plans that ignore the real limits of U.S. military capabilities and military spending. The chairman or his representative may perform ably as an individual at meetings of an NSC subcommittee or with the secretary of defense. But when the need is for a convincing paper to recommend what to do in a developing negotiation or confrontation, the JCS are too likely to make the argument from authority ("the Joint Chiefs of Staff believe . . .") with scant supporting analysis, or with reasons reduced to the lowest common denominator upon which four wary services can agree. Or the JCS simply may be unable to complete staffing before others have taken charge by default. For many years the JCS were criticized for failure to agree on important issues.[42] More recently, the complaint has been that disagreements get papered over.[43] Early secretaries of defense tried to include the JCS in budget discussions, but James Forrestal had great difficulty, and Louis Johnson simply gave up, as did his successors. The chiefs themselves may be too burdened with service responsibilities to devote adequate time to joint matters, even though they have been directed to put those first.

The plans prepared by the joint staff often have dismayed outsiders who had occasion to read them. No "canned" plan, of course, will perfectly fit a real-world situation. But too often it has been discovered when a crisis was at hand that the relevant JCS plans assumed away the hardest problems—by focusing, for example, only on a single contingency involving full-scale enemy invasion; or by assuming that military forces elsewhere would be unaffected and available; or by scheduling reinforcements either too rapidly for available transport or too slowly to arrive before the war was over. Sometimes plans have offered presidents few options between "do nothing" or "shoot the works" by all-out commitment of forces.

There really are two sets of objections to the present JCS system: one goes to the quality of the work product, the other to the institutional behavior of the members themselves. The two complaints are fundamentally related, however, and both stem from a single sensitive source: the division of the U.S. armed forces into four services in three military departments, and the consequent centrifugal pressures that division generates. Any institutional alteration which enhances the influence of the supraservice JCS will almost ipso facto threaten the interests of the individual services, and is likely to be resisted for that reason.[44]

The JCS and the joint staff since their inception have behaved as a "joint" staff of service representatives rather than as a multiservice military staff to the secretary of defense. Difficult policy issues get decided, however, whether or not the JCS have anything helpful to say about them. If the work product of the JCS were more useful, it might find more use. The senior military by the neutralizing procedures of the JCS staff system have tended to reduce their own influence in the national security decision-making process. The balance of this chapter looks at the changes in that system that have occurred lately, and then suggests further organizational changes that might make military advice more effective.

Present Organization—Changes and Trends

The Secretary's Efforts

When Harold Brown became secretary of defense in January 1977, he was well aware of the arguments for and against the present organization of the JCS. He recognized that improvement was needed, but believed that first an effort should be made to achieve it without new legislation or massive reorganizations. Brown set about involving himself in the activities of both the CINCs and the JCS. Officers who could address U.S. defense planning in larger terms than parochial service considerations were given leading roles, and Brown rejected in principle, and sometimes in practice, the notion that some senior positions (like chairman of the JCS) should rotate from service to service, or that others belonged to a single service. He had no intention of trying to manage joint staff activities himself; his objective was to support uniformed leaders who shared some of his perceptions of the deficiencies of the product and wanted to work to correct them. His only formal reorganization move potentially affecting the JCS significantly occurred outside the JCS: the establishment of a new under secretary of defense for policy—a senior civilian who as one duty would work closely with the JCS to tie some activities of the joint staff more closely to actual defense policy.[45]

A dominant theme in Harold Brown's first two years as head of the Department of Defense was an emphasis on jointness. In pressing for a more effective joint staff, in stressing the operational chain of command, in emphasizing readiness of the combat forces, in signaling to the bureaucracy his closeness to and respect for first JCS Chairman George S. Brown and later Chairman David C. Jones, Secretary Brown gave content to the intentions expressed in his address at the commissioning of the U.S.S. *Eisenhower* in 1977. There he predicted that future military operations would involve "coordinated efforts of land, air, and . . . naval forces, in elements functionally, configured . . . led by officers who understand the functions and qualities that our armed services share, as well as the particular capabilities and traditions which enrich each of them." He took as his text Eisenhower's message that "separate ground, sea and air warfare is gone forever."[46]

President Carter in September 1977 signed a memorandum calling for an "unconstrained examination" of the National Military Command Structure as one of four organizational studies in the national security area. The report, prepared by New York investment banker Richard D. Steadman, was released in July 1978.[47] It disappointed those predisposed toward spectacular change. For the most part it made unglamorous but practical recommendations for making the present JCS arrangement work better, emphasizing in particular that many criticisms of the chiefs were traceable to deficiencies in the joint staff. The report urged that a better average quality of officers be assigned to duty on the joint staff, and also that the chairman be given greater authority in its management. Perhaps the most significant part of the report was its last section, which contained an implied threat: If strengthening the joint staff and the chairman did not work, it said, "then solutions of a more fundamental nature directed at resolving the inherent tensions in the current organization, such as separating the joint advice and command functions from those of service administration," would become necessary.[48]

The prescription in the Steadman report, in short, is to give the JCS one more chance. It is not an easy one. Evolutionary rather than revolutionary reform is in some ways a harder course to follow to achieve significant change. This is not to question the ability of those in charge, who are talented men of good will and are probably as likely a group to bring off significant improvement as the JCS ever are likely to have. But often it is much easier for an official in a bureaucracy to make great policy decisions than to try to change the procedures and behavior of the system itself—a change which requires attention to many small systems of reward and punishment, a change which is resisted at every turn, which requires constant attention and vast amounts of time, is likely not to be widely noticed, and for which hardly anyone will ever thank you. Entrusting a task like that to people charged also with the day-to-day safety of the United States does not guarantee that it will get done.

The Chairman's Role

Just a few days before the Steadman report appeared, General David C. Jones had taken office as the ninth chairman of the Joint Chiefs of Staff. Since becoming the highest ranking military officer, General Jones—who had a reputation as one not awed by staff procedures when he was Air Force chief of staff—has been pushing for higher quality and more relevant work from the joint staff.

His authority to work vast changes is limited, however. The law provides that the chairman "may not exercise military command over the Joint Chiefs of Staff or any of the armed forces." The chairman did not even have a vote in the JCS until 1958, although the practical effect of that was negligible, since the JCS operates by consensus and not by ballots, and the chairman, like any member, can get his views to the attention of the decision maker, the secretary of defense.

JCS chairmen of different personal qualities have interpreted their office differently over the years. Some have seen themselves as moderators and consensus seekers, others as champions of the uniformed constituency, others as strategists in a position of definite primacy within the JCS. Admiral Arthur W. Radford was perhaps the first to conceive an independent role for the chairman. General Earle G. Wheeler, whose tenure was the longest, devoted it to the Vietnam War. General George Brown's candor and sense of humor smoothed difficult decisions and won respect from those who worked with him. The present chairman came to the job with a reputation for pragmatism, creativity, and sophistication.

The frustrations he or any new chairman encounters are predictable. He moves usually, if the past is any guide, from being uniformed head of a service to the chairmanship of a committee of equals. He has almost no personal staff and so must depend on the joint staff for much of his support. But the joint staff works for the corporate body, not for him. Although the chairman was told to manage it in 1953, the joint staff remains that of the JCS, which means that in many respects it is run by and for the services. Unless the chairman can call on the joint staff for meaningful help, his position resembles that of the first secretary of defense, who was limited by law to no more than four civilian assistants. Also, the extent of the chairman's freedom to deal on behalf of the JCS is not always clear. Though he has a standing authorization from the JCS to respond on their behalf in emergencies, he runs the risk of exceeding his authority when unexpected issues arise.

Yet the unmistakable trend over time has been toward greater authority for the chairman. And a continued increase of that authority—and particularly his practical control of the joint staff—offers the only possible alternative to a major restructuring of the JCS as a body itself, if an improved product is desired. Secretary Brown, like his predecessors, aided the process here and there by directing that certain offices or agencies in the Department of Defense report to or coordinate with the chairman, rather than to the JCS. The Steadman report suggests that the chairman be given more personal staff—a dubious idea unless the joint staff were shrunk by a corresponding amount—and that the chairman be empowered to select any officers he wants to fill the joint staff. That latter seemingly modest recommendation, incidentally, drew heated opposition from each of the services (and, therefore, from the JCS). The resistance was understandable. Such a power in the chairman could have enormous implications, for it would identify a single officer to whom joint staff officers would look for direction and also would give someone outside a service authority to shape the careers of individuals within it. No action has been taken on these Steadman recommendations.

Secretary Brown, as was recommended in the Steadman report, added the chairman to the Defense Systems Acquisition Review Council (the committee that makes up-or-down recommendations on major new weapons systems (and tried to draw the chairman more and more into serving as an adviser on resource-allocation decisions. General Taylor, a former chairman, worried in that context that "we will ruin the utility of this fellow if we ask too much of him."[49] It might also be urged that he and the JCS should spend much of their time on purely military plans—movements and mobilizations—since no one else does and there are plenty of other players in the budget fights.

The fact is, however, that middle- or long-range planning is impossible without assumptions as to force structure and capabilities, which in turn depend on today's program and budget decisions. The chairman (with his small personal staff) is virtually the only military officer in the Pentagon with supraservice responsibilities to whom the secretary can turn for advice. The CINCs can contribute something from the limited viewpoints of their particular commands, but they are not close at hand. If the chairman cannot advise on program and allocation issues, the uniformed military will abdicate influence on issues of trade-offs that transcend service lines. Surely some of the chairman's time can be allocated profitably to issues of such importance.

The Joint Staff

The Steadman report concluded that joint staff work could be improved, without structural change, by more guidance from senior officers prior to staffing: by less requirement of service unanimity and more analysis of alternatives; and, finally, by assigning more of the most capable officers to the joint staff.

The first two suggestions are difficult to quarrel with. Yet a staff that came up with a sheaf of dissenting views on important issues would be acting differently from the way U.S. military staffs are trained to behave. It would make the task of the JCS more difficult, by leaving more confusion and more differences to resolve. But we are far from that danger point today. The joint staff remains too much in the thrall of the services, a servitude enforced by the individual chiefs themselves and their immediate senior assistants for JCS activities, the operations deputies, or "ops deps," who are not on the joint staff but rather are senior staff officers of the respective services.

If the joint staff were unleashed to think more independently, it still would need persons assigned to it who could deliberate usefully, and not just broker consensus. Today the joint staff has some able officers and some less so. It is not an elite organization. Joint staff duty is not sought after, partly because of the tedious way work is conducted, partly because usually it is not the kind of assignment that enhances a career and helps promotions. That pattern could be broken by assigning more of the most outstanding officers to the joint staff at some point in their careers, and by requiring promotion boards (which are controlled by the services rather than the JCS) to weigh such service favorably. A directive first issued by Secretary of Defense Gates in 1959 was revised in 1978 to tighten the requirement that career officers serve in a joint assignment as a prerequisite to flag rank.[50] The new directive, however, still defines joint service very broadly and provides for waivers by the services. These are loopholes which were fought for by the services' representatives when the directive was being revised, and they still are used too liberally.

For a real change in promotion policies and career patterns to stick, however, the reality of joint staff duty would have to change. It would need to be something that is challenging and meaningful in an officer's development. The proper length of tours of duty on the joint staff should also be considered. Today if an officer served two three-year tours on the joint staff, his future career usually would be jeopardized (and perhaps his mental health as well). Such longer periods—which imply specialization—might be appropriate in certain cases, however. They could also provide the JCS with some of the "corporate memory" that it has been accused of lacking,[51] and without which work already done sometimes gets duplicated three or four years later. Another characteristic of a more permanent joint staff, of course, could well be an ivory tower isolation from the fighting forces, or perhaps after some years a staff-officer elitism.[52]

With regard to planning, some of the deficiencies stem from the isolation of the joint staff. The 1970 Blue Ribbon Panel report criticized the physical separation of the joint staff from other offices in the Pentagon. The drafting of plans is done by officers in the joint staff who often can find little specific direction in the department's general policy and program documents. They have in the past received little guidance from senior military officers, and usually none from the civilians in the Department of Defense.[53] Yet the plans being prepared must make assumptions about the timing and content of decisions which civilian officials in the Department of Defense and elsewhere would take. Lieutenant colonels in cubby holes deep in the Pentagon may have a pardonable lack of understanding of how a president or a secretary of defense would likely behave in the event of a Soviet military gambit in Europe or Iran, or of all the questions for which they would expect answers.

Moreover, JCS plans often are first drafted in the unified commands; a major in EUCOM headquarters in Stuttgart probably will have even less sense than a colonel in Washington of what the highest-level decision makers would need to know in addressing military contingencies in, say, the Middle East. More review and attention by senior officers would likely improve the realism of assumptions underlying planning. Involving the under secretary for policy and other civilians in developing and reviewing the assumptions and the political context of the plans, and testing them with hard questions, would contribute a dimension which the process needs but heretofore has lacked.[54] It remains to be seen whether civilian policy makers will be willing to commit themselves enough to give realistic policy guidance.

A better functioning joint staff more independent of the services almost certainly would, as the Steadman report predicted, enhance the influence of the uniformed military in the decisional process. Today, for instance, subservience to the services has left the joint staff cataleptic when faced with issues of allocating limited defense dollars among the services; the analytical task, and the influence, have passed in many cases—in large part by default—to civilian analysts on the staff of the secretary of defense. If the joint staff could help the JCS face these questions, its role would be enhanced and the quality of ultimate decisions perhaps improved.

All this may make it sound as if joint staff procedures would be easy to fix, that a few simple improvements in staffing and procedures would make structural change in the JCS unnecessary. But it would be a mistake to underestimate the challenge of the task. It is no accident that the joint staff has gone on for this long with little improvement, even though the deficiencies have been recognized for decades. The difficulties have their roots not in lack of management skill, but in the JCS itself and the power balance struck between the forces of jointness on the one hand and the services on the other. Except for the chairman, the chiefs themselves—institutionally, though not necessarily personally—by virtue of their service roles have an interest in *not* having an effective joint staff. The way the joint staff works, or fails to, reflects the existing checks and balances. One has to wonder, therefore, whether vast improvements can be implemented without a change in that equilibrium.

The CINCs

The future of the JCS cannot be gauged without some consideration to the role of the CINCs—at least some of whom, like the JCS, have joint responsibilities and therefore are natural institutional rivals of the services,[55] but who as commanders reporting by statute directly to the secretary are in some respects rivals of the JCS as well.

One of Secretary Brown's early innovations was to require each CINC every ninety days to send him directly a personal letter describing the situation in the writer's command. The secretary's handwritten comments and questions on these reports and the responses created a continuing dialogue and flow of information and actions. Recently Army Chief of Staff General Bernard Rogers agreed to step aside a year early to take the uniquely prestigious CINC assignment in Europe, an office coupled with the post of NATO Supreme Allied Commander and filled in the past by such revered officers as Eisenhower, Norstad, and Goodpaster.[56]

The Steadman report suggested that the chairman should be made the secretary's agent for dealing with the CINCs. That certainly would enhance the chairman's role, but whether it would be a good idea for the secretary is questionable, for it would blur the fact that the chain of command for operations runs to the secretary and that the JCS are not operators, but agents and advisers.[57] Often in the past the CINCs have dealt almost exclusively with the JCS.[58]

Conceivably the CINCs might be brought more directly into resource-allocation issues. At present they submit requests and suggestions to the JCS, and the JCS usually endorse these on the theory that the commander in the field should get what he says he needs. General Alexander Haig as CINC in Europe took the most advantage of this opportunity to define carefully and press for the requirements of his forces.[59] The quarterly reports of the CINCs to Secretary Brown gave them a somewhat greater voice. How independent a view some of the CINCs can take, however, is uncertain, since in most cases the organizations they head are not truly joint; three of the eight commands have units from only one service, and in most of the others a single service dominates. The CINCs can shed light on regional or functional needs but probably can be of little help in tough trade-offs, especially in the case of CINCs dominated by a single service and limited in staff resources.

Future Organization

Prescriptions for the ailments of the JCS range from "take two aspirin" to euthanasia. For those who doubt that the present organization can cure itself, there are some bolder alternatives.

Ending Double-Hatting

Of the possible radical changes in JCS organization, the one most likely to receive serious consideration today is whether to "un-double-hat" the members of the JCS, each of whom now is military head of his service as well as a member of the JCS. Such a change would be designed to cure the problem already complained of by the second secretary of defense, Robert Lovett, to President Truman, and in the Rockefeller report in 1953: The Chiefs have a built-in conflict of interest. The present paradox is that the joint military organization in the Pentagon is headed by a committee for whom joint considerations are not naturally uppermost. Even if the chiefs themselves want to be magnanimous—and most senior government officials tend to be broader-minded than the people who work for them—their staffs keep score of how many the "old man" wins and loses when he goes to the Tank. General Westmoreland, perhaps revealingly, listed among his duties as chief of staff "to serve as *the Army's representative* on the Joint Chiefs of Staff."[60]

General Omar Bradley, the first chairman, had earlier proposed a committee of "superchiefs" freed of service ties. Steadman similarly would, if lesser reforms failed, remove the service chiefs from joint activities and replace the JCS with a body called the national military advisers (NMA). The NMA would have a senior officer from each service, one of whom would be designated chairman. The NMA would perform the functions the JCS perform today, and would have a joint staff to assist them. The four officers who served on the NMA would never return to assignments in their services.

Advantages of splitting the two functions of the chiefs into two separate jobs would include: creation of a senior body able to give military advice uninhibited by service interests; full time for them to spend on joint planning and operations, undistracted by service duties; and consequently a larger role in advising on allocation of resources and other military and geopolitical concerns. Also, filling the highest military assignments might be easier if the duties were split. Some officers may be inspiring field commanders, others good managers, others great strategists. A few are all three, but perhaps a differently organized system could put more talent to use by depending less on finding officers who must try to be universal in their scope.

Impassioned arguments against splitting the dual roles of the chiefs are put forth, however, especially by uniformed people (including the chiefs), nearly all of whom seem to oppose the idea. They warn that the quality of advice would suffer if the senior advisers were not intimately familiar with the current capabilities of their forces, and if they were not personally on the line to come through when they advised that forces be deployed. They worry that splitting the jobs of the chiefs would lead in each case to two positions of lessened influence, and that the NMA would be simply, as one senior officer put it, a panel of "eunuchs."

A more compelling reason to hesitate, however, is that no one can be sure what would happen. To effect such a change in the constitution of civilian-military and intramilitary relationships would be bound to have far-reaching effects. When government alters power balances, the unintended and unforeseen results often turn out to be more significant than the ones planned for. Some might fear, for instance, that a new and more single-minded and efficient group of military advisers would become too influential—would be a modern version of that German general staff which senators denounced during the debates that led to the current system (denounced, it might be added, without in most cases any clear idea of what they were talking about).

If separate national military advisers were established, what would be the effect on military career patterns? Which assignment would be the most desirable and respected—chief of service, CINC, or member of a body like the NMA? An officer might find the most gratification not as an NMA member but rather in the role of paterfamilias of the service he loves and for which he feels responsible and in which he has spent his military career.[61] The present chiefs devote more than half their time to purely service matters; some over the years, like General Westmoreland when he was Army chief of staff, reversed the normal division of labor and left much of the JCS work to the vice chief. No doubt often there must be considerably more satisfaction in addressing matters which one can decide as service chief (subject to approval of the civilian secretary of that service), than in wrangling as a committee member in the Tank.

A question unanswered in the Steadman report is, How would an NMA be staffed? The answer is important, since it is difficult to see how the proposed NMA would make much difference if officers assigned to its staff continued to come from their services and return there for future assignments (and promotions), and remained beholden to their service positions, out of both parochialism and implicit fear for their careers. Essentially the same bureaucratic forces would be in play. Freeing the four officers at the very top from service responsibilities would not automatically free their staff. And if those four officers' roles were to be more than just oracular, a good staff would be essential.

So it might be thought appropriate to remove some or all of the NMA's staff from dependence on their respective services for future assignments and promotions. But if that were done, how would those staff officers receive the senior command experience needed to prepare them to be general officers? Or would the NMA direct assignments within the services? If that were to happen, one of the most valued prerogatives of the service chief (as well as of some service secretaries) would have disappeared. Or would officers entering NMA staff duty thereafter be promoted only to more senior NMA staff assignments? Such an alternative would not likely be attractive to many, given that the staff could not include many high-ranking positions, and that most officers enjoy and develop in command. Such an alternative also would point toward the development of a true, elite general staff corps—one which might indeed begin to lose touch with the grubby day-to-day realities of the services, and which does begin to conjure up shades of Moltke and Schlieffen.

Likely implications of un-double-hatting the chiefs thus include diminution of the importance of the service chief, a greater role for the joint staff, and—ultimately—a move away from separate Army, Navy, Marines, and Air Force, and toward the dreaded (by some) "purple suit." In simplest terms, it is difficult to conceive of an effective totally supraservice senior individual or body, which would not in a short time diminish the roles of the individual services themselves. The shock waves of such a change could in time extend back to the Key West agreement of 1948—the compact blessed by President Truman which guaranteed and defined the roles of each of the four services.[62] And probably it is this perception, dimly or clearly sensed, that lies behind much of the opposition to any proposal for a new national command structure.

A Defense General Staff

The NMA proposal pushes thoughts towards an even more drastic change: to replace the JCS entirely with a single officer (with or without a horse) who, with senior military assistants, would preside over a multi-service Defense General Staff.

That was the sort of proposal urged by Army study groups in the 1940s, before the Department of Defense was formed (and when the Army assumed that it would dominate such an organization). General Maxwell Taylor advocated it in the post-Sputnik era; his Defense chief of staff would be advised by a Supreme Military Council of three four-star officers from the Army, Navy, and Air Force, respectively.[63] Dean Acheson thought that the chairman of the JCS should be made a "Chief of Staff for the Armed Services," though with only staff functions. The Symington report to President-elect Kennedy in 1960 called for abolition of the services as departments and creation of a chairman of the joint staff presiding over a military advisory council of senior officers.

Yet such solutions were rejected by the Congress in 1947[64] and have had little support over the past thirty years. A defense general staff not only calls to mind monocles and spiked helmets, but also threatens vested interests of all the services. No one appears to be campaigning for it today.[65] That does not mean it is not a good idea.

The arguments against establishing a single defense chief of staff are at least threefold. The first is, "we've never tried it before"; stated more respectably, that the unintended and unforeseen consequences of organizational change often dwarf the planned ones. There are, as the Steadman report recognizes, "strengths of the current system and the checks and balances implicit in its design."[66] If those checks and balances are upset, the final outcome cannot be perfectly predicted.

Secondly, the single chief of staff idea, even more than the NMA option (which might evolve into it), implicitly calls into question the continued existence of the Army, Navy, and Air Force, at least as separate military departments. There would be some positive gains from doing away with interservice rivalries, but it would be overkill to try to solve the problem of military headquarters organization by doing away with the individual services. Certainly the Canadian example is not inspiring. If one were designing armed forces from whole cloth today, it might not be immediately appealing to divide them into Army, Navy, Air Force, plus some divisions and air wings of Marines. But that is the division, and those are the traditions, with which we start. Our military personnel still feel a strong tie to the services which they make up. Their pride and competitiveness can produce results which a single service could not; as in Sloan's General Motors, the sum of the parts may be greater than the whole.[67]

At the same time, to say that the service traditions should be preserved does not logically require that the responsibilities assigned to the departments of Army, Navy, and Air Force must be exactly what they are today. Almost certainly with the passage of time they will change, and probably lessen. The burden of proof ought to be on whoever proposes anything that threatens those service traditions and those areas of particular skill. But the existence of the services does not really have to be tied to the continued existence of the JCS.

Finally, there is the worry that a single defense staff under unitary military leadership would become too powerful. This concern should not be dismissed out of hand. Certainly up to now the JCS type of organization has encouraged the military services to trip over one another. A single staff organization probably would be more efficient in whatever it did. More efficiency is likely to mean more influence, and more influence, more power in the government.

On the other hand, today there is much to hold any military staff in check. The JCS designed in 1947 and 1949 has acquired many new rivals over the years to neutralize it. These are not just the many heavily staffed assistant secretaries around the secretary of defense. There are also an unsympathetic political-military bureau in the State Department, a single-issue pressure group in the Arms Control and Disarmament Agency, a large and sometimes erratic staff of the president's National Security Adviser, and of course the CIA. A recent report to the president advocated even more involvement by the staffs of the Office of Management and Budget, State, NSC, and ACDA in what up to now has been internal defense planning.[68] In the councils of government today, the JCS are double-teamed and then some.

So for the short run, one might conclude that it really is a question of balance, and that the military's role in shaping national security policy today is too small; that our defense budgets are inadequate to the role the United States should have in the world; that our military forces are declining relative to the Soviets'. Therefore in the early 1980s a stronger military voice in national policy would be all to the good. For the longer run, however, it certainly would be important to hedge in military leaders, even in a staff role, with safeguards sufficient to maintain unquestioned civilian control of the military in this country. That never has posed a problem, and it should not. Inefficient organization is one way of keeping the military under control, but surely it is not the only way, especially for a military with the traditions of loyalty of ours.

Splitting Functions

Another, less drastic, organizational change would be to split the duties of the JCS planning and advisory responsibilities from its duty to serve as an operations staff for the secretary of defense. The latter task might be given to a single officer with a staff, while the chiefs or a similar body functioned as planners and advisers. In one version, the chairman would still preside over the chiefs but would act alone as head of the operations staff. Variations of such suggestions were prominent among proposals drawn up by military study groups prior to the National Security Act of 1947.

One question these ideas raise is whether planning should be divorced from operational staffing; or, if not whether the chiefs (or some other senior panel), in advising others in the Pentagon who were busy with operations, would be anything more than a neglected council of elders outside the flow of activity. Another consideration is whether splitting the functions might not just double the staffs. Another is, who would prepare contingency plans? Splitting functions seems less attractive in its own right than as a compromise step in evolution toward a single supraservice staff.

Conclusions

Twenty years from now our national security organization will not look the same as it does today. Almost certainly it will be less service-constrained. Will there be something called the Joint Chiefs of Staff? The answer depends partly on what the present chiefs and chairman do now, and partly on the tests to which the present system may be put.

The formal structure of U.S. national security organization has changed little since 1958, or even since 1949. The loci of power within it have shifted considerably. Organizations often adapt to trends and to dominating personalities without shedding old forms. McNamara forever changed the office of secretary of defense by imposing a system of program and budgetary controls. The president's assistant for NSC matters has evolved from a clerk in the 1950s, to a personal adviser, to—probably too often—a public figure.[69] Offices also can diminish. The adjutant general once was the most powerful officer in the Army. The secretaries of the Army, Navy, and Air Force have seen their role in shaping defense policy steadily shrink.

Major changes in U.S. military organization have been associated with the onset or aftermath of wars—the original JCS in 1942, and Secretary Root's design of the Army General Staff after the Spanish-American War are examples. As in so many other ways, the Vietnam War was different. If it provided any novelty in military decision making, it was in greater civilian involvement in the details of military operations, made possible by modern communications.

There is no great external pressure for military reorganization right now, but nevertheless some large and rather steady forces are at work in the defense bureaucracy. Evolution has continued toward more central direction of military activities and away from service distinctions in military planning and operations. It has not been arrested even by those who proclaimed a goal of decentralization. No reason appears to doubt that this trend, which extends back at least to World War II, will persist.

By holding back the joint staff, by insisting on parochial positions, the services cannot keep the forces toward jointness and supraservice concerns from working; they simply risk making the JCS irrelevant. The present secretary of defense constantly is asking the JCS to help him more, not less—but to help with wisdom and analysis rather than corporate *ipse dixits*. Unless the JCS can give the policy makers effective assistance, it will become ultimately of no more consequence than a uniformed House of Lords. Power will flow elsewhere.

Some avenues to improving the present organization are reasonably clear. The most important is a larger role and clearer primacy for the chairman. In addition, a number of small actions—from early guidance to better staffing to more in-dependence from service influence—should be taken to turn the joint staff into the elite military staff of the Department of Defense. The balance of the century is likely to see a continued emphasis on jointness and with it some enhancement, even in peacetime, of the role of the supraservice field commanders, the CINCs. Correspondingly, the policy influence of the separate military departments is likely to diminish. The JCS can go up or down, depending on whether the chiefs can meet the needs instead of standing pat, isolating themselves, and simply letting the stream of decision making flow around them. But whether they evolve and adapt, or rather are simply passed by, the JCS are not likely to remain indefinitely the an-tiquated committee that they are today.

Although they can be moderated, however, the two greatest weaknesses of the JCS cannot be cured within the present structure. These are: first, the dual responsibilities—the built-in conflict of interest—of the chiefs; and second, the nature and composition of the joint staff. Both need to be changed. So does one only slightly lesser failing: the lack of authority in the chairman to tell the chiefs what to do.

The question is not whether the direction of the evolutionary process is good, but whether it can move quickly enough. Militarily, geopolitically, we live in ex-ceptionally dangerous times. The present JCS system is inadequate, not just to our national-security policy-making process, but to performance of some basic, needed military functions. This has been recognized for years. President Eisenhower, who among his many other qualifications had been a JCS member, tried in 1953 to move "toward improving the strategic planning machinery of the Joint Chiefs of Staff, and lead to the development of plans based on the broadest conception of the over-all national interest rather than the particular desires of the individual ser-vices."[70] It didn't work. He gave it another try in 1958, and that didn't work either. Yet in spite of continued obvious inadequacies in the JCS system, no one has done more than tinker with it since.

Notes

1. P.L. 95–485, §807 Oct. 20, 1978. In earlier years such a change, regarded in 1976 as largely formal, would have been controversial. In 1950 the JCS urged that "inclusion of the Commandant of the Marine Corps in the membership of the JCS is unnecessary, undesirable and impracticable" (JCS Memorandum 1977/4. Mar. 21, 1950). The 1976 Senate consideration occupies slightly over one page in the *Congressional Record* (July 11, 1978, pp. S10417–18).

2. General Maxwell D. Taylor. *Precarious Security* (New York: W.W. Norton & Co., 1976), p. 59.

3. Robert F. Kennedy, *Thirteen Days* (New York: W.W. Norton & Co., 1969), p. 119.

4. National Security Action Memorandum no. 55. "Relations of the Joint Chiefs of Staff to the President in Cold War Operations," June 28, 1961. See also testimony of Admiral

Thomas H. Moorer in U.S., Congress, House, Committee on Armed Services, Subcommittee on Investigations, *Hearings on Joint Chiefs of Staff Current Defense Decisionmaking Process* Oct. 12, 1978, p. 20. The plea was not new. Secretary Neil McElroy in 1948 had directed that the Joint Chiefs of Staff" avail themselves of . . . scientific, industrial and economic as well as military" thinking (DOD Directive 5158.8, "Organization of the Joint Chiefs of Staff and Relationships with the Office of the Secretary of Defense," Dec. 31, 1958). The injunction reaffirmed a similar one from Secretary Wilson in 1954, which had reflected recommendations of the 1953 Rockefeller Commission Report.

5. Memorandum for the chairman, Joint Chiefs of Staff, "Relations of the Joint Chiefs of Staff to the President," Sept. 22, 1977.

6. The joint staff proper is limited by statute to four hundred officers 10 U.S.C. §143(*a*). However, the limitation is largely meaningless, since officers can be assigned to the "organization of the Joint Chiefs of Staff" without counting against the ceiling. The Joint Chiefs of Staff currently control about seven hundred officers, including the joint staff.

7. After the 1969 shooting down of a U.S. EC-121 by North Korea, "Secretary Laird directed the OSD staff to assess selected JCS contingency plans because of his dissatisfaction with the contingency options available when the crisis occurred" (Philip Odeen, *National Security Policy Integration* [Washington, D.C.: Office of Management and Budget, 1979], p. 38).

8. General Maxwell D. Taylor, in John Charles Daly et al., *The Role of the Joint Chiefs of Staff in National Policy* (Washington, D.C.: American Enterprise Institute, 1978), p. 16. See also President Eisenhower in Special Message to the Congress, Apr. 13, 1958, *Public Papers of the Presidents of the United States, Dwight D. Eisenhower, 1958* (Washington, D.C.: U.S. Government Printing Office, 1959), pp. 281–82: "The Joint Chiefs of Staff will in the future serve as staff assisting the Secretary of Defense in his exercise of direction over unified commands. Orders issued to the commands by the Joint Chiefs of Staff will be under the authority and in the name of the Secretary of Defense. . . . I think it important to have it clearly understood that the Joint Chiefs of Staff act only under the authority and in the name of the Secretary of Defense."

9. Special Message to the Congress, Apr. 30, 1953, reprinted in *Public Papers of the Presidents of the United States, Dwight D. Eisenhower, 1953* (Washington, D.C.: U.S. Government Printing Office, 1960), p. 234.

10. At present the European, Pacific, Readiness, Southern, and Atlantic commands. The Southern Command is headed by a three-star officer. The Readiness Command includes most of the deployable army and tactical air units based in the continental United States.

11. At present the Strategic Air Command, the Aerospace Defense Command, and the Military Airlift Command.

12. Unified commands generally are geographically oriented and usually contain forces from more than one military service; specified commands have a functional mission and forces from a single service. CINCPAC's area of responsibility extends across the Indian Ocean to the eastern coast of Africa. EUCOM is responsible for the Middle East and the Persian Gulf. No command at present is assigned Africa south of the Sahara.

13. DOD Directive 5100.1, Dec. 31, 1958. This directive assigns functions and authorities to the major elements of the Department of Defense.

14. Blue Ribbon Defense Panel, *Report to the President and the Secretary of Defense on the Department of Defense* (Washington, D.C.: U.S. Government Printing Office, 1970),

p. 35. The Rockefeller Commission Report in 1953 had also recommended removing the Joint Chiefs of Staff completely from a command role in operations.

15. Admiral U.S.G. Sharp, *Strategy for Defeat* (San Rafael, Calif.: Presidio Press, 1978), pp. 35, 33, 38. A chain of operational command depicted in the book shows the JCS in line between the secretary of defense and CINCPAC (ibid., p. 78). When a "JCS Corridor" was dedicated in the Pentagon in 1978, it contained a misleading display of "the chain of command" which included in line both the National Security Council and the Joint Chiefs of Staff.

16. Blue Ribbon Defense Panel, *Report*, pp. 27–28.

17. Admiral Moorer says he saw the President (Nixon) "maybe four or five times a week," presumably not always with the secretary of defense present (House, Committee on Armed Services. Subcommittee on Investigations, *Hearings on Joint Chiefs of Staff Current Defense Decisionmaking Process*, Oct. 12, 1978, p. 28). President Nixon indeed appears to have communicated with Admiral Moorer directly (see *RN: The Memoirs of Richard Nixon* [New York: Grosset and Dunlap, 1978], pp. 500, 734, 735).

18. Memorandum for the Chairman, Joint Chiefs of Staff, "Relations of the Joint Chiefs of Staff to the President," Sept. 22, 1977.

19. "I must say the Secretary of Defense has been very good about sending over to the White House . . . those key memoranda from the Chiefs, and particularly when we ask that the President be informed. I know of no case that the Secretary of Defense has not promptly informed him" (U.S., Congress, Senate, Committee on Armed Services, *Hearings on the Nominations of David C. Jones et al.*, 95th Cong., 2st sess. 1978, p. 99 [testimony of General Jones]; see also pp. 98, 120–21: "Only on important issues will we ask that this be sent to the President, but I know that in those cases . . . that they do go to the President"). When asked in 1978 how often he transmits JCS views to the president, Secretary Brown replied, "Oh, I probably send up one a week" (House, Committee on Armed Services, Subcommittee on Investigations. "Hearings on Joint Chiefs of Staff Current Defense Decisionmaking Process," Oct. 3, 1976, pp. 103–5).

In some other administrations the JCS apparently worried that their memoranda to the president might go unforwarded (see Admiral Elmo R. Zumwalt, Jr., *On Watch* [New York: Quadrangle, 1976], p. 490).

20. Zumwalt, *On Watch*, pp. 288–91.

21. Daly et al., *The Role of the Joint Chiefs of Staff in National Policy*, p. 25. The present chairman said, referring to the same period, that "we have had an unusual degree of access to President Carter" (Senate, Committee on Armed Services, *Hearings on the Nominations of David C. Jones et al.*, p. 97).

22. Zumwalt, *On Watch*, p. 370.

23. Ibid., pp. 494–95, 498. Admiral Zumwalt said he thought individual chiefs were less intended to be "the President's man" than was the chairman (ibid., pp. 370–71).

24. Former Chairman Admiral Thomas H. Moorer has argued that the secretary of defense should be removed from the military chain of command, apparently to avoid the risk of the secretary's civilian staff trying to involve themselves in military operations (House, Committee on Armed Services, Subcommittee on Investigations, *Hearings on Joint Chiefs of Staff Current Defense Decisionmaking Process*, Oct. 12, 1978, pp. 62–63).

25. Wainstein, "Staff Report on Joint Chiefs of Staff Decisionmaking," appendix N to Blue Ribbon Defense Panel, *Report*, p. 8. In 1958 the JCS successfully averted a plan to include language in a DOD directive that would have described the JCS as part of the Office of the Secretary of Defense.

26. General Westmoreland as Army chief of staff observed that "Laird seemed to be concerned that Kissinger was exerting undue influence on policies of the Department of Defense" and "made clear his disapproval of my talking directly with Kissinger" (General William C. Westmoreland, *A Soldier Reports* [Garden City, N.Y.: Doubleday & Co., 1976], p. 387). Kissinger in turn recalls soliciting advice from the chairman, General Wheeler, "which he passed to the President through Haig, thus avoiding the inconvenience of Defense Department channels and the certainty of Laird's wrath" (Henry A. Kissinger, *White House Years* [Boston: Little, Brown, 1979], p. 477).

27. See, for example, Lieutenant General Edward L. Rowny, "Let's Get Back to the Merits of SALT II," *Wall Street Journal,* Oct. 3, 1979.

28. The Congress in 1949 enacted a specific statutory authorization for any member of the JCS to make recommendations to the Congress, after first telling the secretary of defense. This provision is not invoked in practice; President Eisenhower called it "licensed insubordination."

29. General Maxwell D. Taylor, *The Uncertain Trumpet* (New York: Harper & Bros., 1959), p. 112.

30. U.S., Congress, Senate, Committee on Foreign Relations, *Hearings on the Panama Canal Treaties,* 95th Cong., 1st sess., 1977, vol. 1, p. 155. See also Address to the Palm Beach Round Table, Palm Beach, Fla., Dec. 9, 1977 (DOD news release, unnumbered). Those officers who have taken the route of leaving active duty have found a limited audience for their views. General Rowny's SALT II testimony probably changed few minds. General Haig's speechmaking failed to generate a ground swell of support for his becoming a 1980 presidential candidate.

31. Taylor, *The Uncertain Trumpet,* p. 113. General Brown agreed that "the rules are also quite clear that in response to interrogatories before a congressional committee that we answer fully and factually" (Senate, Committee on Foreign Relations, *Hearings on the Panama Canal Treaties,* vol. 1, p. 113). The present chairman also agrees (See Senate, Committee on Armed Services, *Hearings on the Nominations of David C. Jones et al.,* pp. 33–34, 25–27).

32. Admiral Moorer after retirement as chairman of the JCS complained that "the Congress most of the time does not ask the right questions. . . . I think the Congress should ask the professional military people what is your personal opinion, what would you do if you were making the decision solely on your own, and you probably would get a different answer" (House, Committee on Armed Services, Subcommittee on Investigations, *Hearings on the Joint Chiefs of Staff Current Defense Decisionmaking Process,* Oct. 12, 1978, pp. 34, 38). The present chairman has said, "I don't believe it is up to them (military officers) to try to prompt such a situation—to go around and say to people, if you ask me this question you will get a different answer. . . . I don't think it is fair for the person to try to entice such questions" (Senate, Committee on Armed Services, *Hearings on Nominations of David C. Jones et al.,* p. 33).

33. "George Scratchley Brown," *Washington Post,* Dec. 8, 1978.

34. Westmoreland, *A Soldier Reports,* pp. 224–30.

35. Dean Acheson, *Present at the Creation* (New York: W.W. Norton & Co., 1969), p. 243. Secretary of War Stimson called the wartime JCS "astonishingly successful, but . . . incapable of enforcing a decision against the will of any of its members" (Henry L. Stimson and McGeorge Bundy, *On Active Service in Peace and War* [New York: Harper & Bros., 1947], p. 515).

36. Kissinger, *White House Years*, p. 398.

37. Blue Ribbon Defense Panel, *Report*, p. 128.

38. Alain C. Enthoven and K. Wayne Smith, *How Much Is Enough?* (New York: Harper & Row, 1971), p. 336.

39. Eisenhower, Special Message to the Congress, Apr. 3, 1958, reprinted in *Public Papers of the Presidents, Eisenhower, 1958*, p. 282.

40. Zumwalt, *On Watch*, p. 334.

41. Taylor, *The Uncertain Trumpet*, p. 93.

42. See ibid., p. 94.

43. Blue Ribbon Defense Panel, *Report*, p. 128.

44. Indeed, the Navy has not yet managed to pull together, except through compromises, its own semifeudal and often feuding air, surface, and submarine "communities."

45. Secretary Brown also moved each of the ten defense agencies under the line authority of an under secretary or assistant secretary of defense. Some of these agencies were directed to respond also to tasks assigned by the JCS, and the Defense Intelligence Agency reports to both the secretary of defense and the chairman of the JCS.

46. Remarks delivered at commissioning ceremonies of the U.S.S. *Dwight D. Eisenhower*, Norfolk, Va., Oct. 18, 1977 (DOD news release no. 484–77); see *Public Papers of the Presidents, Eisenhower, 1958*, p. 274.

47. Richard C. Steadman, *Report to the Secretary of Defense on the National Military Command Structure* (Washington, D.C.: Department of Defense, 1978).

48. Ibid., at p. 70. For Mr. Steadman's later emphasis on this point, see n. 65. below.

49. Daly et al., *The Role of the Joint Chiefs of Staff in National Policy*, p. 11.

50. DOD Directive 1320.5, July 26, 1978.

51. See Blue Ribbon Defense Panel, *Report*, p. 36.

52. By statute, officers normally may not be assigned to the joint staff for more than three years, or reassigned to it without a three-year interval, though waivers are possible (10 U.S.C. §143[a]).

53. The under secretary of defense for policy is developing a new document with assumptions to be used in developing military plans.

54. For a more detailed discussion of the potential under secretary and JCS roles in continuing General Jones's effort toward more realistic planning, see William K. Brehm, *Evaluation Report of Mobilizaton and Deployment Capability in Connection with Exercise Nifty Nugget* (Washington, D.C.: Office of the Secretary of Defense, 1979), pp. 56–57; see also Odeen, *National Security Policy Integration*, pp. 34–35.

55. However, LANTCOM (the Atlantic command) is composed almost entirely of naval forces, and the three specified commands are exclusively Air Force.

56. By a memorandum approved by President Kennedy and not changed thereafter, the CINCs normally serve two-year terms.

57. The Steadman proposal would have to be adjusted to current law, which forbids the chairman to "exercise military command over the Joint Chiefs of Staff or any of the armed forces" (10 U.S.C. §142[c]).

58. See Sharp, *Strategy for Defeat*.

59. Cf. Daly et al., *The Role of the Joint Chiefs of Staff in National Policy*, p. 15.

60. Westmoreland, *A Soldier Reports*, p. 363 (emphasis added).

61. However, General Maxwell Taylor observed that "I am glad to have had the experience of being chief of staff of the army, but I enjoyed being chairman more. The advan-

tage of the chairman is that he is not responsible for the detailed activities of a service. He can sit back and reflect on the world and its contents" (Daly et al., *The Role of the Joint Chiefs of Staff in National Policy*, p. 11).

62. Currently embodied in DOD Directive 5100.1, Dec. 31, 1958, "Functions of the Department of Defense and Its Major Components," the directive which is the organizational "constitution" of the Department of Defense.

63. Taylor, *The Uncertain Trumpet*, pp. 175–76.

64. The 1949 act, which created the office of chairman, stated that the purpose of the Congress was "not to establish a single Chief of Staff over the armed forces nor an armed forces general staff" (50 U.S.C. §401). The law provides that "the Joint Staff shall not operate or be organized as an overall Armed Forces General Staff and shall have no executive authority" (10 U.S.C. §143[d]): A House Report in 1947 warned that "the Joint Staff must in the future be carefully observed to prevent its possible development into a national general staff" (H.R. Report no. 4214 [1947]).

65. In a later address Steadman went beyond his report to advocate giving powers to the chairman which certainly would move in that direction (see U.S. Military Academy, *1979 Senior Conference Final Report: The Role of the Military in National Security Policy Formulation in the 1950's* [West Point, N.Y.: U.S. Military Academy, 1979], pp. 23–28).

66. Steadman, *Report to the Secretary of Defense*, p. 76.

67. The existence of multiple services with overlapping missions may also result in larger armed forces than the Congress otherwise would authorize. For example, if the Marine Corps were eliminated would its divisions and air wings be added to the other services?

68. Odeen, *National Security Policy Integration*, pp. 16–40. The proposal reflects a valid concern that national security policy is not always made in an effective and orderly manner. But the cure, unless carefully limited, could be far worse than the illness. Unless the proposed staff-level involvement of other agencies in defense programming and budgeting prior to decisions of the secretary of defense were carefully confined—perhaps by channeling all such participation through, say, the under secretary for policy—confusion would abound, and the authority not just of the JCS but of the secretary of defense would be hopelessly undercut.

69. Cf. Karen House, "Mr. Zbig," *Wall Street Journal*, Oct. 3, 1979. Sally Quinn, "The Politics of the Power Grab: Nine Rules of Notoriety," *Washington Post*, Dec. 19, 20, 21, 1979.

70. *Public Papers of the Presidents, Eisenhower*, 1953, pp. 236–37.

Discussion Questions

1. What causes interservice rivalry? Can a mere definition of service roles and missions solve the rivalry problem?

2. What are the structural and procedural limitations on the power of the JCS?

3. What are the weaknesses of the current JCS system? What reform is needed, and what factors would impede efforts to reform the current system?

11

Congressional Power: Implications for American Security Policy

Richard Haass

The Changing Shape of Congress

The terms "Congress" and "President," or "legislature" and "executive," can often be misleading. As David Truman has written:

> the political process rarely, if ever, involves a conflict between the legislature and the executive viewed as two monolithic and unified institutions. The actual competing structures on each side are made up of elements in the legislature and in the executive, reflecting and supported by organized and unorganized interests.[1]

In reality, the picture is further complicated by the influence of coalitions consisting of like-minded individuals and groups from both institutions, who are arrayed against similar coalitions, also based in both institutions, pursuing an alternative policy. This willingness of Congressmen to align themselvs with other members or outsiders underscores a central point: to understand the collective impact of Congress one must understand that its influence is often exerted by one of its many parts.

One can examine Congress through many lenses: parties, the two chambers, committees, sub-committees, joint and conference committees, leadership, staff assistants, outside agencies, issue coalitions and individual members. Such disaggregation *per se* is not new: Congress has never been a simple or single institution. What is new, however, and what is basic to any appreciation of the workings and impact of Congress, is the far greater degree of decentralization that has evolved over recent years. This is in part a result of structural reform designed specifically to democratize the institution; at the same time, it is a product of the explosion of personnel and information sources available to individual members. In both cases, what has been altered is not simply the processes within Congress but also the products which emerge.

Reprinted with minor revisions from Haass, Richard, "Congressional Power: Implications for American Security Policy," *Adelphi Paper 153* (London: International Institute for Strategic Studies, 1979). Copyright © International Institute for Strategic Studies, 1979. Reprinted with permission.

The most powerful administrative units within Congress have traditionally been the committees. Both the Senate and the House of Representatives are divided into more than twenty committees apiece, to which members are assigned by their respective parties in numbers reflecting the overall balance between the parties in Congress. In all cases, chairmen are members of the majority (presently Democratic) party. Each committee has responsibility for a broad area: foreign relations, armed services, energy and so on, and consideration of legislation and other matters by the full membership of each chamber only comes after the relevant committee or committees have had the opportunity to hold hearings and rewrite the legislation. Until recently, committee recommendations would rarely be over-ruled by the full membership; indeed, Woodrow Wilson once described the United States as a "government by the standing committees of Congress."[2]

Today, the situation is quite changed, particularly in the area of foreign and defense policy. Neither the Senate nor the House has a single "National Security Affairs Committee." The principal Senate and House committees in this area—the Foreign Relations and Foreign Affairs Committees respectively—are quite limited in their purview. Their primary legislative responsibilities—the annual foreign military and economic assistance packages—are shared with the appropriations committees, and in many cases are amended heavily by the full membership when the legislation "reaches the floor." Moreover, neither committee has a monopoly on the consideration of most national security matters. Issues in this area are, by one account, dealt with by sixteen Senate and nineteen House committees and an even larger number of sub-committees.[3] What results are two types of jurisdictional tangle: not only are foreign and defense policy issues considered by a large number of separate committees, but often the same matter is considered by two or more committees.

The chief consequence of this structural disunity is to divide the congressional perspective, making the creation of integrated and coherent legislation and policy almost impossible. Compromise becomes the paramount concern: "Legislative conflicts in Congress are resolved more often than not by political pressure, not by any rational presentation of the issues."[4] The tendency is both to isolate and to emphasize the dimension of an issue that comes under the committee's authority; as a result, one dimension of relations between the United States and a foreign country can sour the larger relationship and injure more important interests. In addition, little thought is given to trade-offs—that is, to how the emphasis on one issue might directly affect others, or how bargaining and compromise over one goal may help to achieve another. That the policies emerging from such a system are at times in conflict with the requirements of a sensitive and comprehensive foreign policy should come as little surprise.

The capacity of Congress to produce coherent policy has been further eroded by other trends within the institution. Formal authorities, whether party leaders or committee chairmen, have been successfully challenged and weakened. With neither position nor seniority a guarantee of influence, power has flowed mostly to individual members, *ad hoc* groups and coalitions. There is no central authority capable of co-ordinating the initiatives of these diverse sources. At the same time, the high rate of turnover—more than half the current membership entered Congress this decade—has not only had the effect of removing many powerful members from Congress, but has also brought into office a large number of representatives unwilling to accept the old order within the institution and often unfamiliar with the traditions of American foreign and defense policies. The Congress may be more democratic and decentralized, but it is also less manageable and predictable.

Closely connected with this redistribution of power within Congress has been a growth and redistribution of resources. The expansion of congressional capacity and access to information has been nothing less than spectacular. Three areas stand out: the increase in the staff assistance available to all members, either on their personal staffs or through committees on which they serve; the enlargement of existing "support agencies" as well as the creation of new ones; and the greater capacity of Congress to benefit from the information and expertise of the executive branch.

The increase in staff has been a gradual but accelerating development since the end of World War II. In addition to the provision every member receives for personal staff to serve in Washington and one or more offices in his home state or district, the Legislative Reorganization Act of 1947 authorized each committee to hire four professional and six clerical aides as well as a number of temporary assistants. This Act set the pattern for the next thirty years. By 1947 congressional committee staffs totalled nearly 500 people, and personal staffs 2,000. Twenty years later, in 1967, committee staffs had risen in number to over 1,200, and personal staffs had tripled to some 5,800 people. Today, after additional reforms, committees employ more than 3,000 aides—over six times the post-war figure—and personal staffs number over 10,000 employees. By 1976 the average staff of each of the 100 Senators was thirty-one; some included more than seventy. Allowances for staff and office operations for Senators from the larger states had climbed over $1 million per year.[5]

This sharp increase in the availability of staff has transformed the role of the individual member. With the average Senator serving on ten or more committees and sub-committees, casting thousands of votes every year, serving constituents and working for re-election, it is the staff assistants who do most of the actual work. This includes drafting legislation and amendments, preparing background material for hearings, writing speeches and offering advice. "Senators . . . are functioning more and more like the president or chief presiding officer of a corporation, giving direction to policy and giving staff the responsibility for details."[6]

Members of Congress also have a wide range of congressional support agencies to tap for information, analysis and guidance. The oldest of these is the Congressional Research Service (CRS), established as the Legislative Reference Service under the rubric of the Library of Congress in 1914. With its change of name in 1970 came a redirection of purpose. The CRS was ordered to become a "policy and research arm of the Congress" rather than simply providing more narrow services related to legislation. Today the approximately 700 employees of the nonpartisan CRS answer nearly 200,000 requests annually from members, committees and staffs, and provide a growing number of issue and legislative briefs, background reports and analyses.[7] Similar in function, but both smaller and more restricted is the Office of Technology Assessment (OTA). Established in 1972, the OTA was created to provide Congress with an independent source of scientific and technical expertise.

Like both the CRS and the OTA, the General Accounting Office or GAO is another source of information and analysis for the Congress. Where it differs, however, is in its additional role of "watchdog." In the original 1921 legislation, as well as in the subsequent reforms brought about in 1970 and 1974, the GAO is given the unique mandate to oversee and audit federal government programs and operations. The term "audit" is used broadly. It consists of surveys, detailed reviews and reporting, and covers such matters as federal compliance with laws and regulations passed by Congress, the efficiency and economy of operations and the quality of results. The scope of the GAO is wide. In 1975 nearly one half its staff, or 2,000 people, were located outside Washington and conducted more than 2,000 surveys and reviews of government programs in the United States and seventy-eight foreign countries.[9]

Created by the Congressional Budget and Impoundment Control Act of 1974, the Congressional Budget Office (CBO) is the most recent of the four support agencies. It is also the most closely connected with the day-to-day operations of the Congress, as the CBO is allied with the two new House and Senate Budget Committees. Together, they perform two important functions. On one hand, they provide Congress with an overall budgetary perspective, totalling receipts and expenditures, thereby introducing a measure of fiscal discipline into what had often been an uncontrolled process of considering separate measures with little regard for their composite impact. At the same time the CBO can present analyses of policy options in terms of budgetary implications; for example, their papers on the United States Navy or strategic arms have indicated the kinds of forces the country can choose, the arguments on behalf of each and what each option or mix would cost. But the CBO and the two committees do have their limitations. They can only present analyses of options; they cannot favor one system or alternative. More important, their power is the power of persuasion. They cannot force Congress to adopt or adhere to their spending resolutions; nor can they directly overrule a committee or individual who promotes an initiative in conflict with budgetary guidelines. This latter weakness became obvious during the initial years of the new congressional budget system: while the committees can plead a "disinterested" case along fiscal lines, it can easily be defeated by coalitions designed to promote a particular issue.[10]

The combined resources of the support agencies and both personal and committee staff have gone a long way towards eliminating the "information gap" that many members of Congress felt was basic to executive supremacy in foreign affairs. Thus, the fact that Congress has also turned to the executive itself to help fill this gap is not without its irony. The mechanisms are both formal and informal, authorized and otherwise. Briefings of Congressmen and their staffs are commonplace, and the CIA has been transformed into a fifth support agency by many in Congress. Congressional policy oversight provides members with the right to question executive officials, and the hearing process, with its mixture of testimony and questions, has become an intrinsic part of the policy-making process.

This is not to say that there are no limits to congressional access to executive information. The Supreme Court has lent support to the concept of "executive privilege" and the right of the President to withhold certain information from the Congress, particularly in the realm of military and diplomatic affairs.[11] In addition, certain key officials, including the Assistant to the President for National Security Affairs, cannot be compelled to testify before Congress. In general, though, the trend has favored increased cooperation in maintaining the flow of information, and the Freedom of Information Act in particular has been responsible for increasing congressional (and, more generally, public) access to the documents of the executive branch.[12]

Congress has also turned to legislation to ensure access to certain kinds of information and analysis available to the executive branch. A large number of executive initiatives—arms transfers, nuclear exports, assistance programs—must be accompanied by reports detailing their justification and impact on local stability, nuclear proliferation and human rights respectively. The best-known of these executive reporting requirements, however, are the Arms Control Impact Statements, mandated in 1975. Congress ordered the executive branch to prepare annual statements discussing the arms-control implications of proposed defense programs being sent to Congress for authorization and appropriation. Not only were these statements intended to assist Congress in its consideration of defense requests, but they were instituted as well to force the Administration to consider the arms-control implications of new weapon systems at a sufficiently early stage in their development for either their programs or American policy to be adjusted if necessary. In addition, it was hoped that the statements would enhance the role of the Arms Control and Disarmament Agency (ACDA) within the executive branch. In practice, the exercise has had but a modest effect. Nevertheless, over the years the statements have grown in both number and quality, and have proved useful both as a means of transmitting information to Congress and as a procedure for raising the salience of arms-control concerns within the executive.[13]

Sources of information, analysis and advice outside those mentioned above also exist. A large number of research organizations, universities, constituents, lobbyists and media are actively attempting to influence Congressmen. Indeed, the difficulty now appears to be less a shortage than a glut of information. As Congressman Les Aspin has remarked, "Most congressional offices are deluged with more information than they can possibly absorb."[14] The impact of this fundamental change in the availability of both assistance and information is basic to the under-standing of the influence of Congress. In part, it has brought about a classic demonstration of Parkinson's Law. Congressional activities have increased parallel to the enlargement of congressional capacities. The number of bills and amend-ments considered, the number and length of hearings and reports and the degree of oversight of executive operations—all have increased sharply over the past decade. In the process, Congress has not only placed greater demands on the resources of the executive branch, but it has also overloaded its own members.[15]

The "inputs" to Congress have multiplied many times over, but the institu-tion still consists of 535 members. The congressional bureaucracy has made itself essential at the cost of demanding too much of the members it allegedly serves. Whatever the initial justification for augmenting support capabilities, continued expansion will at best be of marginal use and will more probably be a liability.

The growth of resources has also had the effect of enhancing the role of the in-dividual member, however overloaded he may be as a result. In the past the severely limited resources available to Congress as a whole were reserved largely for the senior members, usually committee chairman and party leaders. Today new provisions for personal staff and guaranteed minority shares in committee staffs, along with the equally available support agencies, have assured individual members of resources adequate for the preparation of initiatives and serious chal-lenges to executive policy. Every member has become a potential source of inde-pendent policy.

Other reforms have also contributed to decentralization. Senators are now limited to a maximum of eleven committee and sub-committee assignments apiece (down from an average of eighteen), and no one may chair more than three com-mittees or sub-committees. As a result, power continues to be distributed more widely. Although the number of committees has been reduced slightly, referrals to more than one committee have become more common, and the allocation of au-thority for considering national security issues less precisely focused. Seniority as the sole criterion for appointment has been successfully challenged, and chairmen have been removed.[16] Again, the institution has traded centralization for democracy. To the extent that the whole can be judged as the sum of its parts, Congress is more ac-tive than ever before; in reality, though, the parts are increasingly autonomous, and there is little or no means of ensuring their integration or moderation.

The Recovery of Traditional Powers

One of the principal means by which the Congress has reasserted its influence over foreign policy has been through the use of its inherent but often dormant powers. To a large extent, this reassertion has centered on the Senate, given its unique constitutional responsibilities for the making of treaties and the approval of certain executive officials. In other areas, however, the recovery of traditional powers has involved both chambers, often resulting more from inferred or inherent powers, both legal and political, than from explicit constitutional decrees. Indeed, in its use of these powers, the "new" Congress most resembles many of its influential predecessors.

The Constitution is characteristically terse in its coverage of the treaty power: The President "shall have power, by and with the Advice and Consent of the Senate, to make Treaties, provided two thirds of the Senators present concur." The power to make treaties, unlike most others, is thus a shared power, forming, in Hamilton's words, "a distinct department . . . to belong, properly, neither to the legislature nor to the executive."[17] Moreover, the power is shared not between President and Congress, but only between President and Senate. Again the *Federalists*, in this case Jay, provide a rationale. Describing senators as "men . . . the most distinguished by their abilities and virtue," he claimed "it was wise . . .to provide not only that the power of making treaties should be committed to able and honest men, but also that they should continue in place a sufficient time to become perfectly acquainted with our national concerns."[18]

Yet although in theory the treaty power is to be shared between executive and Senate, most of the responsibility has devolved on the former. The executive is far better placed and constituted to conduct negotiations with foreign states. After some initial experimentation with a major role for Congress in the negotiating phase, both executive and Senate were willing to accept a division of labor in which the former negotiated and the latter passed final judgment. The constitutional provision for senatorial advice and consent evolved, with the function of advice decreasing and that of granting (or withholding) consent rising.

Consequently, to the dismay of more than one President, the doctrine of automatic or "obligatory consent" grew obsolete as the Senate effectively exchanged its right to assist in the making of a treaty for the right to reject what had been negotiated. Writing at the turn of the century, the powerful senator Henry Cabot Lodge expressed this notion clearly. "The treaty, so called, is therefore still inchoate, a mere project for a treaty, until the consent of the Senate has been given to it."[19] As a result, the Constitution's "Advice and Consent" charge came to refer to the "Senate's action on a treaty which had been submitted to it by the President after negotiations are completed but before ratification."[20]

But whatever the legal right of the Senate to refuse consent, in political terms its refusal would necessarily have a major impact on relations with the foreign state or states involved. As Louis Henkin has noted, "By the time . . . the Senate considers a treaty, negotiations have been held, understandings reached, and commitments made (political if not legal), and Congress [*sic*] is far from free to exercise its independent political judgment.[21] In recent years, however, the Senate has demonstrated a greater willingness to exercise "its independent political judgment" regardless of the risks involved. Moreover, it has also begun to reverse the historical shift in its role towards "consent"; as was perhaps intended by the framers of the Constitution, the Senate is once more offering specific advice on treaty negotiations themselves.

Congressional involvement in the advice or treaty-making phase has taken several forms. The most common is by resolution, which can either "liberate" the executive by urging a particular course of action, as was done before the Partial Test Ban, the Non-Proliferation and the SALT I negotiations, or constrain, an expedient adopted by Congress before the Panama Canal and SALT II negotiations.[22] Although expressions of the latter type are not legally binding, they do warn the President of the unwillingness of Congress to accept terms inconsistent with its wishes. The SALT II negotiations have also been the occasion of other congressional attempts to influence the executive. Fourteen Representatives and twenty-five Senators were appointed "advisers" to the American delegation, while formal and informal communications between the branches, particularly in the early months of the Carter Administration, affected the Administration's proposals as much as they informed Congress of the Administration's intentions.[23]

A more public and dramatic sign of the Senate's using its constitutional powers is reflected in its increased willingness to consider alternatives to either outright approval or nonapproval of proposed treaties. Three classes of option are available to the Senate as it considers the resolution of ratification: the addition of "understandings" or "interpretations," which clarify certain provisions without changing their legal effect; the addition of "reservations," which act to limit rather than simply clarify, the legal effects of the treaty, and which can provoke the foreign state or states to make reservations of their own—or even to repudiate the proposed treaty; and, most serious, the amendment of the terms of the treaty itself, which automatically requires renegotiation with the foreign party.[24] The impact of amendment is obvious; in the case of understandings and reservations, however, the distinction between them is unclear, and it falls to the other state or states involved to decide how to react to them.

All three options have been used; understandings are the most common and least controversial, and actual amendments the least common but potentially the most controversial. Reservations, however, are another matter. The passage in March 1978 of the First (or "Permanent Neutrality") Panama Canal Treaty, with a reservation giving the United States the right "to take such steps as [she] deems necessary . . . including the use of military force in Panama, to reopen the Canal or restore [her] operations," brought forth angry denunciations from the Government of Panama. The entire relationship was salvaged only when the second (or "Basic Treaty") was approved, with a reservation that nothing in the treaties should be interpreted "as a right of [United States] intervention in the internal affairs of the Republic of Panama." Over a decade of careful negotiations, the position of the United States in Latin America and the fate of the Canal itself were thus jeopardized by a single reservation in the Senate.[25]

The differences between the three Senate options to alter a proposed treaty can best be illustrated by using as an example the SALT II Treaty. The insertion of a clause stipulating that no restriction in the Protocol shall continue in force after its expiration (but still during the life of the Treaty) unless formally renegotiated constitutes an understanding and requires no response from the Soviet Union. The addition of a clause stating that nothing in the treaty precludes the introduction by the United States of a particular basing system for new land-based ICBM, however, constitutes a reservation, perhaps requiring formal Soviet acquiescence. By contrast, the terms of the agreement would be altered by an amendment—for example, a demand that the four prototype B-1 bombers be eliminated from American totals, or that the *Backfire* bomber be included in the Soviet force totals—and would require Soviet willingness to reopen the negotiations of the treaty.

These courses of action hold important attractions for critics or opponents of proposed treaties. While a final resolution of ratification for treaties requires that two-thirds of the Senators present approve for passage, the changes described above require approval by only a simple majority, although then any changes are subject, along with the rest of the treaty, to the two-thirds vote at the end of the process. This places initial supporters in the uncomfortable position of voting either for the changed treaty or against what they originally sought, while providing initial opponents with the opportunity to vote in favor of an "improved" treaty, thereby avoiding to some extent the appearance of, and responsibility for, being in opposition. The former was the dilemma of the followers of Woodrow Wilson, who felt forced to vote against the Versailles Treaty and its many reservations; the latter could describe the choices to be made if an amended SALT II Treaty is brought to a final vote.

An additional means by which Congress has sought to recapture its treaty power, and a natural corollary to the others, is the limitation of the executive's ability to terminate a treaty without receiving the approval of a majority of Congress, if not two-thirds of the Senate. The question surfaced recently (in December 1978) with President Carter's announcement of his intention to give notice to the Republic of China (Taiwan), on 1 January 1979, to terminate the Mutual Defense Treaty a year later, the delay reflecting the terms of Article X of the treaty. In defense of this action, the State Department's legal adviser argued:

> The President's constitutional power to give notice of termination provided for by the terms of a treaty derives from the President's authority and responsibility as chief executive to conduct the nation's foreign affairs and execute the laws. . . . The Senate's role in giving advice and consent to the making of a treaty is fulfilled when the treaty is made; thereafter execution and performance of its terms, including terms relating to its duration or termination, are delegated by the Constitution to the nation's chief executive.[26]

This position has been challenged by a number of senators, who have argued that since the Constitution makes no reference of the power of termination, but only sets forth a procedure for sharing the power to make treaties between executive and Senate, then it must be inferred that the power to break treaties must also be shared. Precedent is inconclusive; as a recent study has noted, "In practice no

settled rule or procedure has been followed in the termination of treaties."[27] Although the legal question can only be settled by the courts, in terms of
policy the power of unilateral termination of treaties by either branch appears
potentially undesirable in a context in which the sanctity of the commitments
and treaty guarantees of the United States is critical to her performance as a
global power.

This greater willingness on the part of the Senate to exercise its treaty power
has in part been offset, however, by another development. The role of the treaty as
the accepted form of international compact between the United States and foreign
countries has been steadily declining. Various types of "international agreements
other than treaties" (IAOTT)—in many cases, treaties in every way but name—
have become increasingly common. This development has permitted the executive to enter into arrangements, and in some cases undertake commitments,
either without the Senate's approval or with only a simple majority in both
Houses. Moreover, until recently many of these IAOTT, commonly known as
"executive agreements," were reached and maintained even without the Senate's
knowledge.

There is no constitutional distinction between treaties and executive
agreements, the latter being, in the words of one historian, "one of the mysteries
of the constitutional order."[28] Nor is there any accepted distinction between their
legal standing, although the Supreme Court has ruled that the treaty need not be
used for all international agreements.[29] Distinctions can be drawn, however, between different types of executive agreements. "Congressional–Executive
Agreements" are made by the executive, either under the authority of already existing legislation or subject to congressional approval or legislation, while "Treaty-
Executive agreements" can be made pursuant to an existing and hence senatorially
approved treaty. There are also "Presidential–Executive agreements," based solely
upon the general executive authority allegedly accorded the President by the Constitution. It is this last type that has often been the subject of controversy,
although the first two have also been questioned on occasions when it was claimed
that the President had exceeded his authority.[30]

The use of the executive agreement can be traced back to the 1817 Rush-
Bagot Agreement between the United States and Britain governing the level of
military force on the Great Lakes. Partially pursuant to authorizing legislation
passed two years earlier, the agreement was presented to the Senate in 1818, when
the decision was made to endorse it but not as a treaty. Use of the executive agreement grew slowly throughout the nineteenth century. It was expanded significantly
by McKinley, who used it to conclude the Spanish-American War and to proclaim
the Open Door Policy, and by Theodore Roosevelt, who took the significant step
of using it after the Senate had refused to ratify a treaty placing certain customs
houses under the control of the United States. It was after World War II, however,
during the "imperial presidency," that the use of the executive agreement became
widespread.

The Senate Foreign Relations Sub-committee on United States Security Agreements and Commitments Abroad, established in the late 1960s under Senator Symington—who, by his position on the Committees on Foreign Relations, Armed Services and Atomic Energy, probably had more access to classified information than any other member of Congress—was shocked to discover not only a large number of secret agreements with foreign countries, but also several that were tantamount to security commitments.[31] Indeed, by 1969 the United States recognized her adherence to 909 treaties and 3,973 executive agreements, and during the first Nixon Administration a further 1,087 executive agreements were concluded, as opposed to only eight treaties;[32] what these statistics do not show is the increasing use of the former for the more significant arrangements. As the Senate Foreign Relations Committee wrote in 1969, "We have come close to reversing the traditional distinction between the treaty as the instrument of major commitment and the Executive Agreement as the instrument of a minor one."[33]

Although there was a reaction against the executive agreement in the immediate aftermath of the Second World War owing to fears that human rights undertakings abroad would affect the domestic laws of the United States,[34] the bulk of the resistance began some twenty years later. In June 1969 the Senate passed overwhelmingly the National Commitments Resolution, defining what constituted a "national commitment" from the Senate's perspective.[35] Although the resolution was non-binding, it served as a signal both to the executive and to foreign countries that a commitment by the United States to provide armed forces or other resources on behalf of another country could only come about as the result of a positive action, in the form of a treaty, a statute or a concurrent resolution, involving both branches of government. Thus, it placed in jeopardy those pledges given unilaterally to foreign states by the President. Some three years later, in August 1972, Congress passed the "Case Act," requiring the Secretary of State to transmit the text of any international agreement other than a treaty to which the United States is a party not later than sixty days after it has come into force.[36] If the President so decides, the text can be transmitted under an injunction of secrecy to the two Foreign Affairs committees. For many in Congress, however, the "Case Act" did not go far enough. While it ensured that no agreement would remain secret from Congress for more than sixty days, it failed to guarantee Congress either a voice in the making of the agreement or an opportunity to act upon it once it was negotiated. Moreover, the executive alone could decide whether a particular agreement would be submitted to the Senate as a treaty requiring two-thirds approval or merely transmitted to Congress for its information.[37] Since that time numerous efforts to legislate mechanisms for congressional approval of executive agreements, as well as congressional involvement in the choice of forms some compacts assume, have been defeated. Although Congress retains the power indirectly to affect implementation of certain executive agreements by denying appropriations, it has avoided a more direct role.[38]

One compromise between executive unilateralism and the Senate treaty role is provided by the joint resolution process, in which negotiated agreements are approved by a simple majority of each chamber and signed into law by the President. The instrument is an attractive one: it permits both chambers of Congress a voice in the agreement procedure, but eliminates the severe constraint of the approval of two-thirds of the Senate that is basic to the treaty. Indeed, one constitutional expert has claimed, "It is now widely accepted that the Congressional–Executive Agreement is a complete alternative to a treaty: the President can seek approval of any agreement by joint resolution of both Houses of Congress instead of two-thirds of the Senate only."[39]

This overstates the situation, however, as shown by the Senate's ability to ground the trial balloon floated by the Carter Administration to submit the SALT II Agreement as an executive agreement requiring a joint resolution rather than as a treaty requiring the approval of two-thirds of the Senate.[40] In other cases, though, the joint resolution has been used successfully. It was the instrument of congressional approval of the 1975 "Sinai" Middle East Agreements, as well as the 1972 SALT I Interim Agreement. In the latter case the joint resolution conformed to existing law, which prohibited the President from agreeing "to disarm or to reduce or to limit the Armed Forces or armaments of the United States, except pursuant to the treaty-making power of the President under the Constitution or unless authorized by further affirmative legislation by the Congress of the United States."[41]

Clearly, what has evolved is an atmosphere less tolerant of unilateral executive power to enter into agreements with foreign countries. Whatever the form of arrangement, Congress has tended to demand a greater say in the negotiations and has reserved the right of approval. Not surprisingly, this has had an impact both on the process of negotiations and on the ability of the United States to enter into binding compacts with foreign countries. At least two benefits are readily apparent. First, as Alton Frye has argued, "Congress represents the most potent and credible constraint which the executive can cite in its dealings with foreign powers."[42] Certainly, congressional pressure can enhance the bargaining strength of any American representative. Second, congressional support for commitments can help to lessen doubt in the minds of allies and adversaries alike that the President may lack domestic support and, consequently, the ability to follow through on what he has promised.

Yet these and other consequences of a Congress more active in the process of making treaties and other agreements have certain less desirable implications. While the threat of congressional sanction may induce another party to compromise, the reality of sanction may do just the opposite. Thus, whereas congressional power to deny MFN status and credits to the Soviet Union appeared to prompt an increase in the emigration of Soviet Jews during the 1973 and 1974 trade negotiations, the writing into the proposed agreement of "human rights" conditions caused the USSR to repudiate the entire arrangement. More generally, actual or potential congressional constraints on the policy of the United States can limit the flexibility of negotiators and make compromise more difficult. To bargain in a context where a number of incentives may be or have been denied, and where a number of points are "non-negotiable," is often to burden the process with more than it can carry. At the same time, although congressional support of undertakings can help to reduce uncertainties, the unwillingness of Congress to approve commitments, as well as its power to alter or terminate them, inject new elements of doubt into perceptions of the ability of the United States to play a leading and lasting role on behalf of its allies and interests.

The treaty power, although the most important of the traditional powers, is not the only one. The President "shall nominate, and by and with the Advice and Consent of the Senate, shall appoint Ambassadors, other public Ministers and Consuls, Judges of the Supreme Court, and all other officers of the United States." While nominally similar to the treaty power, in that it is shared between executive and Senate, the power to nominate and appoint ambassadors and other major officials (including the Cabinet) is distinct from the treaty power in two important ways, which emerge from a careful reading of the Constitution. Only a simple majority, rather than a majority of two-thirds, is required of the Senate. In addition, whereas the treaty power is an undivided one—that is, both branches are involved in the making of treaties—the nomination and appointment power is divided. The President alone has the power to nominate; the Senate is only called upon to advise on and consent to appointment.

Although in practice this shared power has been diluted by the increase in the size and influence of the executive branch and the White House staff, many of whom (including the Assistant to the President for National Security Affairs) need not be confirmed in their post and remain outside the purview of congressional scrutiny, in practice it has mostly worked as intended. There are sporadic examples of individuals being refused confirmation, including two of President Nixon's Supreme Court nominees, although usually prior consultation allows for the withdrawal of those nominees likely to be rejected, as occurred with President Carter's first choice to head the CIA, Theodore Sorenson. Two aspects of the process are of indirect importance for security matters, though. The procedure provides the Senate with a good opportunity to examine the qualifications of individuals about to assume great responsibility, and the nomination hearing can be the occasion of a full airing of major issues. In addition, the vote to confirm can be used as a signal or vote of confidence regarding relevant policies. For example, the Senate's confirmation of Paul Warnke as Director of ACDA and Ambassador to the SALT negotiations by a simple and not a two-thirds majority, while legally adequate, indicated its capacity to reject any proposed strategic-arms treaty not to its liking—a signal which was read clearly by the then newly-elected President, by his representative and by the Soviet Union.

Legislating Security

Some fifteen years ago an observer of the American system noted "the increasing tendency to monitor, to establish political parameters of tolerance and expectations, rather than to use power to intervene deeply in shaping the substance of policies, is perhaps the most striking development in congressional behaviour."[43] Although Congress had begun to challenge the Kennedy Administration on the substance of its annual foreign assistance programs, the observation was largely accurate in the context of most of the foreign and defense policy issues of the day. In recent years, however, Congress has turned towards legislation to provide more explicit powers (not specifically denied to it under the Constitution) in six critical areas of foreign and defense policy. This has brought about not only greater control of defense and foreign assistance programs, but also increased congressional authority in the areas of war powers, arms transfers, nuclear proliferation concerns and intelligence activities. The general intent has been to legislate and clarify powers that were often unspecified and unclear in the past and tended to devolve upon the presidency. More specifically, legislation has been used to ensure that the executive provides Congress with adequate information both to permit the execution of its full range of functions and to ensure a more influential congressional role, and a more restricted executive role, in the shaping of policies. To what extent these aims have been fulfilled, and with what effect on American security policy, is the subject of this chapter.

Defense

The Constitution makes no provision for a clear division of labor in the design of the shape and size of the armed forces of the United States. Nevertheless, since the creation of the Bureau of the Budget in 1921 (from 1974 known as the Office of Management and the Budget, or OMB), in the defense budgeting area the initiative has shifted to the executive. As one recent study has stated, "Congressional participation mainly takes the form of acting on proposals or choosing between alternatives presented by the executive branch."[44] Several factors account for this development. First, there are the President's role of Commander-in-Chief, the large executive bureaucracy and the close ties between the executive branch and the uniformed services. Second, Congress has lacked the staff and expertise to compete in this highly complex and important area, and could offer no alternative to the systems analysis capability developed in the early 1960s by the Department of Defense. However, there are also political and even psychological reasons. As Samuel Huntington observed:

> throughout the dozen years after World War II, except when confronted by similar competing programs, Congress never vetoed directly a major strategic

program, a force level recommendation, or a major weapons systems proposal by the Administration in power. . . . During the Cold War Congress was simply not going to assume the responsibility for weapons selection.[45]

Congressman Les Aspin has made a similar point more bluntly: "Playing it safe usually means buying more."[46] Moreover, the bias produced by this tendency to err on the side of approving more rather than fewer forces is reflected in the committees on which members choose to serve: "Liberals who are interested in national security matters tend to seek assignment to the Foreign Affairs Committees where the cosmic issues are discussed. Conservatives tend toward the Armed Services Committee, where the money is divided up."[47]

Recently, however, these patterns have changed to some extent. Committee membership is less directly related to ideological disposition; Congress has reduced both overall and specific budgetary requests; and, most important, Congress has gained a significant degree of influence over the defense budgeting process, at times even taking the initiative. These developments have three basic components.

First, Congress has gradually limited the discretion available to the executive in the spending of defense appropriations. Specifically, limits have been set on executive ability to shift congressionally appropriated funds within or between individual accounts, to impound (or refuse to spend) allocated funds, to carry over unspent funds indefinitely, and to make widespread use of large, undesignated contingency funds.[48] As a result, executive determination of actual defense spending is increasingly confined to what Congress has expressly stipulated.

Second, whereas before 1959 defense budget requests were scrutinized only by the Defense Sub-committees of the House and Senate Appropriations Committees, today approximately one-third of all requests, including those covering the procurement of virtually all weapon systems, research and development and military construction, must be approved, or "authorized," by the two Armed Services Committees.[49] Thus, almost all defense items other than pay must face an annual legislative "double jeopardy": authorization (a process by which programs are designated and costs established) and appropriation (by which the actual monies are approved to fulfill the authorization).

Finally, the extra review provided by the authorization process is but part of the larger increase in the capacity of Congress to affect defense budgets. The 1974 Budget Act, besides establishing a much more disciplined procedure for congressional consideration of defense and other requests, also created a rudimentary systems analysis capability, as the CBO staff is capable of producing life-cycle costs of alternative weapon systems and force postures. Increases in staff, both on committees and in personal offices, and increases in the resources of the other support agencies have similarly extended the capacity of Congress both to examine Administration proposals and to put forth some of its own. These legal and structural changes, along with a greater readiness to challenge the executive in the defense area, have transformed the role of Congress in the process of defense budgeting.

The impact of congressional participation in the budget process can be viewed at two levels. At the total (or macro) level the impact is relatively small. For the past decade congressional appropriations have deviated from administration requests only by some 5 percent on average—and less if certain supplemental requests, financing adjustments and military assistance programs are removed from the equation.[50] Indeed, the conclusion of a recent CRS study, that "Congress has largely confined its budget review actions to identifying areas where waste seems likely to be found rather than to major realignments of the proposed defense program,"[51] resembles that of Huntington's, written nearly two decades before. Yet, if one approaches congressional action at a more specific (or micro) level, it is possible to detect a shift in influence. A number of important programs, including the C-5A and F-111 aircraft, as well as the ABM proposal, have been substantially reduced, while such proposals as the *Cheyenne* helicopter and the MBT-70, or advanced main battle tank program, have been eliminated. At the same time initiatives—the requirement that major surface vessels be nuclear-powered, reforms of NATO, the inclusion of a large nuclear-powered aircraft carrier—have become more common.[52]

These trends, and the annual legislative cycle, can best be illustrated by examining the FY79 Department of Defense Authorization legislation. The authorization bill, introduced in January 1978 following its submission by the Carter Administration, requested a total of $35.5 billion for the procurement of major weapons systems, research, development, testing and evaluation (RDT&E), civil defense and other purposes, for the period 1 October 1978 through 30 September 1979. The bill was immediately sent to the two Armed Service committees, which over the next several months held hearings and considered amendments. Each committee then reported a modified version of the bill to its chamber, where, after further debate and amendment, the House of Representatives passed a $37.9 billion authorization bill in May and the Senate passed a $36.1 billion bill in July. Differences between the passed versions were ironed out in a conference committee, the so-called "third House of Congress," where representatives from each chamber met and agreed to a common compromise version, or "conference report." On the last day of July 1978 a conference report authorizing expenditure of $36.96 billion was issued; not only was this figure nearly $1.5 billion more than the Carter Administration had requested, but the report also sanctioned a large nuclear-powered aircraft carrier specifically rejected by the executive branch, while altering a large number of other program requests. Indeed, in the RDT&E part of the bill alone, while only reducing the overall $12.47 billion requested by the Administration by $210 million, or less than 2 percent, Congress changed over a hundred specific requests, eliminated thirty others, and introduced funding in some fifteen areas for which finance had not even been requested by the Defense Department. This conference report was approved in identical form, and without further amendment, by both chambers and sent to President Carter for his signature. The President, however, exercised his power of veto, claiming, "We cannot have both an adequately balanced defense program and the luxury of an unneeded nuclear-powered aircraft carrier."[53] Several weeks after the 17 August veto, on 7 September, the House failed to produce the necessary two-thirds majority to override the veto; as a result, the Senate did not even try. The authorization legislation then returned to the two Armed Services committees, which amended the conference report by eliminating the funds for the aircraft carrier and inserting some necessary funds to cover shipbuilding claims. Neither committee, however, would consider any other revisions desired by the Defense Department, instead instructing the Administration to include these matters in the regular FY80 authorization bill. Thus, on 4 October, the House passed the changed authorization reported out by the House Armed Services Committee, and three days later the Senate passed a similar bill, followed by a vote to accept the House version and thereby avoid a second conference committee. The identical bill was thus sent to the President, who signed the FY79 authorization of $35.2 billion into law.

This example highlights elements of continuity and change in congressional participation in defense budgeting. Initiative remains largely with the executive, reflecting its greater resources and its sophisticated systems analysis capacity in particular. But although Congress continues to be largely reactive, it is also more able and more willing than previously to challenge the executive on more specific programs. In addition, and perhaps of equal importance, is the increase in general oversight; even where Congress consents to requests, the requests themselves are scrutinized more thoroughly than in the past. The costs and benefits of this increased involvement are difficult to assess: Congress can enhance the quality of American forces through oversight and effective initiative; at the same time its lack of any adequate systems analysis capability, and its particular vulnerability to the domestic political pressures of weapons production, can easily distort its perspective. Budget requests may be increased or decreased, in part or in whole; rarely, however, will they be left alone.

Foreign Assistance

Some similar trends have emerged in the realm of foreign economic and military assistance. Indeed, many appeared in this context some time ago, as shown by the problems the Kennedy Administration encountered in gaining approval for its aid programs. A large number of members have traditionally opposed assistance on grounds of cost, while the lack of clear benefits from often "ungrateful" recipients has made the task of obtaining congressional approval more difficult. In addition, the often less technical and, from the perspective of many, less critical nature of the foreign assistance program has encouraged the participation of many Congressmen and their aides, who are more wary of challenging the armed services or the Defense Department in the defense budgeting process than they are the State Department in the aid process.

Congress has asserted its influence over the assistance process through the establishment of a large number of general and specific conditions. As is the case with defense items, assistance requests are now subject to specific authorization as well as appropriation; in addition, presidential discretion has been limited, in terms of both the adjustment of specific-country programs and the use of general-purpose funds. Military assistance has been particularly affected by these reforms, as in the past it provided the President with a major policy instrument often left unregulated by congressional dictates. Moreover, Congress now requires not only that all military assistance requests be accompanied and justified by presidential determination of national security interests, but it has also declared unequivocally that recipients should not confuse the availability of assistance with the extension of a security guarantee or commitment in any sense.[54]

Challenge by Congress to executive aid requests have not been limited to the amount or the focus of funding; increasingly, legislation has become an instrument by which members seek to alter the domestic or foreign policies of recipients. Nowhere is this as evident as in the area of "human rights." No economic assistance may be provided for any country "which engages in a consistent pattern of gross violations of internationally recognized human rights . . . unless such assistance will directly benefit the needy people in such country." Similarly, security assistance is to be denied unless "extraordinary circumstances exist" which necessitate the continuation of military aid. In both categories, Congress has established a principle or provided a waiver or "escape" clause for the executive, but retained the right of final approval itself. Moreover, in addition to these general approaches on behalf of human rights, Congress has also legislated specific-country restrictions either limiting or prohibiting the availability of assistance (usually security) to some ten countries.[55]

Assistance can also be affected by a host of other actions or policies on the part of recipient countries. Amendments prohibit aid to countries nationalizing American property without adequate compensation, to those defaulting on loans for more than one year, to any countries harboring terrorists, or to states which permit discrimination on the basis of religion, race, national origin or sex against "United States persons" involved in programs. Military assistance requirements also prohibit any retransfer of equipment supplied by the United States to third parties without the prior consent of the United States and limit the permissible use of any item of American military assistance.[56]

It was this last condition, the one that restricts use of equipment, which influenced the controversial decision taken by Congress in early 1975 to terminate military assistance, and especially foreign military sales (FMS) credits, to Turkey in the aftermath of her military action in Cyprus. Although these prohibitions have been relaxed, the low ceiling on credits constrained Turkey's ability to buy arms, while the legislation as a whole angered Turkey and affected both her bilateral relationship with the United States and her position in the Atlantic Alliance. Advocates of the prohibition argued that aid limits provided the only leverage likely to effect a change of Turkish policy towards Cyprus; opponents argued the contrary, claiming that penalties were less likely than incentives to induce moderation and compromise. After repeated but unsuccessful efforts to repeal the "embargo," the Carter Administration finally succeeded in building a majority in both chambers in mid-1978. The repeal was a conditional one: it required not only an initial statement from the President that the resumption of military assistance was in the national interest, but also regular reports to be submitted by the President every sixty days, confirming that Turkey is acting "in good faith" to promote a solution to the Cyprus dispute.[57] In the absence of such a solution, an attempt to reinstate either a partial or a total embargo against Turkey is both within the powers of Congress and politically feasible.

What is certain is that the entire assistance program has become highly politicized and a potential source of friction between the United States and foreign countries. The adjustment of aid levels, whether for the purposes of promoting human rights, changing foreign policy positions or even protecting American industries from aid-assisted foreign competitors, can easily harm relations with actual or potential recipients, who may resent such blatant interference in their internal affairs and such public demonstrations of American power. The alternative option, that of channelling assistance through multilateral institutions such as the World Bank, is increasingly unpopular with many Congressmen; not only does it lessen the control of the United States over the use of the assistance itself, but it weakens her ability (and that of Congress) to use aid for her own ends. But whether the more conditional provision of assistance is likely to enhance the influence of the United States in recipient countries is far from apparent; indeed, what was intended as a means of building strong and friendly states throughout the world could prove counterproductive if manipulated without caution.

War Powers

No single piece of legislation has been as controversial, or as central to the debate concerning the sharing of security powers between executive and Congress, as the War Powers Resolution. One student of congressional foreign-policy influence has hailed it as "a decisive turning-point in the history of legislative-executive relations" and "the cornerstone of the changing structure" of American foreign policymaking.[58] Another observer, however, has offered a rather different perspective: "Having created the myth of presidential usurpation, Congress passed the War Powers Resolution to cure the imaginary disease."[59]

Coming into law on 7 November 1973, after two-thirds of both the Senate and the House of Representatives voted to override President Nixon's veto, the War Powers Resolution (or, more formally, Act) is an attempt, via legislation, to control the ability of the President unilaterally to introduce American armed forces into situations of imminent or actual hostilities, into the territory, air space or waters of a foreign nation while equipped for combat, or in numbers which "substantially enlarge" American forces located in a foreign state and equipped for combat in the absence of a formal declaration of war or specific congressional authorization.[60] The Resolution does not apply in such circumstances as a national emergency resulting from an attack upon the United States, her territories and possessions or her armed forces. If the President introduces forces in situations other than such emergencies, he is required to provide congressional leaders, within forty-eight hours and in writing, with his reasons for so doing, the constitutional and legal authority for his action and an estimation of the scope and duration of the involvement. Moreover, before the forces are introduced the President is required to consult with Congress. The involvement of forces can then continue for sixty days, and for another thirty days thereafter, if the President certifies in writing that the safety of the forces so requires, *unless* Congress passes a concurrent resolution at any time during this sixty- or ninety-day period ordering that the forces be removed. Thus, by a simple majority vote in both chambers which cannot be vetoed by the President,[61] Congress has the power to terminate the involvement of armed forces in a situation whenever it so desires, and potentially before either the sixty-day or the additional thirty-day period is completed. Moreover, after the completion of these periods the involvement cannot be continued unless Congress specifically authorizes it by declaration of war, resolution or legislation. Thus, the President has a "free hand," for a maximum of ninety-two days, to commit American forces abroad to involvement in situations of possible, imminent or actual hostilities; this period of unilateral commitment can be reduced by explicit congressional action and cannot be extended without it.

The Resolution was in many ways the culmination of a debate that had flared periodically during the history of the United States. The Constitution, as ever, was vague, referring only to the "declaration of war" but not to the possibility of using force in situations short of full-scale war, nor to the then already discernible trend of governments resorting to war in the absence of formal declarations. The view of the framers was that "no one wanted either to deny the President the power to respond to surprise attack or to give the President general power to initiate hostilities."[62]

These twin aims posed a dilemma difficult to resolve, and from the outset the war power began to devolve upon the presidency. The armed forces of the United States were ordered into action by early Presidents against pirates and Indians to redress acts committed against property and persons. Lincoln, with both an expanded notion of Locke's doctrine of necessity and self-preservation and a liberal reading of presidential power under the Constitution, responded militarily to the Confederate attack on Fort Sumpter for some three months before congressional approval was obtained. The scope for presidential initiative was further expanded by action taken against Spain toward the end of the nineteenth century, and by the participation of the United States, without congressional approval or protest, in the seige of Peking and the suppression of the Boxer Rebellion. Although these tendencies were reinforced even further by the experience of both world wars, it was the wars in Korea and Indochina, owing to their scope and duration, that marked the Rubicon of the executive's power unilaterally to wage war.

Although it can be argued that the executive did not always act unilaterally, and that various resolutions and authorization or appropriation measures constituted a *de facto* sanctioning of presidential policy,[63] a majority of Congressmen reached the conclusion that the balance of war powers between the branches had become seriously imbalanced and was in urgent need of remedy. This was not the first time frustrated members of Congress turned to legislation to solve this problem; in 1912 Senator Bacon unsuccessfully attempted to deny appropriations for forces sent outside the jurisdiction of the United States without congressional consent, except during emergencies when Congress was not in session. By the 1970s the frustration over presidential power in this area had manifested itself in repeated efforts to curtail the involvement of the United States in Indochina, in an attempt to define the notion of "national commitment" and finally in the War Powers Resolution itself.

To date, the historical record of the War Powers Resolution is a meager one.[64] Four reports have been issued by the executive pursuant to the legislation relating to the transport of refugees from Danang in April 1975, the evacuation of American nationals from Cambodia and the evacuation of American nationals and other persons from South Vietnam, as well as to the *Mayaguez* incident in May 1975, in which President Ford introduced American forces to recapture the ship and crew from the Cambodian authorities. In none of these cases did Congress use any of the Act's mechanisms to affect the policy of the United States; nor is there any evidence the Ford Administration was affected in any way by the existence of the war powers legislation.

This is not to say that no controversy has existed during the Act's lifetime. Two areas concerning its application have been challenged by certain members of Congress. First, they have alleged that the executive has failed to fulfill the intention of the law in terms of its consultation requirement. Consultation in effect has amounted to little more than simply informing congressional leaders of executive decisions, and the reports have contained little information. The executive for its part has claimed that constraints imposed by time and the need for secrecy, as well as the logistical problem of arranging consultations, has precluded more detailed discussion.[65] Secondly, a number of individuals have claimed that on three occasions—the evacuation from Lebanon in June and July 1976, the response of the United States to the Korean "tree-chopping incident" in the DMZ in August 1976 and American participation in Western military actions in Zaire in May 1978—executive actions were such that the procedures of the War Powers Act should have been triggered.[66] Again, the executive has demurred. In the Korean situation, for example, the State Department claimed the Act did not apply as hostilities did not appear imminent, American responses were similar to actions taken frequently under the Armistice Agreement and the additions to American forces were marginal rather than substantial. Similarly, the State Department argued that the American pilots who flew aircraft carrying foreign troops and equipment into Zaire were neither equipped for combat nor within 100 miles of the hostilities.

But if the seven incidents cited above demonstrate that thus far the war powers legislation has failed to guarantee Congress a more significant role in the introduction of American forces abroad, they have also failed to settle the larger controversy surrounding the Act. Indeed, to the extent that a debate on the war powers legislation has taken place at all, it has centered less on its implementation and impact to date than on its implications for American security policy in the future.

Although the Act has been attacked on constitutional grounds, the strongest criticism has focused on its effects on policy. This school of thought is best expressed in the veto message of President Nixon, which argued that its passage

> would seriously undermine this Nation's ability to act decisively and convincingly in times of international crisis. As a result, the confidence of our allies in our ability to assist them could be diminished and the respect of our adversaries for our deterrent posture could decline. A permanent and substantial element of unpredictability would be injected into the world's assessment of American behavior, further increasing the likelihood of miscalculation and war.[67]

Ironically, the Resolution was also attacked by Senator Eagleton, one of its former advocates, who claimed that in its final form the Act actually enhanced presidential ability to go to war in contravention of the intent of the Constitution.[68]

Although the record of recent years has drained much of the enthusiasm of its backers, the Act is still seen as an important symbol of congressional influence and as a real constraint on the ability of the President unilaterally to wage unauthorized war. The former staff chief of the Senate Foreign Relations Committee has written that the legislation "is designed to make it more difficult for Congress to acquiesce in future situations like Vietnam,"[69] while Senator Javits, one of its principal sponsors, argues only that the Act "establishes a procedure by which the Congress can effectively participate and bring to bear the war powers which the Constitution gave us."[70]

On balance, it is interesting to note that the War Powers Act appears to worry its critics more than it pleases its backers; in reality, though, it is likely to be neither as constraining as its opponents fear nor as important as its framers intended and its advocates hope. This is not to say it will have no effect. Senator Church's perspective—that the Act is irrelevant in crises which are over before Congress can act, and unnecessary in longer involvements, as Congress possesses its authorization and appropriation powers through which to affect American military actions—is technically correct but politically incomplete.[71] Even without necessarily going as far as a former senior official, who wrote that the Act "is bound to have a chilling effect on the United States' willingness to use force,"[72] the war powers legislation will to some extent inhibit the executive from contemplating the use of force in those situations where a rapid, low-cost and low-risk solution does not seem assured. Indeed, in some circumstances one can foresee the President having to weigh the risk of not acting militarily against the risk of acting only to have the operation terminated by Congress. Equally, an approaching time limit might lead the executive prematurely to curtail American involvement or to escalate the level of involvement, so as to complete an engagement before Congress is forced to act.[73] At the same time, adversaries could be encouraged to prolong conflicts in the expectation that Congress will refuse support for continued American commitment, while allies must take into account yet another factor affecting the reliability of the United States. For Congress, the impact of the legislation is mixed: it does little if anything to enhance the direct influence of Congress in crises, but the law forces Congress to take a decision after two, or at most three, months of confrontation. A vote to continue operations signifies the sharing of responsibility with the executive; a vote to terminate signifies the assumption of responsibility by Congress alone. In light of current American resistance to another military involvement, this aspect of the law suggests that the United States will in future be less able to assume open-ended commitments.

Nuclear Proliferation

Since the end of World War II, interest in the spread and use of nuclear weapons has been a constant feature of American foreign policy. As such, it has also been affected by the decisions of Congress. Several relatively distinct phases of congressional concern, however, can be defined.[74] After the end of the war, and the United States' use of two nuclear devices against Japan, the emphasis of both executive and congressional policy in this area was on preventing any other state from gaining access to nuclear weapons. Not all efforts were successful: the Baruch Plan to internationalize control of nuclear weapons was still-born, while reluctance to honor wartime agreements with Britain caused serious difficulties in post-war relations between the two allies. From the congressional perspective, the dominant themes were non-co-operation and secrecy. The Atomic Energy Act of 1946 chose an odd approach to the problem, though, by banning exchanges of information regarding industrial uses of atomic energy but not those involving scientific and technical uses alone. While this approach may have slowed the introduction of certain alternative technologies around the world, it actually enhanced the dissemination of information crucial to later military and industrial applications of atomic energy alike.

In the early 1950s these rather strict limits on actual industrial co-operation were relaxed, most probably to ensure American access to uranium supplies in countries desiring access to American technical information. In any case, a fundamental change in the entire thrust of the nuclear policy of the United States came with the announcement of Eisenhower's "Atoms for Peace" program in December

1953, which made little connection between the spread of information and civil technology on one hand and the possible spread of nuclear weapons on the other. This change was authorized by Congress a year later in the Atomic Energy Act of 1954, which ushered in more than a decade of promotion of nuclear projects domestically and nuclear co-operation internationally. Fourteen years later (by which time the nuclear club had expanded to five actual and a host of potential members) the Senate ratified the Non-Proliferation Treaty (NPT). Like American policy, the NPT attempted to square the circle of proliferating nuclear technology and power without proliferating nuclear weaponry.

This optimistic aim dominated American and Congressional interest in non-proliferation matters for the next six years. In 1974, however, everything changed. In April Senator Ribicoff released the "Rosenbaum" report, one of several to appear that warned of the dangers of nuclear theft and terrorism. The French revealed their intention to enter into major nuclear co-operation arrangements with South Korea and Pakistan, while the Federal Republic of Germany announced even more far-reaching plans for Brazil. Most important, the Indian "peaceful nuclear explosion" of May signalled to many Congressmen the inadequacy of the current non-proliferation policy of the United States. Not surprisingly, these events, and the conclusions drawn from them, led to a spate of legislative efforts to fashion a new American policy.

Despite the initial resistance of the Ford Administration and the powerful Joint Committee on Atomic Energy, several efforts reached fruition. Although an amendment requiring congressional approval of all nuclear co-operation agreements was rejected, the International Development Association (IDA) Act of 1974 directed the American representative to the IDA to vote against any loan to a country developing any "nuclear explosive device" unless it was or became a party to the NPT. The FY75 Foreign Assistance Act, passed in December 1974, besides prohibiting the transfer of any funds to Israel or Egypt for nuclear fuel or reactor programs, also specifically authorized additional American contributions to the International Atomic Energy Agency (IAEA) for the strengthening of its safeguard procedures. Most significantly, the so-called "Symington Amendment" (effective 30 June 1976) committed the government to cutting off most forms of assistance to any country receiving sensitive nuclear fuel reprocessing or enrichment facilities unless the President declared in writing the national security reasons for proceeding with an assistance program.[75] Nearly three years later the amendment was implemented for the first time in response to Pakistan's attempts to acquire a uranium enrichment capability.

By the advent of the Carter Administration in early 1977 the atmosphere had changed considerably. In October 1976 the Ford Administration issued a new set of guidelines more responsive to potential problems raised by the transfer of sensitive nuclear technologies.[76] In April 1977 President Carter expanded these in his message accompanying proposed legislation that offered a comprehensive proliferation policy for the United States.[77] Many of the key members of the Joint Committee on Atomic Energy had left Congress by the end of 1976, and non-proliferation advocates took advantage of the Committee's weakened state by transferring authority for nuclear export controls to the foreign affairs committees.[78] In a single year the environment had changed from one of executive and congressional resistance to the introduction of strong non-proliferation measures to one of widespread support.[79]

The passage of the Nuclear Non-Proliferation Act in March 1978 reflected this change. Combining incentives for international co-operation with threats of unilateral American sanctions, the legislation itself is a complicated maze of procedures and conditions governing all forms of nuclear co-operation between the United States and other countries. In addition, the law changed not only American policy but also the role of Congress in overseeing and enforcing that policy.[80]

The law attempts to expand the framework of international agreements and institutions designed to prevent the proliferation of nuclear weapons, while guaranteeing access to the technology relevant for civil uses of nuclear energy. The President is directed to begin negotiations to establish an International Nuclear Fuel Authority, or INFA, which is to provide fuel and treatment services to its customers, thus, it is hoped, alleviating demands for national reprocessing and breeder projects. Similarly, the legislation declares congressional support for the negotiations concerning the promise of alternative but less proliferation-prone fuel cycles, the expansion of the NPT regime, the strengthening of IAEA safeguards and greater co-operation among potential nuclear supplier states.

The more controversial aspect of the law, however, is the guidelines that have been established to govern both new and existing nuclear relations between the United States and other countries. The guidelines principally affect four areas: new Agreements for Co-operation, (that is, agreements that form the foundation of all bilateral nuclear relationships with the United States); existing Agreements for Co-operation, all of which require renegotiation as a result; the licensing procedure for all individual nuclear exports made pursuant to the basic Agreement for Co-operation; and "Subsequent Arrangements," or procedures that recipient states must follow (and on which the approval of the United States is contingent) in regard to a wide range of domestic nuclear activities—including contracts, transfer approvals, physical security arrangements, storage of irradiated fuel, etc.—if more general nuclear co-operation with the United States is to continue.

The Act stipulates terms for entering into or maintaining any form of a nuclear relationship with the United States. These include: the application of IAEA safeguards; a guarantee that exports supplied by the United States will not be used for explosive devices of any kind; assurances that adequate security precautions against theft and terrorism will be taken; an undertaking that all American non-proliferation criteria pertain not only to the items exported from the United States but also to anything generated by or derived from an American export. These four conditions came into effect immediately (as of 10 March 1978), affecting all existing and future co-operation agreements as well as any particular export of fuel, technology or equipment made pursuant to an agreement. In addition, three other conditions—that recipient countries accept "full-scope safeguards," that they do not reprocess nuclear material without the prior approval of the United States, and that they transfer no items to third parties without American approval—are not only applied immediately to all new agreements of co-operation, but also after twenty-four months (10 March 1980) to exports or after only eighteen months (10 September 1979) to license applications made pursuant to co-operation agreements which existed before the new Act came into being. In effect, the legislation provides a two-year breathing space for the renegotiation of agreements which existed before the Act itself. Moreover, should a recipient at any time violate the Act, co-operation must be terminated unless the President determines that "cessation of such exports would be seriously prejudicial to the achievement of United States non-proliferation objectives or otherwise jeopardize the common defense and security." Congress, however, retains the final word: even if the President makes such a determination, he can be overruled by a concurrent resolution.

The Act also empowers the National Regulatory Commission (NRC) to make independent judgments on proposed nuclear exports following an assertion by the Secretary of State that a proposed export is not "inimical" to the interests of the United States. In the absence of NRC approval, the President possesses the power to overrule the Commission and call for the export. Again, though, he in turn can be overruled by Congress if it passes a concurrent resolution of disapproval within sixty days of the presidential order. Similarly, Congress can block by concurrent resolution any general Agreement for Co-operation by the same procedure.

It did not take long for the new law to have an effect. Indeed, even before it was signed, licenses for a large shipment of enriched fuel were approved for export to Euratom countries. After the signing a major diplomatic clash between Washington and the European states was averted, at least for two years, by an agreement to begin renegotiating existing arrangements, thus obeying the letter if not the spirit of the new law.[81] Of more immediate consequence was the failure of the NRC, on 20 April 1978, to approve a license for the export of low-enriched uranium fuel to India's Tarapur plant. Protesting the delay, Indian Prime Minister Desai charged that "the refusal to supply such requirements (pursuant to the 1963 Agreement for Co-operation) would be a breach of the agreement" between the two countries.[82] A week after the NRC vote, and three days after Desai's protest, President Carter approved the export, arguing that "denial of this export would seriously undermine our efforts to persuade India to accept full-scope safeguards, and would seriously prejudice the achievement of other United States non-proliferation goals."[83] While Congress bowed to this logic, and eschewed an override attempt, it also served notice on both the Administration and India that it had not altered its fundamental position and determination to apply the law: "The executive branch and the Indian Government should base their discussions on the anticipation that, if full-scope safeguards are not achieved, it is highly unlikely that a waiver allowing continued exports would be acceptable."[84] The day of reckoning had only been postponed, not averted.

Although it will not be possible to assess the full impact of the Nuclear Non-Proliferation Act until after the eighteen- and twenty-four-month deadlines for renegotiation pass, it is still possible to draw some tentative conclusions. Both the direction and the detail of the legislation appear unlikely to achieve their aims. The law introduces a large amount of unilateralism into an endeavor that can only succeed through international support and consensus. The combination of strict American-determined guidelines and terminations works against development of the trust and co-operation essential to the strengthening of non-proliferation mechanisms in an energy-hungry world. At the same time, not only is the ability of the United States to dictate terms in this area limited by the availability of alternative sources of fuel, technology and equipment, but also the very nature of the Act itself could stimulate efforts by recipients both to locate new sources of assistance and to accelerate their own indigenous capabilities. As one non-American observer has written, "There is a great risk that a strategy of withholding know-how and maintaining dependence could bring about the opposite of what is intended; namely, political disintegration and nuclear self-sufficiency outside the world-wide non-proliferation system."[85] A number of relationships could be injured, if not sacrificed, on the altar of proliferation without furthering either non-proliferation or larger security interests.

Military Transfers

Beginning with "Lend-Lease" just months before the entry of the United States into World War II, and growing after the war through the Truman Doctrine, NATO and other security arrangements, the provision of military equipment and associated services has constituted an integral component of American security policy. In recent years, the advent of strategic parity with the Soviet Union and a marked reluctance on the part of the United States to commit her troops abroad has reinforced this pattern of "indirect" security, achieved at least initially by a mixture of local national forces and a large percentage of American-produced weapons supervised by American advisers.

But while the strategic conception has endured and, if anything, become even more basic to the policy of the United States, the form of its fulfillment has evolved. The Military Assistance Program (MAP), costing as much as $5.7 billion in FY1952, has declined to a level of only several hundred million dollars in recent years; by contrast, the value of military goods and services sold rather than lent or granted has increased tenfold, reaching more than $11 billion in FY77.[86] Economic factors have been paramount in this transition. American economic weakness, coupled with the improved absolute and relative economic strength of allies, have undermined congressional support for the continuation of military programs. The NATO allies, Japan, Australia and New Zealand could afford to purchase weapons by the late 1960s, while credits assisted such states as Israel to do the same. Moreover, the rapid increase in oil prices enabled oil-producing states (Iran and Saudi Arabia in particular) to purchase military goods and services in large quantities after 1973. Arms sales provided jobs for workers, profits for companies and a means of recycling the so-called "petro-dollars," as well as other dollars resulting from recurring American payments deficits, back into the United States. Thus the new economics could be made to fit the old strategy as military assistance gave way to military exports.

Although initial congressional reaction to the shift from assistance to sales was favorable—indeed, it came about in large part because of congressional pressures—the atmosphere quickly and drastically changed. The sheer size and value of the transfers created misgivings, and many Congressmen were sympathetic to the notion that arms sales provoked instabilities both within and between recipients. Others became concerned that an increasingly prominent dimension of American security policy remained beyond effective congressional scrutiny or control. Investigations revealed mismanagement and bribery, which increased doubts about whether the large transfers were serving or harming the interests of either the United States or her allies. As is often the case, investigations led to hearings, and hearings to legislation.[87]

The legislation has sought to make the entire arms-transfer process more considered and more difficult. Reforms in the executive procedure for approving sales have been instituted; impact statements must be prepared and annual statements informing Congress of all intended sales for the current fiscal year must be provided by 15 November each year. More controversially, Congress has increased substantially its capacity to enforce arms-transfer restraint. In 1974 legislation was passed requiring the President to report to Congress every sale of articles or services over $25 million, after which Congress had twenty days to pass a concurrent resolution of disapproval to block the sale. Early experience with this procedure led a majority of Congressmen to vote for reform; legislation approved in 1976 reduced the "trigger" mechanism to any proposed transfer of $25 million or more in defense articles or services, or $7 million or more involving "major defense equipment," while extending the time in which a concurrent resolution of disapproval could be passed to thirty days. In addition, the executive branch has agreed to provide Congress with a further twenty days of informal notification before the formal thirty-day notice begins.[88]

Despite the more than 100 resolutions of disapproval introduced in the past few years, no single sale has been formally blocked by this new legislative procedure. This is not to say that the procedure has not had an effect on specific proposals. In its initial years Congress forced the Ford Administration to pledge that the sale of C-130 cargo aircraft to Egypt would not be followed immediately by other requests for military transfers to that country; in addition, a proposed sale of *Pershing* missiles to Israel was withdrawn and a sale of *Sidewinder* and *Hawk* missiles to Saudi Arabia reduced in number. More difficult were three proposals over which compromise proved elusive. Congress only withdrew its threat to disapprove a proposed sale of fourteen *Improved HAWK* (surface-to-air) missile batteries to Jordan in mid-1975 when the Administration guaranteed that they would be deployed only in a fixed manner, thereby diminishing their potential contribution to offensive operations against Israel. Similarly, the Carter Administration was forced both to modify its sale of 7 AWACS aircraft to Iran in mid-1977 to allay fears in Congress that sensitive technologies might be compromised, and to provide assurances about basing restrictions and future transfers in order to gain support for its package arms sale to Israel, Saudi Arabia and Egypt in the spring of 1978.[89]

Interestingly, the arms-transfer legislation constrains presidential options less in crises than in normal periods. Both the general procedure for disapproval and congressional ability to use concurrent resolutions to block transfers to third parties can be waived by the President in times of emergency, as was done during the March 1979 Yemen crisis. In normal times, however, and as the several cases cited above demonstrated, Congress's use of its disapproval powers (as well as the many other grounds for terminating transfers similar to those found in assistance legislation) can pose a major threat not only to the proposed transfer but also to the entire relationship between the United States and the intended recipient. As then Senator Dick Clark has noted, "Congress gets into the act only after a sale has been promised by the Pentagon. At this stage Congress can reject a sale only at the risk of creating a serious diplomatic incident."[90] Whether provisions of the 1978 legislation which guarantee Congress some influence in the preliminary or "survey" stage of the arms transfer process will prove sufficient to alleviate this problem is doubtful; secrecy will be hard to maintain, and the acquiescence of a handful of Congressmen at the "survey" stage may not guarantee widespread acceptance of a proposed sale as much as five years later in the public domain.[91]

In the long run what may be more serious than difficulties created by the form of congressional involvement are the fruits of a policy clearly biased against arms transfers. Much of the putative linkage between military transfers and instability is unproven, and in many circumstances transfers can enhance stability both militarily and politically. In addition, in the absence of actual or foreseeable co-operation among arms suppliers over the restriction of their wares, it is doubtful that unilateral restrictions on the part of the United States will do much more than provide opportunities for economic and, more significant, political competitors. Similarly, the restriction of conventional arms transfers can both stimulate indigenous production of conventional weapons and increase the desirability of nuclear weapons as a substitute (or security) weapon of last resort. For potential recipients, the certainty of a more restrictive American arms-transfer policy, together with the uncertainty surrounding any particular sale, can only lead to a reassessment both of their security requirements and of their relationship with the United States.

Intelligence

Congress has also moved to gain greater control over the activities of the several intelligence agencies and bureaus within the United States Government. The impetus for this came from several sources: the investigations by both Senate and

House committees of the intelligence agencies during the mid–1970s; the reaction to the discovery of illegal activities; and the growing realization that intelligence operations represented another important dimension of security policy that had largely been exempted from congressional control during the entire post-war era.

Three events stand out along this road to greater congressional participation in intelligence controls. The first has already been mentioned: the dramatic findings of the Church and Pike Committees.[92] Equally important was the so-called "Hughes–Ryan" Amendment of 1974, which prohibited action other than that related to the collecting of intelligence by the CIA in foreign countries unless the President found the proposed action important for American national security and reported a description of the operation and its scope to the two foreign affairs committees. Thus, the amendment not only ended the era of "plausible presidential denial" but it also ensured that Congress would be notified of covert operations through regular channels.[93] Congress went a critical step further, however, during the Angolan controversy of late 1975 and early 1976, by prohibiting "assistance of any kind . . . for the purpose, or which would have the effect, of promoting or augmenting, directly or indirectly, the capacity of any nation, group, organization, movement, or individual to conduct military or paramilitary operations in Angola" unless it so authorized.[94] Moreover, Congress would only consider any authorization after receiving a detailed report justifying and describing the proposed operation.

These three powers—investigation, the right to information and the actual constraint of operations—are incorporated into the 1976 and 1977 Senate and House resolutions establishing select committees on intelligence.[95] The mandate of both committees is a broad one: "to oversee and make continuing studies of the intelligence activities and programs of the United States Government." More specifically, the committees' purpose is twofold: to ensure that intelligence operations are legal and of a sufficiently high quality to meet the demands of American foreign policy. The two committees are empowered to consider all legislation and related matters, including the authorization of budgetary appropriations, for all the intelligence agencies and bureaus; in early 1978 President Carter ordered the Director of Central Intelligence (DCI) and the heads of other agencies and bureaus to keep the two committees "fully and currently informed concerning intelligence activities," to provide any information requested and to report whenever necessary as to illegal activities and measures taken to correct them.[96]

Despite this apparent demonstration of co-operation, executive-congressional relations in the realm of intelligence remain uneasy in two principal areas. The first concerns secrecy and the related matter of congressional right of disclosure. Information of a highly sensitive type reaches not only the two intelligence committees, but also the committees on foreign affairs, appropriations and the armed services. The availability of classified information to virtually all Congressmen and a large number of staff members has increased the risk of unauthorized leaks that could compromise not only the operations themselves but the willingness of other countries to co-operate with the United States in this area. Moreover, the legislation contains a mechanism for unilateral declassification, by which a chamber (but not the committee alone) could, by majority vote, release information against the wishes of the Executive.[97]

A more direct and serious constraint on the ability of the Government to conduct intelligence activities of all types is to be found in the committees' control of the purse. Although both the resolutions and the executive order make clear that notification of operations by the executive to Congress need not precede their implementation, the budgetary power of the committees does give them the ability to prohibit an operation by type or locale through the authorization procedure, either in advance or after it has begun. (The latter was the case with Angola.) Thus, while it would be legal for the executive to initiate an operation before notifying the committees, it would be politically dangerous for it do so as the committees could restrict funding *post hoc*. In addition, too great an exercise of unilateral initiative by the executive could provoke a large number of pre-emptive restrictions and prohibitions placed on operations. As a result, what has evolved thus far in practice is an executive notification to the committees of covert operations prior to implementation, which provides members with an opportunity to voice opposition beforehand.[98]

Constraints Unconstrained?

Speaking on 25 May 1978, in the wake of the participation of the United States in Western military efforts on behalf of Zaire's central government. President Carter called for a full review of congressional restrictions on foreign economic and military assistance programs so as "to preserve presidential capacity to act in the national interest at a time of rapidly changing circumstances."[99] Some sixteen months before, his predecessor had argued that the President and his emissaries "must not be handicapped in advance in their relations with foreign governments."[100] In both instances what was at issue was not simply restrictions on aid, but the more general phenomenon of congressional constraints on the ability of the executive to conduct foreign and defense policy.

While the increased ability of Congress to amend the defense budget is a constraint of another kind, affecting indirectly the relations of the United States with other countries, the other forms of legislated controls—covering assistance, war powers, nuclear exports, arms transfers and intelligence operations—can inhibit presidential discretion and initiative, and therefore foreign policy, more directly. There are, however, important differences between the controls. In the three areas of assistance, transfers and nuclear exports the President in normal conditions can only act if Congress does not prevent the measure, either by refusing to authorize appropriate assistance or by legislative veto, using a concurrent resolution to disapprove an arms transfer or nuclear export. In the areas of war powers and intelligence operations, however, the executive retains full power to undertake action, but then it must notify Congress which can then terminate such action if it so chooses. Although there are exceptions to the above—during emergencies the President enjoys considerable latitude to dispense assistance and arms transfers, while Congress can preclude military or intelligence operations through the authorization and appropriations process—the basic distinctions are still valid.

These distinctions are important, for the concept of constraint is a complex one. In the first three areas the President is confined to negotiating and indicating intent to a foreign country; if Congress then refuses to approve or acts to disapprove his promise, a serious rupture in relations between countries can result, especially (as is often the case) if the congressional action is accompanied by a good deal of publicity and acrimony. A small issue, representing but one dimension of relations, can easily become a test case of the whole. In part this may be alleviated by procedures such as those introduced into the arms-transfer process, but no such parallel opportunity normally presents itself in the other areas; in any case, changing conditions and politics can lead to changing congressional views on a particular action.

Congressional involvement is not without other difficulties as well. Incentives and penalties, or carrots and sticks, must be manipulated carefully and subtly if they are to succeed in effecting desired results; total bans and withdrawals of help are hardly the stuff of which diplomatic compromises are made. Countries spurned by the United States will increasingly be able to locate an alternative source of supply, at home or abroad. Moreover, such penalties tend to affect friends more than adversaries, as the former are more likely to be closely involved with the United States. Last, as was mentioned before, the separate consideration of matters which can directly affect one another often makes for incoherence, with obvious results. War-powers procedures and intelligence controls provide constraints of a different sort. Neither category precludes initial executive action, nor are the effects of either on other states as clear. Yet fear of political or legal investigations, or the threat of congressional termination of some initiative, can inhibit the executive in both thought and deed. Equally, they produce uncertainty among allies and adversaries alike about American willingness and ability to act; the psychology of constraint can in certain circumstances have a powerful effect on decision-making and policy.

This is not to say that legislation in these areas only has the effect of constraining the executive, or that all such constraint is undesirable. Legislation has also increased both executive and congressional scrutiny of policies before the United States commits herself and the flow of information inside and outside the executive branch, to the benefit of many people in and out of government. Moreover, investigations and events have demonstrated all too frequently that a significant number of past executive initiatives would have benefited from congressional oversight and even cancellation. Whether on balance the foreign policy of the United States will benefit from the new legislating of security or not is a question to which the answer will vary with time and perspective.

Conclusion

Tension, even struggle, between executive and legislature over control of the foreign and defense policies of the United States is intrinsic to the political system. The Constitution consciously created it and history has failed to resolve it. Consequently, tension is less a problem than simply a characteristic of the American political process. Yet in recent years it has been argued that in its zeal to curb the abuses of the past, Congress has created a situation that is damaging to the security of the United States and her allies. Indeed, one need not claim that the present relationship between two institutions is worse than before to recognize that today's balance creates its own set of difficulties.

Not surprisingly, a number of solutions have been suggested which can be grouped along structural, political or attitudinal lines. Structural solutions include options designed to improve existing congressional machinery as well as those intended to improve channels of communication between executive and legislature. The most common theme among the former is the creation of an umbrella committee on national security or interdependence.[101] There could either be separate Senate and House committees or a single, joint committee, or both. Whatever the specific form, a committee reform along these lines would ease the present jurisdictional tangle, thereby enhancing efficiency and, more important, reducing the lack of coherence inherent in a system in which a plethora of highly independent committees work their own will.

Problems do stand in the way of such an enterprise, however. If the new committee is to be legislative—that is, if it is to be able to write and amend legislation as well as hold hearings and make recommendations—the workload would be overwhelming for its members. It would encompass work presently performed by a large number of committees, each of which already threatens to demand too much of its members. Moreover, Congress would be most unlikely to establish such a super-committee. Existing committees show a marked tendency to guard their jurisdictions jealously, and most Congressmen oppose concentrations of power in the hands of a few. Indeed, such an omnibus national security committee would constitute a clear challenge to the trends of decentralization and individualism; for this reason it remains unlikely to receive much support within Congress.

On the other hand, the creation of new committees or a single, joint committee with a non-legislative mandate—along the lines of the Joint Economic Committee or Budget committees—might be a possibility. Such a "supra-" rather than "super-" committee, consisting of the congressional leadership and the chairmen and ranking minority members of specified existing committees, could hold hearings on major national security questions as well as providing a focal point for consultation with the executive. In addition, it could assist in co-ordinating separate committee consideration of pending legislation, although standing committees would retain their legislative authority and independence, as would all members.

A supra-committee would not solve the problems of congressional compartment-alization or communication with the executive, but it could mitigate them.

Other structural proposals are concerned with the existing tangle of commit-tees and emphasize the need for joint hearings, concurrent or sequential consid-eration of legislation and, more basically, further realignment of committee juris-dictions.[102] There are also proposals aimed at easing the relations between the two branches. Some are quite modest, urging the upgrading of liaison and congres-sional relations offices, while others would establish some form of a joint execu-tive–Congress or "EXCON" body to oversee national security policy. But whether any such far-reaching reform could be squared with the Constitution, much less receive political support, is doubtful.

On balance, the promise of structural solutions to the dilemma of policy-making appears limited. As a result, political (or policy) solutions have been put forward, predicated on the thesis that institutional harmony can only follow, not precede, agreement over policy. Speaking of executive–congressional relations in 1976, the then Deputy Secretary of State concluded, "What inhibits bipartisan co-operation today is the divisive and chastening experience of Vietnam and Water-gate and the lack of public consensus about America's future role in the world."[103] Thus, if the breakdown of the post-war consensus over American foreign and defense policy was in part responsible for the current institutional crisis, it is often argued that the restoration of consensus would provide a major contribution to its amelioration.

Yet even if this assessment is correct, it holds out little promise. The restora-tion of consensus is a pipedream. As James Chace has written:

> The kind of broad consensus . . . obtained during the post-war era and which became a shibboleth of American foreign policy may no longer be possible to resurrect short of war. American interests are too diverse and American power now much less predominant. . . . Most issues may have to be taken up on a case-by-case basis, and the President will have to look for support for his foreign policies much as he might seek to do for his domestic programs.[104]

Recent evidence supports this theme. Henry Kissinger's "world order" efforts lost domestic support, while President Carter's attempt to build a new consensus, in which human rights played a major part, proved unrealistic and inadequate. In-deed, only success seems to rally widespread support for foreign policy in and out of Congress and then only temporarily.

Some of the more realistic writing on the resolution of executive–congressional difficulties rejects the panaceas of structural overhaul or a revival of consensus, calling instead for a mutual reassessment of the quality of the relationship between the branches:

> The problem facing both Congress and the Executive branch is not so much the necessity to rebuild a new foreign policy consensus as it is the need to achieve a

working relationship between the two branches that will enhance the United States' capability to conduct a democratic and effective foreign policy. . . . Many of the problems affecting legislative–executive relations are attitudinal rather than structural, and no amount of structural innovations will solve them.[105]

Basic to this approach is the need to improve consultation, described by one executive official as the "sacred principle of congressional relations,"[106] a claim likely to be accepted by a majority of Congressmen as long as consultation is understood to mean active participation of Congress in policy-making rather than simply its being informed of executive decisions and initiatives. But in a body of 535 members with whom does one consult? The absence of any clear pattern of authority in Congress diminishes the appeal of this solution. In addition, consultation can involve the forfeiting of secrecy, speed and surprise—all valuable diplomatic assets. Consultation also requires a large element of trust and good faith on both sides if it is not simply to be used by each branch to undermine the objectives of the other. Indeed, the very same factors—congressional decentralization and policy divergence—which militate against both the structural and the policy "solutions" also limit the promise of improving the working relationship between the two institutions. What is more, the entire political process is a bargaining exercise; to the extent that the President requires the support of Congress, the system rewards those who withhold their support. In a world where the squeaky wheel gets the grease, a compliant and co-operative Congress is more likely to be taken for granted than taken into counsel.

One is tempted to concur with Eugene Rostow: "The problem of harmonizing presidential and congressional authority in the field of foreign affairs is not institutional or constitutional, but human and political. It cannot be solved by constitutional amendments, by statutes, or by more institutionalized procedures of consultation."[107] But neither is the problem solely "human and political," for no combination of persons or tactics is likely to bring about a sound partnership. More than anything else, the existence of tension between the two branches reflects a lack of consensus over not policy but power. What is the proper balance between the executive and Congress, and what is the proper role of the latter?

Two opposing concepts exist. There are those who advocate a strong and powerful Congress involved in the details of policy-making. Anything less, it is maintained, will give the executive too much discretion and too much scope to conduct a policy inconsistent either with public opinion or with the Constitution and the law. A number of proposals have been advanced to enhance congressional influence, including a greater capacity for independent defense budgeting; more severe limits on the presidency during crises; positive approval by Congress to sanction (rather than disapproval to prevent) arms transfers and nuclear exports; increased congressional control over the National Security Council system, along with access to its papers and those of the intelligence community; and, in general, a greater role in influencing presidential initiatives before they are launched.[108]

The alternative view of the proper role for Congress offers a very different conception. As expressed by Secretary of State Kissinger:

> The Congress can set broad guidelines and decide basic policies. But the Congress does not have the organization, the information, or the responsibility for deciding the tactical questions that arise daily in the conduct of our foreign relations or for executing a coherent, consistent, comprehensive policy. The President has this responsibility and must be permitted to exercise it on behalf of the entire Nation.[109]

More specifically, it is often maintained that Congress should confine itself to two roles. The first of these emphasizes oversight: "In foreign affairs, Congress probably serves best as discussant, critic, sharp-eyed investigator and watchdog rather than as policy initiator and formulator."[110] In doing so publicly and effectively, Congress would be performing another valuable service. As Woodrow Wilson wrote, "Even more important than legislation is the instruction and guidance in political affairs which the people might receive from a body which kept all national concerns suffused in a broad daylight of discussion."[111]

Congress has the additional responsibility of establishing limits or parameters for policy: "Congress are the rear wheels, indispensable and usually obliged to follow, but not without substantial braking power."[112] This conception receives support from former Senator Fulbright: "This [congressional] role is to participate in shaping broad policies . . . the executive should be left free, within broadly defined limits of scope and direction, to carry out the program and to adapt it to the constantly changing conditions with which we are confronted throughout the world."[113]

The problem, of course, is where to draw the line. How does one ensure adequate congressional involvement without unduly confining the executive? As the preceding discussion indicates, there is little agreement about this at present, nor is there likely to be in the future. As John Lehman has pessimistically but realistically noted, "There are, in short, no frameworks, no cookbooks, no valid models, and no 'golden ages' of administrations past to which we might refer in judging a 'proper' distribution of powers or even 'constitutional' relationship between branches."[114]

Notes

1. David Truman, *The Governmental Process* (New York: Knopf, 1951), p. 433.
2. Woodrow Wilson, *Congressional Government* (New York: Meridian Books, 1956), pp. 55-6.
3. *Congress and Foreign Policy*, Report of the Special Subcommittee on Investigations of the CIR, HR (Washington: USGPO, 1977), p. 20.
4. Les Aspin, "The Defense Budget and Foreign Policy: The Role of Congress," *Daedalus* (Summer 1975):164.

5. See Harrison W. Fox, Jr., and Susan Webb Hammond, *Congressional Staffs: The Invisible Force in American Lawmaking* (New York: Free Press, 1977); see also Michael J. Malbin, "Congressional Committee Staffs: Who's in Charge Here?" and Michael A. Scully, "Reflections of a Senate Aide," *Public Interest*, no. 47 (Spring 1977).

6. Fox and Hammond, *op. cit.*, p. 143.

7. See James D. Carroll, "Policy Analysis for Congress: A Review of the Congressional Research Service," in *Congressional Support Agencies*, A Compilation of Papers prepared for the Commission on the Operation of the Senate (Washington: USGPO, 1976).

8. See E.B. Skolnikoff, "The Office of Technology Assessment," in *Congressional Support Agencies;* also Barry M. Casper, "The Rhetoric and Reality of Congressional Technology Assessment," *Bulletin of the Atomic Scientists* 34 (1978).

9. See Joseph Pois, "The General Accounting Office as a Congressional Resource," in *Congressional Support Agencies*.

10. For discussions of the congressional budget procedure and the performance to date of the new structures, see William M. Capron, "The Congressional Budget Office," in *Congressional Support Agencies;* Richard Burt, *Defence Budgeting: The British and American Cases*, Adelphi Paper 112 (London: IISS, 1974/5), pp. 18–22; Allen Schick, *The First Years of the Congressional Budget Process* (Washington: CRS, LOC, 1976); *Budgeting in the United States Senate*, A Compilation of Papers Prepared for the Commission on the Operation of the Senate (Washington: USGPO, 1977).

11. This concept was recently reiterated in the key Watergate ruling. United States v. Richard M. Nixon, 418 U.S. 683–716 (1974).

12. The Freedom of Information Act, passed in 1966 and significantly amended in 1974, provides the basic authority and procedure for the public to petition the executive branch for unreleased documents and records in its possession. The law as amended places the burden of secrecy on the executive; thus, the individual's "need to know" has given way to the "right to know," although the right is still restricted in certain areas. A full description of the Act can be found in *Freedom of Information Act and Amendments of 1974 (P.L. 93-502)*, a Joint Committee Print of the HR Committee on Government Operations and the Senate Committee on the Judiciary (Washington: USGPO, 1975).

13. See *Analysis of Arms Control Impact Statements Submitted in Connection with the Fiscal Year 1978 Budget Request*, prepared for the CFR, USS and the CIR, USHR by the CRS (Washington: USGPO, 1977); *Fiscal Year 1979 Arms Control Impact Statements* (Washington: USGPO, 1978); *Evaluation of Fiscal Year 1979 Arms Control Impact Statements: Toward More Informed Congressional Participation in National Security Policymaking*, Report prepared for the Subcommittee on International Security and Scientific Affairs of the CIR, USHR by the CRS (Washington: USGPO, 1979); *Statements That Analyze Effects of Proposed Programs on Arms Control Need Improvement* (Washington: GAO, 1977); *Improved Procedures Needed for Identifying Programs Requiring Arms Control Impact Statements* (Washington: GAO, 1978).

14. Aspin, "Defense Budget," p. 164.

15. For a fascinating glimpse of a typical week in the life of an American Senator, see James L. Buckley, *If Men Were Angels: A View from the Senate* (New York: Putnam, 1975), ch. 6.

16. A summary of proposed and realized reforms can be found in *Policymaking Role of Leadership in the Senate*, A Compilation of Papers prepared for the Commission on the Operation of the Senate (Washington: USGPO, 1976): *Toward a Modern Senate*, Final Re-

port of the Commission on the Operation of the Senate (Washington: USGPO, 1976); *Committee System Reorganization Amendments of 1977,* Hearings before the Committee on Rules and Administration, U.S. Senate, on S. Res. 4 (Washington: USGPO, 1977); and the various reports of the Temporary Select Committee to Study the Senate Committee System, published in 1976 and 1977.

17. Alexander Hamilton, *The Federalist Papers,* No. 75, pp. 450–1.

18. John Jay, *The Federalist Papers,* No. 64, pp. 391–2.

19. Quoted in *The Role of the Senate in Treaty Ratification,* A Staff Memorandum to the CFR, USS (Washington: USGPO, 1977), p. 45.

20. Ellen C. Collier, "The Meaning of "Advice and Consent of the Senate" in the Treaty-Making Process," in *Role of the Senate,* pp. 25–6.

21. Louis Henkin, " 'A More Effective System' for Foreign Relations: The Constitutional Framework," in *Commission on the Organization of the Government for the Conduct of Foreign Policy: Appendices,* Vol. 5 (hereafter cited as Murphy Commission 5), Washington: USGPO, 1975), p. 15.

22. In the area of trade Congress has also traditionally "liberated" the President by granting him prior authority to reduce duties within certain limits. See Louis Fisher, *President and Congress* (New York: Free Press, 1972), pp. 146–55.

23. Alan Platt, *The U.S. Senate and Strategic Arms Policy, 1969–1977* (Boulder, Colorado: Westview Press, 1978). See also Stephen J. Flanagan, "Congress, the White House and Salt," in *Bulletin of the Atomic Scientists* (November 1978).

24. *Role of the Senate,* pp. 45–6.

25. See *Senate Debate on the Panama Canal Treaties: A Compendium of Major Statements, Documents, Recorded Votes and Relevant Events,* prepared for the CFR, USS by the CRS (Washington: USGPO, 1979; see also I.M. Destler, "Treaty Troubles: Versailles in Reverse," *Foreign Policy,* 33 (Winter 1978–1979).

26. Memorandum for the Secretary of State of 15 December 1978 from the Legal Adviser, Herbert J. Hansell, and released by the Office of Congressional Relations, Department of State, in January 1979, under the title "Presidential Authority to Terminate Treaties." See especially pp. 6–8.

27. Vita Bite, "Precedents for U.S. Abrogation of Treaties," in *Role of the Senate.* For a full account of this issue, see *Treaty Termination,* Hearings before the CFR, USS (Washington: USGPO, 1979).

28. Arthur M. Schlesinger, Jr., *The Imperial Presidency* (Boston: Houghton Mifflin, 1973), p. 85.

29. In *United States v. Belmont,* 301 U.S. 324–37 (1937), the Supreme Court stated, "an international compact . . . is not always a treaty which requires the participation of the Senate."

30. For discussions of the types of executive agreements and their evolution, see *Transmittal of Executive Agreements to Congress* Hearings before the CFR, USS, on S. 596 (Washington: USGPO, 1971); David M. Sale, *Executive Agreements: A Survey of Legal and Political Controversies Concerning Their Use in United States Practice* (Washington: CRS, 1975); and *Congressional Review of International Agreements,* Hearings before the Subcommittee on International Security and Scientific Affairs of the CIR, USHR (Washington: USGPO, 1976).

31. The findings of the Symington Subcommittee were published in 1971 in two large volumes entitled *United States Security Agreements and Commitments Abroad.*

32. Besides those sources mentioned in n. 30, see Loch Johnson and James M. Mc-Cormick, "Foreign Policy by Executive Fiat," *Foreign Policy*, no 28 (Fall 1977); John F. Murphy, "Treaties and International Agreements other than Treaties," in Murphy Commission 5, pp. 99–115.

33. *National Commitments*, Report of the CFR, USS (Washington: USGPO, 1969), p. 28.

34. This refers to the "Bricker Amendment," which was in fact a series of initiatives proposed by Senator Bricker during the 1950s attempting to ensure that no treaty or IAOTT would have domestic standing in the absence of specific internal legislation.

35. See Ellen C. Collier, *The National Commitments Resolution of 1969: Background and Issues* (Washington: LRS, 1970).

36. The text of the Case Act, or P.L. 92–403, can be found in *Legislation on Foreign Relations Through 1977*, (Washingon: USGPO, 1978), compiled jointly by two foreign affairs committees and updated regularly.

37. A description of the State Department's "Circular 175" procedure can be found in *International Agreements: An Analysis of Executive Regulations and Practices*, prepared for the use of the CFR, USS by R. Roger Majak of the CRS (Washington: USGPO, 1977). The procedure is the means by which the executive branch determines what form an international agreement takes and what role, if any, the Senate and/or Congress plays.

38. Consideration of a more active congressional role in the process can be found in *Treaty Powers Resolution*, Hearings before the CFR, USS on S. Res. 486 (Washington: USGPO, 1976). The most recent debate, during which such a role was rejected by the Senate, is printed in the *Congressional Record* of 28 June 1978, pp. S.9994–10013.

39. Louis Henkin, *Foreign Affairs and the Constitution* (New York: Norton, 1972), p. 175.

40. See works cited in n. 23; also see the discussion in Robert G. Bell, *Implications of Extending the SALT I Interim Agreement* (Washington: CRS, 1977).

41. This stipulation is in Sec. 33 of the Arms Control and Disarmament Act, as amended, and can be found in *Legislation on Foreign Relations Through 1977*, p. 426. Also see the discussion in Bell, *Implications*, esp. pp. 17–25.

42. Alton Frye, *A Responsible Congress: The Politics of National Security* (New York: McGraw-Hill, 1975), p. 153.

43. Holbert N. Carroll, "The Congress and National Security Policy," in David B. Truman (ed.), *The Congress and America's Future* (Englewood Cliffs, N.J.: Prentice-Hall, 1965), p. 151.

44. *Congressional Decision Making for National Security*, A Statement by the Research and Policy Committee of the Committee for Economic Development (New York: Committee for Economic Development, 1974), p. 20.

45. Samuel P. Huntington, *The Common Defense* (New York: Columbia University Press, 1961), pp. 133–4. Compare Huntington's view with Edward A. Kolodziej. *The Uncommon Defense and Congress, 1945–1963* (Athens, Ohio: Ohio State University Press, 1966).

46. Les Aspin, "The Defense Budget and Foreign Policy: The Role of Congress," in *Daedalus* (Summer 1975):157.

47. Ibid., p. 160.

48. See Louis Fisher, *Presidential Spending Power* (Princeton: Princeton University Press, 1975).

49. See Nancy J. Bearg and Edwin A. Deagle, Jr., "Congress and the Defense Budget," in John Endicott and Roy W. Stafford, Jr. (eds.), *American Defense Policy*, 4th ed.

(Baltimore: Johns Hopkins University Press, 1977); Edward J. Laurance, "The Changing Role of Congress in Defense Policy-Making," *Journal of Conflict Resolution* 20, no. 2 (1976).

50. Ibid.

51. Richard P. Cronin, *An Analysis of Congressional Reductions in the Defense Budget: Fiscal Years 1971-1976* (Washington: CRS, 1976), p. 19.

52. Besides the sources listed in notes 49 and 51 above, see Jonathan E. Medalia. "Congress and the Political Guidance of Weapons Procurement," *Naval War College Review* 28, no. 2 (Fall 1975); Richard H. Ichord, "Micromanagement: The Congressional Perspective," *Armed Forces Journal International* (October 1977); and Thomas A. Dine, "Military R&D: Congress's Next Area of Military Penetration," *Bulletin of the Atomic Scientists* 34, No. 2 (1978).

53. The text of President Carter's veto message can be found in *Weekly Compilation of Presidential Documents,* vol. 14, No. 33, 1978, pp. 1447-9. More generally, the route of the FY79 legislation can be traced through reading issues of either *Aviation Week and Space Technology* or the *New York Times* for the relevant period. In addition, the two Armed Services committees published a host of hearings and reports, while full floor debates are in the *Congressional Record.*

54. A summary of existing controls on the provision of military assistance can be found in *United States Arms Transfer and Security Assistance Programs,* prepared for the Subcommittee on Europe and the Middle East of the CIR, USHR, by the CRS (Washington: USGPO, 1978).

55. See David Weissbrodt, "Human Rights Legislation and United States Foreign Policy," *Georgia Journal of International and Comparative Law* 7, no. 231 (1977). In addition, in accordance with Section 502(B) of the Foreign Assistance Act, as amended, the State Department must prepare reports on human rights conditions in every proposed recipient country. These are normally published by the foreign affairs committees in the early spring.

56. As note 34 above.

57. *International Security Assistance Act of 1978,* Conference Report (No. 95-1546, 1978), especially pp. 8-10.

58. Frye, *Responsible Congress,* pp. 212, 223.

59. Eugene Rostow in Murphy Commission 5, p. 34.

60. For background to the war powers debate, see *War Powers Legislation, 1973,* Hearings before the CFR, USS (Washington: USGPO, 1973); *Documents Relating to the War Power of Congress, The President's Authority as Commander-in-Chief and the War in Indochina,* CFR, USS (Washington: USGPO, 1970); and the excellent article by W. Taylor Reveley III, "The Power to Make War," in Murphy Commission 5, pp. 80-98.

61. The concurrent resolution is an expression of congressional sentiment requiring a simple majority in both chambers. Unlike the joint resolution, it requires no presidential signature. Until recently, the concurrent resolution was simply used to express opinion, having no legislative or legal impact; increasingly, however, it is being used as a means of preventing or terminating presidential actions in the spheres of war powers, arms transfers and nuclear exports, thereby constituting a controversial and possibly unconstitutional "legislative veto" against which the executive branch has no recourse. For a full discussion, see John R. Bolton, *The Legislative Veto* (Washington: American Enterprise Institute for Public Policy Research, 1977); Harvey G. Zeidenstein, "The Reassertion of Congressional Power: New Curbs on the President," in *Political Science Quarterly* 93 (Fall 1978), esp. pp.

404–6. President Carter's reservations are printed in *Weekly Compilations of Presidential Documents: Administration of Jimmy Carter* 26 June 1978, pp. 1146–9.

62. Schlesinger, *Imperial Presidency*, p. 4.

63. See the statement by the then Secretary of State, William Rogers, before the Senate CFR on 30 April 1973, reprinted in *Department of State Bulletin* 68, no. 1769 (1973):652–5.

64. See *War Powers Resolution*, Hearings before the CFR, USS (Washington: USGPO, 1977); *War Powers: A Test of Compliance*, Hearings before the Subcommittee on International Security and Scientific Affairs, CIR, USHR (Washington: USGPO, 1975).

65. See especially the exchange between the GAO and Lawrence Eagleburger, then Deputy Under Secretary of State, in *Seizure of the Mayaguez: Part IV*, Reports of the Comptroller General of the United States submitted to the Subcommittee on International Political and Military Affairs, CIR, USHR (Washington: USGPO, 1976).

66. Some of the correspondence between the State Department's Legal Advisor and certain Congressmen is published in the *Congressional Record* of 29 June 1978 (pp. S.10253–4) and 10 August 1978 (pp. H.8414–7).

67. *Weekly Compilation of Presidential Documents*, vol. 9, No. 43, 1973, pp. 1285–7.

68. Thomas F. Eagleton, *War and Presidential Power* (New York: Liveright, 1974).

69. Pat M. Holt, *The War Powers Resolution* (Washington: American Enterprise Institute for Public Policy Research, 1978), p. 40.

70. *War Powers Resolution*, p. 8.

71. Ibid., p. 172.

72. Robert Ellsworth, "New Imperatives for the Old Alliance," *International Security* 2, no. 4 (Spring 1978):137.

73. This view is argued somewhat too forcefully by Paul R. Schratz, "National Decision Making and Military Intervention," in Ellen P. Stern (ed.), *The Limits of Military Intervention* (London: Sage Publications, 1977), p. 360.

74. The initial phases of congressional involvement in nonproliferation policy are summarized by Warren H. Donnelly, "Congress and Nonproliferation, 1945–1977," in Alan Platt and Lawrence D. Weiler (eds.), *Congress and Arms Control* (Boulder, Colorado: Westview Press, 1978), pp. 135–55.

75. Texts are available in *Legislation on Foreign Relations Through 1977*. For a discussion of these measures by an advocate in the Congress, see Clarence D. Long, "Nuclear Proliferation: Can Congress Act in Time?" *International Security* (Spring 1977).

76. Reprinted in *Department of State Bulletin*, vol. 75, No. 1952, 1976, pp. 629–39.

77. *Presidential Documents—Jimmy Carter, 1977*, vol. 13, No. 18, 1977, pp. 611–13.

78. Long, "Nuclear Proliferation."

79. See, for example, *Nonproliferation Issues*, Hearings before the Subcommittee on Arms Control . . . of the CFR, USS (Washington: USGPO, 1977); *Nuclear Nonproliferation and Export Controls*, Hearings before the Subcommittee on Arms Control . . . of the CFR, USS (Washington: USGPO, 1977); and *The Nuclear Antiproliferation Act of 1977*, Hearings and Markup before the CIR, USHR (Washington: USGPO, 1977).

80. Useful descriptions of the main provisions of the Act (PL 95–242 of 10 March 1978) can be found in Frederick Williams, "The United States Congress and Nonproliferation," *International Security* 3, no. 2 (Fall 1978); Pat Towell, "Legislation to Reduce Risk of Nuclear Proliferation Signed by President," *Congressional Quarterly* 36, no. 10 (1978).

81. See Thomas O'Toole and Jim Hoagland, "U.S. Rushed Approval of Uranium Exports," *Washington Post*, 16 April 1978; two articles by Enrico Jacchia, "U.S.-European

Rift on A-Policy" and "Bridging the Nuclear Rift," *International Herald Tribune* of 25 April 1978 and 15–16 July 1978, respectively.

82. Quoted in *India News*, 25 April 1978 (London: High Commission of India); see also "U.S. Decision—A Breach of Agreement," *Statesman Weekly*, 29 April 1978, p. 9.

83. Executive Order of 27 April 1978 (text released by United States Embassy, London).

84. Letter from John Sparkman, Chairman of the Senate CFR to President Carter, 21 June 1978. A full account of the debate over this export can be found in *Nuclear Fuel Export to India*, Hearing before the Subcommittee on Arms Control . . . , CFR, USS (Washington: USGPO, 1978).

85. Gunter Hildenbrand, "A German Reaction to U.S. Nonproliferation Policy," *International Security* 3, no. 2 (Fall 1978):54.

86. For background, see Philip J. Farley, "The Control of United States Arms Sales," in Alan Platt and Lawrence D. Weiler (eds.), *Congress and Arms Control* (Boulder, Colorado: Westview Press, 1978).

87. See, for example, U.S. Arms Sales Policy, Hearings before the CFR, USS (Washington: USGPO, 1977); *U.S. Military Sales to Iran*, A Staff Report to the Subcommittee on Foreign Assistance of the CFR, USS (Washington: USGPO, 1976); *United States Arms Sales to the Persian Gulf*, Report of a Study Mission . . . to the CIR, USHR (Washington: USGPO, 1976).

88. The best summary of the legislation and associated controls is in *United States Arms Transfer and Security Assistance Programs*.

89. See, for example, *Proposed Sales to Jordan of the Hawk and Vulcan Air Defense Systems*, Hearings before the Subcommittee on International Political and Military Affairs of the CIR, USHR (Washington: USGPO, 1975); *Proposed Sale to Kuwait of Air-to-Air Missiles*, Hearings before the Subcommittee on International Political and Military Affairs of the CIR, USHR (Washington: USGPO, 1976); *Sale of AWACS to Iran*, Hearings before the Subcommittee on Foreign Assistance and the CFR, USS (Washington: USGPO, 1977); Richard Burt, "Battle Lines Forming on Carter's Plan to Sell Jets to Arabs," *New York Times*, 31 March 1978, p. A2.

90. Dick Clark, "The Foreign Relations Committee and the Future of Arms Control," in Platt and Weiler, *Congress*, p. 105.

91. See *International Security Assistance Act of 1978*. Conference Report (No. 95-1546, 1978), especially pp. 37–8.

92. See, for example, *Foreign and Military Intelligence*, Final Report of the Select Committee to Study Governmental Operations with respect to Intelligence Activities, USS (Report No. 94–755) (Washington: USGPO, 1976).

93. The full text of the amendment, which forms Section 662 of the Foreign Assistance Act of 1961, as amended, is in *Legislation on Foreign Relations Through 1977*, vol. 1, pp. 162–3.

94. The Angolan restriction forms Section 404 of the International Security Assistance and Arms Control Export Act of 1976 (PL 94–329), the text of which is in ibid., pp. 308–9.

95. See S. Res. 400 (1976) and H. Res 658 (1977).

96. "United States Foreign Intelligence Activities" (Statement on Executive Order 12036 and Executive Order 12036) in *Weekly Compilation of Presidential Documents: Administration of Jimmy Carter, 1978* 24 January 1978, pp. 194–216.

97. See *Rules of Procedure for the Select Committee on Intelligence USS* (Washington: USGPO, 1977), p. 5.

98. See *Annual Report to the Senate of the Select Committee on Intelligence USS* (Report No. 95–217) (Washington: USGPO, 1977). For a different perspective (that is, one that argues that the committees have not done enough to constrain the executive), see Seymour M. Hersh, "Congress Is Accused of Laxity on C.I.A.'s Covert Activity," in *New York Times*, 1 June 1978, p. A2.

99. Presidential News Conference of 25 May 1978 (full text in *New York Times*, 26 May 1978, p. A10).

100. President Ford's Farewell State of the Union message (full text in *International Herald Tribune*, 17 January 1977).

101. Proposals along this line can be found in Graham Allison and Porter Szanton, *Remaking Foreign Policy: The Organizational Connection* (New York: Basic Books, 1976), p. 110; and in *Congress and Foreign Policy*, Hearings before the Special Subcommittee on Investigations of the CIR, USHR (Washington: USGPO, 1976), especially pp. 182–3.

102. See n. 16 above.

103. Robert S. Ingersoll, "The Executive and the Congress in Foreign Policy: Conflict or Co-operation?" *Department of State Bulletin* 74, no. 1911 (1976):148.

104. James Chace, "Is a Foreign Policy Consensus Possible?" *Foreign Affairs* 57, no. 1 (Fall 1978):15–16.

105. *Congress and Foreign Policy*, pp. 1–2.

106. Douglas A. Bennet, Jr., "Congress in Foreign Policy: Who Needs It?" *Foreign Affairs* 57, no. 1 (Fall 1978):45; see also the article by Lee H. Hamilton and Michael H. Van Dusen, "Making the Separation of Powers Work," in the same issue.

107. *Murphy Commission 5*, p. 34.

108. See, for example, nn. 101 and 105.

109. Henry A. Kissinger, "America's Destiny: The Global Context" (speech delivered at the University of Wyoming on 4 February 1976). Similar conceptions of the role of Congress have been expressed by one of Kissinger's predecessors, Dean Rusk (quoted in Richard F. Fenno, Jr. *Congressmen in Committees* (Boston: Little, Brown, 1973), p. 29, and by George F. Kennan, *The Cloud of Danger: Current Realities of American Foreign Policy* (Boston: Little, Brown, 1977), esp. pp. 3–9.

110. Burton M. Sapin, *The Making of United States Foreign Policy* (Washington: Brookings Institution, 1966), p. 54.

111. Woodrow Wilson, *Congressional Government* (New York: Meridian Books, 1956), p. 195. (The work was first published in 1885.) See as well J. William Fulbright, "The Legislator as Educator," *Foreign Affairs* 57, no. 4 (Spring 1979).

112. Henkin, *Foreign Affairs*, p. 123.

113. J. William Fulbright, *Old Myths and New Realities* (New York: Random House, 1964), p. vii.

114. John H. Lehman, *The Executive, Congress, and Foreign Policy: Studies of the Nixon Administration* (New York: Praeger, 1974), p. 214.

Discussion Questions

1. What are the legally prescribed congressional roles in the national security system?

2. What changes in congressional roles have occurred since 1970? What caused those changes?

3. What are the implications of current congressional involvement in the national security system?

4. Do you think Congress is too involved or not involved enough in the determination of U.S. national security policy? Why?

12
The Determinants of Military Weapons

Graham T. Allison
Frederic A. Morris

The Prevailing Simplification and Some Illustrative Puzzles

No public official has been more deeply concerned about the problem of control-ling the strategic-arms race than former Secretary of Defense McNamara. In his annual Force Posture Statements and public speeches, he made a sustained effort to educate the public to the dangers of what he labeled the "mad momentum of the arms race." The crux of McNamara's argument can be found in his own words:

> What is essential to understand here is that the Soviet Union and the United States mutually influence one another's strategic plans. Whatever be their intentions, whatever be our intentions, *actions*—or even realistically potential actions—on either side relating to the build-up of nuclear forces, be they either offensive or defensive weapons, *necessarily trigger* reactions on the other side [emphasis added]. It is precisely this action-reaction phenomenon that fuels an arms race.[1]

According to McNamara, both the United States and the Soviet Union

> have strategic arsenals greatly in excess of a credible assured destruction capabil-ity. [They] have reached that point of excess in each case for precisely the same reason: we each have reacted to the other's build-up with very conservative calculations. We have, that is, each built a greater arsenal than either of us needed for a second strike capability, simply because we each wanted to be able to cope with the "worst plausible case."

McNamara illustrated the action-reaction phenomenon with reference to American deployment of an anti-Soviet ABM.

Reprinted with minor revisions from Graham T. Allison and Frederic A. Morris, "Armaments and Arms Control: Exploring the Determinants of Military Weapons," *Daedalus*, Vol. 104, No. 3 (Summer 1975). Reprinted with permission.

Were we to deploy a heavy system throughout the United States, the Soviets would clearly be strongly motivated to so increase their offensive capability as to cancel out our defensive advantage. It is futile for each of us to spend four billion dollars, forty billion dollars or four hundred billion—and at the end of all the spending, and at the end of all the deployment, and at the end of all the effort, to be relatively at the same point of balance on the security scale that we are now. . . .
If we opt for heavy ABM deployment—at whatever price—*we can be certain that the Soviets will react to offset the advantage we would hope to gain* [emphasis added].

The conceptual simplification employed by Secretary McNamara in analyzing changes in American force posture and predicting reactions in Soviet force posture is not difficult to discover. Each nation's force posture is conceived as the product of governmental choice aimed at achieving well-defined strategic objectives that are threatened by specific changes in the other nation's forces.

In "The Dynamics of the Arms Race," George Rathjens "inquires into the nature of the forces that impel an arms race."[2] With a directness and clarity unusual in discussions on this subject, Rathjens lays out the logic of action-reaction analysis. According to Rathjens' summary of his argument, the "Action-Reaction Phenomenon, stimulated in most cases by uncertainty about an adversary's intentions and capabilities, characterizes the dynamics of the arms race." Reviewing American and Soviet strategic forces since 1960, he finds that:

1) American overreaction to uncertainty at the time of the erroneous "missile gap" in 1960 led to the massive growth of the U.S. missile forces during the 1960's.

2) The scale of this deployment may have led in turn to the recent large Russian build-up in strategic offensive forces and also the deployment of a limited ABM system around Moscow.

3) The U.S. response to the possible extension of the Moscow ABM system into a country-wide system (and to the deployment of a Russian anti-aircraft system which until recently was thought to be a country-wide ABM system) was to equip its Minuteman III and Poseidon missiles with MIRV warheads.

4) A likely Russian reaction to the potential counter-force threat posed by the MIRVs is development of land-mobile ICBMs.

The conceptual basis for these explanations and predictions should be obvious. Weapons are the result of national strategic choice; governmental leaders select specific weapons and total force posture on the basis of precise calculations about national objectives, perceived threats, and strategic doctrine within the constraints of technology and budget. This set of assumptions, which we have identified as the prevailing simplification, is really a variant of a basic conceptual model that most people use when thinking about most problems of foreign policy most of the time.[3] That the "government" is in fact a loose collection of organizations and people is readily apparent. That "choices" of weapons by the United States or the Soviet Union are abstractions for the activities of these organizations and people is certainly no revelation. But explanations and predictions in terms of this simplification nevertheless tend to collect the activities of these people and organizations into one box called "the government," and the mechanism which moves potential weapons systems through the box until they emerge as part of the force posture is called a "strategic choice."

That—"other things being equal"—national decision processes choose weapons designed to implement certain objectives or doctrines is probably true, perhaps even tautologous. The proposition, "If the Soviet Union knows that weapons system X will be less effective in achieving a desired objective than weapons system Y, it will be less likely to purchase weapons system X," is no doubt correct. What is less clear, however, is:

a.   At what level do summary concepts like "the Soviet government," "strategic objectives," and "doctrines" stop being meaningful?
b.   What are the rules of evidence for making summary statements about national goals and intentions?
c.   How can one give an empirical interpretation to such statements by reference, on the one hand, to pressures in the international environment and, on the other, to shared national values and assumptions?
d.   How much of the variance in outcomes can be explained by factors emphasized by the prevailing simplification, e.g., whether strategic forces are determined to the third decimal place, or ten per cent, or one hundred per cent?

These general questions can be applied in specific terms to three major American strategic-weapons systems of the nineteen-sixties. In each case, a juxtaposition of the characteristics of the weapon deployed with the official objectives and doctrines they were said to serve produces a puzzle.

1. *American strategic forces in the nineteen-sixties:* Defense Secretary McNamara's final Force Posture Statement (February, 1968) provided a detailed review of American nuclear strategy. McNamara insisted that the main objective of our strategic forces was "assured destruction," that is, "an ability to inflict at all times and under all foreseeable conditions an unacceptable degree of damage upon any aggressor . . . even after absorbing a surprise attack."[4] When he introduced this concept in 1965, McNamara set the necessary level of damage at one quarter to one third of the Soviet population and about two thirds of Soviet industrial capacity. In his valedictory statement, the Secretary judged that "a capacity on our part to destroy, say, one-fifth to one-fourth of her population and one-half her industrial capacity would serve as an effective deterrent."[5]

Now, compare these requirements with the capabilities actually acquired under McNamara's stewardship. According to McNamara's final force-posture statement, two hundred "equivalent megatons delivered" (EMTs) would meet the assured-destruction objective against the Soviet population projected for 1972.[6] As McNamara spoke, American strategic forces included over 4,000

EMTs on bombers; 1,000 EMTs on ICBMs; 600 EMTs on SLBMs.[7] Factors such as survivability, reliability, and accuracy affect how many of these EMTs would actually destroy their targets under second-strike conditions. But even under very pessimistic assumptions, that figure grossly exceeds the necessary two hundred. This presents our first puzzle: Why did actual strategic forces exceed capabilities required by the doctrine of assured destruction by such a vast amount?

2. *Hardsite defense and ABM:* In September, 1967, Secretary of Defense McNamara announced the Johnson Administration's decision to deploy a light ABM system to defend population areas against the potential Chinese nuclear threat. In March, 1969, President Nixon announced a "substantial modification" of this Sentinel ABM. While using Sentinel components, Nixon proposed a new system (soon designated Safeguard) which revised priorities, the first among them being the "protection of our land-based retaliatory forces against a direct attack by the Soviet Union."[8] A hybrid that combined area-defense and terminal-defense components, Safeguard had quite limited hardsite capability (i.e., ability to defend hardened ICBM silos against attacks). This provides our second puzzle: Given Nixon's decision to defend ICBMs, why did the government choose a system that would defend them so poorly?

3. *MIRV as a response to Soviet ABM:* According to McNamara's analysis of the arms race quoted above, "actions relating to the build-up of nuclear forces, be they either offensive or defensive weapons . . . necessarily trigger reactions on the other side." Rathjens' analysis identified just such a relationship between the Soviet ABM and the American MIRV, asserting that "the U.S. response to the possible extension of the Moscow ABM system to a country-wide system . . . was to equip its Minuteman III and Poseidon missiles with MIRV warheads." Senator Jacob Javits emphasized this point in Senate Foreign Relations subcomittee hearings on ABM: "Is it or is it not a fact," Javits rhetorically asked Deputy Secretary of Defense Packard, "that the MIRV system began to be developed as soon as we had reliable information that the Russians were deploying an anti-ballistic missile system around at least one of their cities?"[9] In 1971, Defense Research and Engineering Director John Foster confirmed the link between Soviet ABM and the need for American MIRV by arguing the converse: "If a ban were placed on the ABM, in the sense of banning a capability to intercept a ballistic missile attack, then as I see it at the moment, there would be no need for the United States to deploy MIRV."[10] The SALT agreement of 1972 banned equipment capable of intercepting a ballistic missile attack. The United States nonetheless continued deploying MIRV. In this case, the puzzle is twofold: If the American MIRV was a *response* to Soviet ABM, why did American research and development on MIRV *precede* Soviet ABM, *and* why did American deployment of MIRV continue *after* Soviet ABMs were effectively banned?

A review of other weapons (including Trident and the F-111 . . .) uncovers similar paradoxes. When examined carefully, weapons systems are found to be "underdetermined" by the prevailing simplification,[11] that is, the factors emphasized by the simplification are not sufficient to explain why one weapon emerged rather than another.

Alternative Overviews and Explanations

The most casual observation shows that the actual weapons process differs rather substantially from the prevailing simplification. Review of the record of predictions and explanations based on the simplification indicates that the latter simply has not adequately summarized the causal impact of relevant factors in the process. What we need is a well-defined, tested causal model of the multiple determinants of military force posture. No such model exists; nor can one emerge without a very substantial research effort. In the meantime, analysts and officials will continue discussing force posture, making judgments and inferences in which force posture plays an important secondary role, and taking action on the basis of such inferences and predictions. These activities could be usefully informed by alternative simplifications that capture other important causal factors in the weapons process. Our aim here is to state two alternative simplifications that, while obviously inadequate and crude, may serve as a stark reminder of the limits to our understanding of the actual determinants of military force posture. The alternative simplifications should make persuasive the importance of causal factors now overlooked or underemphasized. Since both the prevailing simplification and the alternative overviews stress somewhat different causal factors, taken together they may serve as a point of departure for research aimed at an adequate causal map of the process.

These alternative overviews can be developed at considerable length, but will only be summarized briefly here in the form of two series of assertions and questions.[12]

Force Posture as Political Resultant

Assertions

a. Analytic uncertainty: problems of force posture are so complex that reasonable men can disagree about which weapons system the United States should have (and even about which strategic doctrine, or which objective). In fact, the relevant parties do disagree about weapons systems, as well as about doctrines and objectives.
b. Differences of opinion among individuals and groups are organizationally based. Many of the sharp differences reflect—and are highly predictable in the light of—position and organization. (When has a Chief of Staff of the Air Force or a Strategic Air Command officer advocated an end to advanced manned bombers?)
c. Political resolution: differences of opinion among participants who share power must be resolved by bargaining or politics.

Questions

1. Who plays? Who participates in the bargaining? Whose preferences count in shaping the weapons systems that emerge?
2. What determines the participants' preferences?
3. How are preferences combined? Which groups (and interests) are "heavies" and which are "lights" in the process?
4. How stable is the distribution of influence among participants (and what are the sources)?

Force Posture as Organizational Output

Assertions

a. The fact that weapons emerge from a lengthy process of great complexity accents the importance of organizations in determining results.
b. The configuration of organizations that constitute a government changes very slowly.
c. The behavior of organizations at time t is primarily determined by goals and procedures of these organizations at time t-1.
d. Government leaders can disturb the behavior of these organizations, but their behavior cannot be controlled to any great extent by a central authority.

Questions

1. How is the government organized for acquiring weapons, i.e., what organizations and organizational units act on this issue and with what relative influence?
2. How do the goals and procedures of these organizations affect *information* available at various points where decisions are made, choices defined, etc.?
3. How do the goals and procedures of these organizations affect the *alternative* courses of action considered at various points where decisions are made, issues defined, etc.?
4. How do the goals and procedures of these organizations affect the *implementation* of government choices?

These two alternative overviews are obviously not mutually exclusive. Both simplifications are at a level of generalization that permits some reconciliation. For example, the relative stability of the influence of interests in the first alternative overview results in part from the role of military organizations in this process. Still, each overview can be used to provide a relatively straightforward answer to why that particular weapons system appeared in the force posture. The preservation of competing simplifications may help broaden our understanding of the process.

It would be possible at the current stage of research to formulate a single overview of the determinants of force posture, incorporating some of the best features of all the simplifications. We have chosen not to do so because we believe that a single overview might create an impression of understanding greater than that which actually exists. In addition, the competing simplifications serve as a useful point of departure for our own research strategy, which is: first, utilizing the concepts of the simplifications, to examine existing case material in order to make a preliminary determination of the major factors that shape force posture; second, to gather data about these major causal factors; and, third, to formulate and test hypotheses and then, through clustering them, to construct partial models of the process.

In the last few years, students of defense policy have produced a number of case histories of American weapons. In contrast to case studies that simply "tell the story" of a particular development, most of these cases were undertaken to provide answers to more general questions (including some raised by the alternative overviews) and to generate hypotheses that went beyond the particular cases. None of the available studies provides a full, satisfactory explanation of the development of a particular weapon, but the researcher usually succeeded in peeling off at least two or three layers of the weapons-development onion—in contrast to the prevailing simplification, which focuses on the onion as a whole. As it happens, most of the cases divide the government into a number of organizations, treat the organizations as individuals, and then explain the weapon development as the result of bargaining among competing organizational interests. Two layers into the onion, one does understand somewhat more; one's predictions improve. But because the innermost layers of the onion remain intact, each case raises as many questions as it answers. Indeed, this initial division reinforces the view asserted at the outset: the determinants of force posture are not understood; analysts do not even have appropriate categories for investigating the causal factors involved.

American Strategic Forces in the Nineteen-Sixties

By the end of Robert McNamara's tenure as Secretary of Defense, the primacy of "assured destruction" as the central American strategic objective had been established. McNamara's associates had developed a formula for translating that objective into required capabilities. "Indeed," according to Assistant Secretary of Defense Alain Enthoven, "in sharp contrast to most other types of military requirements, those for strategic forces lend themselves to calculation."[13] Yet when one performs the calculation, the answer is unmistakable: American forces have consistently and dramatically exceeded the number of "equivalent megatons delivered" that is required for assured destruction. For example, if one carefully examines McNamara's final Force Posture Statement, one finds that, even if Soviet capabilities surpassed the highest range of national intelligence estimates through 1972 (the standard five-year projection), American strategic missiles alone would be able to deliver six times the number of equivalent megatons (EMTs)

Table 12-1
U.S. Strategy and Forces, 1961–1968

Year	McNamara's Announced Strategic Doctrine	Contemporary Estimates of Soviet Forces Deployed; Retrospective Estimates in Brackets [ ]	U.S. Missiles Planned	U.S. Forces Deployed as of December
1961 (FY '62)	Emphasis on survivability and control. No real strategic doctrine yet articulated.	50 + ICBM [10] 190 long-range heavy bombers	126 Atlas 54 Titan I 54 Titan II 800 Minuteman 656 Polaris	54 ICBM 80 SLBM 600 long-range heavy bombers
1962 (FY '63)	Deterrence through the ability to destroy the enemy's "war-making capabilities" even after the US has absorbed the first blow.	75 + ICBM [40] 200 bombers	54 Titan II 800 Minuteman 656 Polaris	180 ICBM 144 SLBM 630 bombers
1963 (FY '64)	"City avoidance" strategy: maintenance of a "second strike force" capable of (1) striking at both military and non-military targets simultaneously, or (2) striking at military targets first, holding the cities hostage as an incentive for the Soviets not to strike at US cities.	100 + ICBM [80] 100 SLBM 200 bombers	54 Titan II 950–1300 Minuteman 656 Polaris	534 ICBM 160 SLBM 630 bombers
1964 (FY '65)	"Damage limiting" strategy: maintenance of forces capable of (1) destroying Soviet society under all conditions of retaliation, and (2) limiting damage to the US by striking *not only* Soviet cities, but also their unlaunched forces.	200 + ICBM [130] 120 + SLBM 200 bombers	54 Titan II 1000 Minuteman 656 Polaris	907 ICBM 320 SLBM 630 bombers

Year	Strategic doctrine			
1965 (FY '66)	"Assured destruction + damage limitation" strategy: maintenance of forces capable of (1) destroying 1/4 to 1/3 of the Soviet population and 2/3 of its industrial capacity, and (2) limiting damage to the US.	270 ICBM [200] 120 + SLBM 200 bombers	54 Titan II 1000 Minuteman 656 Polaris	854 ICBM 464 SLBM 630 bombers
1966 (FY '67)	"Assured destruction + damage limitation."	300 ICBM [300] 150 SLBM 200 bombers	54 Titan II 1000 Minuteman 656 Polaris	1004 ICBM 592 SLBM 600 bombers
1967 (FY '68)	"Assured destruction," substantial retreat from damage limitation.	520 ICBM 130 SLBM 150 bombers	54 Titan II 1000 Minuteman 656 Polaris	1054 ICBM 656 SLBM 555 bombers
1968 (FY '69)	"Assured destruction."	900-1000 ICBM 125 SLBM 150 bombers	54 Titan II 1000 Minuteman 656 Polaris	1054 ICBM 656 SLBM 465 bombers

Sources: Strategic doctrine: Secretary of Defense's annual Force Posture Statements. Forces deployed: U.S.: U.S. Air Force, Strategic Air Command, *The Development of Strategic Air Command 1946–1973*; U.S. Navy, Strategic Systems Project Office, *Polaris & Poseidon FBM Facts*. USSR: International Institute of Strategic Studies, *Strategic Survey* (1961–1969).

required for assured destruction. The question once again is why United States strategic forces exceeded by such a large factor the capabilities required for their strategic objective. Table 12–1 and figure 12–1 illustrate some of the history of the build-up in American strategic forces during the nineteen-sixties and offer some perspective on the relation between forces and doctrine. Their evidence raises three important questions:

First, were not the size, mix, and character of American strategic forces chosen *prior* to the doctrine of assured destruction and the associated theory of requirements? In 1960 the number of long-range bombers reached 600 and did not vary by more than 100 for the next eight years. In 1961, the Kennedy Administration settled on Polaris submarines carrying a total of 656 SLBMs. The same year McNamara reduced the planned Titan II deployment to 54 missiles; the following year he scheduled the phasing out of Atlas and Titan I, limiting the number of large-payload ICBMs to 54 Titan IIs. The approved number of Minutemen ranged between 800 and 1,300 during 1961–1963. In 1964, the Secretary of Defense established a ceiling of 1,000 Minutemen. But algorithms for calculating the capabilities that were necessary for meeting the stated requirements were not perfected until 1966.[14]

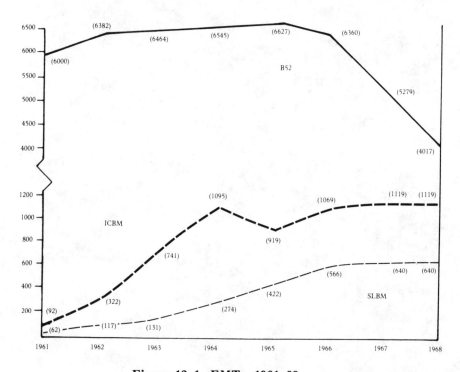

Figure 12-1. EMTs, 1961-68

Second, how did strategic doctrines affect capabilities? Though the McNamara era is remembered primarily for "assured destruction," official strategy shifted a number of times during the nineteen-sixties from deterrence-plus-counterforce (FY 1963), to "city avoidance" (FY 1964), to "damage limitation" (FY 1965), to damage-limitation-plus-assured-destruction (FY 1966), to an increasing emphasis on "assured destruction" alone (FY 1967–FY 1969). Despite this evolution of doctrine, the numbers of launchers programmed in 1961–1962 remained relatively fixed throughout McNamara's tenure, while actual capabilities steadily increased through qualitative improvements.

Third, in what sense were American force levels coupled to Soviet capabilities? The decisions of 1961 and 1962 accelerated our strategic deployments and established target numbers of launchers. But these decisions were taken at the very time that American intelligence had a revelation: the infamous missile gap was a myth, and the Soviet strategic build-up was progressing much more slowly than was previously thought. As early as February, 1961, McNamara made a slip in a background news briefing by discounting the missile gap; and by November, 1961, the government was officially announcing to its allies that the Soviet Union was on the short side of the missile gap. But the dramatic buildup of American strategic forces proceeded apace.

The conclusion that American strategic forces in the nineteen-sixties were being driven by something other than official strategic doctrine and estimates of enemy capabilities seems inescapable. This history even provides some clues as to why our strategic capabilities in 1968 so far exceeded the requirements of assured destruction. The level of American forces was determined in part by choices made prior to the formulation of the assured-destruction doctrine; at the time of the initial decisions, doctrines circulating in the government included some that called for much more than assured destruction. As McNamara has emphasized, the early choices were made when there was considerable uncertainty about Soviet plans and intentions. Thereafter, the number of American launchers was relatively unresponsive to changes either in United States doctrine or in Soviet capabilities.

But why did the United States government initially settle on a missile force of solid-fueled, small payload missiles? Why was the force sized at 1,000 Minutemen and 656 Polaris? And why did the number vary so little during the McNamara era? Desmond V. Ball's study, "The Strategic Missile Programme of the Kennedy Administration, 1961–1963," addresses these questions.[15] It is not possible to do justice to Ball's carefully researched 400-page study here; but the major strands of his argument can be made tolerably clear.

Five major factors seem to have determined the limits within which Kennedy and McNamara could hope to work. First, Kennedy's 1960 campaign pledges to strengthen strategic forces made it politically difficult for him not to enlarge the missile programs in Eisenhower's fiscal 1962 budget. To renege would be to disappoint campaign supporters and to deny expectations generated in Congress, industry, and the military.

Second, in 1960 the political consensus endorsing nuclear "superiority" pervaded all thought about strategic forces among military and civilians, experts and laymen. Having a greater number of missiles than the Soviet Union was a "requirement" that transcended specific strategies. Third, the services had developed their own conclusions as to the level of strategic forces required. Given their allies in Congress and the reluctance of any Administration to argue with the military, their views weighed heavily. These factors seem to have produced defense estimates ranging from about 450 Minutemen and 20 Polaris submarines on the low end (Eisenhower's budget) to 3,000–10,000 Minuteman and 45 Polaris on the high end (the military's "wish list").

In determining the actual ceilings, bargaining with the military figured prominently. As Ball concludes, "The decision by the Kennedy/McNamara Administration to procure 1,000 Minuteman missiles and 41 Polaris submarines was, in essence, the outcome of a 'political process,' involving bargaining, negotiations, and compromise between the various relevant groups and personalities both inside and outside the Administration, each with their own perceptions and interests."[16] The services, and most particularly the Air Force, deliberately inflated their missile "requirements" to gain bargaining leverage. Kennedy and McNamara favored considerably fewer missiles; figures as low as 450 ICBMs were mentioned. But they kept in mind other goals as well, particularly their de-emphasis of manned bombers. Thus they were willing to allow more missiles in exchange for stopping the B-70 and Skybolt, and deferring manned forces.

Recollections of this episode vary. Some Department of Defense civilians recall that McNamara was willing to limit numbers, but that Kennedy was reluctant to alienate Congress (and thus lose support for his other programs) by settling on too low a number. Others recall that Kennedy was willing to agree to a lower number, but that McNamara felt he would "not be able to live with the Pentagon" with the smaller figure. As for the precise number of 1,000, Ball reports that "according to one of the principals involved in setting the programme level, 1,000 was simply the result of a 'visceral feeling' on the part of McNamara and his aides that that figure was a satisfactory and viable compromise."[17]

Third, the shape of the forces—Polaris, small-payload ICBMs and a large bomber force—was not chosen from a blank slate. A number of factors severely constrained the range of possible alternatives. McNamara and his colleagues inherited from the Eisenhower Administration a set of strategic weapons programs at different stages of development and deployment. The decision to deploy had been made on Atlas and Titan I ICBMs, the Polaris SLBM, the Snark air-breathing cruise missile, and B-47, B-52, and B-58 bombers. Weapons at various stages of development included: Minuteman and Mobile Minuteman ICBMs, the Skybolt air-to-surface missile, and the B-70 bomber. Thus the new Administration could not really ask, what strategic forces should we have? Inevitably it asked, what shall we do about strategic programs already in existence?

Fourth, the Kennedy Administration inherited a military establishment of three major services, each with its own role and mission. Choices about the shape of strategic forces would have major consequences for the strength of the Air Force, Navy, and Army, and for the relative positions of subunits within each service. For example, Senator Jackson recalls early Navy resistance to Polaris:

> I was interested in this program from the very outset, going back many, many years I found that in trying to get the Navy to do something about it, I ran headlong into the competition within the Navy for requirements in connection with their day-to-day operational requirements; whatever it was . . . I was told that this strategic system would just eat away and erode their limited funds. . . . The result was the Polaris was not pushed hard until Sputnik came along.[18]

Obviously, Administration questions about strategic needs could not be considered apart from service questions about organizational needs.

Finally, the decisions were made in a hurry. The emphasis on solid-fueled, small-payload Polaris and Minuteman missiles dated from decisions President Kennedy announced in his special defense message to Congress of March, 1961.

Why these programmed levels were not reduced when their excess capacity became apparent is a further question, and one that Ball does not really answer. One rule of thumb suggests that forces-in-being are replaced or improved, but are never eliminated. In strategic debate, a rachet effect seems to be at work: logically, changes in strategic objectives could require a reduction in forces; rhetorically, such conclusions are occasionally drawn; in fact, the reductions never happen. For example, McNamara stated that the forces needed to provide the "no-city option [a 1962 enthusiasm] must be larger than would otherwise be the case" and that, if the option were eliminated, "there would be strong reasons to reduce the forces we are requesting funds to procure."[19] But shortly therafter the option was abandoned, and the forces were not reduced. Similarly, McNamara argued in 1965 that offensive forces beyond those required for assured destruction must be justified on the basis of their contribution to the damage-limitation objective. Damage limitation was later de-emphasized, but the forces were not trimmed. The flexibility of strategic doctrine in justifying programmed (or desired) force levels was illustrated dramatically by the elaborate "Kent Study" of 1962–1964: it analyzed alternative strategies and forces, contributed the concept of "damage limitation," and concluded that "the presently planned inventory of strategic missiles is approximately correct in this time period, whether by accident or good intuitive planning."[20]

Hardsite Defense and ABM

In September of 1967, Secretary of Defense Robert McNamara announced the Johnson Administration's decision to deploy an ABM. Designated "Sentinel," this system was supposed to protect the country's population centers from a primitive

Chinese attack, to catch accidental launches, and to provide some protection for the Minuteman ICBM force against an all-out Soviet attack. In March of 1969, President Nixon announced a "substantial modification" of this Sentinel system. Relegating the mission of population defense to a poor third, Nixon's speech placed primary emphasis on the protection of Minuteman sites. To achieve this objective, the President proposed replacing Sentinel with "Safeguard." But under the "Safeguard" label, one found the same components that had been developed for Sentinel, only now they had shifted to Minuteman sites.

According to numerous experts, including many who applauded Nixon's intention to defend ICBMs, Safeguard provided poor protection for Minuteman. Its interceptors were too few and too slow to foil a determined Soviet attack. Even more critically, Safeguard's "soft" radar made the entire system vulnerable to a single attacking missile. Technology did not dictate Safeguard's deficiencies. An effective system was feasible. The question is, therefore, why did the Nixon Administration choose a system so ill-suited to the defense of the Minuteman?

The explanation must begin with politics. The new Administration faced growing opposition on Capitol Hill. Having pushed ABM into Lyndon Johnson's lap, Congress now threatened to take it away from Richard Nixon. The new President was determined to deploy ABM—for bargaining leverage in the upcoming SALT negotiations and for other reasons—but he needed to act quickly. As a result, exploration of the possible options suffered. Better analysis alone, however, would not necessarily have improved the outcome. The Administration had to select from the available set of hardware alternatives. In 1969, no ABM well suited to the protection of Minuteman had reached the stage of system development. Having decided to deploy *some* ABM, the Nixon Administration was forced to choose from a list that lacked the appropriate item.

But why was the array of options so restricted? Unfortunately no detailed account maps all the twists and turns in the development of ABM. Several related discussions, however, do shed some light on the issue.[21] Drawing on these accounts, we will attempt to explain why no "hardsite" (Minuteman) ABM had reached advanced development, while ABM components designed for population defense were nearing completion.

From the beginning, ABM belonged to the Army. In 1945, the Army initiated Project NIKE, giving contracts to Bell Telephone Laboratories (BTL) and Western Electric. NIKE's mission called for defense of the United States against air attack by enemy aircraft. The means of achieving the mission was a surface-to-air missile system: networks of radar, interceptors, and computers which would identify an incoming target, track it, and fire an interceptor whose warhead would detonate within a lethal radius. In the decade following the original contract, the Army deployed two such systems, NIKE-AJAX and NIKE-HERCULES. Both defended against attacks by conventional aircraft. In 1953, as the prospect of a Soviet missile force appeared, the Army asked BTL to examine the feasibility of defense against ICBMs. By 1956, BTL concluded that appropriate modifications to NIKE-HERCULES would indeed make ABM feasible. Thus the first ABM was conceived as a follow-on to systems already deployed by the Army.

The Army responded favorably to the BTL report. In 1957, Army headquarters established the NIKE-ZEUS project. Hardware development began. From that time, the Army consistently advocated deployment of a large ABM system to defend the population against a major Soviet attack. The Army's determination seems to have stemmed from several factors. First, ABM was following a major service weapon (NIKE-HERCULES) that performed a major service mission (air defense). Second, the Army had surrendered much of its share of the budget to the Air Force and Navy during the nineteen-fifties. President Eisenhower's "New Look" policy emphasized strategic nuclear war capabilities, and the Air Force and Navy captured the strategic offensive missions. In its Jupiter IRBM, the Army had hoped for a small piece of the action, but operational control of Jupiter was given to the Air Force. ABM seemed to be the Army's last chance for a strategic nuclear role. Finally, many within the Army believed ABM could save American lives in the event of nuclear war and could thus make a major contribution to national security.

The Army's strong advocacy (usually with Congressional concurrence) could not alone have secured deployment. That decision rested with successive Presidents and their Secretaries of Defense, and the Defense agencies on whom they relied for information, alternatives, and advice. In particular, while the Army controlled the advanced development of systems hardware, Robert McNamara and the organizations that advised him decisively influenced the character of the systems themselves. Their power to approve or reject deployment, to set standards of acceptability, and to supervise exploratory research and development insured them a major voice. The systems that emerged were the products of Army reactions to these initiatives.

The Directorate of Defense Research and Engineering (DDR&E) and its semiautonomous subunit, the Advanced Research Projects Agency (ARPA), played key roles. ARPA was established in 1958 as a separate agency reporting directly to the Secretary of Defense. Partly a response to Sputnik, ARPA was a low-budget operation charged with performing research that the services handled poorly, especially "quick reaction" and long-range projects. Early assignments included all military and civilian space programs, notably ABM technology beyond the NIKE-ZEUS stage. ARPA conducted research. It did not develop actual hardware. As an ARPA director has explained:

A general principle of ARPA's operation is to work in an area until feasibility has been established. Hardware development for these projects are the responsibility of the services upon assignment by the Secretary of Defense so that those projects can compete against other weapon system elements within the service or services most likely to use them.[22]

Created later in 1958, DDR&E assumed authority over ARPA. DDR&E's mandate called for supervising all Defense Department research and development, including that of the services, and advising the Secretary of Defense on weapons decisions.

From the beginning, the scientists and engineers who manned DDR&E and ARPA questioned the basic feasibility of the Army-development NIKE-ZEUS. Their arguments fueled the skepticism of President Eisenhower. No deployment decision had been made by the time John Kennedy and his Secretary of Defense, Robert McNamara, entered office.

The objections of DDR&E and ARPA, which bridged the two Administrations, centered on the low acceleration of ZEUS's interceptors and the inability of its radars to track a number of incoming warheads at once. ARPA research suggested solutions to these problems in an electronically steered "phased array radar" and an interceptor called Sprint, capable of higher acceleration than ZEUS. At DDR&E's behest, the Army incorporated these advances into its ABM during the period 1961–65. The modified system acquired the name NIKE X.

At the same time, ARPA explored ever more advanced technology, including hardsite defense. As Dr. Jack P. Ruina, ARPA's director, explained in 1963:

> The U.S. program in this field has consisted of two parts. The first is the hardware development of complete systems and this is the responsibility of the Army in its NIKE-ZEUS and NIKE X programs. The second is a broad research and exploratory development program, which is ARPA's Project DEFENDER. . . . Project DEFENDER has an active hardpoint defense system program where we study the technology required for the defense of hardened sites such as missile silos and command posts.[23]

The hardpoint program yielded several components that reached the stage of exploratory development. Thus ARPA both improved the Army's ongoing system for population defense and began designing alternative technology for hardsite defense.

The Army accepted the modifications to the system as their price for improving its chances for deployment. The Army was not interested in hardsite ABM, however. Hardsite defense would have competed directly with the Army's chosen mission, which was large-scale defense of population. The Army Project office did not want such competition. Nor were the Navy and Air Force attracted to ABM. The mere availability of its appropriate technology did not make hardsite defense a genuine option. Development of a complete system would have required service sponsorship, and no service was about to undertake the task without McNamara's forceful intervention. For his own reasons, McNamara did not intervene.

For Robert McNamara, the question was never simply, "Does it work?" He also asked, "Do we need it?" At the beginning of his tenure, McNamara opposed NIKE-ZEUS because he believed it would not work and NIKE X because it was not ready. By 1965, he based his opposition on the twin benchmarks of "assured destruction" and "damage limitation": as a full-scale population defense, NIKE X could not significantly limit damage because the Soviets might easily offset its effectiveness, while it would contribute to assured destruction only at a far greater cost than other, simpler measures. In 1966, McNamara became sufficiently concerned with the Soviet strategic build-up to institute a study called STRAT-X, which was to explore alternative means of preserving the deterrent. He did not, however, support the development of a hardsite ABM system. His failure to do so seems to have been compatible with his goals at the time. By 1967, he opposed ABM in general and hoped that an agreement with the Soviet Union would eliminate the need for deployment. When the Glassboro summit dashed hopes for such an agreement, the pressures of the impending Presidential election left McNamara with little choice but to submit to deployment of NIKE X. However, the question was not, what is the best ABM? but, what is the least provocative rationale for a system that has become unavoidable?

McNamara rejected the defense of Minuteman as a suitable rationale, a suggestion of his advisers in Systems Analysis. NIKE X was a "low confidence" weapon in the hardsite role. Moreover, any system directed against the Soviets might create pressures for a full-scale anti-Soviet population defense. McNamara's immediate concern with the arms race outweighed the consideration of possible Minuteman vulnerability in some future year. A small-scale version of NIKE X directed at the unsophisticated Chinese threat suited his purposes—thus, Sentinel.

This compromise served the succeeding Administration poorly. Sentinel's minimal hardsite capability represented a cheap addition to a modest system for population defense against China. As Air Force Secretary Harold Brown phrases it, "If you are planning to put in an area defense of the population, which would be, say, a $3.5 billion expenditure, then the additional expenditure required to defend the missile complex to a reasonable degree of protection is somewhere between a half billion and a billion dollars. . . ."[24] Obtaining the limited Minuteman defense could be justified by its low maringal cost, given the money already spent on a light population defense. When Minuteman defense became the primary objective of the entire system, the cogency of this rationale diminished.

The implications of this brief sketch seem clear. The Nixon Administration chose an ABM with a relatively poor capability for hardsite defense because the President insisted on immediate deployment, and no other system with a greater capability for this purpose was in a sufficiently advanced stage of development, since it had not previously been required to further the ambitions of any service or strong service subunit. The Army had captured ABM development, and, from the beginning, the Army's ABM Project Office sought only a full-scale population defense. Robert McNamara did not force the issue of hardsite defense, and the Project Office repeatedly rejected suggestions from elsewhere that the Army develop hardsite ABM. Some observers have speculated that the Army's resistance stemmed from apprehension that, should an ABM fit within the fence surrounding a Minuteman squadron, ABM would become the property of the Air Force.

Not only did the Army's control of ABM impede the preparation of hardsite defense, but, equally important, the Army refused to present an alternative—rarely do organizations put forward more than one option. At the outset of the new Administration, presided over by a President who had taken a campaign stand in favor of ABM and a Secretary of Defense who was in favor of giving the Pentagon back to the military, it was not surprising to find the normal short list: one apparently viable option framed by two phony extremes. Since the issue mattered little to the Air Force or the Navy, the Joint Chiefs of Staff were united in support of the Army's position.

MIRV as a Response to Soviet ABM

Arms-race analysts always explain MIRV as being the American response to Soviet ABM. Because the Soviet Union was deploying a defensive weapon that threatened the ability of American nuclear warheads to reach their appointed targets, the United States moved to negate the Soviet advantage by deploying a weapon that multiplied the number of independently targeted warheads aimed at the Soviet Union. Without Soviet ABM, so the argument goes, the United States would not have developed or deployed MIRV.

In fact, American research and development on MIRV *preceded* the Soviet ABM, and American deployment persisted after the ban on ABM. How, then, did the United States come to develop and deploy MIRV? The evidence available is insufficient for a complete explanation,[25] but it is sufficient to make plain the limits to our understanding of American weapons development. First, the lengthy periods required for development complicate the task of distinguishing "actions" from "reactions" in cases such as MIRV. For example, one popular explanation emphasizes Soviet deployment of ABM as the inspiration for American MIRV. But this explanation ignores the central fact about strategic forces, namely, that they take a very long time to develop. The normal incubation period for a strategic weapon, that is, the period between initial research and actual deployment, is seven to fifteen years. MIRV deployment took a decade. Furthermore, in a situation where one nation cannot be sure what weapons the other may be researching or even deploying, the long periods needed for development demand that prudent research *anticipate* threats and requirements. Secretary McNamara emphasized this problem in 1965:

> The weapons we have in being are the result of research and development programs initiated as long ago as 10–15 years. We believe that the programs we have under way are more than adequate to insure our superiority in the years ahead.[26]

If American research were to await evidence of Soviet research before acting, the United States could not be confident of maintaining superiority. Consequently, research pursues any technological possibilities that seem promising to the research community, within given budget constraints. DDR&E Director John Foster testified to Congress: "Our current effort to get a MIRV capability on our missiles is not reacting to a Soviet capability so much as it is moving ahead again to make sure that whatever they do of the possible things that we can imagine they might do, we will be prepared."[27]

To be fully prepared for all contingencies—McNamara's "worst plausible case"—American procurement and deployment of counter-weapons would have to precede Soviet deployment of weapons that the United States wanted to be certain of offsetting. McNamara justified MIRV deployment in 1968 not in terms of what the Soviets *had* done, but as a precaution against what they *might* do:

> Because the Soviet Union *might* [emphasis in original] deploy extensive ABM defenses, we are making some very important changes in our strategic missile forces. Instead of a single large warhead our missiles are now being designed to carry several small warheads. . . . Deployment by the Soviets of a ballistic missile defense of their cities will not improve their situation. We have *already* [emphasis added] taken the necessary steps to guarantee that our strategic offensive forces will be able to overcome such a defense.[28]

But this logic permits "reactions" to precede the action that might provoke them, a possibility that jumbles the action-reaction sequence. Because of such factors as the lengthy period involved in acquisition, uncertainty about the opponent's research, and the consequent necessity for anticipating it, decisions about weapons research, development, and procurement cannot be based on evidence about the opponent's actual weapons programs. Rarely can such evidence be decisive. Thus, the action-reaction hypothesis, which emphasizes tightly coupled, specific, offsetting reactions to particular weapons, seems less important, even logically, than a loosely coupled, general competition in which each nation pursues broad strategic objectives that may be readjusted periodically in light of forces that the other assembles.

When we move from logic to evidence, we observe that each nation pursues its weapons strategy through large organizations for research, development, and use. What drives these institutions are not only estimates of the other side's activity, but also their own internal dynamics. In contrast to the notion of Soviet actions encouraging American research, it appears that, in the case of MIRV, the United States mainly provided its own encouragement. Because research is typically multi-purpose, identifying the moment when research on a particular weapon might be said to have begun poses severe problems. Whatever the date of MIRV's origin, however, the proposition that Soviet ABM provided *the* trigger seems suspect.

In 1957, William Holaday, Director of Guided Missiles for the Department of Defense, established a committee called the Re-entry Body Identification Group and asked it to investigate difficulties for the defense that could be posed by offensive missiles using penetration aides. The immediate spur for this action was the need to elaborate the challenges that American designers of ABM would have to face in meeting an attack that employed penetration aides. He also wanted to identify opportunities for American offensive missiles against a possible future Soviet ABM.

The research agenda established by the committee powerfully influenced American research over the next several years and led directly to MIRV. According to Herbert York, the first Director of DDR&E, the Re-entry Body Identification Group

> ... pointed out the feasibility of greatly complicating the missile defense problem by using decoys, chaff, tank fragments, reduced radar reflectivity, nuclear blackout, and last, but by no means least, multiple warheads. . . . At first, the idea involved a shotgun technique in which a group of warheads plus some lightweight decoys were to be launched along several different paths, all leading to a common target. But shortly after, methods for aiming each of the individual warheads at separate targets were invented.[29]

It is impossible to determine the moment of MIRV's conception. Greenwood identifies at least five independent inventors of the idea. York traces the evolution of technology that built a base for MIRV. By 1962–63, ideas and technology had been combined in research programs for both the Navy and the Air Force aimed explicitly at multiple, independently targeted warheads. It is difficult to escape the conclusion that, at every stage, the reasons for MIRV's development were many. Everyone recognized the possibility that the Soviets had an ABM. Some people worried primarily about that threat; but others had different concerns.

Air Force sponsorship of MIRV research seems to have been motivated largely by the organization's interest in the expanded list of vulnerable targets, which had been acquired by American intelligence in the late nineteen-fifties and reinforced by McNamara's doctrine of counterforce. The Navy's interest in MIRV stemmed in large part from competition with the Air Force for the overall strategic mission, including the expanded target list authorized by McNamara's counterforce doctrine. The technical community seems to have been driven by the "sweetness" of the technology and the researchers' competitive instincts, which were aroused primarily by American ABM research, since so little was known about Soviet ABM activity. This competition, which has characterized much post-war American weapons research, generates what we might call an intra-national action-reaction phenomenon. As York describes it:

> It is most important to note that these early developments of MIRV and ABM were not primarily the results of any careful operations analysis or anything that might be called provocation by the other side. Rather, they were largely the result of a continuously reciprocating process consisting of a technological challenge put out by the designers of our defense and accepted by the designers of our offense, then followed by a similar challenge/response sequence in the reverse direction.[30]

The moral of the story seems to be that the origins of MIRV's research and development were inherently untidy, that it came from many sources, and that, at least in the recent past, American research and development of weapons in general has been as much self-generated as Soviet-generated. As John Foster, the Director of DDR&E during MIRV's research and development, candidly put it:

> Now most of the action the U.S. takes in the area of research and development has to do with one of two types of activities. Either we see from the fields of science and technology some new possibilities which we think we ought to exploit, or we see threats on the horizon, possible threats, usually not something the enemy has done, but something we have thought of ourselves that he might do, we must therefore be prepared for. These are the two forces that tend to drive our research and development activities.[31]

A third strand in the MIRV story concerns the decision in 1965 to deploy MIRV on Poseidon and Minuteman III. Weapons decisions proceed in stages. The 1965 decision to deploy MIRV on Poseidon and Minuteman III flowed naturally from the 1964 decision for its advanced development and engineering. We noted above the disparate and sometimes conflicting interests that converged in this development. Greenwood's conclusion makes the central point:

> MIRV was a program that contributed to the objectives of all organizations and individual decision-makers in the innovation process. . . . These [organizations'] perspectives were quite different and in some cases opposed. But it mattered little whether the different power centers could agree on underlying policy or priorities as long as they were unanimous in support of initiating and continuing research.[32]

The deployment decisions emerged from this same alliance of interests. Air Force officers supported MIRV because it contributed to their central mission, namely fighting strategic wars, and their special interest, namely destruction of "time-urgent" military targets (that is, targets such as missiles and bombers that must be destroyed before they can be launched). Naval interest in MIRV stemmed from judgment about its contribution to the Navy's mission, namely, assured destruction of urban-industrial targets, combined with its competition with the Air Force. The technologists wanted to see MIRV deployed because it had been developed and it worked. DDR&E reflected not only technological fundamentalism, but also the strategic and political preferences of the Secretary of Defense. For McNamara, MIRV wrapped up in a single package a cost-effective, high-confidence, assured-destruction capability against almost any conceivable future Soviet threat, including ABM and the growth of strategic offensive forces. It also increased counterforce capability (in which McNamara retained an interest, even after he had reduced its importance) and targeting flexibility. It provided arguments against Air Force demands for more Minutemen and for a new manned bomber, as well as a defense against critics who charged that growing Soviet expansion of strategic forces threatened the United States. Finally, it provided another argument against our ABM deployment (on the grounds that the Soviets could deploy MIRV and thereby easily overwhelm ABM). President Johnson relied on Secretary McNamara in strategic matters and seems only to have used MIRV as an argument against his domestic critics. The Congressional committees tended to support the services and the Secretary of Defense—whenever the two agreed. So the circle making the decision stopped there. Not until September, 1967, did the public hear its first words about MIRV. All previous decisions about development and procurement were made in secret. Details of the bargaining among these interests show some interesting vacillations, including initial Air Force opposition to MIRV, cancellation of the Mark 17, and mild schizophrenia within the Navy. The central point, however, is Greenwood's: in spite of the disagreements, no one opposed deployment.

A final deployment puzzle stems from the continuation of MIRV installations after the ABM ban. Director of DDR&E Foster testified in 1971 that "if a ban were placed on ABM, in the sense of banning the capability to intercept a ballistic missile attack, then as I see it at the moment, there would be no need for the United States to deploy a MIRV."[33] Shortly after Foster's testimony, a ban of the sort he referred to was established; MIRV deployment continued unabated.

Again, explanation requires more than the official arguments. If full MIRV deployment had been part of the agreement with the Joint Chiefs of Staff for support of SALT, then SALT's ban on ABM would not have affected deployment. The additional capabilities provided by MIRV were seen by some people as a way of offsetting the Soviet advantage in numbers of launchers. But the primary reason MIRV deployment continued was institutional inertia; stopping it simply because its prime rationale had been eliminated would have required strong action by some officials against the interests of others whose commitment to MIRV had always transcended the official arguments. In the absence of a real effort by someone willing to fight, MIRV deployment would continue. None of the people involved was eager for such a battle.

Hypotheses about Determinants of Force Posture and Implications for Arms Control

This brief review documents what we knew at the outset: the array of factors that have an important causal impact on force posture is extraordinarily complex. (Indeed, the attractiveness of the prevailing simplification is precisely that it avoids the messiness of the actual process.) This re-examination of anomalies also illustrates an overwhelming need for many more careful, detailed case histories aimed at developing preliminary causal maps of the weapons-development processes. Each of the cases leaves the reader dissatisfied—demanding much finer detail and analysis than the case-writer provides. (Had we not already overworked the metaphor, we might post a warning sign about the perils of starting to peel an onion.)

But even at this preliminary stage, reflection on the case histories should do something toward stimulating formulation of hypotheses about determinants of force posture. Obviously, the initial statement of such hypotheses will require a great deal of refinement, qualification, and testing. Our aim here is simply to suggest several hypotheses about determinants of force posture, some of which have important implications for arms control.

A major difficulty in the formulation of these hypotheses stems from the fact that force posture, the "dependent variable" (to use a social science term), is not a precise or measurable concept. Sometimes force posture refers to the full inventory of forces deployed and their mix, e.g., American strategic force posture includes ICBMs, SLBMs, and strategic bombers; sometimes it refers to a single weapons system, e.g., ABM or Minuteman III; and sometimes it refers to specific characteristics of a particular weapons system, e.g., range, speed, accuracy, or megatonnage. An effort to draw these distinctions more carefully and to find some crude measures for each is in progress. In the hypotheses that follow, the relevant connotation of the term "force posture" should be clear from the context.

A second difficulty in attempting to generalize about determinants of force posture arises from the "hundred factor problem." Evidently, there are at least one hundred important causal factors (and clusters of factors) involved in the process from which weapons emerge. No one, or group, of these factors dominates the outcome in a normal case. But simple analysis, prediction, and discussion require statements about the impact of single factors or clusters on the weapons outcome. Since other factors change significantly from one weapon to the next, specification of relations between a single factor (or group) and the outcome—"other things being equal"—becomes a difficult and perhaps even questionable enterprise.

A third, though far from final, difficulty in formulating hypotheses about force posture concerns the packaging of such hypotheses. Lists are never satisfactory. But a coherent structure for organizing propositions presupposes a conceptual or theoretical understanding that may only emerge at the end of the research path. Lacking a satisfactory model, or even map of the determinants of force posture, we have fallen back on chronology as an organizing device. Figure 12–2 depicts in a crude, stylized fashion the major stages in a weapon's program from early research, through development, to procurement. Obviously, different weapons have somewhat different histories. The chart presents a "normal" sequence for a generalized weapon.

General Hypotheses and Questions

What follows are some general hypotheses that attempt to identify relationships between factors in the process and force-posture outcomes. The hypotheses are obviously neither exclusive nor exhaustive. Under each hypothesis, we note several examples.

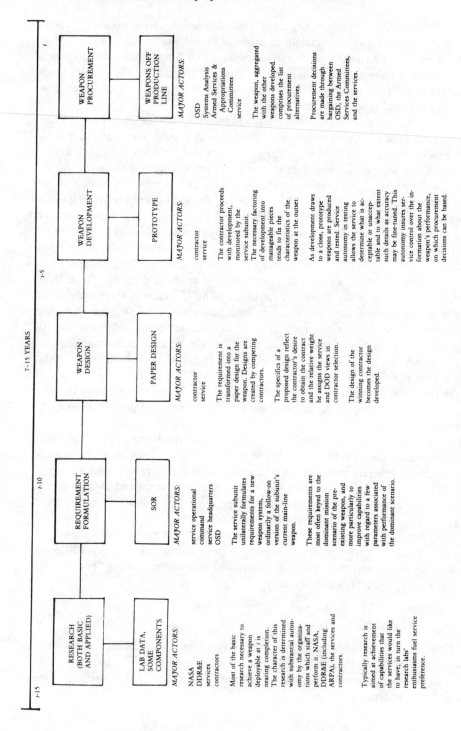

Figure 12-2. Stylized Chronology of Weapons Acquisition

1. The central but persistently neglected fact about force posture is that *weapons are deployed only after a long process* of research, design, and development. Weapons are not selected at a given moment, from off the shelf. As a consequence, the relationship between a weapon and such factors as strategic doctrines, or estimates of enemy capabilities, or central governmental decisions is enormously complicated by assorted lags. This proposition yields a string of related hypotheses.

a. Major decisions about research are made ten to fifteen years before formulation of the strategic doctrine that will be official when the weapon enters the force posture.
b. Major decisions about research are taken ten to fifteen years before the actual Soviet capabilities against which these weapons will operate is known.
c. Major decisions about design and development are made five to ten years before formulation of the strategic doctrine that will be official when the weapon enters the force posture.
d. Major decisions about design and development are taken five to ten years before the opponent's actual capabilities against which these weapons will operate is known.

For example: Decisions about MIRV were made prior to evidence of Soviet ABM capabilities; design and development decisions about ABM were made prior to the choice of hardsite defense as the primary objective; the size of American strategic forces in the nineteen-sixties was chosen before any of the assorted doctrines promulgated to defend it had been invented.

2. The lengthy process from which weapons emerge involves hundreds of important, relatively independent decisions that no one political official can possibly oversee. Given the terms of office of Presidents and Secretaries of Defense, most of the decisions about research, design, and technical specifications of weapons that an Administration might consider procuring will have been made under a previous President and under a Secretary of Defense twice removed from the one occupying the office.

a. The list of advanced development/acquisition choices—i.e., the array of options—from which an Administration can choose is limited by choices settled under previous Administrations.
b. The agenda of weapons choices—i.e., the array of choices that some organization is pushing—that an Administration must face (because programs at an advanced development stage demand decision) is strongly influenced by choices made under previous Administrations. Each item on the agenda has behind it a powerful alliance of advocates.
c. Force posture at any particular time is unlikely to have been substantially shaped by a single specific doctrine, such as assured destruction. It is possible

for an Administration's new strategic doctrine to have some immediate effect on use of previously deployed forces and on current research, development, and procurement outcomes. But the array from which it selects will have been created under a previous Administration, espousing different doctrines. And selections from the choices that it develops will be made by a future Administration with yet another policy.

d. The accountability of political officials for weapons choices is reduced both by the length and by the specific character of this process, for example, Nixon's options for hardsite ABM in 1969, and McNamara's options for a multi-service fighter in 1961.

3. Because of the time involved in the weapons-development process and the number and complexity of the choices involved, no single authority can make all of the important decisions. Organizations play a major role in weapons development in the present weapons-development process, *the services and their subunits are the primary actors in weapons development.* Consequently, force posture is shaped by the goals and procedures and especially the missions and weapons systems to which services (and subunits) are committed. Political officials might disturb this process; only rarely do they control it.

a. Weapons at a given time *t* reflect the structure of service subunits, their relative strengths, and their missions *t* minus five to ten years. For example: the limited numbers of Soviet bombers in the late fifties reflected the weakness of the Soviet Air Force in the early fifties; the limited numbers of Soviet ICBMs in the early sixties reflected the non-existence of Strategic Rocket Forces in the fifties.

b. Weapons systems in the main line of a service's primary mission will be regularly improved by "follow-ons," i.e., successive generations of weapons that make marginal improvements in principal performance parameters. For example: tactical aircraft from the F-86 to F-15; strategic bombers from the B-26 to the B-1; tanks, rifles; submarines from early Polaris to Trident.

c. Weapons systems not in the main-line mission of a service or service subunit tend to develop slowly. For example: hardsite ABM; standoff bombers; Navy mines; "smart" bombs.

d. A mission to which a service assigns low priority (or which is not the primary mission of a service subunit) tends to be poorly performed. This is especially true if performance of the mission is essential not to the service performing it but to a sister service. For example: close air support; airlift; sealift.

e. Weapons requiring coordination of existing services and missions will be poor and will develop slowly. For example: multi-service fighters; anti-submarine warfare.

f. Organizational interests and missions are better predictors of weapon characteristics and uses than are appointed officials' pronouncements. For example: McNamara vs. Army on ABM; McNamara vs. Air Force on MIRV.

4. The current weapons-development process consists of a sequence of bargaining games in which service (and service subunit) preferences are weighed more heavily than other interests. Service preferences about weapons reflect service interests, especially the organization's "health." Service organizational health is seen to depend on maintaining the autonomy of the organization and in preserving what its members view to be the "essence" of the organization, sustaining morale, maintaining or expanding roles and missions, and keeping or increasing budgets.

The *structure* of the current weapons-development process emphasizes the power of weapons developers and users as against that of Executive officials and Congress. This structure allows many small choices to accumulate into formal decisions (e.g., specific operational requirements, requests for proposals, and contracts) by minimizing the number of points at which political officials can make clearly identifiable choices among alternatives. This collection of propositions yields an assortment of related hypotheses.

a. The impact of players (and interests) differs markedly among the various bargaining games in the process of weapons development. Most design and development decisions are made primarily by the services or subunits, design labs, DDR&E, the Secretary of Defense (or other units to whom he delegates authority)—but not the President, the Secretary of State, ACDA, Congressmen, or you and me. The participants in major acquisitions decisions comprise a much wider circle.

b. Somewhere in the advanced development stage, a weapons system picks up momentum. While the causes of this momentum are not well understood, they seem to include pressures from weapon contractors and Congressional beneficiaries. For example: MIRV; ABM.

c. The structure of the current weapon-development process blurs the line between development and procurement. An appropriate strategy for coping with uncertainties of technology and enemy weapons development requires wide-ranging research and development. Many of the resulting weapons should not be procured because a threat fails to materialize or a new technology offers greater promise. But a disproportionate number of systems that reach advanced development are procured in any case.

d. Political leaders tend to concentrate on the variables in the weapons process over which they have nearly total control (e.g., pronouncements about doctrine or descriptions of missions), as opposed to variables that can be changed only with nearly endless bargaining and monitoring (e.g., technical performance specifications of an aircraft).

e. "Secretaries of Defense come and go, but the Navy. . . ."

5. Service-budget shares remain relatively stable. Shifts occur slowly and with considerable noise.

6. Because of the complexity of weapons systems, weapon designs must be broken down at an early stage into interdependent components that can be developed simultaneously. As a consequence, the final weapon that emerges diverges only slightly, say twenty-five per cent, from the technical performance requirements set early in the design stage. For example: the F-111.

7. The *details* of weapons systems (e.g., accuracy of warheads) are determined in large part by the interaction between technical feasibility and organizational interests (in the United States, the services and the research community). (This hypothesis is obviously related to two "laws": *Ruina's law*, "On the issue of guidance accuracy, there is no way to get hold of it, it is a laboratory development, and there is no way to stop progress in that field"; *Brooks' law*, "At least ten per cent of an R&D budget is uncontrollable in detail by a central authority.") For example: ABM, MIRV.

Notes

1. Address to the editors and publishers of UPI, San Francisco, September 18, 1967, reprinted in *U.S. Department of State Bulletin*, October 9, 1967, pp. 443–51.

2. *Scientific American* 220 (April 1969).

3. See Allison, *Essence of Decision* (Boston, 1971).

4. *Statement of Secretary of Defense Robert S. McNamara before the House Armed Service Committee on the Fiscal Year 1969-73 Defense Program and the 1969 Defense Budget* (1968), p. 47.

5. Ibid., p. 50.

6. Ibid., p. 57.

7. See figure 12–1.

8. Statement by President Nixon on Ballistic Missile Defense System, March 14, 1969. *Documents on Disarmament* (Arms Control and Disarmament Agency, 1969), p. 103.

9. United States Congress, Senate, Committee on Foreign Relations, Subcommittee on International Organization and Disarmament Affairs, *Strategic and Foreign Policy Implications of ABM Systems, Hearings,* 91st Congress, 1st session (1969), pp. 317–20.

10. United States Congress, Senate, Committee on Foreign Relations, *Strategic and Foreign Policy Implications of ABM Systems, Hearings,* 92nd Congress, 2d session (1972), p. 248.

11. See W.V. Quine, *Word and Object* (Cambridge, Mass., 1960).

12. These overviews are variants of conceptual frameworks that have been described at greater length as Models II and III in Allison, *Essence of Decision.*

13. Alain C. Enthoven and K. Wayne Smith, *How Much Is Enough? Shaping the Defense Program; 1961-1969* (New York, 1971), p. 176.

14. Ibid., p. 177.

15. Desmond V. Ball, "The Strategic Missile Programme of the Kennedy Administration, 1961–63" (Ph.D. diss., Australian National University, 1972).

16. Ibid., p. 334.

17. Ibid., p. 377.

18. United States Congress, Senate, Committee on Government Operations, *Organizing for National Security, Hearings,* 87th Congress, 1st session (1961), Part 1, pp. 1084–95.

19. United States Congress, House, Committee on Armed Services, *Military Authorizations, Fiscal Year 1964, Hearings,* Force Posture Statement of Secretary of Defense Robert McNamara, 88th Congress, 1st session (1962), p. 332.

20. Ball, "Strategic Missile Programme," p. 291.

21. Edward Randolph Jayne II, "The ABM Debate: Strategic Defense and National Security" (Ph.D. diss., Massachusetts Institute of Technology, 1969); John Newhouse, *Cold Dawn: The Story of SALT* (New York, 1973); Thomas Garwin, ABM papers, untitled, undated. On the Johnson Administration's decision to deploy ABM, see Morton H. Halperin, "The Decision to Deploy ABM: Bureaucratic and Domestic Politics in the Johnson Administration," *World Politics* (October 1972).

22. United States Congress, House, Subcommittee on Department of Defense Appropriations, Committee on Appropriations, *Department of Defense Appropriations for 1963,* 88th Congress, 2d session (1962), Part 5, p. 155.

23. United States Congress, House, Subcommittee on Department of Defense Appropriations, Committee on Appropriations, *Department of Defense Appropriations for 1964,* 88th Congress, first session (1963), Part 6, p. 203.

24. Quoted in Jayne, "ABM Debate," p. 359.

25. Our principal secondary sources are David Koplow, "Modeling the Arms Race: The Case of MIRV" (honors thesis, Harvard University, April 1973); Ted Greenwood, "Qualitative Improvements of Offensive Strategic Arms: The Case of MIRV" (Ph.D. diss., Massachusetts Institute of Technology); and Allison, "Questions about the Arms Race: Who's Racing Whom?" in Robert C. Pfaltzgraff, ed., *Contrasting Approaches to Strategic Arms Control* (Lexington, Mass., 1974), pp. 31–72.

26. "Is Russia Slowing Down the Arms Race?" Interview, *U.S. News and World Report,* April 12, 1965, pp. 52–53.

27. United States Congress, Senate, Committee on Armed Services, Preparedness Investigating Subcommittee, *Status of U.S. Strategic Power, Hearings,* 90th Congress, 2d session (1968), p. 12.

28. *Statement by Secretary of Defense McNamara on the Fiscal Year 1969–73 Defense Program and the 1969 Defense Budget,* pp. 52–53.

29. United States Congress, Senate, Committee on Foreign Relations, Subcommittee on Arms Control, International Law, and Organization, *ABM, MIRV, SALT, and the Nuclear Arms Race,* 91st Congress, 2d session (1970), p. 59.

30. Ibid., p. 59.

31. *Status of U.S. Strategic Power,* p. 12.

32. Greenwood, "Qualitative Improvements, " pp. 80–81.

33. United States Congress, Senate, Committee on Foreign Relations, *Strategic and Foreign Policy, Hearings,* 92d Congress, 2d session (1972), p. 248.

Discussion Questions

1. What factors determine the process by which the United States acquires weapons? What is the relationship between weapons development and strategy?

2. How does the weapons development and acquisition process affect defense policy?

3. Are democratic, bureaucratic, and economic imperatives so strong that they will always overcome strategic/operational considerations? What are the implications?

Suggestions for Additional Reading

Allison, Graham T. *Essence of Decision*. Boston: Little, Brown, 1971.

Betts, Richard K. *Soldiers, Statesmen and Cold War Crises*. Cambridge: Harvard University Press, 1977.

Clark, Asa A. IV, Peter W. Chiarelli, Jeffrey S. McKitrick, and James W. Reed, eds. *The Defense Reform Debate*. Baltimore: Johns Hopkins University Press, 1984.

Destler, I.M. *Presidents, Bureaucrats, and Foreign Policy*. Princeton: Princeton University Press, 1972.

Downs, Anthony. *Inside Bureaucracy*. Boston: Little, Brown, 1967.

Enthoven, Alain C., and K. Wayne Smith. *How Much Is Enough?* New York: Harper & Row, 1971.

Gansler, Jacques S. *The Defense Industry*. Cambridge: MIT Press, 1980.

Gelb, Leslie H., and Richard K. Betts. *The Irony of Vietnam: The System Worked*. Washington, D.C.: Brookings Institution, 1979.

George, Alexander. *Presidential Decisionmaking in Foreign Policy: The Effective Use of Information and Advice*. Boulder: Westview Press, 1980.

——— , and Richard Smoke. *Deterrence in American Foreign Policy*. New York: Columbia University Press, 1974.

Halperin, Morton H. "Why Bureaucrats Play Games." *Foreign Policy* no. 2 (Spring 1971): 70–90.

Kurth, James R. "Why We Buy the Weapons We Do." *Foreign Policy*, no. 11 (Summer 1973):33–56.

Lindblom, Charles E. "The Science of Muddling Through." *Public Administration Review* 19 (Spring 1959):79–88.

Lynn, Laurence E., and Richard I. Smith. "Can the Secretary of Defense Make a Difference?" *International Security* 7, no. 1 (Summer 1982):45–69.

Mueller, John E. *War, Presidents, and Public Opinion*. New York: John Wiley, 1982.

Neustadt, Richard E. *Presidential Power*. New York: New American Library, 1960.

Odeen, Philip. "Organizing for National Security." *International Security* 5, no. 1 (Summer 1980):111–129.

Steinbruner, John, and Barry Carter, "Organizational and Political Dimensions of the Strategic Posture: The Problems of Reform." *Daedalus* (Summer 1975):131–154.

Part V
National Security Policy: The Diplomatic and Economic Dimensions

There are three dimensions of national security policy: diplomatic, economic, and military. The diplomatic and economic components of a nation's security policy are significant because they can be used to achieve national security objectives by providing political leverage on other states. Treaties or alliances can provide credibility to threats to use military force. Economic sanctions can be used to affect a nation's economic well-being and, consequently, influence its foreign policies. Both diplomatic and economic policies also can be used to enhance a nation's own resources. Alliances can increase military capabilities directed against a particular external threat, while economic policies, such as the development of a strategic petroleum reserve, can help decrease vulnerability to economic pressures from other nations. Additionally, diplomatic and economic policies can augment stability, as in the case of strategic arms limitation talks designed to codify nuclear parity, or the use of economic aid designed to improve the internal stability of underdeveloped nations such as El Salvador.

In chapter 1, a wide variety of diplomatic and economic policy instruments available to further national security interests were identified. Diplomatic and economic instruments are the most commonly used policy tools because they usually are less costly than military policy and because much of the interaction between nations involves more cooperation than coercion. Although diplomatic and economic policies have only limited coercive power, they serve as means of communicating interests and resolve. Depending on the circumstances, they are often the most effective means of achieving U.S. national security interests. Even when military policy must be used, diplomatic and economic policies still can serve as valuable complements to military policy and provide additional means of preventing or terminating conflict.

In order to assess the utility of these dimensions of national security policy, we first must analyze how they contribute to national security and identify the factors that limit their contribution. A survey of the major policy instruments will provide the background necessary to understanding the benefits and limitations of diplomatic and economic policy.

Diplomatic Policy

International Organizations

After the enormous destruction suffered during World War II, there arose a hope that nations could find a substitute for military conflict as a means of providing international security and that problems among nations could be resolved by diplomacy and regulation rather than by military force. In 1946 the UN was established to provide a structure for exercising diplomacy in an effort to achieve these goals.

Measured by its level of activity, the UN appears to be an important player in international affairs. Each year the 158-member organization holds approximately 11,000 meetings and produces more than 1 billion pages of documents from its agencies and committees.[1] The UN is involved in a wide variety of issues, ranging from the eradication of disease to the deployment of peacekeeping forces in order to prevent conflict between member nations.

Despite its activity levels, the UN appears to have very limited influence in matters affecting international security. It has come to be regarded as, at best, a "useful place to make statements that resound around the world."[2] Although the UN has deployed military force in efforts to maintain international order on several occasions, such as in Korea in 1950, the Congo in 1960, and Cyprus in 1982, the requirement for consensus in the Security Council makes any such action difficult to implement. As a result, the UN has not played a major role in resolving an international conflict since the 1973 Yom Kippur war, in spite of numerous opportunities to do so. There are even those who argue that the vituperative quality of UN debate has done as much to aggravate conflicts as it has to reduce them.

While unable to enforce universal peace, the UN does provide a forum for communication between potential and active belligerents and as such presents opportunities for negotiated conflict resolution. It also provides an arena for mobilizing diplomatic support for policy actions aimed at resolving international security problems.

Alliances

Although many policymakers view international organizations as making only a limited contribution to national security, its participation in alliances commonly is accepted as a critical facet of U.S. national security policy. The primary basis on which alliances are founded is a sense of common interest. A nation that decides that it cannot defend its interests, achieve its political, economic, or diplomatic objectives, or deter perceived threats solely by mobilizing its own capabilities will seek to alleviate these problems by entering into an alliance with a nation or group of nations with which it perceives a sense of shared interests or common threat. An alliance is a means by which a nation can increase its power relative to that of a potential adversary without having to procure and maintain on its own the necessary military forces. A nation's interests need not be identical with those of its alliance partners (and probably never will be), but the sense of common interest must be sufficient to warrant the acceptance of alliance commitments.

While it is relatively easy to identify the common opponent against which the alliance is oriented, it is much more difficult to define precisely the nature of the threat, the objectives to be sought, and the policies to be pursued by the members of the alliance. In order to be effective, an alliance must be able to ascertain (1) the type of commitments undertaken by alliance members, (2) the situation in which mutual commitments are to become operational (*casus foederis*), (3) the degree of cooperation required of the alliance partners, and (4) the geographic scope of the alliance.[3] The often fractious nature of the relationship between members of NATO is ample evidence of the difficulty involved in getting allies to agree on specific policies or to act in concert.

The U.S. involvement in alliances after World War II represented a major shift in U.S. policy. Prior to 1945, the United States had not taken part in a formal alliance since the Revolutionary War. Traditionally the United States pursued a policy of relative isolation, avoiding the entanglement in foreign affairs that alliances could bring. Its ability to focus on its internal affairs was a function of the insulation and protection provided by the oceans surrounding it and the "Pax Britannica," imposed by the British Navy, that protected U.S. maritime commerce. The exhaustion of the nations of Western Europe at the end of World War II and advances in technology, communications, and warfare combined to place the United States in a much more prominent position in world affairs. The ocean expanses no longer protected it from military threats. The devastation of Western Europe and the disintegration of the British and French colonial empires created a power vacuum that the Soviet Union seemed only too willing and able to fill. In response to this threat, the United States developed a strategy designed to contain Soviet expansion into areas where it had political and economic interests. A key element of this strategy of containment was the development of alliances with nations surrounding the Soviet Union.

In contrast with the earlier reluctance to become involved in alliances, the United States established a series of bilateral and multilateral agreements extending from NATO in the West to South East Asia Treaty Organization (SEATO) in the East. The purpose of these alliances was to increase U.S. military capabilities in response to the Soviet military threat. John Foster Dulles, President Eisenhower's secretary of state, expressed this goal stating, "The cornerstone of security for the free nations must be a collective system of defense. No single nation can develop for itself defensive power of adequate scope and flexibility."[4]

Failure to communicate its interests could cause a potential aggressor to believe that the United States will not respond forcefully to its aggression. Although it is difficult to prove a causal link, five months after Secretary of State Dean Acheson outlined U.S. interests around the world by drawing a perimeter that did not appear to include South Korea, that nation was invaded by the North Koreans.

The principal function of each superpower's alliance structure is to define as clearly as possible the areas that it considers vital and to protect them against encroachment by the other superpower. The United States established alliance relationships with forty-three nations around the Sino-Soviet periphery in the decade following World War II. The purpose was to prevent what the United States perceived as the expansionist tendencies of the communist governments of the USSR and the PRC. While most of these alliance partners contributed only marginally to the military power available to the United States, their membership in a formal alliance served to draw the line beyond which the United States was prepared to resist the expansion of communist influence.

The most important and enduring alliance commitment undertaken by the United States was the formation of NATO. The North Atlantic alliance is fundamentally a political alliance designed to deter Soviet aggression by bolstering the will of the Europeans to oppose the Soviets and by guaranteeing U.S. interest in maintaining a Europe free from Soviet domination. In order to make the alliance commitments of NATO members credible, an extensive cooperative military structure has been established and expanded over the years. NATO has grown to become the primary measure by which its members assess their security efforts and resultant security posture. The dual political and military nature of the alliance inevitably causes tensions. The need for military integration and centralized command in order to respond effectively to a Soviet attack often conflicts with the sovereignty of the members, which have a variety of interests, cultures, economic systems, and political traditions. These differences, and differences in perception of the threat, cause trade-offs to be made between alliance security interests and the domestic interests of its members, thus creating the fundamental problem of the alliance: how to get sixteen nations to agree on common policy.

Regardless of these differences, the key to NATO solidarity has been a shared interest in deterring Soviet aggression. Soviet activity since 1945 has reinforced NATO defense concerns. The Soviet invasion of Hungary in 1956, the invasion of Czechoslovakia in 1968, and the increase in the size of Soviet conventional and nuclear forces all give pause to those who would argue that a strong NATO is no longer important to U.S. security.

While all members have an interest in deterring a Soviet attack on Western Europe, there is a conflict between this and other security interests. Whereas the United States originally was hesitant to be bound by a comprehensive alliance for fear of being drawn into the colonial problems of its European allies, the Europeans are now more concerned about being entangled in U.S. global concerns, such as its involvement in Vietnam or the Middle East.

Doubts about the credibility of the U.S. nuclear umbrella are a major source of alliance tension. This problem and other military issues will be discussed in more detail in part VI. Other issues that cause problems for alliance cohesion include equitable sharing of the economic burden caused by the high cost of NATO defense, the animosity between Greece and Turkey, which weakens NATO's southern flank, and the need to increase standardization and interoperability of military systems. Other factors, such as the emergence of West European economic strength (and independence) and the increased desire by the Europeans to share in the benefits of military production, are more recent. The United States bears approximately 40 percent of the $100 billion cost of the alliance's military forces, thus causing complaints in the United States about burden sharing. In the event of conflict, however, the Europeans would provide 90 percent of the manpower, 80 percent of the aircraft, and 70 percent of the naval forces. Furthermore, the United States sells eight times as much military equipment to its NATO partners as it buys in return, causing European complaints about benefit sharing. Despite these controversies and rising defense costs, U.S. interests in a strong alliance remain.

In chapter 13 David Watt outlines U.S. interests in Europe and analyzes the costs of maintaining the political and military strength of NATO. He discusses some of the changes that will affect the alliance in years to come and assesses how both internal and external pressures will affect the United States. Although U.S. policymakers will be confronted with tough choices, Watt points out that U.S. interests make the abandonment of NATO commitments a poor alternative.

While NATO has been a major focus of U.S. national security interests, the last three wars fought by the United States were conducted completely or in part in Asia. Further, U.S. trade with Asia surpassed its trade with Europe in the 1970s. Among the trends in Asia that are causing increased U.S. concern is the growing Soviet military threat in the region. Although some of this activity is directed against China, the Soviets have improved their capabilities for intervention in Japan and Korea as well.

The evolving economic relationship between the United States and Asian nations such as Japan, Korea, China, and the Philippines is another issue with implications for U.S. security. Increased trade and economic interdependence are creating both new opportunities for security cooperation as well as increased tensions between allies. The increased prosperity of many Asian nations has aided political stability in the region but also has increased competition with the United States on the economic front.

Although the United States pursues a multilateral alliance strategy in Europe, the situation in Asia has resulted in a largely bilateral approach to security problems. The United States has concluded a number of bilateral defense agreements with nations such as Japan, Korea, and the Philippines in the hope of balancing Soviet and Chinese influence in the region. In addition, efforts continue to exploit the Sino-Soviet split and improve Sino-U.S. relations in order to counter Soviet efforts to achieve hegemony in the region. Richard Solomon in chapter 14 analyzes those efforts and assesses U.S. interests in Asia, as well as some of the important regional trends that will affect Asian security in the coming years. His assessment of the problems confronting U.S. policymakers in Asia provides a useful comparison to Watt's analysis of the situation in Europe.

Arms Control

Arms control is an area where diplomatic policy interacts closely with military policy. Successful arms control negotiations can reduce the reliance on military policy and may serve as a potential substitute. Successful negotiations also can complement military policy by reducing uncertainty concerning the threat, reducing the level of the threat, and reassuring ourselves and our allies.

Traditionally arms control has had three major objectives: to reduce the probability of war, to reduce the damages from war should it occur, and to reduce the costs of defense. Reducing the threat of war should be considered the most important of these goals, and an integral part of this objective is the promotion of stability. Arms control agreements can augment stability in several ways. First, they can limit an arms race by restricting the size of opposing forces, thus reducing the need (and domestic pressures) to build new systems to counter those being developed by an adversary. Limitations on the development and building of new weapons can reduce the uncertainty about the level of threat, thus reducing the disparity between perceptions and reality that leads to incentives for worst case planning. Crisis stability can be increased if the invulnerability of nuclear retaliatory systems can be maintained. If deterrent forces are survivable, then there is less incentive to strike first out of a fear of losing the ability to retaliate if the other side attacks.

The primary goal of increasing stability in order to reduce the threat of war is often in conflict with the second goal, that of reducing damage in the event of war. The development of a comprehensive ballistic missile defense system offers the potential benefit of limiting the damage to the civilian population in the event of a nuclear attack. While this appears to be a laudable goal, it actually could increase the possibility of conflict by lowering the perceived costs to a point that might comprise an acceptable risk to the aggressor. While it appears desirable to reduce the costs of defense and the potential damage from war, it should be noted that major force reductions could reduce stability and make war more likely since small quantitative or qualitative force improvements would pose a much greater threat to a small force than to a large one.

Reductions in the size of nuclear forces could contribute to the third objective of arms control, reducing defense costs. Treaties such as the one limiting anti-ballistic missiles can produce savings by preventing the procurement of expensive weapons that could, in turn, elicit additional expenditures by opponents to counter. Arms control may not decrease costs, however. Controlling one segment of the nuclear force may allow other portions to increase. Limiting nuclear forces in general could cause conventional forces, which are more expensive than nuclear forces, to increase. Thus, while the goal of reducing defense costs is attractive, it has not been achieved very often to date. U.S. spending on nuclear forces actually increased slightly after the SALT I treaty was signed, and the USSR continued to modernize its forces. While this situation may seem discouraging, it should be noted that the SALT negotiations were designed to limit rather than reduce the size of nuclear stockpiles, and if one assumes that without SALT nuclear forces would have grown at an even faster rate, the agreement did provide some savings.

Although arms control negotiations seem to offer great potential to improve national security, several problems exist that make reaching significant agreements more difficult. One of the major problems is verification. If limits are negotiated that offer significant constraints on forces, there might be incentives to cheat in an effort to gain a possible advantage in the event of a nuclear confrontation. The need to verify compliance and detect cheating has been one of the greatest stumbling blocks to successful negotiations. Verification can be done by on-site inspection or by national technical means, such as reconnaissance satellites. In effect, verification is hostage to the capabilities of intelligence systems to detect cheating. The level of verification needed is a function, in part, of the type of system being tested and deployed. In the words of one analyst, verification does not require 100 percent accuracy: "A nation need only insure that violations significant enough to pose a threat to its security can be detected in sufficient time to take appropriate counteractions."[5] Further, some systems may be good candidates for prohibition through arms control just because they are difficult to verify. The cruise missile may be one such weapon, due to its small size and the ease with which it can be mounted on a wide variety of platforms. The number and range of cruise missiles deployed will be hard to verify.

Another criticism of arms control is that it often takes on a life of its own and can actually impede solutions to military problems. Efforts by the United States to eliminate defects in its nuclear force posture could be delayed due to exaggerated hopes that negotiations will make them unnecessary. A further concern is that arms control negotiations will be taken as signs of decreased international tension and lower public threat perceptions, even in the face of continuing military competition.

Despite the potential shortcomings, arms control negotiations remain an important means by which potential adversaries can attempt to negotiate limits on military forces. In an era when the nuclear stockpiles of the superpowers number in the tens of thousands, arms control must continue to be a central element of diplomatic policy.

Arms control is only one specific kind of negotiation. In order to understand the role it plays one must have a broader understanding of negotiations in general. Fred Ikle in chapter 15 analyzes the objectives of negotiations, as well as their characteristics, and discusses the results of failure. He also points out that negotiations often are undertaken for the sake of effects other than agreement, such as propaganda or intelligence. His chapter provides a foundation for analyzing arms control negotiations in light of their objectives and side effects.

Economic Policy

Economic policy is an important component of national security because it provides a potential means of gaining political leverage over other nations. Further, it contributes to a nation's own economic development, thus aiding its military capabilities and economic well-being. To the degree that economic policy is successful in achieving these goals, it benefits security by precluding the need to initiate other, more dangerous, actions in order to protect U.S. interests.

Economic Sanctions

The use of economic policy to gain political leverage can take a variety of forms, some designed to reward and some to punish. Policies intended to punish control the flow of goods and technology between nations and often are referred to as economic sanctions. Actions such as tariffs, quotas, embargoes, and boycotts can affect adversely the economic strength of a target nation, thus providing leverage that can be used to influence its political actions.

Tariffs, Quotas, Embargoes, and Boycotts. Tariffs are taxes that are designed to ensure high prices for imported goods. Tariffs affect a target country by damaging its ability to market its exports. If the imposing nation constitutes the major market for a particular good, this policy tool can have significant effects. Another means of reducing the target nation's ability to export its goods is to impose quotas, or quantitative limits, on the amount a nation will import. A more extreme policy that would have an even stronger effect would be to boycott the goods from a target country by preventing firms from importing any goods from a target nation. If the goal is to deprive the target country of goods that it needs, a nation can institute an embargo by prohibiting its own business firms from conducting any transactions with the target nation. Embargoes may be instituted on all goods or restricted to a particular category of commodities, such as strategic materials.

Economic sanctions have four primary goals: to modify behavior of the target nation, to deter further undesirable actions, to communicate resolve, and to demonstrate solidarity with allies.

In order for economic sanctions to be successful in deterring or modifying undesired behavior, two basic criteria must be met. First, the target of the economic sanction must perceive that the policy will prevent the achievement of a vital interest, such as prosperity. Second, the target nation must be unable to neutralize the impact of the sanctions by finding alternative trading partners. In spite of the fact that nations are becoming increasingly interdependent economically, a trend that should add to the effectiveness of sanctions, the record for achieving success is rather dismal. Of eighteen cases between 1918 and 1968 in which total economic sanctions were applied, one analyst concluded that only two were successful in modifying the behavior of the target state.[6] Even the Arab oil embargo, one of the more notorious instances of sanctions, had only limited success. While sanctions do impose hardships, at least in the short term, target nations have been able to restore their trade volume relatively quickly. Sanctions designed to punish the populace, thereby causing people to bring pressure on their government, generally have resulted in the mobilization of the target population in support of their government and therefore have failed.

While sanctions designed to modify behavior appear to be failures, it is more difficult to determine if the other objectives are met. Although the U.S. embargo against Cuba failed to bring down the Castro regime or make it modify its allegiance to the Soviet Union, the sanctions may have been effective in limiting Cuba's ability to export revolution and subversion in Latin America. If the goal of the U.S. grain embargo against the USSR was to force its withdrawal from Afghanistan, then it was a failure. If, however, its primary goal was to demonstrate U.S. resolve to show support for nations attacked by the Soviets, then there was no need for the Soviets to feel adverse effects. They and others only needed to see that the United States was willing to endure hardships in order to communicate its resolve. Willingness to undergo economic hardship in an election year may have convinced the Soviets that President Carter would take more drastic action, to include risking a military confrontation if the Soviets continued their aggression into Iran or the Persian Gulf area, and as a result may have successfully deterred further aggression.

Blockades and Blacklists. More extreme forms of economic policies often are used in conjunction with military action in times of conflict. Blockades may be imposed in an attempt to deprive an opponent of materials needed to continue the war. Blacklists may be used to prevent neutral countries from trading with the enemy by treating such traders as enemies as well. In situations where a blacklist is ineffective, preemptive buying can be used to outbid the enemy for essential materials in order to prevent the opponent from obtaining needed goods. Although the success of these programs is also difficult to measure, they undoubtedly weaken an opponent, as was the case with Germany in World War II, and contribute to the success of prolonged military operations.[7]

Economic Aid

In addition to the capacity to punish other nations, economic policies also provide the option of rewarding them for policies that contribute to U.S. interests. Foreign aid is the primary form of economic reward and there are four main types of aid programs: military aid, technical assistance, technology transfer, and grants, loans, and credits.

Military Aid. Military aid has been used traditionally as a means of reinforcing alliances and as a substitute for committing troops to defend regional interests. It strengthens a nation's security by increasing the military capability of its allies, imposing stability in a region, or creating regional power balances. Military aid adds to the capability of recipient nations to maintain internal stability and can raise the prestige of friendly regimes. Military aid also can improve the donor's political leverage, since recipients are not only dependent on the donor for developing their forces but also for the maintenance, replacement parts, and support needed to sustain those forces. Prior to the fall of the shah, the United States provided Iran with large amounts of modern equipment. Only a few years later, however, most of it became useless because of a lack of spare parts and required maintenance.

The leverage provided by military aid can help influence the use of the recipient's forces to ensure compatibility with the donor's interests.[8] For example, in 1954, South Korea's dependence on U.S. military aid forced it to abandon plans to invade North Korea due to U.S. opposition. Such leverage is limited, however, as has been shown on several occasions. For example, Egypt accepted large amounts of Soviet aid and then ejected all Soviet military advisers. The United States also has had only limited success, such as its difficulty in restraining Israel's military activity, even though Israel is dependent to a significant degree on U.S. aid.

Arms Transfers. Another aspect of economic policy that has important national security implications is arms transfers. In chapter 16, Andrew Pierre points out the growing volume of arms transfers and analyzes its impact on international security. Although he argues that arms do not themselves cause war, he believes that they can exacerbate tensions, spur arms races, and make war more likely. He also addresses some of the rationales used to justify arms transfers, such as a desire to obtain leverage or increase stability, and presents the counterarguments.

Technology Transfer. Technology transfer is a facet of foreign aid of growing importance. Technology transfers to the USSR are especially significant. Opponents argue that allowing the Soviets to gain access to U.S. technology could result in the U.S. losing the qualitative advantages necessary to offset Soviet quantitative superiority in military forces. Proponents argue that transfers increase interdependence and give the United States increased leverage over the Soviets, as well as improving its own balance of trade. Even if the United States attempts to limit transfers of sensitive technology in order to prevent the Soviets from gaining military benefits, problems remain. It is difficult to identify which items are sensitive, and even then embargoed items often are available from alternative sources. There is domestic opposition to restrictions on technology transfers because business interests in the United States suffer losses when they are unable to sell technology abroad. James Golden addresses these issues of economic leverage in chapter 17 and discusses the impact they have on East-West relations. He examines the West's use of trade and credits to achieve political objectives in its dealings with the East and posits an alliance strategy for control of technology transfers. He also analyzes the efficacy of economic sanctions.

Grants, Loans, and Credits. Grants, loans, and credits constitute the remaining type of aid. A shift can be seen from an emphasis on grants in the 1950s to an increased use of loans in recent years. Loans have the advantage of putting strings on aid, as well as providing a source of future income to the donor. The widespread use of loans is reflected in the high debt level of many developing countries and has resulted in many of them having difficulty meeting their payments. The resulting need for new loans to pay off old loans provides creditors with some leverage; however, the size of the debt gives the debtor nations leverage in return due to the potentially adverse consequences of massive defaults.

Many aid programs are designed to achieve security interests as well as serve humanitarian purposes. Successful economic development can improve stability and reduce the susceptibility of recipient nations to political instability. Aid can create opportunities for political leverage and can support friendly regimes that would otherwise be in jeopardy due to economic pressures. It can influence recipients' domestic and foreign policies, reward friendly regimes for joining or maintaining alliances, and minimize opportunities for the expansion of Soviet influence.

As with economic sanctions, the amount of leverage obtained by manipulating aid is a function of the availability of alternative sources and the degree of dependency that exists between the donor and recipient. The record demonstrates only limited success in obtaining leverage, as aid is often used to promote local interests that do not coincide with those of the donor.

It is clear that diplomatic and economic policy tools are critical components of national security policy, both as alternatives and complements to military policy. They send signals to adversaries about the extent of U.S. interests and give credibility to those signals. While they do provide some influence and can aid cooperation, their effectiveness as instruments of coercion is limited. Even so, diplomatic and economic policies remain attractive because the costs associated with their use are low relative to those that accompany military actions.

Notes

1. Richard Bernstein, "The U.N. versus the U.S.," *New York Times Magazine* January 22, 1984, p. 18.

2. Ibid., p. 20.

3. K.J. Holsti, *International Politics* (Englewood Cliffs, N.J.: Prentice-Hall, 1972), p. 114.

4. John Foster Dulles, "Policy for Security and Peace," *Foreign Affairs* 32 (April 1954):355–357.

5. Jerome H. Kahan, *Security in the Nuclear Age* (Washington, D.C.: Brookings Institution, 1975), p. 289.

6. Peter Wallenstein, "Characteristics of Economic Sanctions," *Journal of Peace Research*, no. 2 (1968):248–267.

7. K.J. Holsti, *International Politics: A Framework for Analysis* (Englewood Cliffs, N.J.: Prentice-Hall, 1983), pp. 224–226.

8. Ibid., p. 229.

13
America's Alliances: Europe

David Watt

No man is an infallible judge of his own interests, but for all that, nobody else is likely to be as assiduous or perspicacious in forming the judgement. This rule applies to nations as well as to individuals, and it follows that there is something impertinent about an English commentator being made to prescribe for the future security of the people of the United States. British interests are vested in saying that American interests are vested in Europe, and it would need superhuman detachment on the part of an Englishman to say the opposite. I can only re-emphasize this interest frankly at the outset of this paper, and hope that if American readers detect that I am saddling them (contrary to my intention) with characteristically European calculations and needs, they will find the distortions suggestive rather than merely irritating or sly.

It has been a reality of the American international situation for most of this century that the stability of the European continent is, in the most general sense, important to the well-being of the United States. Another way of putting this would be to say that, after the end of the nineteenth century, the world-wide power of the European empires was so great that any war between them or any undue concentration of power on the continent was bound to affect the Western hemisphere and more particularly to affect U.S. interests—which were themselves widening all the time. American isolationism, before 1900, was a plausible, though decreasingly possible strategy; after 1900, it was self-deception, akin to Gaullism, and—as proved by the preludes to two World Wars—a self-deception which had subsequently to be paid for with considerable blood and treasure.

Since 1947 and the identification of the Soviet threat as the chief menace to American interests, it might be thought that the emphasis had been changed radically from a Eurocentric to a global perspective. Until very recently this has not happened. It is true that the disappearance of the European empires has narrowed somewhat the global significance of European instability as such. And of course the U.S. has acquired many interests elsewhere. But, for nearly the whole of the post-war period, the containment of Soviet Russia has been seen in the U.S.

David Watt, "America's Alliances: Europe", *Adelphi Paper 174* (London: International Institute for Strategic Studies, 1982), pp. 19–26. Copyright © International Institute for Strategic Studies, 1982. Reprinted with permission.

above all in terms of the hard-learned lesson of preventing an undue concentration of hostile power in Europe, which has itself been seen as the central, critical arena in world politics. The broad geopolitical consequences of a Soviet suzerainty of the whole north-Eurasian landmass from the Chinese border to the shores of the Atlantic have of course been regarded as horrific. But it is the huge marginal increase in Soviet power represented by control of the great industrial centers of the West, and the fearful trauma, equivalent to the fall of Constantinople in 1453, that would be caused by the collapse of the European Christian culture that has really haunted the imagination of successive American Administrations since the onset of the cold war.

Whether anything has happened or is soon likely to happen to alter this post-war American perspective radically is the first question of this paper. In theory, two changes—or a combination of them—are possible. The U.S. could decide that Europe is less worth defending either because a free Europe has ceased to be valuable to her, or because the overall cost in terms of men, money and nuclear exposure, or lost opportunities elsewhere, has become too high.

First, then, what is the current "value" of Western Europe to the United States?

America's Interests—The Strategic Stakes

Western Europe is at present a "prize" which it is desirable to deny to the Soviet Union. Western Europe is also a part of the means of its own defense. Its free existence is moreover a thorn in the side of the Soviet empire. The prize is a bit less glittering perhaps from the geostrategic point of view than from the economic; but if the Soviet Union could neutralize (leave aside control) France, Germany and the United Kingdom, she would have achieved some very important ends. What is now an American *glacis* would have been turned into a Soviet *glacis*. Some important actors on the international stage would have been eliminated. And, on the reasonable assumption that NATO had broken up in the process, the Soviet frontiers would have been made markedly more secure. In addition the Soviet Union would have consolidated her existing empire and provided a fillip to her flagging reputation as a power on whose side it pays to third-world countries to remain. To prevent this shift in the balance of world power must clearly be one of the most important aims of U.S. policy, not so much because geopolitics is a zero-sum game (it is not) as because even in positive-sum games an imbalance of power of these proportions between the protagonists is dangerous.

The most reliable and cost-effective means of achieving this end is the preservation and, if possible, the improvement of the North Atlantic military alliance. NATO may have its defects but it has proved an effective and, for Europeans and Americans alike, relatively cheap way of meeting the Soviet military threat. American public opinion naturally, and legitimately, sees the situation in altruistic terms. Americans, from the generosity of their hearts, are defending European interests. The European perspective is equally legitimate, however—the military contribution of the Allies on the Central Front in men, money and materiél, even though given for self-interested purposes, has enabled the U.S. to defend a vital strategic interest of her own for nearly 35 years at a fraction of the cost that would otherwise have been incurred.

Moreover for most of this period two individual members of the Alliance have contributed to the wider purposes of the U.S. as well. The British until 1970 imposed a measure of stability on the Gulf and on large areas of South-east Asia and Africa: the French had a considerable presence in North and West Africa. This contribution has not always been encouraged or appreciated (if one may put it delicately) by American Administrations, but it has now assumed a fresh importance. The increase of Soviet activity outside Europe, coming at the same time as the decline in French–British influence, has left the U.S. with new and unwelcome security problems in the Third World. These are marginally relieved by the residual political links and influences of the old colonial powers as well as by the economic dependence of the developing countries upon Europe, but the U.S. is understandably anxious to share these burdens to a greater extent than in the past. If the European Allies should decline to get involved, or reinvolved, in this responsibility, then the U.S. would have to consider whether this dereliction undermined the importance of her own stake in keeping the Soviet Union out of Western Europe—a "trade-off" to which I shall return later.

Economic Stakes

The U.S. has a profound interest in the maintenance of a prosperous, free-market economic system in Western Europe.

Direct Interest. U.S. economic prosperity is deeply affected by the interpenetration of the American and European economies. The interconnections are myriad and extend to all sections of economic activity. Some general examples must suffice:

> Of all U.S. investment abroad nearly half (or about $90 billion in 1980) is in Western Europe (double the American investment in Canada and four times that in Latin America).

> European investment in the U.S. (about $40 billion) now amounts to more than 70% of all overseas investment.

> The U.S. is currently running a trade surplus with Western Europe of about $20 billion (compared, for instance, with a $38 billion deficit with Asia).

> American exports to Western Europe are worth at present over $50 billion a year, of which a third is in machinery and as much as 10% in agricultural produce.

Indirect Interest. The European economies, taken together, now have as great an influence on the world economic environment as that of the U.S. The U.S. and Europe have about equal shares of the total GNP of the world's market economies. The EEC in 1979 provided 35% of world exports (as opposed to the U.S. 11%), and 36% of world imports (as opposed to the U.S. 13%). In the same year the majority of world reserves were held in dollars (65%) but 31% were held in European currencies or ECUs. From a geostrategic point of view, it is vital to the U.S. that the weight of these economies should be thrown, as at present, broadly behind purposes congruent with American interests. These interests include the maintenance of a free-trade system, close collaboration in the orderly management of the world economy, encouragement of free-market systems in the Third World, and joint economic pressure when feasible and appropriate, against hostile political forces whether in the Communist bloc or the LDCs.

Security Interest. It is important to the U.S. that the European economies should be in a position to support a sustained military contribution to the Alliance. There are political as well as purely economic aspects of this requirement. If the European economies are thrown into difficulties, from whatever cause, there will be problems in meeting the defense budgets simply because of competing pressures on public expenditures. But there will also be difficulties of a deeper kind arising from the turn of public opinion. Times of depression or very high inflation (or both) tend to foster economic and then political nationalism, as well as pressure against defense expenditure. To the extent that this nationalism reflects sharpened competition for employment and growth between the advanced industrial countries, it may pose difficult dilemmas for American policy makers. An uncompromising attack on the problems of the U.S. domestic economy may produce anti-militarism and lower security in Europe.

Psychological Stakes

It is hard to assess what gratification (as opposed to hard strategic or economic advantage) the European Alliance gives to the U.S. Earlier this year, visiting Texas to deliver a lecture on the Atlantic Alliance, I was interviewed separately by two intelligent young television and newspaper reporters who both prefaced their questions with an embarrassed confession that they had not had time to look up what the Atlantic Alliance was. The generation which watched the Alliance win World War II (and win the peace after it) is passing and, as has frequently been observed, domestic power in the U.S. has tilted towards states which have less concern with Europe than do those of the Eastern seaboard. The fact that so many American families are of recent European origin in some ways only seems to increase the distance because they so often make the limited criteria of their ethnic loyalty—Zionism, Irish Republicanism, Ukrainian nationalism, or whatever—the overriding test of the value of the Alliance.

On the other hand, successive American administrations, caught between their global perception of American interests and the tendency of American public opinion to relapse into a narrower continental outlook, have emphasized that the U.S. is acting on behalf of something called "the free world" of which she is the acknowledged leader and of which the European countries are the chief followers and beneficiaries. This claim to responsibility provides not only the moral strand to foreign policy that American people have demanded since the foundation of the Republic, but the consolations of companionship and friendly approval. World power is an ungrateful role, but doubly so for a people that particularly likes to be liked. If what can loosely be called the "moral support" of European governments were withdrawn from the U.S. because the Soviet Union had overrun them, the U.S. would no doubt continue her global mission undaunted (assuming no nuclear Armageddon had made all missions irrelevant). However, if the European Alliance simply melted spontaneously away because Europe no longer believed that the cultural and political values she had hitherto shared with the U.S. were worth defending—at any rate at the economic price implied by a formal military pact—then the blow to American self-confidence would be grave. The political consequences of such a peripeteia are unpredictable, but it is at the very least plausible to suppose that administrations would find more difficulty than ever in mobilizing public opinion behind any foreign policy that was not narrowly nationalistic and therefore ultimately self-defeating.

The "cost" incurred by the U.S. in protecting these interests can to some extent be computed precisely. The material cost of keeping "x" men in Western Europe, providing them with suitable logistic support and reinforcement capability, and developing and deploying weapon systems for them on sea and land and air is known to the last dollar and cent. There is, of course, a methodological problem involved in deciding which military measures the U.S. would think it prudent to take anyway if Western Europe were a neutral bloc, or (to take a more extreme supposition requiring slightly different calculations) if the Soviet Union actually controlled it. The American nuclear missile armory, for instance, or the U.S. fleets now deployed in the North Atlantic and the Mediterranean would presumably be rather different in size and composition under such circumstances, but they would certainly not be eliminated. Nevertheless, making some arbitrary assumptions, we could say that the military defense of Europe is a drain on the real resources of the United States of such and such a size; and if that was all there was to it, we should probably conclude that although this cost was increasing at a considerable rate, it was well worth paying, and indeed that the advantages were cheap at the price.

The problems arise, rather, in the matter of policy costs. Theory proclaims the truism that it is impossible to enter an alliance, even as its leader, without accepting some limitations on one's freedom of action. Where joint operations requiring allied co-operation are concerned, whether in the military, political, or economic fields, nothing can be achieved without agreement, preceded by consultation, debate and persuasions. But even where an individual partner has the possibility of unilateral action it may be wise to refrain, either a) because he wants to trade off his restraint for some long-term reciprocal benefit or b) because his action would attack the interests of his allies so much as to cast doubt in his allies' mind about the value of the alliance or c) because, although he intends to press on anyhow, a postponement may give him time to blunt the edge of his allies' opposition.

All these constraints have a cost in certainty and in time needed for decision-making. But there are also important political costs. In the case of constraint a)—for instance, a tariff cut—there will be the temporary cost of interest which the protagonist hopes will be outweighed later on, but he may have to pay a prohibitively high domestic price within the timescale of democratic elections in the meantime. In the case of restraint b) the cost will be more permanent, and the benefit (namely the continuation of the Alliance) may well be difficult to "sell" to public opinion, and may even be seen by governments as being insufficiently high to warrant the sacrifice.

Rising Costs

Translating this theoretical discussion into the realities of our present situation, we can see that from the point of view of the U.S., the policy costs of the European connection have been rising quite rapidly in the past ten years. The first reason for this stems from the disappearance from within the Alliance (as from the superpower relationship) of the overwhelming preponderance of American power. In a partnership as unequal as, say, the NATO of the 1950s, the West Europeans could argue, but, in the last resort, they had little other choice than to accept American protection on American terms. The Bretton Woods system, the GATT (General Agreement on Tariffs and Trade), and the military structure in NATO itself, were all designed on the assumption of and to some extent to promote, the perpetuation of U.S. supremacy. The oil price increase of 1973 and the collapse of the dollar altered the economic and, more important, the psychological balance of the Alliance. The fact that the American economy was proved as vulnerable and perhaps even more vulnerable than the European, gave Europe new bargaining power in the economic field but also broke the more general European (and in particular German) idea of their dependence and inferiority vis-à-vis the U.S. Since 1973 the European Allies have assumed, what never really sunk in before, that in general the U.S. needs Europe as much as Europe needs the U.S., and in some fields the boot is even on the other foot. They have acted on this assumption by approaching intra-alliance bargaining with the United States in an entirely new spirit of self-assertiveness, even where, as in the case of security matters, their real dependence on America is as great as ever.

The second substantial factor that has apparently raised the policy cost to the U.S. has been the divergence of views that has gradually opened up between the

U.S. and most of the West European governments on how to pursue the central purpose of the Alliance—namely the containment of the Soviet Union.

It is fashionable to see this split in terms of interest and to some extent this is right. The reasons why West European public opinions are encouraged to make a less straightforwardly "worst case" analysis of the Soviet threat than American public opinion include the following:

> Dislike of high defense expenditure has encouraged wishful thinking about Soviet motivation both in Europe and the Third World.

> Economic and cultural links with the Communist Bloc have produced a stake in "détente at all costs."

> Fear of a nuclear war limited to the territory of Europe by an implicit agreement of the super-powers has caused hope to be placed on arms control.

> Fears that sharp military confrontation and super-power rivalry in the Third World will harm European economic interests in those regions.

Nevertheless the fact that these motives are to some degree self-interested does not necessarily mean that they are invalid; nor does it mean that they are exhaustive. There are other differences of perspective arising from historical, cultural, or even purely intellectual causes. The British and French Establishments, for instance, are instinctively conscious of their ability not only to understand the complexities of regional politics in the developing world, but also to react with suitable sophistication to them. They have no similar confidence in the reactions of American administrations, which are bedevilled by the need to placate a cantankerous Congress and a volatile public opinion. In the view of many Europeans (not by any means on the Left) the Reagan and Carter Administrations have been caught in the nationalistic slipstream of Vietnam and Watergate. Until this is past it will be impossible to rely unquestioningly on the international judgment of American leaders, for it will be constantly distorted by two vulgar errors which appear to be embedded in the American collective psyche at this time—first, that virtually all aspects of world politics are to be judged in the terms of the contest between the U.S. and the Soviet Union, and the second, that in order to win this contest it is essential to re-establish military superiority.

European Futures

It is not absolutely necessary for the U.S. to approve, to forgive, or even altogether to understand these European interests and preoccupations, but it is essential that their existence should be recognized, for, taken together, they constitute the most important components in any American cost-benefit analysis of the Alliance.

American policy-makers must also establish a view about how Europeans are likely to develop in the next few years and decide to what extent they can be influenced by American policies and persuasions. This is not an easy computation—depending as it does on many variables in the domestic politics of the European countries, as well as on the behavior of such unreliable actors on the international scene as OPEC and the Soviet Union. My own guesses, on the main points, are as follows:

On the psychological front, I fancy that the American ascendancy is permanently broken. The relationship is and will remain very much a questioning and two-sided one. The EEC may or may not make further advances in economic integration but there will probably be progress in establishing a common European position in a number of political and semi-strategic matters. This position may not always be welcomed in Washington;

Europe is not about to make vast new commitments to defense expenditure in NATO—at any rate unless and until the economic situation improves or the East–West conflict markedly worsens. On the other hand, unless the U.S. grossly mishandles the relationship, they are not about to give up their current levels of defense expenditure or abandon NATO or "go neutralist" in any serious sense of that term. The combination of a Labour Government, led by Mr. Tony Benn, in Britain, a left-wing SPD Government (without Chancellor Schmidt) in Germany, a left-wing socialist regime (without President Mitterand) in France, and a Communist government in Italy, might portend the break-up of the Alliance, but not one of these looks in the least probable. There will, however, continue to be a powerful groundswell of public opinion throughout Europe, especially in Germany and the Low Countries, in favor of détente, East–West trade and arms-control measures; and it will tend to become more powerful and more anti-American if the U.S. frustrates or appears to oppose its ends. A Soviet intervention in Poland would transform the situation in the short run and might perhaps reunite the Alliance in a tough anti-Soviet position; but the underlying ambiguities would tend to reassert themselves before very long.

The vulnerability of Western Europe to the developments in the Third World, especially the oil-producing parts of it, has sunk in in most European countries. On the other hand, most governments, even the British, will remain skeptical about the Soviet capacity to control events in those regions, and will continue to fear that the instinctive reactions of the Reagan Administration will make matters worse rather than better. The most intelligent conclusion to be drawn by Europe from this perception (as well as the most desirable from the point of view of the Alliance) would be that she should accede to American demands for more assistance including military support in trying to control global instability, but use the opportunity to set up a form of consultative machinery that would give them a genuine influence on American policy. The chances are, however, that unless the Administration shows considerably more disposition than at present to allow its freedom of action to be impaired, Europe will conclude that its interests would be better served by maintaining its own freedom in its dealings with the Third World and by not becoming too closely identified with American policy.

Economic issues will continue to be a constant transatlantic irritant, and will provide a perpetual temptation for all parties to play an opportunistic three-sided game with Japan. But there will not be much disposition in Europe to apply direct "linkage" between these and security arrangements—that is (to take an absurdly crude example) to say to the U.S.: "reduce interest rates or we will leave NATO." Nevertheless the indirect linkage will continue to exist in that the largest single economy in the West will be held partly responsible for economic distress; and economic distress is a poor foundation for good security.

A Better Alliance

If these predictions are roughly correct, the U.S. can in theory rely upon having, at the very minimum, a cut-rate economy version of the Alliance throughout the 1980s and 1990s, since Europe is willing to allow itself to be defended on its own territory and to make a contribution in men and money sufficient to make this defense physically possible. This would fulfill the basic geostrategic purpose of keeping the USSR from invading Western Europe, and would continue to protect a vital economic interest. Unfortunately such a model is highly unsatisfactory in several ways. It cannot be relied on to support the wider purposes of the U.S. outside Europe; it does not perform the psychological function required by American domestic politics; and because its psychological base is weak on both sides, it does not provide a satisfactory framework for resolving awkward and inevitable differences of opinion about what really is needed for the defense of Europe, whether in cruise missiles, ERW (Enhanced Radiation Warheads), trade sanctions or anything else.

The crucial question for American policy-makers, therefore, is whether it is possible to procure a more de luxe version of the Alliance at reasonable cost. There is naturally a strong temptation to try to get one on the cheap, mainly by browbeating Western Europe into greater efforts and better behavior. This prescription has proved effective in the past and is being fairly liberally applied at present. The dire reactions of American public opinion to allied sins of omission are constantly cited, and more direct threats of U.S. troop withdrawals from Europe are hinted at. The trouble is that this procedure, though useful and effective up to a point, requires very delicate handling in the U.S. if it is not to excite public opinion to the point at which the prophecy becomes self-fulfilling. It has also proved dangerous in Europe (particularly in West Germany) where it can produce acute neurosis and, by increasing doubts about American credibility, actually provide grist to the neutralist mill.

The alternative course is to attempt to put together a new kind of transatlantic relationship, close enough to co-ordinate a broad strategy for global security between the U.S. and Western Europe, but loose enough to take account of the fact that under the conditions of the 1980s, each side of this dialogue will often find it hard, and at times impossible, to agree. This will not be easy. For one thing, there exists a large establishment with a vested interest in declaring that the existing NATO structure is capable of coping with the problem and in opposing any new machinery for fear it should affect the old. The fact is that NATO, by the will of most of its members, is unsuited to tasks wider than military operations in the European theatre. And, as the cruise missile and neutron warhead controversies have shown, it is even unable to provide the kind of framework in which highly emotive issues relevant to European defense pure and simple can be put into proper perspective. Then there are serious problems about who is to take part in this new dialogue and how. The smaller European countries are understandably resentful of the idea of a "directorate," and to the extent that they are excluded they have a better excuse for limiting their commitment. Yet it is hardly realistic to expect the U.S. to accept limitations of her freedom to pursue her interests as she sees them throughout the world, except when she can expect those with whom she is consulting to accept joint responsibility for the implementation of any decisions that are reached. This difficulty would more or less dictate some kind of "variable geometry"—a structure which has its own drawbacks.

The main difficulties, however, are those that arise from the holistic nature of American foreign policy. American public opinion has always tended to believe that "he who is not with us is against us," and has judged its international relationships in terms of commitment (which is, incidentally, why "linkage" is an almost inevitable element of the American relationship with allies and opponents alike). Its criteria of commitment at present do not make allowances for fundamental differences of opinion about how to cope with the Soviet Union, and the thought of setting up a structure in which the discussion of such differences would be a necessary, protracted, and by no means certain prelude to action is not an appealing one. It is doubly unappealing when most of the putative partners in the discussion have recently been utterly dependent on the United States and are in one crucial respect dependent still. Why *should* the U.S. consult anybody or hold its hand out before giving Colonel Qaddafi a bloody nose, or sending (or not sending) military aircraft to Israel, or supporting guerrillas in Angola, or supplying China with defense equipment, or making contingency arrangements to intervene in the Persian Gulf, or even lifting the grain embargo—especially if all President Reagan hears from his major allies, at any rate at the outset, is a lot of good reasons why he should not do any of them, even though he regards them as being in the American interest?

That is a question to which it is extraordinarily difficult for any European to find a reply that does not, in the present atmosphere, sound like special pleading.

Indeed there is a European school of thought which would argue that one ought not to try. Why not acknowledge that the European nations are now primarily regional powers, with very limited ability to affect the super-powers either in Europe or elsewhere? I hope it will be apparent from what has gone before why I do not agree with this proposition. It would leave the U.S. alone in the world, and the Europeans with little or no influence whatever over American policies that could mean life or death for them. The implications of this stance are ultimately neutralist, which is why the "economy" version of the Alliance is unstable at the European end as well as the American.

It is strongly in the American interest that this minimalist view should not gain ground in Europe, not simply because the U.S. actually needs the political, economic, and to some degree the military co-operation of the Europeans outside Europe, but also because the support of her friends may save her from psychological traumas and consequent errors of a potentially very costly kind. The costs to the U.S. of actually encouraging the Europeans to concert their own foreign policy and of trying to make a new approach to co-ordinated decision-making on a transatlantic basis naturally have to be considered. They represent a considerable investment in time, freedom of action, domestic political capital, and above all patience. On the other hand the price need not necessarily be so very high. There are large tracts of policy where agreement would in practice be perfectly easy, many others where it might eventually be arrived at, and others still where an agreement to disagree harms nobody. The question is whether the ir-reducible number of important disagreements that can be foreseen—for instance, on Israel, on the Gulf, on economic sanctions, on Southern Africa—are thought to make the investment pointless.

Discussion Questions

1. What factors induced the United States to establish the NATO alliance? Are those factors still present today? To what extent?

2. What factors create strains on NATO? How has the economic development of the European members of the alliance contributed to differences within the alliance?

3. How do U.S. alliance relationships in Europe shape U.S. national security policy?

14

American Defense Planning
and Asian Security:
Policy Choices for a Time
of Transition

Richard H. Solomon[1]

Asian Collective Security, Anti-Hegemony, or Détente?

For more than a decade, the premises underlying America's post–World War II involvement in Asian security affairs have been going through a fundamental transformation. The central element in these changes has been the breakdown of the Sino-Soviet alliance and its evolution since the late 1960s into a military confrontation and worldwide geopolitical rivalry.

The Nixon Administration's establishment of a dialogue with Chinese leaders in 1971 symbolically shattered the communist-capitalist lines of conflict in Asia that dated from the Korean War period and established a new political context for an effort to disengage the United States from the Vietnam conflict. The Carter Administration's completion of the process of normalizing relations with the People's Republic of China (PRC), in combination with Tokyo's signing of a Sino-Japanese friendship treaty and China's turn to Japan and the West for development capital and technology, capped a decade of dramatic changes with the potential for a fundamentally new pattern of international alignments in the political, economic, and security affairs of Asia.

These transformations in relations among the major powers were paralleled by no less startling changes in the Asian region itself. History's irony has been most evident in the rapid deterioration of China's relations with Vietnam. What in the early 1970s had been an alliance "as close as lips to teeth" is now a bitter military confrontation, a situation punctuated by the thirty-day Sino-Vietnamese border war in the early winter of 1979. The security implications of the new Chinese-American relationship were highlighted by PRC Vice-Premier Deng Xiaoping's (Teng Hsiao-p'ing's) triumphal normalization visit to Washington in January 1979, just prior to the Sino-Vietnamese military clash—a timing which

Reprinted with minor revisions from Richard H. Solomon, "American Defense Planning and Asian Security: Policy Choices for a Time of Transition," in Richard H. Solomon, ed. *Asian Security in the 1980s* (Cambridge: Oelgeschlager, Gunn, and Hain, 1982). Reprinted with permission.

stimulated questions about U.S. support for Beijing's (Peking's) action and concerns about the possibility of a Sino-Soviet war and its impact on U.S.-Soviet relations.

Less spectacular changes now confront the United States and its Asian allies and friends with major new choices of security strategy and political alignment. These include rapid economic growth in Japan, South Korea, Taiwan, Hong Kong, and Singapore of more than 7 percent per year for most of the 1970s, and the quiet training of generations of scientific and managerial talent that have made East Asia the most rapidly developing region of the world. States formerly dependent on American protection for their security are gradually acquiring the resources to play a substantial role in managing their own defenses.

American awareness of many of these changes was dimmed during the decade of the Vietnam War. With the end of the conflict in the mid-1970s, U.S. interests in the region seemed well-served by a period of inactivity. Policymakers and the public turned their attention to other concerns—domestic inflation, energy and international monetary problems, adverse trends in the strategic military balance and NATO-Warsaw Pact deployments, SALT II, and the Middle East negotiations. These issues had been overshadowed by the divisive and draining Indochina conflict and required attention after a period of neglect. Yet in only three or four years we have come to see new sources of insecurity and conflict in Asia: a growing Soviet naval presence in the Pacific and Indian Oceans; extension of the Moscow-Beijing feud to ravaged Indochina; heightened prospects for nuclear proliferation in potentially volatile areas such as Korea; and the possibility of conflicts over off-shore natural resources that run from the fishing grounds off Sakhalin Island to the oil-rich sea floor of the South China Sea.

The most disturbing aspect of these developments is the prospect they hold for once again involving Asia in the disputes of the great powers. The trend most likely to shape the pattern of Asian security issues in the 1980s is the further extension of the Sino-Soviet conflict into the affairs of the region. Moscow doggedly attempts to build an "Asian collective security" coalition which will give the USSR access to the area and constrain Chinese, and American, power. Its efforts are reinforced by growing Soviet naval and air deployments to the Asian theater and the opportunistic establishment of bilateral political ties and security treaties—most recently with South Yemen, Afghanistan, and Vietnam—in order to create a regional base structure. The Chinese, in response, are making parallel efforts to construct a countercoalition of states allied on the theme of "anti-hegemony," opposed to the further extension of Soviet influence into Asia.

The basic choice in America's security planning for Asia in the 1980s is how to relate to these opposing strategies of the major communist states: Should we join with the Chinese in a global effort to constrain the Soviet Union's imperialistic impulses, and in the process risk polarizing the affairs of Asia around the Sino-Soviet dispute; or should we remain aloof from the Moscow-Beijing feud and seek to account for American interests and the security of our allies—the Republic of Korea (ROK), Japan, the Philippines, and the ANZUS countries[2]—through the strengthening of a "loose Oceanic alliance" of friendly and like-minded states? The alternative chosen will influence many of the specific policy choices that will give shape to America's role in Asia in the coming decade.

At the same time, a clear choice in a regional security strategy will not be ours alone to make. The concerns of our allies will influence many decisions. Difficult choices involving the risk of conflict may be forced upon us by the initiatives of others; and alternatives may be foreclosed by events beyond our control. But in an era of rapid political and economic change, and as yet relatively unstructured responses by the United States and other powers involved, it is important to clarify the major trends affecting Asian security, the policy alternatives that are likely to come before us, and the impact on American and allied interests of different courses of action.

The closest thing to an organizing theme in U.S. Asian policy in recent years has been a derivative of Washington's Soviet-oriented policy of détente: the attempt to normalize relations with former adversaries such as China and Vietnam. At the same time, there has been an uncertainty and lack of coherence to specific American actions which stands in marked contrast to Moscow's persistent, if not highly successful, efforts to contain the expansion of Chinese influence, and Beijing's attempt to engage the United States, Japan, and the NATO countries in a new security alignment designed to counter Soviet "social-imperialism." This reflects a shattering of the policy consensus which had existed in the United States from the Korean War into the 1960s on the need to contain and isolate expansionist Asian communist states allied to the Soviet Union—a major result of our Vietnam agony and the disintegration of the Moscow-Beijing alliance.

Efforts to reestablish a sense of policy direction were part of the process of disengagement from Vietnam. The Nixon Administration's "Guam Doctrine" of 1969 asserted the premise that "the way we could become involved [in another Asian war] would be to attempt withdrawal [from the region] because, whether we like it or not, geography makes us an Asian power."[3] President Ford's "Pacific Doctrine" of 1975 sought to reformulate an Asian policy based on "a balance among the major powers, strong ties to our allies in the region, an easing of tensions between adversaries, the self-reliance and regional solidarity of smaller nations, and expanding economic ties and cultural exchanges."[4]

Conceptualizing and gaining public support for an appropriate set of political, economic, and military policies that would give form to these general assertions, however, has proven to be a difficult task. Despite official pronouncements that "our nation has recovered its self-confidence at home, and we have not abandoned our interest in Asia,"[5] the region has taken third or fourth place in a set of American foreign policy priorities now focused on European security issues, the strategic balance, and the Middle East. There is a profound division of opinion among American leaders about how to deal with the global Soviet challenge and about the place of China in a national security strategy. There is also a feeling among many U.S. officials that American interests, for the moment at least, are relatively well served by conditions in Asia. And although there is ample evidence that the United States remains actively engaged in the political, economic, and security affairs of the region,[6] recent U.S. policy initiatives suggest uncertainty of purpose and a desire to limit American involvement in Asian affairs.

. . . There is a widespread concern in Asia that the United States cannot be depended upon to meet its regional security commitments. This reflects an assumption that the lingering influence of the Vietnam War experience, reinforced by a shifting Soviet-American power balance, continues to immobilize political support in the United States for an activist foreign policy. This perception is also the result of a series of recent American actions that have created confusion or uncertainty about our Asian security policy. Most important of these has been the unilateral announcement in 1977 that all U.S. ground troops would be withdrawn from the ROK, and the subsequent reversal of this decision in the spring of 1979 as a result of Congressional pressures and new intelligence information about North Korean troop strength.

There also has been uncertainty about American intentions toward China. The delay of some years in completing the process of normalizing U.S.-PRC relations suggested to some Asians an inability on the part of the United States to accomplish what most states of the region had already achieved. More recently, a concern has arisen that the development of U.S.-PRC security cooperation on the theme of anti-hegemony will either provoke the Soviet Union or take precedence over America's traditional alliance relationships in Asia. There are also worries that the economic tensions in Japansese-American relations will become so acute as to alienate the Japanese and impel them in the direction of a more independent and nationalistic foreign policy.

An effective American Asian security policy for the 1980s—one which will gain domestic political support and the confidence of our allies—will require greater clarity regarding four issue areas: First, a clear U.S. strategy for dealing with the global Soviet challenge, and greater consensus on the issue of how to relate to China in the "triangular" context of Sino-Soviet relations and the Sino-Soviet dispute. Second, an assessment of regional trends that will affect Asian security in the coming decade. Third, evaluation of American and allied military requirements, as well as economic and political policies, for responding to both global and regional security threats. And fourth, an awareness of the concerns and interests of friendly and allied states in Asia as they will affect American policy choices . . . .

The subsequent discussion seeks to identify the qualities of what will be a time of transition for Asia. By evaluating the major factors that will influence regional security, we can then define the policy choices that the United States and its allies will face as they try to shape a coherent set of political, economic, and defense programs designed to enhance their security and realize other interests in the region.

A Shifting U.S.-Soviet Military Balance

For most of the three decades following World War II, American policy planners saw Asian issues in the context of U.S. strategic military superiority over our primary Cold War adversary, the Soviet Union. They could take some comfort from the knowledge that the United States enjoyed a position of predominance in nuclear and naval forces in Asia. Moreover, the Soviet-American competition was seen by those planners to be centered predominantly in Europe. At the time of the Korean and Vietnam Wars, for example, a major concern was that deep American involvement in conventional military conflicts in Asia would draw U.S. defense capabilities and attention from Europe, where the Soviets had the capabilities and incentives to challenge the United States directly. For this reason, consideration was given to ways of rapidly disengaging U.S. forces from combat in order to be able to respond to possible Soviet challenges in the NATO theater. (Such a disengagement, however, was never effectively implemented.)

The coming decade will require an entirely different set of assumptions about the Soviet-American military balance in both strategic and regional forces, and of the place of Asia in the global U.S.-Soviet rivalry. Many experts believe that for at least several years in the early 1980s America's Minuteman strategic missiles will be vulnerable to a Soviet first strike. This factor, in combination with Moscow's conventional military preponderance in Europe and an active Soviet civil defense program, compromises the assumption that Soviet leaders seek only "strategic parity" or "equal security." Such military trends, if unchallenged, may make the United States more cautious in situations where American and Soviet interests clash.

At the same time, this shift in the pattern of "superpower" military capabilities is likely to make the Soviets more assertive. Recent direct and proxy Soviet interventions in the Third World—from Africa and the Middle East to Indochina—have occurred in circumstances less favorable to the USSR than those Soviet leaders may enjoy in the 1980s.

The Soviet Union's ability to project military force into Asia at all levels of conflict is also growing. The recent deployment to the Soviet Far East of Backfire bombers and SS-20 intermediate-range mobile nuclear missiles is transforming the theater nuclear balance. Soviet ground forces numbering more than 45 divisions, deployed primarily along the Sino-Soviet frontier, are now being supplemented by paratroop and amphibious units in the Maritime Provinces and on offshore islands. These units give Moscow new capabilities for intervention in Japan and Korea, as well as in China.[7] Strengthened Soviet long-range aviation[8] and naval assets in Asia are gradually expanding Moscow's ability to *project* power, to go beyond the missions of threatening the security of U.S. bases in Asia, the Seventh Fleet, and America's ballistic missile submarines. . . . There is growing concern among Asian leaders that the Soviet Union is now creating a capability to threaten the security of the sea lanes and to intervene in support of friendly states and proxy forces—as

Moscow has done recently with Vietnam in its conflict with Kampuchea (Cambodia) and China.

The degree of caution, or assertiveness, that these new military circumstances will induce cannot be predicted—in part because the United States has the ability to remedy some of the presently unfavorable military trends. Moscow's past behavior, however, suggests greater efforts in the future to project the influence of the USSR unless Soviet power is checked by some countervailing capability. There may also be an inclination on the part of regional states to accommodate their policies to the growing Soviet military presence if it is not countered by the United States or some coalition of countries.

Interdependence in Security Affairs

"Interdependence" entered the American vocabulary of international affairs in the 1970s, largely as a result of the oil crisis and economic problems in relations with allies such as Japan. This perspective is likely to gain enhanced significance in the coming decade. As noted above, the shifting power balance between the United States and the Soviet Union is likely to impel greater efforts at coalition-building to compensate for the limited security capabilities of any given country. Indeed, it was such a consideration that led self-reliant China to pursue its opening to the United States, Japan, and Western Europe after the Soviet invasion of Czechoslovakia in 1968 and border clashes along the Sino-Soviet frontier the following year. As Mao Zedong (Mao Tse-tung) rhetorically inquired of Henry Kissinger, "If neither side [the U.S. or China] had anything to ask from the other, why would you be coming to Peking? If neither side had anything to ask, then why . . . would we want to receive you and the President?"[9]

Soviet efforts to isolate China largely backfired, as Beijing succeeded during the 1970s in broadening its international contacts and establishing normal relations with Tokyo, Washington, and the capitals of Western Europe. To date, the antihegemony theme in this proto-coalition of China, Japan, the United States, and Europe is muted and ambivalent, particularly as far as military affairs are concerned. But if Soviet threats to the security of these states continue to increase, it is likely that this emergent entente will acquire a more explicit character as a defense alliance.

The smaller states of Asia, understandably, are reluctant to be drawn into this evolving pattern of great-power contention. Yet events are carrying them in a direction contrary to their desires. The Vietnamese, presumed by all to be fiercely independent, have allied themselves by formal treaty to the Soviet Union in order to gain some protection from Chinese pressures as they pursue the goal of a Hanoi-dominated federation of the Indochina states.[10] In reaction, the countries of ASEAN (the Association of Southeast Asian Nations)—Thailand, Malaysia, Singapore, the Philippines, and Indonesia—contemplate more active forms of security cooperation in order to resist the pressures of an expansionist Vietnam. As with the new pattern of great-power relationships, the evolution of ASEAN as a security coalition will be shaped by the threat the Association faces.

Interdependence will be more than a matter of greater collaboration in security affairs. Evolving economic relationships are reinforcing new patterns of security cooperation—as well as straining old alliances. China's turn to the West and Japan has been motivated, in part, by the desire to gain access to advanced technologies, investment capital, and new markets that will facilitate economic modernization. Continuation of the remarkable growth of the economies of South Korea, Taiwan, Hong Kong, and Singapore, along with the future growth of the ASEAN economies, is highly dependent upon continuing investment from Japan, the United States, and Western Europe, as well as on unimpeded access to their markets for local manufactures. And the stability of the U.S.-Japanese alliance in the 1980s will be tested by the effectiveness with which the two countries cope with the structural economic transformations required to end the massive trade imbalances that have created political pressures for protectionist measures.

The vitality of East Asia will be affected, as well, by developments beyond the region: by the stability of access to Middle Eastern energy supplies; and by the impact of the tide of Islamic fundamentalism on those states with sizable Muslim populations—Indonesia, the Philippines, and Malaysia.

National Interest, Not Ideology, as an Aligning Force

The 1970s has seen the substantial erosion of ideology as an aligning force in international politics, and this has certainly occurred in the affairs of Asia. The normalization of Sino-American and Sino-Japanese relations and the economic rationalization of China's post-Mao Zedong economic and social policies have diminished, at least for the present, the communist-capitalist lines of cleavage in Asian political and economic relations. In contrast, . . . conflict in Asia is now "East-East" rather than "East-West" in character, as former socialist allies China and Vietnam, and China and the Soviet Union, contest the extension of each other's influence with the threat or use of arms.

National interest has replaced ideology as the orienting force of international relationships in Asia. . . . This can be a healthy thing as long as a spirit of independence is tempered by a sense of responsibility for cooperative measures designed to enhance regional security and economic progress. The question for the coming decade is whether the force of nationalism will remain benign, or whether it will fuel territorial disputes, resource rivalry, and destabilizing approaches to security—e.g., through arms races and nuclear proliferation. In this regard, there remains latent concern in Asia about the future evolution of Japanese defense policy in the direction of a more assertive nationalism—a prospect which . . . could be accelerated by the present strains in U.S.-Japanese economic relations and the diminished credibility of the American security presence in Asia.

The Non-Military Determinants of Security

While military factors will, of course, continue to be a major element in regional security affairs, one aspect of the "transitional" quality of current developments in Asia is that emerging social, political, and economic factors will produce new tensions and international alignments which ultimately may lead to regional conflicts.

The economic dynamism of the non-communist Sinitic societies—South Korea, Japan, Taiwan, Hong Kong, and Singapore—has created a stabilizing prosperity. Nonetheless, these states remain vulnerable to recession or dislocations induced by unreliable access to energy supplies or markets in the United States and Europe. If . . . the developed countries of the West are entering a period of economic malaise, current protectionist pressures will only increase. And as economic development proceeds in the multi-ethnic societies of ASEAN, resentment against the more visible wealth of the entrepreneurial "Overseas Chinese" could stimulate communal violence—particularly if Islamic fundamentalism takes hold in Malaysia or Indonesia. Vietnam already has paid a significant economic price for the expulsion of its skilled and commercially active Chinese minority.

Barring a major economic catastrophe, East Asia is likely to remain the world's most dynamic region of growth in the coming decade. And while this will inhibit internal political unrest and contribute to the expansion of constructive trading relationships, the growing scientific and industrial capacities of the states of the region also hold the potential for intraregional arms manufacturing and transfers, and for nuclear proliferation. . . . Regional arms sales are not a matter of concern at present, although failure of the United States to manage economic and security relations with its traditional Asian allies could stimulate disruptive trends toward such transfers and/or proliferation.

The United States retains the capability to shape in a constructive manner emergent economic and defense programs in Asia. Unlike the Soviet Union, which projects its influence in the region almost exclusively through military means, the United States has the political and social access, and the scientific and economic resources, to interact with the countries of Asia on a broad range of issues.[11] To do so effectively, however, will require greater constancy of purpose in security affairs, such as military assistance programs, and a willingness to incur the domestic political costs associated with various structural economic readjustments. For example, a liberal textile import quota for China would enable the PRC to earn the foreign exchange with which to purchase more American industrial goods, although such a policy would affect domestic producers and the interests of our traditional foreign suppliers.

And finally, . . . the 1980s will be a critical period for the states of the region in dealing with population growth and a concomitant sluggishness in agricultural production. Despite decades of effort to solve these problems, the Chinese were unable to sustain per capita grain consumption in 1978 at anything more than a 1957 level;[12] and Indonesia has become the world's major importer of rice as a result of production shortfalls and a population growth rate approaching 3 percent. While the social and political effects of such problems may not be felt in a highly disruptive form for some years, the 1980s may be the last time certain countries can attempt to deal with population and food problems in a manner that does not generate extensive human misery and political turmoil.

New Sources of Regional Instability and Conflict

Apart from the major trends discussed above, East Asian security in the 1980s will be shaped by a range of specific factors, some of which are regional "spillovers" of global trends, and some of which are problems unique to Asia. The eight sources of potential instability or conflict described in the following pages are the factors most likely—in some unfolding combination—to threaten the peace and security of East Asia in the coming decade.

The Sino-Soviet Conflict

The Moscow-Beijing rivalry will be the major "structural" factor shaping the evolving pattern of regional political alignments and prospects for military conflict.

During the 1960s the Sino-Soviet feud was confined largely to political maneuvering within the international communist movement and to the gradual military buildup along the Sino-Soviet frontier which culminated in the border clashes of 1969. The 1970s have seen the feud extended to involve appeals by the Soviets and Chinese to non-communist states from Europe to Asia as the two countries maneuver against each other in a bitter contest of containment and counter-containment.

The first major realignments in the non-communist world associated with this political competition were the opening of Sino-American normalization negotiations in July 1971 and the signing of the Soviet-Indian Peace and Friendship Treaty in the early fall of that same year—just prior to the Indo-Pakistani war of November.[13] Subsequent years saw little progress by Moscow in its persistent efforts to enlist support for an anti-Chinese coalition, although Beijing, once admitted to the United Nations, made significant progress in broadening its political access to the international community. The last two years of the 1970s, however, have seen major developments in the pattern of political realignment around the two communist powers. In August 1978 Tokyo and Beijing signed a Peace and Friendship Treaty that included an expression of common opposition to "hegemony." An agreement on the full normalization of Sino-American relations reached at the end of 1978 contained explicit reference to the same theme. On Moscow's side of the strategic equation, 1978 saw Soviet-oriented coups in South Yemen and Afghanistan and the signing of a Soviet-Vietnamese Peace and Friendship Treaty in the face of serious political and military tensions between Beijing and Hanoi.

These political realignments have not, to date, been accompanied by major military actions, although reports persist of clashes along the Sino-Soviet frontier. Moreover, both sides continue to strengthen their military positions. The Russians are upgrading the weaponry deployed with more than 45 divisions that threaten the Chinese; and Beijing sustains its counterdeployment of more than 70 divisions. The Soviets have positioned SS-20 IRBMs in eastern Siberia in a way that threatens not only China but also Japan and other Asian states as far south as Indonesia. Moscow's construction of the Baikal-Amur Mainline (BAM) Railroad is designed to strengthen Soviet logistical capabilities in the sensitive Chinese border area, as well as to accelerate the economic development of Siberia. And there are persistent reports of Moscow's intention to build a major naval facility at Korsakov on Sakhalin Island as well as Soviet pressures on Vietnam to establish permanent air and naval facilities at Danang and Cam Ranh Bay.

China's military response to the Soviet buildup is only now taking form. A defense modernization program begun in 1975 was sidetracked during the turmoil surrounding political attacks on Deng Xiaoping and the subsequent purging of the "Gang of Four." The Chinese now seem firmly embarked, however, on a broad-scale approach to economic development and the gradual modernization of their military establishment. This effort includes substantial purchases of advanced industrial technology from Japan, the United States, and Europe, and interest in European military hardware such as combat aircraft, anti-tank and air-to-air missiles, and component systems, e.g., aircraft and marine engines. To date, however, no major weapon system has been sold to Beijing.[14]

The question for the 1980s is how far the Russians and the Chinese will proceed in the political and military dimensions of their geopolitical maneuvering. Despite talks initiated between Beijing and Moscow in September 1979 to reduce tensions, the Soviets can be expected to persist in efforts to gain allies on China's periphery. Iran, Afghanistan, Pakistan, and North Korea are likely to be high-priority, if unstable, targets of opportunity. Taiwan and the ASEAN states will be less promising candidates. And it remains to be seen whether Moscow's presently most promising point of access in Asia—Vietnam—will be converted into a permanent Soviet military presence on China's southern frontier.

Similarly, it is not clear how successful Beijing will be in constructing what Deng Xiaoping has termed an "Eastern NATO" in its relations with Japan and the United States, or how far the Europeans (and the Americans) will go in selling military equipment and defense-related technologies to the Chinese. Such developments are most likely to occur in reaction to threatening moves on the part of the Soviet Union. And the possibility of some limited Soviet military action against the PRC during the coming decade—perhaps in the form of large-scale border clashes conducted in a period of heightened Sino-Vietnamese tensions—cannot be ruled out.

. . . The basic policy problem for the United States and its Asian allies in the 1980s is how to conduct relations with Moscow and Beijing in the context of their enduring enmity. A significant reduction in Sino-Soviet tensions resulting from the current discussions would presumably dampen down the Moscow-Beijing rivalry in Asia; and this would contribute to regional stability. Such a development seems unlikely, however, in view of Moscow's penchant for projecting Soviet influence through military power. The Sino-Soviet conflict is most likely to remain bounded by the two extremes of rapprochement and war, with the most likely prospect being an ongoing political rivalry with persistent military tensions.

The U.S.-Soviet Long-Term Competition

As a result of the full normalization of China's relations with Washington and Tokyo, it will become increasingly difficult during the coming decade to separate the elements of global Soviet-American competition from those of regional competition in Asia. The great failure of Soviet policy during the 1960s and 1970s was to have provoked into life a long-feared two-front strategic challenge. The coming decade may see the realization of a Sino-Japanese-American coalition for political, economic, and perhaps even defense cooperation. Although the United States is now unburdened of its "two-front" security problem—at least in the form of a Sino-Soviet alliance—American defense planners must worry about the Soviets redeploying some of their "Chinese" divisions to Europe as reinforcements during a NATO-Warsaw Pact conflict. In sum, the 1980s will see the increasing "globalization" of what thus far have been regional Asian security issues.

As one example of this trend, during the 1970s the gradual strengthening of Soviet naval forces in the Pacific seemed designed to threaten the carrier task forces and ballistic missile submarines of the U.S. Seventh Fleet. While these two missions will remain central to the operations of the Soviet Pacific Fleet, the deployment of the new Kiev-class aircraft-carrying ASW cruiser *Minsk* to the Pacific region in 1979 signifies that Moscow is gradually assembling new and substantial power-projection capabilities. These new capabilities will not only threaten the security of key strait passages that traditionally have been the focus of U.S. and allied naval defense strategy, they already give Moscow some ability to intervene in regional disputes on behalf of client states (as it has done in Vietnam).

These capabilities also mean that the Soviets are building the capacity to threaten the security of the sea lines of communication which are so essential to the commerce of the island nations of the region and their access to energy resources. The growing Soviet military presence will further challenge the ability of the United States to reinforce its Asian deployments in times of crisis. In the coming decade, the United States and its allies will have to consider new approaches to countering the growing Soviet military presence in Asia—a problem which will be substantially compounded should Moscow establish permanent naval and air basing facilities in Vietnam.

Once Again, Indochina

The Indochina Peninsula seems fated to be an area of enduring tension if not overt conflict, and a place in the Asian political landscape where the interests of the great powers converge. It is uncertain how the present military conflict between Vietnam (backed by the Soviet Union) and Kampuchea and China will be resolved, but the outcome will have a significant impact on the security not only of the combatants themselves but also of the ASEAN states. Continuing conflict in Indochina is the factor most likely to poison the Asian security environment and provoke heightened Sino-Soviet tensions in the 1980s.

Hanoi failed in its attempt of late 1978 to wage a quick military campaign which would unseat the Chinese-backed Pol Pot regime in Kampuchea and replace it with a government friendly to Vietnam. And while Beijing's thirty-day punitive border war did not inflict a military defeat on the Vietnamese, it did impose on Hanoi all the military and economic burdens of a two-front security threat and the anticipated political costs of enduring Chinese enmity. It also put the Vietnamese in a position of near total dependence on Soviet security assistance and economic aid for their war-ravaged economy—an international isolation that has been compounded by the collapse of U.S.-Vietnamese normalization talks and international reaction to Hanoi's expulsion of its ethnic Chinese minority and military operations in Kampuchea.

The future evolution of this new phase of the seemingly endless conflict on the Indochina Peninsula is not easily predicted. Vietnam will pursue a new dry-season campaign against the remaining Pol Pot forces, and the Chinese will seek ways of sustaining the guerrilla insurgency against Vietnamese troops in Kampuchea and Hanoi's client Heng Samrin regime. How far the insurgency will spill over into Thailand, already burdened with a major influx of Khmer refugees, will probably be related to Thailand's role as a sanctuary or source of resupply for the Pol Pot forces. If Hanoi succeeds in destroying the insurgency and consolidating control of Kampuchea for Heng Samrin, the Vietnamese could then wage a guerrilla campaign against the Thai in retribution—although Hanoi will have to consider the prospect of a strong reaction from the ASEAN countries and from the United States. Moreover, the Chinese will continue to oppose the extension of Hanoi's influence beyond Vietnam through some combination of support for guerrilla forces in Kampuchea, perhaps the opening of a second insurgent front in Laos, and maintenance of a conventional military threat on Vietnam's northern frontier.

An unlikely prospect at present is for a change in policy and/or government in Hanoi to a regime that is both more inclined to repair relations with China and limit dependence on the Soviet Union. Were such a development to occur, however, Beijing would almost certainly seek to improve its presently poisonous relations with the Vietnamese.

What can be said with some assurance is that a situation of continuing insurgent warfare and military tension in Indochina will be the context most favorable for the Soviet Union to extend its military presence in Southeast Asia. The great danger in the coming years for virtually all states with interests in Asia is that the Sino-Vietnamese conflict will escalate to a point that precipitates a direct Sino-Soviet military clash. The challenge to the PRC and the United States is to attempt to influence events in a direction that will decouple Indochina from further great-power intervention. At present such a development would require the unlikely circumstances of a neutralization of Kampuchea (perhaps under Prince Sihanouk's leadership) or a new regime in Hanoi that is inclined toward establishing a balanced relationship between Beijing, Moscow, and Washington.

Korea: The Shifting Power Balance between North and South

The enduring military confrontation between North and South Korea—a major source of tension in East Asia for the past three decades—will likewise not disappear in the 1980s. However, the coming decade will see a significant transformation in the power balance between the two adversaries. The productivity and technical sophistication of the South Korean economy continues to grow rapidly, in marked contrast to the stagnating, defense-oriented system in the North. Per capita income in South Korea surpassed that of the North in the mid-1970s, and the ROK has developed extensive trading ties abroad. Although the military balance presently favors the North, South Korea should be able to strengthen an effective deterrent military force through its own weapons production capabilities and the continuing presence of American ground forces, aircraft, and naval units. In short, a significant shift will occur in the relative power positions of North and South Korea which, if managed properly, could stabilize the confrontation on the Peninsula. Given the shared interests of the ROK, the United States, China, Japan, and probably the Soviet Union as well, in preventing another Korean War, efforts to achieve such a stabilization are likely to elicit broad support.

There are, however, several factors which will make the coming decade a period of some danger in Northeast Asia. The aging Kim Il-sung could come to believe that he faces a "last chance" opportunity to use military force to reunify the Peninsula, or at least to disrupt the trends toward ever-increasing North Korean inferiority relative to the ROK in political, economic, and even military terms. Should such a view materialize during a time of apparently irresolute or distracted American support for the security of the ROK, political turmoil in Seoul growing from the recent assassination of President Park Chung Hee, and perhaps encouragement of Pyongyang by a Soviet Union so concerned about the evolving pattern of Sino-Japanese-American relations that it wants to stir up trouble, the presently favorable situation could be upset by a North Korean military initiative. Pyongyang's belief that the South was approaching the acquisition of atomic weapons and a delivery system capable of threatening North Korea's existence could also reinforce a "now or never" view of present trends.

As the Korean situation evolves in the coming decade, the "deterrence equation," to use Richard Sneider's term, will require careful management by all parties concerned if the confrontation between North and South is not to become a renewed source of conflict with serious effects on the security of the region. And while military issues will remain central to South Korea's security, the 1980s may well see new opportunities for a negotiated stabilization of relations between North and South. The combination of North Korean economic weakness, political isolation, and unfavorable military prospects could lead Kim Il-sung—or more likely his successors—to accept the temporary reality of two Korean societies in return for broadened political recognition and inclusion of North Korea in the expanding Asian economic community.

China Irredenta

Throughout the 1970s Beijing's concerns about Soviet encirclement led Chinese leaders to set aside certain territorial disputes in order to create conditions for a broad united front against "hegemony." The one exception to this pattern was China's military takeover of the Paracel Islands from South Vietnamese forces in January 1974—an initiative that did much to poison Beijing's relations with Hanoi. Most observers of the Sino-Soviet and Sino-Vietnamese disputes would hold that China's territorial claims in these conflicts reflect political maneuvering more than a determined effort to reclaim lost lands. However, Beijing's presently muted territorial claims on the eastern periphery of the PRC are likely, over the longer term, to be sources of tension if not conflict between China and its neighbors.

Since the early 1970s the Chinese have asserted their claim to the Tiaoyu Tai or Senkaku Islands north of Taiwan in the East China Sea, while at the same time urging Japan to set aside this territorial dispute in favor of unity on other issues. This position was reaffirmed during the negotiations for the Peace and Friendship Treaty in 1978. And although Beijing has warned Japan and South Korea against joint exploitation of undersea oil resources on the continental shelf in the Yellow Sea, the Chinese have indicated that they are prepared to reserve their claim as long as Tokyo and Seoul do likewise.

Although PRC leaders were unwilling to foreswear the use of force in resolving the Taiwan issue as part of a normalization agreement with the United States, in the interest of building a positive relationship with Washington they took an accommodating position on the future of the island (as they continue to do regarding the status of Hong Kong and Macao as well). Deng Xiaoping has asserted that it will take decades, if not longer, to reunify (rather than "liberate") the island with the mainland, and that Taiwan can maintain its social, economic, and political systems so that its people will suffer no loss in their present status. Beijing adopts a similar position of unyielding assertion of a territorial claim with reservation of efforts to enforce it with respect to the Spratly Islands in the South China Sea—territory contested by Vietnam and the Philippines, and lightly garrisoned by troops from Taiwan.

China's currently accommodating position on these residual territorial issues reflects not only a desire to minimize conflicts with the United States, Japan, and certain other neighboring states in the context of the Soviet challenge, but also its limited military capabilities for enforcing claims. However, Beijing's swift air and naval takeover of the disputed Paracel Islands indicates that the Chinese will forcefully pursue their claims when circumstances are favorable and military means are available.

The issue for the 1980s is not whether China will rapidly acquire the military assets to conduct complex offshore air and naval campaigns in support of these unresolved territorial disputes, but whether actions of other parties will force Beijing's hand on issues the Chinese would prefer to reserve for more opportune circumstances. A Taiwanese move to assert their independence of China, or the less likely development of Taiwan turning to the Soviet Union for protection against PRC pressures, could impel Beijing to take ill-prepared and costly actions to the detriment of currently moderate and accommodating policies. Similarly, efforts by neighboring states to exploit offshore resources in areas contested by the PRC would very likely sour the current political atmosphere and provoke Chinese countermeasures.

Territorial Disputes and Resource Rivalry

Paralleling China's unresolved territorial claims are a range of similar disputes which could cause serious tensions in Northeast and Southeast Asia in the coming decade. Among these are the Soviet-Japanese conflict over the four islands of Habomai, Shikotan, Kunashiri, and Etorofu in the Southern Kurile chain off Hokkaido—a dispute that continues to block the conclusion of a peace treaty between the two countries[15]—and associated conflicts over fishing rights in the Seas of Japan and Okhotsk and the Bering Sea. The delimitation of Exclusive Economic Zones of control over continental shelf resources remains contested by China, Japan, and South Korea; and several islands in the Gulf of Siam persist as points of potential conflict among Vietnam, Kampuchea, and Thailand. These territorial claims will acquire heightened salience as efforts to promote undersea oil exploration are expanded during the 1980s. And Indonesia's border differences with Papua-New Guinea could cause problems in Jakarta's relations with Australia and the United States.

While none of these territorial issues is likely in itself to be the cause of major conflict, any of them could catalyze other sources of dispute (e.g., Soviet concerns about the direction of Japanese and PRC foreign policies, or the Vietnam-Kampuchea conflict). In the absence of a successful conclusion of the Law of the Sea negotiations, resolution of associated territorial claims, and delimitation of the boundaries of Exclusive Economic Zones, these issues will remain sources of regional tension and insecurity.

The Strains of Economic Growth

The remarkable economic dynamism of the non-communist states of Asia is not only a source of growing strength and self-confidence, but . . . is also cause for considerable optimism in assessing the future. At the same time, this very dynamism presents certain problems of growth, balance, and the evolution of new relationships which, if not handled properly, could have a negative effect on regional security. Five aspects of the present economic situation are cause for particular attention, if not concern: problems of market competition and related protectionist pressures; competition for available investment capital, technology, and skilled manpower; the securing of energy supplies, especially petroleum, and related sea transportation routes; protection of the economies of the region against the effects of global recession; and prospects for weapons development and arms transfers—including the problem of nuclear proliferation—which come with the growing technological sophistication and industrial productivity of the more advanced states of the region.

As economic growth proceeds, the most natural economic complementarity will be between the advanced industrial states and the less-developed countries (LDCs), between those who can supply natural resources and inexpensive labor and those with the industrial capacity to provide advanced technologies and markets for raw materials and consumer goods. Thus, prospects are favorable for the growth of trade between Japan and China, the United States and China, perhaps between Taiwan and China, and between the industrial superpowers and the ASEAN states. Such economic complementarity will be constrained, however, by the various protectionist measures invoked by the developed countries as they seek to ease the impact on their domestic industries of less-expensive imports from the LDCs—textiles, clothing, electronics, and the products of newly developed light industries. Such protectionism will inhibit structural readjustments in Japan, the United States, and Western Europe that would help these advanced economies "mesh" with those of the developing states of Asia.

We also note . . . concern about the potential for disruptive radicalization of the "North-South" dimension of Asian economic relations as the poorer countries press their quest for a new international economic order that would provide improved terms of trade for their raw material exports, greater control over "common" offshore resources, and more favorable terms of access to development capital and technology.[16] At the present time it is not clear that events in Asia are moving in this direction; but developments beyond the region—such as a radicalization of the oil-exporting states of the Middle East growing from the present turmoil in Iran—could combine with political changes in one or a number of the key countries of Southeast Asia to produce an atmosphere of economic confrontation between the developing and the developed states.

Economic tension will also be evident *between* the developing countries as they contend for export markets, capital, and energy supplies. The prospect of successful offshore oil exploitation in Asia provides some hope for regional protection against the possible disruption of Middle East oil imports. At the same time, the previously noted territorial conflicts raise questions about whether Asian oil can be developed without compounding tensions between China and rival claimants to offshore resources.

As the Korean and Taiwanese economies continue to expand, these two countries will increasingly compete with each other, and with Japan, for American markets currently dominated by the Japanese. And as Beijing pursues its dramatic new economic development program—which various sources estimate could absorb several tens of billions of dollars in foreign investment by the mid-1980s—the ASEAN states will become increasingly concerned about the ability of their new industries to compete with cheap Chinese manufactures and their access to capital and technology from the United States and Japan. A major challenge of the 1980s is to develop a combination of bilateral and multilateral economic institutions, in support of market forces, that can cope with the divisive side effects of economic modernization that is likely to proceed apace.

Among the developed countries, the balance-of-payments problem which continues to burden Japanese-American relations reflects the difficulty of developing complementary market-structures where cultures and social systems are so different. While trade problems have not yet generated a protectionist reaction in the United States strong enough to degrade relations between the two countries, it is not clear that leaders in either Washington or Tokyo will be able to resist the domestic political forces that seek to obstruct the adjustments in economic policy which would resolve trade and related monetary problems. Several authors . . . note concern in Asia that American political and economic pressures on Japan will eventually generate a political backlash among the Japanese which could seriously disrupt U.S.-Japanese relations and drive Japan in the direction of closer ties with either China or the Soviet Union, or impel the country toward a more assertive and nationalistic foreign policy. Such developments can be minimized only by a continuing process of consultation on economic and other issues between Washington and Tokyo.

Security issues deriving from the present phase of economic growth in the region are those related to trends in weapons research and development, production, and transfer. While Japan continues to foreswear an export-oriented arms industry, Korea and Taiwan are establishing a capacity to produce such conventional weapons as light arms, artillery and ammunition, mines, tanks, and light naval craft in quantities that far exceed their own needs. The 1980s could see an increase in weapons sales within the region which would stimulate local arms races. Similarly, Taiwan, South Korea, and Japan each have the scientific talent and industrial capacity to eventually develop advanced military systems such as missiles and atomic weapons.

One of the major challenges to formulating a U.S. security policy appropriate to Asian conditions in the coming decade is the need to sustain a sufficiently credible American defense presence so as to prevent the growth of potentially destabilizing trends in arms research, development, production, and transfer.

Domestic Political Instabilities

As the revolution in Iran of the winter and spring of 1979 illustrates all too clearly, rapid economic growth and defense modernization may generate social and political turmoil that in turn can rapidly undermine regional security arrangements. Apart from the long-term effects of population-growth and food-production problems, which continue to burden several Southeast Asian states, there is the enduring issue of rural-urban social polarization resulting from the uneven distribution of wealth in the early stages of industrialization. Moreover, recently urbanized populations are particularly vulnerable to the disruption of trade-related economic activity and the concomitant prospect of demagogic political appeals by revolutionary political leaders. There is a high probability that the coming decade will witness domestic political instability in a number of key Asian states which could disrupt regional security arrangements. Two factors are particularly relevant in making this assessment: the prospect for leadership-succession crises in states with weakly institutionalized political systems; and the possibility of ethnic or communal tensions exacerbated by political and/or economic developments.

Only three non-communist countries in Asia—Japan, Australia, and New Zealand—have political systems that are clearly capable of smoothly managing leadership successions. Singapore and Malaysia may also be countries in this category. Five states seem particularly vulnerable to disruptive leadership crises in the coming decade: South Korea, Taiwan, the Philippines, Indonesia, and—to a lesser degree—Thailand. In each of these countries the second generation of post-World War II leadership faces the task of managing the transition from highly personal, centralized, and authoritarian rule to more participatory and institutionalized political forms. The assassination of South Korean President Park Chung Hee in November 1979 has already precipitated this problem in the ROK. It seems unlikely that the Chiang, Marcos, Suharto, or Kriangsak leaderships will escape the difficulties of this process, with its attendant potential for domestic turmoil, outside intervention, and disruption of the larger pattern of regional security arrangements.

Ethnic or communal tensions seem particularly likely to develop in four countries: Taiwan, the Philippines, Indonesia, and Malaysia. In Taiwan, the political mobilization of the Taiwanese majority is growing as a result of their substantial economic power. The recent American withdrawal of diplomatic recognition from the Nationalist government is likely to further weaken the legitimacy of the aging "mainlander" ruling elite. While both "mainlander" and Taiwanese communities continue to share an interest in preventing domination of the island by the communist government in Beijing, political and economic developments could impel the Taiwanese to press for self-rule, if not independence. This process may be catalyzed when the strong and visible leadership of Chiang Ching-kuo passes from the scene. Political turmoil on the island, or a Taiwanese move toward independence, could prompt some form of intervention by Beijing and lead to strained relations between the PRC and the United States and Japan.

In Malaysia and Indonesia, enduring ethnic, economic, and political differences between Muslim and Chinese elements of the population could be exacerbated by some combination of growing Islamic fundamentalism, a resurgence in external encouragement of the now-dormant communist insurgencies, and tensions resulting from the process of economic modernization. There is some indication that the Soviet Union may be stimulating such tensions through Arab collaborators in order to disrupt what it sees as an unfavorable trend toward ASEAN solidarity and resulting efforts to limit the Soviet presence in the region.

The communist countries of Asia will also face the prospect of domestic political instability and leadership crises. We have already commented on the possible impact of the anticipated demise of Kim Il-sung on Korean security. China is also likely to go through a period of political instability in the 1980s as the Communist Party continues to adjust to the passing of Mao Zedong. Reports persist of tensions between Party Chairman Hua Guofeng (Hua Kuo-feng) and thrice-rehabilitated Vice-Premier Deng Xiaoping. And while there now appears to be a leadership consensus in support of the national security and economic development policies that have led China to seek close relations with Japan and the West, Beijing's thirty-year history of leadership feuds and abrupt policy changes gives limited confidence that current policies, which are so favorable to the United States and its allies, will long endure. The Soviet Union, as well, will soon experience a period of leadership change holding the potential for political instability and possible modifications in Moscow's policies affecting Asian security.

While it is unlikely that Soviet and Chinese leaders will suddenly repair their enduringly bad relations, a reduction in Sino-Soviet hostility, if accompanied by diminished geopolitical maneuvering by Moscow and Beijing against each other, would be a positive contribution to the security of Asia. Conversely, a deterioration in Sino-Soviet relations to the point of war, or another period of political instability in Beijing which again turned the Chinese "inward" upon themselves, would profoundly alter the present political climate in Asia.

Of all the trends that are likely to shape regional security in the 1980s, the least amenable to American influence—and the most likely to undermine what at present is a relatively promising situation—is the pattern of domestic political instabilities that could emerge in the coming decade.

American Security Policies for East Asia in the 1980s

Beyond consideration of the many factors that will influence Asian security in the 1980s, there remains the problem of the United States—in collaboration with its allies and friendly states—formulating an appropriate set of policies to support their respective and collective interests in the region. Political diversity and the varied nature of Asian problems make it unlikely that one overarching "grand design" for Asia can be formulated. The most fundamental security issue for the United States—how to respond to the regional spillover of the Sino-Soviet dispute in the context of the global Soviet-American rivalry—is a problem that may have limited relevance to the interests of regional allies. And "local" problems may rank low on the U.S. security agenda. In order to identify the major components of an American security policy for the region, the following discussion explores several enduring problems which will shape America's involvement in Asian affairs, suggests certain broad conceptual approaches to a security strategy for the region, and then specifies a set of concrete policy choices.

Problems in Formulating a Coherent American Policy for Asia

Historians of America's relations with Asia have observed several elements of continuity in our approach to the region: a strong interest in commercial development and a fascination with the *potential* of the China market which contrasts with the *reality* of our predominant commerce with Japan; a desire to see Asian nations strong enough to resist the designs of imperialist powers, particularly those who would seek to deny American access to the region; special concern for China's security, its "territorial and administrative integrity" as it was phrased in the "Open Door" Notes of 1899; and efforts to maintain a balance of power in the area, at times through arms control arrangements such as the Washington Conference on Naval Limitations of 1921–22. Of particular significance in contemporary circumstances, America's involvement in Asian security affairs has been characterized by a repetitive or cyclical pattern of periods of reluctance to commit U.S. power in support of self-proclaimed security and commercial interests, followed by deep military involvement—most recently in World War II, Korea, and Vietnam—succeeded by another period of reticence or withdrawal.[17]

Such themes have current relevance as the United States seeks to develop a new defense posture that will reconcile the contradictory pulls of our continuing interests in Asia with a changeable public mood at times inclined to minimize an American security presence and at other times prepared to support forceful intervention in regional affairs. It is not clear that a policy concept can be formulated which will reconcile these conflicting impulses and changing moods, much less one that has the simple coherence of Moscow's vague notion of "Asian collective security" or Beijing's unambiguous appeal for an "anti-hegemony" coalition. America's global and regional security interests are highly varied; and Asia presents a changing and diverse set of defense problems and political relationships which contrast with the U.S. experience in Europe. Moreover, certain characteristics of the Asian environment inhibit the development of a coherent concept for American defense planning which would go much beyond the very general notion of preserving a regional balance of power and preventing domination of the area by one state or a coalition of powers hostile to American interests.

Uncertain Adversaries, Unclear Lines of Confrontation. Since the disintegration of the Sino-Soviet alliance, and with the more recent normalization of

U.S.-PRC relations, the sources of threat to American interests in Asia have diffused. Whereas the sharp political-military demarcation between the NATO and Warsaw Pact states in Europe has been blurred only slightly by détente and American diplomacy in Eastern Europe, the one clear line of military confrontation in Asia toward which defense planning can be oriented is the heavily armed boundary between North and South Korea. The main lines of conflict in the region are now between the communist states—disputes such as the Sino-Vietnamese rivalry, in which Americans have little incentive to become involved.

This situation is likely to change during the 1980s, however. The growing Soviet military presence in Asia—in particular, Moscow's strengthened naval deployment—is becoming a major source of concern in Washington as well as in friendly Asian capitals. New Soviet theater nuclear forces, air assets, and an enhanced capacity to threaten the security of the sea lanes will become major issues in American and allied defense planning. And . . . there has already been a basic reassessment of the notion that U.S. Seventh Fleet assets can be safely shifted from the Pacific to the Persian Gulf, the Mediterranean, or the Atlantic in times of crisis. Aside from the fact that such a naval redeployment would be vulnerable to attack in transit, its greater weakness is that it would substantially degrade the ability of the United States to secure the sea lanes so vital to Japan and our other Asian allies.

Several [authors] note Moscow's difficulty in translating military resources into political and economic influence; and this has led some analysts to question the seriousness of the Soviet military threat to Asia. But such a perspective is unlikely to persist in the 1980s, largely as a result of Soviet actions. The primary source of insecurity in the region, and the driving force behind the political realignments now tending to repolarize Asia, is the heightened political-military rivalry between Moscow and Beijing; and the Soviets are the most powerful and assertive element in the contest. As a result, the Soviet Union is likely to be seen by most Asians as the most threatening and disruptive presence in the region, despite persisting distrust of Chinese intentions in some quarters.

Regional Political and Economic Diversity. In contrast to Europe's post-war political and economic unity, around which the NATO alliance was formed, Asia is a region of considerable geographic and cultural diversity, and limited economic and political integration. States of Northeast Asia with well-developed economic ties and shared security interests, such as Japan and South Korea, are constrained in the development of cooperative defense relations by the burden of past history. Japan and China only recently have begun to explore the security implications of a shared concern about the expansion of Soviet power; and both countries are limited in the development of regional security roles by the legacy of World War II (in the case of Japan) or by support for communist insurgencies and limited military resources (in Beijing's case).

Disparate security requirements further limit the development of integrated defense planning for the region—particularly between the states of Northeast and Southeast Asia. And while ASEAN gives promise of a regional approach to economic development, there is great reluctance to transform this young organization into an instrument of defense cooperation.

For the United States this situation has meant, and will continue to require, a largely bilateral approach to Asian security issues (with the one exception of the ANZUS alliance). The American defense presence in the region will continue to "bridge" states reluctant to deal with each other directly in security matters and will mediate the gradual projection of Japanese and Chinese power beyond their immediate defense needs. In the absence of one clear and present threat to the security of the region, American defense relations will be characterized by diversity of form and varied degrees of involvement.

Three Approaches to an Asian Security Strategy

One remarkable quality of this period of transition is that the United States has real choices in structuring its future role in regional security affairs. Certain alternatives are constrained by public resistance to involvement in distant sources of conflict, but others are reinforced by a concern among government officials that American interests will not permit another period of withdrawal from regional defense responsibilities. The primary sources of choice are changes occurring in the region itself: the heightened capability of various states (especially Japan and Korea) to assume greater security responsibilities; and the interest of others, primarily China, in encouraging a more active American role in global security affairs.

One thoughtful analysis suggests that the United States has three basic choices of strategy in its approach to Asia.[18] The first is a "minimalist" or "limited involvement" pattern in which the United States would restrict its direct security presence to the key alliance with Japan and limit its naval deployments to mid-Pacific island bases from which it can secure the strategic submarine fleet. In effect, this approach would "uncover" America's commercial, cultural, and political involvement in Asia on the assumptions that the security of allies such as Korea and the Philippines is not in serious jeopardy, that there is no real threat to the security of the sea lanes, and that American influence in the region can be limited to economic, political, and cultural activities.

The second choice is to join forces with the Chinese in an active"united front" designed to limit the extension of Soviet influence into Asia and counterweight Moscow's growing military capabilities for strategic and regional action through concerted efforts by the PRC, the United States, Japan, and the NATO states.

The third alternative is to limit America's formal security commitments to its traditional Asian allies but maintain an active "forward" military presence in the region, applying U.S. defense resources in a flexible and responsive way that preserves an equilibrium of power without being provocative to Moscow or seeking to deny Soviet access to the region for non-disruptive purposes of commerce and cultural relations.

While the "limited involvement" strategy reflects a now-changing public mood and the policy positions of a few in official positions, it is largely a straw man against which to test alternatives. It is an unsupportable view, given American interests in Asia; and it is unworkable, given the likely evolution of regional trends in the absence of a mediating American security presence. A viable security strategy is likely to combine elements of coalition activity among the major powers of the region with the flexible application of U.S. defense assets in response to challenges to regional stability. The full significance of these choices, however, can be grasped only by considering in detail the practical policy alternatives we will face in the 1980s.

Notes

1. Richard H. Solomon is director of The Rand Corporation's research program on International Security Policy, and head of the Social Science Department. From 1971 to 1976 he served on the staff of the National Security Council, having previously been a professor of Political Science at the University of Michigan.

2. Australia and New Zealand.

3. Richard M. Nixon, "Informal Remarks in Guam with Newsmen" (July 25, 1969), in *Public Papers of the Presidents of the United States: Richard Nixon* (Washington, D.C.: U.S. Government Printing Office, 1971), p. 546.

4. "President Ford's Pacific Doctrine," Department of State News Release, Washington, D.C., December 7, 1975, p. 3.

5. Secretary of State Cyrus Vance, "United States and Asia," Department of State News Release, Washington, D.C., June 29, 1977, p. 1.

6. Senior U.S. officials have repeatedly asserted in recent years the view that the current situation in Asia is favorable to the interests of the United States and its allies, that America intends to remain an Asian power, and that the United States is strengthening its military presence in the area at a level appropriate to the requirements of regional stability. See, for example, the speech by Secretary of Defense Harold Brown on American defense policy delivered to the Los Angeles World Affairs Council, February 20, 1978, *Los Angeles Times*, February 21, 1978; Keyes Beech, "Mondale Says U.S. Determined to Stay a Pacific Power, Cites 7th Fleet Buildup," *Los Angeles Times*, September 3, 1979; Richard Holbrooke, "East Asia Today and in the Decades Ahead," speech delivered to the Women's National Democratic Club, November 27, 1978.

7. See Russell Spurr, "The Soviet Threat: Ominous Implications of Red Power Plays," *Far Eastern Economic Review*, June 23, 1978, pp. 73–76; and William Chapman, "Japan Reports Soviet Buildup on Disputed Island," *Washington Post*, September 27, 1979.

8. With capabilities for intelligence collection, anti-shipping operations, and transport.

9. Henry A. Kissinger, *White House Years* (Boston: Little, Brown, 1979), p. 1060.

10. Ibid., pp. 468–469, and passim.

11. For example, in 1977 the United States provided a market for 25.7 percent of Asia's exports and furnished 14.6 percent of its imports. The Soviet Union provided only 1.2 percent of Asia's imports and accounted for 1.9 percent of its exports. (International Monetary Fund, *Direction of Trade, Annual 1971–1977.*)

12. "Decisions of the Central Committee of the Communist Party of China on Some Questions Concerning the Acceleration of Agricultural Development" (December 22, 1978), *People's Daily*, October 6, 1979, p. 1.

13. Henry Kissinger has now revealed that in the context of the Indian attack on Pakistan (an ally of both China and the United States), President Nixon communicated to PRC leaders his intention to assist China if Beijing came to Pakistan's aid, and as a result the Soviet Union—India's ally—initiated military action against China. The security aspect of "triangular politics" thus dates from November 1971. See Kissinger, *White House Years*, pp. 910–911.

14. It has been reported that British leaders told PRC Premier Hua Guofeng, during his visit to London in November 1979, that they would sell the PRC about 70 of their Harrier jump-jet fighters. No purchase agreement has yet been signed, however. See Leonard Downie, Jr., "Britain Tells Hua It Is Willing to Sell Harrier Jets," *Los Angeles Times*, November 2, 1979, p. 27.

15. The dispute over what the Japanese call the "northern territories" deepened in 1978 when the Soviets began to garrison the islands. See Henry Scott Stokes, "Soviet Force on Isle Protested by Japan," *New York Times*, October 3, 1979.

16. See Guy J. Pauker, *Military Implications of a Possible World Order Crisis in the 1980s*, The Rand Corporation, R-2003-AF, 1977, especially pp. 10–35.

17. See, for example, A. Whitney Griswold, *The Far East Policy of the United States* (New Haven: Yale University Press, 1964), especially chap. 11.

18. See Robert A. Scalapino, "Approaches to Peace and Security in Asia: The Uncertainty Surrounding American Strategic Principles," *Current Scene*, U.S. Consulate-General, Hong Kong, vol. 16, nos. 8, 9 (August–September 1978).

Discussion Questions

1. What factors shape U.S. alliance relationships in Asia? How have these factors changed over time?

2. How have the roles and influence of the Peoples Republic of China and Japan changed and what is the impact of these changes on U.S. interests and strategy in the Pacific?

3. How does the United States-Soviet competition affect U.S. policy in Asia?

4. How has the emergence of the Peoples Republic of China as a regional power affected U.S. relations with the Soviet Union?

15
Why Nations Negotiate

Fred Ikle

As the richness of diplomatic history illustrates, there is an enormous diversity in international negotiations. Governments are constantly engaged in diplomatic bargaining, ranging from casual contacts to large formal conferences. In order to bring out common traits and render this variety more manageable, one must distinguish among different purposes for which the parties negotiate. The aims or objectives of governments in international negotiations can be classified adequately into five types: (1) extension agreements, (2) normalization agreements, (3) redistribution agreements, (4) innovation agreements, and (5) effects not concerning agreements. In reality, the negotiating parties always pursue a mixture of several of these types of objectives, although one of them may predominate. Moreover, in one and the same negotiation, the dominant objective of one party is often of a different type from that of the other party.

Negotiations for the purpose of an *extension* agreement are meant to continue the "normal"; that is, to prolong existing arrangements which are acceptable to some, if not all, parties involved. Examples are the extension of tariff agreements, the renewal of rights to maintain an overseas military base, or the replacement of important officials in international organizations. Negotiations for the purpose of a *normalization* agreement are meant to terminate the abnormal or to formalize arrangements tacitly arrived at, such as to stop fighting through a cease-fire or truce, to re-establish diplomatic relations, or to end a temporary occupation in exchange for a military alliance and regularize other postwar uncertainties through a peace treaty.

Negotiations for the purpose of a *redistribution* agreement are characterized by a demand of an offensive side for a change in its favor, at the expense of a defensive side, the change consisting of a new distribution of territory, political influence, institutional powers and rights, economic and military assets, or the like. Essentially, what the offensive side gains, the defensive side loses; hence the offensive side has to couple its demand with the threat of causing worse consequences if the demand is refused. Negotiations for the purpose of an *innovation* agreement deal with the setting up of new relationships or obligations between the parties, with

Ikle, Fred, *How Nations Negotiate* (New York: Praeger Publishers, 1964). Reprinted with permission of Kraus Reprint.

the founding of a new institution, or with a new arrangement for controlling objects and areas. In contrast to redistribution, the change supposedly works to the advantage of all parties concerned, though not necessarily to equal advantage.[1] Finally, parties that negotiate for the sake of other *effects not concerning agreement* are interested in such results as propaganda, intelligence, or dissuading the opponent from the use of force.

Extension

The following recent negotiations are examples in which the extension type of objective predominated for both sides: the renewal of cultural exchange agreements between the United States and the Soviet Union, the extension of status-of-forces agreements between the United States and some of its allies, the renewal of the agreement for the sharing of financial burdens with NATO, and the replacement of Trygve Lie by Dag Hammarskjöld as Secretary-General of the United Nations. The outcome of such negotiations may be an agreement that simply confirms the status quo or one that makes slight changes in the existing relationship. (If there are major changes, the outcome represents a redistribution or innovation.) The initiative to negotiate might be taken by any one of the parties or by an international institution.

If no agreement is reached, the result is a change from the status quo; that is, there will be an interruption of customary relations between the parties or a discontinuation of the existing arrangements that were based on earlier agreements. Sometimes this interruption is avoided by a tacit understanding to extend the status quo temporarily; or to put it differently, the negotiatons result in a tacit extension. The principal incentives to agreement are the disadvantages of interrupting existing arrangements, as for example, the economic losses from an expired trade agreement, the inconvenience of an unfilled vacancy in an international organization, or the military disadvantage to one side and financial loss to the other if an agreement for a foreign base is not extended.

An important characteristic of negotiation for an extension is the strong influence exercised by the previous agreement. The old agreement limits the area of dispute, introduces weighty precedents, and may even provide specific means for settling differences regarding the renewal. For the replacement of officials in an international organization, for example, the institutional framework often circumscribes the choices and methods of negotiation quite narrowly. Sometimes there are arbitration procedures to bring in third parties if the original parties fail to reach agreement among themselves.

Normalization

Examples of negotiations where the main objective of all parties was a normalization agreement, are Litvinov's talks in Washington in 1933 leading to American recognition of the Soviet Union, the negotiations for the peace treaty with Japan in 1951, the negotiations between Egypt, Israel, and United Nations mediators on the armistice of 1949, the Panmunjom conference on the Korean armistice, and (to a large extent) the 1961–62 Geneva conference on Laos. At peace conferences, however, the principal parties frequently have other objectives, apart from normalization. The Paris Peace Conference of 1919–20 and the Potsdam Conference with its sequels from 1945 through 1946, for example, served purposes of redistribution and innovation as well as normalization. The League of Nations, an important issue at the Paris Peace Conference of 1919, is an example of an innovation.

In situations where fighting will continue to threaten to resume unless agreement is reached, public opinion and other domestic forces may exert considerable pressures on the negotiators to agree. Often, there are important asymmetries in the susceptibility to such pressures. American negotiators at Panmunjom and their superiors in Washington felt very strongly the yearning back home for an end to the fighting, but their Chinese and North Korean opponents—while sensitive to the military weakness of their side—remained relatively immune to popular sentiment in their countries.

Apart from these pressures for agreement, negotiations for the purpose of normalization are strongly influenced by the *instability* of the "abnormal" situation they are supposed to settle. If fighting continues while negotiations are prolonged, one side may gain through force what it failed to gain through bargaining. Or, at least, it may shake the opponent's confidence in his ability to defend his military position and thus make him anxious to reach an agreement. After a temporary suspension of fighting, however, the threat of a resumption of hostilities tends to become less effective for bargaining purposes, unless supported by existing military capabilities or preparations that make a new offensive both likely and dangerous to the opponent.

The Korean armistice negotiations would probably have led to an agreement much sooner, or on terms more favorable to the United Nations side, if the latter had been able to demonstrate to the Communist side that it might launch a major offensive. In the spring of 1953, when General Mark Clark as the UN Commander in Korea met President Dwight D. Eisenhower, he had prepared "a detailed estimate of the forces and plans required to obtain military victory in Korea should the new administration decide to take such a course." But according to General Clark, the newly elected President showed no interest in using the threat of such an offensive to exert pressure on the truce negotiations: "The question of how much it would take to win the war was never raised."[2]

In the event that no normalization agreement is reached, the "abnormal" situation will initially continue; but because of its instability, further changes usually ensue in short time. After the failure of cease-fire negotiations, continued fighting will change the fortunes of war; after the failure of truce negotiations, the cease-fire may erupt again into fighting. Conversely, hostilities may gradually subside despite the failure of negotiations, so that a tacit truce will in fact be established.

Redistribution

Negotiation for the purpose of redistribution is characterized by a clear and permanent division between an offensive side and a defensive side. The demand by the offensive side is often directed against one of the weaker or more exposed allies on the defensive side. In the most acute form of this type of negotiation, the offensive side presents its central demand in the form of an ultimatum (that is, a position put forward as final), with only ancillary issues left for bargaining, and it not only makes its threat highly specific but also announces that the threat will be carried out at a definite date unless the central demand is satisfied.

If the offensive side is successful, agreement in this type of negotiation will lead to a change in the status quo, as the defensive side complies with all or part of the demand. The classic illustrations are the Munich agreement and its sequel in March, 1939, when President Hácha of Czechoslovakia was forced to surrender the rest of his country to Hitler. There are other illustrations, however, of a far less aggressive character and an entirely different political tenor. For example, Iceland's claim in 1958 to a twelve-mile zone for exclusive fishery was backed up by the threat of force against British vessels. After some resistance, Great Britain, as the defensive side, essentially complied with the Icelandic demands.

If the offensive side is unsuccessful, an agreement may still result, whereby the defensive side consents to exchange some face-saving formula for a formal withdrawal of the demand. For example, the negotiations for the lifting of the Berlin blockade of 1948–49 resulted in an agreement by which the Western powers consented to a Foreign Ministers' conference with the Soviet Union, which was to start eleven days after the termination of the blockade and discuss problems regarding Germany and Berlin. (This conference reached no agreement of substance.) However, if either side is stubborn, redistribution negotiations may end without any agreement. In this case, there are two basic outcomes: either the status quo is preserved tacitly, which means that the offensive side gives in completely, or the offensive side carries out its threat or part of it. When the Soviet-Finnish negotiations in the fall of 1939 failed to induce Finland to cede the territories demanded by Russia, the Russians carried out their threat and attacked Finland.

There are some distinguishing features between negotiations for a redistribution and those for an innovation. In redistribution, the conflicting interest is the principal topic of negotiation, whereas the common interest remains tacit or is shunted into peripheral bargaining. The conflicting interest simply stems from the demand by the offensive side. The common interest lies in the mutual desire to avoid violence; that is, the offensive side would rather keep its gains more modest than carry out its threat, and the defensive side would rather relinquish something than challenge the threat. Occasionally, a complementary interest in an exchange is added to this basic common interest, such as the formal withdrawal of a threat in exchange for a face-saving formula, or the preservation of long-term friendship in exchange for a modest concession. (This was the idea of the British government when Mussolini demanded a free hand in Abyssinia: to buy Italy's friendship by granting Mussolini part of what he asked for.)

In negotiations for an innovation, on the other hand, it is the common interest, or alleged common interest, which constitutes the primary topic, while the conflicting interests are relegated to the details. Threats are scarcely used for innovations. But for redistributions, the offensive side must always threaten, or at least issue strong warnings.[8]

A demand for institutional changes in an international organization may have the objective of a redistribution of political power. In contrast to institutional innovations, such changes are clearly to the disadvantage of the defensive side. They are the issue of conflict, while the common interest, if any, is extraneous to them. An example is the Soviet demand that the United Nations Secretariat be headed by a "troika" instead of by a single, independent Secretary-General. Since this change was firmly opposed by many UN members, including all the other permanent members of the Security Council who had the power to veto it, the Soviet negotiators had no chance of success unless they could find an effective threat.

After the sudden death of Dag Hammarskhöld in 1961, it seemed as if the opportunity for such a threat had come. As expected, the Soviet negotiators tried to tie their demand for a "troika" to the threat they would veto the replacement of the single UN Secretary-General. In other words, they tried to link a redistribution agreement on the "troika" with an extension agreement for the staffing of the UN Secretariat. In the former they were opposed by parties that could veto the redistribution; in the latter they, in turn, could veto the kind of staffing that the same parties wanted. In principle, a tie-in between an extension and a redistribution agreement can be very effective—the offensive side trades its consent to the extension in exchange for the demanded redistribution. (This is the essence of labor-management negotiations.) In this particular case, however, the tie-in could have been used for a compromise only, since the "troika" could not be traded for the replacement of a *single* Secretary-General, the two being incompatible. As it turned out, the Soviet negotiators lacked the skill to advance their cause significantly by a compromise. (They might have succeeded, for instance, in obtaining a "troika" of powerful Deputy Secretaries, in exchange for their consent to the election of a single Secretary-General.)

There is an interesting difference in the reaction of public opinion to negotiation for normalization and for redistribution. A cease-fire, armistice, or peace treaty—the ostensible goal of negotiation for normalization—is usually supported by public opinion on both sides, and the publicized dispute concerns only the terms for settlement. (An exception is the propagandistically important opposition of Egypt and other Arab countris to a peace treaty with Israel.) In negotiations for redistribution, on the other hand, the offensive side usually appears in the public eye as the disturber of peace—unless the redistribution is aimed at the liberation of occupied areas or colonies. In modern times, if liberation or decolonization can be neither the true objective nor a plausible pretext, it takes someone as bold as Hitler to admit unashamedly that he is making a demand for a change entirely to his advantage. Although Hitler still used the pretense of liberating the Sudeten Germans in the Munich conference, he felt no embarrassment that he had to do without a pretext in the subsequent negotiations with Hácha.

Characteristically, Khrushchev says that his demands for West Berlin aim not for a change of the status quo to his advantage but for a normalization of the aftermath of World War II. As part of this tactic to enlist public support, Khrushchev argues that what he is after in West Berlin is merely to clear up old business: "The need to do away with the vestiges of World War II by signing a German peace treaty."[4] On the surface, Khrushchev's demands for a "free city" of West Berlin could be viewed as a normalization. But the Western powers fear that Khrushchev's real goal is a redistribution: to detach West Berlin from the Federal Republic of Germany—the ally of the West—and gradually to incorporate the city into the Communist bloc. The history of Eastern Europe since World War II gives ample ground for this interpretation.

Why Does the Defensive Side Negotiate at All?

In examining the motives of the defensive side for entering redistribution negotiations, one must distinguish two possibilities. In certain cases, the defensive side may have concluded that it is better to yield, for if it did not, the offensive side would in all likelihood carry out the threat, and this would result in greater losses than yielding would. Here negotiation has the purpose of cutting the losses—for instance, by obtaining a face-saving arrangement or some small compensation, or by improving the prospects for friendly long-term relations with the offensive side.

A recent example is the transfer of West New Guinea in 1962 from Dutch administration to Indonesia. It appeared very likely to the Netherlands and the United States (the latter being largely responsible for the settlement) that Sukarno would carry out his threat and attempt to take West New Guinea by force. Sukarno might, in fact, have welcomed a "war of liberation" to rally his people and cover up economic mismanagement at home. Although the Dutch might have successfully defended the territory (certainly if given American naval help), the losses from doing so seemed greater to the American government than the losses from giving up the territory, because West New Guinea was an economic burden for the Netherlands, and a war with Indonesia would have been costly and might have driven Sukarno closer to the Communists. (Of course, as in all appeasements, there was the question whether it might not do greater harm by setting a bad precedent and encouraging Sukarno to make further territorial demands.)

On the other hand, in many redistribution negotiations the defensive side has concluded that it is better not to yield, either because the costs of yielding seem greater than the costs from whatever the offensive side threatens or because it seems unlikely that the threat will be carried out. In such situations, why should the defensive side want to negotiate at all?

This very question has been a source of prolonged differences between Washington and London on one side and Paris on the other in connection with Khrushchev's demands for Berlin. The French government maintained that it was unwise for the Western powers to enter into or show interest in negotiations. In a speech to the French Parliament in December, 1961, the Foreign Minister, Couve de Murville, explained some of the objections to negotiating on Berlin:

> This problem, paradoxically, is whether the French, the Americans, and the British should take the initiative to propose to the Russians the setting-up of a four-power conference. I say "paradoxically" because, after all, it is the Russians who have raised the question of a change of status quo. Looking at it differently, it would mean that we should ask them to discuss their conditions for our staying in Berlin; that is, to discuss the concessions we would have to make to them so that they agree, to a certain extent and perhaps for a certain time only, that our troops can stay and that the freedom of West Berlin thus will remain more or less guaranteed.[5]

One can be more specific about the risks that the defensive side runs by negotiating on a redistribution demand. First, the negotiators of the defensive side might feel they ought to demonstrate flexibility; therefore they offer concessions that go some way toward satisfying the offensive demand. Second, they might lower their expectations and adapt their image of the status quo so as to bring it closer to the opponent's position (a process to be discussed later). Third, their view of the character of the negotiations may gradually change from a redistribution to a normalization. That is, they may come to regard a situation that has been the subject of prolonged negotiations as abnormal. Ergo, they will deem it appropriate to change the status quo so as to normalize it.

Despite these risks of negotiating, the governments of the defensive side may have countervailing reasons for meeting with their opponents, even though they conclude that they need not yield. They may be in favor of negotiation because they think that it has certain advantageous effects unrelated to any agreement. That is, they pursue side-effects. In addition, some Westerners when faced with certain offensive demands favor negotiation in order to find out what the opponent "really" wants. Thus they imply that the opponent could not be so brutish as to want what he in fact keeps demanding. They feel the opponent's true goal must be more reasonable or more realistic, and then a solution satisfactory to both sides could be found.

Innovation

Negotiations with the objective of innovation are meant to create a new relationship or new undertakings between parties. They are exemplified by the conferences on the Treaties of Rome to set up the Common Market and Euratom, the discussions on the treaty demilitarizing Antarctica, the conference for the statute for the International Atomic Energy Agency, and the marathon talks for a nuclear test ban. Disarmament negotiations normally pursue a mixture of objectives in which this type predominates.

As to the initiative, it is usually quite clear which party has made the first move proposing the innovation. Sometimes, this initiator continues to push for agreement; at other times, the initiative for the innovation may shift from one side to the other (in contrast to redistribution negotiations, where it is always the offensive side that wants the change). For example, in the nuclear test-ban negotiations it was at first clearly the Soviet Union that was pressing for a ban while the United States remained reluctant; but since 1960 or 1961 these roles have been reversed.

What pressures are available to the parties primarily interested in an innovation, to induce reluctant partners to agree? An important way of exerting pressure is the mobilization of domestic political support among the prospective partners. Jean Monnet's Action Committee for the United States of Europe has been instrumental in rallying the support of important political groups among the Six behind the Treaties of Rome and subsequent steps toward European integration. One of the important functions of the European Parliamentary Assembly in Strasbourg (the parliament of the Six) is the domestic support that it can generate within the member states to strengthen the hand of the European Executives on innovations advancing integration.[6] For innovations in the disarmament field, the initiators seek to exert pressures through public opinion within the countries of reluctant opponents as well as through neutral countries. (In part, these pressures may be designed to make the opponent disarm unilaterally, rather than to force an agreement on him.)

To win over those who hesitate to go along with an innovation, the warning of exclusion is often more effective than pressures of public opinion. A party that is at first reluctant or indifferent toward an innovation may join merely because it is afraid of becoming an outsider.

When President Eisenhower first proposed the creation of an International Atomic Energy Agency in December, 1953, he said that "the United States would be more than willing—it would be proud to take up with the others 'principally involved' the development of plans [for such an agency]. Of those 'principally involved,' the Soviet Union must, of course, be one."[7] The United States government followed up this invitation in a diplomatic exchange with Moscow, but the Soviet government took a negative attitude. Nine months after his initial proposal, President Eisenhower therefore declared: "Although progress in this plan has been impeded by Soviet obstruction and delay, we intend to proceed—*with* the cooperation and participation of the Soviet Union if possible, *without* it if necessary."[8] This warning was given weight by a number of American initiatives: among them the exploratory talks with seven other friendly nations and the rapid expansion, early in 1955, of bilateral agreements between the United States and twenty-four countries for aid on peaceful uses of atomic energy. A year later, the Soviet Union joined in establishing the International Atomic Energy Agency, after it obtained certain concessions modifying the original American design.[9]

In April, 1945, when Molotov came to see President Truman a few days before the United Nations was to be launched at San Francisco, it seemed uncertain whether the Russians would cooperate in creating the new world organization, since deep differences had already arisen over the Yalta agreements. President Truman told Molotov that the United States was determined to go ahead with plans for the world organization, or as the President put it privately to his advisers, that he "intended to go on with the plans for San Francisco and if the Russians did not wish to join us they could go to hell. . . ."[10]

The warning of exclusion, however, is ineffective against a government which thinks the innovation will not be successful (or would not succeed without its participation). A cardinal error of British foreign policy during the 1950s was the belief that European integration would not succeed. In 1950, the British turned down the Franco-German invitation to participate in the negotiations which translated the Schuman Plan into the Coal and Steel Community, and in 1955 they stayed away from the Conference of Messina which established the principles for the European Economic Community and Euratom. Subsequently they sent only an observer to the committee of experts which, on the basis of the Messina principles, prepared the report that led to the Treaties of Rome. And they soon withdrew their observer again when pressed to assume a positive attitude toward European integration.[11]

While the initiator of an innovation will want to have essential parties included, he has to be careful lest his efforts to win over reluctant participants jeopardize his basic goals. In the negotiations for the implementation of the Schuman Plan, Jean Monnet removed the principle of a supra-national authority as a topic of dispute and compromise by making its acceptance the condition for participation in the negotiations. The British refused to meet this condition.[12] It has occasionally been said that such a condition is contrary to diplomatic practice among friendly nations. With perhaps more validity, however, it might be argued that, without violating diplomatic standards, initiators of a new proposal who invite others to discuss its implementation may define the agenda so as to exclude alternatives incompatible with their proposal.

There are many situations where the initiator of an innovation cannot use the warning of exclusion to win over reluctant parties. The participation of certain countries may be so essential that their exclusion would make negotiations meaningless. In any diarmament negotiation of a global scope, the United States and the Soviet Union, of course, play such a role. So would Communist China and several other powers, if disarmament progressed beyond the initial phase.

Other situations do allow the warning of exclusion to be used against essential parties. An interesting example is the Antarctica treaty. In spite of the fact that Soviet participation was essential for an agreement to *demilitarize* the region, the

United States, as the initiator, did have a warning of exclusion available. If the Soviet government had obstructed agreement (for example, by objecting to inspection), the United States could have switched from the demilitarization project to a project for *regional security* based on the exclusion of the Soviet Union. (The only countries close to Antarctica are U.S. allies and South Africa, and all claims to Antarctic territory were made by allies, with the only unclaimed sector generally recognized as a potential U.S. claim. Given allied cooperation—an important qualification!—the Soviet Union could have been effectively excluded, for example, through a condominium.) This possibility never came into the open during the negotiations, in part because the conflict of interest was relatively mild—unlike the usual feeling in disarmament negotiations. Nonetheless, as a latent threat it may have contributed significantly to the successful conclusion of the Antarctica treaty.

The warning of exclusion can be ineffective for two reasons: either the innovation is meaningless without the participation of those who oppose it, or it requires approval by an international organization in which the opponents have a veto. It is for the latter reason that initiatives for revising the United Nations Charter have made so little headway.

There are cases, however, when even the obstacle of the veto has been overcome. The treaty of the European Economic Community provided that a common agricultural policy be gradually established according to certain principles, but it left all the important details to future negotiations. France expected to be the chief beneficiary of the integration of agriculture, while Germany stood to lose; and without German consent, agricultural integration would have been held up.[13] Initially it seemed that the French negotiators had no leverage to win German consent. But when the transition of the Common Market from its first to its second stage came up for negotiation in 1961, the French refused to agree to it unless agricultural integration was included. This created sufficient pressure on the Germans, since they were generally interested in the transition to the second stage (as were the other members of the Common Market). This *iunctim*, as the Germans call such a tie-in, combined two innovations: one (the transition to the second stage) in the interest of all the parties, and another (agricultural integration) in the interest of only some of the essential parties.

The French government was less interested than the other members of the Common Market in the transition to the second stage as such, apart from the integration of agriculture. Or at least it gave the appearance of being less interested, which was made easy by its well-known coldness toward the majority voting provided in the second stage. This lack of interest was an essential aspect of the *iunctim*, because it made credible the French threat to veto the transition. The *iunctim* also had the advantage of offsetting the domestic strength of the German farmers, who were opposed to agricultural integration, with the strength of industrial and other groups in Germany that wanted to have the Common Market move into its second stage.

Incidentally, the history of the provision in the Common Market treaty which enabled France to veto the second stage illustrates how negotiators sometimes acquire a bargaining advantage by accident or for the wrong reason. This provision was requested by France and reluctantly accepted by the other five member-countries in 1956 in the belief that the French economy might need an escape from rapid integration. But in 1961 the French could use this escape clause for almost the opposite purpose: to prevent the Germans from escaping a more rapid integration of agriculture.

As a sidelight on the types of objectives for negotiation, it is worth noting that domestic groups opposed to an innovation always picture it as a redistribution to the detriment of their own country. This happened with the various moves in European integration, where at one time the Germans were supposed to gain at the expense of the French, at another time the French or Italians at the expense of the Germans. Similarly, the nuclear test ban has been criticized by some Americans as resulting in military gains for the Soviet Union with no offsetting advantages for the United States.

Side-Effects

The very process of negotiation can have important effects which do not concern agreement. These "side-effects" may be one of the reasons—or sometimes the only reason—why governments engage in diplomatic talks. Indeed, side-effects may provide the motive not only for going along with negotiations started by others but even for *initiating* negotiations. Proposals and speeches at the conference table, contacts with the opponent's diplomats, and the interest aroused among third parties may all contribute to various foreign-policy aims without leading to a settlement of the issues ostensibly discussed. For example, the negotiating process (or its simulation) can launch propaganda, produce intelligence, or modify political attitudes of nonparticipants.

If Western governments are engaged in negotiations where agreement appears highly unlikely or even undesirable, they frequently stress certain benefits from such side-effects. Of course, these side-effects may not materialize, or if they do, they may not meet the expectations of the parties that pursued them. Also, it is sometimes doubtful whether these alleged benefits are the real reason for negotiating or whether a government advances them to rationalize what it is doing out of habit or to conceal the fact that it clings to unrealistic hopes for a satisfactory agreement.

Side-effects are such an essential aspect of negotiation that they must be discussed more fully. Before going on, however, it may be worthwhile to scrutinize the five types of negotiation objectives as a group in Table 15-1.

Table 15-1
Five Objectives of Negotiation

	Extension Agreement	Normalization Agreement	Redistribution Agreement	Innovation Agreement	Side-Effects
Subject of negotiation	Continuation of normal (renewals or replacements).	Termination of abnormal (cease-fire, truce, resumption of diplomatic relations).	New distribution in favor of offensive side (surrender of territory, liberation of colonies).	New institutions or other arrangements of mutual interest.	
Main characteristics of negotiating process	Strong influence of previous agreement: as a precedent, and in limiting area of dispute.	Strong influence of situation at time of negotiations. Domestic or third-party pressures toward normalization.	Continuous division between offensive and defensive side. Continuous open threat of offensive side.	Inducement of mutual benefits, and risk of exclusion. A specially interested party may act as initiator.	The less likely the agreement, the more important the side-effects.
In case of prolonged negotiations	Both sides lose.	In case of continuing hostilities, stronger party may win by force instead of negotiation.	Defensive side postpones loss, but redistribution may begin to look like normalization.	Interest in innovation may shift from one side to the other.	Side-effects continue to flow from negotiating process.
In case of *no* agreement	Interruption of customary arrangements.	*Either* continuation of fighting (or of abnormal relations) *or* subsiding of fighting (tacit truce).	*Either* status quo *or* implementation of threat by offensive side.	Continuation of status quo	Side-effects nonetheless materialize and may be used to vindicate negotiations.

Notes

1. Thomas C. Schelling (*The Strategy of Conflict*, [Oxford: Oxford University Press, 1960], p. 21) introduces the distinction between the "efficiency" aspect of bargaining and the "distributional" aspect: the former consists of exploring for mutually profitable adjustments; in the latter the better bargain for one party means less for the other. Innovation negotiations are clearly dominated by "efficiency" bargaining, while redistribution negotiations are dominated by "distributional" bargaining. In extension and normalization negotiations, these two aspects are usually mixed. There are, of course, many gradations between a pure redistribution and innovation negotiation, ranging from exclusively "distributional" negotiation, through mixed "distributional-efficiency" bargaining, to purely "efficiency" cases.

2. Mark W. Clark, *From the Danube to the Yalu* (New York: Harper, 1954), p. 233.

3. A distinction between "threats" and "warnings" is developed in Fred Ikle, *How Nations Negotiate* (New York: Praeger, 1964), chap. 5.

4. *Tass* statement of July 12, 1962. This is a constantly recurrent theme in the Soviet statements on Berlin.

5. *Journal Officiel de la République Française* (Sénat), Dec. 5, 1961, p. 2297.

6. These three Executives (the High Authority of the Coal and Steel Community and the Commissions of the Common Market and Euratom) use resolutions by the European Parliament to defend their position in the Council of Ministers (which represents the six governments). The ministers normally do not want to disregard the views of the European parliamentarians, who are also members of their home parliaments.

7. Address by President Eisenhower to the United Nations, Dec. 3, 1953.

8. The President's press release at the signing of the Atomic Energy Act, Aug. 30, 1954.

9. In the fall of 1955 the Soviet Union entered the negotiations on the preparation of the statute for the Agency, and in October, 1956, the revised Statute was finally adopted by 81 nations. For an excellent history see Bernard G. Bechhoefer, "Negotiating the Statute of the International Atomic Energy Agency," *International Organization* 13 (Winter 1959): 38–59.

10. Harry S. Truman, *Memoirs* (Garden City, N.Y.: Doubleday, 1955), I, 80; and Walter Millis (ed.), *The Forrestal Diaries* (New York: Viking, 1951), p. 50. Three days earlier, however, the President was less sanguine; when Harriman asked him whether America would go ahead with the United Nations plans even if the Russians dropped out, Truman replied the truth of the matter was that without Russia there would not be a world organization (*Memoirs*, I, 72).

11. Karl Kaiser, *EWG und Freihandelszone* (Leiden: Sythoff, 1963), p. 37.

12. According to Anthony Nutting (*Europe Will Not Wait* [London: Hollis & Carter, 1960], p. 29), this condition merely provided the British government with the excuse it wanted for staying out.

13. After the first two stages of the Common Market, the agricultural policy could have been adopted by majority vote. From the French vantage point in 1961, not only would this have meant considerable postponement, but in view of the possible entry of Great Britain and other countries, the opposition to agricultural integration might also have become stronger.

Discussion Questions

1. Are there any special attributes that make arms control negotiations different from other types of negotiations? Are side effects more or less important?

2. How would you analyze current arms negotiations using Ikle's categories?

3. Do you feel that any of Ikle's objectives are more likely or desirable than the others? Why or why not?

16

The Global Politics of Arms Sales

Andrew Pierre

Arms sales have become, in recent years, a crucial dimension of international affairs. They are now major strands in the warp and woof of world politics. Arms sales are far more than an economic occurrence, a military relationship, or an arms control challenge—*arms sales are foreign policy writ large.*

The dramatic expansion in arms sales to the developing world during the 1970s is by now widely known. Less clear is what judgment to make of this important phenomenon.

To some observers, the arms delivered feed local arms races, create or enhance regional instabilities, make any war that occurs more violent or destructive, and increase the tendency for outside powers to be drawn in. The arms received are often seen as unnecessary to the true needs of the purchasing country and as a wasteful diversion of scarce economic resources. The remedy often proposed is drastic curtailment of arms sales, with tight international controls as the best means for achieving this.

To others, the recent increase in arms sales is no cause for particular concern. Sovereign nations have every right to the weapons that they deem necessary. By giving or selling arms the supplier country acquires political influence or friendship. It receives economic benefits. Regional peace and stability may be advanced rather than hindered by the transfer of arms. In any case, there is little that can be done about the international trade in arms. If one country does not sell the weapons, some other state will be only too happy to oblige. Accordingly, seeking international restraints is a will-o'-the-wisp.

Neither judgment is fully right or wrong. In order to be better understood, the arms trade phenomenon must be viewed in the wider context of the transformations under way in world politics.

Arms sales must be seen, essentially, in *political* terms. The world is undergoing a diffusion of power—political, economic, and military—from the industrialized, developed states to the Third World and the so-called Fourth World (poor and without oil). The acquisition of conventional arms, often sophisticated and usually in far greater quantities than the recipient state previously had, is a critical element of that diffusion.

Arms are a major contributing factor to the emergence of regional powers such as Israel, Brazil, South Africa, or, until recently, Iran; their purchase makes a deep impact upon regional balances and local stability. The diffusion of defense capabilities contributes at the same time to the erosion of the early postwar system of imperial or hegemonic roles formerly played by the major powers around the globe. Thus the superpowers, and even the medium-sized powers such as Britain and France, are losing the ability to "control" or influence events in their former colonies or zones of special influence. And the transfer of conventional arms is only one element of the diffusion of military power. Another, of prime importance, is the trend toward nuclear proliferation. As we shall see, the relationship between the two is intricate and complex.

Arms sales must also be seen in the context of North-South issues. They constitute a form of redistribution of power whose significance in certain cases may be equal to or greater than that of some of the well-recognized economic forms. Certainly the withholding or granting of arms can have a great political and psychological impact. Arms transfers can also be a form of transfer of technology; an increasing number of states do not want the weapons fresh out of the crate but the technology that will enable them to build, or "co-produce," them at home.

Finally, arms sales remain a key element of the continuing East-West competition. Indeed, they may now be the prime instrument available to the Soviet Union, and a significant one for the United States, in their rivalry for the allegiance of much of the world. The condition of mutual deterrence at the nuclear level, and the risk that a conventional conflict could quickly or uncontrollably escalate to the nuclear level, make a direct military confrontation between the two superpowers unlikely—hence the tendency toward competition by "proxy" in the Third World, with the superpowers supporting friendly states or regimes, or (in the case of the Communist states) assisting "movements of national liberation." Sometimes alliances and the identification of "friends" alter quickly, as happened in the Horn of Africa where the Soviet Union initially supported Somalia with arms and the United States supported Ethiopia, only to see their respective roles reversed. A contributing factor to the emerging importance of arms transfers as an instrument of the East-West competition has been the relative decline of ideology as an element in the continuing struggle, because of the diminishing attractiveness of both the United States and the Soviet Union as models. Yet another factor has been the declining size and role of economic and developmental assistance. Both the United States and the Soviet Union now give less in economic assistance than the value of their arms sales.

Arms do not of themselves lead to war. The causes of war are manifold and complex, but the underlying roots are usually found in political, economic, territorial, or ideological competition. Yet arms sent into a region may exacerbate tensions, spur an arms race, and make it more likely that, as Clausewitz taught us, war will emerge as the continuation of politics by other means. Once war has started, the existence of large and sophisticated stocks of weapons may make the conflict more violent and destructive. And if the arms have been acquired from abroad, often with the establishment of a resupply relationship and sometimes including the presence of technical advisers from the producing country, they may have a tendency to draw the supplier into the conflict. Yet these undesirable developments need not be inevitable. Arms may deter aggression, restore a local imbalance, and generally enhance stability. All depends upon the specifics of the case and the perceptions that exist about it.

Nevertheless, the people of the world can take little comfort from the trend toward a higher level of global armaments. Total world military expenditures have grown from $100 billion in 1960 to $500 billion in 1980. Measured in constant prices this is an increase of 80 percent. The rise in arms spending in the developing world has been especially acute. Since 1960 military expenditures in the Third World have risen over fourfold (in constant prices), while those in developed countries have gone up a more modest 48 percent.[1] (Note 1, this chapter, discusses fully the data base for this study.)

For all these reasons, we need a more complete and sophisticated understanding of the global politics of arms sales. We also need to think more creatively, as well as realistically, about developing some type of international management for the process of transferring weapons.

Neither of these aims is easy to achieve. What we term the global politics of arms sales involves an enormous number of variables: the foreign affairs of close to 150 nations; their economic affairs, ranging from their industrial or development policies to questions of balance of payments and trade; their approach toward the acquisition or sale of technology; their perceptions of the threats to their national security and what must be undertaken to maintain it. This involves, in turn, a very large number of bilateral and multilateral relationships. Arms are usually sought because of the desire to maintain security vis-à-vis one's neighbors, or to enhance one's role and status within a region—hence the importance of a regional approach to both comprehending and controlling arms transfers. This regional emphasis is reinforced by the present diffusion of political, economic, and military power away from the principal postwar centers of power and influence.

Beyond the task of better understanding the arms transfer phenomenon is the need to manage or regulate it But this is uncommonly difficult because of the lack of norms by which to measure restraints and controls, or even of agreement on the basic necessity for them. With regard to the spread of nuclear weapons capabilities, a general consensus has been reached in the world that nuclear proliferation is undesirable. There are some exceptions to this agreement but they are quite negligible. The nuclear non-proliferation debate today, significant as it is, is about the means for preventing or retarding proliferation, not about the widely accepted end goal. No equivalent consensus exists on the proliferation of conventional arms.

With regard to conventional arms three general points of view can be identified. Some persons perceive arms to be inherently wasteful or even evil. They seek a maximum curtailment of their production and distribution. At the opposite end of the spectrum are those who make no moral judgment on arms and who view their sale abroad as essentially a commercial activity. They would prefer to have a minimum of regulation by governments, with the arms trade left to the forces of the marketplace. A third perspective—and the one reflected in this study—is primarily concerned with the impact of arms transfers upon regional stability and international security. Arms transfers, it is argued, should be managed so as to prevent or contain conflict and enhance the forces of moderation and stability.

But how are such laudable purposes to be achieved? Assuming that some restraints or controls over arms transfers are desirable in principle, how are they to be created in practice? Underneath the practical aspects of the problem is the difficulty in making normative judgments that have universal applicability.

A particular sale may be destabilizing, or it may restore a balance. It may promote an arms race in a region, or it may act so as to deter a potential conflict. Moreover, what is true in the short run may not hold true for the longer term. Who is to say how a weapon transferred now could be employed in ten years' time? And who can vouchsafe that the political leadership of a country will be as sober and "responsible" about the use of weapons in the future as it appears at present? Or that the alliances and foreign policy alignments of today—upon which the prospective supplier must base his decision—will be the same tomorrow?

Arms sales are fraught with policy dilemmas. There are no easy answers to the above questions. There are no "simple truths" to guide policy makers. Even when a supplier country has adopted general policy guidelines, each weapons transfer decision will involve complex judgments and trade-offs. Long-term risks must be weighed against shorter-term benefits. The prospective economic advantages of a sale may have to be balanced against potentially disadvantageous political or arms control consequences. One foreign policy goal, such as strengthening an alliance relationship or a nation's capacity for self-defense, may run counter to another goal, such as promoting human rights. As the debates of recent years on individual arms transfers show, one can almost take for granted that every decision will involve competing objectives.

Trends In Transfers

It is, of course, the major increase in both the quantity and the quality of arms sent to the Third World that has given this problem its current salience. Complete and reliable data on arms transfers are not readily available. Governments are not inclined to release data that could prove to be embarrassing either at home or abroad. Nevertheless, enough is known to give a reasonably accurate impression of the trends. [See figures 16–1 and 16–2.]

Shares by Suppliers

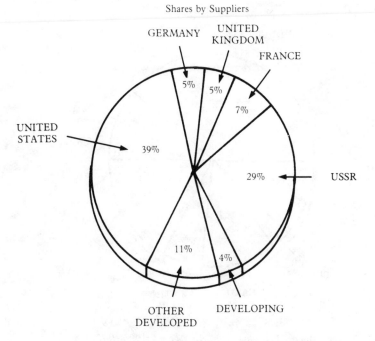

Source: ACDA, *World Military Expenditures and Arms Transfers 1968–1977,* p. 10.
Figure 16–1. World Arms Exports, 1977

In worldwide terms, arms transfers have more than doubled in the past decade, having grown from $9.4 billion in 1969 to $19.1 in 1978 (in constant dollars).[2] At the beginning of the 1980s most estimates of arms sales worldwide were on the order of $21 billion per annum.

The United States has been the largest supplier of conventional arms and has had the greatest increase in sales. American foreign military sales (the accounting for these sales includes items other than weapons, such as training and logistical assistance, which can account for 40 percent of the total) totaled $1.1 billion in 1970 and rose sharply to $15.8 billion in 1975.[3] They have since remained above $10 billion per annum, with a projected all-time high for 1981 of $16 billion. As sales went up, however, there was a decline in grant aid through military assistance programs. Equally significant has been the more than quadrupling of the French and British export of arms since 1970, as well as a marked increase in the level of Soviet transfers.

Changes in the qualitative dimension of the arms trade have been as significant as its quantitative expansion. [See table 16–1.] In the past, most arms transferred to less developed countries were the obsolete weapons of the major powers which

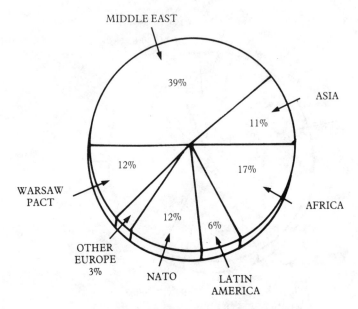

Source: ACDA, *World Military Expenditures and Arms Transfers 1968-1977*, p. 8.

Figure 16-2. World Arms Imports, 1977

Table 16-1

Imports of Arms by Developed and Developing Nations, 1969-1978

(billions of constant (1977) U.S. dollars)

Year	Developed Nations	Developing Nations	Total
1969	3.2	6.2	9.4
1970	2.7	6.4	9.1
1971	2.5	6.9	9.4
1972	4.4	10.3	14.7
1973	4.6	13.0	17.6
1974	4.1	10.2	14.3
1975	3.9	10.1	14.0
1976	4.4	12.9	17.3
1977	4.1	15.2	19.3
1978	3.6	15.5	19.1

Source: Calculated from ACDA, *World Military Expenditures and Arms Transfers 1969-1978*, p. 117.

they wanted to eliminate from their inventories to make room for new, more advanced ones. Often they were gifts from surplus stocks of over-age, technologically inferior equipment. Thus many of the arms transferred to the Third World prior to the 1970s were still of the World War II, or early postwar, vintage. Even in the early 1960s, the aircraft transferred to the developing world more often than not were ten-year-old American F-86s and Soviet MiG-17s rather than the first-line planes of the period (such as F-4s and MiG-21s). In contrast, today many of the arms being sold are among the most sophisticated in the inventories of the supplier states. This is strikingly evident with certain advanced fighter aircraft. The F-15, the most sophisticated plane of its type, is being sold to Saudi Arabia and Israel, and plans are in progress to have it co-produced in Japan; the Soviet MiG-23 is being exported to several nations in the Middle East, as is the French Mirage F-1. It is less evident, but equally significant, in smaller yet very advanced systems such as the TOW anti-tank missile, which was not released from the American inventory until the critical stages of the Yom Kippur War but has now been approved for sale to more than a dozen countries. As was the case with the $1.3 billion sale of the Airborne Warning and Control System (AWACS) aircraft to Iran, foreign orders have been accepted while the producing country was still deciding about procurement for its own armed forces. Foreign orders have occasionally been given higher priority than domestic ones or have become the necessary element in a favorable decision to start a production run to equip the supplying country's own armed forces.

Another dimension of the qualitative change has been the significant growth in the transfer of arms through co-production agreements. These enable states to acquire through licensing arrangements the knowledge to manufacture or to assemble a weapons system. More than two dozen developing countries now participate in such arrangements. As a result of this trend, there has been a spread in sophisticated weaponry around the globe.

The acquisition of a new weapon by one country in a particular region creates strong pressures in the surrounding countries for the acquisition of comparable weapons. In 1960 only four developing nations had supersonic combat aircraft; by 1977 the total had risen to forty-seven. There has been a similar proliferation with respect to long-range surface-to-air missiles, from two nations in 1960 to twenty-seven by the mid-1970s.[4]

A third change has been in the direction of the arms flows. Until the mid-1960s most weapons transferred went to developed countries, usually the NATO allies of the United States or the Warsaw Pact allies of the Soviet Union. It was not until the war in Southeast Asia in the second half of the decade that the dominant portion went to the developing world. Nor was the trend reversed by the end of the Vietnam War. During the late 1970s the Persian Gulf and Middle East countries received by far the largest portion of arms. Iran, Saudi Arabia, and Israel were the major recipients of Western arms, while most Soviet weapons were shipped to Syria, Iraq,

Libya, and, a little earlier, Egypt. The importation of weapons by Third World countries rose from $6.2 billion in 1969 to $15.5 billion in 1978 (in constant dollars).[5] [See table 16–2.] Over three-quarters of the global arms trade now goes to the Third World. No area has not seen some growth in its imports; after the Persian Gulf and Middle East, the most notable increases have been in arms sent to Africa and Latin America.

Quite interestingly, only a very small number of countries constitute the principal suppliers of arms, thereby maintaining the pattern of the past twenty-five years. Four states accounted for 87.5 percent of the value of the major weapons transferred to the developing world during the decade of the 1970s: the United States (45 percent), the Soviet Union (27.5 percent), France (10 percent), and Britain (5 percent). When one adds a few members of the NATO alliance (West Germany, Canada, Italy, the Netherlands) and the Soviet Union's Warsaw Pact ally Czechoslovakia, the figure is raised to 94.3 percent. The largest supplier not included in one of the two alliances is the People's Republic of China, but it only accounts for slightly more than 1 percent of transfers.[6] Other industrialized countries that export arms, such as Sweden and Switzerland, are still relatively minor suppliers.

There are a number of new arms manufacturers within the so-called Third World (a misnomer for which there is no satisfactory alternative) such as Brazil, South Korea, India, South Africa, and Israel that are developing their industries and actively seeking export markets. This is a relatively recent phenomenon. Two decades ago almost none of the states in Asia, Africa, and Latin America could

Table 16–2
Weapons Delivered to the Third World by Category, 1972–1978

Equipment Description	United States	U.S.S.R.	Major West European Nations
Tanks and self-propelled guns	6,110	8,570	2,090
Artillery	3,715	6,310	955
Armored cars and personnel carriers	9,735	6,975	2,430
Major surface combatants	83	7	17
Minor surface combatants	157	94	247
Submarines	24	9	20
Guided missile boats	0	60	15
Supersonic combat aircraft	11,160	1,990	355
Subsonic combat aircraft	925	390	35
Helicopters	1,730	575	1,180
Other aircraft	1,520	260	855
Surface-to-air-missiles (SAMs)	6,240	15,745	1,065

Source: U.S., Congress, Senate, Committee on Foreign Relations, *Prospects for Multilateral Arms Export Restraint*, Staff Report, 96th Cong., 1st sess., April 1979, p. 11.

produce arms indigenously. Arms production in the Third World is likely to continue to expand at a steady rate and is a new dimension of world politics. But . . . because these countries are mainly dealing in second-echelon technology, and in most cases cannot provide the political support the principal suppliers do, which is often part of the attraction of doing business with them, these new arms producers are unlikely to present a serious challenge to the four major suppliers. From 1969 to 1978 arms exports by developing countries grew from $276 million to $837 million (in constant dollars), but this only accounted for 4.4 percent of world arms exports.[7]

This configuration of the suppliers becomes significant when one considers opportunities for developing some form of arms control or international management for arms transfers. . . . The domination of the arms trade by the Big Four should facilitate efforts in this direction because they are but four and, in effect, have an oligopoly. Moreover, they all have experience and past involvement in the pursuit of common objectives, either in East-West arms control negotiations or in intra-Western alliance diplomacy. As much as 67 percent of arms transfers to the Third World were undertaken in 1978 by members of NATO, while the Warsaw Pact accounted for another 29 percent.[8]

Uncertain Rationales for Arms Sales

The dilemmas created by the international trade in arms, which face decision makers presented with an arms transfer request, arise from the difficulty in reaching a judgment as to whether a given transfer would be "good" or "bad." This can best be illustrated by examining some of the justifications traditionally given for making weapons sales or grants. We do this here in general terms, postulating the justifications and questioning or examining their validity, before turning in the following sections to some of the more specific situations and dilemmas that exist in particular countries and regions.

Influence and Leverage

A major political rationale for arms transfers has been the influence the supplier gains in dealings with the recipient nation. Arms can be an important symbol of support and friendly relations and thereby create influence. Arguments for the sale of weapons to China have been based not so much on the need to enhance its military capabilities against the Soviet Union, for the Chinese will remain comparatively weak under any circumstances, as to demonstrate American friendship and further the normalization of relations. After the invasion of Afghanistan, pressure on the Soviet Union became an additional objective. Similarly, the Soviet Union has transferred arms to Arab states and to national liberation movements as a demonstration of ideological support or affinity. Moscow sold weapons to Peru on a long-term, low-interest basis in order to establish a base of influence in South America. American arms sales to Saudi Arabia have been justified by the need to maintain a "special relationship" with that country.

Arms may provide access to political and military elites. This has been the traditional justification for many of the U.S. military assistance programs to Latin American nations, where often there was no serious military threat or need for arms. The continuing contacts between defense establishments, which accompany arms transfers through training missions and the sending of Latin American military officers to U.S. military schools, is thought to be important because of the political role played by the military on the continent. Similarly, the Soviet Union has competed with China for access to foreign elites through the sale of weapons to countries such as Indonesia and India.

When countries are dealing with established allies, arms can give substance to treaty commitments. NATO and the Warsaw Pact are the most obvious cases. But in a more fluid situation where there is no formal alliance, and when a prospective recipient may turn to one side or the other, the argument for an arms transfer has often been made on preemptive grounds: to deny the transfer, and the influence that presumably flows with it, to the competing side. Many recipient countries have become adept at this game. Faced with American reluctance to provide a modern air defense system, King Hussein of Jordan discussed such a purchase with the Soviet Union in 1975 before being able to get from the United States the 500 Hawk surface-to-air missiles that he wanted. Preemptive selling is not limited to the East-West competition but often occurs between Western states, although the motivations in such cases are more commercial.

The most important political benefit of arms transfers may be leverage over other countries' sensitive foreign policy decisions. In the Arab-Israeli conflict, the offer of arms has been used to make difficult political and territorial decisions more acceptable. Former Secretary of State Henry Kissinger, who was especially inclined to use arms transfers as an instrument of foreign policy, promised Israel substantial amounts of new weapons (including the first sale of the F-15 to another country) in exchange for its leaders' approval of the 1975 Sinai disengagement agreement. The Carter administration's decision in 1978 to sell F-5E fighters to Egypt was strongly influenced by the need to buoy up Anwar Sadat in order to dissuade him from breaking off the peace negotiations after the initiative he had launched seemed to be going nowhere. Implicit in the large-scale provision of arms to Iran and Saudi Arabia was the belief that this would make it less likely that the Shah or King Khalid would support an OPEC embargo cutting off the supply of oil.

Yet one must be very cautious in accepting some of the generalized justifications for arms transfers. Influence and leverage are transitory phenomena: they can be lost even more quickly than they are acquired. The Soviet Union developed a close relationship with Egypt when it began supplying arms in 1955; after it refurbished the Egyptian armed forces following the 1967 war it gained the use of naval facilities in Alexandria for its Mediterranean fleet and access to air bases, and greatly augmented its physical presence in the country. Still, the very existence of this arms supply relationship led to friction between Cairo and Moscow. Sadat expelled the Soviet advisers in 1972, and after the Yom Kippur War changed the orientation of Egypt's foreign policy toward close ties with the United States. To take another example, the United States brought promising military officers to the States for training as part of its Latin American military assistance programs, partially in order to indoctrinate them with the democratic values it sought for the Western hemisphere; yet the leaders of most of the military juntas that today exercise repression and violate human rights in Latin America are graduates of these programs.

The most vivid demonstration of the uncertain nature of the influence that arms can achieve is the course of events in Iran. Because the United States sold large quantities of sophisticated arms to Teheran, it was seen by many Iranians as a strong supporter of the Shah—to some he was even an "American puppet," with the arms the most visible symbol of American support. Came the revolution, the United States was thoroughly discredited. Not only did it lose all influence, but America became *the* enemy against which conflicting groups within Iran rallied so as to achieve a common goal. If arms sales have the effect of closely associating the supplier with a certain regime in a country, and that regime is overturned, the former association can have serious negative consequences. Local conditions can always change, and general assumptions that underpin the sought-after influence or leverage are always subject to being undermined.

One can also question the essence of the leverage that arms provide over specific foreign policy decisions. The United States used its arms relationships with success in deterring a war between Greece and Turkey in 1967, but in 1974 it was powerless to prevent Turkey's invasion of Cyprus. Nor, it should be noted, did the subsequent arms embargo legislated by the Congress succeed in bringing about Turkish concessions; on the contrary, Ankara responded by placing restrictions on NATO bases in the country. Western largess in making arms available to Iran (in some cases delaying the equipping of the supplier state's armed forces) did not persuade the Shah to help keep oil prices down; Iran was a consistent advocate within OPEC for higher oil prices—in part, to help pay for the weapons it was purchasing.

Indeed, the provision of arms can even give the recipient "reverse leverage" over the supplier. Perhaps the most striking example of this occurred during the Vietnam War when America's deep commitment to that country was played upon by the Thieu government in vetoing various peace proposals. A different kind of reverse leverage can exist when arms have been made available in exchange for base rights. In the Philippines, for example, Washington has been limited in the extent to which it can make known American disagreement with the internal human rights policies of the Marcos government. Washington's continued dependence on U.S. bases for its Pacific strategy encouraged Manila to demand substantial military and economic assistance in return for the use of bases on Philippine soil.

The transfer of arms can go so far as to make the supplier hostage to the recipient. As a 1976 report to the Senate Foreign Relations Committee on American arms sales to Iran noted, the large-scale sales to Teheran invariably involved a commitment to provide support for the weapons. The United States could not abandon its arms-support activities without provoking a major crisis in Iranian-U.S. relations (and such a crisis, were it to occur, could have a major consequence for the supply of oil). If Iran had become involved in a war then, it would have been difficult to keep American personnel uninvolved. Thus the 24,000 American personnel in Iran at the time, whose number was expected to increase substantially in the coming years as more arms were scheduled to be delivered, could physically become hostages at a moment of crisis. The report concluded that because of the political symbolism that stems from a close supplier-client arms relationship, "it is not clear *who really has influence over whom* in time of an ambiguous crisis situation."[9] Although events did not proceed exactly as foreseen—they rarely do—the warning was prescient. Reverse leverage of another type came into play in the spring of 1981 when the level of Saudi oil production was linked to arms sales. Speaking on American television Sheik Ahmed Zaki Yamani, the Saudi oil minister, stressed the importance that his country attached to the planned sale of five AWACS planes in the context of a discussion on both the price and the future output of Saudi oil.

In short, it is clear that the provision of arms may provide influence and leverage. Arms sales can be important tools of foreign policy. As such, they are attractive to policy makers who are in immediate need of instruments to help implement their strategies.

But experience suggests that the politial value of arms sales in global politics can be overrated. Creating an arms supply relationship is not sufficient to cement relations between two countries and entails certain risks. The influence acquired may be of surprisingly short duration. The amount of leverage will depend upon the alternatives available to the recipient state. If there are other suppliers, then the degree of leverage will be less than if the recipient has little or no choice. The supplier may find that there are incalculable political costs in applying leverage. The recipient may come to regret his dependence and the implicit conditions attached to a sale. In short, the transfer of arms can often create an uncertain and symbiotic supplier-recipient relationship which ends up limiting the freedom of action of both.

Security and Stability

Another traditional rationale for supplying arms is to help fulfill the security requirements of allies and friends. From the early postwar period until the mid-1970s, when most U.S. arms transfers were in the form of military grants, this was the basic reason for transferring arms to NATO and to other allies such as Japan and South Korea. As the danger thought to be posed by internal subversion in South Vietnam and elsewhere came to occupy the attention of the Kennedy administration, arms for purposes of counterinsurgency were deemed to be important. Later, the Nixon Doctrine expanded the reliance upon arms transfers by emphasizing the role of U.S. weapons for indigenous forces as a replacement for the direct presence of American military personnel. Only in recent years as arms transfers have become predominantly sales rather than grants, and the bulk of U.S. transfers has gone to the Persian Gulf and Middle East, have they become controversial and have the presumed benefits become more difficult to identify with certainty.

Providing military support for allies and friends has also been an important Soviet motivation in countries such as North Korea, North Vietnam, Syria, Iraq, Somalia, and Cuba, as well as in the Warsaw Pact countries. Arms have been transferred to Cuba to encourage and enable it to become or remain involved in conflicts in Angola and elsewhere on the African continent. France and Britain, as they withdrew from their colonies, often transferred some of their remaining arms or undertook to provide new ones for the new states; but most of their more recent sales have been essentially commercial rather than political or security related in nature.

Arms for allies are often perceived as being transferred within the context of creating, or maintaining, a regional balance of power. This is most evident in the Middle East, where additional arms from both East and West have been justified as necessary to maintain the Arab-Israeli balance. Similarly, arms for Chile and Peru, or for India and Pakistan, have been viewed in this manner in the past.

But one nation's perception of balance may be another nation's "*im*balance." The risk of a process of competitive acquisition, leading to a local arms race, is often present. Local arms races exist in the Latin American and South Asian cases just cited. In Africa, Kenya and Tanzania felt impelled to build up their own capabilities with Western assistance after Idi Amin's Uganda received arms from the Soviet Union. Sometimes the question whether or not an arms race even exists is open to interpretation. The Shah insisted that Iran's massive defense buildup was not aimed at such Persian Gulf states as Saudi Arabia and the United Arab Emirates, but was the consequence of the need to respond to, and deter, his immediate neighbors, the Soviet Union, Iraq, and Afghanistan. Saudi Arabia also disclaimed being in an arms race with Iran. Yet the Saudis were deeply concerned with the Shah's military aggrandizement, and this concern had a major impact on their decision to increase and modernize their armed forces. Moreover, as their request for the F-15 demonstrated, even if they did not intend or wish to match Iran fully, for reasons of both pride and politics they sought clear assurance of equal access to American arms.[10]

Other classical military concerns are often cited as rationales for making arms transfers. One of these is the right to establish a military base in the recipient country. As far back as 1940 President Roosevelt offered fifty destroyers to Britain in exchange for base facilities in the Caribbean. Following World War II, as the United States came to rely upon a global network of overseas bases for its bombers and for monitoring the Soviet Union, arms were often transferred as a quid pro quo for the availability of bases. The United States received base rights in Pakistan, Ethiopia, and Libya and naval facilities in Spain and the Philippines with such understandings. More recently, after the Soviet move into Afghanistan, Washington promised arms to Oman, Somalia, and Kenya in exchange for access to bases. Arms were an even more important instrument for the Soviet Union as it sought to expand its strategic reach and break out of its continental isolation through achieving access to various military support facilities in South Yemen, Somalia, Syria, and Cuba, among other locations. Moscow in the late 1970s gained valuable strategic access to the American-built bases at Cam Ranh Bay and Danang in Vietnam in exchange for arms and economic aid.

Although the total number of U.S. bases abroad has declined (because of the reliance upon long-range intercontinental ballistic missiles and missile-firing submarines, new satellite observation techniques, and shifting international needs), overseas bases are likely to remain an important component of American and Soviet strategic planning. This is certainly the case in the Persian Gulf and Middle East, where both superpowers seek to improve their on-the-spot presence. Given the critical necessity of protecting the oil flow from the region, American planners would like nothing more than a military base in the area. The granting of any such facility is certain to include arms as part of the deal.

Closely related to the need for overseas military bases is the need for intelligence facilities for such activities as electronic eavesdropping and surveillance flights, as in the case of the famous U-2 flights over the Soviet Union. Here, too, the supply of arms can be an invaluable quid pro quo. In early 1980 Egypt was promised forty F-16 fighers as part of a military equipment package totaling just under $1 billion at a time when the United States began flying AWACS aircraft from Egyptian bases. But no bargain is without some risk: when the United States placed its embargo on arms to Turkey following the invasion of Cyprus, Turkey retaliated by restricting the use of American intelligence activities, saying, in effect, "no arms, no intelligence."

Another justification for arms transfers, popular with military establishments, is based on the assumption that they are more likely to be tested in combat earlier by the receiver than by the supplier. New American precision-guided anti-tank weapons were first employed in conflict by Israel during the Yom Kippur War; the lessons learned and the experience gained in 1973 through their use had a profound impact upon military planners thereafter. The testing of new weapons also appears to have been one of the Soviet motivations in selling some arms to Iraq that were used in the Kurdish rebellion. The fighting in Afghanistan in 1980, in which some Soviet arms were used by regular Afghan forces, provided another opportunity to test them.

There are several possible military costs or disadvantages that any government must take into account before it sends arms overseas. Once they are in the arsenal of another country it becomes difficult, if not impossible, to control their use. Thus the arms sent may one day be transferred by the recipient country to a third party, as happened when French Mirages, sold to Saudi Arabia, found their way to Egypt. Most arms transfer agreements now have a clause forbidding retransfer without the supplier's permission, but such prohibitions may be difficult to enforce in a crisis. This also applies to any stipulation as to the circumstances in which the arms are to be used. Washington objected at one point, but to no avail, to Morocco's use of F-5 fighters, based in Mauritania and intended for defensive purposes only, in the Western Sahara. A similar "defensive purposes only" provision was attached to the sale of F-15 fighters to Israel; their use against Lebanon in 1979, which led to the shooting down of six Syrian MiG-21s, may have violated existing agreements, according to Secretary of State Cyrus Vance. Another violation took place when Israel in 1981 bombed the Osirak nuclear reactor outside Baghdad with American-built aircraft. Moreover, there can be no guarantee that the arms will not fall into enemy hands as a result of conflict, thereby creating a boomerang effect. Here the most notable case occurred in South Vietnam when U.S. arms in the possession of the South Vietnamese army were captured by the Viet Cong and North Vietnamese and were then used against American forces. These same arms were used again in Cambodia in 1979. Israel acquired in 1973 Soviet arms that had been sent to Arab countries; some of these weapons provided valuable new knowledge on Soviet equipment for the Pentagon.

Another concern arises out of the fact that a nation's professional military will always want to give priority to the equipment and readiness of its own armed forces. Yet there is the risk that large arms transfers, rapidly made, may reduce the supplier state's own inventory and diminish its military preparedness. This occurred in the months immediately following the Yom Kippur War when substantial quantities of arms were taken from U.S. forces and shipped to Israel, much to the dismay of the Joint Chiefs of Staff. To judge from the Soviet Union's ability to send large quantities of arms to distant places rapidly (as demonstrated in the Horn of Africa) without any visible strain on its own armed forces, it appears to have a larger stockpile of arms permanently available for such purposes; hence this consideration may be less relevant to the Soviet Union.

There is always the danger that unforeseeable political changes may make past transfers of arms unfortunate, if not tragic, in retrospect. Who is to know where, or when, irrational leaders such as an Idi Amin or Colonel Qaddafi or Ayatollah Khomeini may suddenly seize power in a country that has received arms from abroad? Likewise, shifts in political alignments and alliances cannot be predicted. In the Horn of Africa, the United States supplied to Ethiopia, over two decades, close to half a billion dollars worth of weapons, making it the largest recipient of U.S. arms in black Africa. Similarly, the Soviet Union sent large numbers of advisers and arms to neighboring Somalia. Yet the American investment did not prevent Ethiopia's shift from a conservative monarchy to a radical socialist state with close ties to Moscow, just as Soviet military assistance to Mogadishu did not forestall its break with Moscow and its turn to the West. In the end, these arms from outside suppliers were employed in a manner completely opposite from that originally intended.

Finally, mention should also be made of the concern that the supply of arms will set off a chain of events that will ultimately drag a nation into war. This fear reflects the history of the Vietnam involvement which began with U.S. military assistance to Saigon. Entry into war is, of course, a highest-level political decision based upon broad foreign policy considerations. But there is always the risk that direct involvement through the supply of arms will encourage the creation of a parallel supplier relationship on the other side, thereby introducing an arms competition which can then become an issue of political will and resolve; or that a supplier will come to the conclusion that it must participate more directly because it cannot affford to let its partner be defeated. Concerns of this sort were part of the arguments for restraint as Washington was faced with the question of how to respond to events in Angola and whether to send military equipment to Zaire.[11] Among the arguments made in early 1981 against sending U.S. arms to El Salvador was that such a course might lead to a deeper American involvement.

Economic Benefits

The third cluster of rationales for arms transfers comprises the economic advantages they are thought to bring. Arms sales have come to be viewed as an important earner of foreign exchange and contributor to the balance of payments. This was particularly true with respect to weapons sales to the Persian Gulf following the quintupling of the price of oil. After the 1973–1974 price rise, the Nixon administration appointed an interagency task force headed by Deputy Secretary of Defense William P. Clements, Jr., the purpose of which was to stimulate exports, especially of arms. At that time the French government also adopted a new sense of urgency about weapons sales to Saudi Arabia and Iran as a way of paying for higher oil costs. And the Soviet Union took a new interest in selling arms to countries that could pay in cash from oil revenues, principally Libya and Iraq.

Arms sales are also thought to provide significant employment in the defense industries of the producers. In addition, the export of arms is seen as an excellent way to create economies of scale, thereby reducing the per-unit costs of arms to be manufactured for the armed forces of the producer country. Exports are also a way of spreading out, or recouping, some of the research and development expenses.

These are all important considerations, especially at a time when the Western world is in an economic slump and is faced with the prospect of higher energy costs. Defense budgets are under continuing and growing pressure, in part because of the rising expense of ever more sophisticated weapons. Such countries as France and Britain have a smaller domestic market for their arms manufacturers than has the United States and are therefore more dependent upon overseas sales. Indeed, in 1977, 41 percent of French-built arms were exported, and approximately 35 percent of Britain's. Certain industries, such as naval construction and tank manufacture in Britain, or aeronautics in France, are even more export dependent than the above percentages would indicate. For these reasons the advocacy within defense establishments for new weapon systems, especially advanced aircraft such as the F-16 or the Mirage 2000, has often been phrased in terms of which system will be most successful in foreign markets.

It may be, however, that the economic importance of arms sales—the "explanation" most often given for their existence and expansion—is not so great as it is often believed to be. The widespread perception that high levels of arms sales are necessary for the national economies of the principal suppliers is based upon vague, general notions rather than on hard data. Closer investigation . . . suggests that the economic benefits are less than is generally assumed. Accordingly, limited restraints on sales may have a relatively small economic impact, except for the particular companies or regions directly affected.

Reliable data are not available on all dimensions of this question. According to the U.S. Arms Control and Disarmament Agency, in 1978 French arms exports came to 1.7 percent of total exports, British to 1.5 percent and American to 4.7 percent.[12] A Library of Congress study estimates that arms exports accounted for 2.7 percent of France's and 2.0 percent of Britain's total exports of "machinery, transport equipment, firearms of war and ammunition" in 1975 while the American figure was 10.2 percent.[13] According to still another study, for the same year French military exports accounted for 0.9 percent of total exports, British for 0.8 percent, and American for 4.5 percent.[14] These estimates seem low for the Europeans and vary greatly for the United States. Through discussions with officials in a position to know in the three countries, the author has arrived at an estimate for 1980 of 4 to 5 percent for the United States, approximately the same for France, and 3 to 4 percent for Britain.

Two important conclusions emerge, whatever the variations in the available figures. First, arms exports are relatively small in terms of total exports, and are only a small fraction of what is needed to pay the increased oil import bill of recent years. In fact, the most rapid adjustment to the higher oil prices has been made by Germany and Japan, countries whose sales of arms are relatively insignificant. Arms exporters must also consider the risk that oil prices will be raised to pay for the purchase of costly weapons. It is no accident that the largest purchaser of arms in the late 1970s—Iran—was one of the leading advocates within OPEC of higher oil prices. Second, and contrary to accepted wisdom, the principal European suppliers are *not* more dependent than the United States is on arms exports for balance of payment purposes.

Additional economic indicators support the hypothesis that none of the major suppliers is heavily dependent upon arms exports. According to a special study completed in 1977 by the Bureau of Labor Statistics of the U.S. Department of Labor, foreign military sales provided 277,000 jobs in 1975. Since total employment in the United States came to 80 million, arms exports accounted for only 0.3 percent of national employment.[15] As to the savings generated through enlarged production runs and recoupment of research and development expenses, a Congressional Budget Office study has estimated that arms exports of $8 billion per year produce savings of only $560 million.[16] This amounted to 0.5 percent of the 1977 defense budget. A study prepared by the Department of Defense found that "there is only a loose relationship between production readiness and cost economies on the one hand, and the total dollar volume of transfers on the other."[17] A similar conclusion was reached by a parliamentary committee in Britain. . . .

In France, of a total work force of 22 million, only 90,000 are engaged in manufacturing weapons for customers abroad; in Britain it was 70,000 to 80,000 in 1975.[18] Comparable figures for the Soviet Union are unavailable—some scholars at institutes in Moscow suggest that the data do not even exist—but we do know that in the policy followed for many years of granting long-term, low-interest loans to purchasers of arms, the USSR traditionally emphasized the political significance rather than the economic benefits of arms sales. More recently, the USSR has sold arms at higher prices to countries that could afford to pay, such as Libya. As the Soviet Union has sought hard currencies to pay for its import of Western technology and grain, it has placed a higher reliance on weapons sales as a source of revenue.

We do not mean to conclude that the economic importance of arms exports is as trivial as some of the data seem to suggest. Arms exports for the European countries may, in some years, make the difference between a trade balance that is in deficit and one that is in surplus. The data on direct employment only tell part of the story, for they say nothing about the multiplier impact of jobs in one industry upon those in another. Specific companies may be particularly dependent on arms exports, although this is not the case for many American companies. Relatively minor economic benefits, in statistical terms, may be perceived to be of great importance by a country that is trying to climb out of a recession. Such minor benefits from exports may also be seen to be of considerable value by particular interest groups that may have a significant influence on policy. As indicated earlier, overseas markets are more important for the European suppliers than for the United States or the USSR, because the Europeans require fewer arms for their own armed forces. Moreover, the maintenance of viable national defense industries is perceived—especially in France where it is linked with images of independence and sovereignty, and to a lesser extent also in Britain—as an important political goal. Yet for none of the main suppliers do arms exports occupy as important a role in the national economy as is often assumed by those who believe that economic imperatives must overrule any attempt to restrain arms sales.

Notes

1. *World Military and Social Expenditures, 1980,* comp. Ruth Sivard (Leesburg, Va.: W.M.S.E. Publications), p. 20.

2. U.S. Arms Control and Disarmament Agency (ACDA), *World Military Expenditures and Arms Transfers 1969-1978,* p. 117.

3. U.S. Department of Defense, *Foreign Military Sales and Military Assistance Facts* (December 1979), p. 1. This is a retroactive figure; the 1975 total was $10.1 billion according to comparable 1976 data in ibid., December 1976, p. 13.

4. SIPRI *Yearbook, 1976* (New York: Humanities Press, 1976), pp. 18–19; ACDA, *World Military Expenditures and Arms Transfers 1968–1977*, p. 16.

5. ACDA, *World Military Expenditures and Arms Transfers 1969–1978*, p. 117.

6. SIPRI *Yearbook, 1980*, p. 65. ACDA figures are based upon shares of the total world arms sales market, rather than transfers to the developing world. United States (39.2 percent), Soviet Union (29.5 percent), France (7.4 percent), United Kingdom (4.7 percent), and West Germany (4.5 percent) for 1977. ACDA, *World Military Expenditures and Arms Transfers 1968–1977*, p. 18.

7. ACDA, *World Military Expenditures and Arms Transfers 1969–1978*, p. 21. According to SIPRI, Third World suppliers account for 3 percent of arms exports to Third World countries. SIPRI *Yearbook, 1980*, p. 62.

8. SIPRI *Yearbook, 1979*, p. 173. ACDA, for the same year (1978), gives NATO 53 percent of arms exports globally (not just Third World) and the Soviet Union 34 percent. *World Military Expenditures and Arms Transfers 1969–1978*, p. 9.

9. U.S., Congress, Senate, Committee on Foreign Relations, *U.S. Military Sales to Iran*, A Staff Report to the Subcommittee on Foreign Assistance, 94th Cong., 2d sess., July 1976, p. xi.

10. Andrew J. Pierre, "Beyond the 'Plane Package': Arms and Politics in the Middle East," *International Security* (Summer 1978):148–161.

11. For an excellent further analysis of the military benefits and costs of arms transfers see Geoffrey Kemp with Steven E. Miller, "The Arms Transfer Phenomenon," in Andrew J. Pierre, ed., *Arms Transfers and American Foreign Policy* (New York: New York University Press, 1979), pp. 50–59.

12. ACDA, *World Military Expenditures and Arms Transfers 1969–1978*, pp. 132, 155.

13. Congressional Research Service, Library of Congress, *Implications of President Carter's Conventional Arms Transfer Policy*, September 22, 1977, p. 67.

14. Anne Hessing Cahn, Joseph J. Druzel, Peter M. Dawkins, and Jacques Huntzinger, *Controlling Future Arms Trade* (New York: McGraw-Hill Book Co., 1977), p. 66. These figures are based upon compilations from several sources.

15. U.S., Department of Labor, Bureau of Labor Statistics, *Foreign Defense Sales and Grants, Fiscal Years 1973–1975: Labor and Material Requirements* (July 1977), p. 17.

16. U.S., Congress, Congressional Budget Office, *Budgetary Cost Savings to the Department of Defense Resulting from Foreign Military Sales*, Staff Working Paper, May 24, 1976, p. ix.

17. U.S., Congress, Senate, Committee on Foreign Relations, *Arms Transfer Policy*, 95th Cong., 1st sess., July 1977, Appendix 3, p. 94.

18. According to Minister of State for Defence William Rodgers, in the Commons, Great Britain, *Parliamentary Debates* (Commons), July 8, 1975, col. 416.

Discussion Questions

1. Why does Pierre feel that arms transfer policy is of increasing importance?

2. How do arms transfers affect weapons procurement decisions in the United States?

3. How much leverage do arms transfers convey to the United States? Is this a cheap way to project power without risking lives of Americans?

4. Are arms transfers simply a form of foreign aid? What other dimensions do they have?

17
East–West Trade and Technology Control

James R. Golden

National economic and security policies overlap in a number of important areas. At the domestic level, military production claims a substantial share of national resources and has important impacts on national output, research and development, employment, and prices. The structure of the defense sector, with few producers and one domestic buyer, inevitably means important departures from the more competitive market system that characterizes a substantial portion of the U.S. economy. At the international level, economic transactions constitute by far the largest volume of contacts with foreign citizens and are simultaneously a source of national security interests and a mechanism for influencing their attainment. Market efficiency argues for free international trade and capital flows, but national security objectives occasionally suggest restrictions on international economic relationships.[1]

The importance of economics to national security has long been acknowledged, but economic policy rarely has been integrated effectively in overall national security policy formulation. The primary reason for this policy separation is the commonly accepted premise that unfettered economic markets produce the most efficient allocation of resources, achieve the greatest national output, and therefore most clearly generate the industrial capacity required for defense. Thus, perceived conflicts between economic and security objectives are the exception rather than the rule. The traditional view of international transactions underscores this point.

Economic theory emphasizes two dimensions of international trade—efficiency and equity—and gives lip-service to the national security argument. Traditional trade theory emphasizes efficiency arguments and concludes that free trade will generally raise the incomes of both trading partners. There is, however, no generally acceptable way of making judgments about changes in the distribution of income, either within a country or between countries, that might result from trade. Economists can attempt to forecast or describe the distributional impacts of trade, but judgments on equity must be left to the political arena. Similarly economic theory concludes that there may be legitimate national security reasons for limiting free trade, such as potential trade blockages in wartime, but the theory provides no neat formula for comparing security impacts with efficiency or distributional arguments.

Economic theory therefore tends to support free international trade and to emphasize the advantages of international specialization based on comparative advantage. Moreover, the theory concludes that specialization and trade are not only desirable, they are also virtually inevitable because strong market forces based on individual advantage naturally will tend to produce such specialization. Market forces, based on price and profit signals, will allocate resources to their most efficient use, and attempts to block those forces are likely to be self-defeating in the long run.

These conclusions led one political scientist to conclude that economists always will contend that whatever does happen should have happened. This remark, made in the context of a discussion of East-West trade, reflected a frustration with the inability of the United States to harness its tremendous economic strength in its dealings with the Soviet Union.

East-West trade relationships illustrate the interaction of economic and national security policies and the problems inherent in balancing conflicting interests both among domestic U.S. constituencies and within the Western alliance. The alliance disagreements follow from fundamental differences in economic interests, varied experiences concerning the interaction of economic and military factors in meeting national security objectives, conflicting assessments of the balance of leverage and vulnerability involved in various economic transactions, different views of the appropriate roles of government in influencing world trade patterns, and different assessments of the nature and importance of the Soviet threat to Europe and the rest of the world. Technical disputes over specific export controls and credit conditions in East-West trade are the symptoms of more fundamental disagreements. Alliance policy debates on issues such as the Siberia-Europe natural gas pipeline raise numerous technical issues that dominate official exchanges. Outcomes, however, are driven more by perspectives on the long-run role of East-West trade than by the technical merits of individual cases.

Trade with the East always has been characterized by high levels of government participation. Trade with a potential enemy raises questions of direct and indirect contributions to military capabilities. Moreover, the potential gains from trade can be important bargaining chips in other negotiations. Trade with the East means interaction with state monopolies and calls for a larger government role in coordinating the activities of private firms, a function that the United States ignored at its peril in the great grain robbery of 1972–1973. Private grain exporters, isolated by competitive secrecy, sold their grain to the USSR at bargain prices. Had those firms known the extent of Soviet purchases, their pricing decisions would have reflected true market conditions. In addition, the shortage of hard currency in the East means that credit arrangements and political guarantees play a critical role in trade, a role far more similar to trade with developing nations than with other industrial nations.

Security considerations, the structure of Eastern trade monopolies, and the key role of insured credit all guarantee that governments will play a major role in

East-West trade. For some governments—France, for example—that role is typical of all trade arrangements. For other members of the alliance, the requirements for government intervention in trade arrangements contrast with normal practice. Trade with the East inevitably must be managed. The question is what form that management should take and, more important, what objectives that management should pursue.[2]

Economic theory offers some limited light on the impacts of intervention in East-West trade. Four implications stand out. First, both sides have higher incomes as a result of trade, and trade restrictions will reduce the incomes of both sides. Second, trade restrictions will tend to redistribute incomes within each country and between the trading partners. Third, there is no formula for assessing the security impacts of trade or even determining the direction of impact of such trade. Economic interaction may increase security by expanding on joint interests, providing extended contacts, and helping to develop mutual confidence for other negotiations. On the other hand, trade may permit a greater diversion of activity to military production, either through its general impact in increasing national income or through its more direct contribution to specific military capabilities. Economic analysis can help to estimate some of these impacts, but in the final analysis political assessments will dominate. Finally, attempts to block trade must deal with enormous market pressures to exploit the potential gains from trade. This situation does not mean that trade restrictions will be futile, but it does suggest that effective controls will require large commitments of economic and political resources.

Trends in Export Policy

U.S. export policy toward the East in general and the Soviet Union in particular has been characterized by denial, with exceptions. The premise is that exports, particularly industrial exports, most-favored-nation (MFN) tariff status (granting the lowest import tariff charged to any trading partner), and governmental credits should only be granted as concessions based on favorable Soviet actions. From the passage of the Export Control Act of 1949 through the Export Administration Act of 1969, few exceptions were granted. Controls were aimed at restricting economic growth in the East, based on an assessment that economic strength of any kind could be converted into military strength in the long run.

The Harmel Report to NATO in 1967 suggested a new dual approach to the Soviet Union based on defense and détente. Economic interaction and broader negotiation might complement military strength rather than erode it. Both the emerging balance of strategic nuclear strength and U.S. commitments in Vietnam suggested fertile areas for negotiation with the Soviet Union. The 1969 Export Administration Act provided more flexibility in economic arrangements with the East by limiting controls to items with direct military significance, rather than broad economic potential, and by endorsing the promotion of exports.

From 1969 to roughly 1976 the United States experimented with a one-sided form of economic linkage; economic concessions would be made to provide incentives for negotiation. Computer exports became a key component of this policy, including sales for the Kama River truck plant. The concessions clearly were linked to progress on the SALT I negotiations and probably were linked to assistance in negotiations over Vietnam as well. The policy, however, was stymied by the Jackson-Vanik amendment to the Trade Act of 1974, which made the granting of Soviet MFN tariff status contingent on the emigration of Soviet Jews and, more important, by the Stevenson restrictions on the Export-Import Bank passed in December 1974 that denied the Soviet Union access to government trade credits.

In 1976 I chaired a task force for President Ford that was aimed at streamlining the export controls process and eliminating processing delays.[3] The climate for promoting East-West trade already was shifting. Soviet military spending had apparently not slowed in the period of détente, despite the U.S. drawdown after the Vietnam war. Moreover, the evidence was mounting that the Soviets were attempting to expand their influence on a global scale, particularly on the Horn of Africa, in Angola, and in the Persian Gulf region. The world energy situation increased the perceived risk of those developments.

In the Carter administration, linkage became negative linkage in the form of sanctions for unacceptable behavior. Although advisers such as Samuel Huntington called for an aggressive policy of "competitive engagement" with both carrots and sticks, in practice only the sticks were used.[4] The 1979 trials of Soviet dissidents Alexandr Ginsburg and Anatoly Shcharansky brought restrictions on computer exports. Studies on the possibility of controls on the export of energy technologies bogged down until the Soviet invasion of Afghanistan in late 1979 demanded some response. The response was further export restrictions and a partial embargo on grain sales. In a situation where U.S. military strength did not provide effective leverage, the administration resorted to sanctions to demonstrate the extent of U.S. concern.

The Reagan adminstration extended the policy of negative linkage but with some new twists. Agricultural embargoes were seen as imposing asymmetrical costs on the United States in general and on one portion of the U.S. economy in particular. The Reagan policy focused on tightening the export controls process to include technologies that might have indirect military applications and on limiting Soviet foreign currency earnings that could be used to purchase that technology. In the wake of the declaration of martial law in Poland, the administration sought sanctions that would help implement that policy, taking specific aim on the Siberia-Europe natural gas pipeline deal that implied business-as-usual with the Soviet Union, threatened to increase Soviet economic leverage, in Europe, and risked alleviating Soviet hard currency shortages.[5]

The U.S. position on Polish sanctions brought it into direct conflict with its European allies, who favored some sanctions but not an interruption of the long-planned natural gas pipeline deal. In their view, the pipeline would reduce energy dependence on risky Middle East sources, would provide important export sales of pipeline equipment, and would not expose Europe to Soviet leverage. The Soviets, they argued, needed European technology as much as, or more than, the Europeans needed gas, and the Europeans already had developed contingency plans for the unlikely event of any disruption.[6] The debate, however, was less over the specifics of the pipeline deal than on the longer-run thrust of economic relations with the East. While the United States had pursued economic linkage throughout the 1970s, most European states had rejected that approach. In the Federal Republic of Germany, for example, Ostpolitik rejected a political role for trade with the East and pursued a normalization of trade relationships based on the traditional pattern of German industrial exports to the East and raw material imports. Complementary trade interests, in the German view, were far more likely to promote political concessions than economic sanctions.[7]

Since World War II the U.S. strategic position has changed dramatically. The economic and military development of its allies has been a tremendous advantage in countering the military strength of the Soviet Union, but at the same time the problems of coordinating policy within the alliance also have expanded. Although the United States still holds important leads in some technology areas, it cannot avoid the necessity of developing a common East-West economic policy with its allies if the policy is to have any hope of success. Moreover, a failure to develop an integrated economic policy could have important implications for the solidarity of the alliance, solidarity important to developing effective military deterrence. The prospects for developing an effective economic policy are not bright, but they will be improved if the policy expands on current areas of alliance consensus and recognizes the institutional and political constraints on nuance and fine-tuning.

Dimensions of Export Policy

Export Controls

In the East-West context, export controls may be differentiated based on five major characteristics: the presumption of control, the objective of broad economic or narrow military impact, emphasis on end products or technology transfer, variations based on export destination, and restrictions concerning end use and reshipment. In the United States the presumption is that trade to designated communist states is prohibited unless a license is obtained. In the Federal Republic of Germany, the presumption is that trade with the East is unrestricted unless specific controls are imposed. Differences in presumption shift the burden of proof in determining whether items may be exported.

The objective of East-West export controls has been specified in various legislation, but in practice political agreement on objectives has been less apparent. Until 1969 the objective in the United States was to limit Soviet economic potential and thereby to restrict military development. After 1969 the emphasis shifted to limiting exports with direct military impact. In practice, however, this distinction is difficult to apply because all products have some conceivable military implication. Most of these have dual civilian and military uses, and controls policy must decide how such dual-use products will be treated. Those decisions tend to be very sensitive to the political climate, and thus the actual objectives of export controls tend to shift over time.

The controls may be applied to the transfer of technology, to the sale of products, or both. The Bucy Report of 1976 argued that controlling technology transfer was most important because the major problem in the East was production know-how and quality control. In this view, turnkey sales, in which a Western firm constructed a plant and turned the keys over for operation, were the most damaging form of transfer. End products, the report argued, were less important because of the difficulty of reverse engineering—that is, determining production designs from the end product. This conclusion on reverse engineering remains controversial, particularly concerning the extent of generalization that can be made from the specific products studied in the report.[8]

Export policy is defined further by the treatment of different destinations. Three levels of differentiation in the East-West framework are communist states, Western allies, and other nations. Control differentiation on exports to allies and other nations is becoming more and more of an issue as concern for reshipments to the East increases. Many critics have suggested that even technology transfer to U.S. allies, particularly in the form of coproduction agreements on weapons systems, ultimately makes such technology more available to the East.[9] The same argument has been made with respect to the sale of advanced military systems outside NATO. U.S. controls policy has long made clear differentiations among shipments to various communist states, with concessions based primarily on the currently perceived political distance between the Soviet Union and the export recipient.

End use and reshipment restrictions are applied to permit exceptions to general export control policies. For example, items that are embargoed for shipment to the East may be released to other destinations if the end use is clear and the recipient agrees that the item will not be reshipped. End use agreements also are used in cases of possible dual civilian and military applications.

Export Credits

The volume of East-West trade clearly is dependent on the extent of controls on specific products. It is perhaps even more sensitive to credit arrangement used to finance sales. Despite enormous reserves of natural resources, the location of those reserves, a weak capital infrastructure, and poor standards of production seriously have restricted the availability of hard currency in the East. Sales to the East typically depend on the availability of credit from the West. This situation is particularly true in the case of resource development projects that are pursued based on the long-term prospects of hard currency earnings.

The risks inherent in such projects—commercial as well as political—mean that major investments only will be pursued with substantial diversification over a number of firms and clear government guarantees. Private insurance for such ventures is available, but it is relatively expensive, and private insurers insist that firms carry a substantial portion of the risk. Government programs designed to promote international trade in general through credit guarantees are available in some cases to finance East-West trade as well. Credits may be advanced as direct government-to-government loans, or guarantees may be provided to private lenders to insure against potential losses. Such credits provide a subsidy to the importer in the East. In the case of direct loans, the subsidy would be the difference between the interest rate on the loan and the cost of funds to the government (the treasury bill rate in the United States). In the case of guaranteed loans, the subsidy is the difference between the insurance premium paid to the government and the private insurance rate that would have been paid in the absence of a government guarantee. Such a subsidy is clearly more difficult to measure.[10]

Import Restrictions

Import restrictions on exports from the East are far less significant in the current context of East-West trade. Eastern exports, particularly from the Soviet Union, fall primarily in areas with low import tariffs. Although much publicity has been given to the issue of granting MFN tariff status to countries in the East, that status has greater political than economic significance. In particular, the Stevenson restrictions on credits granted by the Export-Import Bank were tied to MFN status, and the Jackson amendment to the Trade Act of 1974 tied MFN status to Soviet policies concerning Jewish emigration.

Machinery of Export Policy

The elements of trade policy—export controls, credits, and import tariffs—are linked to broader East-West policy through complex institutional arrangements. In the United States the institutions dealing with the various dimensions of policy tend to be more independent, based on traditions of limited government involvement in trade, restrictions on interlocking control of banking and industrial organizations, and the normal division of powers within the federal government. In Europe, with traditions of closer interaction among industry, banks, and government and less separation of power, the various dimensions of export policy are far more integrated.

Administration of Export Controls

The implementation of policy through a large federal bureaucracy is difficult at best. The president can control political appointments at the top of the bureaucracy, but even if those officials actively pursue the president's policies, they must do so through a bureaucracy that will endure from administration to administration. Policy implementation requires not only consensus among relevant cabinet officials but also clear, consistent signals to the bureaucracy. Therefore policy is implemented by campaign. In the economic arena, this means a clear choice between major alternatives such as fighting inflation or unemployment. That one decision provides signals for the bureaucracy on thousands of subordinate issues. Similarly, export control policy tends to be managed by campaign. Does the president want to expand or restrict East-West trade? The answer to that question will determine the pace and form of numerous export decisions.

Nuance and shifts in direction are therefore difficult to implement. After the 1969 Export Administration Act changed the criteria for export controls, officials in the Office of Export Administration were slow to change the criteria they applied in licensing. Applications to export items with potential dual military and civilian uses routinely were denied, and long delays were encountered in getting licensing decisions. Ambiguous policy direction also can slow down the process. The machinery works best when policy is consistent and precedents can be applied.

The political balancing involved in the licensing process suggests the difficulty of adjusting policy to changes in the international situation. Items are placed into restricted export categories through three published control lists, and firms wishing to export restricted items must apply to the Department of Commerce for an export license. Roughly 92 percent of the applications received are for non-communist countries, and those routinely are approved based on reshipment restrictions. Those applications are processed by the Office of Export Administration without any need for interagency consultation. The remaining cases require interagency approval, primarily from the Departments of Commerce, Defense, and State. An operating committee reviews the more difficult cases. The most controversial cases are passed to the cabinet-level Export Administration Review Board for a decision or ultimate referral to the president. Each agency conducts its own review of the military significance of the export, the safeguards available against diversion to military applications, and the political consequences of the transfer.[11]

The interagency debates over the broad objectives of controls policy are reflected in more detailed debates over specific exports. Within the Reagan administration, the secretaries of state generally have favored a more liberal stance on controls, while the Department of Defense and the National Security Council staff have supported tighter trade restrictions.[12] As a result, adjusting controls policy to changes in the international environment requires substantial time and political effort.

The availability of similar products and technology overseas means that licenses must be coordinated with allies. An informal coordinating committee (COCOM) with representatives from Japan and NATO countries, except Iceland, meets in Paris to agree on restricted items and grant waivers. The COCOM arrangement reflects the political sensitivity of controls. There is no formal treaty arrangement, and it would be very difficult to forge one. Compliance with COCOM restrictions is voluntary, and some countries simply have bypassed COCOM in controversial cases.[13] Weaknesses in enforcement in COCOM and transfers through countries that are not members, such as Sweden, are major problems that have been noted by virtually every study of export controls over the past decade.[14]

Credits and Guarantees

Promotion of international trade through government-supported credits is a standard practice. In some cases, the exporter arranges for insurance directly with the government agency. In others, the foreign importer first arranges a loan with a bank in the exporting country to cover the invoice value of a shipment. The bank arranges insurance with a government agency to cover the amount of the loan. In either case, the exporter or the bank normally pays a fee of roughly 2.5 to 3 percent of the invoice value.

In the United States, for example, the Export-Import Bank directly guarantees private bank loans and loans by the Private Export Funding Corporation. It also reinsures the Foreign Credit Insurance Association, a private consortium that insures commercial risks. In the Federal Republic of Germany, a private corporation, Hermes Versicherungs AG, insures sales to private buyers; a public firm, Treuarbeit, insures sales to public buyers; and a public firm, Treuarbeit, insures sales to public buyers such as the Soviet Union. In France, export insurance is arranged by the Compagnie Française d'Assurance pur le Commerce Exterior, in Japan by the Export Insurance Division of the Ministry of International Trade and Industry, and in the United Kingdom by the Export Credits Guarantee Department.[15]

Competition for exports through credit concessions led the OECD to coordinate interest rates on long-term loans beginning in 1976. The consensus rates are based on the income category of the importer—rich, intermediate, and poor—and the maturity of the loan. The longer the term and the richer the importer, the higher the interest rates must be. The top consensus rate stayed at 8¾ percent from 1976 to 1981, rose to 11¼ percent in December 1981, jumped to 12.4 percent in July 1982, and was cut back to 11½ percent in the spring of 1983.[16]

In the East-West context such credits pose two central questions. Should subsidies be given to potential adversaries? Could Western loans become a source of leverage by the East? Export controls address the issue of blocking the market forces for trade, but credit subsidies actually increase the pressure for trade. An effective policy must clearly integrate each of these dimensions.

The credit issues are complicated by a number of factors. First, since credit subsidies are common in international trade, agreements to restrict such credits to the East would constitute a departure from normal competition for markets. In other words, credit subsidies are not viewed as concessions made to the East.

Second, the interlocking activities of governments, banks, and exporters, particularly in Europe, make it very difficult to establish just what the terms of credit were in any specific case. For example, there was considerable controversy in establishing the terms of credit under which the Soviet Union was financing its purchases for the Siberia–West Europe natural gas pipeline. The Soviet negotiators attempted to obtain a favorable combination of interest rates, subsidies, and flexibility by negotiating for credit with many European countries in excess of their actual needs. In 1980 and 1981, as market interest rates rose, European governments reduced their credit offers and demanded higher interest. The Soviets resisted interest rate increases but made concessions on the size of down payments and the price of pipe. For example, the Federal Republic of Germany ultimately guaranteed $1.13 billion in market rate loans to West German manufacturers, which then loaned the funds to the Soviet Union at 7.8 percent interest. At the same time, however, Soviet payments for pipe were raised by 20 percent, making the effective rate of interest 11.2 percent, a rate far more consistent with then-current market conditions.[17]

At the Versailles economic summit in the summer of 1982, the role of preferential credits to the Soviet Union became a major source of transatlantic contention. The ensuing flurry of credit studies highlighted the difficulties of identifying effective interest rates and placing East-West credit arrangements in the broader context of routine trade subsidies.[18] Rising market interest rates and soaring debts in the East were far more effective in coordinating credit policies than formal government agreements, as OECD exports to Council for Mutual Economic Assistance (COMECON) countries dropped for the first time in a decade in 1981 and fell again in 1982. Preliminary indications, however, suggest that trade and credit flows expanded in 1983, including a 1 billion DM loan from the Federal Republic to East Germany.[19] Credit terms in East-West trade inevitably will become more controversial as credit flows expand.

Toward an Integrated Alliance Strategy

Attempts to develop a coordinated economic approach to the East must deal with the realities of substantial differences within the alliance concerning the objectives and instruments of economic policy. There is indeed a great deal of irony in committing enormous resources to defense while at the same time pursuing trade policies that help buttress the economy of the potential enemy. However, both sides gain from trade, the domestic consequences of trade disruption can be significant, unilateral actions without alliance support are usually ineffective, and trade does provide for expanded contacts that may reduce tensions or at least provide conduits for negotiation. In searching for an alliance consensus on these matters, commitments should first be reached and strengthened on the points of common agreement, with the understanding that lowest-common-denominator solutions will not be completely satisfactory to anyone, but they may be far superior to the alternatives of unilateral action.

Case for Tighter Military Restrictions

The broadest consensus within the alliance lies in the area of controls on exports directly relevant to military potential. President Reagan has called for renewed emphasis on blocking the transfer of such technology, and the COCOM members have been negotiating a revised list of controlled items since October 1982. The debate centers on narrowing the list and tightening enforcement—the European and Japanese view—or expanding the list of controlled technologies—the U.S. view. There is little time to waste. New technologies for conventional weapons could have dramatic impacts on alliance strategy over the next decade. Control of those technologies is essential to provide NATO time to close the conventional gap in Europe.

The evidence on end use agreements, reached to permit the export of items with potential military use for civilian purposes, is not good. The trucks built in the Kama River plant, the showpiece of detente linkage of the early 1970s, have appeared in army inventories and have been used by Soviet forces in Afghanistan. The export of technologies with even indirect military implications, such as advanced computers, is not worth the risk.

Extending this argument to include technologies important for Soviet industry in general, such as drills and compressors, runs the risk of weakening the alliance consensus for tightening controls. Europeans clearly do not accept the objective of weakening Soviet economic potential. The domestic consensus in the United States for tightening export controls also weakens when the argument is pushed away from items with direct military relevance, as indicated by the current debate over the revision of the 1979 Export Administration Act. The act expired in September 1983 but was extended to the end of February 1984 to permit further discussion of long-term policy.

Enforcement of controls has seen significant improvement. Operation Exodus, a U.S. effort to tighten enforcement on arms and technology sales, was initiated in 1981, and there have been some impressive successes. To date over 100 cases of technology smuggling have been prosecuted, and a large computer bound for the USSR through Sweden was confiscated in Germany in the fall of 1983. In December 1983 British officials intercepted computer equipment valued at $750,000 en route to the East.[20] Such successes, however, remain a drop in the bucket compared to the estimated flow of illegal transfers through sales and espionage.

The first task is to press for strict enforcement of restrictions on technologies that everyone agrees have military relevance. This goal will mean not only pressing through COCOM channels but also tightening less formal lines of potential transfer. Much work needs to be done on the simple tasks of cataloging the critical technologies that are embodied in different industrial products, identifying various sources of those technologies in the United States and overseas, and improving the exchange of information required for effective enforcement.

Case for Linkage

The policies of denial and confrontation on the one hand, and a laissez-faire free market approach on the other, are both inconsistent with the realities of strategic competition. Adjustments in economic relationships based on the political and military behavior of the Soviet Union are inevitable and desirable. They are inevitable because free markets will react to perceptions of increased risk when international tensions mount. They are desirable because inconsistent economic and military policies in the alliance can undermine the rationale for defensive strength, and the Soviet Union should be forced to pay for aggression. Linkage between economic relations and Soviet military actions may influence Soviet behavior, but this potential impact should not be overstated. Military spending in the Soviet Union clearly has top priority, and there is little evidence that other domestic objectives will divert funds from military programs. Linkage conceivably could affect Soviet behavior if trade were seen as essential to long-run military strength, but even so, short-run military objectives would have to be sacrificed for long-run potential; such trade-offs are unlikely.

Even if Soviet behavior is not affected by economic linkage, linkage still serves important alliance objectives. The need is to develop forms of linkage that can strengthen alliance solidarity. Variations in export control policy based on Soviet behavior are not an effective means for establishing linkage. Controls are most effective when they emphasize direct military impacts. Therefore variations in controls must occur on technologies with less military relevance, or concessions must be made on items with military potential. In either case, the fragile consensus for controls would be weakened by linkage. Adding items to the controls list as potential bargaining chips weakens the rationale for controls in general. Cutting items with military relevance based on short-term shifts in Soviet behavior would be dangerous. Although in the past changes in export controls have been used to signal policy shifts, the machinery for doing so is cumbersome, and the process draws the entire controls program into question.

Variations in credit policies are a far more fertile field for linkage. Shifts in the political climate automatically will produce shifts in the credit market.[21] The issue then becomes whether governments will continue to grant and insure credit on favorable terms despite the shifts in the market. Although determining effective rates of interest is difficult because of the complex interactions among exporters, banks, and governments, the OECD consensus rate policy provides a format for general guidelines. Shifting loans to the East from the developing-nation rate to the high-income-nation category clearly would raise credit rates. Alliance consultation could produce agreement on the rate category to be applied, and this rate could be adjusted based on the political climate. Monitoring national compliance with the policy would be difficult, but the criterion would be to measure behavior against export policies in force in that country for different regions. In other words, there would be less emphasis on comparing French and German interest rates and more on comparing French and German approaches to the Soviet Union with their approaches to other nations.

Case against Sanctions

The pressure to shift economic relationships in the short run based on specific Soviet actions is intense. Governments must respond to acts such as the invasion of Afghanistan, the declaration of martial law in Poland, and the destruction of the South Korean civilian airliner that strayed over Soviet airspace. In such situations military retaliation would carry excessive risks of escalation, and mere speeches could be interpreted at home and abroad as signs of weakness. Economic sanctions appear to be a reasonable mechanism for at least sending a clear signal of national disgust and concern or at best actually deterring similar behavior in the future.

To be effective, sanctions must impose a cost on the target country, but they need not change behavior. It may be enough if they carry a clear signal. The reality has been that sanctions against the East frequently have transmitted a signal of weakness rather than strength. The partial grain embargo against the Soviet Union after the invasion of Afghanistan was withdrawn in the face of domestic pressure in the United States. The debate over sanctions against martial law in Poland produced sharp disagreements within the alliance and generated a counter-productive debate over the Siberia–Europe natural gas pipeline and sharp European reactions to U.S. assertions of extraterritorial controls on exports.

Sanctions inevitably fall on one group of producers and exporters in alliance countries. In industrial trade, long planning periods are typical for major projects, and interrupting those projects at the last minute has serious political and economic implications. Short-run variations in export controls policies again draw the very basis of controls into question, and cumbersome government bureaucracies are incapable of such short-run policy reversals. Financial and trade policy instruments are inappropriate for nuance and precise policy control.[22]

Assessing the Prospects for an Alliance Consensus

The agenda proposed here is modest but achievable within the substantial constraints of maintaining alliance consensus. First, export controls policy must be strengthened by clearly defining the military relevance of various technologies, tightening COCOM enforcement of technology transfer, and substantially improving the data base on critical technologies. Second, linkage of economic policies with Soviet political and military behavior should be made an explicit element of alliance strategy. That linkage should emphasize credit arrangements rather than variations in export controls policies. Finally, economic sanctions should be used only when the domestic political pressures for some action are overwhelming, and then only after extensive alliance consultation. The duration of sanctions should not be linked to modifications in Soviet behavior because such modifications are unlikely, and termination could then be seen as a sign of weakness. Announcing the term of the sanction at the outset could avoid such problems.

The potential impacts of economic linkage are limited in comparison with the impact of military strength on deterrence. In the early 1970s economic linkage often was viewed as a substitute for strength as the U.S. defense budget declined in real terms. The recovery of U.S. military strength in the 1980s should reduce the pressure for placing such a strategic burden on limited financial instruments. Yet, East-West economic relationships remain an important part of overall U.S. strategy. Even the lowest-common-denominator program outlined here could make an important contribution to the solidarity and strength of the alliance.

Notes

1. For an overview of the interrelationships of economics and national security policy, see Lee D. Olvey, James R. Golden, and Robert C. Kelly, *The Economics of National Security* (Wayne, N.J.: Avery Publications, 1984), pp. 1–12.

2. For an elaboration of these points, see James R. Golden, *The Dynamics of Change in NATO: A Burden Sharing Perspective* (New York: Praeger Publishers, 1983), pp. 162–168.

3. For the results of that study, see James R. Golden, "Testimony on the Administration of Export Controls," *Extension and Revision of the Export Administration Act of 1969*, Hearings before the Subcommittee on International Economic Policy and Trade of the Committee on Foreign Affairs, House of Representatives (Washington, D.C.: Government Printing Office, 1979), pp. 265–276.

4. Samuel P. Huntington, "Trade, Technology, and Leverage: Economic Diplomacy," *Foreign Policy* 32 (Fall 1978): 63–80.

5. The U.S. position actually predates the imposition of marital law in December 1981, but the situation in Poland strengthened U.S. opposition. For a summary of the official U.S. view, see Bureau of Public Affairs, "Soviet-West European Natural Gas Pipeline," *Current Policy*, no. 331 (Washington, D.C.: Department of State, October 14, 1981).

6. For example, see Friedemann Mueller, *Die Ost-West-Beziehungen im Energiebereich: Zwischen Abhaengigkeit und Verflechtung* (Ebenhausen, FRG: Stiftung Wissenschaft und Politik, October 1980).

7. For an excellent summary of the reversal in the German view of trade between the 1960s and the 1970s, see Angela Stent Yergin, *East-West Technology Transfer: European Perspectives*, Washington Papers, no. 75 (Beverly Hills: Sage Publications, 1980), pp. 23–28.

8. Defense Science Board Task Force on Export of U.S. Technology, "An Analysis of Export Control of U.S. Technology—a DOD Perspective," (Washington, D.C.: Office of the Director of Defense Research and Engineering, February 4, 1976.)

9. For example, see Michael T. Klare, "The Unnoticed Arms Trade: Exports of Conventional Arms-Making Technology," *International Security* 8 (Fall 1983): esp. 78–80.

10. For rough estimates of the extent of such subsidies, see Daniel F. Kohler and Kip T. Fisher, "Subsidization of East-West Trade through Credit Insurance and Loan Guarantees" (Santa Monica, Calif.: RAND, January 1983). For a German reaction and argument that export credit guarantees provide little subsidy, see Klaus Schroeder, *Die Ost-West-Finanzbeziehungen* (Ebanhausen, FRG: Stiftung Wissenschaft und Politik, November 1983), pp. 23–26.

11. For a more complete discussion of the licensing system see Olvey, Golden, and Kelly, *The Economics of National Security*, pp. 324–327.

12. For one assessment of the positions within the administration, see Clyde H. Farnsworth, "The Doves Capture Control of Trade," *New York Times*, October 23, 1983, pp. F1, F12, F13.

13. For example, the United Kingdom sold 150 jet engines and the technology to build them to the People's Republic of China in 1973, despite COCOM opposition.

14. For one of the earlier studies of these problems, see Comptroller General of the United States, *The Government's Role in East-West Trade: Problems and Issues* (Washington, D.C.: General Accounting Office, 1976), p. 47.

15. For a discussion of the practices of these organizations and the typical terms of the insurance granted see Kohler and Fisher, "Subsidization of East-West Trade," pp. 63–67.

16. "Export Credits: The Consensus Agrees to Differ," *Economist*, April 23, 1983, pp. 94–95.

17. Nil Ozergene, "Lessons of the Pipeline Negotiations," ACIS Working Paper no. 40 (Los Angeles, Calif.: Center for International and Strategic Affairs, University of California, Los Angeles, July 1983), p. 68.

18. For example, see OECD, *The Export Credit Financing Systems* (Paris: OECD, 1982).

19. "East-West Traders Raise the Curtain," *Economist*, January 7, 1984, pp. 64–65.

20. "COCOM: Stemming the Tide," *Economist*, December 17, 1983, p. 41.

21. Freidemann Mueller, "Der Zusammenhang von Politischem Klima und Wirtschaftskooperation," in *Sanktionen in den Ost-West-Beziehungen*, ed. Friedemann Mueller (Ebenhausen, FRG: Stiftung Wissenschaft und Politik, August 1982), p. 168b.

22. For a similar conclusion on economic sanctions in other contexts, see Margaret Doxey, "International Sanctions: Trials of Strength or Tests or Weakness?" *Millenium: Journal of International Studies* 12 (Spring 1983):79–87.

Discussion Questions

1. Trade benefits our economy; technological superiority is an important aspect of national security. Must we sacrifice one to maintain the other?

2. What are the alliance implications of technology transfer? Can we achieve consensus within NATO on trade restrictions with the East?

3. How would you evaluate the efficacy of economic sanctions?

Suggestions for Additional Reading

Bucy, J. Fred. "Technology Transfer and East-West Trade." *International Security* 5, no. 3 (Winter 1980–1982):132–151.

Bull, Hedley. *The Control of the Arms Race.* London: Weidenfeld and Nicolson, 1961.

Hoffmann, Stanley. "New Variations on Old Themes." *International Security* 4, no. 1 (Summer 1979):88–107.

Huntington, Samuel P. "Trade, Technology and Leverage: Economic Diplomacy." *Foreign Policy,* no. 32 (Fall 1978):63–80.

Olvey, Lee D., James R. Golden, and Robert C. Kelly. *The Economics of National Security.* Wayne, N.J.: Avery Publications, 1984.

Osgood, Robert. *NATO: The Entangling Alliance.* Chicago: University of Chicago Press, 1962.

Talbot, Strobe. *Endgame: The Inside Story of SALT II.* New York: Harper and Row, 1979.

Wolfe, Thomas. *The SALT Experience.* Cambridge, Mass.: Ballinger, 1979.

Part VI
National Security Policy: The Military Dimension

Military policy is usually the instrument of last resort because of its high risk and cost. Nonetheless, military power is an important commodity "in a world where the institutions and rules of law are honored mostly in the breach and where force is often the final arbiter of conflicting claims."[1]

Purposes of Military Policy

Military policy contributes to national security in four ways. First, a nation may use military power to deter aggression, either against itself or other nations. Military power gives a nation the ability to punish an adversary, an essential requirement of deterrence. Despite the fact that deterrence focuses on the threat to use military power rather than its actual employment, a country must have both the military capabilities and the requisite strategies if deterrence is to be credible.

Second, a nation may employ military policy to defend itself or its interests should deterrence fail and aggression occur. Defense may be limited to denying the attacker its objectives or may be expanded to achieve the attacker's unconditional surrender or destruction.

Third, a nation may use military policy to coerce other nations to comply with its desires. As we pointed out in part III, coercion is based on the threat to use force. Coercion is an important aspect of military policy, and it serves as a complement to diplomatic and economic policy. The threat of force often has served as a backdrop and impetus to diplomacy.

Fourth, military policy can increase the prestige of a nation or regime through displays of military might. Although such displays may serve deterrent or coercive functions as well, the flexing of military muscle often is done to increase prestige or to gain respect. History provides numerous examples of rulers and governments parading their forces in order to impress their allies and adversaries, as well as their own publics. The Soviet May Day parade is an example of this use of military policy.

Just as different purposes require different applications of military power, a particular type of force structure may not achieve each purpose equally. Offensive nuclear forces currently are the foundation of deterrence. But despite their tremendous capacity for destruction, they have little utility for preventing damage in return. Alternatively, a developing nation's desire to add to its prestige may be achieved through the purchase of sophisticated jet combat aircraft, yet they may be of little use in combating insurgency, the type of conflict such nations are most likely to face.

The spectrum of military policy can be divided into four basic categories: strategic nuclear, theater nuclear, conventional and low intensity. Although these categories are not meant to be precise divisions, they do differ in terms of the size, intensity, scope, and types of forces employed.

The most destructive form of conflict is strategic nuclear war. Not only could the United States and the USSR completely destroy each other's society, but the destructive power of nuclear weapons is so enormous that some scientists claim that even a limited nuclear war between the superpowers could result in a nuclear winter, ending human life on the planet.[2] Because strategic nuclear war would be characterized by massive destruction, nations have a strong incentive to prevent its occurrence. As long as neither adversary feels it is immune to nuclear destruction, there is little utility in starting such a conflict since the costs would far outweigh the benefits.

Since 1974, however, there has been increased discussion of limited nuclear war. War can be limited in terms of the objectives sought, forces used, the geographic scope of the conflict, or the nature and location of the targets. The most commonly considered ways of limiting nuclear war would be to limit the types of targets (military forces rather than cities), the number or types of weapons used (demonstration strikes of one or a few nuclear weapons or use of tactical nuclear weapons only), or geographic limitations (restricting use of nuclear weapons to areas outside the borders of the superpowers). While some argue that limited nuclear war has the advantage of being less destructive than strategic nuclear war, and therefore of some possible use as a means of achieving political objectives, it presents a danger of escalation to general nuclear war and may actually increase the possibility of conflict by making nuclear war appear winnable.

Theater nuclear war is a form of limited nuclear war in which nuclear weapons are limited to use in a particular geographic area. For example, nuclear weapons could be used to defend Europe against a Soviet attack, but their use could be limited to the European theater in order to reduce the risk to the superpowers of nuclear destruction. While this view is consistent with the theory of limited war, it is easy to understand why the Europeans are not very sanguine about this possibility, since a nuclear war limited to Europe would be devastating to them.

Whereas the fear of the possible consequences has prevented nuclear conflict to date, it has not prevented the occurrence of major conventional military conflicts. The possession of vast nuclear arsenals by both the United States and the USSR has resulted in a form of nuclear stalemate in which these tremendous forces appear to have little utility except to prevent each other's use of nuclear weapons. Beneath the umbrella of nuclear stalemate, a wide variety of conventional warfare can and does continue to take place. These conflicts range from small-scale interventions of relatively short duration (such as the U.S. invasion of Grenada), to prolonged, intense, and costly military conflicts (such as the Soviet invasion of Afghanistan), to large-scale conventional wars (such as the Iran-Iraq war).

Low-intensity warfare is perhaps the most difficult category to define; it includes such diverse elements as counterterrorist operations, insurgency, guerrilla warfare, and border skirmishes. The belligerents in such conflicts may be nations, political parties, hordes of religious fanatics, or small groups of terrorists. Although on an international scale their size is usually quite small, these conflicts still can threaten the stability of a nation or even a region. Because the opponent is difficult to identify, the application of massive amounts of military force often has limited utility. The U.S. experience in Vietnam reflects the difficulty that even a superpower has in achieving its objectives, despite tremendous military superiority.

The wide variety of possible levels of conflict makes the development of military policy difficult at best. Forces that are useful in one context may be of very little use in another. For example, nuclear warheads are of little utility in guerrilla warfare. Adding to the difficulties faced by policymakers is the fact that they must give priority to the most dangerous possibilities, yet these may be the least likely to occur. The United States has spent billions of dollars on nuclear forces in order to deter nuclear war but has lost over 110,000 soldiers in two major conflicts in which its vast nuclear arsenal was of little use. Since resources are limited, there are insufficient funds to provide forces to cope properly with all possible types of conflict, especially on the lower end of the spectrum. As a result, the military forces of the United States often seem inadequately structured to deal with conflicts that actually or seem most likely to occur.

Military policy has two basic components: strategy and force structure. While strategy traditionally has been defined as the use of military engagement to achieve the object of war, a more appropriate definition in modern times may be the employment of the national armed forces to secure national policy objectives by the application or the threat of force. The people and equipment organized to execute military policy constitute force structure. These two components combine to determine a nation's military policy.

Typically, analysis of military policy is divided into considerations of strategic nuclear forces and conventional forces; however, this approach is inappropriate since the two are inextricably linked in terms of strategy and force structure. An evaluation of one type of force without considering the others poses an artificial distinction that does not exist in the world of military policy and that hampers effective analysis. Consequently, we divide military policy not into different types of forces but into strategy and force structure in order to illuminate the linkages which exist along the spectrum of military policy.

Military Strategy

Military strategy is distinct from national strategy in that it focuses on military means to achieve military ends. Nonetheless, in order for military strategy to serve national security policy usefully, military ends must be linked to political objectives. Although military policy emphasizes the use of armed force, the use of military force should never be separated from the political objectives it is meant to serve. Further, military strategy, the plans for the use of armed force, should be consistent with the national strategy and should assist the nation in meeting its national interests and maintaining its values.

From this perspective it follows that military strategy may be changed while the national strategy remains unchanged. Military strategy may be changed as a result of a shift in emphasis to diplomatic and economic policy components or to emphasize different capabilities along the spectrum of military policy in order to meet changes in the international or domestic environments. For example, the United States changed the emphasis of its military strategy in 1961 from a reliance on nuclear weapons to flexible response while maintaining a national strategy of containment.

Military strategy has a number of components, and any analysis of military strategy must look beyond statements of declaratory policy. Analysis of nuclear policy must include considerations of the nuclear balance, as well as targeting and deployment plans. Analysis of the conventional force components of military strategy must include considerations of the balance of forces as well as the employment and deployment plans. Since military strategy is designed to meet military ends, it is most directly a function of the military balance along the entire spectrum of force.

The Nuclear Balance

The relative nuclear balance affects strategy in two ways. Militarily, a major imbalance in favor of the Soviets could jeopardize the survivability of U.S. forces. This condition would violate an important precept of nuclear deterrence, crisis stability. Crisis stability is achieved when neither side has the incentive to attack first due to confidence in the ability of its arsenal to be able to accomplish its mission even after absorbing an all-out nuclear attack. Without crisis stability, one or both sides could have an incentive to strike preemptively in order to gain an advantage. The deployment of U.S. nuclear forces is designed to hedge against breakthroughs that could threaten crisis stability.

Politically it is important that the United States maintain at least essential equivalence with the Soviet Union—that is, a rough balance in nuclear capabilities. There should be no significant asymmetry in the basic elements that determine force effectiveness, such as survivability, flexibility, penetrability, and secure command, control, and communications. If the Soviets attain an advantage, it is possible they could use it to coerce or intimidate the United States or its allies. Even though essential equivalence may remain unaffected, the appearance of a Soviet advantage could affect political perceptions and influence.

In order to measure effectiveness, one must look at more than a comparison of total force levels, since qualitative as well as quantitative measures also are important. Survivability, accuracy, reliability, throw-weight, yield, warhead capacity per launcher, and equivalent megatonnage are all as significant as the number of launchers. Conclusions regarding the balance can differ depending on the measures used to compare the two forces. While the Soviet Union outnumbers the United States in strategic nuclear launchers, the United States outnumbers the Soviets in strategic nuclear warheads. Although the Soviets possess an advantage in total throw-weight (a measure of launcher payload), the bulk of U.S. systems are more survivable. Comprehensive analysis of the nuclear balance must be based on all of the measures of force effectiveness, not just one or two.

The Conventional Balance

In any attempt to assess the balance of conventional forces between the United States and the Soviet Union, it is important to be aware of the difficulties inherent in comparing forces. As with the nuclear balance, mere comparisons of the quantities of equipment are inadequate. Such comparisons do not take into account such important factors as differences in quality of equipment, technology, training, geographical advantages, deployment, and even morale.

To take one statistic as an example, the Soviet Union has 191 divisions in its army, while the United States has only 19 active divisions, including the marine corps. This comparison implies that the Soviets outnumber the Americans by more than ten to one. But this comparison is misleading since many Soviet divisions are not at full strength (approximately 100 of them are manned at 30 percent strength or less). Further, U.S. divisions typically have 16,000 soldiers each, while Soviet divisions contain approximately 10,000 soldiers.

Any assessment of the balance of forces must reflect the circumstances of the specific contingency. Geography always plays an important role in determining the balance of military power. The distance to the theater, quality of lines of supply, and mobilization rates all become important. For example, NATO is outnumbered by the Warsaw Pact only slightly (1:1.23) with respect to tanks in Europe. Nonetheless, the Soviets can reinforce quickly their units in Europe, while the United States must transport heavy equipment 5,000 miles, an enormous reinforcement problem that takes a considerable amount of time.

A major issue in comparing forces concerns the quality of weapons systems. The West traditionally has relied on qualitative advantages to offset the Soviet quantitative edge; however, the value of the quality differential is difficult to determine. While efforts are made to compare systems (for example, the U.S. Air

Force maintains a small unit that flies and tests Soviet fighters obtained from other nations), it is difficult in peacetime to measure the impact of qualitative differences.

There are some conclusions that can be drawn from an assessment of the conventional balance. The Soviets have maintained an overall quantitative advantage in most conventional forces since World War II. A disturbing trend is that the quantitative gap seems to be widening as a result of the higher rate of Soviet production and investment in weapons systems. In addition, the qualitative advantage enjoyed by the Western allies is being challenged by advances in Soviet technology. Recently the Soviets have made major improvements in their navy and increased their ability to project military power worldwide. The increased ability to project power is enhanced by a considerable geographic advantage, since many areas of U.S. interest such as Europe, Northeast Asia, and the Persian Gulf are much closer to the USSR than to the United States.

Deployment Policy

Nuclear. In order to be able to retaliate and inflict unacceptable damage, at least a portion of U.S. nuclear forces must be able to survive a Soviet nuclear attack. An essential requirement for successful deterrence is survivability. This need for survivability has a major influence on deployment policy. The deployment of U.S. nuclear forces is based on the maintenance of three independent systems, each capable of inflicting unacceptable damage. These three systems—ICBMs, SLBMs, and intercontinental bombers—make up what is commonly called the triad. The purpose of the triad is twofold. First, maintenance of a nuclear triad bolsters deterrence by complicating Soviet attack planning, making it extremely difficult for the Soviet Union to plan and execute a successful attack on all these components at the same time. Further, although each system is designed to be independently survivable, the redundancy provided by the triad hedges against a technological breakthrough that could threaten any one system. For example, should advances in Soviet ICBM accuracy cause the U.S. land-based ICBMs to become vulnerable, as some analysts suggest they are, the United States still can assure destruction of the Soviet Union with SLBMs and bombers while solutions are sought to the problem of ICBM vulnerability.

Merely having survivable nuclear weapons is not enough to guarantee effective retaliation, however. In order to use those systems, an effective command, control, and communications (C^3) system is necessary. This system must perform several functions: warn of an attack, assess the results of an attack (so an appropriate response can be determined), determine what U.S. forces remain, identify Soviet targets, order retaliation, assess results of the retaliatory attack, and provide a means of terminating the conflict.

While maintaining a capability for assured destruction may be sufficient to deter nuclear attacks on the United States, it is less clear that such a policy would have sufficient credibility for extended deterrence, since the all-or-nothing approach implied by assured destruction lacks flexibility in the event deterrence fails.

It may be that a military strategy of flexible response that develops options other than the total destruction of the other side is more effective for extended deterrence. If deterrence fails, it is argued, flexibility would increase the possibility that the United States could terminate the conflict on favorable terms and reestablish deterrence at the lowest possible level.

Anthony Cordesman discusses nuclear force structure and doctrine in chapter 18. He describes the various components of the nuclear triad and elaborates on the characteristics of each one. He analyzes the different doctrinal approaches to nuclear weapons and points out some of the difficulties in attempting to extend their deterrent value to our allies.

Conventional. Due to the threat posed by Soviet force in Europe and the difficulties in quickly transporting the heavy forces necessary to counter such a threat, the U.S. Army stations four and two-thirds divisions in Europe. To counter immediate threats in Asia, one army division is located in Korea and another in Hawaii, and one marine division is stationed in Okinawa. The bulk of the remaining U.S. ground forces are stationed in the United States, available for deployment anywhere overseas.

In addition to the divisions stationed in Europe, the United States also prepositions heavy equipment in Europe sufficient to equip four additional divisions. By placing the heavy equipment in Europe, the air and sealift required for initial deployment is cut drastically, and the ability of NATO to defend itself without having to resort to nuclear weapons is improved significantly.

Part of the need for rapid deployment to Europe is due to the strategy adopted for its defense. The adoption of flexible response caused the Europeans to be concerned about the possibility that a destructive conventional war would be fought in Europe. The West Germans were especially concerned that their country would be overrun or devastated. As a result, the doctrine of the alliance is to defend as far forward as possible (hence the name, forward defense) and to rely on the threat of rapid escalation to nuclear retaliation in order to deter aggression. This strategy requires rapid reinforcement from the United States if NATO is to stop a Soviet attack without using nuclear weapons. Given the distances involved and the limited amount of airlift and sealift available, rapid reinforcement will be difficult, especially if another confrontation has occurred in some other region of the world.

U.S. deployment policy is largely a function of the time available for deployment and the airlift and sealift assets available to transport forces to the threatened theater. The short warning time expected in Europe and the size of the deployment needed to counter the threat impelled the United States to deploy troops and equipment to Europe on a permanent basis. While the level of the threat is less in Asia, the tremendous distances and lack of lift also influence U.S. deployments there. Whereas flexibility is augmented by keeping forces stationed in the United States, as William Kaufmann points out in chapter 19, the advantage of increased flexibility gained by stationing forces in the United States must be balanced against the time required to deploy those forces against varying levels of threats overseas.

The location and nature of potential threats and the limited size of U.S. conventional forces make flexibility and mobility crucial aspects of force design. The army is making efforts to increase the strategic mobility of its forces (though some argue at the expense of their combat power) by lightening them to reduce the strategic lift required to move them. A significant requirement for strategic lift remains, however. Mobility forces do not receive priority in the air force and navy; they compete with other missions that these services consider more important.

Targeting Policy, Nuclear Forces

Since nuclear forces have not been employed since World War II, it is more appropriate to look at the targeting policy for those forces—that is, how they would be employed should the occasion arise. Targeting policy affects flexibility just as deployment policy does. The countervalue targeting policy that is a basic part of assured destruction provides little flexibility. It could force the United States into an all-or-nothing situation, with the only U.S. response to a Soviet attack being a counterstrike against Soviet cities, thus eliminating any reason for the Soviets to refrain from attacking U.S. cities. An alternative approach, counterforce targeting, is to attack military targets in order to destroy the instruments of aggression and to reduce the aggressor's capability to inflict damage on the United States. The adoption of counterforce targeting is not essential for assured destruction; rather it is more consistent with a controlled war-fighting strategy.

While counterforce targeting, like other flexible nuclear options, may add to the credibility of deterrence by making a nuclear response more likely, there are those who argue that this increased likelihood makes nuclear war itself more likely by appearing to lower the level of destructiveness. Further, since nuclear war may be impossible to control, such a response could escalate to countervalue attacks, thereby negating any benefits of such a policy.

Nonetheless, the tremendous proliferation in the numbers and types of potential targets since 1961 has resulted in more and more emphasis being placed on flexible nuclear options. Military bases and forces, transportation facilities, the industrial infrastructure, and the instruments of political control of the communist party are all examples of the types of targets included on the target list. The proliferation of targets and options also gave rise to new requirements for command and control and for more accurate weapons, although it is difficult to tell which came first, the policy or the technology.

Employment Policy, Conventional Forces

Conventional forces can protect vital interests from attack or seize resources considered vital to the United States. For example, President Carter stated that the United States would intervene in order to protect Persian Gulf oil resources, and President Reagan threatened to employ U.S. forces to keep the Strait of Hormuz open. Both are examples of declaratory employment policy. As an example of actual employment policy, the British and the French employed troops in an attempt to protect the Suez Canal from Egyptian takeover, and the British sent troops to the Falkland Islands to recapture them from the Argentines. Missions such as the 1948 Berlin airlift, the military intervention in the Dominican Republic, and the invasion of Grenada are examples of employment of U.S. force to protect U.S. interests.

Second, employment of military forces can demonstrate national resolve to stop aggression, thereby deterring future aggression. In chapter 6, Glenn Snyder points out that by responding firmly when peripheral interests are threatened, a nation can lend credibility to threats to contain higher levels of aggression, thereby enhancing deterrence. This view, as part of the strategy of flexible response, was responsible in part for U.S. employment of troops in Vietnam. The employment of military forces in retaliation for acts of an adversary, as in the case of Israeli air strikes in retaliation for Palestinian terrorism, is a form of deterrence in that it may deter further acts for fear of reprisals.

Third, a policy of horizontal escalation can preclude the need to escalate vertically to the use of nuclear weapons should efforts to defend against a conventional attack fail. The flexible response strategy yields several advantages to a potential aggressor. The aggressor can choose when, where, and how to attack and can formulate a detailed plan for its operations in order to maximize its strengths and exploit U.S. vulnerabilities. Rather than fighting at the place and time of the aggressor's choosing, horizontal escalation entails responding to an attack by conducting an attack against the aggressor's interests in another region, where the United States has the advantage. This responding attack can be intertheater or intratheater in nature. A U.S. invasion of Cuba in response to Soviet aggression in Iran would be an example of intertheater horizontal escalation. An example of intratheater horizontal escalation can be seen in proposals that suggest that NATO should respond to a Soviet attack in Western Europe with a counteroffensive into Eastern Europe.

Finally, U.S. forces can be employed to maintain stability in a region or in a nation. The landings of marines in Lebanon in 1958 and 1982 were examples of U.S. efforts to accomplish this goal.

There are, however, potential problems with the employment of military forces to accomplish the purposes set forth here. There is always the risk of escalation, resulting in a possible superpower confrontation that could lead to broader conflict and nuclear war. There is also the risk of entanglement, where the U.S. commitment becomes larger and more costly than originally envisioned, as occurred in the case of U.S. intervention in Vietnam and to some extent in Lebanon. While entanglement is a major concern, a comparison of Vietnam and Grenada could lead to the conclusion that the American people are not opposed to the employment of force; rather they merely do not have a high tolerance for sustained conflicts with ambiguous objectives and limited success.

Force Structure

Force structure is the second component of military policy. It is the prime determinant of what military forces are available to be used and the prime constraint on how they can be used. For example, the presence of airborne units, coupled with sufficient strategic airlift, means that light infantry divisions can be delivered quickly to virtually any part of the globe. On the other hand, heavy armored divisions, although of high utility in an armored warfare environment, cannot be deployed quickly from peacetime locations, even should the requisite amount of strategic sealift be in the force structure.

Force structure is, in theory, determined by a nation's military strategy. In practice, however, military force structure is shaped by service parochialism, congressional interests, bureaucratic inertia, industrial pressure, and public opinion. Further, because of the long lead times required to develop, produce, and deploy new weapons systems, military strategy can change faster than force structure.

Military force structure reflects, nonetheless, the relative emphasis that strategy places on nuclear versus conventional forces. A military strategy that seeks to meet expanded U.S. interests usually will emphasize conventional forces. A strategy more concerned with central deterrence will emphasize nuclear forces. Further, since conventional forces are labor intensive, they are relatively more expensive than nuclear forces. Thus, while nuclear forces include some costly items, overall nuclear forces typically take only 15 to 20 percent of the defense budget. Therefore, cost also can play a significant role in determining force structure.

Force structure has two major aspects: manpower and weapons. Together they determine the numbers, types, sizes, and capabilities of military units. Manpower policy, especially with an all-volunteer force, is particularly critical since personnel-related defense costs can consume nearly half of the defense budget, thereby reducing the resources available for new weapons. The Soviets' significantly lower manpower cost is a major factor in the Soviet Union's ability to produce more weapons than the United States. Nonetheless, conscription carries a societal cost, which Americans have been unwilling to pay since 1972.

Attempts to buy more manpower within existing manpower budgets can result in less-than-competitive wages being offered and consequently can result in recruiting lower-quality soldiers. This result can have an adverse impact on trainability, morale, leadership, and discipline in the forces and can severely degrade combat readiness.

Throughout the twentieth century, the U.S. armed forces have sought to capitalize on U.S. technological expertise to increase combat capabilities, hoping to save U.S. lives on the battlefield by substituting firepower for manpower. There is an even greater premium placed on this substitution when manpower is cost constrained to the degree that it is in an all-volunteer force.

As a result, the weapons we buy often seem to attempt to incorporate every conceivable technological advantage. This approach risks degrading overall effectiveness by driving up unit costs for equipment and therefore reducing the quantity of weapons available for the force structure. Such an approach also can require the reduction of operating and maintenance budgets in order to finance weapons procurement, thereby reducing combat readiness.

Additionally, more advanced weapons can necessitate a higher-quality soldier, if not to operate then certainly to maintain those weapons. This situation sets up a tension between the manpower budget, which attempts to hire smart soldiers, and the procurement budget, which attempts to buy advanced weapons. This tension is difficult, if not impossible, to resolve without large increases in defense spending.

An even greater problem affecting force structure is that although combat operations are typically joint operations involving all the services, the budgeting and procurement of manpower and weapons is done by each individual service with little or no leveling across the services. Thus, one can find duplication of effort on the one hand and inadequate numbers of specific forces on the other.

Finally, we find that the desirable force structure characteristics of strategic deployability, battlefield mobility, sustainability, and lethality often are at odds with each other. Attempts to rectify deficiencies in one area can exacerbate difficulties in another.

It is apparent that military policy often can display incongruity and discontinuity since strategy and force structure are formed by different processes and are shaped by different influences. Nonetheless, despite such deficiencies, military policy continues to be a vital component of national security policy.

Notes

1. William W. Kaufmann, "Defense Policy," in Joseph A. Pechman, ed., *Setting National Priorities: Agenda for the 1980s* (Washington, D.C.: Brookings Institution, 1980), p. 293.

2. Carl Sagan, "Nuclear War and Climatic Catastrophe," *Foreign Affairs* 62, no. 2 (Winter 1983–1984): 259.

18

American Strategic Forces and Extended Deterrence

Anthony H. Cordesman

T here is nothing new in Europeans questioning the credibility of the American nuclear commitment to the defense of Europe, or the willingness of the United States to risk using her strategic forces to halt a successful Warsaw Pact attack on NATO. Both Europeans and Americans have publicly and privately questioned U.S. resolve to defend Europe since the date when the first Soviet test of a thermonuclear weapon became public.

This questioning has naturally increased in intensity since the Soviet Union began to deploy large numbers of theater nuclear weapons and intercontinental ballistic missiles (ICBM). Ironically, several European defense experts and commentators expressed strong doubts about U.S. ability to extend deterrence during the year before the Cuban missile crisis. Although the resolution of that particular crisis eased European fears, it scarcely stilled all uncertainty and doubts.

The Multilateral Force (MLF) debate of the mid-1960s was largely a product of continued European questioning of extended deterrence. Although the MLF was never deployed, this was more the result of the vicissitudes of the politics of the day than of European confidence in the assignment of some U.S. submarine-launched ballistic missiles (SLBM) to the Supreme Allied Commander Europe (SACEUR) and the creation of a NATO Nuclear Planning Group (NPG).

Similar European doubts were exposed during the debate over the *force de frappe* and French withdrawal from NATO's military command, during the British debate over the creation of Britain's *Polaris* force, in various German debates over changes in the basing of theater nuclear weapons on German soil, and during many of the high-level NATO discussions that went into the planning of the Military Committee document MC 14/3 and NATO's discussion of flexible response. Such fears delayed the conversion of NATO's dedicated nuclear strike aircraft to dual-capable or conventional missions by half a decade longer than was otherwise required.

During the last three years, however, the basis of European uncertainty about the U.S. commitment to extended deterrence has changed fundamentally in character:

First, it has become obvious that the USSR has achieved full parity with the U.S. in her ability to achieve assured destruction against civil and economic targets.

Second, it has gradually become clear that the USSR may acquire a temporary superiority in counterforce exchange in the early 1980s if she launches a first strike against U.S. ICBM forces.

Third, the Soviet Union is acquiring increasingly superior numbers of long-range SS-20 IRBM and *Backfire* medium bombers, and could be moving towards a credible first-strike capability to virtually disarm NATO's land and air forces in Europe.

Fourth, data gradually becoming public on Soviet nuclear plans indicate that the Soviet military appears never to have accepted mutual assured destruction. Instead, it seems to have focused on developing a doctrine of war-fighting capability which is in part based on disarming nuclear first strikes which will, in effect, achieve a practical decoupling of U.S. strategic forces from NATO.

Finally, the quality of U.S. leadership during the last few years, and such incidents as President Carter's handling of the "neutron bomb" have raised serious doubts about U.S. resolve.

Unhappily, many of the doubts raised about America's ability to extend deterrence to Europe are essentially political arguments based on theoretical descriptions of strategy and military capability that are divorced from the reality of the U.S. forces now in being or in procurement. (For a full presentation of these arguments, see Henry A. Kissinger, "NATO: The Next Thirty Years," and McGeorge Bundy, "The Future of Strategic Deterrence," both in *Survival,* November/December 1979.) They may well lead Europe to seek the wrong kind of American assurances and American and NATO force improvements. This becomes clear when one looks at the criteria that American and NATO forces must meet to make extended deterrence effective in the 1980s and at how American capabilities for extended deterrence have evolved during the last twenty years.

The Criteria for Extended Deterrence

It is important to note in beginning this examination that there is no hard and fast definition of "extended deterrence," nor any fixed method of evaluating U.S. strategic forces, plans and doctrine, and saying whether they do or do not provide extended deterrence.

"Extended deterrence" is the result of *Soviet* perceptions of both U.S. and NATO capabilities, and not the result of the relative total size of U.S. and Soviet strategic forces. It is the result of the ability of U.S. strategic forces to contribute to the deterrence of Soviet or Warsaw Pact aggression at the theater level, to limit the intensity of such attacks, and to terminate them on terms favorable to the U.S. and her Allies. To a lesser degree, it is the result of the ability of theater forces to contribute to the deterrence of Soviet strategic attacks on the U.S. by increasing the difficulties of launching successful attacks, and by increasing the risk of unacceptable retaliation by a combination of strategic and theater forces.

In any given scenario, Soviet perceptions of extended deterrence will be largely determined by the mix of strategic nuclear, theater nuclear, and conventional capabilities on each side as they apply to the particular scenario and objective involved. "Extended deterrence" thus covers a necessarily broad and uncertain range of force characteristics, contingencies, and United States' national security objectives. It can be applied to virtually any military theater in the world. For NATO, "extended deterrence" covers those situations where the Soviet objective would be serious enough to make escalation to theater nuclear war credible. In other parts of the world, it covers any situation where the objective is important enough for the United States to undertake the risk of using strategic forces.

In both cases, the common element will be that a limited use of U.S. strategic forces could alter the outcome favorably for the West, and that the resulting risk of all-out strategic conflict would be proportionate to the value of the theater objective being defended. This means that the degree of deterrence extended in any given contingency is shaped by an extremely complex mix of factors. However, it will always depend upon the Soviet perception that U.S. strategic forces have the particular capabilities needed to intervene in a given conflict, and that the required level of force is one that the U.S. has both the incentive and will to use.

This means that extended deterrence can function at very different levels of military capability. If the U.S. has sufficient flexibility to use her strategic forces in limited theater strikes without degrading her overall ability to attack Soviet countervalue targets, then extended deterrence can be credible, provided always that the U.S. has convincingly demonstrated that she plans to employ her strategic forces, has the will to do so, and values the objective enough to take the risk. Conversely, even a weak U.S. possessing inferior and relatively inflexible strategic forces, might provide a convincing degree of extended deterrence against a massive Soviet theater nuclear first strike on NATO forces in Europe, simply because of the importance of the objective and the large-scale prior involvement of U.S. theater forces. Obviously, a vast range of contingencies exists between these extremes where the credibility of extended deterrence will depend entirely on the circumstances.

At the same time, extended deterrence does become steadily more convincing as theater capabilities and nuclear forces are improved. The credibility of extended deterrence in Europe is not simply a function of U.S. strategic capabilities but of NATO capabilities as well. This is particularly true as NATO theater nuclear forces improve their range and capability and become more and more capable of attacking those Soviet and Warsaw Pact targets currently covered by U.S. strategic forces. For example, NATO's plans to deploy land-based cruise missiles and *Pershing* II MRBM inevitably blur the distinction between U.S. strategic and NATO theater forces. This makes it more credible that any large-scale conflict in Europe which involves theater nuclear weapons will escalate to a level where U.S. strategic forces become involved and that limited uses of U.S. strategic forces would be made to cover any gap in NATO forces, because of the limited levels of escalation involved.

No simple equation exists between the strategic balance and U.S. ability to provide extended deterrence, nor is extended deterrence inevitably tied to the risk of all-out strategic conflict or its outcome. Its extent will be determined by whether the combination of U.S. strategic and NATO (or other) theater capabilities offers an overall range of military options that makes U.S. willingness to use the required number of strategic forces credible to the USSR. Where both strategic and theater forces are well suited to the defense of Europe, and where U.S. forces are strong enough to limit any Soviet incentive to escalate to even broader levels of conflict, then the level of deterrence extended is likely to be high.

For similar reasons, there can be no simple definition of the particular U.S. strategic forces or types of strike that may be employed in support of extended deterrence. Bombers, ICBM, SLBM and cruise missiles can all be employed with different degrees of flexibility. The particular mix of targets will be chosen to fit the situation and forces available. It might involve anything from demonstrative strikes on Warsaw Pact air bases in Eastern Europe to counter-city strikes to deter further Warsaw Pact nuclear attacks on urban areas in West Germany. It could involve a strategic strike on the major Other Military Targets (OMT) (i.e. targets of military significance but excluding strategic weapons) facilities in the Western Military Districts of the USSR, or SSBN attacks on a Soviet fleet operating against Norway.

Finally, extended deterrence does not simply apply to the prevention of war. It also applies to limiting its scope and intensity, and to its termination. Extended deterrence can thus be measured according to a number of different operational standards. The most critical is how far U.S. strategic and NATO theater nuclear capabilities deter any form of war and eliminate any incentive for the USSR to expand her forces and improve her warfighting capabilities. The second in priority is how far these capabilities deter large-scale confrontations or attacks. The third is how far the active employment of Western nuclear forces in war can terminate a conflict, once it has begun, on terms acceptable to NATO. For obvious reasons, the least important operational standard is the ability actually to inflict unacceptable levels of massive damage on the Soviet bloc once deterrence of war has failed.

Given this definition, it should be clear why it is difficult to establish firm criteria for measuring the degree of extended deterrence that any given balance of forces provides. Nevertheless, there are at least some criteria that U.S. and NATO forces must meet, and others which, if not essential, are desirable.

Essential Criteria

U.S. and NATO nuclear forces must meet four criteria to make extended deterrence credible to the USSR and to be effective in limited nuclear wars:

> The risk of escalation resulting from the use of U.S. strategic forces, in addition to NATO theater nuclear forces, must be limited enough to avoid the U.S. running an unacceptable risk of mutual civil and economic annihilation with the USSR. The U.S. cannot afford to rely on extended deterrence options which target Soviet cities and populations, or which expose her strategic forces to massive counterforce strikes. She must have limited nuclear options for her strategic forces which "blend" into the escalation ladder created by NATO conventional and theater nuclear forces, and which can pose an unacceptable risk of additional damage to Soviet and East European facilities and military forces without having to rely on a large-scale strategic exchange.

> The U.S. must have sufficient survivable strategic forces so that even large-scale exchanges in defense of NATO will not lead to an unacceptable "run down" of U.S. strategic capabilities against the USSR, needed as the ultimate defense. There must be no incentive for a Soviet strike against the remaining U.S. strategic forces.

> The U.S. must have the flexibility of rapid targeting capability and ability to control collateral damage. She must have flexibility to tailor her attacks rapidly to the most significant targets in the specific scenario she faces, and to minimize the height of each step in escalation. The more flexible, rapid-reacting, accurate and limited the U.S. options for response, the greater the credibility of use and conflict termination on an acceptable level.

> U.S. determination to use any combination of strategic and theater nuclear forces in the defense of Europe must be credible. Once U.S. and NATO forces have met the previous criteria, the U.S. must do everything in her power to convince the USSR that she will not accept a defeat in NATO, and that close links exist between the U.S. strategic forces and the defense of Europe. This linkage is partially assured by the deployment of some 300,000 U.S. forces in Europe and by the deployment in Europe of a substantial portion of the total U.S. inventory of nuclear weapons. However, it is also determined by the explicitness and determination with which the U.S. states her commitment to extended deterrence, by the ability of U.S. strategic forces and war plans to execute limited strikes if deterrence fails, and by the extent to which NATO theater nuclear weapons provide a smooth and survivable ladder of escalation which couples to the capabilities of U.S. strategic forces.

These four criteria are necessarily somewhat vague in terms of the precise forces and plans required to meet them. Many different mixes of U.S. and NATO nuclear capabilities are adequate to provide a substantial degree of extended deterrence, and there is room for a wide range of legitimate political and philosophical difference over how large and diverse a range of capabilities is required. This is one of the reasons why experts can so disagree regarding the adequacy of U.S. forces to carry out extended deterrence, and it may be a reason why men who think in largely political terms tend to ignore the details of force changes.

Non-essential Criteria

This uncertainty as to the minimum criteria that U.S. and NATO forces must meet has also led many to insist that *additional* force improvements must be provided, or that additional criteria must be met, if the West's nuclear forces are to be capable of extending deterrence. While many of the proposed force characteristics are unquestionably desirable, they are not essential to the success of extended deterrence. This has become clear in many analyses over the last fifteen years, and an understanding of the relative merits of such additional force capabilities is also important to an understanding of the evolution of U.S. forces.

In strictly military terms, the U.S. does not require strategic superiority. The increase in U.S. strategic warhead numbers to over 9,000, combined with the capabilities of U.S. and Allied theater nuclear forces, creates a situation where the U.S. can credibly strike large numbers of Warsaw Pact targets using only a relatively few strategic systems. Large numbers of survivable warheads are desirable, however, to minimize any Soviet incentive to launch limited counterforce attacks, or to strike the U.S. in some other limited way. Further, perceptions regarding relative superiority have an undeniable political and deterrent effect.

The U.S. does not have to have the capability to launch counterforce strikes against Soviet strategic nuclear forces. There are several thousand OMT in Eastern Europe and the Western USSR which the U.S. can strike with her strategic forces, and whose destruction would inflict serious damage to the USSR's ability to fight, while avoiding any major collateral damage to Soviet civilians. The Soviet Union cannot credibly launch counterforce strikes in retaliation for such U.S. strikes without risking an all-out exchange. Similarly, there are large numbers of key Eastern European economic or "counter-value" targets which the U.S. can hit without striking the USSR. The East European population associated with such non-Soviet Warsaw Pact (NSWP) targets varies from negligible to levels high enough to give the U.S. the ability to enforce equivalent population damage to the Warsaw Pact for any damage to Western Europe without striking at the USSR. Putting it bluntly, Eastern Europe's human and economic survival are now inevitable hostages to Western nuclear power. There are also a significant number of key economic targets on Soviet territory, distant from population centers which are inevitably in the same hostage category.

The U.S. therefore has many options between "assured destruction" (counter-city) targeting of the USSR and counterforce strikes. In fact, even the desirability of a large-scale first-strike counterforce attack capability is questionable, given the risk of Soviet launch under attack to protect the Soviet ICBM force. However, many argue that since the USSR also possesses a counterforce capability, such a threat by U.S. and NATO nuclear forces would have a deterrent value and an impact on Soviet perceptions worth its war-fighting risk.

Although it is semantically something of a contradiction in terms, the U.S. does not need a "war-fighting" capability to conduct and win all-out strategic nuclear exchanges. U.S. strategic and NATO theater nuclear forces do not have to be able to fight and conclude a war, in the sense of being able to destroy the Warsaw Pact's ability to attack or to remain a military force-in-being. In fact, such a capability is probably impossible to achieve, given the size of the forces on each side and the number of nuclear weapons that would remain after any conceivable strike, and may lead to intensities of conflict which are far more damaging to both sides than a process of politically-oriented strikes and exchanges. The U.S. can instead extend deterrence by threatening to inflict high levels of damage, by being in a position to terminate conflicts on terms favorable to NATO, and by demonstrating her willingness to increase the damage she inflicts until the Warsaw Pact in a war accepts NATO's terms for a cessation of hostilities. This may well involve strikes against the Warsaw Pact military forces which are threatening to defeat NATO, since this may be the least escalatory response in many contingencies. However, modern nuclear forces can nevertheless deny the Warsaw Pact "victory" by threatening to inflict damage to any aspect of its existence as a set of modern industrialized states.

The U.S. does not have to have large numbers of highly accurate, low-yield, or long-range strike systems. While such force characteristics are unquestionably desirable, she can use relatively inaccurate and high-yield systems like *Poseidon* to strike at Warsaw Pact other military and economic targets, and to inflict carefully escalated and controlled levels of damage. She can do the same with existing NATO theater systems. There are plenty of targets in the Warsaw Pact for the use of high-yield weapons in air bursts with relatively low-accuracy and reliability. Many of these targets are not time sensitive.

There is no requirement for the U.S. to have flexible and survivable C^{3}I, targeting, damage assessment and retargeting capabilities. Again, these force characteristics are desirable, but attack options which are relatively insensitive to the detailed dynamics of a given conflict can be pre-planned. There is also considerable doubt as to how rational or sophisticated nuclear bargaining can be in the real world. Moreover, it is not clear whether NATO gains from a Warsaw Pact perception that it will use nuclear forces highly flexibly and surgically nor whether NATO and the U.S. can in fact buy such capabilities at any reasonable price.

The U.S. and NATO do not need a clear strategy for the threatened use of U.S. strategic systems in extended deterrence. Experts are sharply divided over the relative merits of an explicit strategy compared with uncertainty, and of rational compared with irrational action in a crisis, whether as a means of improving deterrence in peacetime or of encouraging Soviet willingness to terminate a conflict. At least one former Commander of U.S. Strategic Air Command has argued privately that the U.S. should have many options but no strategy; that the U.S. and NATO must in any case react to the Warsaw Pact; and that the USSR will be most deterred if she has no way of predicting how the U.S. would use strategic weapons.

The use of U.S. strategic forces does not need to be guaranteed. It is obvious that extended deterrence benefits in credibility both from being a declared U.S. strategy, and from every improvement in the capability of the U.S. to execute such a strategy. At the same time, however, there is no obvious need for a NATO finger on the trigger nor for some kind of automatic U.S. response in order to render U.S. forces highly threatening to the USSR.

There is obviously a large gap between the four *essential* criteria discussed earlier and these merely desirable force characteristics, and this gap has been endlessly debated both inside and outside the United States. The advocates of stronger nuclear forces have often vehemently stated the absolute necessity of some, or all, of such desirable characteristics. In practice, however, they are optional, and each United States' Secretary of Defense and every set of nuclear planners since the early 1960s has had to consider the fact that providing the desirable characteristics would involve billions of dollars of expenditure which must be traded off against other United States' force capabilities.

Extended Deterrence and Mutual Assured Destruction: 1950–1968

The rather slow evolution of Western capabilities to meet these criteria was not the result of a failure to perceive what kinds of forces might be necessary or desirable. Several senior U.S. military officers and civilians raised many of the same points about extended deterrence in the late 1950s, and similar ideas were extensively debated and analyzed within the Office of the Secretary of Defense and in NATO from at least 1962 onwards. Rather, the development of capabilities for extended deterrence has been slowed by other factors. These have changed significantly over time, but they have included a U.S. concentration on maintaining strategic superiority, the search for arms control, a focus on other NATO problems and priorities, and the rate at which the technology could be made available to implement the more sophisticated concepts of using strategic forces to support extended deterrence. The history of these changes still shapes the state of extended deterrence today, and a knowledge of it is essential to understanding both current Western capabilities and the West's potential capabilities in the 1980s.

From the 1940s to the Cuban Missile Crisis

The U.S. has always been faced with the need to formulate four different types of strategic doctrine and plans which affect her ability to extend deterrence. First, a declared doctrine for public debate and to provide messages to the Soviet Union. Second, a weapons acquisition or force development doctrine which shapes her future capabilities. Third, an internal doctrine which the Department of Defense can use for planning. And, fourth, a targeting or war-plan doctrine which translates current capabilities into strike plans.

All four of these doctrines involve different groups of U.S. planners and different levels of political sensitivity. As a result, each can differ, broadly or in detail, although in theory they are co-ordinated by the National Security Council and the Office of the Secretary of Defense. This range of difference can be particularly great in the case of declaratory doctrine. Declaratory doctrine has often been manipulated to meet the needs of American foreign policy and domestic politics, and has often departed very significantly from operational doctrine and war plans.

This gap between declared doctrine and the reality of U.S. war plans and military capabilities has been particularly important in the case of extended deterrence. During the late 1940s, for example, the U.S. had virtually no capability to launch successful nuclear attacks on the Soviet Union. The operational U.S. stockpile then consisted of less than 80–120 weapons, most of which were of doubtful reliability and even potentially defective. Moreover, the U.S. lacked all-weather accuracy and combat-ready and experienced bomber forces. The *only* U.S. strike option then would have been to strike at the major Soviet cities, and the outcome would have been highly uncertain because of the total inability to predict the resulting damage to the USSR. Yet most historians now feel that the *image* of American nuclear strength exercised a powerful deterrent force in limiting Soviet action during this period.

During the early 1950s, crash efforts to improve the U.S. strategic forces reversed this situation. When Secretary of State Dulles announced the doctrine of massive retaliation on 12 January 1954, the U.S. had a virtual strategic monopoly. Although the Soviet nuclear effort had received extensive publicity, and the Soviet Union had deployed significant theater nuclear forces, the U.S. could have extended deterrence in terms of almost any mix of damage she could threaten to inflict upon the Soviet Union and Eastern Europe without a major risk to herself. Further, the bomber forces of the day gave her a long period in which to react. She could have had days in which to pick a mix of OMT or other limited targets without the complications or time pressures inherent in the 15–25 minute flight times of the ICBM and SLBM of today.

The U.S. also increased her relative strength in the late 1950s because she initially overestimated the rate at which the USSR could deploy new bombers and ICBM. This, and the relative vulnerability of the Soviet strategic forces at this time, had the effect of moving the U.S. towards a true counterforce capability. During the Cuban missile crisis she had approximately 1,500 B-47s and 500 B-52s, and had already deployed over 200 of her first generation of ICBM. In marked contrast, the Soviet strategic missile threat consisted of a few token ICBM whose unreliability was so great that it was uncertain exactly whom they threatened. Soviet long-range bomber forces consisted only of 100 Tu-20 *Bear* and 35 Mya-4 *Bison*, whose range and flight characteristics forced them to fly at medium and high altitudes where they were extremely vulnerable to U.S. fighters and surface-to-air missiles. Although the USSR also had over 100 Tu-16 *Badger*, these medium-range bombers were largely a threat to Europe and Japan.

Once Secretary of Defense McNamara finished evaluating the notorious "missile gap," he found that the U.S. was so superior that she did not need to rely on massive retaliation and, during 1961–2, he briefly shifted her to a declared counterforce strategy. In practical terms, this shift in strategy had several effects. The Single Integrated Operational Plan (SIOP) was adjusted to emphasize Soviet strategic systems and OMT. The U.S. developed "limited war" options in the form of a number of pre-selected strike options that so far as possible avoided Soviet cities and population centers, although they still involved the release of at least several thousand U.S. and NATO nuclear weapons. In Europe, U.S. and NATO planners at least examined the possibility of using U.S. and NATO forces to launch a pre-emptive disarming first strike against Warsaw Pact theater nuclear forces that were then unprotected and slow to react.

The first three years of the 1960s can thus be described as the zenith of extended deterrence—at least in the sense that the U.S. could have put the SIOP and NATO Nuclear Strike Plan (NSP) into operation to defend Europe with near impunity. It is extremely doubtful whether the combined use of strategic and theater nuclear forces could in fact have protected Europe, in the sense of avoiding the use of nuclear weapons against European targets, but until late in 1961 they did have a significant damage-limiting capability. This gave the West overwhelming strength in terms of its overall mix of strategic and theater force capabilities.

McNamara and Extended Deterrence

However, McNamara's somewhat tentative declaration of a counterforce strategy was quickly overtaken by political and military events. The USSR had solved most of the initial teething problems which had limited her ICBM capabilities by late 1963, and in the mid-1960s she began rapidly to build theater and strategic forces which the U.S. then had no way of successfully attacking. Even though the Soviet ICBM forces were not originally sheltered and so were very soft targets, and although they had very long reaction times in preparing for flight, the counterforce capabilities of contemporary U.S. ICBM were even more limited and uncertain. The U.S. had her own reliability problems: severe C^3 limits, poor missile accuracy and missiles with only one re-entry vehicle (RV) each. She was also limited by her ability to launch restricted numbers of missiles at one time, and was thus faced with the prospect that the USSR could increase her ICBM forces faster than the U.S. could expand her capability to target and destroy them. The growth of the Soviet ICBM threat also meant that U.S. air defenses could now no longer limit the damage it could do to U.S. cities, and that the warning time in which U.S. civil defenses could implement a shelter and evacuation program had vanished.

The trends and interactions involved are shown in figure 18–1, as is the growth in Soviet capabilities against Europe. This shows that, by 1965–6, the U.S. began to face a significant assured destruction (counter-city) capability from the USSR, and that Europe faced a similar threat from Soviet intermediate- and medium-

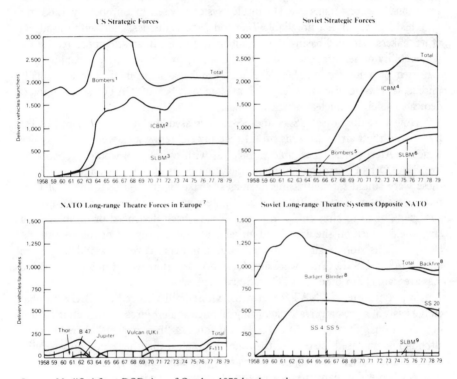

Source: Modified from DOD data of October 1979 by the author.

[1]B-47 and B-52 bombers, excluding B-47 based in Europe.

[2]*Atlas, Titan* and *Minuteman.*

[3]Number of tubes on U.S. *Polaris* and *Poseidon* SSBN. Includes SLBM dedicated to SACEUR.

[4]SS-7, -8, -9, -11, -13, -17, -18 and -19.

[5]*Bear* and *Bison.*

[6]SLBM tubes on active submarines.

[7]Does not include French Forces or 400 *Polaris/Poseidon* warheads assigned to SACEUR or British SLBM.

[8]Excluding naval versions.

[9]SLBM tubes directed against NATO.

Figure 18–1. Delivery Systems Affecting Extended Deterrence

range ballistic missiles from roughly 1961 onwards. These trends obviously presented serious problems for both overall U.S. strategic planning, and for extended deterrence. Long before the U.S. faced anything approaching strategic parity—which did not occur until the early 1970s—she faced both a major Soviet strategic threat to herself and a Soviet capability which could destroy virtually all European population centers, large-scale industrial complexes and major NATO military targets.

These same shifts also made NATO's theater nuclear posture increasingly vulnerable (and so destabilizing) and put pressure on the link between U.S. strategic forces and the long-range NATO theater systems based in Europe. By 1963, the U.S. had phased out her unreliable *Thor* and *Jupiter* missiles, and—with the advent of jet tankers—stopped basing B-47 bombers in Europe in an attempt to reduce the vulnerability of her strategic forces. NATO's only long-range strike capability then consisted of a limited number of British bombers, some ineffective and totally unreliable U.S. cruise missiles, and a large number of NATO strike fighters dedicated solely to nuclear attack missions.

However, the Soviet SS-4s and SS-5s increased the vulnerability of NATO fighters on their airfields. This meant that any fighters which were not on Quick Reaction Alert (QRA) (i.e., able to take off within minutes) would probably be lost. NATO had less than 200 main operating bases at this time, and only 70 of these were suited for the basing of nuclear strike fighters. The number of U.S. nuclear weapons storage sites for these fighters was far smaller (less than a third) and many of these sites could in any case have been destroyed or disabled by a large-yield attack on the associated airbase. Moreover, several of the central nuclear weapons storage sites contained large numbers of weapons and they were known to the USSR. They were also located where they would in addition cause massive damage to other NATO military targets.

In practical terms, NATO's growing vulnerability forced SACEUR to plan on the basis of a pre-emptive strike, using all nuclear alert forces, under attack warning conditions. This gave NATO's nuclear forces a "hair trigger" character and, although no one used the term at the time, it was clear that they could only survive if NATO launched its weapons on warning of impending attack. At the same time, such NATO plans meant that the SIOP had to be based upon the assumption that *any* major NATO nuclear conflict would involve the initial release of over 1,000 long- and medium-range theater nuclear strikes. These had to suppress and interdict Warsaw Pact conventional and theater nuclear forces as effectively as possible in the first day of conflict, and NATO therefore had little or no ability to avoid massive collateral damage to Warsaw Pact civilians or economic facilities.

The result of this was to make any restraint by the U.S. in shaping her extended deterrence options almost impossible, and to give both the SIOP and NATO's NSP an automaticity which was highly undesirable. Both NATO and the Warsaw Pact faced a situation where there was an extremely strong incentive to strike first, where both sides had to launch their initial strikes in such large numbers that they were likely to cause strategic escalation, and where any restraint might well lead to a catastrophic increase in damage. While this led NATO Headquarters to become increasingly concerned about the risks inherent in any delay in nuclear release caused by NATO's political authorities, it had the opposite effect in Washington. It convinced many Americans that reliance on nuclear strike aircraft in Europe to provide extended deterrence was unacceptably dangerous to both the United States and to Europe.

From "Countervalue" to "Assured Destruction"

The U.S. reaction to these trends in Soviet strategic and theater nuclear capabilities was to adopt the declaratory strategy of assured destruction and to reduce NATO's vulnerability by reducing her QRA forces and emphasizing conventional options as an alternative to reliance on theater nuclear weapons.

Secretary of Defense McNamara examined a wide range of other options. These included both changing U.S. strategic forces to provide more sophisticated strike options in support of NATO, and deploying a large and less vulnerable long-range theater nuclear missile force in Europe to provide a sounder linkage between U.S. strategic forces and NATO theater nuclear capabilities.

There were many political and budgetary reasons why the Secretary rejected these options, but there were also some important technical considerations. The command-and-control capability of U.S. strategic forces was then comparatively primitive in its ability to implement limited nuclear options. Every aspect of conflict management, from retargeting to damage assessment, took too long, and the information that planners could count on was so limited as to make it almost impossible to manage nuclear forces in anything other than large-scale predetermined attack options. Long bomber flight times, and low ICBM and SLBM numbers—plus low accuracies and yields—also restricted what the U.S. could do with her strategic forces. It is certain that the U.S. could then have developed a much better capability for extending deterrence to Europe, but it would have been extremely costly to create and it would still have had serious limitations.

Similar technical problems affected any attempt to upgrade NATO's long-range theater nuclear strike forces. The U.S. was already in the process both of deploying the *Pershing I* missile and attempting to develop options for a NATO Multi-lateral Force, but neither option seemed likely to solve NATO's vulnerability problem. Any extended-range missile with accuracy and reliability superior to the *Pershing*, with its range of 450 nautical miles (nm), would then have been as costly as additional U.S. ICBM. It would also have presented serious command-and-control, nuclear safety and basing problems for the technology was not available to provide effective and survivable C^3I support for a mobile missile, and any land-based missile which could be used flexibly in a wide range of strikes would virtually have had to be silo-mounted, again raising its cost to the ICBM level.

The problems inherent in deploying a mobile missile are illustrated by the *Pershing* I. This could only strike at a very limited range of pre-selected targets and could only be fired from predetermined sites. Co-ordination of strikes for the entire *Pershing* missile force and aircraft took months. Even with this pre-planning there was a good chance that the Soviet forces could locate the *Pershing*, for the road movement of the system was so visible that Soviet agents could track individual missiles to their sites. The reliability and accuracy of the missile was also sharply degraded by road movement for this affected both the guidance platform and missile frame. *Pershing* I had to carry warheads with yields of 100KT and above and could only attack soft area targets.

The basing problem was even worse. An adequate NATO force had to consist of at least several hundred missiles in order to provide a useful range of attack options. (The relevant Soviet target base then consisted of about 500 Soviet missile sites, up to 400 Warsaw Pact airbases, and some 200 additional facilities.) In the case of silo-based missiles, Europe would have had to accept several hundred silos, and there was no guarantee that these could be made hard enough to ride out strikes by the SS-4 and SS-5 force. The cost of silos would have been very high, and there would have been substantial manpower and sub-system costs. The situation was no better for mobile missiles. The missiles could only solve the vulnerability problem if they were not concentrated in bases in peacetime—as was *Pershing*—because NATO could not count on sufficient warning for dispersal. This meant that any mobile missile force would have had to be scattered around 200–300 sites in Europe, giving rise to great cost and serious security problems.

Although the MLF offered an alternative solution to some of these problems, the accuracies of the proposed surface-ship-mounted missiles were substantially worse than those of the already inadequate land-based mobile missile option. Although the MLF could have reduced vulnerability to pre-emptive missile attack, it opened up other equally serious vulnerabilities to Soviet Naval counteraction. It would thus have lacked true survivability, and would have been even less flexible for actual employment in a NATO conflict than U.S. SLBM.

Secretary McNamara ultimately chose a fundamentally different set of options. On 18 February 1965 he announced that the U.S. would rely on "assured destruction" to deter any Soviet strategic strike against the U.S. In effect this meant that the U.S. had decided to seek a stable strategic balance with the USSR by convincing her that no conceivable action she could take would eliminate the U.S. capability to devastate the USSR, and that extended deterrence would be effective because the risk that any nuclear conflict in Europe would start a process of escalation which would ultimately trigger such a U.S. attack on the Soviet population and economy.

This new declaratory strategy was not based on any very sophisticated military strike plan so much as on the then overwhelming U.S. lead in strategic nuclear delivery vehicles (SNDV). There was then no indication that Soviet ICBM forces would suddenly surge upwards, and the U.S. lead seemed so great that assured destruction hardly required detailed planning. It was clear that the effect of U.S. retaliation would be devastating, inflicting damage on the USSR in greater orders of magnitude than a Soviet strike could inflict on the U.S. It was also clear that, once the destabilizing aspects of NATO's posture were reduced, the size of the U.S. conventional and nuclear forces in Europe would create a situation where any initial Soviet attack would have to be so large that it ran a severe risk of triggering the SIOP. By the standards of the time, that seemed planning and strategy enough. As a result of these factors, and sharp resistance by the Joint Chiefs of Staff (JCS) and Strategic Air Command (SAC) to any further changes in U.S. war plans, Secretary of Defense McNamara did little to reduce the minimum threshold of attacks on the SIOP. He concentrated instead on making the ultimate threat to Soviet cities more convincing, and he adopted a procurement strategy for U.S. strategic forces based on maximizing delivery systems and warhead numbers, and reducing the future vulnerability of the triad.

The U.S. solution to NATO's vulnerability problem, following the collapse of the MLF negotiations, was equally simple. The U.S. sought to shift NATO from reliance on a thin screen of conventional forces, designed only to defend against "incursions and other local hostile actions" and to force the Soviet Union into making an attack sufficiently large to trigger a NATO nuclear response (the "sword and the shield" concept enshrined in the document known as MC 14/2), to an emphasis on major NATO conventional defense options supported by existing short-range theater nuclear systems and backed by U.S. strategic superiority. This new U.S. policy became the strategy of "flexible response," and one of the key elements of this strategy came to be to reduce NATO's reliance on dedicated QRA nuclear strike aircraft in favor of more conventional use of air power. Nuclear-capable aircraft were retained to deter the Soviet Union from launching a massive nuclear first strike on Europe.

The U.S. succeeded in getting NATO agreement to this shift, although it took far longer than simply announcing the shift to "assured destruction." NATO's adoption of flexible response involved hard negotiations from 1964, and it was 1968 before NATO ministers agreed to the document known as MC 14/3 and to plans which emphasized conventional options. The reduction of the QRA strike aircraft force took even longer and came only after the U.S. had assigned a large number of *Polaris* SLBM warheads to SACEUR for longer range targeting by NATO to make up for the reduced QRA posture and the failure of the MLF.

Adding "Mutual" to "Assured Destruction"

McNamara's adoption of Assured Destruction meant more, however, than simply a rejection of counterforce options and of sophisticated U.S. and NATO capabilities for extended deterrence. Even though it was conceived at a time when its authors believed U.S. strategic superiority would continue indefinitely, assured destruction was founded on the assumption that U.S. superiority would steadily decline in absolute terms and had already lost much of its meaning in terms of protecting the U.S. economy and population. As a result, McNamara and the planners around him began to see less and less value in a massive effort to achieve strategic superiority in a military sense, and became steadily more interested in some form of arms control that would stabilize the balance.

The shift in viewpoint was compounded by the rapid changes in Soviet forces which began to take place between 1965 and 1967. As figure 18–1 shows, it was during this period that the growth in the number of Soviet ICBM began to really move towards "parity," demonstrating a rate of growth which previously had been badly underestimated by the majority of the U.S. intelligence community. This confronted McNamara with the fact that the USSR would before long be able to hit over 1,000 U.S. targets, and was increasing its force at a rate where U.S. superiority in assured destruction had already disappeared.

As a result, McNamara added the word "mutual" to his declared strategy of "assured destruction" in an interview on 18 September 1967. He did so with several goals in mind. First, he wished to persuade the USSR that the U.S. accepted its vulnerability and would not seek to eliminate it. Second, he wished to place a tighter cap on the cost of U.S. strategic programs and to set a clear policy goal of not seeking a damage-limiting or war-winning strategy. Third, he wanted to define the number of targets necessary to assure destruction on both sides at so low a level that no conceivable counterforce exchange would ever eliminate either side's retaliatory credibility and no arms-control effort would become tied to large numbers of systems. And fourth, he wished to notify the USSR formally that the U.S. accepted the fact that *any* significant use of either strategic or theater nuclear weapons could result in a process of escalation that would effectively destroy the Soviet Union.

It seems fair to state that, as he neared the end of his term as Secretary of Defense, McNamara regarded the balance of risk as so high on both sides that he saw no real need for highly sophisticated strike options. While he and his staffs did discuss such options, they had low priority relative to such pressing issues as the Vietnam War and, once President Johnson had quietly eased McNamara over to the World Bank, no one in the last year of the Johnson Administration had time for nuclear strategy.

Extended Deterrence in 1967

In summary, therefore, the U.S. ended its era of superiority in assured destruction capability without any clear plan for executing strategic strikes in support of extended deterrence. If anything, she regarded the improvement of NATO conventional forces as a much higher priority for ensuring the overall deterrence of Warsaw Pact aggression than any possible action she could take to improve the capability of either her own nuclear forces or NATO's. The U.S. also continued to rely on the risk of strategic nuclear war to deter the Soviet Union without having any limited options in the SIOP beyond demonstrative use.

This had serious implications during the early 1970s as U.S. forces began to deploy warheads equipped with multiple independently targetable re-entry vehicles (MIRV) and the total number of U.S. strategic warheads increased dramatically. While it is true that assured destruction had never meant that the U.S. had no option other than hitting at populations or civil economic facilities, there was a natural tendency, as the number of her warheads increased, to use them to target more and more Soviet military facilities. The United States did stress counterforce targeting in the sense of striking at more and more Soviet military targets; what it did not stress was flexibility and restraint.

It is also relevant to point out that the NATO weakness in the theater balance, shown in figure 18-1, and the Soviet shift towards strategic parity, were both relative. By 1967, the U.S. had over 3,000 strategic nuclear delivery vehicles (SNDV), and 7,000 U.S. tactical weapons were deployed in Europe. These presented a massive threat to the Warsaw Pact, even allowing for probable losses resulting from a Soviet first strike. The U.S. also still enjoyed considerable superiority in accuracy, survivability, and many other key force characteristics. While the balance had changed by 1967, it still did not appear to threaten either U.S. superiority in most measures of the strategic balance or the credibility of the assumption that any Soviet attack on Europe would lead to the use of U.S. strategic forces.

Extended Deterrence in the First Nixon Administration

The U.S. did little to improve her plans for extended deterrence between 1968 and 1974, although experts did begin to pay more and more attention to the options for making such improvements. The major concerns of U.S. policy-makers were Vietnam, the overall buildup in Soviet military capabilities, détente and arms control, and the slow pace of NATO's effort to build up its conventional options.

During this period, however, the U.S. and USSR did have to cope with two major changes in the structure of strategic forces: the competition over ABM; and over the introduction of MIRV. These two competitions led the Nixon Administration in very different directions, one of which was to change U.S. capabilities to support extended deterrence radically.

On the one hand, the U.S. lead in ABM technology created at least the possibility that one side or both could create a damage-limiting capability by some time in the early 1980s, and raised the spectre of a trillion-dollar arms race with the USSR to be the first to create such a capability. On the other hand, the number of delivery systems shown in figure 18-1 came to mean less and less as the introduction of the first U.S. and then Soviet MIRV drastically changed the ratio of delivery systems to strike capability.

The resulting growth in warhead numbers on each side, shown in figure 18-2, reveals that between 1970 and 1974 the number of U.S. ICBM and SLBM

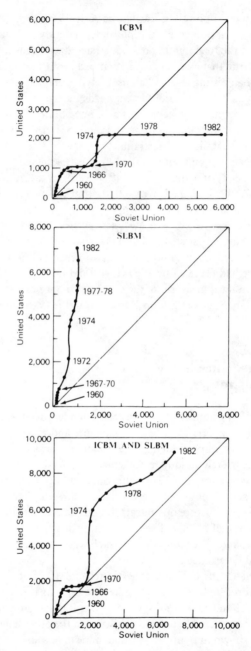

Source: Santa Fe Corporation. Measures and Trends of U.S. and USSR Strategic Force Effectiveness, March 1978, pp. 34, 36, and 38.

Figure 18–2. U.S. and Soviet MIRV Strength

warheads targetable on the Warsaw Pact increased threefold, from less than 2,000 to about 6,000, and they have since risen to about 9,000. The growth in Soviet warheads was much slower, and only began to reach truly significant proportions in 1974.

Figure 18–2 also shows that the U.S. initially used her lead in MIRV technology to deploy large numbers of SLBM warheads with high survivability but limited yield and accuracy. In contrast, once the USSR began to deploy MIRV, she concentrated on ICBM. This initially permitted the USSR higher yields and, as MIRV accuracy increased, also allowed her to move towards a counterforce capability against U.S. ICBM. It should be noted, however, that ICBM represent only 24 percent of the U.S. ICBM/SLBM warhead mix.

Initial Assumptions about MIRV and ABM

The Nixon Administration initially interpreted these trends in the strategic balance as leading to an increased U.S. advantage in all major contingencies, although it concluded that it would never be in a position to avoid massive Soviet retaliatory damage to the U.S. As a result, the U.S. went into the first Strategic Arms Limitation Talks (SALT I) with the impression that she held two key cards. The first was MIRV technology—since at that time she grossly underestimated the speed with which the USSR could introduce MIRV—and the second was in ABM, where she had a clear lead in technology, although it was far from certain that she could create an effective defense system for either her cities or her military forces.

This analysis of the balance had several major effects for extended deterrence. First, the perceived U.S. lead again reassured a new Administration that there was no real urgency about further improving either the strategic or theater nuclear balance, particularly in the absence of any doctrine for making use of the latter capabilities. Second, it reinforced President Nixon's initial view on coming to office that NATO theater nuclear systems did little more than increase the risk of accidental war or threaten loss of U.S. strategic control. Third, it meant that the Administration felt it was free to concentrate on SALT I and the Vietnam issue.

A practical result of these trends was that the U.S. military, which had to write U.S. war plans, was faced with the problem of loading more and more missile warheads into roughly the same set of SIOP strike options. This posed a number of problems. The accuracies of the new missile systems did not permit effective attacks against the 1,500 or so Soviet ICBM, and there were only about 100 Soviet bomber bases and submarine ports that could be attacked with SLBM and ICBM forces. Further, although the number of U.S. warheads steadily increased, the total megatonnage of U.S. warheads (including bomber forces) had dropped by 60 percent, and the total number of weapons including bombs had gone down by 25 percent because of cuts in the bomber force. The net effect was that the military had to concentrate on preplanned missile strikes against the target set containing 25,000 targets (excluding Soviet ICBM), while the marginal value of directing yet more weapons against Soviet cities decreased sharply after approximately the first 200–350 strikes.

With her ICBM and SLBM missile force the U.S. could therefore cover more and more Other Military Targets, together with additional military and quasi-military production and research and development facilities distant from large population centers. This focus on fixed preplanned strikes on OMT reached the point where even the ultimate assured destruction option in the SIOP directed nearly 70 percent of U.S. strategic weapons to non-strategic Soviet and Warsaw Pact military targets.

In theory, therefore, the U.S. acquired both the prompt invulnerable delivery capability and the targeting necessary to support extended deterrence. However, this was not supported by the development of the required command, control, communications and intelligence (C³I) capabilities, by war planning that would have allowed her to use these capabilities effectively, or by any serious joint planning with NATO. In fact, one effect was to thicken up the existing SIOP options by adding more warheads, rather than to improve the range and flexibility of the SIOP by adding new options. According to one Pentagon expert, until 1974 the lowest SIOP attack option (other than "demonstrative use") involved the release of at least 2,500 weapons and was so closely linked to the Priority Strike Program (PSP) in SACEUR's Nuclear Operations Plan (NOP) that it would have almost automatically triggered an additional 1,000 NATO fighter or missile strikes.

Accordingly, until at least 1974, the ultimate effect of deploying U.S. MIRV and the shift from bombers to missiles, was to raise the level of conflict that would have resulted from *any* attempt to use U.S. forces and to increase the risk of escalation to all-out war. From the European point of view, it is also important to realize that by then the USSR had at least 2,000 relatively high-yield bombs and warheads threatening Europe, the accuracy of which was not suitable for discriminate strikes against small military targets, and which could launch in the face of a U.S. attack but could not ride out such an attack with any confidence. These facts are generally ignored in talking about extended deterrence and the era of U.S. strategic superiority. They should be remembered before showing any nostalgia for this period.

After SALT I: Soviet MIRV and No ABM

As in 1964 and 1967, however, the U.S. gradually discovered that she was basing her declarations and plans on a major underestimation of Soviet capabilities. Shortly after the signature of the ABM Treaty and SALT I in May 1972, she began to realize that she had seriously miscalculated the trends. Broadly speaking, in the months after the 1972 election U.S. policymakers began to discover that the Soviet Union was modernizing her delivery systems, introducing MIRV and improving system accuracy faster than either U.S. scientists or the U.S. intelligence community were predicting.

This process is a now familiar aspect of the history of strategic planning, but in 1972–4 the failure to predict the growth of this aspect of the Soviet threat still came as a major shock. The Nixon Administration discovered that the USSR could introduce MIRV far more quickly than it had expected. This meant not only that the Administration lost the advantage that it had counted on to preserve the U.S. lead through the late 1970s, but also that the Soviet advantages in ICBM throw-weight suddenly took on a whole new meaning, because Soviet ICBM could carry many more warheads than U.S. ICBM.

This interaction between the discovery of the real extent of Soviet MIRV programs and the growing importance of the qualitative differences in U.S. and Soviet strategic forces is shown when one compares figure 18–2 and 18–3. Figure 18–2 shows that the year 1974 marks a sharp, even dramatic, change in the rate of increase in Soviet ICBM warheads. Figure 18–3, however, shows that, long before 1974, the U.S. had begun to fall behind in such total measures of strategic force capability as equivalent megatonnage and total numbers of delivery vehicles and was soon to fall behind in throw-weight.

The trends shown in figure 18–3 did not matter so long as the U.S. appeared to have a very marked lead in MIRV technology, accuracy and other aspects of missile technology. However, the sudden Soviet "break-out" in fitting MIRV created a very different picture. It meant that, although the U.S. could retain a

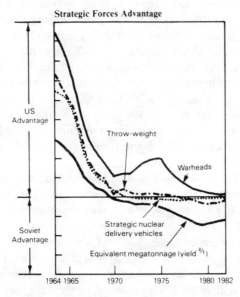

Figure 18–3. Changes in Strategic Capabilities, 1964–1982 (Rumsfeld Estimate)

major lead in the number of targets she could attack, the Soviet Union came to lead in assured destruction capability against the U.S. civil and population base, and moreover had delivery systems in being which, if fitted with MIRV, could ultimately launch far more warheads than the United States.

This change in the rules of the game occurred when the second Nixon Administration was just beginning, and made it almost certain that U.S. policymakers would begin to re-examine U.S. nuclear strategy. This was reinforced by the fact that the American withdrawal from Vietnam freed American policymakers to think about other aspects of defense, and by the appointment of James R. Schlesinger as Secretary of Defense. Schlesinger had stressed the need to improve U.S. capability to employ limited nuclear strike options since 1968. Accordingly, the early 1970s began a steady process of improvement in the way the U.S. thought about extended deterrence and about the need to include options for lower thresholds of conflict in the SIOP, although this thinking initially did little more than improve the co-ordination of the SIOP and SACEUR's Nuclear Strike Plan (NSP) so as to eliminate some conflicts of timing and emphasis.

Limited Strategic Options and the Rise of the Counterforce Threat

The primary catalyst in initiating the new U.S. strategy was the Office of Program Analysis and Evaluation (PA&E), reporting to the Secretary of Defense, which faced the problem of trying to readjust the long-term defense program for strategic forces to the changes taking place in U.S. policy and in the balance. It conducted several in-house studies which indicated that U.S. forces had become dangerously imbalanced toward large-scale options even before Schlesinger became Secretary. As a result, it began a joint study of new targeting options with the Joint Chiefs of Staff. This study was originally confined to a narrow circle, not only to avoid disturbing the arms-control negotiations going on at the time, but because the defense officials involved were afraid of interference from the National Security Council, the Arms Control and Disarmament Agency and the State Department on political and diplomatic grounds.

By late 1972, however, this planning had reached the point where the JCS had completed a preliminary re-examination of the SIOP, and the whole future of U.S. strategy was beginning to be re-examined on an inter-Agency basis. Soviet progress in MIRV and other increases in Soviet capability, kept this inter-Agency effort going at a comparatively intensive level, and by mid-1973 it had produced a broad consensus in favor of a new U.S. approach to strategic planning.

As a result, Schlesinger began to hint at the coming changes in U.S. strategy in November and December 1973. These changes received the President's approval in January 1974 and were issued in the document filed as NSDM-242. The Administration then approved its public release as declared strategy, and Schlesinger announced the change in his testimony in Congressional hearings in March 1974.

Schlesinger's testimony shifted the United States away from a declared but unimplemented strategy of assured destruction to one which formally stressed the need to seek to destroy the USSR's long-term capability to recover as an advanced industrial economy under her current regime, and the use of strategic and theater nuclear weapons in carefully graduated responses. The new doctrine emphasized the targeting of Soviet strategic forces, OMT in the USSR, and Soviet or Bloc military targets in other countries.

The words Schlesinger used both in his original March 1974 testimony and on subsequent occasions were often confusing, even to their authors, because of the continuing debate inside the Pentagon as to precisely how the U.S. would implement the doctrine, and because of technical uncertainties affecting U.S. forces. The key message, however, was to communicate to the USSR that the U.S. would develop the capability to use her nuclear forces in limited nuclear options (LNO), so that escalation control would exist all the way from the most limited use up to an all-out exchange.

New Strike Options for Extended Deterrence

The U.S. was, in effect, formally announcing to the USSR that she was ceasing to focus the planning of her strategic forces on deterring large-scale strategic conflicts, and that she was adding a range of lower-level options that could be used to deter or "win" a wide range of other types of wars. In practice this involved the development of the following kinds of nuclear strike options:

Countervalue Options were strike options against non-military targets. They could be of two kinds: strikes on transport, production and other targets with immediate impact on Soviet ability to fight in the particular crisis or conflict at issue; or strikes at any non-military target in the Soviet Bloc which might be a reasonable exchange for the losses being suffered by the U.S. or its Allies. Consistent efforts were made to find counter-value targets which minimized any loss of life. Although a number of studies performed for the Department of Defense by private contractors which became public presented such options as targeting only the Russian population of the USSR, or "surgical" strikes against key concentrations of the Soviet leadership and intelligentsia, these reflected little more than the normal tendency of researchers to explore every option, and they were never part of formal U.S. plans to implement the new strategy.

Counterforce Options were strike options against Soviet or Soviet Bloc military targets of any kind. These included strategic forces, theater nuclear forces, conventional forces and fixed military facilities. One of the key features of the new strategy was that the counterforce target mix should be the one most likely to persuade the USSR to terminate a conflict. That implied options for attacking relatively small numbers of targets or fixed facilities of the kind not previously used as targets for U.S. strategic forces. Included were options for limited or demonstrative strikes on Soviet strategic forces.

Limited Nuclear Options (LNO) originally meant strikes against carefully selected targets on Soviet territory, but later were often used to describe all limited strike options in most public discussion. They involved both counterforce and countervalue targets in the USSR, but emphasis was placed on counterforce options.

Regional Nuclear Options (RNO) included the entire mix of countervalue and counterforce targets in areas like the Warsaw Pact or Persian Gulf that might be attacked by U.S. strategic and theater nuclear forces. In many parts of the world, the same type of options were most logically targeted on Soviet territory. Planning again stressed counterforce options, and particularly OMT.

Theater Nuclear Options (TNO) included all the military targets in the theater of operations directly involved in the conflicts. They could involve many different types of "theater" throughout the world, and they often overlapped RNO when the theater involved conflicts as large as the entire Central Region. More attention was also devoted in TNO than in the other options, although it was clear that theater weapons could be employed in LNO and RNO as well.

All of these options fit under the broad heading of limited strategic or Limited Strike Options (LSO). They also had the common characteristic that they created a need for new intelligence, targeting, C^3 and damage-assessment capabilities to increase the flexibility with which the U.S. could use her strategic forces in this wide range of options. These capabilities later became lumped under the acronym C^3I (Command, Control, Communications and Intelligence). They also made increases in accuracy desirable, and argued for flexibility of yields and the ability to retarget rapidly.

Other Key Factors

There are several other aspects of the new strategy which deserve careful attention. First, Schlesinger explicitly rejected the notion of being able to develop a significant damage-limiting capability with U.S. strategic forces. He did so both on cost grounds and on the basis of an almost universally agreed series of inter-Agency analyses which indicated that any advance in strategic defense technology—even if permitted by the ABM treaty—would simply lead to a matching increase in Soviet defensive and offensive capabilities.

Second, Schlesinger accepted the fact that both sides could escalate to a virtually unchallenged assured destruction capability. His references to counterforce targeting did not mean the use of such strikes to develop any kind of "war winning" capability for all-out strategic exchanges but rather that such strikes could help the U.S. to "win" at lower levels of nuclear conflict. He stated in effect that both sides had the option of limited exchanges against the other's strategic forces as an alternative to strikes on cities and populations, and declared that this was part of U.S. strategy.

Third, Schlesinger explicitly rejected strategic competition in terms of gross static measures of military capability such as throw-weight, equivalent megatonnage (EMT), counter-military potential, and numbers of delivery vehicles. He established a doctrine based on "essential equivalence" in terms of the ability to attack the Soviet and Bloc target base allowing for the loss or degradation of U.S. and NATO forces in prior exchanges.

The USSR initially seemed genuinely afraid that the U.S. was seeking to develop a pre-emptive counterforce capability, a fear reinforced by the then superior U.S. accuracy and hardening technology and the fact that so much of the Soviet force was loaded on ICBM and bombers. Yet Schlesinger was simply responding in kind to the fear that the USSR might be able to develop a strike capability that would enable her to destroy a significant portion of the U.S. ICBM force at the cost of as few as 15,000 to 150,000 prompt civilian casualties. Schlesinger was also concerned that, although the ICBM force then only carried 23 percent of U.S. warheads, roughly 50 percent of U.S. warheads were vulnerable to pre-emptive attack including those aboard bombers, which could not take off on alert, and submarines in U.S. and foreign ports. Accordingly, Schlesinger was seeking to deter such Soviet limited-strike alternatives to assured destruction by creating strikes options which ensured that U.S. forces could retaliate in kind without escalating to attacks on Soviet cities.

The Counterforce Strategy

U.S. officials and experts also tended to become confused over what Schlesinger was saying about counterforce capability, and this may have been partly responsible for the Soviet misinterpretation. Many confused the distinction between military targets of any kind and civil targets by using the term "counterforce" to refer only to strikes against Soviet strategic offensive forces. In fact, virtually all of the resulting U.S. "counterforce" targeting was against non-strategic Soviet and Soviet and Bloc military forces, and this was dictated by the fact that the targeting of Soviet ICBM was both extraordinarily provocative and tended to produce unfavorable exchange ratios in terms of the residual numbers of warheads on both sides. Furthermore, U.S. strikes at Soviet ballistic missile nuclear submarine (SSBN) ports would involve large-scale collateral damage, as would Soviet retaliation in kind. Moreover, OMT strikes do not invite confusion over whether the U.S. is carrying out a first strike against Soviet strategic forces, and this is critical because, although Soviet ICBM silos are now probably hard enough to render impractical a mass U.S. attack with existing ICBM, major uncertainties must still exist for Soviet planners over the actual outcome of such a strike.

The more detailed aspects of the planning for Schlesinger's new strategy were never heavily publicized and did not result in quite the same level of confusion and debate. They included a broad effort to find ways of limiting civil or collateral damage from attacks on military targets, to try to fill the gap between NATO's reliance on short-range theater nuclear systems and the use of U.S. strategic systems, to reduce the vulnerability of all nuclear forces, to find credible regional LSO for the defense of areas like Iran and South Korea, and to structure U.S. limited strike plans to emphasize counterforce targets, in the sense of striking at mixes of Soviet and Warsaw Pact military forces and facilities rather than "countervalue" economic and civil facilities such as East European cities or steel complexes.

These were reasonable extensions of a fairly moderate shift in U.S. strategy and policy, although the words used in some policy papers and studies regarding these aspects of the "Schlesinger Strategy" which reached the press often lacked the pragmatism and restraint of the U.S. officials who actually made the decisions involved.

Deficiencies of U.S. Capabilities

It is one of the ironies of the resulting public debate over Schlesinger's new strategy that comparatively little of it focused on the fact that U.S. forces were in no position to implement it without major improvements. This is partly because many of the key aspects of U.S. strategic forces required to execute LSO had never received much public attention, and partly because changes taking place in strategic forces were then so new that they received only limited attention.

However, the declared strategy of NSDM-242 highlighted the following deficiencies in U.S. capabilities:

The entire U.S. warning and command-and-control system was oriented around large-scale exchanges. The U.S. warning system could only warn against a mass Soviet attack. It provided very poor and unreliable attack characterization capability for many types of limited exchange and was virtually unable either to assist in identifying and targeting exactly which Soviet forces were used in a given attack—which is highly desirable in limited counterforce retaliation—or to provide precise measures of the level of Soviet escalation involved. The system was particularly bad at analyzing Soviet actions at precisely the low levels of escalation where the U.S. strategy sought to control or terminate the conflict.

U.S. and NATO defense communications systems were unlikely to survive in war, and U.S. systems particularly were poorly integrated between the services, between civilian and military intelligence, between the National Command Authorities and the theater and at tactical command level. They were also extremely unreliable and too automated. The U.S. communications system had evolved from the assumption that the SSBN, ICBM and bomber forces would have at least 16 hours to effect any change of targets, and would generally expect to have up to 48 hours. Nor could it provide the President with timely and accurate information on what was happening or allow him to choose a controlled response, consult with allies as necessary, or quickly execute his plan.

The U.S. and the NATO allies had virtually no means of rapidly directing weapons onto targets more than 50 miles behind the forward edge of the battle-field (FEBA) in NATO, and lacked the ability to direct nuclear weapons in many other regions in less than 48–96 hours. The U.S. also had an extremely poor ability to assess precisely and rapidly the damage done to either side. This gap between the declared strategy and actual capability led to some ludicrous situations during this period. U.S. planners would spend days arguing over very precise strike op-tions and bargaining arrangements with the USSR, or gaming real time exchanges based on perfect knowledge in Washington and the Kremlin, when in fact the U.S. lacked any real ability to obtain virtually any of the required data at anything like the rate required.

The U.S. emergency command-and-control system for strategic war consisted then mainly of relatively primitive aircraft whose equipment and data handling facilities limited them to the management of large-scale retaliatory attacks. The so-called "hardened" National Command Authority (NCA) facilities were in fact dis-tinctly vulnerable to attack by Soviet ICBM. This meant that a Soviet attack on her facilities could blind the U.S. at any time, and that she had therefore to assume that the USSR would not attack Washington or nearby installations.

The bulk of U.S. warheads were survivable. However, while most of the *Minuteman* missiles then took 16–28 hours to reprogram, the U.S. did not even have a C^3 system for reprogramming her SLBM in a way that suited their use in LSO. Moreover, no real effort had been made to establish a reporting system for the NCA that could check the availability and functioning of particular groups of ICBM, SLBM or bombers. There was therefore a high risk that a limited employ-ment could misfire or give the wrong signal. Finally, bomber and SLBM system accuracies were relatively poor—much less than the theoretical missile accuracies or systems performance specifications quoted in most literature.

These technical problems were compounded by the human problems of shift-ing from mass strikes to politically-oriented LSO. A large organization involving thousands of decision-makers had to agree on such options and transform them into specific plans. It quickly became apparent that practical war planning re-quired the selection of very conservative options which were restricted in number, and which could get broad enough Pentagon and Administration support to avoid constant changes in concept and a high probability of being implemented in a crisis. This process, however, was so agonizing that virtually everyone was unhappy with the result—from the President down to the lowest staff officer involved. It also took years to achieve, and had constantly to be revised to match U.S. capabilities and changes in procurement policy.

It also gradually became apparent that in the real world there are no "fire-breaks" between TNO, RNO and LNO. The strategic and tactical nuclear capabilities on both sides were then, and are now, so great that either side can retaliate to its potential advantage regardless of the LSO it must respond to. Further, virtually any firebreak between types of systems and targets which is based on American or Allied perceptions not only may, but probably will, be different from the firebreak perceived by the USSR.

None of these factors invalidated the new U.S. emphasis on Limited Nuclear Strikes, but, to return to the minimal criteria for extended deterrence discussed earlier, they meant that when such a strategy was announced in 1974, it was announced with the knowledge that the U.S. could not really have the force to carry it out until the late 1970s or early 1980s.

The Problem of NATO Nuclear Forces

The U.S. announced her emphasis on LSO and conducted discussions within the NATO Nuclear Planning Group (NPG) without having reached any clear recommendations as to what should be done about NATO theater nuclear forces. Certainly there was much debate on the matter and many ideas were proposed and discussed, but there were a number of reasons why selecting some combination of these ideas and putting them into practice had only limited priority.

The immediate focus of American attention was to preserve the U.S. troop presence in Europe in the face of major congressional pressures for its withdrawal. The Administration had to emphasize the need for conventional forces and was even prepared, at the Mutual and Balanced Force Reduction (MBFR) talks in Vienna, to offer reductions in U.S. theater nuclear forces in return for Soviet troop reductions in Central Europe as a means of trying to prove to the Congress that the U.S. could create a significant conventional defense capability.

The cruise missile was still a concept only, and advances in missile guidance and C^3 technology had not yet reached the point where the broad problems we discussed earlier of long-range theater missile C^3 basing, accuracy, reliability and vulnerability could be solved. The *Polaris*, and later *Poseidon* warheads allocated to SACEUR seemed to offer better capability than the available theater systems, and the Soviet long-range theater threat had not evolved to the point where their lack of visibility on European soil seemed to be a political and strategic problem.

Any effort in theater nuclear forces seemed likely to occur only at the cost of improvements in NATO conventional forces. NATO conventional forces were then relatively weak, and this created such vulnerability at the lowest levels of escalation that the U.S. gave priority to their improvement and put her energies into trying to redress the conventional imbalance through negotiations with the USSR.

Soviet long-range theater nuclear forces (LRTNF) were still composed of aging bombers and SS-4 and SS-5 missiles. The U.S. had deployed a limited number of F-111s to Europe in 1969 and had committed more significant numbers of U.S.-based F-111s to SACEUR. This reinforcement capability gave NATO "quasi-survivable" long-range forces which were backed by the increase in assigned U.S. SLBM warheads resulting from fitting the missiles with MIRV. Any further U.S. initiatives to improve NATO forces seemed likely to do little more than lead to a Soviet response in kind.

Schlesinger found it expedient to push a U.S. offer to reduce the number of nuclear warheads in Europe in return for a reduction in Soviet conventional forces. This allowed him more domestic and foreign flexibility in dealing with MBFR, and he preferred to focus on strategic systems where the U.S. had unchallenged control, rather than on NATO forces, where LSO and RSO (NATO SEP, or Selective Employment Plans) required a formal and complex process of agreement by the Alliance.

The shift in Soviet capabilities that created a near-term counterforce threat to the United States was not yet apparent. Accordingly, the U.S. superiority in warheads seemed so great that a balanced range of escalatory capabilities, including survivable NATO-based long-range theater nuclear strike forces, did not seem critical to the credibility of the new American strategy or to extended deterrence.

The result was that only limited advances were made in the quality of United States' and NATO theater nuclear war planning, and theater force improvement plans. The U.S. Army recognized a need to modernize the warheads for its artillery and *Lance* short-range missiles, and to upgrade the *Pershing* longer-range missile to correct some of its severe limitations in targeting and deployment flexibility. Tactical nuclear bomb yields and tactical missile yields were also cut back to levels more proportionate to the size of Warsaw Pact targets. NATO also adopted new Nuclear Operations Plans (NOP) to reduce collateral damage, and changed the Priority Strike Program (PSP) within the NOP to provide additional lower-threshold strike options. However, no major changes were planned in NATO long-range theater nuclear forces, and the result was little more than tinkering in the absence of any clear conceptual framework for modernizing them.

The Rise of the Counterforce Threat

During 1975–8 it steadily became clear that the USSR would create a major counterforce capability against the *Minuteman* force by the early 1980s. Virtually every three months during this period the U.S. discovered yet another significant improvement in Soviet ICBM design and deployment, missile accuracy, missile reliability and fractionation capability. As figure 18–3 shows, by the time Secretary Rumsfeld wrote his FY 1978 *Annual Report*, the U.S. was projecting inferiority in several key measures of the balance and therefore a major risk that the USSR could "win" a counterforce exchange.

The fact that the Soviet Union could "win" any kind of exchange with the U.S. came as a major shock to many of the U.S. policy-makers involved. However, the nature of such a "victory" needs careful qualification. The war-gaming of a so-called "counterforce run-down" depends on the Soviet Union being able to launch her forces with theoretical efficiency and effectiveness in a first strike against 1,054 U.S. ICBM silos. The game goes on to assume that the United States is then forced to launch her surviving ICBM in a retaliatory strike against 1,469 Soviet ICBM silos, an unknown number of which are empty. Not surprisingly, the end result of the game, under these assumptions, is that the remaining American strategic forces are smaller than the remaining Soviet forces, and that further counterforce exchanges against ICBM make this situation still worse for the United States.

Such a war game is definitely a worst-case scenario for the U.S. in that there is no conceivable reason for her to retaliate for such an attack by striking Soviet ICBM silos, given the range of Soviet OMT that she could attack without significantly running down her residual ICBM forces. It also ignores the massive asymmetries in the triad on each side.

Figure 18–4 shows the relevant differences in the mix of U.S. and Soviet strategic offensive forces. While about 50 percent of U.S. strategic delivery vehicles are on ICBM, ICBM carry only 24 percent of U.S. warheads and 33 percent of

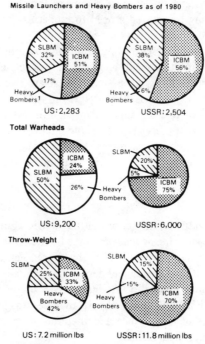

Missile Launchers and Heavy Bombers as of 1980

SLBM 32% | ICBM 51% | 17% | Heavy Bombers[1] | US: 2,283

SLBM 38% | ICBM 56% | Heavy Bombers 6% | USSR: 2,504

Total Warheads

ICBM 24% | SLBM 50% | 26% | Heavy Bombers | US: 9,200

SLBM 20% | 5% | ICBM 75% | USSR: 6,000

Throw-Weight

SLBM 25% | ICBM 33% | Heavy Bombers 42% | US: 7.2 million lbs

SLBM 15% | 15% | ICBM 70% | Heavy Bombers | USSR: 11.8 million lbs

Source: Adapted from DOD FY 1981 Annual Report. Tables 5–3 and 5–6.
[1]Includes approximately 220 B-52 in deep storage.

Figure 18–4. Composition of Forces (1980)

throw-weight. Although not shown in the diagrams, ICBM carry 44–49 percent of megatonnage. Accordingly, the U.S. would retain virtually 75 percent of her ability to strike at other Soviet targets even if she lost all her ICBM force. In marked contrast, ICBM represent 56 percent of Soviet delivery vehicles and carry 75 percent of warheads, 70 percent of throw-weight and, although not shown, 85 percent of megatonnage. Any major counterforce run-down of Soviet ICBM immediately threatens the credibility of Soviet retaliatory capability.

Nevertheless, the fact that this contingency was possible began the complex debate over U.S. "counterforce inferiority" which still continues. It also shifted attention away from how the U.S. could use her strategic superiority to win conflicts at low levels of escalation and towards guarding against a worst-case defeat by Soviet limited counterforce first strike. This in turn meant a rapid shift in focus away from the problem of making extended deterrence effective to a concentration on the B-1, *Trident*, MX and cruise missile. While efforts to give U.S. strategic forces a full range of LSO and capabilities did not stop, the high priority that LSO activity had enjoyed under Schlesinger dropped sharply under Rumsfeld, who concentrated more on trying to make qualitative improvements than on planning.

Extended Deterrence since 1977

While the Ford Administration had sought to continue to compete from strength, President Carter and his closest advisers initially questioned whether such competition would result in anything more positive than larger nuclear forces and even larger defense budgets. As a result, the new Administration concentrated on trying to find some arms control arrangement with the Soviet Union that would produce far lower levels of nuclear forces and halt the trends that were producing a first-strike counterforce capability on both sides. The period 1976–8 was therefore one of drift, in which only limited changes took place in actual U.S. strategy, war plans and procurement strategy. The President did make some major decisions, such as the cancellation of the B-1, but these were prompted more by the budget and problems in the bomber's development program than by any new concept of how he wished to shape the U.S. strategic forces. Most of the other force improvement programs begun under Schlesinger and Rumsfeld continued, although some major new delivery system programs were delayed. The new Administration did show more interest in some aspects of C^3 capabilities than its predecessor.

Re-examining U.S. Nuclear Strategy

Yet the Administration did start a general review of U.S. strategy in the spring of 1977. Presidential Review Memorandum 10, or PRM-10, received major publicity because of its discussion of changes in U.S. policy regarding NATO and the defense of the Far East. Its major effect on extended deterrence was to call attention to the fact that the U.S. had so far made only limited progress in translating the strategy and targeting policy announced in NSDM-242 into war plans and capabilities. As a result of PRM-10, the President issued a Presidential Directive, PD-18, in August 1977, which called for six major policy studies, including one on nuclear targeting policy which was the key one for extended deterrence.

This broad mix of studies did not lead to any major shifts away from the basic strategy which Secretary Schlesinger had set forth in NSDM-242, or in the basic structure of SIOP 5, which had grown out of NSDM-242. The work on the nuclear target policy review did, however, lead to the development of a highly complex matrix of "building block" options that could be flexibly combined to suit a given crisis or war. It also led to the development of strike option concepts designed to divide the Soviet Union by forcing the regionalization of its population and economy and potentially destroying the ability of its ruling Russian majority to survive as a governing and social elite. It led to new priorities for both limited and large-scale military strike options against both residual Soviet strike forces and Soviet OMT—some of which were specifically designed to defend NATO and to counter the Soviet long-range theater nuclear threat. It led to the development of carefully constrained population strike option concepts which could be used in limited wars or in combinations which would have a far more serious impact on Soviet recovery capabilities than striking at cities or fixed economic facilities. It led also to new targeting concepts for strikes at the Soviet economy which focused on the critical links that the country would need during the initial months of a post-nuclear exchange if it was to recover. It was found that, by concentrating strikes on these links, rather than trying to hit the entire base of major Soviet economic facilities, the U.S. could vastly increase the lethality of her strategic attacks.

All of this work had an obvious impact in increasing the flexibility with which the U.S. could use her strategic nuclear forces to execute limited strikes and support extended deterrence, and it had important effects in several related areas. The combined re-examination of U.S. targeting strategy and ICBM modernization resulted indirectly in the first serious debate over the future of the triad that had taken place since the early 1960s. By mid-1979, the U.S. had run through virtually every feasible basing and force improvement option for the 1980s. By the time the President reached his MX "decision" in the Summer of 1979, the U.S. had even seriously examined the option of shifting to a "dyad" emphasizing SSBN. This debate was reopened, as the Reagan Administration reviewed the Carter basing decision, but during the Carter Administration it was resolved in favor of the triad for many reasons. These ranged from the need to gain political support for SALT II to a gradual shift in the Administration's views which led the President to doubt whether the USSR would ever provide reciprocal restraint, and to believe that the U.S. had to match the rate of Soviet force build-up to achieve either substantial arms control or security. Accordingly, the main effect of this aspect of the PD-18 debate was to impose a delay in the deployment of MX, to delay the decision to develop the *Trident* II (D-5) SLBM with counterforce accuracies, to limit the upgrading of SLBM C^3 links, and to increase relatively the emphasis on the cruise missile.

It was also accompanied by a growing debate over the implications of Soviet civil defense and the level of assured destruction that each side could inflict on the other. This led the Administration into the somewhat contradictory position of supporting major increases in the future number and yield of U.S. strategic war-heads while actively seeking limits on the numbers of delivery systems. It also led to a public debate (which still continues) over a possible "recovery gap" with the USSR which is taken to mean that the USSR might be able to regenerate herself after a war faster than the U.S. However, this civil defense recovery gap debate has so far had only peripheral impact on extended deterrence. Soviet capabilities in this respect simply do not seem to be great enough to produce an asymmetry in population damage capability significant enough to confront the U.S. with the risk that LSO would involve levels of U.S. casualties unacceptably higher than those produced in the USSR, or that the Soviet Union could somehow prevent her population and economic facilities from being the assured destruction hostage that limits Soviet willingness to escalate any limited strategic conflict.

Finally, during the PD-18 exercise, separate initiatives by the Administration led to an initially rather subdued effort to re-examine NATO theater nuclear forces. This aspect of the NATO Long-Term Defense Programme (LTDP) grad-ually began to take on real meaning in 1978, at the urging of some NATO nations (like Germany and Britain) and SACEUR, then General Alexander Haig. The Europeans pressed heavily for improvement of NATO's long-range missile capabilities as a counter to the *Backfire* and SALT II, and the Administration's original reluctance to take such an effort seriously gradually shifted to support as it became clear the Europeans wanted this as tacit *quid pro quo* for support of SALT, as the true scale of the Soviet SS-20 and ICBM build-up became clear, and as experience with the USSR indicated that SALT III was likely to have far better results if the U.S. actively supported such TNF improvements. This ensured a closer relationship between U.S. strategic planning and theater nuclear planning than might otherwise have been the case. The whole issue of the targeting became enmeshed in the debate over the MX and, after the President's decision to deploy the MX in May 1979, the draft targeting directive was quietly shelved.

In June 1980, under the shadow of the election campaign, it seemed to senior White House and Pentagon officials that declaring the changes taking place in U.S. planning would provide a clear signal to the USSR that the U.S. was taking a stronger tone, had not rejected the concepts declared by Secretary Schlesinger, had plans to deal with ICBM vulnerability, and was improving—rather than reducing—the linkage between U.S. strategic force and NATO.

The President actually signed the document, Presidential Directive (PD) 59, on 25 July, but the White House arranged to have the document leaked to the press almost immediately to counter the attacks being made on the Administration's defense policy by the challenger for the Presidency, Ronald Reagan. This timing meant that the strategy was published two weeks before Secretary Brown was ready to deliver a speech explaining it, and it caused a flood of misunderstanding, ranging from Soviet claims that the U.S. was seeking a first-strike capability and supremacy to press reports claiming that the U.S. had just rejected Mutual Assured Destruction (MAD) as a strategy (she had actually rejected MAD in 1974). It also inevitably forced a public debate over the fact that Secretary of State Muskie had not been consulted.

In any case, issuing PD-59 did not mean changes in the basic strategy that Schlesinger had declared, in the continuing development of LSO in the SIOP, or in force improvements that were designed to give the U.S. a full range of LSO capabilities. If anything, the entire PD-18 effort, the continuing work on SIOP 5 and Administration policy after 1978, accelerated the implementation of NSDM-242, although it did delay or cancel some developments in strategic warheads and delivery systems. Secretary Brown's speech of 20 August 1980 was explicit on all these points:

> At the outset, let me emphasize that PD-59 is *not* a new strategic doctrine; it is *not* a radical departure from U.S. strategic policy over the past decade or so. It *is*, in fact, a refinement, a codification of previous statements of our strategic policy. PD-59 takes the same essential strategic doctrine, and restates it more clearly, more cogently, in the light of current conditions and current capabilities.

This is particularly important in the light of Ronald Reagan's election, because the continuity of this aspect of U.S. strategy since 1974 has been a powerful factor in ensuring that it would not change with a given Administration. In fact, the Reagan Administration is—if anything—even more committed to the rapid implementation of NSDM-242 and PD-59 than the Administration of President Carter.

Improvements in U.S. Capabilities

While the debate over SALT II and U.S. strategy received more attention than the Carter Administration's efforts to improve U.S. strategic capabilities, the actions of the Carter Administration and the Reagan Administration, coupled to the programs begun under Presidents Nixon and Ford, produced a wide range of force improvement programs which affect both U.S. capabilities to execute limited strikes and enhance extended deterrence.

C³I Systems. In 1974, the Department of Defense estimated that it would cost between $300 million and $800 million to provide the minimum upgrading of its C³ and warning systems necessary to support a suitable range of LSO strikes. Since that time, the U.S. has spent several billion dollars in making relevant improvements. The strategic force improvement program which President Reagan announced on 2 October 1981 will add billions more.

These improvements include the development of Command Data Buffer System (CDBS) for the 550 *Minuteman* III ICBM. This system, which started to become operational in 1977 and was completed in 1980, allows instantaneous selection from a number of pre-stored targets and the introduction of new targets in 25–36 minutes per missile, as against the previous 16–24 hours required to change tapes. This means that at least the *Minuteman* III force now has much of the targeting flexibility needed to provide a suitable range of LSO options. The associated electronics in the silos are also being hardened, provided with independent power supplies for sustained stand-alone operation, made resistant to electromagnetic pulse (EMP) and given new suspension systems.

Major improvements are planned in the Airborne Command Post (ABCP) Program to harden the system against EMP and to improve its ability to deal with complex attacks and provide LSO retargeting. Six advanced E-4B aircraft will be deployed by 1983, and the first entered service in early 1980. Several of those aircraft will include the Phase III airborne launch control system (ALCS). This will provide a jam-resistant secure data link to allow Strategic Air Command (SAC) crews to determine the status of each *Minuteman* III missile and the extent to which it has survived an attack, and it will allow encrypted rapid retargeting of *Minuteman* III missiles under attack conditions.

The Phase III system will be ready for 200 *Minuteman* III in 1982, and the USAF is now seeking to upgrade the remaining 350 *Minuteman* III, and possibly 450 *Minuteman* II, during 1983–4. Combined with the CDBS and improved B-52G/H capabilities, it will allow reprogramming and launch during a Soviet attack, and give the U.S. a major launch under attack (LUA) capability.

The E-4B will also have a mix of UHF, SHF, satellite, LF and VLF communications which will improve the flexibility, reliability, and survivability of the U.S. National Command Authority (NCA) in executing ICBM, bomber, ALCM and SLBM LSO even under trans-attack conditions, and it will have far longer airborne endurance. Coupled to the improvements in *Minuteman*, the B-52 force, and C³I links to SSBN, this will give the U.S. an improved Secure Reserve Force (SRF) capability that will survive any foreseeable Soviet counterforce strike on U.S. C³I facilities.

The deployment of the USAF satellite communications system (AFSATCOM) netted *Minuteman* launch sites, B-52G/H and FB-111 bombers, KC-10 tanker aircraft, SAC Wing Command Posts, ICBM launch control centres, the E-4B, and the existing airborne command centres on EC-135 and EC-130 TACAMO aircraft by the end of 1980. As part of the strategic program that President Reagan announced on 2 October 1981, the EC-135 airborne command posts serving military commanders will be hardened against nuclear effects, and will be equipped with upgraded satellite and VLF/LF communications.

This will also improve airborne warfighting capability, and greatly reduce the need to withhold a given number of U.S. strategic systems from strike missions in support of NATO. Further, the U.S. will acquire five mobile survivable ground terminals for AFSATCOM by 1985, and these will have considerable flexibility to conduct sophisticated LSO strikes and manage joint U.S. and NATO strike plans even under worst case conditions. These measures will sharply reduce Soviet estimates of the probability that an all-out strike could somehow decouple NATO theater and U.S. strategic forces.

Other advances will take place in LF communication systems by December 1983, and high-speed encrypted digital land lines (SACDIN) will be established as a back-up between selected bomber and missile facilities during 1984–5. This will not only improve LSO flexibility and survivability, but again reduce any need to hold back warheads and launch vehicles from the support of NATO under attack conditions to avoid losing SIOP options because of the inability to retarget rapidly. Phase II of the AFSATCOM program will also net the strategic satellite communication system into the Defense Satellite Communications System (DSCS) used for the theater and tactical forces, and provide immediate worldwide communication and status coverage for planning, executing, and assessing extended deterrence and LSO.

Related improvements include the integrated operational nuclear detection system (IONDS) which will provide worldwide reporting on the location and yield of nuclear detonations, and provide far more rapid and accurate damage assessment information for LSO planning in the mid-1980s, plus deployment of satellite communications to theater nuclear units in Europe. This will greatly improve U.S. capabilities for launching through attack and will reduce the present vulnerability of the European Command and Control Console System (ECCCS). This system's nuclear C^3 links are currently dependent on the survival of five fixed HF broadcast control stations, and help to integrate globally U.S. strategic and theater nuclear forces in much the same way that U.S. strategic forces are being netted by AFSATCOM. The Carter Administration also completed a long term C^3I plan for TNF forces in late 1980, which is going forward in a reinforced form under the Reagan Administration.

Although the revised 56-mile-long extremely low frequency (ELF) *Seafarer* System which President Reagan decided to deploy on 8 October 1981 has a communication rate which is far too slow to allow flexible strike commands to be sent to U.S. SSBN, this will be compensated for by other improvements in the quality and number of Navy EC-130 TACAMO aircraft, worldwide LF systems, fleet communications satellites, SSBN antennae and on-board communications. Taken together, these improvements will greatly improve LSO-capable communications with U.S. SSBN by the mid-1980s and will allow a substantial increase in the ability to use *Poseidon* and *Trident* I SLBM in LSO against those fixed area targets which are in use by the Warsaw Pact. Combined with the Reagan Administration's tentative decision to deploy the *Trident* II (D-5) SLBM in the late 1980s, these systems will also eventually allow the U.S. to employ SLBM in LSO strikes even at the lower levels of escalation where preplanned targeting is often inappropriate.

Other new features of the U.S. C³I system announced on 2 October 1981, include:

Deploying mobile ground terminals for processing data from U.S. warning satellites, and upgrading the satellites to improve their survivability. This will increase the speed and survivability of the command structure that would carry out a retaliatory strike and provide a better basis for linking U.S. strategic and NATO LRTNF forces.

The attack characterization capabilities of warning satellites and ground-based radars will be improved as well as their reliability. This will improve the ability to characterize the limits and intended target of Soviet strikes and to fight LSO conflicts. It will also provide a steadily improving launch-through-attack (LTA) capability.

Additional *Pave Paws* surveillance radars will be deployed to improve coverage of Soviet submarines operating to the south-east and south-west of the U.S. This will improve bomber survivability, attack characterization and warning.

VLF/LF communications receivers will be deployed and installed on strategic bombers to ensure the receipt of orders and retargeting capability under attack and trans-attack conditions.

A new satellite communications system will be developed providing EHF communications channels to ensure two-way communication between commanders and forces. This will further improve LSO capabilities, and the ability to link U.S. strategic and NATO theater nuclear forces in the future.

An extensive R&D program will be initiated to provide a survivable C³I system that can fight an extended war, and force the USSR to face a situation where no Soviet strike could eliminate U.S. or NATO capability to tailor long-range strikes to the nature of the Soviet strike or to desired tactical objectives. In effect, the USSR could not limit the U.S. to the alternatives of mass strikes or nothing by attacking U.S. C³I facilities.

This does not mean all the C³I problems affecting extended deterrence will be solved during the 1980s. Continuing delays in the Space Shuttle may cause some of these plans to slip, and there will continue to be severe gaps and problems in this mix of battle management systems, particularly in the ability to characterize and assess attacks on Western Europe and to assess damage to both Western and Eastern European targets. However, the U.S. now has, or will soon acquire, many of the elements needed in terms of rapid communication and data management between U.S. theater forces, strategic forces and the National Command Authorities, to manage all but the smallest- or largest-scale strike options that might be used in defense of Europe. While their reliability and the netting of U.S. C³I systems is still somewhat weak, the situation is much better than it was in 1974, and it will improve sharply over the next five years.

ICBM Forces. There has also been a considerable increase in the capabilities of the ICBM force. The somewhat unreliable NS-17 inertial guidance system in *Minuteman* III has already been replaced with the NS-20. This has vastly improved U.S. ability to use specific ICBM in selective strikes with predictable results, and has increased the predicted lethality of each warhead against its target (single-shot kill probability, or SSKP) from 0.19 to 0.55 for hard targets. The U.S. silo-hardening program has raised the resistance of *Minuteman* silos to blast overpressure from 300 to 2,000 psi. While this is no defense against mass strikes from Soviet ICBM, and compares somewhat unfavorably with 3,500–4,500 psi for Soviet ICBM silos, it makes it difficult for the USSR to predict the results of attacks with only small numbers of warheads.

The deployment of the improved NS-20 guidance system on *Minuteman* III is further reducing its Circular Error Probable (CEP) from 400 to 200 meters and will improve its reliability. The effect will be a six-fold increase in lethality against semi-hard targets over the NS-17, and a further rise in SSKP against Soviet missile silos or other similarly hard targets from 0.55 to 0.70. Adding the Mark 12A warhead to 300 of the 550 *Minuteman* III missiles will double their yield from 170 to 335 KT, and raise their hard target SSKP even more—to 0.83.

Although, as we discussed earlier, the actual operational SSKP would be significantly lower, it would still be high enough to make a "two-on-one" attack on most Soviet hard targets credible (also called "cross-targeting," this involves aiming two RV—normally from different missiles—at one silo to give a high assurance of destruction). It will also allow the expansion of soft area target coverage for each RV from 50 to 88 square miles. Coupled with the fact that much of the force will retain warheads of lower yield, this provides a better mix of escalation capabilities with far less risk of a major miss. The Mark 12A improvement has, in fact, been so successful that SAC is pressing for all 550 *Minutemen* III to be upgraded, and consideration is being given to deploying this warhead in the *Trident* II (D-5) SLBM.

Similar improvements may take place in the 450 *Minuteman* II during the early 1980s, although the Reagan Administration has not yet chosen to fund this option. The NS-17 guidance system in these systems has already aged to the point where it is prone to failure, and SAC will also have to replace it with some variant of the NS-20. The boost motors in the *Minuteman* II missiles have already been replaced for the most part, and the missiles have been reconditioned to cure many of the problems of propellant and liner aging. Further, 300 of the 450 *Minuteman* II missiles have had the same silo hardening, improved suspension and improved launch control upgrades as *Minuteman* III.

Serious study is also under way to improve the ballistic performance of the *Minuteman* RV to reduce the vulnerability of the warhead to various electronic effects. Finally there are plans to improve the ability to launch through heavy dust and residual radioactivity that might be expected over the silo after an attack. These improvements, if accomplished, will greatly improve the survivability and effectiveness of the U.S. ICBM force against large area targets and very hard targets and in counter-value missions.

The deployment of at least 100 MX missiles will provide a major increase in LSO strike capability over *Minuteman*. The MX will be ready for deployment in 1986 and will have four times the throw-weight of *Minuteman* III, although it weighs only 2½ times as much. It will carry 10 RV and will have the potential for carrying 12. The warhead package has space to allow the incorporation of precision guidance or homing features and the ability to arm or disarm after launch.

The MX will also have approximately ten times the EMP hardness of *Minuteman*, and far greater reliability. Its computer will offer substantially greater capability to store target data and much greater speed and reliability in retargeting, particularly under attack conditions. The new inertial guidance system, AIRS, coupled with improved RV and platform design, will offer far better operational accuracy.

President Reagan's deployment decision of 2 October 1981 called for an interim deployment of 100 MX in a mix of *Titan* II and *Minuteman* silos, subsequently amended to *Minuteman* silos only. This is only half the size of the force the U.S. had previously planned to deploy by 1989, although a 200-missile force would still be possible. It will also mean the phasing out of the obsolete and unreliable *Titan* II missile and temporary reliance on reconstructed silos with perhaps improved hardening through the mid-1980s.

The President has also announced, however, that by 1984 the U.S. will select one or more improved MX basing options from among Continuous Airborne Patrol Aircraft (survivable long-endurance heavy-lift aircraft that could launch the missile), Ballistic Missile Defense (active defense of land-based MX), and Deep Underground Basing (deployment in survivable locations deep underground). While all of these concepts have their problems, they have gradually emerged as more cost-effective than the variants of the Multiple Protective Shelter (MPS) scheme, all of which would need some kind of ballistic missile defense by the late 1980s, and most of which would have proved prohibitively expensive. Equally important, the improvements being made to U.S. C³I systems offer a high potential for reliable launch under attack by the mid-1980s, with any large-scale attack being characterized about 10–14 minutes after the launch and target options being selected according to its nature. While the Reagan Administration did not announce this option, it is steadily improving in technical feasibility, and a number of experts in the Department of Defense now believe that it will emerge as the preferred solution to ICBM vulnerability.

SLBM Forces. Improvements in the SLBM force will also improve U.S. capabilities for extended deterrence. Although the total number of on-line warheads will drop slightly in the mid-1980s, the three last *Polaris* submarines are now being phased out of the force. This will create an SSBN force of 31 *Poseidon*-carrying submarines, of which 12 will be converted to carry the *Trident* I C-4 missile.

The C-4 missile increases SLBM range from 2,500 to 4,230 nm and thus increases ten-fold the area Soviet anti-submarine forces must cover in order to attack the SSBN. It will also have a nominal CEP of about 1,000 feet, or about 17 percent better than *Poseidon*, and will eventually have stellar mid-course correction. This increased accuracy, together with an increase in yield from 40 KT to 100 KT, will greatly increase the ability to use the system in LSO strikes against semi-hard OMT or industrial targets.

At the same time, the U.S. plans to deploy up to 15 *Trident* SSBN. Although the program has experienced considerable slippage and cost escalation, President Reagan announced in October 1981 that the U.S. would continue to lay down *Trident* ballistic missile submarines at a steady rate of one per year, including one in 1981, one in 1982, and one per year in 1983-7. The contract for the 1981 submarine is underway, and the 1982 submarine has been partially funded. *Trident* SSBN will have 24 missile tubes, against 16 for the *Poseidon* boats, and will be able to carry the *Trident* II (D-5) missile.

The Reagan Administration announced at the same time that it would also accelerate deployment of the D-5 missile and begin deployment in 1989. This weapon will be able to carry a nominal 14 RV per missile, against 8 for the C-4, and will provide a further increase in SLBM range to 5,000 nm at full payload. The most important features of the D-5 missile, however, result from its being 10 ft longer and 50,000 lbs heavier than the C-4 and having a throw-weight of about 6,000 lbs. This increase in throw-weight allows the increase in warhead numbers to be accompanied by the development of a precision-guided RV.

The D-5 can thus for the first time enable the U.S. to use SLBM against the full range of LSO and Soviet hard targets, eliminating the present need to rely on ICBM, bombers or cruise missiles. This, in turn, would mean the U.S. would have no need to withhold ICBM from LSO missions because of their superior accuracy, or to rely on aircraft, ALCM and SLCM which lack a swift strike capability. Since the *Trident* D-5 warhead package is highly flexible and can hold even larger numbers of small RV, the U.S. can also reduce yield to limit collateral damage while increasing the number of SLBM warheads available to react to any Soviet breakout in RV numbers.

Although the U.S. has not announced it publicly, the *Trident* will also allow her to retaliate for a strike on her land-based ICBM force by using her SLBM. It will eliminate any possibility that the USSR could destroy so many of her ICBM that the U.S. could only retaliate with slow-flying bombers or cruise missiles or by launching relatively inaccurate SLBM at area targets with large populations. Further, she could deploy the D-5 missile in a mobile land-based mode or on surface ships if forced into such an arms race by the USSR. This offers an important option in addition to the MX, and creates an added Soviet incentive to agree to arms control in the late 1980s.

Surface and Attack Submarine Forces. The Reagan Administration has further plans to improve the LSO capabilities of the U.S. Navy, announced on 2 October 1981. It had already announced in the Spring of 1981 that it was planning to deploy substantial numbers of submarine-launched cruise missiles (SLCM) in modular launchers on major surface vessels. These would equip each such ship with 32–60 SLCM, and 75 percent of these missiles would be designed for strikes against land targets, having the same precision and LSO strike capability as the air-launched cruise missile (ALCM). They would have an initial range of 1,500 nm and a potential range of 2,000 nm.

The first such SLCM missiles were to have conventional warheads and were to be deployed as early as mid-1983 on DD-963 destroyers. Others were to be added to the CG-47 *Aegis* fleet air defense cruisers in 1987. The initial deployments on the DD-963 would be limited in number, but armored 32-missile canisters would be deployed from 1985. In addition, the Reagan Administration announced that it would reactivate two battleships and refit them with 60 SLCM each, and these could be deployed as early as 1983–4. The two ships would have the growth potential to carry 320 missiles each, and two more battleships might be activated by the mid-1980s.

While the Administration did not say whether such ships would also acquire SLCM with nuclear warheads, this was under study in the Pentagon and created a major new option for expanding U.S. LSO strike capability. As a result, when it became clear that it would not be possible to solve the MX vulnerability problem in the near term, and that the *Trident* submarine building program would have to be limited to one per year, the Administration decided to put nuclear-armed SLCM on existing attack submarines. This decision means that U.S. attack submarines will carry up to 12 SLCM each, and will act as LSO strike platforms without degrading their anti-submarine capabilities. Given these plans, the U.S. opened five new land attack mission planning centers by the end of 1981. These are located at U.S. commands in the Pacific, the Atlantic, Europe, Britain and at SAC. They have a capability for terrain contour matching (TERCOM) planning and are able to launch a wide range of LSO.

The Strategic Bomber Force. While much has recently been made of the age of the B-52 force, the B-52 is undergoing a comprehensive upgrading that should keep it functioning through the 1980s and will improve its survivability, accuracy and weapons delivery capability. The improvements include a comprehensive upgrading of all aspects of the B-52G/H offensive avionics systems (OAS) and the conversion of the B-52G to an AGM-86B ALCM carrier.

The first B-52G with ALCM is now available for standing alert with external cruise missiles, and the first squadron should become operational late in 1982.

The 196-bomber force will then steadily convert to the ALCM, with the B-52G initially carrying twelve missiles externally before being converted to carry eight more internally. The conversion program is now scheduled to be complete by FY 1990.

The B-52G will also be greatly hardened against EMP to prevent "barrage" type nuclear defense by the USSR, and will have the option of carrying short-range attack missiles (SRAM) for penetration missions. Although the ALCM aircraft will have very long mission flight times (12–16 hours), they can accommodate changes in the political and military situation while ensuring high survivability. They will also be able to achieve very high accuracy in LSO missions. (Under ideal circumstances, the ALCM will have accuracies of 300–600 ft. with a 180-KT warhead, and should normally have a CEP better than 3,000 ft.)

The Reagan Administration announced on 2 October 1981 that it would convert an unspecified number of the remaining 96 B-52H to ALCM. In the interim, both the B-52G and B-52H are being provided with modern computers to improve accuracy. Terrain mapping/avoidance radar, necessary to correct the aircraft's current problems in low-altitude penetration missions, are also being improved. The aircraft will also have new data cartridge systems. These will allow data preparation centers on each base to program new strike options rapidly and, in conjunction with central data centers at SAC, cut the time necessary to prepare a bomber for new LSO missions by hours. The OAS package will also increase the accuracy of the B-52H in dropping nuclear bombs by up to three times. The remaining B-52D will be retired in 1982 and 1983.

These capabilities of the B-52 force will be supplemented by those of the FB-111 forces based in the U.S. The FB-111 can fly low-altitude penetration missions at half the height of the B-52H, and can use the SRAM in LSO missions, firing up to six missiles within a short period of time. Its terrain-following radar and navigational packages already provide much of the accuracy that is to be added to the B-52, and the communications links to the FB-111 are being improved to enhance control in flight.

In October 1981, the Reagan Administration also announced a decision to produce 100 improved B-1 bombers, with deployment of the first squadron in 1986, and "vigorously" to pursue development for the early 1990s of a more advanced "stealth" bomber which would be relatively invisible to Soviet radar. The "simplified" B-1 that will be deployed as a result of this decision will have a limited-sweep wing and will be ideal for LSO and other extended deterrence missions. It will be tanker-independent and will have much more advanced defensive avionics and high multi-role payload capabilities. Even without an aft bomb bay, it could carry 22 ALCM—8 externally and 14 internally. With an aft bomb bay it could carry 30 ALCM, 38 SRAM, 28–30 nuclear bombs, 142 500-pound conventional bombs, or 38 2,000-pound bombs. In combination with the B-52 force, the B-1 force will allow the United States to deploy over 3,000 cruise missiles.

These conventional and theater nuclear mission capabilities are particularly relevant because, if the "stealth" technology on the B-1, combined with low-power ECM, can keep its radar detectability low after prolonged service, the U.S. could use it in NATO support missions with minimum risk of attrition and would have little need to withhold it so as to preserve it for strategic missions. (The B-1, while not a "stealth" bomber, does have greatly reduced detectability and will be produced with several advanced features.) The B-1 variant is the Reagan Administration's choice for this role, and it is likely to enter service in 1987.

Finally, satellite navigation systems will improve the accuracy and reliability of all U.S. bombers in LSO attacks during the mid-1980s, and advanced multispectral and enhanced imaging techniques, communications and data processing will also improve targeting and damage assessment.

Strategic Defense. While strategic defense has only a marginal impact on extended deterrence, it seems worth noting that the Reagan program, announced on 2 October 1981, also included:

a. Replacing five obsolescent F-106 squadrons with F-15s;
b. Expanding the ballistic missile defense R&D program;
c. Bringing space-based missile defense to the development stage;
d. Buying at least six additional AWACS air-borne surveillance aircraft to augment ground-based radars in peacetime and to provide surveillance and control interceptors in wartime;
e. Expanding the U.S. civil defense and continuity of government programs;
f. Improving the U.S.–Canadian air surveillance network by buying some combination of *Over-The-Horizon Back-scatter* (OTH-B) and other improved ground radars.

War Fighting Capabilities and Extended Deterrence

The rationale behind these force improvements is summarized in figure 18–5, which shows the estimate of the balance that former Secretary of Defense Harold Brown used in his SALT II testimony to the Senate Foreign Relations Committee in July 1979. Although both U.S. force plans and the estimated capabilities of Soviet forces have changed somewhat since then, these estimates are important because they reveal the Carter Administration's thinking when it shaped the basic structure of the U.S. ALCM, *Trident*, MX and bomber programs, and the "balance" the Reagan Administration considered in making its October 1981 decisions.

The U.S. increased her force loading from 3,950 warheads in 1969 to 9,200 in 1980, while the USSR increased hers from 1,659 to about 5,100. Under the Carter program, the U.S. would have further increased her on-line warheads to about

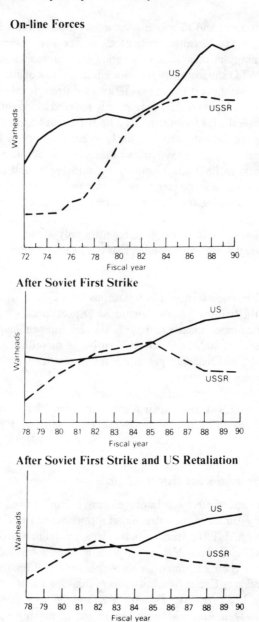

On-line Forces

After Soviet First Strike

After Soviet First Strike and US Retaliation

Source: Secretary of Defense Harold Brown, Testimony to the Senate Committee on Foreign Relations, 9 and 11 July 1979.

Figure 18–5. Counter-force Exchange Capabilities (warheads)

15,000 by 1990, while the USSR would have a maximum of 10,000–12,400, if she continued to modernize within the limits set by SALT II. It was also shown at the time that deployment of the ALCM, *Trident* I, and MX were estimated to maintain rough parity in hard-target capability, and gradually to give the U.S. significant superiority in soft-target kill capability, provided that the USSR did not respond with radical new force improvement initiatives.

It was also demonstrated that, if the U.S. carried out all the force improvements programmed under the Carter Administration, and, if the Soviet Union did not change her force mix radically from that predicted by U.S. intelligence, the U.S. would never suffer significant inferiority in the number of targets she could hit. This estimate is particularly important for extended deterrence because it means that the Carter Administration had concluded that no set of worst-case Soviet strike options could pre-empt the American ability to conduct limited-strike options in the 1980s. Even after an all-out Soviet attack on U.S. ICBM and a U.S. response in kind, she could carry out extended deterrence options involving several thousand weapons while still preserving at least three times the number of warheads required for the civil-economic recovery targets in the SIOP assured destruction option.

The Reagan Administration's decisions of 2 October 1981 change the force mix underlying the U.S. data in figure 18–5, but they do not change the essence of the balance. They emphasize bombers and ALCM over ICBM, and they slightly slow the rate of MX and *Trident* submarine deployment. At the same time, they could lead to an even faster MX deployment in the late 1980s, and they add SLCM and two additional bomber types to U.S. strategic forces, and confirm deployment of the *Trident* D-5 missile. The net result should be to strengthen the U.S. by comparison with the estimates shown in figure 18–5.

As has been discussed earlier, a pure counterforce retaliation against Soviet ICBM of the type shown in figure 18–5 would also be an unrealistic worst-case response to an attack on U.S. ICBM. As the supporting analyses for PRM-10, PD-18 and PD-59 revealed, a much better response to a Soviet counterforce first strike would involve some mix of the several thousand key Soviet economic and military facilities which are critical to both Soviet sustained war-fighting and recovery capabilities but involve no significant increase in the population damage than would result from a Soviet strike on *Minuteman*. The U.S. thus has almost no incentive to retaliate by striking Soviet ICBM where the exchange ratio is relatively unfavorable.

Secretary of Defense Harold Brown hinted at this in his long discussion of countervailing strategy in his FY 1980 *Annual Report*. He also made several points about counterforce targeting (pp. 75–9) which need careful attention. He stressed that such retaliatory targeting would require at most one warhead per remaining Soviet silo, command bunker, nuclear weapons storage site and soft strategic facility. In practical terms, this would mean that the U.S. would need at most 2,000 warheads even if she could not determine whether or which silos were empty and yet felt that she could risk an all-out launch on all residual Soviet strategic capabilities.

Over 7,000 of the approximately 9,000 U.S. warheads are on relatively survivable SLBM and bombers. Although these systems have the wrong mix of yields, cannot react quickly and lack the desirable degree of accuracy, surviving U.S. forces could still carry out extensive extended deterrence strikes without jeopardizing either the option of OMT retaliation or assured destruction strikes. Further, as U.S. attack characterization capabilities improve, it will become extraordinarily difficult for the USSR to launch large-scale counterforce attacks without the U.S. locating many of the empty Soviet ICBM silos. This means that the U.S. will need to reserve steadily fewer residual warheads for retaliatory counter-silo strikes each year, while simultaneously increasing the total number of survivable warheads she has available.

The "Counterforce Gap"

It also cannot be overstressed, given the attention that the "counterforce gap" has received, that this scenario was never intended to be a basis for sizing U.S. forces, but rather to be the worst-case test for measuring Soviet capabilities. The gap applies only to U.S. ICBM, non-alert bombers, and SSBN in port, and only if all the Soviet ICBM used launch at the proper time and perform according to the theoretical predictions, with no significant cumulative degradation for any of the anticipated readiness and C^3 problems caused by the "law of large numbers." It requires the U.S. to accept a minimum of 5–10 million casualties, and to reject "launch through attack" despite her steadily improving C^3I capabilities.

The gap also occurs only because of the asymmetries in the U.S. and Soviet triads, which have the effect of making it easier for the USSR to attack U.S. ICBM because they are a much smaller portion of the triad. Further the gap only becomes serious if it is measured in aggregates like effective megatonnage; these are poor measures of each side's ability to destroy targets, given the lethality of even a 100 KT weapon against 90 percent or more of the unhardened targets on each side.

There have been many different unclassified assessments of the consequences of a Soviet counterforce first strike on U.S. ICBM but none are entirely satisfactory. Obviously the alert status of U.S. forces is critical but it is now generally assumed that the U.S. could cope with even a major increase in the rate of Soviet expansion in on-line warheads by either deploying more MX or accelerating *Trident* II, and could do so even under conditions where SALT I and SALT II constraints no longer apply.

The MX or *Trident* II programs are clearly important if the U.S. is to avoid inferiority in the middle and late 1980s. However, the U.S. can also offset much of her inferiority in a pre-emptive Soviet counterforce strike by either increasing her alert rate or converting to a launch-under-attack posture. While such a shift to LUA retaliation would be far more risky than deploying new delivery systems and continuing to plan to ride out any Soviet attack, the new C^3I systems described earlier will massively reduce the risk of a "false alarm" or overreaction by the mid-1980s. This will again help to ensure that the U.S. can maintain a suitable margin of retaliatory capability to execute LSO even under worst-case conditions. In short, the "counterforce" gap does not seriously threaten U.S. capability to employ strategic forces in extended deterrence missions during the 1980s.

Extended Deterrence and the Uncertainties of the 1980s

Existing and planned U.S. strengths and capabilities do not mean, however, that the U.S. and NATO do not face major challenges from the USSR. Specifically, there are a number of problems which the U.S. and NATO must deal with if extended deterrence is to be secured in the 1980s.

The USSR is clearly outspending the U.S. on strategic forces and now has equal overall technical capability and a vastly superior production base. The details of this Soviet lead are shown in figure 18–6 (although some of the data on Soviet spending in the figure are the subject of an intense debate within the strategic studies community, the broad trends seem certain to be correct). While it is difficult to translate a superiority in expenditures into military superiority, it is clear that the USSR has the potential ability to improve her nuclear forces faster than the U.S.

The U.S. must be ready to deal with a far greater range of Soviet force improvements than those projected in figure 18–5. While U.S. plans seem adequate to cope with the known trends in Soviet forces, the USSR has the initiative in many areas, and the U.S. must be prepared to respond. Moreover, U.S. strategic forces still lack a number of highly desirable capabilities which, though not essential to meet the minimum criteria for extended deterrence, provide insurance against miscalculation or uncertainty.

The gap between NATO's present theater nuclear capabilities and those of U.S. strategic forces has taken on a different character since the mid-1970s. It now presents serious problems of both range and capability in ensuring a proper spectrum of deterrent options, and NATO long-range theater forces must be improved, as must the mid-range capabilities against fixed targets (and their associated air defense weapons) and against mobile or imprecisely located targets in the various echelons of Warsaw Pact forces. Nor has the U.S. developed adequate forces suited for limited nuclear strike options in other areas of the world such as Korea and the Persian Gulf. The actual need for such forces may be arguable, but the inadequacies of current and programmed U.S. capabilities are not.

Finally, the U.S. has failed adequately to explain her strategy and capabilities to her European allies and to declare her intentions in a way that would help to restore the belief that a U.S. President would implement extended deterrence in a crisis.

1. Cumulative: 1971–1980 (billion 1979 dollars)

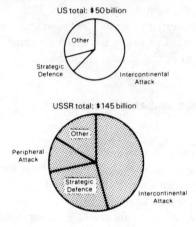

US total: $50 billion

USSR total: $145 billion

Source: These comparisons use *U.S. Defense Planning and Programming Categories* of November 1980 with minor adjustments to attain comparability. Investment includes all costs for the procurement of military hardware and the construction of facilities. 'Other' category includes nuclear weapons and strategic control and surveillance. Costs for pensions and RDT&E are excluded. Procurement excludes construction and nuclear weapons materials.

2. Trend: 1970–1979

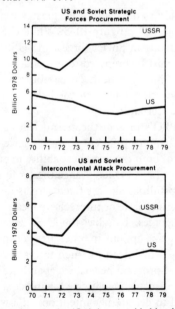

Source: Adapted by the author from unclassified data provided by the Central Intelligence Agency.

Figure 18-6. Comparative Investment in Strategic Forces

Uncertainties in the Soviet Threat

It is clear that even conservative estimates about the improvements taking place in the Soviet threat will mean that the USSR will lead the U.S. in some major measures of total force strength during the 1980s, although she will have only parity or inferiority in others. Estimates could shift substantially further in favor of the USSR if additional Soviet and Warsaw Pact force improvements take place.

Soviet Strategic Forces. Even if the SALT II limits were implemented in some form, the USSR could greatly improve her bomber forces, the warhead loading and overall reliability of her ICBM and the number of warheads in her SLBM forces. There have been strong indications recently that the USSR may be moving in this direction. She has increased the tempo of her R&D effort to develop five new ICBM and may be developing improved variants of the SS-18 and SS-19. She can certainly deploy 8–10 RV per missile, and her ICBM accuracy has now reached 0.15 nm for SS-19, with Soviet ICBM in general now being expected to reach 0.08 nm by 1985. This would reduce or eliminate the Soviet need to allocate two RV per U.S. ICBM in counterforce strikes. While the initial SLBM launches for the new SS-NX-20 missile to be used on the *Typhoon* SSBN were failures, the SS-N-18 missile in *Delta* 3 submarines has demonstrated the Soviet ability to give her SLBM 7 MIRV and a range of 6,500 nm with high accuracy; and the USSR has since deployed the *Typhoon* SSBN and seems to be making enough progress with the SS-NX-20 to deploy an SLBM with 12 RV, an 8,300-nm range and accuracies substantially higher than 0.3 nm by the mid-1980s. Work is also proceeding now on two new Soviet strategic bombers—a large supersonic bomber and a low altitude penetrating aircraft—and ALCM tests have shown that the weapon load of a heavy bomber (plus *Backfire*) could be raised to 8–10 systems per aircraft by 1985.

Under worst-case conditions, such developments would allow the USSR nearly to double the number of warheads she could deploy by 1990 to a total of over 20,000. This is important because the estimates in figures 18-4 and 18-5, and in current U.S. strategic analysis, depend upon the assumptions that the Soviet Union:

a. Will not quickly load her ICBM to the 10 RV permitted in SALT II;
b. Cannot quickly improve the fractionation of her SLBM or bring them up to the 14 RV permitted by SALT II in the near future;
c. Cannot greatly improve the bomber loadings with larger cruise missile numbers;
d. Will not introduce a less vulnerable ICBM basing mode;
e. Will not have any kind of SLBM with depressed trajectory and precision-guided RV capability before 1990.

Unfortunately, there is no firm intelligence evidence that the USSR will not do any of these things, and strong recent indicators show that she may. The real exchange curves of the 1980s could thus be very different from those shown in the previous figures. In fact, the balance could shift in favor of the USSR as early as 1983.

However, as Part 2 of figure 18-6 has shown, the U.S. does have a number of rapid countermeasures she can take to such Soviet actions. She could deploy more MX missiles into the presently planned basing structure and increase *Trident* SSBN production to one to two submarines per year. She could speed deployment of the *Tomahawk* SLCM in the 8 *Polaris* submarines being replaced by *Trident*, produce FB-111 variants to increase her bomber strength, increase B-1 bomber production and ALCM loading, and add ALCM capability to the 96 B-52H as well as the 169 B-52G.

It seems unlikely, therefore, that Soviet actions could greatly affect U.S. strategic capabilities for extended deterrence before the United States could react with longer-term and more intensive force improvements, or that unanticipated increases in Soviet capability could threaten a substantially greater portion of the U.S. ICBM force or civil population than the Soviet force improvements currently planned. Nevertheless, unless the United States acts decisively the perceived balance—in terms of static measures of force strength—might be much worse, and this could have significant political effects.

Soviet Theater Nuclear Forces. The USSR is in the process of deploying large numbers of *Backfire* bombers and SS-20 missiles. Over 70 *Backfire* were deployed with her Long Range Aviation in mid-1981, with a matching number in her Naval Aviation. Most were the improved *Backfire* with a payload of more than 5,500 kg, an unrefuelled range of over 8,900 km and the ability to fit a probe for in-flight refuelling. By July 1981 the USSR had deployed over 250 SS-20 launcher/missile combinations, with one reload missile per launcher, which put more than 1,500 SS-20 warheads on line. About 175 of the launchers were deployed where they could be used against NATO. The resulting force had more than 350 missiles or 1,050 warheads.

The *Backfire* is being produced at a rate of 30 per year, and the rate of SS-20 production is accelerating. Since January 1981 the pace of SS-20 base construction opposite NATO has increased sharply, and bases now under construction will add 65 launch positions and 390 warheads to the force. As many as 100–150 additional launchers, or 600–900 warheads including re-loads, may be deployed before the end of the program. An improved version of the SS-20 may also be in the process of deployment, and a follow-on version may now be reaching advanced development.

The USSR is also starting to deploy the shorter-range SS-21 and SS-22 and is completing final testing of the SS-23a—all of which have superior range and performance capabilities to *FROG, Scud* and *Scaleboard* that are presumed to be obsolescent. She is also greatly improving the capability of the fighters that can be used for nuclear strike missions. Accordingly, the balance of Soviet theater systems in the 1980s could be very different from that currently projected by U.S. intelligence in figure 18-1.

This could affect extended deterrence quite profoundly in two ways. First, there are indications that the Soviet Union may have targeted SS-11 ICBM on Europe in the past, and may now employ SS-19s extensively when Warsaw Pact exercises simulate "counterattacks" against NATO. As the overall mix of Soviet theater systems improves, she could either shift these SS-19 warheads to targets in the U.S. or combine them with a vastly greater theater first-strike and escalatory capability against NATO. All SS-20 in the USSR can also be fired against NATO (and not simply those normally counted as targeted against Europe), and the relatively short-range SS-22 and SS-23a have sufficient range to cover 70 to 90 percent of NATO's European military target base. Major improvements may also occur in the Soviet submarine-launched cruise-missile (SLCM) and naval bombers forces. All currently deployed Soviet submarine-launched missiles and naval aircraft with a nuclear capability, except the SS-N-6 and SS-N-8, have been used in exercises in simulated strikes against European land targets as well as in naval roles.

Such improvements in her theater systems also allow the USSR to deploy her mix of systems with far greater flexibility than can the U.S. in potential limited nuclear options against NATO's flanks, the Middle East, the Persian Gulf and Asia. Recently published maps of SS-20 deployments show that the Soviet Union is already taking such options seriously by orienting her SS-20 forces to maximize coverage in areas beyond China and the NATO Central Region.

Soviet C³I and Warning Systems. The Soviet C³I and warning systems have always been oriented towards fighting a nuclear war, rather than triggering retaliation. Unlike the U.S., the USSR had a system that could put limited strategic options into effect in the early 1970s, and she has been steadily improving that system ever since. The U.S. currently estimates that she has a greater ability to conduct limited strikes in the 1980s because of her superior computer, satellite and communications technology. However, such superiority is extremely difficult to predict or to prove. There is no real way at this point to determine which side will lead in the targeting, damage-assessment and battle-management capabilities which could be more important in a limited strategic exchange than the size and capability of the nuclear forces on each side.

Soviet Strategic Defenses. A Soviet breakout in either passive or active strategic defense cannot be ruled out, though it does not now seem likely. However, anti-ballistic missile (ABM) and anti-submarine warfare (ASW) technologies and other aspects of strategic defense are evolving rapidly and the USSR has active programs in all these areas. "Breakthroughs" are by definition not predictable, and there is growing uncertainty about the progress the USSR is making in ABM and ASW technologies. It is clear from table 18–1 that she already has a major lead over the U.S. in strategic defenses, and this is certain to continue, given the fact that the U.S. has gradually reduced her constant dollar spending on strategic defenses from nearly a third of total expenditure on strategic forces in FY 1971 to token amounts from FY 1976 onwards.

Table 18-1
U.S. and Soviet Strategic Force Strengths, 1977–81

	1 January 1977		1 January 1978		1 January 1979		1 January 1980		1 January 1981	
	U.S.	USSR	U.S.	USSR	U.S.	USSR	U.S.	USSR	U.S.	USSR
Offensive										
Operational ICBM launchers[1]	1,054	1,550	1,054	1,400+	1,054	1,400	1,054	1,398	1,054	1,398
Operational SLBM launchers[1,2]	656	800	656	900+	656	950	656	950	576	950
Long-range bombers(TAI*)[3]										
Operational[4]	419	190	349	140	348	150	348	156	347	156
Others[5]	184	170	225	0	221	0	225	—	223	—
Variants[6]	—	—	0	120	0	120	—	—	—	—
Force loadings[7] weapons	8,400	3,300	9,000	4,000+	9,200	5,000	9,200	6,000	9,000	7,000
Defensive										
Air defense surveillance										
Radars[8]	59	6,000	59	6,500	59	7,000	88	7,000	91	7,000
Interceptors(TAI*)	416	2,590	324	2,600	309	2,500	327	2,500	312	2,500
SAM launchers	—	10,000	—	10,000	0	10,000[9]	0	10,000	0	10,000
ABM defense launchers[9]	—	64	—	64	0	64	0	64	0	64

Source: Adapted from DOD Annual reports FY 78–FY 82.

[1] Includes on-line launchers as well as those being built, overhauled, repaired, converted and modernized. Excludes test and training launchers and 18 launchers of fractional orbital missiles at Tyuratam test range.

[2] Includes launchers on all nuclear-powered submarines and operational launchers for modern SLBM on Soviet G-class diesel submarines. Excludes 48 SALT II-accountable launchers on 3 Polaris submarines now used as attack submarines.

[3] 1981 figures exclude 65 U.S. FB-111 and over 100 Soviet Backfires, about 120 Bison tankers and Bear ASW and reconnaissance aircraft.

[4] Includes deployed, strike-configured aircraft only.

[5] Includes B-52s used for miscellaneous purposes or in reserve, mothballs or storage and 4 B-1 prototypes; includes Bears and Bisons used for test, training and R&D.

[6] Includes, for USSR, Bison tankers, Bear ASW and reconnaissance aircraft. U.S. tankers (641 KC-135s) do not use B-52 airframes and are excluded.

[7] Total force loadings reflect independently-targetable weapons associated with the total operational ICBM, SLBM and long-range bombers.

[8] Excludes radars and launchers at test sites or outside North America.

[9] These accommodate about 12,000 SAM interceptors. Some launchers have multiple rails.

*TAI: Total Available Inventory.

The importance of this Soviet strategic defense effort is illustrated by the fact that recent data on the Soviet surface-to-air missile (SAM) threat has evidently led Strategic Air Command to reconsider using the B-52H as a penetrating bomber for the 1980s. It is also clear that the USSR is carrying out extensive R&D efforts in SAM, ABM and anti-satellite (ASAT) weapons. Many of the advanced Soviet C^{3}I and warning systems—such as *Cat House* and *Dog House* defense radars—could be used rapidly to expand the Soviet ABM force, although they do not now seem to offer much potential for a "breakout" or a massive rapid deployment of ABM defense.

Successors or modifications to virtually all the air defense radars, interceptors, and SAM launchers shown in table 18–1 are now being deployed. These may significantly degrade the penetration capability of all NATO fighters and medium and heavy bombers and may offer a significant defense capability against NATO's older LRTNF missiles. U.S. experts expect about 1,700 new early-warning radars to be added to the totals in table 18–1 by 1989, including *Over-The-Horizon* and phased-array systems with ABM capabilities, plus major improvements in C^3 systems to integrate radar, missile and fighter forces and provide the command center and integrated defense management capabilities that Soviet forces now lack.

The obsolete Tu-126 *Moss* airborne warning aircraft is being replaced by a variant of the Il-76 *Candid* with a capability similar to the American AWACS. The SA-10 SAM will provide greatly improved low-altitude coverage; it accelerates beyond Mach 5, has greatly improved electronic counter-counter-measures (ECCM) compared to the SA-3, and will have a significant theater anti-ballistic (TABM) capability. The SA-11 and SA-12 SAM will probably replace the SA-2, and the resulting system promises to have far better range and ECCM capabilities against U.S. bombers flying at high altitudes. Finally, modifications to the MiG-25 *Foxbat* will give it a deployed "look down/shoot down" capability by 1982, and advanced Sukhoi (Ram-L) and MiG (Ram-K) strategic defense fighters are expected to be deployed by 1985 with greatly improved ECM, radars, look down/shoot down capability and air-to-air missiles.

While the USSR now has only 32 obsolete *Galosh* ABM in the Moscow area, there are indications that she has recently begun to upgrade this force, and she can still deploy up to 100 launchers under the ABM Treaty. This would allow her to test several aspects of an ABM defense of her ICBM forces in the field, and permit much more rapid deployment of such defenses if she chose to abrogate the ABM Treaty. The USSR is known to have a hypersonic exoatmospheric ABM and associated radars under development; she has also recently tested an anti-satellite weapon successfully after several failures, and there is firm evidence of an intensive effort to develop laser missile defense technology.

Soviet Planning and Doctrine. All of these uncertainties are compounded by the uncertainty over how the Soviet Union views extended deterrence, and how she would react to the limited use of strategic weapons by the U.S. It is clear from

Soviet literature that the USSR does in fact practice limited strategic exchanges in her games and exercises, although she uses very different terminology. However, she has publicly taken a strong line against the feasibility of such options. She has shown a far greater tendency, in her discussions of nuclear warfare, to focus on the value of massive pre-emption or escalation than have U.S. or NATO planners confronted with the same sort of military situation. There are also disturbing hints that some Soviet planners may believe that full-scale and rapid escalation is an inevitable result of any limited nuclear strike and act accordingly. Yet such a belief would cut two ways. It could make the USSR afraid of a U.S. strategy of extended deterrence and its escalatory consequences.

It is true that there does seem to have been some shift in Soviet planning and doctrine over the last five to seven years. Particularly in recent years, the Soviet Union has analyzed a wide range of conflicts against NATO involving some limited use of strategic weapons, and she has discussed the use of steadily lower yields. She now seems to be tailoring her strikes to minimize collateral damage and the risk of escalation, and to be deploying improved theater forces at least partly so as to be able to fight a broad range of limited nuclear wars.

However, major uncertainties remain as to whether Soviet and Western perceptions are sufficiently alike to allow extended deterrence to operate in a crisis, and there are good indications that the USSR may seek to improve her combined strategic and tactical nuclear capabilities against NATO to the point where she could try to force some kind of decoupling between the U.S. strategic deterrent and NATO forces.

Limitations in U.S. Capabilities

Perhaps the most serious potential limitations in American and NATO capabilities for sustaining extended deterrence lie in the fact that so many of the key improvements in existing U.S. strategic forces are still being implemented or are uncertain to receive full programming support and to reach deployment, notwithstanding the new impetus the Reagan Administration is giving to improving U.S. strategic forces. There is also no way to assess the probable success of each system, or how they will interact. Many operate at the leading edge of technology, and such efforts have often fallen far short of their predicted performance in the past.

Doubts also exist about whether the U.S. can bring in new systems like the cruise missile, MX, *Trident*, B-1 and "stealth" bomber at anything like the rate now projected in her plans. Some slippage in operational date or performance is almost inevitable, and the problem of cost escalation and competition for funds is serious enough, even under the new Reagan defense budget, to threaten cut-backs in all the major efforts now underway. This compounds the risks of comparing U.S. plans against observed Soviet trends.

The current emphasis on upgrading U.S. ICBM and SLBM forces to increase their assured destruction capabilities and the counterforce retaliatory capabilities of U.S. ICBM will significantly raise the yields of weapons in the U.S. strategic forces.

The deployment of cruise missiles will not ease this situation, since they also have comparatively high yields. This could tend to limit U.S. targeting flexibility, although it is easy to exaggerate the impact of such changes because the number of targets where truly low yields are necessary to limit collateral damage is restricted. Moreover, the effect of a given strike can be reduced very sharply by raising the height of burst of the warhead, and the cumulative damage effect of doubling or tripling the yield of a weapon detonated on or over a soft or area target is much smaller than the increase in yield implies.

Any delay in developing precision-guided RV technology for strategic missiles could deprive the U.S. of the ability to deploy a *Trident* II (D-5) force with low yields and extremely high accuracies in the mid-to-late 1980s, despite the recent Reagan decision to accelerate D-5 development. This force would be an important addition to U.S. extended deterrence capabilities since it would provide a launch platform which was not on U.S. soil and which was not vulnerable. A delay or problem in the D-5 program might be critical if the vulnerability of U.S. ICBM increased strikingly. Nor has the U.S. yet matched the improvements being made in the ability of strategic C³ systems to retarget and manage LSO strikes with suitable improvements in survivable intelligence and theater systems. The U.S. C³I system will be unbalanced in the mid-1980s by an overemphasis on the ability to execute strikes and a relative inability to decide what to shoot at, or to measure the effect.

President Reagan's 2 October 1981 decision to deploy 100 MX in existing silos also leaves the issue of U.S. ICBM vulnerability undecided. While he announced that the U.S. would decide on some mix of ABM defense, deep silos and airborne MX launchers by 1984, it is unclear whether she will actually fund and deploy a survivable basing mode for her ICBM in the 1980s. This may well force the U.S. to convert to a launch under attack mode if she detects a very large-scale Soviet attack on land targets in the U.S. This could reduce her ability to restrict herself to LSO under worst-case conditions.

The fact that most of the changes necessary to make extended deterrence effective are still in the process of completion has ensured that almost no real U.S. planning and exercise testing of these capabilities has yet taken place. This has been compounded by the long-standing tendency of senior officials to delegate virtually all exercise participation to comparatively junior members of their staffs. It does little good to plan such force capabilities, and even to have effective plans at the level of SAC, if the U.S. National Command Authority (NCA) is made up of people who would have to learn how to operate extended deterrence under wartime or crisis conditions. For similar reasons, only a few European officials have ever paid any really serious attention to their NATO crisis management or wartime responsibilities. The NATO battle staffs that would exercise operational control over theater nuclear forces are not permanently established, nor do they have the capability to adapt or adjust plans using up-to-date intelligence. The success of extended deterrence, however, would greatly depend upon the quality of the link between U.S. and European authorities and the depth of their understanding of U.S. strategic and NATO theater capabilities. Delegation of such European responsibilities to SACEUR might partly compensate for such a lack of national capability, but the spectacle of United States' and NATO officials trying to deal with the cabinets of European governments undergoing a crash course in nuclear war is a real possibility. Much needs to be done to make NATO staffs more capable and NATO's national leaderships more cognizant of the need for effective crisis management.

Coupling Strategic and Theater Nuclear Forces

The problems in strategic capabilities cannot be separated from the trends in NATO theater nuclear forces. The ability to sustain extended deterrence is determined both by U.S. strategic capabilities and by those of NATO theater forces—and particularly by the extent to which U.S. strategic capabilities to execute LNO overlap, and are reinforced by, NATO theater capabilities to execute long-range strikes. While extended deterrence is not absolutely dependent upon the existence of such NATO capabilities, it is obviously reinforced by them, and they can be of major value in insuring against the uncertainties or weaknesses in the relative capabilities of U.S. strategic forces.

The Current Trend in Force Capabilities

The overall trends in the relevant LRTNF capabilities of each side, as projected by the U.S., are shown in table 18–2. The first part of the table shows the U.S. estimates on 1 January 1981. The second shows the latest trends as projected in U.S. intelligence estimates. Both show that the LRTNF balance has shifted sharply in favor of the Warsaw Pact, yet the table understates the extent of this shift and the problems it creates for extended deterrence.

Table 18–2 does not count either the Soviet SS-19 warheads which may be targeted in support of the Warsaw Pact, or the roughly 400 *Poseidon* warheads assigned to SACEUR. However, the Soviet ICBM form a highly precise system with rapid retargeting capability which links well to a full range of Warsaw Pact theater systems. In contrast, *Poseidon* has comparatively poor true system accuracy, and, while it has some retargeting capability, the *Poseidon* SSBN lack the C^3 links to make effective use of this. This situation will not change materially if the *Poseidon* SLBM are replaced with the *Trident* I, since the near-term improvements in the *Trident* I's CEP and retargeting capabilities will still limit it to roughly the same strike options.

The USSR therefore has large strategic land forces in Europe to supplement her theater forces which are better suited to creating a smooth spectrum of escalation between strategic and theater forces. The U.S. SLBM on the other hand act as a residual deterrent which is oriented towards comparatively rigid, preplanned and large-scale strike options against fixed area targets like Warsaw Pact air bases.

Table 18-2
Estimated U.S./NATO and Soviet On-Line Land-Based Long-Range Theatre Nuclear Forces[1]

	Missile Range/ Aircraft Radius (km)	*Weapons Per System*	*January 1981*				*Mid-1980s (Estimated)*			
			Total Launchers/ Aircraft Worldwide	*Total Launchers/ Aircraft Europe[2]*	*Total Warheads Worldwide*	*Total Warheads Europe[2]*	*Total Launchers/ Aircraft Worldwide*	*Total Launchers/ Aircraft Europe[2]*	*Total Warheads Worldwide*	*Total Warheads Europe[2]*
Soviet										
SS-20 launchers	≥ 4,400	3	180	110	540	330	300+	[4]	900[3]	[4]
Backfire bombers[5]	4,200	4[6]	65–70	40	260–280[8]	160	150	[4]	600	[4]
Older missiles	1,900–4,100	1	400	400	400	400	50–200[7]	50–200[7]	50–200[7]	50–200[7]
Older bombers[5]	2,800–3,100	2[6]	450	350	900	700	400	300	800	600
NATO										
UK *Vulcan* bomber	> 2,000	—[8]	56	56	—[8]	—[8]	0	0	0	0
U.S. F-111	1,800	2[6]	360	170	720	340	330	170	660	340
U.S. GLCM	> 2,000	1	0	0	0	0	464[9]	464[9]	464[9]	464[9]
U.S. *Pershing* II	> 2,000	1	0	0	0	0	108[9]	108[9]	108[9]	108[9]

Source: Adapted from *Department of Defense Annual Report Fiscal Year 1981*, p. 66.

[1] Soviet systems that can unambiguously hit targets in Western Europe from bases in the USSR, and NATO systems that can unambiguously hit the USSR from bases in Western Europe. Aircraft radii are illustrative for European missions.

[2] Inventory normally based in, or within striking range of, Europe.

[3] Because of the continuing construction program, the SS-20 force may be larger than estimated here.

[4] Two-thirds of worldwide inventory could be deployed against NATO.

[5] Strike-configured bombers and ASM carriers only; excludes comparable numbers of *Backfire* and older bombers currently assigned to Soviet Naval Aviation.

[6] Illustrative weapons load. Actual load would vary according to mission and type of weapon (ASM or bombs).

[7] Numbers shown reflect uncertainties about the future status of the older missile launchers.

[8] Unclassified data not available.

[9] After completion of LRTNF modernization.

Virtually every NATO theater nuclear system is now outranged by its Warsaw Pact counterpart, and NATO systems are deployed in highly vulnerable and concentrated sites. There are only about 70 major NATO theater nuclear targets in peacetime, and no more than 200–300 in war. The only long-range NATO theater system which can truly disperse on alert is *Pershing* IA, and this system suffers from an array of targetability, reliability and flexibility problems which seriously limit its effectiveness. Moreover, NATO has still taken only limited steps to improve its C^{3}I capabilities for nuclear war. Its C^{3}I systems are even more vulnerable than its long-range nuclear forces—the loss of less than ten C^3 centers in Europe (many of which could be destroyed with conventional weapons) could virtually "blind" all NATO nuclear war management. Limited improvements in C^3 capability, such as AWACS and at Boerfink (NATO's wartime HQ), will improve NATO's capabilities in some areas, but these will not be enough for dynamic nuclear planning in a crisis. The improvement of key targeting, damage assessment, intelligence and battle management capabilities are not even called for in current NATO force improvement plans. While there is no question that these weaknesses would not prevent NATO from fighting, they would sharply limit its ability to support extended deterrence with accurate and timely information, to draw up carefully measured response plans and to conduct accurate damage assessment. These difficulties are compounded by the fact that NATO cannot rely on survivable nuclear delivery systems.

Overall, NATO TNF have only a very inadequate first strike posture. Their vulnerability invites Warsaw Pact pre-emption in peacetime, and NATO has left a large gap between its largest or most capable systems and the smallest strategic system the U.S. could employ in extended deterrence. This posture creates both an incentive for a Soviet first strike early in any conflict in the Central Region and the risk that such an attack could be so successful that the U.S. use of strategic systems for extended deterrence would lose credibility or effectiveness.

Improvement of NATO Long-Range Systems

As has been described earlier, the Carter Administration did not initially believe that these problems would be serious enough to require significant improvements in NATO forces. In fact, President Carter showed as much initial opposition to improvements in NATO's nuclear strength during 1977–8, as he did to many of the efforts to improve U.S. strategic forces. Although a number of senior European leaders and politicians sought U.S. support for providing cruise missiles to NATO in that Administration's early days, it still proposed the temporary protocol on cruise missile deployments in SALT II. When West German Chancellor Schmidt made his speech at the IISS calling for stronger NATO nuclear forces in the Autumn of 1977 (see *Survival*, January/February 1978, pp. 2–10), the Carter Administration continued to hold to the dogma of previous Administrations, taking the position that large-scale attacks on Western Europe by Soviet medium-range forces were deterred (or countered) by the U.S. strategic deterrent, especially those *Poseidon* forces at sea that were committed to NATO.

During 1978, however, there was a significant shift in President Carter's views as he came to feel that such a U.S. policy met neither Europe's political or military needs. The initial catalyst was political. Repetition of U.S. strategic guarantees through 1977 and into 1978 had little effect on European expressions of concern about the unrestrained growth of Soviet long-range TNF and the extent to which the U.S. might be limiting her long-range TNF options in SALT. Accordingly, despite U.S. concern that the European Allies would lose their political enthusiasm when faced with the reality of missile deployments on their soil, the Carter Administration began to look seriously at the question of modernizing long-range TNF in mid-1978. It is also fair to say that the neutron warhead debacle had some influence on this decision.

In the process, U.S. planners went beyond the politics of NATO TNF and began seriously to re-examine the military aspects of the theater balance in Europe. After about five months of study in 1978, they produced estimates which concluded that there was indeed a military problem, although its dimensions were not universally agreed within the Government. Elements of the State Department viewed the problem as mainly political, and certain elements of the U.S. military viewed the problem (and continue to view it) in terms of a perceived need to cover SACEUR's entire target list in a theater equivalent of the SIOP.

In broad terms, however, the new U.S. planning effort reached the following conclusions:

Strategic parity had changed European and Soviet perceptions of the credibility of an American strategic nuclear response, even a limited one, to Soviet nuclear attacks on Europe. Although this was a perceptual problem, it was not one that could be rectified simply by resorting to rhetoric or structural solutions.

In addition to achieving strategic parity, the USSR had developed capabilities for a variety of military responses at conventional and nuclear levels. The nuclear improvements were striking, not so much in their numbers as in their quality. These changes also suggested that the USSR was moving towards being able to dominate escalation at all levels, even if this were not the preferred Soviet strategy. Since it had been U.S. strategy since NSDM-242 to dominate the process of escalation, this change suggested that the NATO strategy of flexible response, already vulnerable at conventional level, was now vulnerable throughout the nuclear spectrum. Thus the military/strategic problem was not simply the SS-20, but the range of nuclear modernization, of which the SS-20 was an important part.

NATO's most serious deficiency in this connection was seen to be in LRTNF based in continental Europe and capable of striking Soviet territory. The Alliance had almost no LRTNF—only the 156 F-111s based in the U.K., which were dual-capable and also had important conventional tasks, and the 50 British *Vulcan* bombers, which were practically at the end of their operational availability, were in the inventory. The vigorous Soviet modernization, represented not only by the SS-20 and *Backfire* but also by fighter aircraft such as the *Fencer* and the shorter-range ballistic missiles (SS-21, -22, and -23a), suggested the possibility of Soviet efforts—in conflict or in peace—to decouple Europe from U.S. strategic forces in the sense that the USSR could attack or threaten attacks with her LRTNF, and the Alliance would have no response other than to resort to U.S. strategic forces.

To these military/strategic conclusions was added the political assessment that some new LRTNF capability was needed to reassure the Allies that the American nuclear commitment to Europe remained firm. The SS-20 had become a symbol of the potential weakness of NATO nuclear forces, and something was needed on the ground to "counter" the SS-20. (Unfortunately, the "countering the SS-20" argument became the predominant theme in the ensuing political debate, which, since 1979 has thus tended to overlook the overall requirements of NATO and U.S. strategy, and Soviet across-the-board improvements in nuclear capability and ability to dominate theater nuclear escalation.)

There was an additional political dimension. The Europeans felt left out of the SALT process. They saw the U.S.—whether justifiably or not—bargaining away theater systems (i.e., the ground-launched cruise-missile) in SALT II, while the Soviet strategic threat to Western Europe remained unconstrained and was in fact being vigorously modernized. It was clear that any SALT negotiations beyond SALT II would have to grapple with the Soviet strategic threat to Western Europe. It was similarly clear that the politics of defense in Western Europe would make it impossible to obtain Alliance agreement to deploying U.S. LRTNF in Europe, no matter how much they were needed, unless that deployment was accompanied by negotiations to reduce and limit LRTNF on both sides. This led to the ultimate decision by the U.S., with Alliance backing, to make an arms-control proposal to the Soviet Union in the context of SALT.

Most U.S. analysts felt, however, that the Soviet build-up did not require the sort of "force matching" solution recommended by some military authorities which involved deployment of 1,000 to 3,000 warheads to provide a "theater balance" and to be able to execute a theater-level SIOP against SACEUR's targets without relying on U.S. strategic forces for help. There was a conscious decision at the higher levels of the Carter Administration that NATO did not need to "match" Soviet LRTNF warheads one-for-one, at least in its initial *Pershing* II and cruise missile deployments. The Administration also felt that the chances of achieving an Alliance consensus on deployment of 1,000–3,000 warheads were virtually nil, and that any U.S. effort to seek it would ensure that no new LRTNF systems would be deployed at all.

The Carter Administration also rejected views within the Government calling for small deployments, such as simply replacing the *Pershing* I with *Pershing* II, mainly because such a force would be so small as to be viewed for what it was—a token—and because a small deployment of a single system would not hedge sufficiently against vulnerability problems. Many in the Administration also feared that such proposals would have adversely affected perceptions of the U.S. nuclear commitment to Europe and would raise again the old fears that the U.S. wanted to be able to fight a nuclear war in Europe without harm to U.S. territory.

The end result was the development of a LRTNF improvement package designed to provide a strong "bridge" between NATO's existing TNF and U.S. strategic forces. While not replacing U.S. strategic forces in any way, this package was felt to be large enough to counter the developing Soviet long-range threat and to force a level of Soviet escalation which would eliminate any doubt in the minds of Soviet planners (and perhaps of Western planners as well) as to whether the U.S. would be willing to employ strategic forces in the improved mix of LSO capabilities being developed as a result of the PD-18 studies.

The Impact on Extended Deterrence

On the positive side of the ledger, NATO's decision of December 1979 could provide it with the LRTNF necessary to establish a far stronger link between its current theater forces and U.S. strategic forces, and with much improved military capabilities that would greatly reinforce extended deterrence. NATO plans to deploy a force of 464 ground-launched cruise missiles with 2,500-km range, and 108 long-range *Pershing* II medium-range ballistic missiles (MRBM), with initial procurement of the GLCM beginning in FY 1981 and its initial operating capability (IOC) in Europe being December 1983. About 160 systems would be deployed in Europe by the end of FY 1985, and all 464 GLCM would be deployed in hard shelters by the end of FY 1988. Virtually all of these missiles would be deployed on NATO airbases, with 160 in Britain, 112 in Italy, 96 in the Federal Republic, 48 in Belgium and 48 in the Netherlands. All of the 108 *Pershing* II missiles would be deployed in West Germany and would replace the present U.S. *Pershing* IA systems by the end of FY 1985.

Also as a result of the Carter Administration's reappraisal of the TNF balance, the U.S. is already improving her F-111 training and deployment, and the F-111 force will soon have operational experience in Norway, Turkey, Italy and Greece in addition to the Central Region. Other improvements are being made in U.S. C^3 systems, and U.S. forces in Europe will acquire AN/MSC-64 UHF satellite communications channels during FY 1981-4 to improve their links to the U.S. National Command Authority. A comprehensive C^3 improvement plan is now being developed to link U.S. theater and strategic forces as part of the preparation of the FY 1983 defense budget.

Britain has also committed herself to enhance these U.S.-sponsored improvements by buying *Trident* missiles as a successor system to her existing *Polaris* weapons. This will increase the weapons loading on British SLBM from 3 multiple re-entry vehicles (MRV) per missile to 8 MIRV, and warheads carried will increase the total weapons of the British force of four submarines with 16 launch tubes each from 192 MRV to 512 MIRV. This is a much greater threat to the Soviet and Warsaw Pact target base, and the improvements in accuracy and retargeting capability would allow much more flexible use of the British force. The *Trident*'s longer range will give British SSBN the same increase in patrol area and survivability that it provides for U.S. forces, and British SSBN will be able to take full advantage of the improvements in U.S. C³I systems without affecting their independent targeting in their dual role as a national deterrent.

British nuclear capabilities will be further improved by conversion of British strike aircraft forces to the *Tornado*, although there will be range penalties. The present strike aircraft, *Vulcan* and *Buccaneer*, are both comparatively obsolete in terms of reliability, delivery accuracy in long-range missions, attack mission computers and other offensive avionics, and low-level penetration capabilities. The *Tornado* should substantially increase the speed with which the RAF can change its targets, allow at least some reduction in yields or collateral damage, and increase the chances of any one bomber reaching a target by 50 percent or more.

These improvements are partially reflected in the estimates in table 18-2. They indicate that NATO as a whole should have sufficient delivery and warhead capability to maintain a broad spectrum of extended deterrence in the 1980s.

Continuing Uncertainty

There is also a negative side of the ledger. For a variety of reasons, there has been little serious European attention paid to how LRTNF can be made effective by providing either a range of new strike options for NATO or firmer links between NATO and U.S. strategic forces. The various West German, Belgian, Dutch and British debates over LRTNF modernization have so far tended to focus on its impact on arms control and detente, rather than on forging a sound mix of employment capabilities to strengthen its deterrent value. While NATO certainly discusses the need for such plans and concepts, it has made little real progress in developing them.

The GLCM has experienced serious recent development problems. There are difficulties in warhead design and reliability, and the guidance system is proving far more sensitive to mapping problems and other anomalies than had been hoped. The GLCM delivery date may have to slip 1-3 years, or it may have to be put in service with poor overall systems reliability. Furthermore, few U.S. experts are happy about the present basing, deployment, C³I and targeting concepts for the cruise missiles. There is a fairly broad consensus that hard shelters on air bases leave the systems far too vulnerable to pre-emptive attack for effective survival and flexible employment at the levels of nuclear combat necessary to link theater and strategic forces. Many planners feel that the current basing concept tends to invite a Soviet first strike and to act as an incentive to Soviet planners to develop dedicated forces to attack the GLCM bases and facilities.

Underlying this lack of attention to survivability is a continued attachment by the NATO military to SACEUR's existing target list and a history of reserving long-range systems for a general nuclear response in concert with the SIOP. Unfortunately, it has proved easier for the NATO military to demonstrate a need for more forces on the basis of a growing list of targets and SACEUR's inability to cover them all without assistance from strategic forces than to take limited nuclear option planning seriously and build the options and capabilities to support such a strategy.

Although French nuclear forces are improving in numbers and capabilities, and inevitably reinforce extended deterrence to some degree, they remain largely isolated from NATO. They also lack the kind of warning, C³I and targeting systems that would allow their effective employment in limited strikes in concert with NATO. Current and programmed French forces also lack survivability, and the French government has made it clear that it has little interest in joint planning for extended deterrence. The result is that French forces tend to retain a "trigger force" character. They are potentially large enough to force NATO to join France if she should choose to escalate unilaterally or to force NATO into the position of attempting formally to decouple itself from any Soviet attack on France. At the same time, they increase the Soviet incentive to conduct large-scale theater strikes against them by being significant and rather vulnerable.

As a result, even if NATO does implement its agreement to deploy the *Pershing* and GLCM systems, and France and Britain do upgrade their national nuclear forces, table 18–2 shows that it is still not clear that this will close the gap between NATO and Warsaw Pact LRTNF quickly enough, and no convincing basing options have yet been advanced to ensure the survivability of NATO's theater nuclear forces in conventional or nuclear war. To put this in perspective, the USSR now has 275 SS-20 launch positions, of which at least 175 are targeted on Europe. This will perhaps rise to a total of 350–500 launch positions in the future. These now have two missiles per launcher, but may well increase to 3–5. At three warheads per missile, the USSR now has 525 SS-20 warheads ready to launch against Europe at any given time, and 1,500 including reloads and missiles with dual targeting capability. These numbers could, on worst-case assumptions, rise to a staggering 3,150–7,500 SS-20 warheads targetable on Europe if all missiles, including those normally aimed at China and Japan, are counted. And this does not include the SS-22 or SS-23. In contrast NATO is discussing the introduction of new systems with only 572 warheads, and then only in the mid-1980s.

Demonstrating U.S. Intentions

The Carter Administration had obvious problems in trying to determine how it should express a declared U.S. strategy for extended deterrence. There is no doubt that it strongly repeated its commitment to extended deterrence on every suitable occasion, nor that it backed the necessary improvement of NATO nuclear forces even at the cost of raising problems with the USSR and rejecting Brezhnev's recent arms-control initiatives. Nor is there any doubt that it set out to procure many of the necessary improvements in its strategic forces, and that the Reagan Administration is as firmly committed to this policy and will accelerate these force improvements.

At the same time, the issue of how the U.S. would actually extend deterrence to Europe has tended to be left hanging in the air, and little public reference has been made to the changes that have been introduced in American LSO capabilities or to the impact of the other relevant changes taking place in the nuclear balance. Secretary Brown, for example, made reference to LSO in his FY 1980 *Annual Report* (pp. 84–5), but simply in order to discuss the problems affecting their implementation. He explicitly rejected U.S. reliance on "assured destruction" to implement extended deterrence: "Our allies, particularly in Europe, have questioned for some time whether the threat of assured destruction would be credible as a response to nuclear threats against them. . . . it is little wonder in the circumstances that for many years we have had alternatives to counter-city retaliation in our plans, and a posture substantial and responsive enough to permit the exercise of these options."

Yet Secretary Brown went on to state that the American ability to protect Europe may be weakening, and devoted most of his twelve page discussion of strategic and theater nuclear capabilities to the problems of deciding what to do about U.S. strategy, rather than to what the U.S. had decided to do (*Annual Report*, pp. 74–86). More American leadership is obviously required, and this may well be the Reagan Administration's greatest challenge in its dealings with NATO's European leaders over nuclear affairs. The United States cannot simply say to Europe that it is investigating the problems of implementing extended deterrence; she must declare the details of her capabilities, and her willingness to act. She must also state what her strategy is, and what concrete programs are in hand for accomplishing this strategy, in far stronger and more precise terms than just using ritual reassurances. She must communicate to both Europe and the USSR just how great American capabilities are becoming, and she must show convincingly why these capabilities will not be threatened by improvements in Soviet strategic forces.

Conclusions

The United States and her European Allies face major challenges in making extended deterrence effective in the 1980s. If the West is to be successful, it must complete the transition begun in the early 1970s and end its reliance on U.S. strategic superiority. It must develop an effective mix of strategic and theater nuclear capabilities that can influence Soviet perceptions—and reinforce deterrence—in the face of the major improvements taking place in Soviet strategic and theater nuclear forces.

The United States and NATO are already making major progress towards completing this transition. The United States has made many of the improvements that are required in her strategic forces, and the force improvement program announced by the Reagan Administration in October 1981 will lead her to make most of the others. She is beginning to implement properly the strategy of limited strategic strike options which former Secretary of Defense James Schlesinger enunciated in 1974, and the Carter Administration added the missing focus by improving the link between U.S. strategic forces and NATO's theater nuclear delivery systems. Although NATO's collective progress is more halting, the deployment of GLCM and *Pershing* II forces can provide it with the long-range delivery systems needed to improve the coupling of theater and strategic forces, and Britain is planning independent improvements in long-range strike capabilities that should tend to further reinforce extended deterrence.

Yet this level of progress provides no firm guarantee that the West will continue to meet all of the basic criteria necessary for the United States to extend deterrence to Europe, or that it will develop a sound mix of capabilities to reinforce its credibility and stability. While the U.S. and NATO are now in a far better position actually to execute the nuclear strikes that extended deterrence implies than they were in 1972, the Soviet threat has also increased sharply, and the West faces a broad spectrum of problems that both the U.S. and Europe are still not prepared to deal with.

Extended Deterrence in the 1980s

The extent to which the joint ability of U.S. and NATO forces is adequate to sustain extended deterrence is best illustrated by the extent to which these forces do and do not meet the criteria set forth on pp. 455–458.

Meeting the Minimum Criteria. The West should have a relatively high capability to meet the minimum criteria for extended deterrence in the 1980s, if the U.S. continues to improve her strategic forces at the pace necessary to match the changes taking place in the Soviet strategic threat. The central criterion must be that the risk of using U.S. strategic forces in addition to NATO theater forces ought, in terms of the resulting escalation, to be limited enough to avoid the U.S. running an unacceptable risk of mutual civil and economic anihilation with the Soviet Union. U.S. strategic forces and plans do now offer major alternatives to mutual assured destruction. The United States can plan to employ her strategic forces in many types of LSO where the risk of escalation to all-out war seems acceptable. If anything, the steady increase in the total strategic and long-range theater forces on each side should reduce the incentive to escalate to all-out war if limited uses are made of strategic forces, and should reduce any tendency to over-react to limited strikes without fully assessing their nature.

The second criterion is that the U.S. must have sufficient survivable forces that even large-scale exchanges in defense of NATO will not lead to an unacceptable "run down" of her strategic capabilities against the USSR. The present mix of strategic delivery systems in the U.S. triad, and their current and planned warhead loading, offer the ability to launch far larger strikes in support of NATO—without degrading U.S. strategic capabilities—than are ever likely to be required. The discussion of U.S. counterforce vulnerability has shown that this capability is unlikely to be affected by the vulnerability of U.S. ICBM even under worst-case assumptions, given the thousands of weapons on survivable U.S. SLBM, bombers and attack submarines. Further, U.S. capability to target OMT and civil facilities essential to the conduct of Soviet military operations has steadily improved since the early 1970s. By the mid-1980s the U.S. should be able to draw on her satellite sensors and other intelligence capabilities to provide a significant amount of timely data for use in limited strategic strikes in direct support of NATO tactical forces. She can already use these capabilities to attack many Warsaw Pact targets which are in the US. target base or for all-out strategic war. Such strikes in support of NATO do not by definition degrade U.S. strategic retaliatory capabilities.

Third, the U.S. must have flexibility in terms of rapid targeting and the con-trol of collateral damage. The improvements in her intelligence systems have un-questionably given the U.S. great flexibility in targeting, and she has steadily in-creased the sophistication of her target planning over the last two decades. The improvements to the *Minuteman* force will give very rapid retargeting capability, and the U.S. SIOP contains literally thousands of Warsaw Pact targets of major military importance to the USSR where collateral damage to civil population is below the threshold that would be inevitable in any large-scale nuclear exchange. While the U.S. may not yet have adequately planned to use this flexibility in a suffi-ciently wide range of LSO in her war plans, and does not now plan to provide her SLBM and bomber forces with enough rapid retargeting and C^3 capability to give them the highest possible retargeting and damage-limiting capability for use in theater combat, she does have enough current capability to sustain extended deter-rence, and her programmed C^3 improvements will substantially improve this capability by the mid-1980s.

Finally, U.S. determination to use strategic forces in the defense of Europe must be credible. Soviet knowledge of U.S. capabilities and war plans is suffi-ciently great for the USSR almost certainly to accept the fact that any large-scale theater conflict might lead the U.S. to use her strategic forces in limited nuclear strike options. If anything, the USSR may be frightened by the lack of flexibility in combined U.S. and NATO plans and capabilities, and the possibility these would lead the U.S. to escalate too quickly or to over-react. While there is a clear gap between U.S. military plans and capabilities and the lack of any well-defined NATO declaratory strategy, the USSR is likely to shape her perceptions on the basis of those military capabilities and not on the conflicting and uncertain statements of U.S. and European political leaders.

Accordingly, the problem does not seem to lie with the *credibility* of extended deterrence, which is likely to be continuously reinforced by Soviet intelligence as the U.S. improves her capabilities, plans and exercising. It seems instead to lie in the lack of any clear Soviet belief that the West can manage such conflicts with skill and restraint, and in the Soviet perception that NATO currently has a mix of forces whose vulnerability and limited command-and-control capabilities have sufficient first-strike characteristics to create a strong Soviet incentive to launch large-scale disabling strikes in an initial attack, or to pre-empt at the first rough indicators that NATO may be bringing its forces to readiness.

Meeting Other Criteria. U.S. and NATO forces seem equally likely to meet many of the non-essential, but desirable, criteria for extended deterrence in the 1980s, although both the U.S. and NATO need to improve their capabilities. This is particularly true of NATO theater forces, although a number of relatively low-cost improvements in the U.S. forces could have major benefits. For example, there is no need for the U.S. to be able to launch counterforce strikes against Soviet strategic nuclear forces. However, while she will not be able to launch counterforce strikes in the sense of being able to degrade Soviet capabilities to strike at an unacceptably large number of U.S. urban industrial complexes and OMT targets, she will, nevertheless, be able to strike selectively at those Soviet strategic forces which are employed in theater conflicts, and to strike at Soviet strategic forces as an option in conducting LSO strikes.

Although it is semantically something of a contradiction in terms, the U.S. does not need a "war-fighting" capability. Yet, while there is no expectation that U.S. strategic forces can develop a "war-fighting" capability that can "win" an all-out conflict with the USSR while acceptably limiting damage to the U.S., they can certainly "fight" wars at many different levels of escalation. Moreover, the U.S. can certainly extend deterrence by threatening to inflict high levels of damage, by seeking to terminate conflicts on terms favorable to NATO, and by demonstrating her willingness to increase the level of damage she inflicts until the Warsaw Pact accepts NATO's terms. There is little question that the U.S. will have this capability during the 1980s. There are some major rigidities inherent in her present forces and force improvement plans, but these are not such as to leave large gaps between the levels of escalation (or intensity within those levels) that the USSR seems likely to be able to exploit. Most of these rigidities lie in U.S. and NATO C³ systems, and not in the force size or force structure now planned for the mid-1980s. They can, therefore, be largely eliminated at comparatively low cost.

Although there is no requirement for the U.S. to have highly flexible and survivable C³I, targeting, damage assessment and re-targeting capabilities (for the

U.S. can rely on pre-planned strikes, given her vast peacetime targeting capability and the dependence of the USSR on fixed facilities and the inherent value of the entire Warsaw Pact fixed target base), she does in fact possess such capabilities in some degree. The cost of substantially upgrading U.S., NATO and European national capabilities is in any case low enough to be feasible in the 1980s, and there are strong indications that such capabilities may be funded by the Reagan Administration. They could perhaps be on line by the mid-1980s.

It can also be argued that the U.S. and NATO do not need a clear strategy for the use of U.S. strategic systems in extending deterrence to Europe. While the U.S. strategy may not be clear in the sense of reflecting a single approach to the problem—it has been declared in broad terms, and this declaration is supported by strike options and military capabilities which are known to the USSR. Nevertheless, the lack of any cohesive NATO doctrine, the confusing and shallow nature of the current debate over extended deterrence, and the problems in NATO theater nuclear planning and force structures create difficulties for the convincing application of the doctrine of extended deterrence. While the links between U.S. strategic forces and the defense of NATO are not now "guaranteed"— indeed cannot be guaranteed—the U.S. has clearly done more than utter empty reassurances to her European Allies. She has made those changes in her doctrine, plans and forces which are essential if she is to maintain extended deterrence in spite of the changes now taking place in the balance of strategic and theater nuclear forces, and she continues actively to pursue the development of more effective links between strategic and theater forces.

Further Desirable Steps

There are six relatively low-cost steps which the U.S. and Europe could take which would greatly strengthen extended deterrence in the 1980s.

Rejecting Reliance on Strategic Superiority. U.S. and European political and military leaders must fully accept the fact that extended deterrence can never again be tied to U.S. strategic superiority. There is no possibility that the U.S. can regain enough "superiority" in fighting a general strategic war to allow any lowering of the threshold of nuclear deterrence. The steady increase in the number of strategic warheads available to both sides will make it less and less likely that the threat to escalate to general war can serve to protect interests. The USSR, for example, will probably at least double her deployed strategic warheads over the next decade even if she fully complies with SALT II. The U.S. will probably increase her own warhead numbers enough to retain her lead in total numbers of deliverable weapons, but this will not make the threat of all-out war more credible.

The U.S. must continue to seek strategic parity with the USSR to preserve an ultimate deterrent to ultimate war, and to influence world perceptions of U.S. military and political power. However, this search for parity cannot by itself provide the bridge the West needs between theater and strategic forces. This can only be accomplished by a dedicated American effort to develop all the force capabilities necessary to employ strategic forces effectively in a suitable range of limited nuclear options and by ensuring that the U.S. force improvement plans previously described are implemented. The new Administration seems firmly committed to this course of action.

Similarly, the NATO military authorities (SACEUR and SHAPE in particular) must reject the thesis that NATO nuclear war plans can consist primarily of a series of limited short-range theater options linked to large-scale strike options in the SIOP. The Joint Strategic Target Planning Staff (JSTPS) and SHAPE must jointly develop war plans which fully implement the rethinking begun in NSDM-242, PRM-10, PD-18 and PD-59 and symbolized by U.S. support of the GLCM/*Pershing* II force. NATO plans are now far too rigid, involve initial thresholds of nuclear conflict which are far too high, and owe too much to the threat to escalate to all-out war. It is unclear whether the Reagan Administration has yet recognized the extent of this problem.

At the same time, NATO and European military planners must accept that they will not get theater nuclear forces large enough to "match" Soviet long-range strike capabilities or to replace U.S. strategic superiority. The issue for NATO military planning is not to justify more and more long-range theater systems as a substitute for strategic parity, but rather to make the available and planned long-range theater systems effective, and to establish a convincing bridge between NATO's shorter-range systems and U.S. strategic forces. This may or may not require somewhat more theater nuclear forces than are currently planned in U.S. and British force improvements, but it definitely does not mean trying to establish a force of several thousand new long-range NATO systems simply because the Warsaw Pact has them.

In short, both U.S. and European leaders must fully accept that what is needed is a mix of strategic and theater war-fighting capabilities for limited nuclear conflict which will deter the USSR at all levels of theater conflict and which will provide as seamless a continuum of nuclear options as possible so as to limit any conflict that does occur as much as possible. NATO must also seek to deprive the USSR of any incentive to sustain conflict at a given intensity or to escalate it to some higher level of violence.

Joint Strategic and Theater Nuclear Planning. The steady increase in the complexity of strategic forces and in the ways in which they can be employed requires that both Europeans and Americans carry out joint and continuous nuclear planning and analysis that must be far more comprehensive than in the past. European defense authorities will have to become involved in the details of strategic forces and war-planning in the 1980s if Europe is to understand American capabilities and limitations well enough to place the proper degree of trust in the American ability to extend deterrence and pursue the required improvement in European-based nuclear forces.

Above all, European officials and military officers and the NATO Military Commands must be brought fully into the process of U.S. LSO planning. There is no longer a place for "tokenism" or largely symbolic NATO nuclear planning activities such as the NPG. The U.S. must allow Europe to participate fully, and Europe must take that participation seriously. The current (largely *pro forma*) NATO institutions for nuclear planning must be made effective. Nor will it be enough just to develop the right plans at SHAPE. Nuclear war plans for the 1980s must be fully understood by national defense ministries and commands. Again, the intentions of the Reagan Administration remain unclear in this area.

Improving Command and Control. NATO should provide the range of improvements in C^3 systems and in intelligence, targeting and damage assessment capabilities that would convince the USSR that NATO could, if necessary, employ a mix of theater and strategic forces proportionate to the theater attacks which the West wants to deter. There are obviously many different levels at which such capabilities are needed if the U.S. is to extend deterrence to NATO Europe. At present, European national authorities and NATO headquarters are so poorly provided with secure and durable communications and are so vulnerable that they are not adequate for any substantial theater nuclear conflict. Only U.S. theater nuclear forces are now programmed to acquire some of the command-and-control links to U.S. strategic forces that would improve their ability to operate in common.

These improvements do not seem likely to require massive increases in the funding of either European national command-and-control capabilities, or in the NATO infrastructure program. They do require, however, that existing levels of investment in NATO C^3I be adjusted and improved to support both conventional forces and NATO theater and U.S. strategic forces without reliance on large-scale or pre-planned attacks. The Reagan Administration is seeking some of these improvements, but there is as yet no adequate European plan for such improvements.

Improving U.S. Support Capabilities. The U.S. should fund all the improvements in her military satellites necessary to allow them to be used in conducting effective LSO and long-range theater strikes, and she should share more of her national intelligence. Such a sharing of upgraded U.S. strategic C^3 systems may be the only method by which NATO can collectively conduct LSO planning and the management of joint strategic/theater nuclear strikes. Sharing U.S. intelligence systems also seems increasingly more feasible as much of the more sensitive classified data relating to U.S. reconnaissance satellites and SIGINT sensors have become known to the USSR. There would also be substantial benefits for NATO's conduct of conventional operations.

It would be equally desirable to upgrade the retargeting capability of the U.S. strategic forces, and to improve American ability to use all of the triad of strategic forces in limited strategic strikes. The U.S. may, for example, be underfunding both the relevant C^3 and retargeting capabilities of *Minuteman* and MX, and the link between her strategic command posts and NATO. She may also have failed to provide enough flexibility for employing her B-52G and ALCM in limited strikes, either in concert with the GLCM to be deployed in Europe or to compensate for Soviet theater strikes against them.

At the same time, it would be desirable for the U.S. to accelerate efforts to give the *Trident* II program a capability to launch accurate strikes in support of NATO, tailored to specific theater requirements. Similar capabilities might be given to U.S. SLCM. This would fully decouple U.S. capabilities for extending deterrence from the ICBM vulnerability issue and would reduce any need to use U.S. strategic systems based on U.S. soil.

While these improvements may not be essential for deterrence to be extended to Europe, they would greatly increase U.S. capability to support NATO, greatly complicate Soviet planning and ensure that U.S. LNO capability was not affected by changes in the vulnerability of any given part of the triad.

Improving Survivability. NATO also needs to make further reductions in the vulnerability of its theater nuclear strike forces. It is true that reducing the number of dedicated nuclear strike aircraft will reduce the Soviet incentive to launch nuclear strikes at NATO air bases, and that GLCM and *Pershing* II should be substantially less vulnerable once dispersed. However, neither the *Pershing* II nor GLCM basing concepts reduce the incentive for the USSR to strike at their peacetime bases if she can do so before NATO's long-range systems are dispersed as the result of an alert.

The GLCM basing concept seems not entirely satisfactory. Current NATO plans envisage the basing of the 464 GLCM in hard shelters on a limited number of U.S. airfields in Europe with the missiles truck-mounted and dispersable, given warning. However, the associated C³I links seem likely to be inadequate and such peacetime basing of the GLCM tends to reinforce the Soviet perception that NATO still focuses on a general release of long-range weapons and a first-strike posture, giving the USSR a continued incentive to escalate.

It is true that keeping the GLCM and *Pershing* II systems dispersed in peacetime and moving them often enough to disrupt Soviet targeting could double the operating costs of the force and the manpower required. This, however, may be a comparatively small price to pay for assured survival of the force, and it would imply that NATO could use its theater nuclear forces with restraint. Certainly, the Permissive Action Links (PAL) and C³I technology is available to allow such basing with safety. Such improvements in basing might also eliminate any subsequent need to increase system numbers to compensate for future increases in Soviet warheads and targeting capabilities, and that would improve the prospects of both European acceptance and TNF arms control.

Influencing Soviet Perceptions. Finally, both U.S. and European policymakers need to pay more attention to the fact that they should be attempting to deter the USSR by influencing Soviet perceptions, rather than winning arguments with each other. Much of the present debate over extended deterrence and theater nuclear force modernization never mentions whether or not Soviet planners are likely to find the resulting capability convincing enough to be deterred by it. The West must begin to regard the USSR as a highly sophisticated opponent. The Soviet Union has never enjoyed the luxury of being able to keep her planning of strategic and theater nuclear forces separate, and she has long focused on what kinds of long-range theater forces and strikes are practical and credible. For all her declaratory rhetoric, she has always tended to look at capabilities rather than at the symbols of military strength, and she has enjoyed distressingly good and timely access to classified data on United States and NATO capabilities and war plans.

It follows that extended deterrence will be shaped in large part by capabilities and not simply by rhetoric. The USSR will also tend to judge the credibility of the United States to extend deterrence by highly demanding standards and to be more fully aware perhaps than most European NATO governments of any weaknesses or vulnerabilities that she can exploit. At the same time, the USSR is far less likely to be concerned with American will to use strategic forces or to risk escalation to general war if she sees tangible evidence that the U.S. and NATO can jointly use strategic and theater forces in a wide range of options and at several different levels of escalation.

In this regard, it is interesting to note that the USSR probably reacted more strongly to Schlesinger's initial announcement of an LSO strategy in 1974, to U.S. plans to modernize NATO long-range theater nuclear systems, and to the implications of PD-59 than to any other improvements in U.S. strategic and NATO theater forces over the last two decades. It is obvious that the USSR takes such developments with great seriousness when it looks as if the West will develop real capabilities.

If the U.S. and Europe can take these six steps, this should provide a high assurance that the West can deal with any Soviet force improvements that seem possible through the mid-1980s. It would also demonstrate that the West has the unity to respond to Soviet actions and provide the basis for developing the coherent plans and doctrine to cope with unanticipated threats or new Soviet challenges in the 1980s. These changes in official plans and doctrine need to be supported by improvements in the efforts of the strategic studies community to analyze extended deterrence, and by changes in the character of the present debate over strategic and theater nuclear forces.

In particular, the West needs to correct a tendency to polarize the debate about nuclear force improvements. On one side is the "force size" or pro-nuclear camp. This camp structures many of its arguments for nuclear force modernization in such a way as to shift NATO from conventional options to greater reliance on nuclear forces and seeks to match every major aspect of Warsaw Pact nuclear forces, regardless of the need to do so. On the other side is the "conventional" camp, which fears that any major improvement in theater nuclear forces will come at the expense of improvements in conventional forces. It tends to oppose TNF improvements, not out of a conviction they are not necessary but rather from the unstated perspective that they are less necessary than conventional improvements. These two camps do little more than obscure the issue of what needs to be done, while pushing discussion of extended deterrence towards impractical extremes—over-reliance on conventional and strategic forces or seeking unachievable and unnecessary increases in theater nuclear forces.

American capabilities to extend nuclear deterrence are only one essential link in the whole process of deterrence. They can certainly reinforce conventional capabilities at high levels of conflict, but it does not look likely that NATO conventional forces will ever reach the levels where feasible trade-offs can be made between conventional forces and nuclear forces. It would, of course, be cheaper to rely to a greater extent on nuclear systems, but that is no longer an option open to NATO.

A balanced combination of NATO theater and U.S. strategic capabilities can make both the U.S. and Europe safer. The Warsaw Pact could come to see that any attack on Europe could result in unacceptable loss, and an appropriate mix of theater capabilities would greatly increase the problems that the USSR would face in contemplating any attack on U.S. strategic forces. There is no point, however, in increasing either U.S. or NATO forces beyond what is planned. Such increases would not significantly enhance NATO capabilities, and the USSR is more likely to be influenced by capability than by size.

Finally, although political relations between the U.S. and Europe are not the subject of this chapter, it is obvious that the NATO Allies need to do a far better job of communicating with each other and with their respective citizens. The recent split between the U.S. and Europe over the "twin track" approach to pursuing arms control and the LRTNF improvement program could grow far more serious in the future. If the West is to develop a coherent approach to strengthening extended deterrence, that approach must be fully understood on both sides of the Atlantic and be understood by the public as well as the politicians. The current almost totally unrealistic debates about large-scale nuclear wars being fought over the heads of Europe or on European soil while excluding the U.S., grow out of a degree of ignorance that stems largely from a past failure even to try to communicate the reality of extended deterrence. If there is to be a "strategic consensus" within NATO, this situation must change in the future. Europe must pay as much attention to U.S. strategic developments as to those in theater forces. Similarly, the U.S. must recognize the linkage, and that it cannot unilaterally plan U.S. strategic forces which are Europe's ultimate defense.

Discussion Questions

1. Which characteristics of nuclear weapons are most significant militarily? Politically?

2. What is the current nuclear balance between the U.S. and the Soviet Union?

3. What are the advantages and disadvantages of each leg of the triad?

4. How important is targeting policy? What are its implications? How does it fit with U.S. force structure?

19
Planning Conventional Forces, 1950–1980

William W. Kaufmann

orce planning is a military art more practiced than studied in the United
States. Techniques for assessing the costs and effectiveness of competing
nuclear and nonnuclear forces have been developed over a number of years,
largely by or at the instigation of the defense establishment, but their respective
merits are rarely evaluated. The ideas that inspire them are hardly ever recorded,
much less recalled. Yet as John Maynard Keynes once wrote about economic planning, "Practical men, who believe themselves to be quite exempt from any intellectual influences, are usually the slaves of some defunct economist. . . . It is
ideas, not vested interests, which are dangerous for good or evil."

Lord Keynes's remark seems to hold true for defunct force planners as well.
The ideas behind current defense programs therefore deserve to be understood,
and their assumptions and logic need to be reviewed. Some grasp must be obtained
of what does and does not work, and under what conditions. The planner should
know what has proved more or less operational and feasible. In short, it would do
no harm if a little recollection and assessment preceded further action.

Reflection is especially in order before further programs are launched to
strengthen U.S. conventional forces. The United States ended World War II with
about ninety-five Army and Marine Corps divisions, 1,167 warships, and nearly
70,000 combat aircraft. It probably had more men and women under arms than
the Soviet Union. Approximately 36 percent of its gross national product went to
defense in 1944, the peak year of its war effort. Twice since then it has set out, in
conjunction with its allies, to create a more modest but still credible nonnuclear
deterrent to conventional attack, with the Soviet Union as its main putative opponent. Twice that effort has fallen short of its goals in important respects. Now that
a third attempt is getting under way, it may not be amiss to recall briefly the first
two efforts and ask why the United States has encountered such difficulties in
reaching what, in relation to its World War II posture, have not been especially
demanding objectives.

Kaufmann, William W., *Planning Conventional Forces: 1950–1980*, (Washington: D.C.: The Brookings Institution, 1982), pp. 1–26. Copyright © The Brookings Institution, 1982. Reprinted with permission.

NSC-68

The first effort began in 1950 as an outgrowth of the Korean War and a National Security Council memorandum known as NSC-68.[1] Before NSC-68, Department of Defense planning had concentrated on the strategy and forces needed for a general nuclear war. This was not because the planners ruled out the possibility of conventional probes and attacks. Rather, budgetary constraints before the Korean War were so severe that they saw no choice but to focus resources primarily on the development of the Strategic Air Command. NSC-68, however, assumed that "within four years the Soviet Union would have enough atomic bombs and a sufficient capability of delivering them to offset substantially the deterrent capability of American nuclear weapons." The memorandum went on to emphasize "the inadequacy of the Western capability to meet limited military challenges due to lack of conventional forces, shortcomings in the Western alliance system, and the military and economic weaknesses of western Europe."[2]

NSC-68 itself did not recommend any particular concept or size for U.S. conventional forces. Instead it argued the case for an across-the-board buildup of capabilities to be completed by 1954, when it was estimated that a nuclear stalemate between the United States and the Soviet Union would be reached. The Joint Chiefs of Staff were left with the responsibility to give form and substance to the buildup. They did so by dividing the world into regions and estimating U.S. military requirements by geographic area. When their estimates were added up, they proved too large for any conceivable budget. Accordingly, they were scaled down to about twenty-seven Army and Marine Corps divisions, 408 warships, and a tactical air force of about forty-one Air Force and Marine Corps fighter attack wings.[3] Some of the ground and tactical air forces were to be stationed in Europe. But as General Omar N. Bradley, then chairman of the Joint Chiefs of Staff, later testified before the Senate Appropriations Committee, "It is now evident that we must have an even greater flexibility of military power in the United States itself not only for our own protection, but also to give us a ready, highly mobile standing force which we can bring to bear at any threatened point in the minimum time."[4]

Thus emerged the precursor of what came to be known as the concept of flexible response. Its life was exciting but brief. By 1960, the conventional forces, which had been increased rapidly during the Korean war, were back close to where they had been during the austere years before the war. In all, they consisted of seventeen Army and Marine Corps divisions, 376 warships, and twenty-four Air Force and Marine Corps fighter-attack wings. The fiscal policies of the Eisenhower administration and the mystique of nuclear weapons had virtually eradicated the concept of flexible response—at least temporarily.

Despite repeated nonnuclear clashes in various parts of the globe, the prevailing view in Europe and America was that the wars of the future (and their deterrence) would or should be the province of nuclear weaponry. This was the era of the "New Look," of a U.S. defense establishment symbolized by the Strategic Air

Command and the rhetoric of massive and, later, selective nuclear retaliation, and of efforts by the Army and Navy—fearful of budgetary extinction—to prove that they too could survive and fight to some purpose in a nuclear conflict.

Conventional forces retained few constituents in these circumstances. Of the Army's fourteen remaining divisions, only eleven retained much combat effectiveness. Of these, five were deployed in Europe and two in South Korea. The strategic reserve (not to be confused with reserve forces) consisted of one division in Hawaii and three in the continental United States. General Maxwell D. Taylor, while Army chief of staff, continued his struggle to salvage something from the ruins, but his success, at best, was modest. As he later testified, "I based the limited war requirement of the Army on being able to close a corps of three divisions in an overseas theater in 2 months, and to have the necessary logistic backup to fight these divisions until a supply pipeline was established. That was taken merely as a commonsense objective, something more than we could do, but a goal far enough in advance to give us something to strive for regardless of whether it was theoretically adequate or not."[5]

Multiple Options

The second attempt to develop a coherent conventional strategy began in 1961 with the inauguration of John F. Kennedy as president and the confirmation of Robert S. McNamara as secretary of defense. Both men and their closest advisers had come to maturity during the cold war. The doctrine, if not the practice, of containment was their main foreign-policy heritage, and both remained wedded to it for at least a few more years. Their view of the Soviet Union as an implacably expansionist power allied with Communist China was fortified by the crisis over Berlin, by Nikita Khrushchev's endorsement of wars of national liberation, and by the growing turmoil in Southeast Asia, which was seen as inspired by the Sino-Soviet conspiracy. Their approach to defense policy was dominated by skepticism about nuclear capabilities as the prime instrument of military containment. It was a skepticism forged by the admissions of the Eisenhower administration that a nuclear stalemate already existed, by their own sense that nuclear weapons did not deter very much, and by their conviction that threats of nuclear retaliation were not a credible way to deal with the dangers that seemed to lie ahead. Whatever the relevance of massive retaliation and its codicils for the turbulence of the 1950s, the problems of the 1960s, as they saw them, would require new ideas and a revived emphasis on U.S. and allied conventional forces.

Exactly how to reconcile containment, conventional forces, and acceptable defense budgets, however, was not immediately apparent. The military establishment, for once, could hardly complain of lacking clear-cut objectives. The problem was that it had accumulated so many of them. Apart from the primary responsibility to defend the United States itself, there were nine formal treaty commitments to more than forty allies (twenty of them in the western hemisphere), and informal but no less weighty obligations to several others. While the Soviet Union and Communist China were seen as the main prospective threats, North Korea, North Vietnam, and Cuba were also considered likely sources of future challenges. Furthermore, roughly half the states to which commitments had been given were on or near the borders of the Soviet Union and China. Most of them had only recently recovered from the effects of World War II. All of them were skeptical about the feasibility of a conventional defense against what were then (as now) advertised to be the Red Hordes, presumably being held in check only by the increasingly incredible threat that any aggression would be met by a prompt U.S. retaliation with nuclear weapons. Even with significant contributions from these allies, the burden on the United States looked as though it would be impossibly large. Or so it appeared at first glance, even without any firm numerical estimates of the size and composition of the U.S. forces that would have to be provided.

A second glance did not materially improve the prospects. In 1962, at Secretary McNamara's request, the military planners undertook a study of the need for conventional ground and tactical air forces. Although the study itself is not in the public domain, enough has been said about it so that its results can be reproduced with standard planning techniques. As in 1950, the planners studied all the places related to the United States by a commitment of one sort or another that could be threatened more or less plausibly by hostile conventional forces. They determined that about sixteen separate theaters of conflict could develop, ranging around the periphery of the Soviet Union and China from Norway to Japan.

To determine the need for U.S. forces, the planners first calculated what might be expected from relevant allies in the way of nonnuclear capabilities. They then assumed that the United States would contribute whatever additional forces would be required to check the hypothetical enemy attack. They concluded that American ground and tactical air forces would have to be provided in eleven of the theaters. In addition, Alaska and Panama would require their traditional garrisons. The original sixteen theaters, the eleven in which U.S. contributions would be made, the size of the estimated contributions, and the other demands that would be made on U.S. forces are listed in table 19–1.

According to this estimate (which probably does not correspond precisely with the results of the 1962 study), the total of U.S. requirements was substantial: the eleven separate theaters, the garrisons, and a strategic reserve were expected to take fifty-five divisions and eighty-two fighter-attack wings. Of this total, fifty-two of the divisions would be Army and seventy-nine of the tactical wings Air Force; the remaining three divisions and air wings would come from the Marine Corps, as required by a statute passed in 1952. For the first time since taking office, Secretary McNamara had some idea of how much conventional capability was thought to be enough. But enough proved to be far more than he could expect the president and Congress to provide.

Table 19–1
Reconstruction of the 1962 General-Purpose Forces Study

Theater	Number of U.S. Divisions	Number of U.S. Fighter-Attack Wings
North Atlantic Treaty Organization region		
Norway	1	1
Germany	15	23
Greece, Turkey	1	1
Central Treaty Organization region		
Iran	4	6
Pakistan	0	0
Southeast Asia Treaty Organization region		
Thailand, Laos	9	14
South Vietnam	8	12
Australia-New Zealand-United States Treaty Organization region		
Australia	0	0
New Zealand	0	0
Other theaters		
Israel	3	4
India	0	0
Philippines	0	0
Republic of China	0	0
Republic of Korea	8	12
Japan	0	0
Cuba	3⅓	4
Alaska	⅓	1
Panama	⅓	1
Continental United States (strategic reserve)	2	3
Total	55	82

Source: Author's estimates.

There were, in any event, good grounds for acquiring fewer divisions and tactical air wings than had been estimated by the study. Among the factors that had influenced its results, none was more important than the assumption that all eleven theaters would come under attack more or less simultaneously. However, it was considered highly unlikely that such a conflagration could occur short of a massive and long-term mobilization by the Soviet bloc. In that event, the United States and its allies would have the warning in which either to take comparable countermeasures or to prepare a nuclear response. Short of such preparations, the Soviet Union seemed capable of launching no more than one major attack, with the northern, central, and southern parts of Western Europe as both the most logical targets and the theaters in which Russia and its Warsaw Pact allies could bring the largest force to bear. Similarly, China might be able to undertake a fairly large-scale campaign in Korea or Southeast Asia, but not both. It was also thought that military action would be required at the same time but on a much smaller scale against one of the lesser troublemakers such as Cuba. In short, three rather than eleven simultaneous contingencies seemed not only a more manageable but also a more plausible basis on which to plan the conventional forces.

With these more modest assumptions, the requirements developed by the 1962 general-purpose forces study no longer looked overwhelming. A recapitulation of the requirements, as shown in table 19–2, suggests that a total of twenty-eight and one-third divisions and forty-one fighter-attack wings would be needed by the United States, in conjunction with its allies, to deal with what were considered to be the three most serious and plausible contingencies. Such a total was by no means out of reach provided that parts of the National Guard and Reserve forces could be made to count as the equivalent of active-duty forces.

A more challenging problem was how to cope with a real world in which emergencies other than those planned for arose. It was all well and good to develop a conventional posture based on three more-or-less simultaneous contingencies in Western Europe, Korea, and Cuba. But what if trouble broke out instead in the Middle East, Southwest Asia, and North Africa? Where would the forces come from for these theaters? Would additional forces have to be created, or would it be possible to draw on the forces generated by the planning contingencies?

The answer to these questions was based on several considerations. It was becoming increasingly evident that stationing U.S. forces in threatened areas such as Western Europe and Korea not only made them less available for service elsewhere, but it also imposed heavy economic and political costs on the United States. The more units that could be brought back to the continental United States, the greater their potential availability for worldwide use and the lower the total cost. Instead of having conventional forces dedicated to every theater of any consequence, as had in effect been postulated by the 1962 study, with staggering implications for force size and cost, a strategic reserve could be established at home. From that

Table 19–2
Forces Required by the "Flexible-Response" Concept

Theater of Possible Conflict	Number of U.S. Divisions	Number of U.S. Fighter-Attack Wings
Norway	1	1
Germany	15	23
Greece, Turkey	1	1
Korea, South Vietnam	8	12
Cuba	3⅓	4
Total	28⅔	41[b]

Source: Author's estimates.

[a]The total consists of sixteen and one-third active Army divisions, three active Marine Corps divisions, eight reserve Army divisions, and one reserve Marine Corps division.

[b]The total consists of twenty-six active Air Force wings, three active Marine Corps wings, eleven reserve Air Force wings, and one reserve Marine Corps wing.

favorable geographic position, specially tailored expeditionary forces could be dispatched quickly to trouble spots wherever they might be, if they could be given the necessary long-range mobility. Fortunately, the advent of intercontinental, high-speed, large-payload, wide-bodied jet aircraft seemed to solve the problem. Combined with a minimum of overseas deployments, some pre-positioning of materiel in sensitive theaters such as Western Europe, and fast deployment logistic ships that would serve as floating and mobile depots for heavy equipment and supplies, a large fleet of cargo jets would ensure that intercontinental mobility could substitute for having forces frozen into all the theaters of primary interest to the United States.

Thus were articulated the main elements of what has come to be known somewhat inaccurately as the "two-and-a-half-war" concept. The unclassified references to it have been sketchy,[6] but the planners of the time would probably not have been astonished to receive policy guidance such as this about the design of the conventional forces:

1. Assume that no more than two major nonnuclear contingencies and one lesser contingency will arise simultaneously.
2. Use the most demanding contingencies—in Europe, Korea, and Cuba—as the basis for developing the U.S. conventional force posture, but do not plan on committing the resulting forces only to those specific theaters.
3. In planning the U.S. posture, take allied contributions as given, though always encouraging the allies to do more, and assume that U.S. forces will make up any deficit between the attacker and the defender.
4. For political as well as military reasons, plan where appropriate on the basis of a forward defense. Trading space for time is inefficient because the war would be lengthened and larger forces would be required to recover any territory lost during the early stages of a conflict.
5. Design the forces to cope with the initial and largely defensive stages of the war (from three to six months, depending on the theater), the assumption being that mobilization will provide the larger forces needed for later and more decisive operations.
6. Because of the uncertainty about the duration of potential conflicts, plan war reserve stocks on the principle of D-to-P (D-day to Production-day). That is, stockpile enough combat consumables (excluding ships and aircraft) to maintain intense operations until production rates are adequate to supply combat needs—a period of about six months.
7. On the assumption that the 1962 study was correct in its estimate of the threats and allied contributions, and hence that total U.S. ground and tactical air requirements will amount to twenty-eight and one-third divisions and forty-one fighter-attack wings, depend on the National Guard and Reserve forces for nine of the divisions (eight Army and one Marine corps) and twelve of the fighter-attack wings (eleven Air Force and one Marine Corps).

8. In organizing this high-priority reserve force, require designated divisions and wings to be ready for overseas deployment from two to four weeks after a presidential call-up.
9. Design the forces so that they will be versatile enough in equipment, training, and supplies to operate in more than one theater and against more than one type of opponent. At the same time, keep them ready for rapid deployment.
10. Although the forces can be stretched to failure if more than three contingencies occur simultaneously or if attacks on them are heavier than anticipated, the lower-priority reserves constitute a hedge against these unlikely events. To preserve that hedge, plan on calling up the reserves in the event of an emergency.

To make the flexible-response concept work with a ground and tactical air force structure of this size, the forces themselves would have to become highly versatile and they would also have to be deployed and supported so as to maximize their worldwide flexibility. Accordingly, planning guidance on deployment and strategic mobility might have read something like this:

1. Because of the sizable Warsaw Pact forces deployed in East Germany, Poland, and Czechoslovakia (including twenty-two Soviet divisions), the relative weakness of the non-U.S. forces of the North Atlantic Treaty Organization (NATO) in the central portion of Western Europe, and the possibility of surprise attacks by Warsaw Pact forces, for the time being leave the five U.S. divisions in Germany and the seven U.S. fighter-attack wings in the region. Continue to pledge three other divisions to NATO.
2. In Korea, because of the heavy fortifications along the demilitarized zone and the strength of South Korean ground forces, withdraw the remaining two U.S. divisions deployed there and use them to strengthen the strategic reserve in the continental United States. Leave several squadrons of fighter-attack aircraft in South Korea as symbols of the continuing U.S. commitment. Continue to maintain one Marine Amphibious Force (a division and its air wing) on Okinawa, the 25th Infantry Division in Hawaii, and a brigade each in Alaska and Panama.
3. Expand the uncommitted strategic reserve in the continental United States to approximately nine active-duty and nine high-priority reserve divisions. Also provide roughly fourteen active-duty and twelve high-priority reserve fighter-attack wings for the strategic reserve. Since fast amphibious lift will be provided for two Marine Corps divisions (of which one will be in Okinawa), plan on a rapid deployment capability for the three heavy divisions in the continental United States that are pledged to NATO and for seventeen of the eighteen divisions in the strategic reserve (the eighteenth being a Marine Corps division with its amphibious lift).

4. In designing this rapid deployment capability, assume that the United States and its allies will obtain thirty days' warning of enemy buildups, but owing to ambiguities in the signals and political hesitations about responding, will have only twenty-three days for their own mobilization and deployment.

5. Pre-position three sets of division equipment in Germany to which the NATO-committed divisions can be flown by the Civil Reserve Air Fleet. Otherwise, plan on a mix of fast deployment logistic ships stationed in key waters overseas and in home ports with divisional equipment and supplies on board, and wide-bodied aircraft capable of lifting both units and their equipment to threatened overseas theaters.

A number of studies were subsequently commissioned to determine specifically what should be the composition of the airlift and sealift forces. It was eventually concluded that the optimum mix would consist of thirty-one fast deployment logistic ships and a heavy airlift force comprising 280 C-141s (already in procurement) and 129 C-5As (wide-bodied aircraft capable of transporting all Army tanks and tracked vehicles). These mobility forces, as shown in table 19-3, could be expected to give the United States the capability in twenty-three days to deliver nearly 300,000 tons (or eight divisions of varying size and weight) by airlift over a distance of 4,000 nautical miles, and to station another 300,000 tons (or about nine divisions) anywhere in the world depending on how the fast logistic ships were deployed. Indeed, even the logistic ships held in U.S. home ports could, in twenty-three days, reach theaters as many as 11,000 nautical miles distant. This should have been enough capacity to deploy forces to Europe, the Far East, and a third destination, in accordance with the flexible-response concept and the assumptions that went with it. Whether the ground forces would be ready enough to exploit the lift and the pre-positioned materiel was and remains uncertain.

Table 19-3
Rapid Deployment Capabilities Programmed for the "Flexible-Response" Concept

Deployment Status or Mode	Number of Divisons	Tonnage	Destination
Already deployed	5		Europe
Pre-positioning and Civil Reserve Air Fleet	3		Europe
Airlift (C-5As and C-141s)	8	300,000	4,000 nautical miles
Sealift	9	300,000	Worldwide (or 11,000 nautical miles)

Source: Author's estimates.

None of these studies dealt in detail with how the Navy was to be related to the concept. The reason for the omission is quite simple. For all practical purposes, the Navy managed to escape from the discipline of having to shape its forces to the planning contingencies postulated by the new concept. It did so by arguing that to whatever degree land warfare might be limited by the geography and other constraints of particular theaters, naval warfare would have to be treated as a seamless and worldwide phenomenon. Naval planners also asserted that, following the traditions of earlier centuries and such episodes as the War of Jenkins's Ear, a war at sea might develop independently of and even without any prior clashes on land, and that such a war should be treated as a separate and additional contingency. It followed that naval forces should be planned and programmed on a worldwide basis without regard to the constraints of the concept.

Despite these arguments, the navy was bound to become smaller than it had been in the early 1960s. It should be stressed in this connection that what constitutes the size of a navy is to an important degree a matter of definition. It depends on what is to be counted. If the count includes only ocean-going surface warships, carriers, and submarines, for example, the fleet will obviously be smaller than if it includes everything that floats, active and reserve, in operation and in mothballs. If the U.S. Navy is counted by one definition, and the Soviet Navy by another (not an uncommon practice), the differences between the two fleets can be startling.

According to one of the standard counting definitions, the U.S. Navy consisted of 971 active and reserve ships as late as 1964. However, many vessels dated back to World War II. With the time coming to retire them, it was certain that they would not be replaced on a one-for-one basis, especially since the replacements would be larger, more capable, and a lot more costly (even after adjusting their nominal costs for inflation). The issue confronting the planners thus was not whether the Navy would shrink, but by how much. That was well understood, despite subsequent nostalgia for a thousand-ship fleet.

It was equally well understood, at least within the Navy, that fleets do not simply cruise about for the purpose of showing the flag and remaining a peacetime presence. Like other military forces, navies can perform one or more wartime missions in specific parts of the globe against particular enemies. But they cannot perform all such missions everywhere at once. Among the most critical of naval missions are the following:

1. Attacks on enemy naval forces in their ports, one of the primary justifications for attack carrier battle groups.
2. The equivalent of long-range blockades of enemy ports and naval forces made possible by geographical features favoring the United States and by barriers made up of mines, submarines, surface warships, and aircraft deployed so as to intercept enemy submarines, surface ships, and aircraft.

3. Close-in protection of U.S. and allied convoys by escort warships, aircraft, helicopters, and (possibly) submarines.
4. Amphibious assault supported by gunfire from surface warships and carrier-based aircraft.
5. Air support of land-based operations with carrier-based aircraft.

The appropriate size and composition of U.S. naval forces can be estimated by specifying theaters and missions, by analyzing hypothetical but plausible naval campaigns, and by determining the number of theaters to be dealt with simultaneously—and the U.S. Navy, of course, has often made such estimates. Given that the number of modern, large-deck carriers would remain at fifteen, and that the U.S. Navy would be structured, in conjunction with allied navies, to perform all or all but one of the key missions against Soviet forces in the North Atlantic, Mediterranean, and Western Pacific (but not yet the Persian Gulf), a representative estimate—shown in table 19–4—indicates that naval requirements would run to slightly more than 600 ships. Whatever the precise estimates of the times, certainly such a force, consisting of modern ships and first-line nuclear-powered attack submarines, would be compatible with the flexible-response concept.

These force objectives, it should be stressed, were never cast in concrete. As analysis proceeded and the performance as well as the cost of new weapons increased, refinements and even reductions in force goals were made. The concept itself underwent some modification as well with the advent of the Nixon administration. However, despite frequent but undocumented charges that the forces were incompatible with the original concept, it would be difficult to argue that the force goals were less than faithful to the spirit of the concept. Despite a planned dependence on the reserves—a dependence that is never popular with the

Table 19–4
Rapid Deployment Capabilities Programmed for the "Flexible-
"Flexible-Response" Concept

	Number of Vessels by Type of Mission				Total
Type of Vessel	*Multi-purpose*	*Barrier Operations*	*Amphibious Operations*	*Convoy Escort*	*Number of Vessels*
Attack carrier	15	—	—	—	15
Surface warship	150	—	36	80	266
Nuclear-powered attack submarine	30	60	—	—	90
Amphibious ship	—	—	102	—	102
Mine countermeasure ship	—	—	18	—	18
Underway replenishment ship	60	—	—	—	60
Auxiliary ship	26	6	16	8	56
Total	281	66	172	88	607

Source: Author's estimates.

services in peacetime—the total size of the forces and of the proposed airlift and sealift capacity was consistent with military estimates of what it would take to deal with the three planning contingencies. In principle, all the elements necessary to a powerful and highly flexible conventional capability had been identified and were on order.

The Inheritance

In practice, that may indeed seem like the kind of conventional capabilitity the United States has acquired. The current nonnuclear posture compared with the approximate force objectives of the 1960s is shown in table 19–5. The only apparent differences are in naval forces and mobility capabilities. However, the table only begins to describe what has happened since the mid-1960s and how far practice has diverged from plan.

The flexible-response concept called for minimizing overseas deployments and building up in the continental United States a large strategic reserve with

Table 19–5
Conventional Forces Planned During the 1960s and Existing in 1981

Force Component	Planned	Existing
Divisions		
Active Army	16⅓	16
Active Marine Corps	3	3
Reserve Army	8	8
Reserve Marine Corps	1	1
Fighter-attack wings		
Active Air Force	26	26
Active Marine Corps	3	3
Reserve Air Force	11	11
Reserve Marine Corps	1	1
General-purpose naval forces		
Attack carriers	15	12
Surface warships	266	188
Nuclear-powered attack submarines	90	82
Underway replenishment ships	60	56
Amphibious assault ships	102	59
Mine countermeasure ships	18	3
Auxiliary ships	56	40
Rapid deployment capabilities		
Pre-positioned sets of division equipment	3	4
C-5A aircraft	129	70
C-141 aircraft	280	234
Fast deployment logistic ships	31	7

Sources: Author's estimates and *Department of Defense Annual Report Fiscal Year 1982* (Government Printing Office, 1981), pp. 132, 154, 174, 199, 204, 205, and A-3–A-4.

worldwide responsibilities. Reality, as reflected in table 19–6, has been otherwise. The Nixon administration actually succeeded in removing one of the two divisions from South Korea. But despite all the efforts of the Carter administration, the other division, minus a battalion or two, is still stationed there, the number of fighter squadrons in South Korea has been increased, and the Marine Amphibious Force remains anchored in Okinawa. In Europe, two brigades were withdrawn from Germany in the 1960s, leaving four and one-third divisions, two armored cavalry regiments, and a brigade in West Berlin. But that small decrease has been more than offset by the subsequent addition of three brigades and six fighter squadrons.

The strategic reserve, though smaller than originally planned, remains an impressive force on paper, especially considering how large U.S. divisions actually are. The appearances, however, are somewhat deceptive. Out of twenty Army and Marine Corps division-equivalents, nine are in the high-priority reserves. However, those nine lack sufficient equipment and training to achieve anything like the early deployment goals set by the original concept. Several of the active-duty Army divisions are under strength; they are short of maneuver battalions and must depend on the reserves for roundout and augmentation in the event of an emergency. All the active-duty divisions in the continental United States depend on the reserves for combat service support units. At best, no more than eight divisions out of the twenty are likely to be available for early deployment.

Table 19–6
Ground Force Deployments Planned during the 1960s and Existing in 1964, 1968, and 1980

Area of Deployment	Planned Number of Division Equivalents	Existing Number of Division Equivalents		
		1964	1968	1980
Germany	5	5	4⅓	5
Republic of Korea	0	2	2	1
Japan (Okinawa)	1	1⅓	0	1
Hawaii	1	1	0	1
Panama[a]	⅓	⅓	⅓	⅓
Alaska[a]	⅓	⅓	⅓	⅓
Continental United States, active duty	12⅓	10	7	11
Continental United States, reserve	9	9	9	9
Subtotal	29	29	23	28⅔
South Vietnam	0	0	10	0
Total	29	29	33	28⅔

Sources: Author's estimates and *Department of Defense Annual Report Fiscal Year 1981* (Government Printing Office, 1980), p. 151.

[a]Units stationed in Panama and Alaska are not included in the usual count of Army units. Neither are other separate units, including the brigade in Berlin and armored cavalry regiments in Germany.

The original concept called for genuinely general-purpose forces; that is, forces with the versatility and sustainability to operate effectively in any theater of the world. But in truth, the active duty forces are rather specialized and short-winded. Most of them are trained for and oriented toward combat in the European theater. The war reserve stocks on hand for them vary in both quantity and quality. Older munitions are fairly plentiful; the expensive and "smart" munitions remain in short supply. No doubt the forces would fight wherever ordered, just as they did in Southeast Asia. But how well and how rapidly they would adapt to conditions for which they had not been trained is uncertain. How long they could fight would depend not only on the opposition and the intensity of the conflict but also on whether other campaigns were going on simultaneously and competing for resources. At present, the logistical system might have trouble supplying their needs in the interval from the outbreak of hostilities to full-scale war production partly because the U.S. war production base has shrunk.

The greatest discrepancy between concept and reality is in the capability for rapid deployment. Plans developed under the original concept assumed that, of the twenty-one active and reserve divisions in the strategic reserve, three would be moved to Europe and the remaining eighteen to one or more other theaters by amphibious shipping and airlift within twenty-three days. By contrast, the Carter administration hoped that sometime in the late 1980s it would be able to reinforce the European theater with nine divisions in fourteen days. As of 1981, only two of the planned mobility programs bore much resemblance to what was originally intended. More than 230 C-141 aircraft have been acquired, and their fuselages are being lengthened to accommodate greater tonnages. The C-5A aircraft also exists, and remains the only carrier of the largest Army equipment. However, four rather than six squadrons were bought and payloads of the current fleet must be restricted until the C-5A wings can be modified. Only a pale shadow of the old fast deployment logistic ship program remains in the form of seven tankers and cargo ships, hastily acquired in 1980 and stationed in the Indian Ocean off Diego Garcia with equipment and supplies for 10,000 Marine Corps troops.

As mobility has declined so, perversely enough, has the officially allowed time in which to deploy from the continental United States. Until the mid-1970s, the number of warning days remained fixed at twenty-three. It was decreed thereafter that only fourteen days would be available. This meant that in central Europe the United States would have exactly two weeks in which to respond to a massive mobilization and deployment by Warsaw Pact forces (a mobilization that would allegedly be completed in the same amount of time). To compensate for the shortage of airlift, the Carter administration pushed vigorously for pre-positioning more materiel in Germany to which the troops could be flown. By 1981, the equipment for a fourth division was being put in place, and if the Carter program is continued, heavy materiel for a total of six and possibly nine divisions will be pre-positioned in Europe.

As a consequence of these developments, the strategic reserve is now badly out of balance with the capacity of the mobility forces to deploy it worldwide. The only theater to which forces could be moved quite rapidly (assuming that the combination of passenger airlift and equipment pre-positioning would work as intended) is central Europe. And even there the best that could now be done by way of reinforcement is no more than six divisions in two weeks or so, even if all heavy airlift capacity were committed to the task. Whatever else might happen to the forces positioned in South Korea, Okinawa, and Hawaii, four Army divisions would be stranded in the continental United States. In other words, central Europe would receive fewer divisions than the planners consider essential, and the occurrence of a second and simultaneous emergency (outside of Korea) would find those four divisions in the continental United States partly ready for it but unable to move.

For this reason, it has been proposed from time to time that the Army deactivate four divisions, and use the personnel to strengthen twelve others. On paper, at least, this would bring the forces and the deployment capabilities back into balance. But even such surgery would, for all practical purposes, leave the United States still short of rapid reinforcement capability. If all the airlift were committed to a European deployment, the forces designated for Korea would have to wait at least two weeks (and probably more) for their turn to deploy. If all the airlift first went to a rapid reinforcement of Korea, European reinforcements would be delayed for some time, despite all the pre-positioning.

What Went Wrong

It is easy—and it may even be accurate—to attribute the various discrepancies between the actual conventional posture and that implied by the original concept more to acts of God than to any defects in the concept itself. The strategic mobility program almost immediately encountered difficulties in Congress, in part because of the cost overruns on the C-5A aircraft, and because so much potential cargo capacity in the form of military airlift and sealift seemed to threaten the commercial carriers of lucrative military cargoes. But a more important influence was the war in Southeast Asia, which had its damaging effects in this realm as elsewhere. Arguments were advanced that presidents would act recklessly in distant places if they had military forces mobile enough to reach them. Hence, these arguments ran, military mobility should be curtailed so as to lessen presidential temptation. Conscription was destroyed as an instrument of defense policy, and the permanent peacetime military establishment had to shrink in order to accommodate the Gates Commission's quite accurate projection of no more than two million volunteers at reasonable pay scales. Defense budgets were reduced in real terms, first by the executive branch and then by Congress, both to mollify opponents of the war and to pay for social programs mandated by the Great Society.

At the same time, to reassure allies in Europe and Asia, overseas deployments had to be maintained despite periodic demands in the Senate that they be greatly reduced.

A fundamental review of defense policy in early 1969 supposedly caused the Nixon administration to modify the original conventional concept by dropping a major planning contingency and requiring "general purpose forces adequate for simultaneously meeting a major Communist attack in either Europe or Asia, assisting allies against non-Chinese threats in Asia, and contending with a contingency elsewhere." Among the reasons for the change, according to the president, was that "the prospects for a coordinated two-front attack on our allies by Russia and China are low both because of the risks of nuclear war and the improbability of Sino-Soviet cooperation. In any event, we do not believe that such a coordinated attack should be met primarily by U.S. conventional forces. . . . [7] Whether the Ford and Carter administrations agreed with this reasoning, they went along with the change. At the same time they laid great stress on the increasing Soviet military threat.

Presumably, the dropping of a major nonnuclear contingency should have resulted in a substantially reduced need for U.S. conventional forces. Divisions, tactical air wings, and naval capabilities were in fact cut back. Whether the cuts were the effect or the cause of the modified concept is less clear. In any event, not all of them lasted. By 1975, Congress proved willing to restore the active-duty forces of the Army and the Air Force to at least the appearances of sixteen divisions and twenty-six fighter-attack wings. However, it still balked at returning to the original goals for strategic airlift and sealift. It even resisted subsidies to commercial airlines for modifications in the wide-bodied civilian cargo aircraft dedicated to the Civil Reserve Air Fleet—modifications that would enable those aircraft to load and transport oversized military cargoes. By the end of 1980 only three modifications had been funded. As a substitute, Congress accepted the use of war reserve stocks for pre-positioning divisional equipment in Europe, a program which, despite assertions to the contrary, was bound to reduce the flexibility of the posture. The result, in short, was if not a caricature at least a distorted version of what had been planned under the concept of the 1960s.

The Concept Reviewed

It is at least conceivable that under the more propitious conditions of the 1980s, a workable facsimile of the original plan can be produced. There is even some reason to think that the Carter administration, while still in office, was going to make just such an attempt. It planned to add dramatically to the airlift fleet with approximately 130 new wide-bodied aircraft (known as the CX) capable of transporting the Army's largest equipment. It proposed the acquisition of eight fast sealift ships and planned to build at least fifteen maritime pre-positioning ships, the modern version of the fast deployment logistic ships. The Rapid Deployment Joint Task Force was also created to manage lesser contingencies. Although no forces were assigned to it, presumably its commander had drawing rights on the strategic reserve in the continental United States, as did other and more powerful commanders. Thus the assumption remained that elements in the strategic reserve would become versatile enough to operate on short notice in the area of the Persian Gulf as well as in Europe, Korea, or elsewhere.

Perhaps this time it will be demonstrated that there is nothing wrong with the concept and that it can be made to work as visualized in the 1960s. However, grounds for skepticism remain about the realism of the concept itself. For one thing, while the positive aversion to conventional forces that existed in the 1950s and even into the 1960s has diminished, questions remain as to whether the very large expenditure needed to make the original concept operational will yield compensating benefits. Such doubts are understandable. Pessimism about adverse trends in the military balance of power continues to deepen. Soviet conventional capabilities are invariably described as larger, more modern, and more powerful than comparable capabilities of the United States and its allies. Despite all the difficulties the Soviet Union has encountered in Eastern Europe and Afghanistan, it has become bad form to suggest that the Warsaw Pact is less than invincible on the ground. Despite well-known instances of slow and chaotic military buildups by the Soviet Union in preparation for its various "police actions," the Red Army is credited with the ability to mobilize and deploy its understrength divisions so rapidly that it is virtually impossible for NATO, or U.S. forces near the Persian Gulf, not to be caught totally by surprise. Even though Soviet forces appear to be bogged down in Afghanistan and seem to operate with such poor logistics that larger capabilities cannot be supported, the USSR is loudly proclaimed to have secured a vastly improved strategic position relative to Iran and all of Southwest Asia.

As if this news were not grim enough, it is asserted as incontrovertible fact that the Soviet Union has now acquired a usable superiority over the United States in strategic and theater nuclear capabilities. Even so, the argument is still made that the United States and its allies can compensate for the weaknesses of their conventional forces by an early initiation of nuclear war, especially with neutron bombs. These devices are seen as having the advantage that at one and the same time they would stop an attack and fool an enemy into believing that he had not been hit with "real" nuclear weapons. Hence, if he lacked enhanced radiation weapons of his own, he would not dare to respond with more "conventional" nuclear explosives.

In the face of so much pessimism and so many contradictions, the investment of large-scale resources in the nonnuclear enterprise hardly seems to make a great deal of sense. Suppose, however, that conditions become more favorable to a conventional-force renaissance. Suppose even that the more hysterical claims about Soviet military prowess are recognized for what they are. Still a nagging question remains: Can the original concept for the conventional forces ever be made operational?

Central to the effectiveness of the concept in its current form are three requirements: minimal forward deployments overseas and a strategic reserve in the continental United States; considerable versatility on the part of the units in this reserve in terms of both equipment and training; and strategic mobility capabilities sufficient to move about 300,000 tons of equipment and supplies to overseas bases in a matter of a few weeks. In the abstract these requirements sound plausible. Operationally they are not easy to meet.

There should be no particular trick in pulling U.S. units back from their overseas stations and adding them to a strategic reserve. Practically speaking, however, the process has proved extraordinarily sticky in both Europe and Asia. The garrisons in Germany and Korea, much more than any treaties, are seen as the real guarantee that the United States will come to the aid of its allies. Thus, any major change in their size and composition almost automatically sets the alarm bells ringing in friendly chancelleries.

The reasons for this reaction are not psychological only. Surprise attacks by deployed forces in East Germany and North Korea are almost certainly low-probability events short of a major crisis. It would be foolish, however, not to insure to some degree against them. Admittedly, the 2nd Infantry Division in South Korea and the 3rd Marine Divison in Okinawa may constitute excessive insurance in view of South Korean strength and the fortifications along the demilitarized zone. But the U.S. divisions in Germany (nearly six of them now) cover an important part of the front in NATO's Central Region. Without them, this front would be vulnerable to sudden attacks on a relatively small scale.

These eight divisions are not the only ones essentially committed to specific theaters. The 25th Infantry Divison in Hawaii cannot seriously be considered part of an uncommitted strategic reserve. If it goes anywhere in a major crisis, its destination will almost certainly be the Far East as part of the three-division force deemed necessary to shore up South Korean defenses in the event of an attack from the North. At least the equivalent of another two heavy divisions in the continental United States remains part of the annual force commitment the United States makes to NATO. Furthermore, if a surprise attack in the region of the Persian Gulf is to be treated as a serious contingency, a minimum of one brigade from a Marine Corps division will probably have to be put on station in the Arabian Sea. In sum, of the nineteen active-duty divisions in the Army and Marine Corps, eleven and one-third would have quite specific responsibilities. Only seven and two-thirds divisions can therefore be considered seriously as making up an uncommitted strategic reserve. If regular units alone are counted as available, that total is not quite half of what was deemed desirable in the planning of the 1960s.

Admittedly, the concept of those years assumed a capability for three simultaneous contingencies, whereas one of the planning contingencies has now been dropped. But the earlier planning also assumed that nine high-priority reserve divisions would be part of the uncommitted pool of forces. By contrast and despite the changes in the concept, current planners have been for all practical purposes struggling with the possibility of three more or less simultaneous contingencies—in the Persian Gulf, Europe, and Korea—on the basis of a much smaller uncommitted reserve, all of which could, in a crisis, be rapidly claimed by the European Command.

This tight situation is not likely to change short of a substantial increase in the ground and tactical air forces. Furthermore, it is bound to raise the issue of whether, with all the obligations the United States has undertaken to other countries, it will ever prove feasible to acquire a large uncommitted reserve over and above the forces oriented toward and practically committed to specific theaters. The prospects for obtaining such a reserve are not promising. It is already proving difficult to juggle a two-contingency capability among the demands of three possible theaters, and one consequence of the strain seems to be that the United States has a Rapid Deployment Joint Task Force, but not much of a rapid deployment force. Another may turn out to be that what looks like economy of force in peacetime may prove to be a force deficit in a crisis.

Force versatility is equally difficult to achieve. As has become evident from the *Mayaguez* and *Desert One* operations, even small units with a great deal of experience have difficulty adapting rapidly to new conditions and the demands of specific missions. It is no disparagement to say that large military units are like elephants in a ballet company. Their repertories are bound to be limited and they are not very adept at rapid change. Since most of the units sent to Vietnam were not originally trained or equipped for that environment and type of warfare, the marvel is not that they fought in an elephantine fashion, but that they fought at all.

Obviously some types of units can adapt to new conditions more rapidly than others. But all-purpose forces are unlikely to perform well on any given mission. With time, and knowledge of what a specific task is to be, units can be reequipped and retrained. However, the necessary foreknowledge and time are explicitly precluded by assumptions of short warning and the concept of flexible response.

The advocates of versatility thus have a second major obstacle to hurdle. If they manage to withhold forces from specific theaters and commitments, they must solve the problem of how to equip and train them. Specialization may ensure superb performance combined with low adaptability. Attempts to combine great versatility in repertories with rapid responses may simply foster operational dilettantism—with the appearance, but not the reality, of economics of force.

Finally, a well-oiled system of rapid deployment has proved remarkably elusive despite years of admittedly intermittent effort. If one believes that the Soviet Union, with only a few days of effort, can mobilize and deploy large assault forces in a particular theater, the only suitable response is to have the entire defending force in the theater and ready for action at all times. Not only is this impractical on a number of grounds; it also precludes the flexibility and economy of force that supposedly go with holding a strategic reserve in the continental United States. In any event, no one really believes either that the Soviet forces are capable of such blinding speed in their preparations or that evidence of major activity on their part could be concealed.

The difficulty with the evidence has proved twofold. First, while warning has tended to come early in the mobilization and deployment process, it has rarely permitted its consumers to say with confidence whether Soviet forces would in fact attack or, if so, when precisely they would move. Second, in the face of these ambiguities and uncertainties, Western statesmen have proved reluctant to initiate countermeasures at an early stage of the crisis. It is precisely this reluctance, rather than surprise, which has led strategic mobility to become synonymous with rapid deployment.

Strategic airlift capable of moving troops with all their equipment over intercontinental distances is the system most compatible with economy of force and rapid deployment. But it is expensive, and even the large fleet of C-141 and C-5A aircraft planned in the 1960s could not have manged to transport much more than 12,000 tons a day to Europe. So far, the United States has not been able to come close to that level of effort. Furthermore, while airlift delivers a few combat units early in the deployment process, it requires (as the daily tonnages indicate) a substantial number of days to provide major reinforcements.

Modern, fast sealift, with a relatively modest number of ships, could deliver an equal amount of tonnage to a port such as Antwerp after about two weeks. But, of course, it could not deploy any intermediate tonnage or even modest reinforcements before then. Thus, despite its low ton-mile cost, sealift has received little consideration for rapid deployment.

The combination of airlift and pre-positioned heavy equipment, while it limits flexibility (unless equipment is pre-positioned at or near every trouble spot in the world), appears to permit the most rapid buildup of forces in a given theater. However, its speed has probably been exaggerated because all the pre-positioned equipment may not be properly stored or in good working order (despite large monitoring crews on the spot), and because it takes time to match men with equipment and then move units to their wartime positions. Moreover, the process itself is a difficult one to rehearse on a large scale. Annual *Reforger* exercises are held in which units of up to a division in size are airlifted from the United States to Germany. But advance notice of the exercises is always given, units have ample time to prepare for them, and all the maintenance and supply assets of the U.S. forces in Germany are at their disposal. Such exercises are a far cry from a multidivision deployment undertaken without any prior notice—a deployment, incidentally, that could probably never be practiced in peacetime owing to fears about its effects on allies and opponents alike. To depend on a system of this character is effectively to accept low confidence in the ability of the United States to deploy its strategic reserve with flexibility and great speed.

Lessons

Do these difficulties mean that conventional force planning has been off on a wild goose chase for the last twenty years? It is all well and good to compare U.S., allied, and opposing tanks, antitank weapons, artillery pieces, helicopters, aircraft, and warships. But such comparisons are not a sufficient basis for force evaluation and planning or judgments about the military balance. In fact, no one has yet devised a serious planning substitute for (a) the development and analysis of plausible but hypothetical campaigns in specific theaters, (b) for the determination of the forces needed to bring about the desired military outcomes in those specific theaters, and (c) difficult judgments about the number of contingencies for which U.S. conventional forces should be prepared. What is more, when careful analyses are done and sober judgments are made, they strongly suggest that current conventional threats can be contained by conventional means at costs that are quite bearable to the United States and its allies.

The use of these traditional military methods naturally does not mean that the forces needed for a specific contingency, or the number of contingencies for which forces should be acquired, will not change as the threat changes. Both issues deserve more examination than they have received in light of the furor about the Soviet military buildup. Nor do the difficulties with the original, flexible-response concept mean that multipurpose forces and the effort to create an uncommitted strategic reserve have no military value. Rather, what these difficulties may signify is that the economies of force sought under the original concept are false economies after all, and that it may be necessary to expand the force structure in order to ensure, at a minimum, that forces are available for and dedicated to those theaters in which the United States has a bedrock interest. In short, flexibility may have to take second place to the ability at all times to defend certain specific and vital theaters.

Finally, while strategic mobility will remain an essential component of the U.S. conventional posture, it is by no means clear that rapid deployment as currently defined is the only solution to ambiguous warning. Only recently has there been any acquisition of fast sealift, and even then it has been regarded as a stopgap measure and not a true substitute for additional airlift, although it may take a decade to obtain substantially more aircraft. As yet, very little thought has been given to other measures that can be taken on warning. Yet there are actions that do not commit cautious policymakers to what they may regard as premature, irrevocable, and provocative action. There are also routines such as frequent but randomly timed deployment exercises that will accustom an opponent to the practice but leave him uncertain about his ability to achieve surprise. Best of all, there are measures—field fortifications are one example—that make an early response to warning less critical to a successful defense.

George Santayana once declared that "those who cannot remember the past are condemned to repeat it." A look at the last thirty years suggests that the need for strong conventional forces is an idea whose time has finally come. The same look also implies rather strongly that the kind of flexibility sought by the particular concept of the 1960s is currently beyond the grasp of the U.S. military establishment.

No doubt the ways in which the conventional posture has diverged from the requirements of the old concept during the last fifteen years reflect to some degree the special conditions of the time. But the divergence also represents a gradual (if tacit, mechanical, and hit-or-miss) recognition of the difficult demands inherent in the concept. Large and uncommitted strategic reserves, units with worldwide missions, and smoothly operating rapid deployment capabilities are not easy to acquire even when generous defense budgets are available. The maintenance of overseas deployments; the inexorable orientation of units to specific theaters and particular missions if they are to have any proficiency at all; the creation of a Rapid Deployment Joint Task Force with the facade of a worldwide charter but immediate responsibility only for the Persian Gulf: these are not aberrations. They are acknowledgements of the practical limits on conventional force flexibility. Surely the time has come to review the whole concept and its implementation in the light of these developments.

Notes

1. This account is largely based on Paul Y. Hammond, "NSC-68: Prologue to Rearmament," in Warner R. Schilling, Paul Y. Hammond, and Glenn H. Snyder, eds., *Strategy, Politics, and Defense Budgets* (New York: Columbia University Press, 1962), pp. 267–378.
2. Ibid., p. 306.
3. Ibid., pp. 342, 358.
4. Ibid., p. 352.
5. Quoted in William W. Kaufmann, *The McNamara Strategy* (New York: Harper and Row, 1964), p. 34.
6. See, for example, *The Fiscal Year 1969–73 Defense and the 1969 Defense Budget*, Statement by Secretary of Defense Robert S. McNamara (Washington, D.C.: Department of Defense, 1968), pp. 78–79.
7. See *U.S. Foreign Policy for the 1970's: A New Strategy for Peace*, A Report to the Congress by Richard Nixon, President of the United States, February 18, 1972 (Washington, D.C.: Government Printing Office, 1970), p. 129.

Discussion Questions

1. What factors determine the structure of U.S. forces?

2. How does strategy interact with weapons acquisition and the policy process to produce the U.S. force structure?

3. In view of previous discussions regarding NATO, strategy, and the Soviet threat, how well are U.S. forces structured to defend Europe?

Suggestions for Additional Reading

Ball, Desmond. "Targeting for Strategic Deterrence." *Adelphi Paper No. 185.* London: International Institute for Strategic Studies, 1983.

European Security Study. *Strengthening Conventional Deterrence in Europe.* New York: St. Martin's Press, 1983.

Huntington, Samuel P., ed. *The Strategic Imperative.* Cambridge, Mass.: Ballinger, 1982.

Kahan, Jerome H. *Security in the Nuclear Age.* Washington, D.C.: Brookings Institution, 1975.

Kaufmann, William W. *Defense in the 1980s.* Washington, D.C.: Brookings Institution, 1981.

————. *The McNamara Strategy.* New York: Harper and Row, 1964.

Mako, William P. *U.S. Ground Forces and the Defense of Central Europe.* Washington, D.C.: Brookings Institution, 1983.

Rosenberg, David A. "The Origins of Overkill: Nuclear Weapons and American Strategy, 1945–1960." *International Security* 7, no. 4 (Spring 1983):3–71.

Steinbruner, John D. "Nuclear Decapitation." *Foreign Policy,* no. 45 (Winter 1981–1982):16–28.

Treverton, Gregory F. "Managing NATO's Nuclear Dilemma." *International Security* 7, no. 4 (Spring 1983):93–115.

U.S. Office of Technology Assessment. *The Effects of Nuclear War.* Washington, D.C.: Government Printing Office, 1979.

Part VII
Conclusion

20
Appraising U.S. National Security Policy

The Editors

A national leader once remarked that the people have a right to expect efficiency from their government, even if they should not expect imagination. Yet administrations often are criticized for not having efficient policies and programs, and national security policy is no exception. Various criticisms include charges that administrations have no guiding strategy, fail to realize how the world really is, overemphasize military solutions, or try to solve national security problems by throwing dollars at them. Such criticisms invariably reflect a sense that U.S. national security policy fails to protect its interests adequately, a sense that it often encapsulated in phrases like *capability-interest gap* or *strategy-structure mismatch.* These disjunctions can be termed vertical discontinuities, since they are areas in our analytical framework where the results of the policy formulation process seem not to follow logically from the preceding step. We say *seem not to follow* since an examination of the entire analytical framework may explain why the discontinuity occurred.

The second type of discontinuity is horizontal; it occurs as changes over time. Since national security policy is the product of ever-changing factors in the international and domestic environment, it should be no surprise that policies change over time. However, not all changes in the environments result in policy shifts. National security policy displays a surprising degree of continuity in this sense, for better or worse.

This chapter describes U.S. national security policy in each administration since World War II. The framework for analysis is used to identify vertical and horizontal continuities and discontinuities and to explain how and why they occurred. The chapter makes some observations about future national security policy, the problems the United States may need to address, and the prospects of doing so efficiently.

Truman Administration, 1945–1953

The death of Franklin Roosevelt brought to office a man little versed in foreign affairs. Indeed, some people have claimed that in his eighty-three days as vice-president, Harry Truman had never set foot inside the White House War Room, an interesting enough situation in peacetime but a nearly appalling one in war. Nevertheless, Truman did not need to wage a world war; by April 1945, it was practically over. Instead Truman had to reconstruct a shattered world, face a new adversary in the Soviet Union, define a new U.S. role in international affairs, and restore the U.S. economy to a peacetime footing.

With peace at hand, security interests no longer dominated the political scene. Prosperity and the return to normalcy were the most important goals, as exemplified by rapid demobilization, the push for a balanced budget, and the use of the remainder method for defense budgeting. Tax revenues were calculated, all other federal programs funded, and the remainder went to defense. As a result, by 1949 the defense budget totaled only $13 billion.

In a world where the new UN was seen as the protector of international peace, $13 billion seemed adequate. Since diplomacy was to be the major instrument of national security policy, the armed forces were reduced quickly from 12 million men in 1945 to 1.6 million in 1947. Arms control initiatives advanced by the United States in the Baruch Plan and the Acheson-Lillienthal Plan would have placed nuclear weapons under the control of the United Nations.

George Kennan argued that as long as the other power centers in the world, which he identified as the United States, United Kingdom, Germany, and Japan, could be kept out of Soviet control, international peace and order could be maintained. Kennan's characterization of these nations as being U.S. vital interests and, by exclusion, other areas of the world as being of peripheral interest was to hold sway until 1950.

In an attempt to institutionalize the success achieved in World War II, a need made even greater by the constantly decreasing defense budget and armed forces, Congress enacted sweeping organizational reforms in the National Security Act of 1947. The act created the NSC, the Department of Defense, the JCS, the air force, and the CIA. Problems remained, however, and for the remainder of the Truman administration, these fledgling agencies still were sorting out their proper roles in the national security process. Truman saw the creation of the NSC in particular as an effort by the Republican-controlled Congress to constrain his freedom of action as president. Consequently he attended only twelve of the fifty-seven council meetings held before the Korean war. As a result, Secretary of State Dean Acheson, and his department, proved to be the most influential actors in the national security system during these years.

Events were unfolding that were to cause a major shift in U.S. national security policy. Communist activity in Greece and Turkey in 1947 prompted the United States to provide $400 million in aid and to proclaim the Truman Doctrine, a call for protecting free countries everywhere. The establishment of communist governments in Czechoslovakia and Poland in 1948 and the Soviet blockade of Berlin in the same year were signs that the UN could not be counted on to protect important U.S. interests. The European nations began pressuring the

United States for a security arrangement outside the UN that would allow them to continue the rebuilding process begun in 1947 with the Marshall Plan. In 1949 the United States agreed, and NATO was formed. Soviet acquisition of the atomic bomb and the fall of China to the communists in that same year seemed further proof that the United States faced a global threat to its interests, a threat not met adequately by Kennan's strategy of containment.

Paul Nitze, Kennan's replacement as director of the State Department's Policy Planning Staff, drew up a plan in 1949 for refurbishing U.S. conventional and nuclear forces to meet the communist threat. Designated NSC 68, the plan based its proposals on a redefinition of U.S. interests. No longer were Kennan's five power centers the only areas of interest. Rather, anywhere the communists attempted to expand their influence, the United States would have to contain them. To do otherwise, it was argued, would undermine the credibility of the U.S. commitment to Europe and would make the rest of the world vulnerable to Soviet "salami" tactics of biting off a little bit of the free world at a time.

Nonetheless, at the time NSC 68 was completed, it stood little chance of being implemented. Congress had cut taxes (over a presidential veto) in 1948, U.S. forces were withdrawn from Korea in 1949, and in 1950 Secretary of State Acheson, in a public speech, defined a defensive perimeter for the United States that corresponded very little with NSC 68's vision of U.S. interests—and seemed to exclude Korea.

The Korean war provided the impetus for the implementation of NSC 68 and the strengthening of the military component of national security policy. In part, this reaction was for domestic reasons. Heavy criticism had been leveled at the Truman administration for losing China the previous year, and Senator Joseph McCarthy was conducting his witch hunts for communists in (and out of) government. Failure to react strongly to a clear case of communist aggression would have been politically unwise in a congressional election year. Nonetheless, the reaction also was due in part to a concern that in fact the North Korean invasion was just one more step in a plan for communist world domination. If true, then communist expansion obviously had to be stopped.

The defense budget was increased rapidly until by 1952 it reached $50 billion. Selective service was expanded, and the armed forces increased from 1.4 million in 1950 to 3.6 million in 1952. Interestingly, the bulk of this military buildup was committed to Europe, not to Korea. This priority was the result of two concerns. First, some officials felt that the Korean invasion was a ruse designed to draw the U.S. into an Asian land war, leaving the Red Army free to roll across Western Europe. After all, by 1948 the Soviets had thirty divisions in Europe, while the best the United States, Britain, and France could muster collectively was a mere ten divisions. Even the creation of NATO in 1949 (a NATO without Germany, Greece, or Turkey) had done little to rectify that imbalance.

Second, the United States was interested in keeping the Korean conflict limited. Although the United States was fighting with allied support under a UN flag (due to a Soviet walkout from the UN Security Council), the commitment of too large a force was seen as risking Chinese or Soviet military intervention.

By 1952, the American people had become disillusioned with the war. After the sweeping victories of World War II, limited war seemed an unacceptable option. The war in Korea was stalemated, and public opposition to the war effort was growing. Congress, reflecting the growing public dissatisfaction, rejected the administration's 1952 proposal for universal military training and cut the fiscal year (FY) 1953 defense budget by $4 billion.

Eisenhower Administration, 1953–1961

The Eisenhower administration inherited the continuing war in Korea and inflation at home (caused by deficit federal spending to finance the military buildup). As the first Supreme Allied Commander, Europe (SACEUR), Eisenhower had seen the economic and political support for the 1952 NATO-adopted force goal of ninety-two divisions evaporate in less than a year. It was clear to him that neither the resources nor the will were present to continue a policy of maximum military confrontation with communist countries. Instead, Eisenhower felt, a sound economy, based on a balanced federal budget and a stabilized (and reduced) defense budget, would provide the prosperous domestic environment necessary to win the long struggle between communism and democracy.

For the first three years of the administration, it looked as if Eisenhower's New Look policy might succeed. Although he did not scale back U.S. interests from the global ones enunciated in NSC 68, he was able to cut back U.S. military expenditures for at least three reasons. First, Stalin died in 1953, and his successors seemed interested in reducing tensions between the United States and the Soviet Union. In fact, between 1953 and 1956, Soviet armed forces were reduced by 1.8 million men. Second, due to the Korean war buildup, Eisenhower had a much higher baseline to work from than did Truman. Even though Eisenhower reduced the defense budget to about $40 billion by 1955, this level was a far cry from the $13 billion it had been before the Korean conflict.

Finally, technology provided him with a vastly superior nuclear weapon. The hydrogen bomb, a thousand times more powerful and substantially smaller (hence more deliverable) than the atomic bomb, meant that Eisenhower could substitute relatively cheaper nuclear weapons for more expensive ground troops and get "more bang for the buck." Consequently the army was reduced from 1.5 million men to 1 million men by 1955; strategic and theater nuclear forces were increased greatly. By the end of Eisenhower's administration, the United States had approximately 2,500 theater nuclear warheads in Europe, warheads that were to be used, in Eisenhower's words, "just like a bullet" should war occur. This capability, when coupled with an employment policy of massive retaliation, was felt to be adequate to deter Soviet aggression around the world. The NATO allies formally adopted the military strategy of massive retaliation in 1956.

Eisenhower did not rely completely on nuclear weapons to achieve his security objectives. He increased reserve forces from 580,000 in 1953 to 913,000 in 1956 in order to be better prepared to fight what he felt would be a long war, should war occur. He expanded the budget and operational latitude of the CIA, which provided such victories as putting the shah on the throne in Iran in 1953 and helping depose the communist-oriented Arbenz government in Guatemala in 1954. After the French defeat at Dienbienphu in 1954, he sent U.S. military advisers to South Vietnam to assist its efforts to resist pressure from Hanoi. All of these relatively inexpensive activities were designed to help the United States meet global interests while relying primarily on nuclear capabilities.

Eisenhower, and his secretary of state, John Foster Dulles, also pushed hard on the diplomatic front. Although arms control proposals such as Atoms for Peace (a modified revival of the Baruch Plan) went nowhere, the United States was more successful in strengthening alliance relationships. The Federal Republic of Germany (rearmed) joined NATO in 1955, thereby providing a tremendous and immediate boost to the alliance's capabilities. SEATO was formed in 1955. Although the United States was not a member of the Central Treaty Organization (CENTO), that alliance did receive active U.S. support. Bilateral security arrangements were signed in 1953 with South Korea and with Taiwan. Even though not deserving of the "pactomania" appellation often given it, the Eisenhower administration clearly saw alliances as a less expensive way of meeting U.S. security interests.

Like Truman, however, Eisenhower saw events occur that undercut the efficacy of his national security policy. At home, a $7.4 billion tax cut in 1954, coupled with increases in domestic programs (rising by 50 percent from 1956 to 1960), started a cycle of inflation and recession rather than achieving Eisenhower's goal of a constantly growing economy. Abroad Soviet detonation of their own hydrogen bomb and their acquisition of intercontinental bombers undermined the credibility of massive retaliation. Further, the creation of the Warsaw Pact in 1955 seemed more than to offset any gains NATO had made in balancing Soviet military power in Central Europe. American opposition to the actions of its British and French allies during the Suez crisis in 1956 demonstrated the conflicting interests of the NATO allies. Finally, the lack of NATO response to the Soviet invasion of Hungary in 1956 indicated that NATO was not prepared to challenge Soviet hegemony in Eastern Europe.

The Soviet launching of Sputnik in 1957 was a critical blow to the U.S. feeling of security. If the Soviet Union could put a satellite in orbit, it also could deliver an unstoppable thermonuclear strike on the United States. A 1957 report by the Gaither Committee recommended acceleration of the U.S. ICBM, IRBM, and SLBM programs, plus increased civil and air defense efforts in response to this new threat. Eisenhower accelerated the ICBM program and deployed the first of the SLBM fleet. Yet the concern engendered by Sputnik remained, and the resulting fears of a missile gap became a major issue in the 1960 presidential campaign.

Events such as the 1958 Lebanon crisis, the Berlin crisis of 1958–1959, and the revolution in Cuba in 1959 demonstrated that a military policy that relied primarily on nuclear weapons for deterrence was not effective in preventing conventional provocations. Eisenhower's New Look in his second term did modify the reliance on nuclear weapons somewhat, but fiscal constraints precluded a significant increase in conventional forces. Critics of Eisenhower's military policy argued for a strategy capable of dealing with a wider range of threats. This criticism provided the basis for the new strategy of flexible response adopted by the Kennedy administration in 1961.

Kennedy Administration, 1961–1963

The Kennedy administration held basically the same global perspective of U.S. interests as did its predecessor. The general feeling, however, was that the national security policy adopted by Eisenhower did not protect those interests adequately. Increased military capabilities were needed across the entire spectrum of force, from unconventional warfare forces to strategic nuclear forces. Such an expansion would provide the president with flexibility by providing additional options for reacting to security threats and would bolster U.S. credibility by avoiding over-reliance on a single aspect of military policy, such as nuclear forces. Thus, a president would be able to respond to any threat with an appropriate level of force.

There were other reasons for expanding military capabilities besides the much-publicized missile gap. The European countries had completed the economic rebirth that the Marshall Plan had started, and their decreased economic dependence meant increased political independence from the United States. Further, France developed and deployed its own independent nuclear capability, throwing a wild card into NATO's nuclear planning. Finally, Khrushchev's proclaimed support for wars of national liberation, Castro's successful revolution, and the crisis in Laos all seemed to dictate a need for increased conventional and unconventional warfare forces.

Such a military buildup obviously could not be accomplished by following Eisenhower's balanced budget and steady defense spending approach. Deficit spending was required initially, and Kennedy's economic adviser, Walter Heller, argued this deficit spending also would lead to economic growth. This line of reasoning prevailed, and by FY 64 the defense budget had increased to the Korean war level of $50 billion, 8.2 percent of a rapidly expanding gross national product.

To oversee this military buildup, Kennedy persuaded Robert McNamara of Ford Motor Company to be defense secretary. Capitalizing on the increased authority of the secretary of defense granted by the 1958 amendments to the National Security Act of 1947, McNamara set up the planning, programming, and budgeting system (PPBS) in the Pentagon. The PPBS was intended to rationalize military policy by using systems analysis to determine the most cost-effective weapons systems and force structures and by firmly linking both of those to military and national security policy objectives. The pre-NSC 68 Truman administration and the Eisenhower administration had employed a bottom-up approach to military policy. Fiscal limits determined the size of the defense budget, and the services based their force structure and procurement decisions on those limits. Such an approach is obviously susceptible to vertical discontinuities between national interests and security policy. Alternatively, the PPBS approach was intended to determine defense budgets from the top down. National interests and security policy were to drive military policy, weapons acquisition, and force structure.

The impact of this new system on military policy varied. There was only a slight increase in conventional forces, reaching 2.7 million men by FY 64. Nuclear forces grew quickly, however. President Kennedy increased the size of the Polaris submarine program by 50 percent and accelerated its production schedule by 100 percent. This buildup, coupled with slower-than-expected Soviet strategic nuclear force deployments, soon laid to rest fears of a missile gap. Kennedy's pet project, the Green Berets, also enjoyed an increase in size, many of whom were in the vanguard of the advisory group buildup in South Vietnam (which numbered 18,000 men by the time of Kennedy's death).

Kennedy also was intent on using to the utmost other instruments of national security policy. The creation of the Agency for International Development (AID) was meant to organize and give impetus to aid programs to Third World countries. Special economic programs were targeted for specific areas, such as the $2 billion Alliance for Progress program designed to assist Latin American economic development.

In the diplomatic arena, the Cuban missile crisis, while proving the adequacy of U.S. conventional forces, had brought the world too close to the brink of a nuclear disaster. Consequently, the United States and the Soviet Union established the hot line in 1963 to provide for rapid communications to each other's capital, with an aim toward minimizing misunderstanding during future crises. The United States and the Soviet Union also signed the Limited Test Ban Treaty in 1963, prohibiting nuclear tests in the atmosphere.

Kennedy proved less willing to use the CIA in the same manner as Eisenhower, primarily because he had lost confidence in that agency as a result of the Bay of Pigs debacle.

By the time of Kennedy's assassination in 1963, flexible response was fully implemented, but it had yet to meet its biggest test, Vietnam.

Johnson Administration, 1963–1969

Lyndon Johnson's first concern as president was to project an image of continuity and political stability in order to ease uncertainties at home and abroad. To this end, he quickly announced that his administration would continue to follow the policies of his predecessor, and he kept Kennedy's senior national security advisers in place.

This arrangement reinforced Johnson's own career-long orientation on and interest in domestic politics and policy. Thus, at least until 1966, Kennedy's principal advisers, such as McGeorge Bundy in the White House and Robert McNamara at Defense, exerted even more influence on U.S. national security policy than they had while Kennedy was alive. To this group soon was added McGeorge Bundy's brother, William, assistant defense secretary for international security affairs. Walt Rostow, director of State's Policy Planning Staff, also joined the group and enjoyed a great deal of influence with Johnson. When McGeorge Bundy left the White House in 1966, Rostow moved in as the new national security adviser. William Bundy also moved, from Defense to assistant secretary of state for the Far East. Both of these personnel changes were significant in that they put in positions of power individuals convinced that a military solution was possible in Vietnam.

This viewpoint seemed to be vindicated by the successful U.S. military intervention in 1965 to stop the civil war in the Dominican Republic. The insertion of marines and the Eighty-second Airborne Division between the warring factions created a stabilized environment in which Ambassador Ellsworth Bunker was able to bring about a negotiated political solution. As in World War II, democracy had been brought to another country on the point of a bayonet. If it could work in the Dominican Republic, why not in Vietnam?

Until 1964, CIA analysts agreed that U.S. involvement could successfully bring about the establishment of democracy in Vietnam. After 1964 the analysts reversed themselves. No longer did the domestic support exist in Vietnam for the national government. Without such support, they concluded, any U.S. efforts would prove futile.

This shift by the CIA was more than offset, however, by the support McNamara and General Maxwell Taylor gave for U.S. involvement. McNamara was convinced that systems analysis would allow the government to calibrate its commitment and achieve the desired results at the lowest costs. The JCS, which previously had opposed military involvement in an Asian land war, saw Vietnam as a test case for the concept of limited war, a concept in which General Taylor believed quite strongly. The JCS maintained this view even after General Earl Wheeler replaced General Taylor as Chairman of the Joint Chiefs in 1964. Both Defense and the JCS saw Vietnam as the proving ground of the flexible response strategy.

As in the Truman administration's response to North Korean aggression, a threat to U.S. interests in Asia resulted in a massive military buildup. By 1968, U.S. armed forces were increased by nearly a million men, to 3.5 million. But unlike the earlier period, when the bulk of the increases went to Europe, this time most of the buildup was committed to the Asian conflict. Between 1964 and 1965,

U.S. forces in Vietnam increased tenfold—from 18,000 to 180,000. They were increased another 250 percent—to 480,000—by 1967.

Also unlike the previous period, there was no clear and present danger to U.S. interests in Vietnam. Despite Johnson's use of the Gulf of Tonkin incident in 1964 to get congressional support for commitment of forces to Vietnam, there was no clear-cut military aggression to spark public support. This situation made Johnson reluctant to call up the large number of reserve and National Guard forces created during the Eisenhower years. Doing so, he feared, would cause public opposition to his policies because of the effect it would have on communities throughout the nation. Rather, Johnson relied on selective service, as Truman had done, to provide the manpower for the expanded force structure. In an effort to minimize the public impact of the draft, the administration limited tours in Vietnam to one year rather than keeping soldiers there for the duration of the conflict. This policy, however, undercut Johnson's objective of minimizing the public impact. First, the policy meant that as the war continued, more men would have to be drafted to replace those coming home. Second, the large number of Vietnam returnees meant there were numerous Americans throughout the nation who had seen first-hand and usually disliked, the war. By the time large-scale military aggression did occur in the Tet offensive of 1968, public opinion was already against the war. Consequently, rather than serving as a catalyst for public support, Tet served to fuel further public opposition.

Exacerbating this situation was the economic impact of increased defense expenditures. Primarily in order to finance the war effort, the defense budget was increased from $50 billion in 1964 to $78 billion in 1968, a sum that absorbed 9.4 percent of the gross national product. This increase, coupled with Johnson's insistence on funding large increases for social programs to implement his Great Society and war on poverty, was an effort to have both guns and butter. The result was inflation at home and increased pressure on the dollar abroad. By 1968, the United States was forced to loosen the dollar's ties to the gold standard. A two-tier system was established, with fixed exchange rates continuing between governments but with private sales and purchase prices allowed to float according to market forces.

This halfway measure only partially mollified U.S. European allies, which were being forced to hold dollars and consequently suffer inflation in their economies. They saw U.S. involvement in Vietnam as being the primary culprit for this economic situation. A sense that the United States had no vital interests in Vietnam, coupled with the increasingly difficult economic consequences of the U.S. efforts there, led the Europeans to become critical of U.S. policy in Southeast Asia. Moreover, this criticism was only one issue that affected U.S.-European relations.

Since 1961, the Kennedy and Johnson administrations had been pressuring NATO allies to replace massive retaliation with flexible response as the official NATO strategy. The Europeans were reluctant to bless this change, as a decreased reliance on nuclear weapons for deterrence could make a conventional war in Europe more likely, and, as World War II had proved, even a conventional war would be catastrophic. Further, the buildup of U.S. theater nuclear weapons in Europe, from 2,500 warheads in 1960 to 7,000 in 1967, seemed to pose the worst of both worlds: a nuclear war limited to Europe. Moreover, despite the large increase in U.S. strategic nuclear forces with the deployment of over 1,000 ICBMs and 656 SLBMs, the increase in Soviet strategic nuclear forces made it less clear that the United States could deter a Soviet attack on Europe by threatening a nuclear strike on the Soviet Union, since the United States was sure to suffer a devastating strike in return. This declining belief in the credibility of the U.S. nuclear umbrella led France to withdraw from the NATO military command structure in 1966 and set about to construct its own strategic nuclear deterrent force.

Furthermore, Khrushchev's successor, Leonid Brezhnev, seemed to offer the West (and Europe in particular) the possibility of reaching a new political relationship, which would deemphasize confrontation and increase political and economic ties. Thus, it seemed that the threat might be diminished politically, obviating the need for a new NATO strategy. Of course, the fact that flexible response also would require a buildup in costly conventional forces made it even less attractive to the Europeans. Not surprisingly, the NATO ministers adopted the 1967 Harmel Report, "Future Tasks for the Alliance," which called for a twin policy of deterrence and detente with the East. This emphasis on detente was in large part a result of Willy Brandt's success in 1966 as West Germany's foreign minister in gaining the adoption of Ostpolitik as FRG policy. The decreased economic and political European dependence on the United States was beginning to be translated into European political leadership.

Nonetheless, McNamara finally was successful in getting NATO to adopt the flexible response strategy in 1967. He was able to do so for a variety of reasons. Three major arms control initiatives in 1967—the Nonproliferation Treaty and treaties banning nuclear weapons from outer space and Latin America—eased European concerns about U.S. adoption of nuclear war-fighting policies. Further, since 1962, McNamara had declared that U.S. nuclear forces were meant to deter by threatening the assured destruction of Soviet cities and industrial centers. Although in practice U.S. nuclear forces were targeted on Soviet military forces and although there was uncertainty about what percentages of destruction were necessary to assure deterrence, nonetheless McNamara's continued emphasis on assured destruction as the basis of U.S. policy calmed European fears. (Assured destruction also provided McNamara with an argument for capping U.S. nuclear forces rather than facing a never-ending arms buildup.) Finally, it was argued that theater nuclear forces should be seen not as instruments of nuclear war fighting but as a means of linking or coupling U.S. strategic nuclear forces with the conventional forces in Europe, thereby guaranteeing escalation in case of conflict and reinforcing the credibility of the U.S. strategic nuclear deterrent. These arguments, along with the removal of France's opposition from NATO's nuclear councils, contributed to European acceptance of flexible response.

The initial 1968 agreement between the United States and the Soviet Union to initiate strategic arms limitation talks was derailed by the Soviet invasion of Czechoslovakia later that year. The Tet offensive of 1968 appeared conclusive proof that despite years of effort and thousands of lives, the war in Vietnam was not being won. McNamara stepped down as defense secretary, and Johnson declined to run for a second term as president. Systems analysis and flexible response seemed to have been dealt a mortal blow by American failure in Vietnam.

Nixon and Ford Administrations, 1969–1977

Richard Nixon and his national security adviser, Henry Kissinger, came to office convinced that the United States had neither the economic nor political wherewithal to build the military forces necessary to meet adequately the global interests inherent in the flexible response strategy. What was needed, they felt, was a scaling back of U.S. interests, a decreased emphasis on military policy, and an increased emphasis on diplomatic and economic policy to meet those interests. These changes resulted in a horizontal discontinuity in U.S. national security policy.

This redefinition of interests was remarkably similar to those interests outlined by George Kennan during the early years of the Truman administration. U.S. vital interests dictated that a balance of power be maintained among the Soviet Union, Europe, the United States, Japan, and the People's Republic of China (added to Kennan's original list). As long as such a balance could be maintained, Kissinger argued, the Soviet Union could be contained and U.S. interests protected. The rest of the world, which was witnessing the proliferation of nation-states, was of peripheral interest. As enunciated in the Nixon doctrine, the United States would provide those countries economic assistance and weapons to defend themselves but would not provide U.S. troops. Further, providing aid and arms to certain countries, such as the shah's Iran, would result in strong regional policemen to maintain regional order and, concomitantly, protect U.S. interests. Consequently U.S. arms exports increased from $3.5 billion in 1969 to $5.2 billion in 1976.

To maintain a balance of power among the five power centers in the face of domestic constraints on military policy required détente with the Soviet Union and rapprochement with the PRC. Opening the China door, which Nixon accomplished with his 1972 trip to the PRC, would capitalize on the now-clear Sino-Soviet split. The new China policy would force the Soviet Union to be more concerned about its eastern flank, cause the Soviets to commit more resources to the defense of its border with China, and be more reluctant to initiate aggression in the West for fear of facing a two-front war. Implementing détente required following the European lead by creating a seamless web of economic and political relationships between the United States and the Soviet Union that were of such immense benefit to the Soviet Union as to make it unwilling to threaten those benefits by committing an act of aggression.

Economically, détente meant increased trade, and from 1969 to 1976 Soviet exports to the United States increased from $61 million to $264 million and imports from the United States rose from $117 million to $2.6 billion. Total trade figures fail to give the complete picture, however. Most of the trade was from the United States to the Soviet Union since the Soviets had few goods that the United States desired. Further, the significance to the Soviets of increased trade was not in total amounts but in purchases of agricultural goods and, especially, Western technology. They were, for example, eager to acquire the technology to build the Kama truck factory (those trucks were later used in the Afghanistan invasion) and the Bryant ball-bearing precision grinders (used to increase the accuracy of their ICBM warheads). Further, increased economic relationships provided the Soviets increased access to Western credits, always a problem for the Soviet Union, since by their choice, the ruble is not convertible to Western currencies and hard currency is difficult to obtain. The 1974 passage of the Jackson-Vanik amendment linking MFN status for the Soviet Union to Jewish emigration and the Stevenson amendment sharply limiting the level of U.S. credits reduced the effectiveness of economic policy in achieving détente.

It was in the diplomatic arena where Nixon and Kissinger were able to achieve the most success. Besides establishing closer diplomatic ties to the PRC, Nixon picked up the SALT initiative from the Johnson administration, and negotiations commenced in 1969. The interim agreement on limiting offensive nuclear weapons (SALT I) and the antiballistic missile (ABM) treaty were signed in 1972. This event seemed especially significant since the Soviets had achieved a rough nuclear parity with the United States by then, and it was doubtful that as a result of the antimilitary sentiment in the United States due to the Vietnam war, the United States could build more systems to keep its nuclear advantage. SALT I seemed the first step of a process destined to reinforce the new political relationship between East and West. As Kissinger put it, SALT was the centerpiece of détente.

By 1973 the mutual and balanced force reduction (MBFR) talks were underway between East and West with the stated purpose of achieving conventional force reductions on the central front in Europe. Despite Helmut Schmidt's hopes that "MBFR would be the proving ground of détente," the Nixon administration had entered the talks primarily to stop efforts such as those mounted by Senator Mike Mansfield to reduce unilaterally U.S. forces in Europe by 50 percent.

Détente and diplomacy seemed a better way to cap U.S. nuclear forces than McNamara's unilateral declaratory policy of assured destruction. Consequently Nixon adopted a nuclear policy of sufficiency, although what was sufficient was not made clear. What was clear was that banning ABMs, as the 1972 treaty practically did, would preclude an expensive arms race in defensive weaponry started during the Johnson administration. With SALT I constraining strategic nuclear weapons launchers, however, concern mounted that in a crisis, a president would be left with no choices except suicide (mutual assured destruction) or surrender. In an effort to provide more options, Defense Secretary James Schlesinger proposed a policy of limited nuclear options, capitalizing on the increased number of ballistic missiles warheads available as a result of putting multiple independently targetable reentry vehicles (MIRVs) on each missile. The idea was to provide an increased capability to control escalation and limit damage should nuclear war occur. Further, developing MIRVs was a relatively cheap way to expand nuclear capabilities compared to building more missiles, an option constrained in any event by SALT I.

The picture was somewhat different for conventional forces. Nixon had inherited a huge U.S. military involvement in Vietnam and, although having campaigned on withdrawing those forces, sought some way to achieve what he termed "peace with honor." Failure to do so, he argued, would undermine the credibility of commitments elsewhere in the world, such as in Europe, and would make the United States susceptible to additional challenges. As a result, U.S. forces were not withdrawn until 1972. Even then the withdrawal came only after Nixon sent military forces into Cambodia (hitherto off limits to U.S. ground operations) in order to strike Vietcong and North Vietnamese forces operating from there with impunity.

In deemphasizing military policy, Nixon eliminated the draft and instituted the all-volunteer force in 1972. The armed forces were reduced by 1974 to 2.1 million men: the number of ground divisions cut by one-quarter, air force squadrons reduced by one-third, and the navy shrunk by nearly half. The defense budget, however, remained nearly constant at $78 billion a year. Nonetheless, in real terms the defense budget declined by nearly one-third from 1968 to 1973 (also shinking from 9.4 percent to 6 percent of the gross national product) due to the spiraling inflation caused by the 1971 collapse of the gold standard and the 1973 OPEC oil embargo. President Ford was able to reverse this trend and gain a real increase in the defense budget between FY 75 and FY 76.

Under Kissinger, the NSC reached its apogee of influence. As the chairman of every major interagency group, the president's most trusted adviser, the administration's back channel link with Moscow, and the conductor of shuttle diplomacy in the Middle East, Kissinger ensured that every national security policy was his or at least bore his imprint. When William Rogers left as secretary of state in 1973, Kissinger assumed that position while retaining his job in the White House. It was not until Nixon resigned and Ford became president that Kissinger relinquished the national security adviser position to his former deputy, Brent Scowcroft. Kissinger nonetheless remained the primary force in the national security process until the Carter administration came to office in 1977.

Even Kissinger's power was not unlimited, however. Although no cabinet officer would challenge his policy positions (except Schlesinger during his brief tenure as defense secretary), Congress was asserting itself to a remarkable degree in national security policy during this period. In reaction to the superior number of nuclear missile launchers granted the Soviet Union in SALT I, Senator Henry Jackson spearheaded a congressional amendment calling for equal limits in SALT II. In 1973, Congress passed the War Powers Act proscribing the president's power to commit military forces without congressional approval. The Arms Export Control Act of 1974 gave Congress the final approval authority on arms transfers exceeding $25 million. The Hughes-Ryan Amendment in the same year restricted the CIA from undertaking covert operations unless the president certified to the two congressional foreign relations committees that such operations were necessary to protect U.S. national security interests. Further, in 1974, Congress imposed an embargo on arms to a NATO ally, Turkey, as a result of Turkey's invasion of Cyprus. In 1975 the Clark amendment prohibited both overt and covert aid to the anti-Marxist guerrillas in Angola.

By the end of the Ford administration, despite the massive 1975 airlift of Cuban troops to Angola and the 1975 invasion and conquest of South Vietnam by North Vietnam, it was still commonly accepted that détente was appropriate as the basis for U.S. policy. The 1974 Vladivostok accords indicated that the Soviets would accept equality in nuclear weapons in a SALT II treaty. The 1975 Helsinki accords included a commitment by the Soviet leadership to respect human rights in the Soviet Union (in exchange for which the West recognized as legitimate the Soviet occupation of East Europe). With these events as background, the Carter administration came to office intent on carrying détente to its logical conclusion, moving from confrontation to competition to cooperation.

Carter Administration, 1977–1981

Jimmy Carter came to office convinced that U.S. national security policy was badly in need of a reordering of priorities. Détente should be pursued not as a means of containing the Soviet Union but as the proper way of conducting one's international affairs. Further, the long involvement in Vietnam had made the U.S. public skeptical of the utility of force in furthering U.S. national interests around the world.

Proclaiming that the United States had overcome its inordinate fear of communism, Carter set about to construct a truly cooperative relationship with the Soviet Union that would reduce the risks of war, reap economic benefits, and above all lead the Soviets, and others, to exhibit proper international behavior by following the U.S. example.

Respect for human rights by all nations became a policy objective. Declaring that the United States would no longer be the merchant of death, Carter made conventional arms transfers an exceptional instrument of national security policy with an aim toward capping, if not reducing, those transfers. He also linked arms transfers to the observance of human rights in the requesting country. Consequently, U.S. delivery of arms to Third World countries declined from $5.7 billion in 1977 to $3.4 billion in 1980.

Carter also moved to tighten U.S. control of nuclear proliferation. The 1978 Nuclear Nonproliferation Act set even more stringent requirements than had the 1967 Nonproliferation Treaty (NPT). Specifically the act prohibited the transfer of nuclear technology to countries that were not signatories to the NPT and did not accept international safeguards. Although Carter waived its provisions in order to supply fuel for India's Tarapur nuclear reactor, he did enforce the provisions of the act against France and Germany.

In the economic arena, Carter worked at improving economic relations with the Soviet Union. By 1979 Soviet imports from the United States reached $3.8 billion, and exports to the United States totaled $535 million.

Carter emphasized the diplomatic component of national security policy. The return to Panama of control over the canal demonstrated that the United States was interested in and would meet the concerns of Third World countries. The establishment of full diplomatic relations with the PRC completed the process set in motion by Nixon and indicated that the United States continued to be willing to work with communist and noncommunist countries alike. The mediating role Carter played at Camp David in bringing about a peace treaty between Israel and Egypt proved that his administration saw diplomacy as being a primary instrument in resolving world problems.

This diplomatic emphasis was felt to be especially crucial in U.S.-Soviet relations. Desirous of "ridding the face of the earth of nuclear weapons," Carter sent Secretary of State Cyrus Vance to Moscow after only two months in office with a set of comprehensive proposals to reduce sharply the strategic nuclear forces of both sides. The Soviets rejected the initiative out of hand as violating the Vladivostok agreement, and Carter was forced to search for an agreement that would cap those forces at existing levels. The result was the SALT II treaty signed in June 1979.

Carter was disinclined to use the military component of national security policy. Although he had campaigned on enacting cuts of $5 billion to $7 billion in the defense budget, the NATO goals set in the 1977 long-term defense program of 3 percent real growth precluded substantial cuts. Further, his administration worked out with the NATO allies a plan to modernize U.S. theater nuclear forces in Europe by deploying new ground-launched cruise missiles and Pershing II missiles in order to counter the growing threat to Europe posed by increased deployment of Soviet intermediate-range SS20 missiles.

The armed forces were stabilized at approximately 2 million men, prepositioned equipment in Europe nearly doubled, 8,000 troops were added to U.S. forces in Europe, and withdrawal began of U.S. forces in Korea. All of these actions indicated a military policy focus on Europe and NATO despite Soviet-sponsored military actions elsewhere in the world, such as its continuing support for the Angolan Marxist government and the airlift of Cuban troops to Ethiopia in 1977–1978.

The Soviet invasion of Afghanistan in 1979 sparked a reversal in U.S. policy. Hitherto Vance's arguments for negotiations with the Soviet Union and for deemphasizing U.S. military policy had prevailed. Afghanistan resulted in Carter's being more receptive to the advice he was receiving from his national security adviser, Zbigniew Brzezinski, who was more willing to emphasize the military component of national security policy.

The Afghanistan invasion, the disclosure of what was thought to be a new Soviet brigade in Cuba, the fall of the shah of Iran, and CIA estimates predicting Soviet military expenditures comprising 13 to 15 percent of GNP combined to force Carter to reevaluate and change his national security policy. In a presidential election year, Carter could ill afford to let such international events go unchallenged. As a result of instability in Southwest Asia, he announced the Carter doctrine, which proclaimed U.S. willingness to use military force in the Persian Gulf if outside powers (for example, the Soviet Union) were to use force there. To cut down the mobilization time required should the United States go to war, he pushed through legislation requiring draft registration. Further, he withdrew the SALT II treaty from the ratification process, imposed economic sanctions on the Soviet Union in the form of a grain embargo, and withdrew the United States from the Olympics in Moscow. Additionally, Carter submitted requests for higher defense spending in FY 81 and FY 82.

Carter also issued a new presidential directive, PD 59, which called for targeting Soviet military forces and military and political command structures as those items the Soviets prized the most and would hate most to lose, thereby increasing Soviet reluctance to undertake activities that would risk losing those items and consequently enhancing deterrence. While nuclear doctrine had been under study by the Carter administration for a number of years and PD 59 was not so dissimilar from the limited nuclear options advocated by Schlesinger, it did refine U.S. nuclear doctrine and emphasized that nuclear weapons would be used to preclude the attainment of any meaningful political objective. The nature and timing of PD 59, and the fact that it was drafted by Brzezinski's NSC staff, seemed further proof that influence in the Carter administration had shifted from the State Department to the NSC and that Carter's world view had changed dramatically.

By 1980, the U.S. public seemed more willing to support active involvement in the protection of national interests. High inflation (fueled in part by the second oil shock in 1979) and demonstrations of limitations on U.S. power, such as the seizure of hostages in Iran and the unsuccessful attempt to rescue them, led to public dissatisfaction, which resulted in the election of Ronald Reagan.

Reagan Administration, 1981–

Ronald Reagan came to office convinced that U.S. military strength had been allowed to deteriorate dangerously over the course of the previous decade and that its armed forces needed to be strengthened to meet its global interests. A revitalization of containment was necessary to stop the expansion of Soviet influence in the world.

Reagan also was determined to reduce the visibility and influence of the NSC, believing that the role Kissinger and Brzezinski had played there was detrimental to the formulation of coherent national security policy. He subordinated his national security adviser, Richard Allen, to his counselor, Ed Meese, and gave more latitude to his cabinet officers, especially Secretary of State Alexander Haig, Secretary of Defense Caspar Weinberger, and CIA director William Casey. By 1982, it had become clear that an effective national security policy was difficult to control without strong guidance from the White House. Consequently Reagan replaced Allen with William Clark, a long-time friend, elevated Clark to cabinet level, and granted him direct access to the Oval Office.

Reagan felt that before he could focus on national security policy, he had to address inflation, rising unemployment, and declining productivity in the U.S. economy. Failure to do so would undercut any effort to refurbish U.S. military forces. Domestic tax cuts and supply-side economics were enacted. This fiscal approach was basically one of deficit spending, as Kennedy had practiced, and Reagan was able to obtain a defense increase of $26 billion (13 percent) for FY 82. By FY 84, projected multibillion-dollar deficits made Congress reluctant to continue funding large defense increases, and, as a result, the Reagan administration's request for a 10 percent real increase was cut in half.

The defense buildup focused on the procurement of modern military equipment. The B1 bomber (which Carter had cut) was resurrected, and two new nuclear aircraft carriers (which Carter had opposed) were planned as part of the goal of reaching a 600-ship navy. Carter's plan for a mobile MX system was scrapped, and Reagan planned on placing 100 MX in Minuteman missile silos. It took three years, three presidential commission reports, and intense negotiations with Congress before a smaller number of MX were authorized to be procured and installed in fixed silos as an interim step toward deploying a new small, mobile, single-warhead ICBM.

Reagan's nuclear doctrine, as declared in National Security Decision Directive 13, was a continuation of Carter's targeting policy laid out in PD 59. The United States would continue to emphasize targeting Soviet military forces and command and control structures as the best way of deterring Soviet aggression. However, Reagan challenged the traditional notion of nuclear deterrence in 1983 by proclaiming the strategic defense initiative (SDI), an effort to eliminate the nuclear balance of terror. Despite public opposition and fear that it would make nuclear war more likely, SDI was funded at the very high level of $26 billion over five years, a top priority project to find a way to defend the United States through the deployment of advanced systems designed to destroy incoming ballistic missiles before they could reach their targets.

In Europe, U.S. nuclear warhead stockpiles were reduced by 1,000, as mandated by the 1979 NATO decision on theater nuclear force modernization. NATO's Nuclear Planning Group decided in 1983 that the stockpile could be reduced further by 1,400 warheads, bringing the inventory down from its 1967 peak of 7,000 to 4,600 weapons. Reagan also worked at getting the NATO allies to stand by the 1979 deployment decision, and in 1983 the first Pershing II missiles went in to Germany and the first ground launched cruise missiles GLCMS were deployed in Great Britain. Reagan reversed Carter's cancellation of the enhanced radiation warhead (neutron bomb) but because of Allied sensitivity agreed to stockpile those warheads in the United States.

Total military manpower increased only slightly, despite the program for expansion of the navy. Light ground forces, with increased strategic deployability, were emphasized. Additional strategic airlift, a long-standing deficiency in the U.S. force structure, has been programmed. All of these program changes indicated a desire to increase U.S. power projection capabilities to meet global interests. This increased capability was soon put to the test, first as part of a multinational peace keeping force in Lebanon and then in an invasion of the Caribbean island of Grenada.

In the diplomatic area, Reagan began the intermediate-range nuclear force (INF) negotiations with the Soviets in 1981 in fulfillment of the requirements of the NATO 1979 decision on Pershing II and GLCM deployment. The West hoped that the INF negotiations would establish parity between new U.S. systems and the Soviet SS-20s aimed at Europe, but when the first U.S. missiles were deployed in 1983, the Soviets broke off the negotiations.

Reagan had campaigned against the SALT II treaty as being "fatally flawed" since it codified a number of Soviet advantages in strategic nuclear weapons. As president, he did nothing to resurrect the SALT II treaty Carter had shelved and instead proposed one-third reductions by the United States and the Soviet Union in ballistic missile warheads in new strategic arms reduction talks (START). The START talks began in 1982 and ended in 1983 when the Soviets walked out of the negotiations.

The Reagan administration's use of economic policy was two-fold. First, efforts were increased to control the transfer of technology from the United States and its allies to the Soviet Union, as it was felt that such transfers would undermine the compensating qualitative advantage of U.S. outnumbered military forces. As for East-West trade, Reagan lifted the grain embargo Carter had placed on the Soviet Union, arguing that the embargo served no purpose and was hurting the United States more than the Soviet Union. The United States also opposed the construction of the natural gas pipeline from the Soviet Union to Western Europe, fearing it would make allies overly dependent on, and thus responsive to, the Soviet Union. Although the U.S. allies went ahead with the project and even provided credits to the Soviet Union so it could build the pipeline, U.S. pressure was successful in getting the Europeans to drop plans for a second pipeline.

The second focus of Reagan's economic policy was on arms transfers and economic assistance. Contrary to Carter's view that arms transfers were destabilizing and the source of conflict, Reagan felt that arms transfers would assist other nations in meeting legitimate security concerns and could contribute to regional stability. As a result, a multibillion-dollar arms agreement was made with Pakistan, and Saudi Arabia received F-15 fighters and early warning aircraft (over intense political opposition in the United States). Earlier restrictions on arms transfers to the PRC were lifted, and by 1984 an agreement was reached whereby the PRC would receive dual-use (civilian and military) equipment and technology. In Central America, arms and aid were combined to provide Honduras and El Salvador the wherewithal to resist Nicaraguan-sponsored insurgents. Even though Congress refused to fund the $350 million dollar Carribbean Basin initiative, economic and military aid to Israel and Egypt was continued, and new aid programs for Lebanon and Jordan were sponsored. As a result, foreign assistance requests by the administration grew to $14.5 billion in FY 84: $9.2 billion in security assistance and $5.3 billion in economic assistance.

Reagan also set about to reinvigorate the CIA. It had been severely reduced in the 1970s, with the clandestine services cut in half between 1971 and 1975 and additional deep cuts made in October 1977. By 1984, the number of CIA operatives had been restored. The agency was assisting anti-Sandinistas in Central America and enjoyed increased influence in the government, in part due to the close personal relationship between Reagan and the CIA director, William Casey.

Conclusions and Outlook

U.S. national strategy has displayed a marked degree of historical continuity. Except for a brief period in the Carter administration, containment of the Soviet Union has always been the foundation. But the identification of interests that the containment strategies were to protect has varied. Early in the Truman administration, a differentiation was made between vital and peripheral interests. The Korean war and NSC 68 obliterated that distinction, and U.S. interests became global. They were to remain that way until the Nixon-Ford years, when again a distinction was made between vital and peripheral interests. Carter eliminated the distinction, and once again U.S. interests were expanded to global dimensions. Reagan continued this global view.

The national security policy used to meet national interests has also varied, in part because of shifts in interest characterization, in part because of changes in the international and domestic environments, and in part because of changes in the national security systems that have formulated and implemented those policies. In the pre-NSC 68 Truman administration, the emphasis was on diplomatic and economic policy. With the outbreak of the Korean war, the emphasis shifted to military policy. Throughout the Eisenhower administration, military policy was deemphasized, only to be the major focus again in the Kennedy and Johnson administrations. Under Nixon and Ford, military policy reverted to a supporting role, a role it continued to play under Carter until the invasion of Afghanistan. After that event, military policy was predominant and emphasized even more in the Reagan administration.

Three basic conclusions can be reached based on this analysis of postwar U.S. national security policy. First, national security policy goes in cycles. Interests alternatively expand because of threat and contract because of resource constraints, thus forcing shifts in national security policy. Further, when interests expand, the emphasis typically is on military policy to meet the threat; when interests contract, military policy is subordinated to diplomatic and economic policy.

Second, the national security system, due to conflicting interests of policymakers and organizations, can fail to develop the policies required to implement fully the national strategy. For instance, the strategy of flexible response called for a military capability to respond to threats throughout the world. Yet the air force has been indifferent to strategic airlift because it only marginally contributes to the air force's organizational essence. The result was a vertical discontinuity—a military policy inadequate for implementing the strategy and protecting U.S. interests as they were defined.

Finally, military policy is more likely to be the policy instrument of adjustment when administrations seek to change U.S. national security policy. This approach is based on three factors. First, military policy is more controllable than diplomatic and economic policy, since it is less subject to influence by other nations. Second, the impact of changes in military policy is more immediate than the effects of economic and diplomatic policies. Third, military policy changes have a larger impact at home in terms of effects on the population, the budget, and the national economy.

What issues lie ahead for U.S. security policy to address? The role of nuclear weapons, the types and targets, and the efficacy of relying on nuclear deterrence will certainly be a major one. The numbers, types, and application of conventional forces around the world in limited war situations will be another. North-South economic issues, especially arms transfers, will raise political problems at home, while East-West economic relations, especially in the area of technology transfer, will continue to pose problems for the NATO alliance. Maintenance of NATO's cohesion will prove more difficult in the face of continuing independence on the part of European allies of the United States. The entire question of the proper relationship of the United States with the PRC will not be resolved in the short run.

In sum, there will continue to be a whole host of security issues that national security policy must attempt to meet. Recognition of the factors at work can help in the creation of coherent policies; however, because so many factors are uncontrollable, it may be too much to expect that national security policy will demonstrate consistency. What we should expect, if not imagination, is efficiency—that is, formulation of national security policies that meet national interests as much as possible.

Index

About the Contributors

Graham T. Allison is dean of the John F. Kennedy School of Government at Harvard University.

Harold Brown is director of the Foreign Policy Institute, Johns Hopkins School of Advanced International Studies.

Anthony H. Cordesman is a journalist who writes on national security issues.

I.M. Destler is a senior associate at the Carnegie Endowment for International Peace.

James R. Golden is professor and deputy head, Department of Social Sciences, U.S. Military Academy.

Richard Haass is deputy for policy, Bureau of European Affairs, Department of State.

Morton H. Halperin is the director, Center for National Security Studies, Washington, D.C.

Fred Ikle is under secretary of defense for policy.

William W. Kaufmann is a professor at the John F. Kennedy School of Government, Harvard University.

John G. Kester is a lawyer in Washington, D.C.

Frederic A. Morris, at the time his article was written, was a student at the Harvard Law School and the Harvard Public Policy Program.

Robert E. Osgood is a member of the Policy Planning Council, Department of State.

Andrew Pierre is a senior fellow at the Council on Foreign Relations.

Glenn H. Snyder is a professor of political science at the University of North Carolina.

Richard H. Solomon heads the Social Science Department of the RAND Corporation.

Edward L. Warner III is an analyst at the RAND Corporation.

David Watt is director, Royal Institute for International Affairs, Chatham House, London.